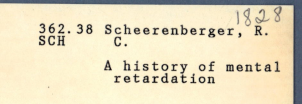

A
History
of
Mental
Retardation

A
HISTORY
OF
MENTAL
RETARDATION
A QUARTER CENTURY
OF PROMISE

R. C. Scheerenberger, Ph.D.

1828

·P A U L·H·
BROOKES
PUBLISHING CO

Baltimore • London

Paul H. Brookes Publishing Co.
P.O. Box 10624
Baltimore, Maryland 21285-0624

Typeset by The Composing Room, Grand Rapids, Michigan.
Manufactured in the United States of America by
The Maple Press Company, York, Pennsylvania.

Permission to reprint the following quotations is gratefully acknowledged:

Pages 44–45: Quotations from Jensen, A. (1969). How much can we boost IQ and scholastic achievement? *Harvard Educational Review, 39,* 108, 115, 117. Reprinted by permission.

Page 45: Quotations from Shockley, W. (1972). Dysgenics, genecity, raceology: A challenge to the intellectual responsibility of educators. *Phi Delta Kappan, 53,* 306, 307. Reprinted by permission.

Page 99: Quotation from Roos, P. (1974). Human rights and behavior modification. *Mental Retardation, 12*(3), 3–4. Reprinted by permission.

Pages 99–100: Quotation from Whiteside, M. (1983, September 12). A bedeviling new hysteria. *Newsweek,* p. 13. Reprinted by permission.

Page 146: Quotation from Freeman, R. (1968, July 8). Schools and the elusive ''Average Children'' concept. *Wall Street Journal,* p. 10. Reprinted by permission.

Page 154: Quotation from Dunn, L. (1968). Special education for the mildly retarded—Is much of it justifiable? *Exceptional Children, 35,* by permission.

Pages 224–225: Quotation from MacAndrew, C., & Edgerton, R. (1964). The everyday life of institutionalized idiots. *Human Organization, 23,* 312–314. Reprinted by permission.

Page 243: Quotation from Tarjan, G. (1966). The role of residential care—past, present, and future. *Mental Retardation, 4*(6), 5–6. Reprinted by permission.

Permission to reprint the following photographs is gratefully acknowledged:

Pages 121 and 131: Wolf Wolfensberger and Burton Blatt. Copyright © D. Blatchley, Syracuse D.S.O. Reprinted by permission.

Page 132: Herschel W. Nisonger. Courtesy of Photo Archives, The Ohio State University. Reprinted by permission.

Page 252: Special Olympics. Courtesy of Wisconsin Special Olympics. Reprinted by permission.

Library of Congress Cataloging-in-Publication Data
Scheerenberger, R.C.
   A history of mental retardation.

   Bibliography: p.
   Includes index.
   1. Mental retardation—United States—History—20th century. 2. Mentally handicapped—Services for—United States—History—20th century. 3. Mentally handicapped—Services for—Government policy—United States—History—20th century. I. Title. [DNLM: 1. Mental Health Services—history—United States. 2. Mental Retardation—history—United States. 3. Public Policy—history—United States. WM 11 AA1 S31h]
RC570.5.U6S34   1987   362.3'8'0973   87-675
ISBN 0-933716-80-X

CONTENTS

PHOTOGRAPHS

FIGURES

TABLES

PREFACE

THIS VOLUME COVERS the historical period of mental retardation from 1960 through 1984, 25 years replete with new concepts, new directions, and new aspirations. Though it stands alone in terms of content, it also serves as a sequel to *A History of Mental Retardation* published by Paul H. Brookes Publishing Company in 1983, which, for all practical purposes, ended with the year 1959. Since the two texts follow a similar format, the interested reader may historically track any area of interest.

As with the original volume, the purpose was again to set forth in a straightforward manner some of the major decisions, events, and personages of the times. It was not intended to advance any particular position, school of thought, or philosophy. While every effort was made to be as free of bias as humanly possible, it must be remembered that for nearly every sentence or paragraph of historical summary, numerous books and articles have been written. Thus, many of the nuances and subtleties of each situation are missing; and since there is always a selection factor as to what shall be included, some omissions may have occurred. Any major omissions, however, were entirely unintentional.

Again, as with its predecessor, this text was written as a documented history to permit the more curious or venturesome reader to examine the original sources of information or research cited. It was also hoped that some of those readers might take an interest in the history of mental retardation and prepare their own reviews. In that event, the documentation should prove both useful and time saving. Historians in the future, possessing a much clearer picture as to which of the many presented events were of long-term significance, may also find the documentation valuable.

Unfortunately, with rare exception, the text focuses on activities in the United States. To do otherwise would have commanded a linguistic skill and time element beyond that of the author. Nevertheless, it is regrettable that the outstanding contributions of such individuals as Eloisa de Lorenz of Uruguay, Jack Tizard and Neil O'Connor of England, and Jean Vanier of France, as well as many others, are not included. In essence, there were many advances in providing services for or understanding persons who were mentally retarded throughout the world; some of the innovative thinking, especially from a philosophical perspective, had a significant impact on the United States.

The text is divided into two primary sections: Understanding Mental Retardation, and Social Care and Treatment. These correspond roughly with the major chapter divisions in *A History of Mental Retardation,* and since mental retardation is always part of a larger social consideration, a short political overview of the times has again been included.

A brief note about style: one of the hallmarks of the quarter century under review was the increased sensitivity toward all persons who were mentally retarded or otherwise developmentally disabled. This was reflected in a series of linguistic transpositions from ''the retarded'' to ''the mentally retarded'' to the ''mentally retarded person'' to the ''person who is mentally retarded.'' While the latter phrase is most appropriate, for purposes of readability and literary conservatism, the phrase ''mentally retarded person'' or ''mentally retarded individual'' has been used occasionally. This in no way disparages either those who are mentally retarded or contemporary ideology.

Many people contributed to this text. Though it is impossible to acknowledge each of them, I would like to express particular gratitude to John Toussaint, M.D., William Adkins, M.D., Paul Harris, J.D., Miles Santamour, Lee Gruenewald, Ph.D., and Orv Karan, Ph.D. for their advice and/or assistance; to Kathy Reiner, Mary Celentani, Ruth Mertens, and Terry Hummel for their help in preparing the manuscript; to Gerry Matthews, Ph.D., for locating critical books and articles; and to Jacquie Kennedy, Wisconsin Special Olympics; Richard Pauli, M.D., University of Wisconsin–Madison; Joan Frumkies, Albert Einstein School of Medicine, New York; Eranell McIntosh-Wilson, Partlow State School and Hospital, Alabama; David Blatchley, Syracuse Developmental Services Office, New York; Mike Guralnick, Nisonger Center for the Mentally Retarded and Developmentally Disabled, the Ohio State University; and Richard McVicar, Central Wisconsin Center for the Developmentally Disabled, for providing the various photographs used.

To my wife, Emilie, my perpetual gratitude for her support, for tolerating the mess, and for forgiving the all-too-frequently-missed weekend outings.

Finally, I wish to express my sincere appreciation to Paul Brookes for both his continued interest in the history of mental retardation and his patience in awaiting the manuscript; to Melissa Behm, for her continued support and counsel, which was always delivered in a most pleasant manner; and to Susan Hughes Gray for her outstanding editorial skills.

ABOUT THE AUTHOR

During his distinguished career, Dr. R.C. Scheerenberger has received more than 20 awards and honors for his work in the field of mental retardation, has been published more than 100 times, and has held 8 editorships. He is currently Director of the Central Wisconsin Center for the Developmentally Disabled (Madison) and a lecturer at the University of Wisconsin–Madison; he is also a member of the Advisory Committee to the Rehabilitation Research and Training Center of the University of Wisconsin–Madison, the publications committee of the American Association on Mental Deficiency, and the Board of Directors for the National Association of Superintendents of Public Residential Facilities for the Mentally Retarded. He has also served on the Advisory Committee to the School of Education, University of Wisconsin–Madison and on the National Program Services Committee of the Association for Retarded Citizens of the United States. Dr. Scheerenberger is past president of both the American Association on Mental Deficiency and the National Association of Superintendents of Public Residential Facilities for the Mentally Retarded.

To
Rose Maren
Emily Lynn
Samantha Louise

May you walk through life with joy in your hearts,
and like the ancient poet, Ou-Yang Hsiu,
find that each bird has its own song
and each flower its own smile.

Introduction

THE POLITICAL YEARS

THE QUARTER CENTURY under consideration was filled with years of unparalleled activity in the field of mental retardation, and at no time in the history of the United States had the federal government—in all its branches—taken a greater interest in promoting the rights and welfare of persons who were disabled. Therefore, prior to discussing some of the major gains in understanding and service, let us review briefly the political course of events.

While 25 years in the universe of time is at best a momentary blush, in the history of a young country constantly striving to realize its philosophical premises in an everchanging society with increasing aspirations and expectancies, 25 years is an interval of both length and substance. For the United States, 1960 to 1985 was a period of tumultuous change, with many of its numerous achievements periodically overshadowed by social unrest, violence, political controversy, a changing economy, and troubled international entanglements.

The sixties began rather quietly with an aging Dwight David Eisenhower—distinguished soldier, conservative leader, and to many a respected father figure—serving his eighth and final year as president. The country was beginning to stir, however. Change was in the air: "At periodic moments in our history," wrote Arthur Schlesinger, Jr. in January, 1960, "our country has paused on the threshold of a new epoch in our national life, unable for a moment to open the door, but aware that it must advance if it is to preserve its natural vitality and identity. One feels that we are approaching such a moment now—that the mood which had dominated the nation for a decade is beginning to seem thin and irrelevant; that it no longer interprets our desires and needs as a people, that new forms, new energies, new values are straining for expression and release. The Eisenhower epoch—the present period of passivity and acquiescence in our national life—is drawing to a close."[1]

In November of that year, the people of the United States narrowly elected as their 35th president, John F. Kennedy, Democrat and Roman Catholic. Though his tenure in office was tragically brief, he was universally recognized, in the words of Republican Senator Everett Dirksen, as "young, vigorous, aggressive and scholarly—one who estimated the needs of his country and the world and sought to fulfill that need—one who was wedded to peace and vigorously sought this greatest of all goals of mankind—one who sensed how catastrophic nuclear conflict could be and sought a realistic course to avert it—one who sensed the danger that lurked in a continuing inequality in our land and sought a rational and durable solution—one to whom the phrase 'the national interest' was more than a string of words—one who could disagree without vindictiveness—one who believed that the expansion of the enjoyment of living by all people was an achievable goal—one who believed that each generation must contribute its best to the fulfillment of the American dream."[2]

Kennedy infused the country with a new spirit, a renaissance of humanitarianism, and a

1

rededication to fundamental human and societal values. The challenge was eloquently set forth in his inaugural address:

> We observe today not a victory of party but a celebration of freedom—symbolizing an end as well as a beginning—signifying renewal as well as change. For I have sworn before you and Almighty God the same solemn oath our forebearers prescribed nearly a century and three-quarters ago.
>
> The world is very different now. For man holds in his mortal hands the power to abolish all forms of human poverty and all forms of human life. And yet the same revolutionary beliefs for which our forebears fought are still at issue around the globe—the belief that the rights of man come not from the generosity of the state but from the hand of God.
>
> We dare not forget today that we are the heirs of that first revolution. Let the word go forth from this time and place, to friend and foe alike, that the torch has been passed to a new generation of Americans—born in this century, tempered by war, disciplined by a hard and bitter peace, proud of our ancient heritage—and unwilling to witness or permit the slow undoing of those human rights to which this nation has always been committed, and to which we are committed today at home and around the world . . . .
>
> Now the trumpet summons us again—not as a call to bear arms, though arms we need—not as a call to battle, though embattled we are—but a call to bear the burden of a long twilight struggle, year in and year out, "rejoicing in hope, patient in tribulation"—a struggle against the common enemies of man: tyranny, poverty, disease, and war itself . . . .
>
> And so, my fellow Americans: ask not what your country can do for you—ask what you can do for your country . . . .[3]

Prior to his world-stunning assassination on November 22, 1963, Kennedy promoted many new programs for powerless people in need. His direct interest in mentally retarded and other disabled persons is well known, and some of his activities on their behalf are reviewed in subsequent discussions in this book.

Of equal importance to disadvantaged and disabled persons over the years to come was his commitment to abolish discrimination, primarily viewed as racial in his day. It was Kennedy, utilizing the authority and power of the federal government. who assured the admission of James Meredith to the University of Mississippi on September 30, 1962, and two black students to the University of Alabama on June 11, 1963. It was Kennedy who applauded the dream of the Reverend Martin Luther King, Jr., "that one day on the red fields of Georgia, sons of former slaves and the sons of former slaveowners will be able to sit down together at the table of brotherhood, [and that] my four children will one day live in a nation where they will not be judged by the color of their skin but by the content of their character."[4] It was Kennedy who introduced civil rights legislation to Congress, but it fell to Lyndon Baines Johnson to assure its passage—a task entirely consistent with his own aspirations for a Great Society and his intended War on Poverty.

In his very first address to Congress, President Johnson implored, "No memorial oration or eulogy could more eloquently honor President Kennedy's memory than the earliest possible passage of the Civil Rights Bill for which he fought so long."[5] Pass it did, on July 2, 1964, but not before 3 months of heated and often acrimonious debate, as well as one of the longest filibusters in Senate history, lasting over 306 hours. Its final passage required all the expertise, experience, and political acumen that the unusual team of Democratic Senator Hubert Humphrey and Republican Senator Everett Dirksen could muster to resolve the conflicts and bring the matter to successful closure.

The Civil Rights Bill of 1964 forbad discrimination on the grounds of race, color, or national origin in most places of public accommodation and by employers and unions; permitted the withholding of federal funds from programs where discrimination existed; set forth new standards against discrimination in registering voters; permitted the Attorney General of the United States to intervene in suits; created a Community Relations Service; and guaranteed jury trials in contempt cases.[6] It also provided the foundation for subsequent federal and state legislation as well as federal court decisions that, over the next 20 years, broadened the included classes to age, race, creed, color, handicap, marital status, sex, national origin, ancestry, and sexual orientation. Its positive impact on the rights and services to individuals who were developmentally disabled was immeasurable.

President Johnson was also effective in promoting two other Kennedy priority programs: aid to schools, realized through the Elementary and Secondary Education Act of 1965; and medical assistance to the aged, realized through the Medicare amendments to the Social Security Act in 1966. Both represented historic landmark actions by Congress, and both would prove of critical import to persons who were mentally retarded.

Uniquely his own, however, was Johnson's War on Poverty, initiated through the Economic Opportunity Act of 1964. This legislation included expanded educational assistance, special efforts to help the distressed areas of Appalachia, a youth program, broader food stamp plans for the needy, a youth employment program, a national service corporation, more public housing, improved minimum-wage coverage, and more modern mass transit facilities.[7] Passed by the 88th Congress and generously funded by the 89th, Johnson's Office of Economic Opportunity launched a wide-ranging series of programs to assist the economically disadvantaged, including community action, Head Start, the Neighborhood Youth Corporation, and Volunteers in Service to America (VISTA). Though not all programs proved as successful as hoped, they did provide considerable direct and indirect assistance to mentally retarded persons and their families.

The years 1961 through 1966 were the most socially progressive in the history of this country, but the thrust of Kennedy's New Frontiers and Johnson's Great Society, as well as the latter's political future, became enmeshed in riots, protests, and what had become an ugly war in Vietnam. While the passage of the Civil Rights and Economic Opportunity Acts were a marked departure from the political past and were dedicated to assisting those in need, they could neither solve all the country's problems nor alter the course of history overnight. Delight and hope soon turned to despair and disillusionment, and racial rioting raged across the country: Harlem, Brooklyn, and Philadelphia, 1964; Watts, Nashville, Detroit, Tampa, and Chicago, 1965; Dayton, Chicago, Atlanta, and San Francisco, 1966; Newark and Detroit, 1967; 125 cities coast to coast, 1968; City College of New York, 1969. The sights and sounds of unrest became all too familiar: barking dogs, wailing fire engines, looting adults, and terrified children.

The Vietnam War, especially after the bogus Tonkin Bay incident in 1964 and Johnson's resulting expansionist resolution, convulsed the country, dividing it into two hostile camps: the ''hawks'' and the ''doves.'' What had begun as an advisory program in the fifties became an all-out war during the late sixties with nearly 500,000 military personnel serving in Vietnam. Forgotten was Eisenhower's last admonition to the country and its leadership, ''In the councils of government, we must guard against the acquisition of unwarranted influence, whether sought or unsought, by the military-industrial complex. The potential for the disastrous rise of misplaced power exists and will persist.''[8]

Few understood the war; many rejected it. Anti-war protests—marches, ''sit-ins,'' draft-card burnings, and riots—were common in most cities and on most university campuses throughout the United States from 1965 until the death of an innocent victim by bombing at the University of Wisconsin and the equally tragic confrontation at Ohio's Kent State University in 1970.

Vietnam was not, however, the sole military involvement of the United States at this time. There was also the Bay of Pigs (1961); the Berlin Wall crisis (1961); the Cuban Missile crisis (1962); the Dominican Republic invasion (1965); the Pueblo incident, involving North Korea (1968); and perpetual unrest in the Middle East.

In response, many young people—lower, middle, and upper class—simply dropped out of the mainstream of society, adopting new and frequently extreme life-styles: group living on the margin of absolute poverty, heavy drug usage, and unbridled sex. Hippies, yippies, flower children, LSD, mescaline, cocaine, pot, grass, and psychedelic celebrations became all too familiar to the American public. The music of youth reflected the change—the Beatles, hard rock, and contemporary folk singers, some of whom asked, with musical poignancy, "Where have all the flowers gone?" Old values and traditions were tested by the young and were, in their judgment, often found wanting.

The sixties had an effervescent beginning—a true moment of "Camelot"; it ended with a legacy of tragedy, strife, and dissension, a country divided against itself. Even the great achievement of the world's first moon landing by Neil Armstrong, Edwin Aldrin, and Michael Collins on July 20, 1969, could not dull the ache of assassinations and senseless killings—John F. Kennedy, Medgar Evers, Martin Luther King, Jr., Robert F. Kennedy, the young men and women serving in Vietnam, and four girls quietly attending church in Birmingham, Alabama.

In 1968, an exhausted citizenry, war-weary and frustrated, turned to Richard M. Nixon and Spiro Agnew to alter the course of events and seek new avenues to peace. Most people were more than willing to comply with the President's inaugural request "to lower their voices, to search for unity instead of divisiveness, for harmony instead of disorder."[9]

During his first years in office, Nixon supported a variety of programs for expanded Social Security benefits, stiffer affirmative action requirements, and day care services for an additional 450,000 children. Still, in 1970, he enjoyed one of the rarest of twentieth century federal phenomena—a budget surplus of over $3 million.

In 1970, the president, Congress, and the people in general were confronted with an old demand raised with renewed vigor and support: women's rights. Growing slowly throughout the sixties with the appearance of Betty Friedan's popular book, *The Feminine Mystique* in 1963, and the formation of the National Organization of Women (NOW) in 1966, women's concerns received increasing visibility. In 1970, Kate Millett's book, *Sexual Politics,* and its well-heralded theme that relations between men and women were political—men held all the power, dominating and controlling women in every aspect—added a forceful, militant note to the movement. Not surprisingly, on June 20th of that year, the U.S. Department of Justice filed the first federal lawsuit charging job discrimination against women. Several years later, the Equal Rights Amendment to the Constitution—"Equality of rights under the law shall not be abridged by the United States or by any state on account of sex"—was approved by the Senate but failed to be ratified by the required number of states. Nevertheless, regardless of the Amendment's failed ratification, the entire action represented another marker in the progress toward equalization of all citizens.

During the remainder of his first term, Nixon and Congress continued to increase social welfare spending, adding developmentally disabled persons to those covered by the Social Security Amendments of 1972. Public job programs, pollution control, child abuse, and family planning were just a few areas that received attention and funding. As president, Nixon also committed the nation to: reduce "the occurrence of mental retardation by one-half before the end of the century," return "one-third of the people in mental institutions to useful lives in their communities," and assure "those who are retarded their full status as citizens under the law."[10] Internationally, the Strategic Arms Limitation Talks (SALT I) resulted in the first successful effort to limit the number of nuclear weapons deployed by the United States and Russia. In 1973, American participation in the Vietnam War ended, as did 20 years of hostile relations with the People's Republic of China.

In 1972, a grateful public, including the vast "silent majority," presented Nixon and Agnew with one of the greatest election landslide victories in history, winning 49 of 50 states and 62% of the popular vote. Then, with the discovery of Watergate, it began to fall apart. On October 10, 1973, Spiro Agnew resigned and was later placed on 3 years probation and fined $10,000 after pleading *nolo contendre* to income tax evasion.* Gerald Ford, senator from Michigan, was selected to serve in his stead.

Ten months later, on August 9, 1974, President Nixon addressed a terse note to Secretary of State Henry Kissinger: "I hereby resign the office of President of the United States." The first president to so resign was replaced by Gerald Ford, the country's first non-elected president.

During his brief tenure, President Ford, confronted with a rapidly increasing national debt accompanied by creeping inflation, attempted to control federal spending by vetoing high cost programs. Congress, however, overrode his veto affecting education and health services. In 1975, Title XX was added to the Social Security provisions, providing extra support for poor, disabled citizens. In the same year, and with considerable presidential reluctance, the Education for All Handicapped Children Act (PL 94-142) was signed into law.

Beginning in the mid-seventies, millions of Americans enjoyed bicentennial celebrations. The festivities were, however, marred by yet another federal scandal: the Central Intelligence Agency (CIA) was found to have engaged in numerous illegal activities. Also, but viewed with little concern at the time, the Oil Producing Exporting Countries (OPEC) raised their oil prices by 10%.

In 1976, Gerald Ford lost his bid for a continued presidency to Democrat James Earl (Jimmy) Carter, "a Georgia peanut farmer, former state governor, ex-navy officer, and 'born-again Christian' whose trademark [was] a perpetual smile."[11] A man of goodwill and compassion, Carter fought fervently for the recognition of human rights throughout the world, appointed many minority persons to high governmental positions, and was suc-

cessful in mediating the historic Camp David peace accord between Israel and Egypt. Also, in response to the expressed interest of many, in 1979, Carter elevated the U.S. Office of Education to the cabinet-level Department of Education, lending it and educational programs for those who are mentally retarded increased visibility and authority. In general, however, his was a perpetually troubled administration: double-digit inflation; 20% loan interest rates; exponentially accelerated oil prices by OPEC; a fiscally insecure Social Security system; a growing and effective Japanese industrial offensive; and Iran—the Shah Mohammed Reza Pahlavi, the Ayatollah Khomeini, the hostage crisis, and an aborted rescue attempt. Social welfare spending increased at a quickened pace, primarily as a result of indexing Social Security entitlements to inflation, a practice initiated in 1972. As a result, by 1980, the country found itself with a national debt approaching $1 trillion, the interest alone of which exceeded Kennedy's first year's total budget. Public trust in government fell from over 60% in the early sixties to 20% in 1978.[12]

Not all critical decisions during the seventies were made by the people's elected representatives, however. The federal court system and federal regulators became increasingly powerful and active. Political commentator Theodore White offered this explanation for what had transpired:

No one can draw a straight line of cause and effect through the bewildering chain of events that changed American politics. All the main actors were caught in the same cultural climate of demands and moralities. But one must go, inescapably, to the Congress of the United States. To leave out the role of the Congress in the transformation would be as unreasonable as to leave out the role of the United States Air Force in the Second World War. Congress, in its 20 year course, dropped one bomb burst after another on the nation—and then left it to the courts and regulators to clean up in their wake, as did the infantry and occupying armies that

---

*Spiro Agnew was not the first vice president to resign. In 1832, John Calhoun stepped down, but for a substantially different reason. He chose to fill a vacant senate seat from South Carolina.

followed the air force into the terrain of the enemies.[13]

Regardless of the reason, the federal court system rendered many decisions that positively affected the rights of persons who were mentally retarded and the services they were offered.

In 1980, the citizenry turned down Carter's presidential re-election bid, preferring instead the oldest person ever elected to that office, Ronald Reagan. Former actor and governor of California, Reagan's philosophy was simple and straightforward: "Family, neighborhood, work, peace, freedom . . ." less federal government, and lower taxes—"we are taxing ourselves into economic exhaustion and stagnation, crushing our ability and incentive to save, invest, and produce. This must stop. We *must* halt this fiscal self-destruction, and restore sanity to our economic system."[14]

Nearly every president since Lyndon Johnson made an effort to control federal spending, but neither public sentiment nor Congress offered much support. Ronald Reagan, however, vigorously campaigned against big government, favoring less regulation, less taxation, less spending, and less governmental interference in the daily lives of the citizenry. He argued with equal fervor for a balanced budget and a strong defense program. As indicated, the voters responded favorably, and he received 489 of 535 electoral votes, signaling a call for a more conservative approach to government. Over the next several years, social programs, which had grown from $25 billion in 1960 to $307 billion in 1980, were altered in several ways: reductions were made in financial aid to families with dependent children, and in food stamp allowances; 40 social welfare programs were collapsed into seven block grants with a funding reduction of 20%; stricter qualifying criteria for various benefit programs were established; and great effort was made to reduce the rate of fiscal growth associated with Medicare and Medicaid programs.[15] Federal spending on such programs continued to grow, however, increasing to

$459 billion by 1985. At the same time, Congress approved President Reagan's proposed 25% decrease in personal income tax spread out over 3 years. Due to the combination of increased federal spending and the implemented tax cuts, the country encountered its largest budget deficits in history, acquiring a national debt in excess of $1 trillion by 1981.[16]

Nevertheless, during President Reagan's first term in office, the country saw: a marked decrease in loan interest, inflation, and unemployment rates; a reasonably stable economy; a growing national sense of well-being; the appointment of Sandra Day O'Connor as the first woman justice of the Supreme Court in 1981; and the magnificent flight of the first space shuttle, Columbia. These trends, plus the tremendous personal appeal of the president, resulted in the 1984 landslide re-election victory of Ronald Reagan and his running mate George Bush over their Democratic opponents, Walter Mondale and Geraldine Ferraro, the first woman to be selected by her party to run for the office of vice president.

Over the 25-year period under consideration, the United States had gone through the struggles of an unpopular war; established a greater respect for all human and civil rights; recognized the need for widespread social reform; witnessed the greater participation of all three branches of the federal government in the affairs of the country; and made the transition from international economic dominance to open competitiveness, relying more on technology and service than "smokestack" industries.

The majority of these changes were well received and numerous gains were made by the citizenry as a whole. Despite such advances, however, the country still faced a large number of social problems: the dissolution of the nuclear family; increased poverty among children and youth, often as a result of the growing number of single-parent families; the appearance of 10 million "latchkey" children or those who came home to nothing but a TV set; an epidemic of drug use; the tripling of homicides, suicides, and illegitimate births among adolescents and young adults; and a geometric rise in private violence.[17]

Throughout the world, civil conflict and international strife remained common. Fortunate indeed was the rare country that lived in peace and harmony with itself and its neighbors.

For persons who were mentally retarded, the quarter century was one of promise, progress, and uncertainty.

Part

I

UNDERSTANDING
MENTAL RETARDATION

Chapter
1

DEFINITION, MEASUREMENT, AND LABELING

OLD CONCEPTS AND NEW VISIONS

THE HUMAN CAPACITY TO GROW IN knowledge and understanding, if not always in wisdom, is a unique and marvelous attribute, and, owing in part to new and sophisticated technology, the gains realized over the quarter century under consideration, in nearly all areas of endeavor, were frequently astounding and of great significance. Yet, additional information often compounded the difficulties and complexities associated with conceptualizing and defining those human abilities and characteristics that could not be physiologically situated and precisely measured. So it was with the notion of mental retardation.

DEFINITION AND CLASSIFICATION

AMERICAN ASSOCIATION ON MENTAL DEFICIENCY

After years of grappling with the problem of defining mental retardation, the American Association on Mental Deficiency set forth a widely adopted concept in 1961:

Mental retardation refers to subaverage general intellectual functioning which originates in the developmental period and is associated with impairment in adaptive behavior.[1]

"Subaverage general intellectual functioning" referred to performance greater than one standard deviation below the population mean for any given age group, and "the developmental period" extended from birth to approximately 16 years of age. The criterion of "impairment in adaptive behavior" constituted the unique and essential feature of this definition. As Heber observed in 1962, the critical factor in this concept of mental retardation was inclusion of the dual criteria of reduced intellectual functioning and impaired social adaptation. Impaired adaptive behavior was considered to be reflected in: 1) maturation, or the rate at which an individual develops his basic motor and self-care skills; 2) learning, or the ability with which an individual gains knowledge from his experiences; and/or 3) social adjustment, or the ability with which the individual is capable of independently sustaining himself in a manner consistent with the standards and requirements of his society. The need to consider both measured intelligence and adaptive behavior was emphasized. Thus, a person with an IQ of 75 or 80 who revealed no significant impairment in adaptive behavior was not to be judged mentally retarded.[2]

The triparite division of mental retardation—moron, imbecile, and idiot—was abandoned in favor of a five-part structure based on the number of standard deviations from the mean. New terminology was introduced to avoid the negativism that had come to surround earlier classifications. The five levels and IQ ranges based on Stanford-Binet norms were: Borderline (IQ 83–67), Mild (IQ 66–50), Moderate (IQ 49–33), Severe (IQ 32–16), and Profound (IQ 16).

As noted, the new concept promulgated by the American Association on Mental Deficiency placed priority on adaptive behavior in determining mental retardation. One major problem associated with adaptive behavior at that time was the absence of measuring devices. While Doll's Vineland Social Maturity Scale was helpful in scaling developmental behaviors among youngsters, no similar technique existed for older persons that took into consideration the multifarious aspects associated with successful adult living. Intent, in other words, was not matched by psychometric technology.

The Association's definition also represented a marked departure from Doll's frequently cited six criteria of mental retardation: 1) social incompetence, 2) due to mental subnormality, 3) which has been developmentally arrested, 4) which obtains at maturity, 5) is of constitutional origin, and 6) is essentially incurable.[3] Significantly, the Association's terminology did not include the criterion of constitutional (physical) origin, nor did it assume mental retardation to be essentially incurable.

While the Association's definition was generally accepted, it was not without its critics or lingering concerns. In spite of the general trend to view mild mental retardation as a consequence of various sociocultural phenomena, some of which would be amenable to treatment or training, a number of professionals

remained uncomfortable over the omission of "incurability."[4] Others felt that the definition and related subcategory "Psychogenic mental retardation associated with psychotic (or major personality) disorder" might lead to the erroneous classification of emotionally disturbed youth as mentally retarded, thus denying them appropriate treatment. Many users were hesitant about extending the potential range of mental retardation to include persons with IQs between 70 and 83, regardless of the need for substantiation through adaptive behavior. Garfield and Wittson, for example, recommended that ". . . if an individual's level of functioning is not clearly that of the retarded and is thus seen as borderline, he should not necessarily be given a diagnosis of mental retardation."[5]

In 1973, the American Association on Mental Deficiency published a slightly revised definition:

> Mental retardation refers to significantly subaverage general intellectual functioning existing concurrently with deficits in adaptive behavior, and manifested during the developmental period.[6]

Herbert Grossman, editor of the manual, clarified the intent and conceptual nature of this definition by stating that mental retardation, as defined, "denoted a level of behavior performance without reference to etiology. Thus, it does not distinguish between retardation associated with psychosocial or polygenic influences and retardation associated with biological deficit. Mental retardation is descriptive of current behavior and does not imply prognosis. Prognosis is related more to such factors as associated conditions, motivation, treatment and training opportunities than to mental retardation itself."[7]

While this concept continued to emphasize both measured intelligence and adaptive behavior, the borderline classification was dropped. Thus, mental retardation was psychometrically redefined as being greater than two, rather than one, standard deviations from the mean. In turn, the levels of mental retardation were reduced from five to four in number. These levels, based on Stanford-Binet norms, were: Mild (IQ 67–52), Moderate (IQ 51–36), Severe (IQ 35–20), and Profound (IQ 19 and below).

Adaptive behavior—defined as "the effectiveness or degree with which the individual meets the standards of personal independence and social responsibility of his age and cultural group"—received more attention in this revision as greater knowledge and additional measuring devices became available.[9] Deficits in adaptive behavior were more definitively outlined by age and degree of mental retardation. To illustrate, the manual noted that during infancy and early childhood, deficits would be reflected in sensorimotor skill development, communication skills, self-help skills, and socialization; during childhood and early adolescence such deficits would relate to the utilization of basic academic skills in daily life activities, the application of appropriate reasoning and judgment in mastery of the environment, and social skills. Vocational and social responsibilities and performances became critically important during adolescence and adulthood.[10]

The 1977 revision of the manual retained the same definition and quaternary levels-of-retardation classification with the editor, again Herbert Grossman, noting that it was difficult to develop a precise classification system for several reasons. First, "mental retardation is not a single disease, syndrome, or symptom; it is a state of impairment, recognized in the behavior of the individual, and its causes are many."[11] Second, "individuals with the same medical diagnosis and the same level of measured intelligence and of adaptive behavior may still differ widely in patterns of ability, in signs or stigmata, and in a variety of characteristics not included in the medical and psychological evaluations used to arrive at classifications." Third, it is difficult to agree "on the dimensions which distinguish mental retardation from autism, emotional disturbance, and learning disability."[12]

While the 1973 and 1977 nomenclatures satisfied many critics by removing the borderline category, the same action created problems for the special educator. In 1979,

the Committee on Definition and Terminology of CEC-MR (Council for Exceptional Children–Mental Retardation) urged the American Association on Mental Deficiency to raise the upper IQ limits of mental retardation to 75 ± the standard error. The Committee argued that under the current definition, "school-age persons scoring Binet 68 or higher (or equivalent) cannot even be considered for special education programs and services for the mentally retarded."[13] Consequently, "many school-age persons of significantly subaverage cognitive functioning who need special education for the 'educable' mentally retarded [were] being 'drowned' in the 'mainstream' and/or being misclassified and misplaced in programs for persons with specific learning disabilities where the methodology used, that of remediation, is appropriate for LD but not for MR."[14]

In 1983, the American Association on Mental Deficiency published a slightly revised definition of mental retardation for purposes of clarity and currency:

Mental retardation refers to significantly subaverage general intellectual functioning resulting in or associated with concurrent impairments in adaptive behavior and manifested during the developmental period.[15]

In addition to restating the need for measures of both intelligence and adaptive behavior, the Association again emphasized that the definition carried "*no connotation of chronicity or irreversibility and, on the contrary, applies only to levels of functioning*." Further, mental retardation implied a "*substantial handicap*."[16]

In response to persons concerned with the previous elimination of the borderline category of mental retardation, the Association did recognize that schools probably were classifying "mentally slow-learning children as learning disabled if they are not mentally retarded," and did offer a modified version of "significantly subaverage":

Significantly subaverage is defined as IQ of 70 or below on standardized measures of intelligence. This upper limit is intended as a guideline; it could be extended upward through IQ 75 or more, depending on the reliability of the intelligence test used. This particularly applies in schools and similar settings if behavior is impaired and clinically determined to be due to deficits in reasoning and judgment.[17]

Despite these advances and modifications in the concept of mental retardation, many age-old problems persisted, frequently aggravated by growing social sensitivities. Mild levels of mental retardation remained ever elusive, by definition and certainly by measurement.

The fine distinction between the emotionally disturbed youngster functioning as mentally retarded and the mentally retarded person with emotional disturbances also remained a difficult judgment. Addressing an international audience in 1972, Tarjan and Eisenberg observed:

> It is not uncommon to find children in the United States who sequentially, and in any combination, acquire a series of diagnoses that include early infantile autism, mental retardation, childhood schizophrenia, brain damage, early childhood autism, and minimal brain dysfunction. At times the clinical pictures in these patients are further complicated by a variety of organic or functional sensory impairments . . . .
>
> It is unquestionable that severe mental disturbances in infancy and early childhood impair intellectual adaptive performances. As a consequence, such patients fulfill the requirements of the diagnosis of mental retardation by both AAMD and APA [American Psychiatric Association] standards. Moreover, measurable IQ in such patients functions as the best single prognosticator of outcome. On the other hand, one might argue that the primary disease in these children is the psychosis or the emotional disorder, with mental retardation being one of the severe manifestations of the severe emotional pathology. At the present time, no firm scientific conclusions can be drawn on the basis of etiologic research. The argument, although often heated, therefore remains a philosophic and semantic one.[18]

Twelve years' additional experience did little to ameliorate this difficulty.

OTHER DEFINITIONS AND CLASSIFICATIONS

Other definitions were posited, though they neither received the visibility nor attained the level of application as did that of the American Association on Mental Deficiency. The President's Panel on Mental Retardation offered the following concept:

> The mentally retarded are children and adults who, as a result of inadequately developed intelligence, are significantly impaired in their ability to learn and to adapt to the demands of society . . . . The term 'mental retardation' is a simple designation for a group of complex phenomena stemming from many different causes, but one key common characteristic found in all cases is inadequately developed intelligence.[19]

Masland preferred to define mental retardation in a cultural context:

> Mental retardation [refers] to a condition of intellectual inadequacy which renders an individual incapable of performing at the level required for acceptable adjustment within his cultural environment.[20]

Though Masland's definition per se did not have a significant impact, the cultural component, as is later reviewed, became a dominant issue in terms of diagnosis and classification.

New theoretical definitions also appeared. Sidney Bijou, one of the country's outstanding developmental psychologists, defined mental retardation in terms of the operant conditioning model: a person who is mentally retarded is one "who has a limited repertory of behavior evolving from interactions of the individual with his environmental contacts which constitute his history."[21]

Europeans, on the other hand, tended to perpetuate the dual connotation of mental retardation (mild category) and mental deficiency (moderate, severe, and profound). England, for example, preferred to apply the term "educationally subnormal" to their school-age mildly retarded population, a practice consistent with the recommendation of the World Health Organization. Labeling the least affected "feebleminded" also remained a common practice in other countries.[22]

In Russia, mental retardation was defined not only in terms of characteristics but also of cause: "Mentally retarded children," wrote famed A.R. Luria in 1963, "have suffered from a severe brain disease while in the uterus or in early childhood and this has disturbed the normal development of the brain and produced serious anomalies in mental development . . . its consequence is an anomalous development of brain function. The mentally retarded child is sharply distinguished from the normal by the range of ideas he can comprehend and by the character of his perception of reality."[23] Thus, mental retardation was dependent upon the occurrence, or suspected occurrence, of brain injury.

This concept of mental retardation was not independent of sociopolitical implications. Luria continued his discussion by describing the approach to mental retardation in such countries as the United States and England:

> In order to separate this group of children (mentally retarded) in the Capitalist countries, all children between 10 and 11 years of age undergo short psychological tests—tests of intellectual ability. These consist of a series of tests requiring shrewdness and general knowledge. Those children who do well in these tests are placed in class "A" where pupils pursue an advanced programme and later transfer to an advanced type of school. The second group, placed in the middle by the test, are put in class "B" and the third group which has the lowest marks, are treated as having inferior ability and put in class "C."
>
> Pupils in this last group are considered incapable of receiving a complete education; they are sent to a lower type of school and when they are finished they cannot progress further and have to remain unqualified workers. It is quite clear that such a system of selecting children—as though they were of "low intellectual level"—openly carries a social class bias.[24]

Regardless of such sentiments, John W. Tenny, following a visit to Russia in the late fifties, noted that special class "children observed seem to be comparable to a cross-section of mentally retarded children in America."[25]

In addition to setting forth a generally accepted definition of mental retardation, another critical concept gained favor during the early sixties—"learning disabilities." As defined by Kirk and Bateman in 1962,

> a learning disability refers to a retardation, disorder, or delayed development in one or more of the processes of speech, language, reading, writing, arithmetic, or other school subjects resulting from a psychological handicap caused by a pos-

sible cerebral dysfunction and/or emotional or behavioral disturbances. It is not the result of mental retardation, sensory deprivation, or cultural or instructional factors.[26]

This concept collected under one educational umbrella a diverse group of medically labeled disturbances, such as autism, dyslexia, minimal brain injury, neurological disorganization, and various aphasic disorders. Many persons continued to assume, however, that most learning disabilities involved some organic insult, even though so slight as to be undiagnosable.[27] Though not so intended, some students who previously had been or would have been classified as mentally retarded were now subsumed under the category of learning disabled.

A corollary definition developed by the federal government for purposes of funding was "developmental disabilities." In its initial version promulgated in the Developmental Disabilities Services and Facilities Construction Amendments of 1970 (PL 91-517), developmental disabilities included mentally retarded persons along with those with cerebral palsy, epilepsy, and other neurologically handicapping conditions.[28] The Developmentally Disabled Assistance and Bill of Rights Act of 1975 (PL 94-103) offered a slightly modified interpretation:

> The term "developmental disability" means a disability of a person which (A)(i) is attributable to mental retardation, cerebral palsy, epilepsy, or autism; (ii) is attributable to any other condition of a person found to be closely related to mental retardation because such condition results in similar impairment of general intellectual functioning or adaptive behavior to that of mentally retarded persons or requires treatment and services similar to those required for such persons; or (iii) is attributable to dyslexia resulting from a disability described in clause (i) or (ii) of this subparagraph;
>
> (B) originates before such person attains age 18;
>
> (C) has continued or can be expected to continue indefinitely;
>
> and
>
> (D) constitutes a substantial handicap to such person's ability to function normally in society.[29]

In 1978, the Rehabilitation Comprehensive Services and Developmental Disabilities Amendment (PL 95-602) substantially revised the concept in an effort to encourage functional rather than categorical judgments. Thus, a developmental disability was redefined as: 1) severe and chronic, 2) attributable to a mental or physical impairment, 3) manifested before age 22, 4) expected to continue indefinitely, 5) resulting in substantial functional limitation in three of seven specified areas of major life activities, and 6) reflecting the need for life-long and individually planned services. The seven areas of life activities were self-care, learning, mobility, self-direction, economic sufficiency, receptive and expressive language, and capacity for independent living. This concept substantially broadened the base-line of service and included some intellec-tually borderline persons who may not have been categorized as mentally retarded.[30] As the 95th Congress noted, "the definition is intended to cover everyone currently covered under the definition and it is also intended to add other individuals with similar charac-teristics . . . . It is not the intent to exclude anyone who legitimately should have been in-cluded under the definition in current law."[31]

The term "developmental disabilities" was intended to serve only as a qualifier for fund-ing and *not* as a clinical determination. Yet, in time, it began to assume the properties of a clinical classification, thus creating consider-able confusion as to the exact nature of the population being served or studied. In the words of Herbert Grossman:

> Sometimes new terminology, invented to clar-ify and address problems, will tend to obscure or confuse the issues they are intended to ad-dress . . . . More recently the term "develop-mental disabilities" has been used and misused frequently. Mental retardation and developmen-tal disability are not synonymous. Mental retar-dation is a clinical term, the term used to de-scribe certain clinical manifestations which can be assessed clinically. Developmental disabil-ities, on the other hand, is not a clinical term. It includes individuals who have a variety of phys-ical and clinical disorders, each with different implications for clinical care, education, and program planning. In assessing our patients or clients, it is important that we use terminology as precise as our clinical evaluation will allow, in

order that we can plan treatment and remedial programs designed to help each individual.[32]

Independent of any clinical considerations, federal reports concerning programs and fund-ing for the developmentally disabled often failed to identify the various groups affected, thus leaving one with little information as to how those who were mentally retarded were actually faring. Further, when such reports did mention mental retardation, rarely were its various subgroups delineated.

A SOCIAL SYSTEMS CONCEPT

To many persons, the American Association on Mental Deficiency's definition and classifi-cation system, even with subsequent modifi-cations, remained basically clinical and psy-chometric in orientation. A new school of thought, that of social systems, appeared dur-ing the sixties. Over the next 2 decades, com-bined with the authority of the courts, it sig-nificantly affected both the concept of mental retardation and procedures used in so classify-ing persons.

The first inkling members of the American Association on Mental Deficiency had of this new view of mental retardation appeared in several articles by Lewis Anthony Dexter in 1958 and 1960, in which he set forth many of the rudimentary notions that would, in time, be found in the social systems work of Jane Mercer and in the normalization theory as conceived by Wolf Wolfensberger. In 1958, for example, Dexter hypothesized that "a substantial proportion of the cost and trouble resulting from the presence of mental defect in our society is a consequence, not of the bio-logical or psychological characteristics of mental defectives, but of their socially pre-scribed or acquired roles . . . ."[33] Again, in 1960, he stated that "mental retardation may, in large measure, be a social role, acquired as a result of experience, by high-grade retar-dates, who have been assigned certain statuses as a result of manifest psychobiological char-acteristics. And the major characteristics of the role may have as little necessary relationship to the psychobiological base as, for example, the Victorian conception of 'Woman' had to the actual differences between the male and the female of *Homo Sapiens.*"[34]

Dexter also drew attention to the fact that mental retardation had different meanings and expectancies not only in society as a whole but within an individual's personal subsociety:

> So, also, it is perfectly possible to imagine a retarded child brought up in some society or situation where his retardation does not matter much; the record seems to show subsocieties where behavior that most U.S. school psychologists would classify as "retarded," with some skill at hunting or athletics, are not socially handicapped . . . . Vice versa, a child of "normal" abilities, born into a family and community (for instance, a university town) where there is great achievement in and emphasis upon intellectual skills, might be sociologically "retarded," as might a clumsy child in a family of horse-trainers.[35]

Dexter's presentations did not substantially influence the course of history. First, he was not directly associated with the field, being an employee of the Depositor's Trust Company, Lewiston, Maine. Second, and more important, his audience simply was not attuned to such ideas.

In a few years, however, the social systems concept was successfully reintroduced to the field, primarily through the efforts of Jane Mercer of the School of Sociology at the University of California–Riverside and research specialist with the California Department of Mental Hygiene and the Pacific State Hospital. She maintained that the American Association of Mental Deficiency's classification system, being clinical in nature, was "relatively unproductive in providing illuminating insights."[36] She, and others, contended that insufficient attention had been paid to people's functioning within their particular cultural subgroup. In her judgment, the latter should constitute the point of reference rather than any broadly based national numerical norms or expectancies reflective of a predominantly white middle-class culture.

From a social system perspective, she wrote:

> . . . mental retardation is not viewed as individual pathology but as a status which an individual holds in a particular social system and a role which he plays as an occupant of that status. In this context, mental retardation is not a characteristic of the individual, but rather, a description of an individual's location in a social system, the role he is expected to play in the system, and the expectations which others in the system will have for his behavior. Mental retardation is an achieved status. It is a position in the group that is contingent upon the performance or, in this case, the lack of performance, of the individual. Thus, mental retardation is specific to a particular social system. A person may hold the status of a mental retardate in one social system and may play the role of a mental retardate in that system, yet may also participate in other social systems in which he is not regarded as mentally retarded and does not hold that status. If a social system does not place a person in the status or role of mental retardate then he is not retarded in that system, although he might qualify for the status of mental retardate if he were participating in some other system.[37]

Highly respected behavioral researcher Alfred Baumeister and his colleague, John Muma, also criticized the Association's approach for similar reasons:

> Thus, intellectual assessment is not just a matter of assessing an individual's capacities, as we might measure the size of one's think tank, but refers more appropriately to the interactive effects of the individual and his environment. Accordingly, it seems to us that the appraisal process should extend to various constraining and facilitating influences of the environment rather than being limited to an individual's formal test performance. It is our judgment that the AAMD definition does not adequately provide for measures that meaningfully reflect the interactive effects of psychological and social systems.[38]

In the final analysis, both concepts were used, since no one system could satisfy all needs. However, many constraints were placed on labeling a person mentally retarded solely, or even primarily, on the basis of intelligence test data.

DEFINITION AND PREVALENCE

Ever since Howe reported his survey of the "idiot" population in Massachusetts in 1846, the incidence and prevalence of mental retardation and its associated conditions in the United States have been periodically studied or estimated, often with little overall agreement. During the sixties, it was generally estimated that approximately 3% of the population was mentally retarded. In 1962, the President's Panel on Mental Retardation, for example, prefaced its proposed program of national action to combat mental retardation with the judgment that "3 percent of the population, or 5.4 million children and adults in the United States, are afflicted [with mental retardation] some severely, most only mildly."[39] Further, mental retardation "afflicts twice as many individuals as blindness, polio, cerebral palsy, and rheumatic heart disease, combined. Only four significant disabling conditions—mental illness, cardiac disease, arthritis, and cancer—have a higher prevalence, but they tend to come late in life while mental retardation comes early."[40] Of the total mentally retarded population, approximately 87% were estimated to be mildly mentally retarded, 10% moderately mentally retarded, and 1% severely or profoundly mentally retarded.

The President's Panel added an essential qualification to its estimate, one that was often overlooked: "At some time in their lives," the members wrote, "3 percent of the population would be judged mentally retarded." As the Panel recognized, the 3% estimate could not be applied to the total population at any given time since this would require at least four conditions that would not exist: 1) the diagnosis is based essentially on an IQ below 70, 2) mental retardation is identified in infancy, 3) the diagnosis does not change, and 4) the mortality of mentally retarded individuals is similar to that of the general population.[42]

As research conducted in both England and the United States clearly demonstrated, social agencies applied different standards, and the upper limit frequently exceeded an IQ of 70.[43] In 1976, for example, Luckey and Neman noted the information provided by 39 state offices on mental retardation and the District of Columbia and reported the upper IQ limit varied from 64 to 85, with corresponding prevalence rates ranging from .36% to 5%.[44] This lack of uniformity among states was also evident in their estimates of the total developmentally disabled population, which again varied from .4% to 6.7%.[45]

Further, it was known that most instances of mental retardation were not diagnosed during infancy nor did the diagnosis necessarily remain unchanged. While developmental lags and other clinical signs among profoundly, severely, and moderately mentally retarded youngsters were usually evident from an early age and persisted throughout life, the same was not true for those deemed to be mildly mentally retarded. Their visibility tended to fluctuate markedly with age. Most were not determined to be mildly mentally retarded until attending school since they adapted most readily to the challenges of their preschool years and, as very young learners, performed well within a primarily perceptually oriented world. In school, however, they were confronted with learning situations demanding increasingly higher levels of abstract reasoning and thus were most likely to be identified in that setting.

The fact that mental retardation among those less severely affected was most evident during school hours gave rise to the notion of the "six-hour child" by the President's Committee on Mental Retardation in 1970.[46] In essence, "six-hour retarded children" were usually from a depressed socioeconomic environment and placed in a special class for the mildly mentally retarded on the basis of low IQ scores. After school hours, as indicated, they often performed normally in their home community settings. Upon leaving school, many mildly mentally retarded persons, no longer faced with an abstract verbal world, were believed to live a productive and satisfying life in a less intellectually demanding environment with little or no assistance, and the label "mentally retarded" was often abandoned or simply forgotten.

Did this imply that mildly mentally retarded persons in late adolescence and adulthood acquired or attained normal levels of intellectual performance and hypothetical reasoning? Probably not. Though few studies were reported concerning adult intelligence among persons deemed mentally retarded while adolescents, in 1965, Miller was able to retest 15 subjects originally studied by Baller in 1935 and later by Charles in 1951.[47] Re-examination of these former special class students in mid-life revealed "no statistically significant difference between the 1950 and 1961 Wechsler-Bellevue full-scale weighted scores for the total group tested, for the institutional subjects, and for the noninstitutionalized."[48] The most definitive statement concerning mental retardation in adulthood in direct relation to the "six-hour child" was provided by Kogel and Edgerton in 1984 after completing a study of 12 mildly mentally retarded adults living in a large city:

> First, none of these 12 persons has "disappeared" into his or her community as a normal person. All 12 are seen by others close to them as limited or handicapped, sometimes in terms of a particular skill such as reading, at other times in terms of a more fundamental deficit such as being slow to learn or possessing limited intelligence. With greater or lesser willingness, most of these 12 persons acknowledge their own limitations.
>
> A second theme that emerges repeatedly from the experiences of these 12 individuals is that the deficiencies which troubled them in school—inabilities to read, write, and use numerical concepts—are the same deficiencies which most obviously trouble them in their everyday lives as adults. . . . Compared to those around them and judged on the basis of the standards of their own communities, they are found lacking, not only in their academic skills but in their basic intelligence and general adaptive skills as well.
>
> The lives and self-concepts of these 12 persons only partly fulfill the expectations one would reasonably have of "six-hour retarded children" who have become adults. Their everyday lives sometimes parallel those of nonretarded adults in their neighborhoods, but only sometimes and never completely. Regardless of whether or not they have disappeared from the official attention of the service delivery system, they continue to face the same kinds of problems which first brought them to the attention of school professionals.[49]

Other studies also confirmed that mental retardation, statistically defined, was evident among an adult population. In 1965, Imure, for example, in a rather comprehensive survey of a Maryland county, found that 8% of persons 20–34 years of age and 8.12% of persons 35–39 years of age could be classified as mentally retarded based on intelligence test data with an upper IQ limit of 70.[50]

Further, it was difficult to assume that mentally retarded persons were not among the 23 million functionally illiterate adults in the United States; among the 19% of over 10 million white males between the ages of 18 and 26 who, as of 1966, failed the "Armed Forces Qualification Test"; or among the 15.4% of adults who lacked vocational opportunities because of severe educationally related skill deficiencies.[51]

Finally, in regard to the fourth factor affecting prevalence estimates, that of mortality, it had been long recognized that the age at death was related to the degree of mental retardation. Despite numerous advances in medical treatment, the more severely and profoundly mentally retarded person's life expectancy still remained less than that of the population in general.[52]

It was also learned that mental retardation and giftedness were not equally represented on the normal curve. Research conducted during the sixties found marked discrepancies between expectancy and realization. The number of more severely affected persons (profoundly through moderately retarded levels) was discovered to exceed that that would be anticipated; in fact, that group tended to form its own miniature "normal" distribution curve at the far left of the continuum. Further, the number of mildly mentally retarded persons also exceeded general expectancies.[53] Conversely, a number of studies found that the prevalence of gifted children and adults was appreciably less than one would expect on the basis of normal distribution.[54] All these factors—age of diagnosis, changing diagnosis, IQ levels used, variances from theoretical expectancies, the addition of adaptive behavior, and disparate mortality rates—significantly influenced prevalence estimates.

Taking into consideration all these factors,

Tarjan estimated that the prevalence rate would decrease from 3% to approximately 1%. In his judgment, if the 3% prevalence rate were evident at all, it would only be so during the school years. Parenthetically, the 1%, as opposed to the 3%, estimate of mental retardation in the general population brought the United States more in line with the projections of such countries as Denmark (1%), Sweden (1.8%), and Russia (1%). The lower estimate subsequently received additional support from other American researchers.[57]

In the final analysis, no one could posit a clear, precise, and irrevocable estimate of the prevalence of mental retardation. The purpose for such estimates, philosophical orientation, tests and procedures used, cultural considerations, and all the factors mentioned influenced any final judgments. Nevertheless, it was still believed by many that while it was probable that approximately 3% of the population at some time during their life would be identified at least as functioning as mentally retarded, in terms of lifelong visibility and program planning, the general estimate of 1% would prove more valuable.

INTELLIGENCE AND ITS MEASUREMENT

Since 1908, when Goddard first introduced the Binet-Simon Intelligence Scale for use in the United States, many persons—professional and lay alike—constantly questioned and debated the adequacy of intelligence tests in terms of content, structure, practices in administration and interpretation, and their very relationship to intelligence. The operational notion that intelligence is what is measured by an intelligence test had few sophisticated adherents.

CONCEPTS OF INTELLIGENCE

New theories and research not only elaborated upon the many facets of intelligence but also challenged the frequent presumption that intelligence was fixed or its development predetermined. "Intelligence is not a unique entity," observed master test developer David Wechsler in 1971, "but a composite of traits and abilities recognizable by the goals and ends it serves rather than the character of the elements that go into it."[58] To the behavioralist, intelligence equaled the "entire repertoire of acquired skills, knowledge, learning sets, and generalization tendencies considered intellectual in nature that are available at any one period of time." To Raymond Cattell, there was both "fluid" and "crystallized" intelligence.[59] Fluid intelligence involved the capacity for insight into complex relations independent of the sensory or cultural experiences. Crystallized intelligence, however, reflected judgment skills dependent on previous learning.[60]

In 1966, J.P. Guilford presented his expanded model of intelligence, noting that 80 abilities had then been identified. These were distributed according to operations (cognition, memory, divergent production, convergent production, and evaluation); products (units, classes, relations, systems, transformation, and implications); and contents (figural, symbolic, semantic, and behavioral). Most authorities also recognized, by one label or another, abstract or symbolic intelligence, social intelligence, and physical or motor intelligence.[61]

Of equal, and perhaps greater import, there was a growing acceptance of the notion that intelligence was neither predetermined nor permanently set. Two leading proponents for this perspective during the sixties were Jerome S. Bruner of Harvard University and J. McViker Hunt of the University of Illinois. While both scholars recognized that there is some physical or biological limit to human ability, people's potential to learn and grow as a consequence of experience was inestimable. In his 1965 presidential address to members of the American Association of Psychology, Bruner contended:

> What is most unique about man is that his growth as an individual depends upon the history of his species—not upon a history reflected in genes and chromosomes but, rather, reflected in

a culture external to man's tissue and wider in scope than is embodied in any one man's competency. Perforce, then, the growth of mind is always growth assisted from the outside. And since a culture, particularly an advanced one, transcends the bounds of individual competence, the limits for individual growth are by definition greater than what any single person has previously attained. For the limits of growth depend on how a culture assists the individual to use such intellectual potential as he may possess. It seems highly unlikely—either empirically or canonically—that we have any realistic sense of the furthest reach of such assistance to growth.[62]

Similarly, J. McViker Hunt disavowed any notions concerning fixed intelligence or predetermined development:

In view of the conceptual developments and the evidence coming from animals learning to learn, from neuropsychology, from the programming of electronic computers to solve problems, and from the development of intelligence in children, it would appear that intelligence should be conceived as intellectual capacities based on central processes hierarchically arranged within the intrinsic portions of the cerebrum. These central processes are approximately analogous to the strategies for information processing and action with which electronic computers are programmed. With such a conception of intelligence, the assumptions that intelligence is fixed and that its development is predetermined by the genes are no longer tenable . . . . The problem for the management of child development is to find out how to govern the encounters that children have with their environments to foster both an optimally rapid rate of intellectual development and a satisfying life.[63]

In presenting his arguments, Hunt called upon the developmental theory and epistemological tenets of Jean Piaget.

Jean Piaget and His Theory of Development

Jean Piaget (1886–1980) introduced both an original concept of intelligence and innovative techniques for studying human behavior. He was a remarkably creative person who possessed the talent and curiosity to examine human development from a different perspective and had the persistence to pursue his interest throughout a long and productive life.

Born in Neuchatel, Switzerland, Piaget, as

Jean Piaget

a very young and gifted lad, was fascinated with biology, and at the tender age of 10, published his first scientific paper, describing the characteristics of an albino sparrow. By age 21, he could claim 20 scientific articles on zoological subjects. His contributions were so impressive that while only enrolled in secondary school, he was offered the position of curator of the mollusk collection for a Geneva museum.

Completing his doctorate in the natural sciences in 1918, Piaget turned his attention to psychology and epistemology, and in a few years was offered the position of Director of Studies at the Institute J.J. Rousseau, later renamed the Institute des Sciences de l'Education. In addition to his administrative duties and research at the Institute, Piaget founded the Centre d'Epistemologie Genetique and became the Director of the Bureau International de l'Education, an affiliate of the United Nations Educational, Scientific, and Cultural Organization, which provided him diplomatic status. Throughout the years he received many awards, including honorary doctorate degrees from the Sorbonne, Brussels, Brandeis, Harvard, and other universities. By 1966, he and his collaborators had produced over 20 full-length books and 180 studies.[64]

Despite his numerous publications, Piaget's

thesis did not receive much attention in the United States until the sixties for a variety of reasons, including his unfamiliar style of writing and terminology, which were often rendered nearly obtuse by translators. However, two books—*Intelligence and Experience* by J. McViker Hunt in 1961, and *The Developmental Psychology of Jean Piaget* by J.H. Flavell in 1963—presented to a growingly receptive American audience a relatively clear picture of his developmental theory and research. Other of his publications soon became readily available.

Piaget's work deviated from that of American experimental psychologists in a number of ways. First, he "was primarily interested in the theoretical and experimental investigation of the qualitative development of intellectual structures."[65] His concern for the "qualitative" as opposed to the "quantitative" was contrary to American procedures, as was his reliance on observation. Second, he adhered to his early training by maintaining that the inchoate principles of zoology also applied to epistemology. Third, as stated above, he adopted many terms from other fields that proved to present problems to both translators and readers unfamiliar with his writing style and choice of terms. He was, as summarized by his long-standing and best-known collaborator Bärbel Inhelder, "a zoologist by training, an epistemologist by vocation, and a logician by method. Accordingly, his conceptions and unusual terminology derived from this triple orientation—biological, epistemological, and logico/mathematical."[66]

When speaking of intelligence, Piaget was not concerned with response repertoires, informational knowledge, or any form of statistical notation. Rather, to him, intelligence was reflected in intellectual operations or, in other words, logical structures. In fact, "intelligence" would not be manifest by children of normal ability until approximately age 6, when they could begin to perform the five basic logical operations of combinativity, reversibility, associativity, identity, and tautology or special identities.[67]

While it was impossible even to introduce Piaget's theories, the following quotes illustrate his basic concepts and his emphasis on active children interacting with their environment. "Life," he wrote, "is a continuous creation of increasingly complex forms and a progressive balancing of these forms . . . . Intelligence constitutes an organizing activity whose functions extend that of the biological organization, while surpassing it due to the elaboration of new structures . . . . If the sequential structures due to intellectual activity differ among themselves qualitatively, they always obey the same functional laws."[68] This developmental process involves two invariant operations—organization (internal) and adaptation (external)—and two invariant functions—assimilation (intake and interpretation of environmental experiences) and accommodation (adaptation of experiences to the realities of one's environment). Intelligence then is an active process used by active people interacting with and adapting to their environment.

Piaget was able to define four categorical periods in the development of intelligence:

I. The Sensorimotor Period (0–2 years of age)
II. The Preoperational Period (2–7 years)
III. The Period of Concrete Operation (7–11 years)
IV. The Period of Formal Operations (11 years and upward)

These periods, each of which was divided by stages and/or subperiods, took the newborn from reflex modification to late adolescence and hypothetico-deductive reasoning. A few brief comments concerning the preoperational period, which relates most closely to the intellectual functioning of most moderately retarded persons, offers at least a glimpse of Piaget's thinking and approach. It is during this period that children begin to internalize and symbolize their experiences and reality. They are beginning to establish a cognitive system capable of transcending concrete reality; in other words, children can think in terms of the past, the present, and, in a limited sense, the future. They are capable of distinguishing between the real and the hypothetical. Of equal importance, children now begin to communicate with others, testing the adequacy of their social responses, as well as their feelings, attitudes, and emotions.

There are still, however, a number of restrictions and limitations with respect to pre-operational children's thinking:

1. Pre-operational children are basically egocentric (i.e., they think and act primarily in terms of their needs).
2. Pre-operational children remain unable to adopt various points of view concerning a particular problem. They are concerned neither with the consistency of their thought processes nor whether their ideas adhere to any particular social or logical norms. Subsequently, they feel no great need to defend their opinions or to justify their thinking.
3. Though pre-operational children are beginning to think in terms of signifiers (internal words or images), their internal representations still remain at the level where everything is exactly as perceived.
4. Pre-operational children also tend to focus their attention, or "center," on the most interesting aspect of any stimuli or stimulus situation. Their lack of ability to "decenter" means simply that they cannot see or understand the integral parts that a situation or task may comprise.
5. A further limitation involves the inability of pre-operational children to reverse their thinking without producing some major distortion. In other words, these children think and proceed from one instance, or particular, to another in an irreversible sequence. Piaget believed that this phenomenon of "irreversibility" was the most important characteristic associated with the pre-operational period.
6. Pre-operational children's thinking is very rigid; they have yet to see the "grays" of a situation. This is exemplified by their rigid concepts of justice and morality, their difficulty in discriminating between fantasy and reality, and their naive and inadequate notions concerning time, space, number, and quantity.[69]

While Piaget's developmental theory was elaborate and complex, it consistently stressed human activity and logical structures rather than subject content or skill acquisition, or in simpler terms, process rather than product. Intelligence was never viewed as either fixed or static, but as a dynamic phenomenon that develops over time, primarily as a function of interactive experiences. Nearly every behavioral aspect of mental retardation was, in some manner, influenced by Piaget's contributions, including intelligence and its measurement, imitation, play, arithmetic, language, concept formation, moral reasoning, and social/emotional development.

Though the preceding review barely touched upon the highlights of intelligence as a perpetually expanding field of inquiry, it does illustrate the diversity of thinking surrounding this hypothetical construct as well as an increased sensitivity to its ramifications and subtleties. It also indicates that much had yet to be learned about this most elusive human attribute.

ASSESSMENT OF INTELLIGENCE

The course of mental testing, with rare moments of respite, has never been smooth. As previously observed, and despite continuing improvements, many professional and lay persons alike often objected to their nature, their emphasis, and their use, or more correctly, their misuse. As summarized in 1967 by Anne Anastasi, renowned authority on individual differences, psychological tests were condemned as an invasion of privacy, as invalid, as unreliable, and as generally meaningless avenues for understanding and predicting human behavior.[71]

This does not imply, however, that testing was abandoned. Quite the contrary, more than 250 million standardized tests of academic aptitude, perceptual and motor abilities, emotional and social characteristics, and vocational interest and aptitudes were used yearly in the public schools.[72]

Individual Tests of Intelligence

During the years under consideration, old and trusted individual tests of intelligence were revised and new ones were introduced. In 1960, the Stanford-Binet Intelligence Scale was modified by combining select items from the two 1937 Forms L and M into a single scale, simply identified as Form L-M.[73] In 1972, updated norms were added to the new scale based on the performance of both white and nonwhite subjects.[74] In 1974, 25 years after its introduction, the Wechsler Intelligence Scale for Children was revised. Sixty-four percent of the old items were utilized in the new scale and, once again, both verbal (Information, Similarities, Arithmetic, Vocabulary, Comprehension, and Digit Span) and performance (Picture Completion, Picture Arrangement, Block Design, Object Assembly, Coding, and Mazes) items were included. The revised scale was standardized on the performances of over 2,000 white and nonwhite American children representing a population distribution consistent with 1970 U.S. census data.[75]

In addition, a number of new tests appeared, many of them concerned with the intellectual functioning of infants and young children. In 1967, David Wechsler introduced a scale intended for youngsters 2–6 years of age: The Wechsler Preschool and Primary Scale of Intelligence.[76] Consistent with Wechsler's usual format, the scales provided both verbal and performance items. In 1969, Nancy Bayley, who for many years had studied infant behavior, introduced her Bayley Scales of Infant Development, intended to cover the age range of 2 months to 2½ years. This widely used and often-favored infant scale provided two standard scores: a Mental Development Index and a Psychomotor Developmental Index.[77]

Utilizing the developmental theory of Piaget, Ina Uřgiris and J. McViker Hunt published their Infant Psychological Development Scale in 1975.[78] This scale, which empha-

sized the sensorimotor period, was intended for infants 2 weeks–2 years of age, and included ordinally scaled items related to such Piagetian stages as the development of visual pursuit and the permanence of objects, the development of means for obtaining desired environmental events, the development of vocal and gestural imitations, the development of operational causality, and the construction of object relations in space. This instrument was also widely accepted and utilized in a variety of settings.

Another popular test developed in the early seventies was the McCarthy Scale of Children's Abilities, intended for youngsters 2½–8½ years. The 18 subtests were grouped according to six scales: verbal, perceptual-performance, causative, memory, motor, and general cognitive. Though no IQ scores were available, a general cognitive index was provided.[79]

Additional general tests of intelligence made their appearance during these years. In 1963, Slosson, for example, published his intelligence test for children and adults, ages 5 months–27 years. This short test, requiring only 10–30 minutes to administer, had an age scale format and included items similar to those found on the Stanford-Binet.[80] Other approaches were also used to measure intelligence. Illustrative of this was J. French's Pictorial Test of Intelligence, first published in 1964, which purported to measure vocabulary, form discrimination, information and comprehension, similarities, size and number, and immediate recall for youngsters 3–8 years of age.[81]

Of wide interest, but not accepted fully in the psychological community, was the System of Multicultural Pluralistic Assessment (SOMPA), developed by Jane Mercer and June Lewis during the late seventies. This approach, intended to provide a more accurate assessment of intellectual performance among disadvantaged or minority youngsters 5–12 years of age, incorporated medical, social, and pluralistic information in the evaluation of cognitive, perceptual-motor, and adaptive behavior. The test yielded an Estimated Learning

Potential score. In 1978, its authors contended that "SOMPA is most useful in laying the broad diagnostic foundation on which specific interventions can be built. It is most enlightening in those situations in which there are large sociocultural differences between the family background of the child and the culture of the school."[82] Though SOMPA was of marked interest to many persons, especially to those vitally concerned about labeling disadvantaged or minority youngsters, there still remained some question as to the validity of utilizing the Estimated Learning Potential score, and whether the system was less biased than other standardized tests of intelligence and development.[83]

Each of the preceding measurements possessed unique properties and each was duly assessed and criticized by knowledgeable persons in the field of mental measurement. The revised Stanford-Binet, for example, in the opinion of Kennedy and associates, was too heavily weighted with verbal content; Sattler believed its abstract material was low and rote memory too high.[84] In brief, perfection was not attained; but as Edward Zigler once observed, "What should be remembered is that many less than perfect measures have proven to be useful in psychology . . . ."[85]

Measurement of Adaptive Behavior

No one should be classified mentally retarded solely on the basis of intelligence test data. So stated the American Association on Mental Deficiency in conjunction with its 1961 definition. Remarkably, when that position was adopted, the only structured measure of adaptive behavior was the rather limited 1953 version of the Vineland Social Maturity Scale, developed by Edgar A. Doll, father of all such devices.[86] This situation changed dramatically and rather rapidly: by 1980, there were well over 100 published adaptive behavior scales, formal and informal.[87]

The most commonly accepted definition of adaptive behavior was that of the American Association on Mental Deficiency, which referred to "an individual's effectiveness in meeting the standards of maturation, learning, personal independence and/or social responsibility that are expected from his or her age level and cultural group, as determined by clinical assessment and, usually, standardized scales"[88] Nevertheless, adaptive behavior, like intelligence, was a rather loose construct subject to wide interpretation, adhering only to some dimension of socially defined age-related behavior.[89]

The proliferation of adaptive behavior scales resulted from a number of influences. First, there was the need to develop measures capable of satisfying the definitional requirements of the American Association on Mental Deficiency. In response, two related scales were developed: the AAMD Adaptive Behavior Scale (ABS) by Nihira and his associates in 1969, and the AAMD Adaptive Behavior Scale–Public School Version by Lambert and her colleagues in 1975.[90] The 1974 version of the AAMD Adaptive Behavior Scale consisted of two parts.[91] Part I provided for 10 behavioral domains; Part II was concerned with 14 domains related to personality and behavior disorders (see Table 1.1).

The original AAMD Adaptive Behavior Scale was constructed for and normed on an institutionalized mentally retarded population. In 1975, Lambert and her colleagues re-standardized the scale on a sample of 2,600 children in 14 school districts in California, thus producing the school version applicable to an educational setting and for children in the approximate age range of 7–13 years of age or in the second through sixth grades. These two behavior scales plus the Vineland Social Maturity Scale were most commonly used.[92]

In 1984, the long-awaited revision of the Vineland Adaptive Behavior Scale by Sparrow, Balla, and Cicchetti became available. The new Vineland Social Maturity Scale consisted of three versions: a survey form containing 297 items, an expanded form containing 557 items, and a classroom edition containing 244 items. The Scale, which provided for the four primary domains of communication, daily living skills, socialization, and motor skills, was intended for both handicapped and nonhandicapped youth and, like other test

Table 1.1.   Parts I and II of the 1974 version of the AAMD Adaptive Behavior Scale

PART I		PART II (continued)	
		VII. Vocational activity	
I. Independent functioning		VIII. Self-direction	
A. Eating		A. Initiative	
B. Toilet use		B. Perseverance	
C. Cleanliness		C. Leisure time	
D. Appearance		IX. Responsibility	
E. Care of clothing		X. Socialization	
F. Dressing and undressing		PART II	
G. Travel		I. Violent and destructive behavior	
H. General independent functioning		II. Antisocial behavior	
II. Physical development		III. Rebellious behavior	
A. Sensory development		IV. Untrustworthy behavior	
B. Motor development		V. Withdrawal	
III. Economic activity		VI. Stereotyped behavior and odd mannerisms	
A. Money handling and budgeting		VII. Inappropriate interpersonal manners	
B. Shopping skills		VIII. Unacceptable vocal habits	
IV. Language development		IX. Unacceptable or eccentric habits	
A. Expression		X. Self-abusive behavior	
B. Comprehension		XI. Hyperactive tendencies	
C. Social language development		XII. Sexually aberrant behavior	
V. Numbers and time		XIII. Psychological disturbances	
VI. Domestic activity		XIV. Use of medications	
A. Cleaning			
B. Kitchen duties			
C. Other domestic activities			

Adapted from Fogelman (1974).

modifications, included a larger and more representative sample for purposes of standardization.[93]

Other frequently applied standardized, wide-range adaptive behavior scales included the Camelot Behavioral Systems Checklist, the Minnesota Developmental Programming System, and the Progressive Assessment Chart, the latter developed by England's H. Gunsburg.[94] Not only did such devices assist in rendering decisions concerning mental retardation; ultimately, they aided in satisfying federal educational and civil rights requirements to assure the utilization of nonbiased diagnostic techniques.

Another motivating influence in the development of adaptive behavior scales was the increased need to satisfy the diagnostic and programmatic requirements of special sub-groups. While the previously mentioned assessment devices served a vital function, by design they were intended to cover a wide range of youngsters. Subsequently, the intervals between scaled items were quite large, failing to provide critical points for purposes of programming and assessing gains in very small increments. In order to overcome that problem, Leo Cain and his colleagues released the Cain-Levine Social Competency Scale in 1963.[95] This device was created for use with youngsters enrolled in the then recently formed classes for trainable children. Its purpose was to assess those skills that would enable such students to achieve self-sufficiency and to engage in interpersonal relationships with other children and adults. It consisted of 44 items in a rating scale format collated around four major areas: Self-Help, Initiative, Social Skills, and

Communications. This scale, as well as their TMR School Competency Scales, was released in 1976.[96]

Further, as professionals turned their attention to providing more than custodial services for the most severely affected, appropriate adaptive behavior scales were again designed, beginning with Ross's Fairview Self-Help Scale in 1969.[97] Other, often more sophisticated scales, soon appeared for use with severely and profoundly retarded persons, including the Balthazar Scales of Adaptive Behavior I: Scales for Functional Independence; the Balthazar Scales of Adaptive Behavior II: Scales of Social Adaptation; and the Wisconsin Behavior Rating Scale edited by Song and Jones.[98] Similarly, when the need for adult programming became increasingly visible, appropriate adaptive scales again were constructed, as exemplified by the appearance of the San Francisco Vocational Competency Scale in 1968.[99]

Last, and often of a less formal basis, adaptive scales or small portions thereof were used or prepared by psychologists and educators employing behavior modification techniques. This practice was consistent with the essential prerequisite of behavior modification programming that there be clearly defined, sequential, and measurable steps associated with an individually designed task.

It should be noted that when first announced, not all members of the professional community received the addition of adaptive behavior as a welcome supplement. Johs. Clausen of the Institute for Basic Research in Mental Retardation was skeptical and preferred retaining a priority on intelligence testing.[100] "With respect to validity," he commented, "the intelligence scales are probably the best tool available—as compared to subjective estimates of developmental potential, or judgment of social inadequacy, which by necessity may vary with examiner and circumstances . . . . Instruments for obtaining measures of general intellectual functioning are readily available. Adaptive behavior, however, is ill defined; guidelines are poor; and for all practical purposes one is still limited to a subjective evaluation of "social adequacy."[101] Others, such as MacMillan and Jones and Adams felt quite the contrary. They believed that adaptive behavior was not only critical, but that it should receive greater emphasis than intelligence testing since it was valuable to both diagnosis and programming.[102]

Researchers, such as Baumeister and Muma, were quite concerned about the limits of adaptive behavior as then measured. They believed that adaptive behavior must be viewed in the context of broader social elements and that further research and test development take into consideration the interaction of persons with the contingencies of their living environments, such as home, school, and job.[103] While both Mercer and Buck basically concurred, they recommended reducing the significance of the education or school component of adaptive behavior.[104] Marc Gold, the ever-delightful, inveterate innovator, also recommended that adaptive behavior of parents, workshop supervisors, educators, and others interacting with mentally retarded persons be evaluated.[105] Over the years, many of these initial disagreements were resolved; a number of adaptive behavior scales began to take into consideration a variety of societal aspects; and most examiners wholeheartedly supported the use of adaptive behavior scales in diagnosis, program planning, and evaluation.

INTELLIGENCE TESTS, DISCRIMINATION, AND THE COURTS

As noted, professionals in the field of mental testing had, for years, winnowed and weighed the advantages and limitations of intelligence testing and attempted to increase the efficacy of such measurements, fully recognizing that intelligence is always inferred from performance. In doing so, they revised their tools frequently; included more nonwhites in standardization procedures; examined subtest relationships; made numerous efforts to enhance each test's reliability and validity; and, at the same time, set forth cautionary guidelines for their use.

Also, during the early sixties, leaders in the field of mental retardation and special education repeatedly cautioned educators and others to view intelligence testing and intelligence test data circumspectly. In 1960, Ivan K. Garrison wrote:

> We are concerned that measures of ability (such as IQ, achievement scores, physical development scales) have been assigned more predictive value than they were designed to provide or than can be supported by research . . . .
>
> We are concerned that in spite of evidence that indicates that individuals can learn new and more efficient ways of meeting and dealing with their environment, experience and opinion are more influential in determining teachers' methods than this research evidence.
>
> We are concerned about these matters because a program which is planned for a child as though his abilities were his potentials is less than realistic; it is without Hope; it is sterile, stifling, and a dead end.[106]

In 1964, Gallagher and Moss emphasized:

1. Intelligence scores are not stable in individual children but can fluctuate widely during the first ten years of life.
2. The same intelligence test may measure different cognitive abilities at different age levels.
3. Each test, no matter what its label, measures only a limited amount of the total complex that we refer to when we talk about "intelligence."
4. Intelligence tests may have three major functions that are often confused—the prediction of future school performance, the patterning of abilities in an individual child or giving information leading to classification.

[They further declared:] It is time to assess the functional value of the IQ tests for each type of exceptional child. Such assessment will not result in the complete discarding of the IQ test or concept. What is most likely is that it will change the emphasis in test construction and produce instruments of greater functional use than to monopolize space in the files where their sole function is to give the teacher or administrator false confidence that "At least we know something about this child."[107]

In 1965, Maynard Reynolds persisted in his efforts to persuade the professional communi-

ty that every child—mentally retarded, normal, or gifted—possesses many capacities, noting:

> A faulty concept of capacity has permeated a great deal of educational thinking and practice. Especially has there been a tendency to use the modest degree of academic prediction afforded by intelligence tests as a basis for specifying expectancy or capacity. Exceptional children, in particular, have been subject to easy classification and placement on the basis of tests presumably predictive of their achievement . . . . Teachers need to stop thinking so often and so much about the capacity of the child and more about making proper educational decisions.[108]

In 1967, Bluma B. Weiner addressed the need for assessment to go beyond the limits of psychometry, prefacing her comments with the following observation:

> Concern about the evaluation of handicapped children is really not of recent origin. For many years conscientious professional workers, especially those who have been involved in the rearing and educating of mentally retarded children, have been disenchanted with the prevailing modes of arriving at decisions about them. On too many occasions, the traditional manner and means of judging capacity and achievement have culminated in dead end diagnostic labeling. The apparent futility of efforts to translate psychometric data into applicable educational prescriptions has led to much discouragement and sometimes to resentment and outright rejection of the whole idea of testing.[109]

These same arguments persisted during the seventies:

> Outside the prediction of academic achievement, intelligence tests probably should not be used at all, especially for the prediction of social adjustment and ultimate success in living in communities.[110]

And:

> . . . behavioral classification (measured intelligence and adaptive behavior) as presently assessed do not specify educational treatment and disposition. To classify a child and attach a label cannot be justified unless the child demonstrably benefits from the process.[111]

Despite the ingenuity of test developers and the admonitions of professional leaders in the field of mental retardation, the use of tests became increasingly suspect, especially when confronted with the volatile issue of discrimination. In the minds of many, psychological tests—personality, achievement, and intelligence—were inherently discriminatory and extremely deleterious to the development and self-concept of minority children and to the educational and occupational aspirations of their parents.

Yet, the first political challenge to psychological examinations involved neither children nor intelligence. It concerned the use of personality tests with federal employees. The all important Civil Rights Act of 1964 contained the following provision:

> It shall not be an unlawful employment practice for an employer to give and to act upon the results of a professionally developed ability test, provided that such test, its administration or action upon the results thereof is not designed, intended, or used to discriminate because of race, color, religion, sex, or national origin.[112]

In the same year the Civil Rights Act was passed, Senator Sam Ervin, who later, in the seventies, received national visibility as chairperson of the Senate Select Committee on Presidential Campaign Activities (better known as the Watergate hearings), claimed the use of personality tests with federal employees represented an invasion of privacy. During the very hot June of 1965, both the Senate and the House held hearings on this subject and mutually concurred that such examinations, which delved into a person's sexual attitudes, religious beliefs, and family life, violated employees' right to privacy and so curtailed the use of such measurements.[113]

The first judicial challenge to the use of tests involving school children occurred in *Hobson v. Hansen* in 1967.[114] In brief, the multiple educational tracking system employed by the Washington, D.C. public school system was legally questioned since there was a significantly disproportionate number of black students in the lower tracks and fewer than expected in the upper tracks. The tracking system was found to be unconstitutional since it did not provide equal educational opportunities for all blacks and whites. Further, Judge Wright declared that tracking classifications based on the use of group ability tests were invalid and constitutionally inappropriate since:

> The evidence shows that the method by which track assignments were made depends essentially on standardized aptitude tests which, although given on a system-wide basis, are completely inappropriate for use with a large segment of the student body. Because these tests are standardized primarily on and are relevant to a white middle class group of students, they produce inaccurate and misleading test scores when given to lower class and Negro students.[115]

By 1968, the battle over tests and discrimination had reached the point where the Association of Black Psychologists presented a mandate to the American Psychological Association to declare a moratorium on the use of psychological and educational tests in schools with students having disadvantaged backgrounds. In response, the American Psychological Association's Board of Scientific Affairs appointed an ad hoc committee to study the educational use of tests with disadvantaged students. Their report fundamentally supported tests (but neither their misuse nor misinterpretation), clearly recognized the need for further research and interpretation models, and concluded by urging the development of normative data for disadvantaged groups and further research in understanding predictability:

> The development of normative data for disadvantaged groups also deserves attention. It appears likely that until massive educational intervention on behalf of the disadvantaged has taken place, they can be expected to show appreciable deficits, on the average, on present ability tests. It would be desirable to document the facts for at least two purposes: (a) so that the extent of the need for intervention could be better understood and (b) so that the tests employed with the disadvantaged might be more appropriately selected.
>
> With respect to the first purpose, it is desirable for the educational system and for society as a whole to understand the handicaps under which the disadvantaged must compete. Documentation is necessary to persuade society of the magnitude of the task, and accordingly of the magnitude of necessary costs. The development of separate norms should not be used, however, to award higher percentile rankings to students than

they would receive from comparison with combined norms groups if prediction for mixed groups is the goal.

The development of subgroup norms should result in the selection of tests that are at appropriate levels of difficulty for the disadvantaged. For some administrative purposes, it may be necessary to administer a single level of achievement tests to all pupils at a given grade in a given system; indeed, it is probably desirable to do so, especially if one of the administration's goals is to find out where and how much educational intervention is needed. For other purposes, however, a more flexible utilization of test levels is greatly preferred. Thus, if most of the students in a single class or grade score below the 10th or 15th percentile, the teacher is learning too little about the students from the tests, and the students have had one more unhappy experience of defeat inflicted on them. The use of a lower level of the test would provide more information (and more psychometrically sound information, because of better reliability) about the students while avoiding a needless defeat for them. The availability of separate norms for the disadvantaged would permit greater wisdom in the selection of appropriate levels of tests to be used with them.

Among studies that might be helpful in permitting more fruitful use of present tests are those that seek out student characteristics that make given students more or less predictable. Although the use of race has not been of much utility as a moderator variable, it is still possible that personal characteristics may be found that identify those for whom predictions are more likely to be accurate and those for whom prediction is less accurate. It may be that such characteristics differ between the disadvantaged and advantaged groups. Whether or not there is such a differentiation should be subject to empirical investigation; the results of such investigations would be of benefit to all students because more informed counseling would be the happy by-product of any solid data which might be found. In general, more and better data are recommended as one of the most desirable elements in a program concerned with better and fairer use of tests.[117]

In spite of its mediative tone, the report was rejected. The Association of Black Psychologists rejoined, "Again, we repeat: we need *more* than a moratorium now—we need government intervention and strict legal sanctions. In taking this position we are not unmindful of the role government has played in relationship to minority groups. However,

coupled with other mechanisms as in the entrance of the government into civil rights, some benefits must accrue."[118]

The use of intelligence tests to classify minority and/or disadvantaged students as mentally retarded soon found its way into the courts, where their application for such purposes usually was rejected. The first and most celebrated of these cases was *Diana* v. *State Board of Education*.[119] In 1970, a suit was filed in the Federal District Court for Northern California on behalf of nine Mexican-American children, whose ages ranged from 8 to 13 and whose IQ scores ranged from 30 to 72, and who had been assigned to special classes for the mentally retarded in Monterey County. The suit alleged that these placements were based on inappropriate procedures since the tests used required facility in the English language, questions were culturally biased, and items were standardized on white, native-born Americans. It was noted that children of Spanish surname were overly represented in special classes. In resolution, an agreement was reached by the parties, which stipulated in part that:

1. Children were to be tested in their primary language, as well as English. Interpreters were to be provided when a bilingual examiner was not available.

2. Mexican-American and Chinese children who had been placed in special classes for the educable mentally retarded were to be retested and evaluated.

3. Special efforts were to be extended to assist misplaced children to readjust to their regular classroom placements.

4. The State of California was to undertake efforts to develop and standardize appropriate IQ tests intended to reflect the abilities of minority children.

5. The performance of minority children had to be compared only with that of their own peer group and not with the non-minority population group.[120]

In a seemingly unrelated case, *Griggs* v. *Duke Power Company* (1971), a critical judgment was reached:

Each person using tests to select among candidates for a position or for membership shall have available for inspection evidence that the tests are being used in a manner which does not violate 1607.3 of the Civil Rights Act of 1964 . . . . Evidence of the test's validity should consist of empirical data demonstrating that the test is predictive of or significantly correlated with important elements of work behavior which comprise [sic] or are relevant to the job or jobs for which candidates are being evaluated.

Thus, the court made it incumbent upon those sanctioning the use of tests or other screening devices to be able to demonstrate their validity most clearly. This requirement was called upon frequently in subsequent cases involving the use of intelligence tests among minority and disadvantaged children, and would be incorporated into the regulations of the Education for All Handicapped Children Act of 1975 (PL 94-142).[121]

The importance of *Griggs v. Duke Power Company* was soon realized, when, in 1972, California was again confronted with a test discrimination case; this time, however, it was brought on behalf of black youngsters. In *Larry P. v. Riles,* Chief Judge Peckham used the reasoning of Griggs to enjoin the San Francisco school system from administering intelligence tests for purposes of placing black youngsters in classes for the educable mentally retarded, even though all California guidelines were observed.[122] The plaintiffs had successfully argued that the burden of proof as to why there was a disproportionate number of black children in such classes rested with the school system. Regardless of the school's posture that nutritional and other factors adversely affected black children's development and that a variety of testing devices had been used, the judge still maintained that the primary placement criteria placed too much emphasis on IQ data.

This case continued to be debated until 1979 when Judge Peckham once again denied the use of intelligence tests based on the Civil Rights Act of 1964, the Rehabilitation Act of 1973, and the Education for All Handicapped Children Act of 1975. He concluded that "defendants have utilized standardized intelligence tests that are racially and culturally biased, have a discriminatory impact against Black children, and have not been validated for the purpose of essentially permanent placement for Black children into educationally dead-end, isolated, and stigmatized classes for the so-called educable mentally retarded."[123] Judge Peckham remained firmly convinced that "the history of the IQ test is not a history of neutral scientific discoveries . . . but a history of racial prejudice, social Darwinism, and the use of scientific 'mystique' to legitimate such prejudices."[124]

Intelligence tests were not the only standardized examinations to be criticized, and efforts were also made to terminate their use. In 1973, for example, the National Education Association called for a moratorium on *all* standardized tests, again in the belief that they were biased, "potentially damaging to a student's self-concept," and "used in an exploitive manner by the media."[125] In 1983, however, the Association modified its stance by recognizing "the need for periodic comprehensive testing for evaluation and diagnosis of student progress." Tests, it was now contended, could help students assess their own strengths and weaknesses, provide "ongoing diagnosis," and identify "appropriate learning experiences.[126]

As indicated, the implications of the court cases involving test usage, as well as that of the *Griggs* v. *Duke Power Company* decision, were incorporated into the federal regulations of the Education for All Handicapped Children Act of 1975. The final regulations required:

Testing and evaluation materials and procedures used for the purposes of evaluation and placement of handicapped children must be selected and administered so as not to be racially or culturally discriminatory. [Further,] State and local educational agencies shall insure, at a minimum, that:

  (a) Tests and other evaluation materials:
  (1) Are provided and administered in the child's native language or other mode of communication, unless it is clearly not feasible to do so;
  (2) Have been validated for the specific purpose for which they are used; and

(3) Are administered by trained personnel in conformance with the instructions provided by their producer;

(b) Tests and other evaluation materials include those tailored to assess specific areas of educational need and not merely those which are designed to provide a single general intelligence quotient;

(c) Tests are selected and administered so as best to ensure that when a test is administered to a child with impaired sensory, manual, or speaking skills, the test results accurately reflect the child's aptitude or achievement level or whatever other factors the test purports to measure, rather than reflecting the child's impaired sensory, manual, or speaking skills (except where those skills are the factors which the test purports to measure);

(d) No single procedure is used as the sole criterion for determining an appropriate educational program for a child; and

(e) The evaluation is made by a multidisciplinary team or group of persons, including at least one teacher or other specialist with knowledge in the area of suspected disability.

(f) The child is assessed in all areas related to the suspected disability, including, where appropriate, health, vision, hearing, social and emotional status, general intelligence, academic performance, communicative status, and motor abilities . . . .

[Even then, placement procedures require that] each public agency shall;

(1) Draw upon information from a variety of sources, including aptitude and achievement tests, teacher recommendations, physical condition, social or cultural background, and adaptive behavior;

(2) Insure that information obtained from all of these sources is documented and carefully considered;

(3) Insure that the placement decision is made by a group of persons, including persons knowledgeable about the child, the meaning of the evaluation data, and the placement options; and

(4) Insure that the placement decision is made in conformity with the least restrictive environment . . . .

(b) If a determination is made that a child is handicapped and needs special education and related services, an individualized education program must be developed for the child . . . .

[Finally,] each State and local educational agency shall insure:

(a) That each handicapped child's individualized education program is reviewed . . . .

(b) That an evaluation of the child . . . is conducted every three years or more frequently if conditions warrant or if the child's parent or teacher requests an evaluation.[127]

Several testing-related court cases followed the issuance of these federal regulations. In *Mattie T.* v. *Holladay,* the judge once again upheld that IQ tests could be culturally biased.[128] This assessment, however, was not upheld by another judge. In *Parents in Action on Special Education (PSE)* v. *Hannon,* a case in Illinois in 1980, Judge Grady did not concur that the tests administered by the Chicago Board of Education were culturally biased against black children.[129] "I conclude," he wrote, "that plaintiffs have failed to prove their contention that the Wechsler and Stanford-Binet IQ tests are culturally unfair to Black children, resulting in discriminatory placement of Black children in classes for the educable mentally handicapped. Plaintiffs, however, claimed that it is not their burden to show the tests are culturally biased against Black children. Rather, they claim the defendants just prove the tests are culturally fair to Black children. They based this argument on a provision of the Education of the Handicapped Act . . . . I do not read the statute as relieving plaintiffs of the burden of proof . . . ." His concluding judgment read, "Intelligent administration of the IQ tests by qualified psychologists, followed by the evaluation procedures defendants used, should rarely result in the misassessment of a child of normal intelligence as one who is mentally retarded. There is no evidence in this record that such misassessments as do occur are the result of racial bias in test items or in any other aspect of the assessment process currently in use in the Chicago Public School System."[130]

The single divergent opinion did not, of course, override the common consensus nor did it, in any way, influence the requirements of the Education for All Handicapped Children Act. Subsequently, by 1985, the provisions of that Act were being met in most school systems with the net effect of reducing the significance of individual test data.

In brief, the prevailing arguments against intelligence testing were:

1. There was a disproportionate number of minority children in special classes; ergo, criteria and tests must be biased.
2. Examiners had a greater tendency to classify more minority than white youngsters as mentally retarded.
3. Minority children were ill prepared to take tests for a variety of reasons, including motivational factors, test practice, reading skills, ethnic cultural differences, and inadequate familiarity with the English language.
4. National norms were inappropriate.
5. Minority children did not perform well for nonminority examiners.
6. IQ tests had a white, middle-class bias.

Underlying these concerns was the dread of labeling, of self-fulfilling prophecies, and of the alleged disastrous consequences of special class placement, which Judge Peckham declared to be "educationally dead-end, isolated, and stigmatized."[131]

Through it all, a number of psychologists firmly maintained that some of the arguments presented in court were erroneous. As summarized by Sattler in 1982, "Research suggests the following: (a) There is little, if any, evidence to support the position that intelligence tests are culturally biased, using either external or internal procedures to evaluate bias. (b) Although pluralistic norms may have a limited use, national norms are important because they reflect the performance of the population as a whole. (c) While there is some evidence that ethnic minority children may have motivational deficits that interfere with their test performance, it is not known to what extent these deficits lower their test scores. (d) There is no evidence that white examiners impair the intelligence test performance of black children. (e) There is no evidence that special ed-

ucation classes are necessarily harmful or that test results create self-fulfilling prophecies."[132]

Further, many psychologists contended that tests could be used effectively with minority children. Again quoting Sattler, "Arguments for the use of intelligence tests in assessing ethnic minority children include the following: (a) Test scores are useful indices of present functioning. (b) Tests provide good indices of future levels of academic success. (c) Tests are useful in obtaining special services. (d) Tests serve to evaluate the outcomes of programs. (e) Tests help to prevent misplacement of children. (f) Tests serve as a stimulus for change. (g) Tests provide a universal standard of competence. (h) Tests help to reward individual efforts to learn."[133]

Nevertheless, as indicated, by 1985, the general posture of the federal government, the federal court system, as well as various state departments of special education remained with the constrained use of intelligence testing, at least among minority and disadvantaged children. The overriding considerations and prevailing attitudes were perhaps best summarized by James Dick in an article prepared for the *Stanford Law Review* in 1974 concerned with equal protection and intelligence classifications: "Regardless of their legal effect, the two levels of discrimination—explicitly on the basis of intelligence and implicitly on the basis of race—inevitably reinforce each other, hastening the downward spiral of self-confidence and self-esteem. The potentially dangerous consequences generated by the creation of a racial group stereotype based on low intelligence gives greater force to this stigmatic effect."[134] Or, in the words of the liberal, internationally recognized anthropologist and author Stephen J. Gould, in his scathing review of intelligence theories and tests in *The Mismeasure of Man*—"We pass through this world but once. Few tragedies can be more extensive than the stunting of life, few injustices deeper than the denial of an opportunity to strive or even to hope, by a limit imposed from without, but falsely identified as lying within."[135]

LABELING

Classification systems, though they cannot serve all purposes and are always subject to debate on their respective merits, are entirely neutral when an individual is involved. As stressed by Grossman, "classification systems deal with population groups (not individual cases), are fundamental to the study of any phenomenon, and form the basis for all scientific generalization. Clinicians deal with individual diagnoses that collectively provide *population* data; however, classification systems are concerned only with the latter. Population-based information provides statistics on incidence, prevalence, and related conditions that are essential to program planning and service-delivery systems."[136]

Labeling, as indicated, is an individual matter; and labeling someone as mentally retarded—especially mildly mentally retarded—has always been difficult, primarily since society has tended to view those so identified as less than worthy, less than desirable, and on occasion, less than human. This was well recognized from the beginning of special programming. In 1884, long before intelligence testing became popular, Isaac Kerlin, superintendent of a residential facility for mentally retarded persons, cautioned, "So, in social and governmental dealings with the defective classes it is all-important that a right interpretation be made upon observed phenomena; for, if a mistake be made in the premises, the sequences of the relief or correction administered may be detrimental."[137] In 1908, Binet and Simon noted that their newly devised test should be used with great care since, "It will never be to one's credit to have attended a special school. We should at least spare from this mark those who do not deserve it."[138] During the forties and fifties, Edgar Doll and Seymour Sarason were among those who fought diligently to discourage labeling except in the most clearly documented instances.[139]

During the late sixties and early seventies, this issue again became one of earnest discussion and often presumptive speculation as a result of increased input from social theorists, challenges to special classes, and the growing sensitivity to minority groups and their status in American society. The effects of labeling, in the judgment of many, could be devastating and long lasting. "Where the judgment is mental retardation," wrote Robert and Cecil Edgerton in 1973, "the influence will last a lifetime."[140] The previous year, Burton Blatt cautioned that labeling was dangerous since it tended to "dehumanize and stigmatize these children and their families."[141] Mercer, Rowitz, and other social scientists hypothesized that once an individual was labeled mentally retarded, he would assume the perceived behavior of a mentally retarded person; thus, the mere existence of the label could conceivably "cause" or foster mental retardation.[142] As explained by Mercer, "When a person has been assigned the status of retardate by a professional diagnostician and has been systematically socialized to the role, it is difficult for him to escape the status even in thinking about himself."[143]

In the judgment of those quoted, the professional assignment of "mental retardation" to a youngster would be manifest in low self-esteem and, ultimately, a poor self-concept. Some authorities also held that such labels would prove self-fulfilling, as the result of lowered expectancies by both the individual and others.

It was for these reasons that the design of new classificatory systems capable of specifying problems but avoiding labels were encouraged. In 1972, special educator Blatt recommended:

> . . . appropriate state agencies should develop a system of regulations that define the special needs of children in ways which would emphasize each child's developmental needs rather than his "deviancy."[144]

Psychologists Baumeister and Muma advocated:

> . . . a theory-guided approach to the definition of human adjustment that focuses upon the developing organism and its interactions with a dynamic environment. It is not only important to identify significant personal, social, and en-

vironmental variables, but also to cast these into a hierarchical and interdependent system. We should choose our variables from our best understanding of the processes of learning, development, and socialization. In such a system there would not be "MR" but rather a complex and continually changing profile of an individual's adjustments to the constantly changing exigencies of his environment. All of us would have a place in such a system.[145]

Such a system would be ideal, but inordinately difficult to realize; and at the end of 1984, such proposals, even though they had been made during the seventies, had not translated into new, commonly adopted nomenclatures.

Labels, however, were not totally devoid of value. Most persons challenging their use also benefited from them, for mental retardation as a category and mental retardation as a sociopolitical concern produced billions of sorely needed federal and state dollars for special services, professional training, and research. These, in the words of James Gallagher, represented the "sacred" application of labels, in contrast to "profane" uses that provided a means:

1. For tranquilizing professionals by applying labels . . . to children without following with subsequent differentiated programs of treatment, merely fulfilling a need for closure on a difficult diagnostic issue.
2. To preserve a social hierarchy by using labels to keep minority group children from opportunities and to force them to remain at the bottom of the social ladder.
3. To delay needed social reform by focusing the problem on the individual, rather than on complex social and ecological conditions needing specific change and repair.[146]

The primary question, however, still concerned the overall effect of placing the label "mental retardation" upon an individual. Though frequently a subject of research throughout the years, no absolute answers were forthcoming. First, since many of the studies concerned mentally retarded youngsters in school, or from an institution, or were based on an artificial noncontact situation, most of the results, at best, were judged indicative rather than affirmatory. To illustrate,

when, in 1974, MacMillan, Jones, and Aloia critically reviewed a number of research reports published to that time, they concluded, "Few studies were found in which labelling was isolated thus enabling differences between labelled and unlabelled groups to be attributed to the label, per se. The evidence uncovered failed to provide support for the notion that labelling has long-lasting and devastating effects on those labelled."[147] This did not mean, however, that the label might not have an impact, rather that the research data did "not reflect sufficient appreciation for the complexity of the dynamics of how the label operates."[148]

Guskin, during the same year, concurred with the interpretation of MacMillan and his colleagues. He approached the subject from a slightly different perspective, noting that the significance of labels depended upon the images they generate.[149] In developing his response, he called upon his previous work, which indicated that while a label could result in negativism, it did "not invariably do so."[150] First, he found that the individual's behavior ("relevant cues to his subnormality") was essential to any strong assessments. In another study, conducted shortly thereafter, he found there was a tendency for both college students and other people from the community to form stereotypes of individuals stated to be mentally retarded, reflecting such characteristics as "quiet," "timid," "unintelligent," "abnormal," "strange," "helpless," "and clumsy." There was, however, an important variable affecting such stereotypes. The severity of the label was highly contingent upon the information respondents were given; that is, moderate statements resulted in little or no negative reaction.[151]

In 1967, Robert B. Edgerton wrote one of the most widely read and frequently cited books of the decade, *The Cloak of Competence.*[152] In doing so, he not only prepared an intriguing study of 48 former Pacific State Hospital residents, but also introduced the field to the thinking of an anthropologist. The overall intent of the investigation was to determine how formerly institutionalized, mildly mentally retarded men and women managed their lives and perceived themselves when left to their own devices in a large city. The generic goal was further defined by design when interest was focused on seven major areas: 1) where and how the ex-resident lived; 2) making a living; 3) relations with others in the community; 4) sex, marriage, and children; 5) "spare time" activities; 6) perception and presentation of self; and 7) practical problems in maintaining himself or herself in the community.

Of immediate concern were Edgerton's results and interpretations as they related to labeling. First, he found that the mentally retarded men and women spent a great deal of time and personal energy in attempting to "pass" themselves in the community as "normal" and in engaging in a perpetual self-denial of mental retardation. Through the use of these two techniques, his subjects strove both to accept and to project themselves as normal, or, in the author's words, to surround themselves with a cloak of competence. Though Edgerton concluded that "an accusation of stupidity has a shattering effect," he also discovered and duly recorded that "true typicality is largely fiction."[153] His four detailed portraits depicted four uniquely different people, reacting in their own way to the circumstances in which they found themselves. Fred, a man in his early 30s, for example, assumed different roles with different people according to their perceived status in his eyes: with former residents he was domineering and occasionally arrogant; with normal persons, he displayed behavior characterized as "happy, carefree competence"; with "important" or "big" people who had befriended and/or protected him, he was "passive, deferential," and "almost reverential."[154] Thus, it would appear that be one normal, gifted, or mentally retarded, the world still remains, in the words of William Shakespeare, a "stage" upon which "one man in his time plays many parts." Edgerton's overall conclusion was important since it demonstrated that it was frequently the behavior of the individuals that focused attention on their level of functioning.

Twelve years later, Edgerton and his colleague, Sylvia Bercovici, reinterviewed 30 of the original 48 subjects, evenly distributed according to sex, and discovered a number of significant changes. In marked contrast with the early results, adult concerns with stigma and passing were now far less evident.[155] Most of the subjects felt that the "issue was behind them; never completely forgotten, perhaps, but not an everyday concern, either".[156] What the interviewers did find was that the subjects now had a vital interest in enjoying life and were highly concerned with their recreation, hobbies, leisure, good times, friends, and family. This led to the conclusion that the adults surveyed were now much happier than in previous years and "however deleterious labelling may be, its effects are not necessarily permanent."[157]

The fact that mentally retarded persons, regardless of professional labeling, were identified by their peers and neighbors as mentally retarded, or at least slower than normal, cannot be denied. Not only was this obvious in Edgerton's research, it was quite evident in an interview with a young married couple reported in the *Hartford Courant Special*. The wife, who often came home from school in tears, clearly remembered being called "retard" and "stupid" by her fellow students, though she did not attend any special program until high school. Similarly, her husband, who had never been labeled mentally retarded, also acquired such nicknames as "hedge head" and "block head."[158]

Though other studies in the area of labeling and expectancy are reviewed later in this book when considering historical developments in special education, it is obvious that the 25 years under consideration witnessed a significantly heightened sensitivity to questions concerning the desirability of and need to label a person mentally retarded, especially those mildly affected. Though the ultimate impact of labels on individuals appeared contingent upon a host of influences and any negative effects of such labels might diminish over time, increased caution was exercised by all.

Chapter

2

Etiology, Prevention, and Growing Issues in Medical Treatment

O F THE MANY remarkable advances in knowledge during the historical period under review, none was more impressive than those involving the human being in terms of physical functioning and genetic influences. Consequently, many advances in diagnosis, classification, and treatment were made, but, at the same time, new treatment techniques, changing societal attitudes, federal court decisions, and a country increasingly sensitive to health-related costs posed a threat to those who were born mentally retarded or otherwise disabled.

ETIOLOGY AND ETIOLOGICAL CLASSIFICATION

Ever since man first recognized deviance in ability and its occasional relationship to peculiar physical attributes, an ever-growing number of probable etiological influences and conditions associated with mental retardation were noted and described. Thus, by 1961, when the American Association on Mental Deficiency formally published its medical nomenclature, most of the "common" visible syndromes were identified and could be classified, though not without some degree of un-

certainty and error. The original classification consisted of eight primary categories (see Table 2.1).[1]

Table 2.1. Etiological classification of mental retardation by the American Association on Mental Deficiency (1961): Eight primary categories

I

Mental Retardation Associated with Diseases and Conditions Due To Infection

Encephalopathy, congenital, associated with prenatal infection (e.g., congenital rubella, syphilis, and toxoplasmosis)

Encephalopathy due to postnatal cerebral infection (e.g., viral or bacterial)

II

Mental Retardation Associated with Diseases and Conditions Due to Intoxication

Encephalopathy, congenital, associated with toxemia of pregnancy

Encephalopathy, congenital, associated with other maternal intoxications

Bilirubin encephalopathy (Kernicterus)

Post-immunization encephalopathy

Encephalopathy, other, due to intoxication

III

Mental Retardation Associated With Diseases and Conditions Due to Trauma or Physical Agent

(continued)

Table 2.1.   (*continued*)

Encephalopathy due to prenatal injury

Encephalopathy due to mechanical injury at birth

Encephalopathy due to anoxemia at birth

Encephalopathy due to postnatal injury (e.g., contusion, hemorrhage of brain, porencephaly, vascular occlusion, postnatal anoxemia)

IV

Mental Retardation Associated With Diseases and Conditions Due To Disorder of Metabolism, Growth, or Nutrition

Cerebral lipoidosis, infantile (Tay-Sach's disease)

Encephalopathy associated with other disorders of lipoid metabolism (e.g., cerebral lipoidosis, late infantile, Bielschowsky's disease; cerebral lipoidosis, juvenile, Spielmeyer-Vogt disease; cerebral lipoidosis, late juvenile, Kuf's disease; lipid histiocytosis of kerasin type, Gaucher's disease; lipid histoicytosis of phosphatide type, Neimann-Pick's disease)

Phenylketonuria

Encephalopathy associated with other disorders of protein metabolism (e.g., hepatolenticular degeneration, Wilson's disease; porphyria)

Galactosemia

Encephalopathy associated with other disorders of carbohydrate metabolism (e.g., glycogenosis, Von Gierke's disease; hypoglycemosis)

Arachnodactyly

Hypothyroidism

Gargoylism (Lipochondrodystrophy)

Encephalopathy, other, due to metabolic, growth, or nutritional disorder

V

Mental Retardation Associated with Diseases and Conditions Due to New Growths

Neurofibromatosis (Von Recklinghausen's disease)

Trigeminal cerebral angiomatosis (Sturge-Weber-Dimitri's disease)

Tuberous sclerosis

Intracranial neoplasm, other

VI

Mental Retardation Associated With Diseases and Conditions Due to (Unknown) Prenatal Influence

Cerebral defect, congenital (e.g., not further specified; anencephaly; malformations of gyri;

(*continued*)

Table 2.1.   (*continued*)

porencephaly, congenital; multiple congenital anomalies of the brain)

Cerebral defect, congenital, associated with primary cranial anomaly (e.g., craniostenosis); hydrocephalus, congenital; hypertelorism, Greig's disease; macrocephaly; microcephaly)

Laurence-Moon-Biedl syndrome

Mongolism

Other, due to unknown prenatal influence

VII

Mental Retardation Associated With Diseases and Conditions Due to Unknown or Uncertain Cause With the Structural Reactions Manifest

Encephalopathy associated with diffuse sclerosis of brain (e.g., acute infantile diffuse sclerosis, Krabbe's disease; diffuse chronic infantile sclerosis, Merzbacher-Pelizaeus disease; infantile metachromatic leukodystrophy, Greenfield's disease; juvenile metachromatic leukodystrophy, Scholz's disease; progressive subcortical encephalopathy, Schilder's disease)

Encephalopathy associated with cerebellar degeneration (e.g., spinal sclerosis, Friedreich's ataxia)

Encephalopathy associated with prematurity

Encephalopathy, other, due to unknown or uncertain cause with the structural reactions manifest

VIII

Mental Retardation Due to Uncertain (or Presumed Psychologic) Cause With the Functional Reaction Alone Manifest

Cultural-familial mental retardation

Psychogenic mental retardation associated with environmental deprivation

Psychogenic mental retardation associated with emotional disturbance

Mental retardation associated with psychotic (or major personality) disorder (e.g., autism)

Mental retardation, other, due to uncertain cause with the functional reaction alone manifest.

Adapted from Heber (1961).

Throughout the years, the nomenclature was revised and updated to provide for greater precision and/or utility. The 1983 version reflected heavily upon the advances made in understanding the biogenetics of human existence (see Table 2.2).[2]

Table 2.2. Etiological classification of mental retardation by the American Association on Mental Deficiency (1983)

0
Infections and Intoxications

Prenatal infection (e.g., Cytomegalic inclusion disease, congenital; Rubella congenital; Syphilis, congenital; Toxoplasmosis, congenital)

Postnatal cerebral infection (e.g., viral, bacterial)

Intoxication (e.g., toxemia of pregnancy; maternal; other maternal disorders, such as maternal PKU; hyperbilirubinemia; lead; post immunization; fetal alcohol syndrome)

I
Trauma or Physical Agent

Prenatal injury

Mechanical injury at birth

Perinatal hypoxia

Postnatal hypoxia

Postnatal injury

II
Metabolism or Nutrition

Neuronal lipid storage diseases (e.g., ganglioside storage diseases, lipofuscin storage diseases, other glycolipidoses with neuronal involvement)

Carbohydrate disorders (e.g., galactosemia, glycogenoses [Glycogen storage disease], fructosemia [Hereditary fructose intolerance], hypoglycemia)

Amino acid disorders (e.g., Phenylketonuria)

Other and unspecified disorders of metabolism

Mineral disorders (e.g., Wilson disease, Idiopathic hypercalcemia)

Endocrine disorders (e.g., thyroid dysfunction, congenital)

Nutritional disorders

III
Gross Brain Disease (Postnatal)

Neurocutaneous dysplasia (e.g., Neurofibromatosis (von Recklinghausen disease)

Trigeminal cerebral angiomatosis (Sturge-Weber-Dimitri disease), tuberous sclerosis

Tumors

Cerebral white matter, degenerative (e.g., sudanophilic leukodystrophy, sudanophilic leukodystrophy of Pelizaeus-Merzbacher type)

Specific fiber tracts or neural groups, degener-

(continued)

Table 2.2. (continued)

ative (e.g., Huntington disease, Spinocerebellar disease)

Cerebrovascular system

IV
Unknown Prenatal Influence

Cerebral malformation (e.g., anencephaly)

Craniofacial anomaly (e.g., holoprosencephaly, Cornelia de Lange syndrome, microcephalus, macroencephaly, Crouzon syndrome, Apert syndrome, craniostenosis, other, including Rubenstein-Taybi, Oral-Facial-Digital; Laurence-Moon-Biedl syndrome)

Status dysraphicus (e.g., meningoencephalocele, meningomyelocele)

Hydrocephalus, congenital

Hydranencephaly

Multiple malformations (specify)

Single umbilical artery

V
Chromosomal Anomalies

Down syndrome

Patau syndrome

Edwards syndrome

Autosomal deletion syndromes (e.g., Cri-du-chat syndrome)

Gonadal dysgenesis, ovarian dysgenesis, Turner syndrome, XO syndrome

Klinefelter syndrome

Other conditions due to sex chromosome anomalies

Additional sex chromosome (e.g., Sex chromosome mosaicism, Triple X syndrome, XXX syndrome, XYY syndrome)

Conditions due to anomaly of unspecified chromosome

VI
Other Conditions Originating in the Perinatal Period

Disorders relating to short gestation and unspecified low birthweight (e.g., prematurity)

Slow fetal growth and fetal malnutrition

Disorders relating to long gestation and high birthweight

Maternal nutritional disorders

VII
Following Psychiatric Disorders (Specify)

VIII
Environmental Influences

(continued)

Table 2.2.   (*continued*)
Psychosocial disadvantage
Sensory deprivation

IX

Other Conditions

Defects of special senses
_____
Adapted from Grossman (1983a).

GENETIC DISORDERS
AND MENTAL RETARDATION

The quarter century realized many gains in understanding chromosomal and gene disorders that undoubtedly would have astounded an earlier generation of genetic researchers. In order to appreciate such advances, especially as they relate to mental retardation, it is necessary to return to the fifties and those critical discoveries that opened the doors to expanded knowledge, theories, and speculations.

In 1953, Hsu and Pomerat devised a technique—karyotyping—that represented a major improvement over any preceding method for the examination of human chromosomes. This effort soon led to the discovery by Tijo and Levan in 1956 that the normal number of human somatic cells was 46 instead of 48 as previously presumed. Shortly thereafter, in 1959, Lejeune, Gautier, and Turpin reported that Down syndrome youngsters had 47 chromosomes. In the same year, Jacobs and Strong discovered that Klinefelter's syndrome involved an extra sex chromosome, and Ford and associates identified the XO chromosome complement in Turner's syndrome.[3] By 1963, 23 different chromosomal aberrations had been documented.[4] These included such conditions as trisomy D (Patau's syndrome, 1960), trisomy E (Edwards's syndrome, 1960), and the cri-du-chat (cat-cry) syndrome, 1963.[5]

While karyotyping enabled the examination of pronounced chromosomal defects, the development of banding techniques during the seventies permitted the close scrutiny of each chromosome, including relatively small aberrations. This, in turn, resulted in an explosion of newly recognized syndromes related to mental retardation. By 1981, Warkany and his associates were able to outline 64 autosomal defects and 8 sex chromosomal abnormalities, all of which were associated with mental retardation. Of the autosomal disorders, eight involved conditions where three similar chromosomes were found when only a pair was expected—trisomy 8, 9, 13, 14, 18, 20, 21, and 22. The remainder of autosomal disorders involved duplications or deletions of chromosomal segments. Of these conditions, trisomy 21, which is associated with Down syndrome, was by far the most prevalent.[6]

Thus, much of the historical mystery surrounding Down syndrome was finally resolved. For generations, scientists had attempted to explain the occurrence of this relatively common condition. What was known and well documented was that it tended to occur among infants of women of relatively advanced childbearing age. Given the extra chromosome, subsequent research revealed that 95% of the cases resulted from a meiotic error, while the remaining 5%, which occurred independent of parental age, was due to direct inheritance. Why meiotic errors occurred remained unresolved, but it was determined that on occasion the chromosomal anomaly could be attributed to the father.[7]

Lionel Penrose

Regrettably, in the early seventies, the field of mental retardation lost one of its most famous genetic researchers: Lionel Penrose (1899–1972). Penrose, educated at Leighton Park School, the University of Cambridge, and St. Thomas' Hospital in London was, for over 40 years, one of the world's major contributors to understanding the etiology of mental retardation, being particularly interested in children with Down syndrome. In addition to his pioneer work in dermatoglyphics, biochemistry, and cytogenetics, he designed nonverbal intelligence tests and was among the early researchers to apply statistical methods to the resolution of biological problems. His text, *The Biology of Defect*, was a mainstay in many classrooms throughout the world. A re-

Lionel Penrose

cipient of numerous honors, in the words of J. Berg of the Mental Retardation Centre in Toronto, Canada, Penrose always maintained "an unswerving interest in this relatively neglected and often unfashionable segment of human disability. In no small measure are the advances in knowledge and the more dignified status appertaining to this area, in our time, due to him."[8]

X-Linked Disorders

Though it had been recognized for years that more males than females were judged to be mentally retarded, most researchers, including Penrose, did not believe this variance was due to any sex-related genetic factor. Research proved them wrong; and, by 1983, Turner could estimate that sex-linked gene defects probably accounted for approximately 25% of intellectual problems among males and 10% of learning problems among females.[9]

Usually defects of this nature were not found to involve any obvious chromosomal anomalies. This was not true, however, as concerns a condition discovered among males during the late sixties and early seventies. The peculiar characteristic—a visible fragile site on the end of the long arm of the X chromo-

some, identified as a "marker" rather than a defect—was labeled the fragile X syndrome.

Affected males were characterized as having rather large foreheads, ears, and jaws, and following the onset of puberty, enlarged testicles (macro-orchidism). Behaviorally, affected males were often hyperactive, autistic, and frequently engaged in hand biting. Though the associated mental retardation varied from profound to mild degrees of severity, most males were considered to be within the moderate range.[10]

Discovery of the fragile X syndrome confirmed an earlier suspicion. In 1943, Martin and Bell reported the first documented X-linked kindred study involving mental retardation. They observed that a number of males in a particular family were mentally retarded while the mother and daughters were not, but the mother had mentally retarded brothers and the daughters ultimately gave birth to several mentally retarded sons.[11] From this evidence, Martin and Bell concluded there must be an X-linked relationship. During the sixties, the Canadian pediatric neurologist, Henry Dunn, also studied such a family and found 20 X-linked males living in western Canada; his results were replicated by John Opitz who found five X-linked kindreds in Wisconsin.[12]

Person with fragile X syndrome

At that time, it was not possible to determine any peculiar chromosomal anomaly; however, in 1969, Lubs, without the benefit of banding techniques, identified the fragile site. Other researchers, however, could not consistently confirm his findings. Finally, the mystery was clarified—quite by accident. The fragile X site became readily visible when an improper culture mix was used, one low in folic acid. With that information, Sutherland provided a formula that consistently revealed the fragile phenomenon.[13] By 1985, numerous researchers held that the fragile X syndrome was second only to Down syndrome in terms of chromosomal differences associated with mental retardation, even though the relationship was not understood.[14]

Although reported as early as 1965 by Andreas Rett, a lesser-known similar chromosomal anomaly may affect females. In Rett syndrome, a suspected fragile site on the X chromosome may result in severe mental retardation. Not apparent at birth, the effects have their appearance between 7 and 12 months of age, when the infant begins to regress. Within 18 months, the brain begins to atrophy and the child withdraws to a form of autism in which she quits talking and appears to be blind and deaf. Nervous hand wringing, hypersalivation, teeth grinding, atrophy of the lower extremities, severe scoliosis, shunting of growth, and acquired microcephaly were common. Though only 100 cases were reported in the United States by the end of 1984, Rett contended that this chromosomal anomaly could account for as high as 20% of severely or profoundly mentally retarded or autistic girls.[15]

The previously mentioned chromosomal disorders, with the probable exception of fragile X, were quantitative in nature; that is, there were either too many chromosomes or there was too much or too little of a given chromosome. In addition, there were many disorders associated with genes of which tens of thousands are located on each chromosome. Often these involve a qualitative, rather than a quantitative difference, and, despite their numerousness, one small defect can be most severe

Young girl with Rett syndrome

in terms of limiting intellectual or physical abilities.

Like chromosomal anomalies, most clinical conditions associated with genetic metabolic disorders and mental retardation were recognized by 1960. Among the new ones reported were homocystinuria in 1962, and the Lesch-Nyhan syndrome in 1964.[16] The latter, somewhat unusual syndrome involved both mental retardation and a most difficult-to-control self-mutilating behavior. Such conditions, however, represent rare reproductive events, as illustrated by the tabulation prepared by Hugo Moser, Director of the John F. Kennedy Institute for Handicapped Children, in 1982 (see Table 2.3).[17]

Molecular Genetics

While the previously discussed gains in understanding were both remarkable and significant, with the few exceptions to be discussed, they did not yield direct measures of prevention or treatment. Yet, many believed that this situation would change in the near future as the result of the exciting discoveries and movements in those areas related to molecular genetics. Once again, in order to appreciate such advances and trends, it is necessary to return to the fifties.

First, there was the Nobel Prize-winning

Table 2.3. Clinical conditions associated with genetic metabolic disorders and mental retardation

Condition	Frequency
Congenital hypothyroidism	1:3,500
Phenylketonuria	1:11,000
Sanfilippo syndrome (MPS III; Netherlands)	1:24,000
Metachromatic leukodystrophy (Sweden)	1:40,000
Fabry's disease	1:40,000
Gaucher disease (Ashkenazi Jews)	1:2,500
Tay-Sachs disease	
Ashkenazi Jews	1:5,600
General population	1:500,000
Arginosuccinicaciduria	1:60,000
Hunter syndrome (MPS II)	
Ashkenazi Jews	1:67,500
British Columbia	1:150,000
Galactosemia	1:75,000
Hurler syndrome (MPS I)	1:100,000
Maple syrup urine disease	1:120,000
Homocystinuria	
Ireland	1:40,000
General population	1:200,000

From Moser, H. (1982). Mental retardation due to genetically determined metabolic and endocrine disorders. In I. Jakob (Ed.), *Mental retardation* (p. 9). New York: Karger; reprinted by permission.

achievement of James Watson and Francis Crick of Cambridge University, which involved the development of a model of the molecular structure and manner of replication of deoxyribonucleic acid (DNA) in 1953. In 1956, Kornberg discovered the pathway leading to the biosynthesis of DNA, and Grunberg-Manago and Ochoa synthesized a number of simplified models of ribonucleic acid (RNA) that would serve to transport and transfer the DNA message.[18] The combination of these findings gave birth to an entirely new era for those researchers dedicated to the far-reaching and extremely complicated study of biogenetics. In the most elementary of terms, it became recognized that heredity involves a complex biochemical process and that the gene is a bundle of DNA molecules that possess and transmit the biochemical code that controls the structure of enzymes, which are vital to life—they control, or regulate, the metabolism and structure of the cell.[19] The

absence or inactivity of a single enzyme, as in those cases involving gene disorders, may result in severe mental retardation.

During the seventies and early eighties, biogenetics evolved into a major scientific and commercial concern, with increasingly larger budgets and resources devoted to its study. Not surprisingly, this produced some significant gains in a relatively short period of time—gains that held future promise of preventing or at least modifying some forms of mental retardation. By the mid-seventies, the genetic code was fairly well understood, and scientists soon discovered recombinant DNA, which permitted the splicing of one type of cell to another. This technique, in turn, opened the doors not only to the specific study of genes and their location but also to the entire field of genetic engineering, which, in all probability, will eventually affect nearly every aspect of human life, positively or negatively.

By the mid-eighties, scientists could deter-

mine both the exact sequence of the four nu-
cleotides (adenine, cytosine, quanine, and
thynine) and the precise chromosomal sites of
approximately 730 genes, including those giving rise to Huntington's chorea, phenylketonuria, and the Lesch-Nyhan syndrome.[20] Of
equal import, a spliced gene could be re-
produced through the use of a bacterial medium. Thus, as of late 1984, scientists could
isolate, study, and reproduce short segments
of DNA. What they could not do was reinsert
the spliced gene into the human system to correct or modify a given disorder. While some
felt the genetic cure for phenylketonuria and
the Lesch-Nyhan syndrome was just around
the corner, others were less sure:

> Certain inherent difficulties exist when consider-
> ing gene therapy as a tool to prevent disease. For
> example, there is a need to establish a prenatal
> diagnosis in the embryonic phase of pregnancy.
> Quite possibly, genetic cures may have to wait
> for technological refinements that allow the sam-
> pling of a few or even single embryonic cells.
> Only then, with diagnoses made just prior to or
> immediately after implantation, will active inter-
> vention with "gene therapy" provide an oppor-
> tunity for the successful prevention of mental
> retardation due to genetic causes. In addition,
> important questions about gene therapy still have
> to be answered. Will the added gene function? or
> will it be able to act only in concert with other
> genes not provided? Will a higher frequency of
> birth defects or malignancy be associated with
> such manipulations? With what certainty and
> precision will individual genes be tailored so that
> not only their structure but also their function is
> retained?[21]

Thus, while gene therapy for humans appeared to hold great promise, it was neither a
reality by 1985 nor without its potential hazards. Further, most of the advances in knowledge were related to those defects that account
for only 10%–15% of mental retardation,
which, in most instances, involve the more
severely affected. As concerns mild mental
retardation, biogenetics had little to offer.
This fact, however, in no way influenced the
historical heredity-environment controversy,
which remained a frequent topic of debate,
often accompanied by hostility and recrimina-
tion.

HEREDITY, POVERTY, AND CULTURE

In 1969, at the very time when the country
was re-examining its racial policies and practices and attempting to forge a new spirit of
oneness and equality, Arthur Jensen published
his 123-page controversial article, "How
much can we boost IQ and scholastic achievement?" in the prestigious *Harvard Educational Review*. His intent was to review all
possible factors that might account for the disappointing results of Head Start and similar
programs for culturally deprived/low-income
youngsters as they related to increments in
measured intelligence.[22] In doing so, he examined the nature and inheritance of intelligence, environmental influences, the effectiveness of intensive educational intervention,
and the "learning quotient" versus the intelligence quotient. As part of his deliberations,
he speculated that 80% of intelligence was in-
herited, 20% a consequence of environmental
experience, and that black youngsters tended
to score approximately one standard deviation
below white children on tests of intelligence.
Also:

> . . . ordinary IQ tests are not seen as being "un-
> fair" in the sense of yielding inaccurate or inval-
> id measures for the many disadvantaged children
> who obtain low scores. If they are unfair, it is
> because they tap only one part of the total spec-
> trum of mental abilities and do not reveal that
> aspect of mental ability which may be the disad-
> vantaged child's strongest point—the ability for
> associative learning.[23]

And:

> The evidence so far suggests the tentative con-
> clusion that the pay-off of preschool and com-
> pensatory programs in terms of IQ gains is
> small. Greater gains are possible in scholastic
> performance when instructional techniques are
> intensive and highly focused, as in the Bereiter-
> Engelmann program. Educators would probably
> do better to concern themselves with teaching
> basic skills directly than with attempting to boost
> overall cognitive development. By the same
> token, they should deemphasize IQ tests as a
> means of assessing gains, and use mainly direct
> tests of the skills the instructional program is
> intended to inculcate. The techniques for raising
> intelligence per se . . . probably lie more in the

province of the biological sciences than in psychology and education.[24]

Finally,

> If diversity of mental abilities, as of most other human characteristics, is a basic fact of nature, as the evidence indicates, and if the ideal of universal education is to be successfully pursued, it seems a reasonable conclusion that schools and society must provide a range and diversity of educational methods, programs, and goals, and of occupational opportunities, just as wide as the range of human abilities. Accordingly, the ideal of equality of educational opportunity should not be interpreted as uniformity of facilities, instructional techniques, and educational aims for all children. Diversity rather than uniformity of approaches and aims would seem to be the key to making education rewarding for children of different patterns of ability. The reality of individual differences thus need not mean educational rewards for some children and frustration and defeat for others.[25]

Jensen's conclusions were interpreted by many to mean that black children were innately and impermeably intellectually inferior to white youngsters and should have a less cognitively oriented curriculum. His study received widespread publicity under such sensational headlines as "IQ: God-Given or Man-Made?," "Born Dumb?," and "Can Negroes Learn the Way Whites Do?," and also found its way into the *Congressional Record*.[26]

Public and professional response ranged from support to rage and denial, with many in both camps contending the report simply should not have been published at all. William Shockley, Nobel Prize co-winner for inventing the transistor, not only supported Jensen's 80:20 genetic-environmental ratio, but also proposed a voluntary sterilization program. In brief, he wrote:

> The thought-blockers . . . that reject the relevance of genetics to social problems arise, I propose, because the theory that intelligence is largely determined by the genes and that races may differ in distribution of mental capacity offends equalitarian-environmentalism. . . . The preponderance of the world's intellectual community resist the fact that nature can be cruel to the newborn baby. Babies too often get an unfair

shake from a badly loaded parental genetic dice cup. At the acme of unfairness are features of racial difference that my own research inescapably leads me to conclude exist: Nature has color-coded groups of individuals so that statistically reliable predictions of their adaptability to intellectually rewarding and effective lives can easily be made and profitably be used by the pragmatic man in the street.

> If, as many thinking citizens fear, our welfare programs are unwittingly, but with the noblest of intentions, selectively down-breeding the poor of our slums by encouraging their least foresighted to be most prolific, the consequences will be tragic for both blacks and whites—but proportionately so much worse for our black minority that, as I have said, the consequence may be a form of genetic enslavement that will provoke extremes of racism with agony for all citizens.

> My position is that humanity has an obligation to use its intelligence to diagnose and to predict in order to prevent agonies that lack of foresight can all too easily create.[27]

He further proposed, as a *"thinking exercise,"* a voluntary sterilization bonus plan:

> Bonuses would be offered for sterilization. Payers of income tax would get nothing. Bonuses for all others, regardless of sex, race. or welfare status, would depend on best scientific estimates of hereditary factors in disadvantages such as diabetes, epilepsy, heroin addiction, arthritis, etc. At a bonus rate of $1,000 for each point below 100 I.Q., $30,000 put in trust for a 70 I.Q. moron potentially capable of producing 20 children might return $250,000 to taxpayers in reduced costs of mental retardation care. Ten percent of the bonus in spot cash might put our national talent for entrepreneurship into action.[28]

While Jensen and Shockley argued with vigor and unction that genetic factors were primarily responsible for mild levels of mental retardation, others—most others—argued with equal vigor and unction that mild retardation, in most cases, was attributable to cultural deprivation or disadvantage. These two terms, both of which were quite popular during the sixties, basically referred to "children with a particular set of educationally associated problems arising from and residing extensively within the culture of the poor."[29] There were a large number of such children in the United States, including at least one in three youngsters living in cities, migrant children, the rural poor, and Indian youth.[30] Demographic researchers continued to reveal that large numbers of educable mentally retarded children in public school classes were from families of low intelligence, poor schooling, and/or inferior economic status.[31] Many of these families were representative of minority groups, and most were poor: in 1968, 59% of nonwhite children lived in poverty as compared to 15% of white children.[32]

Poverty was a major concern to John F. Kennedy and was a crusade to Lyndon Johnson. Subsequently, the sixties saw a renewed interest in and a vigorous attack on poverty and related conditions that had the potential to affect adversely a child's development and intellectual functioning. The results of such efforts soon demonstrated that the entire questions of poverty and poverty-related issues were many, complex, and often interactive.

From the physical standpoint alone, there were many factors that could significantly reduce the intellectual potential of young children. In their scholarly review of the literature, Herbert Birch and Joan Dye Gussow documented a long series of interconnected health problems associated with mental retardation and other developmental disabilities. Major reproductive complications were all too common among low-income women, including maternal malnutrition, absence of adequate medical attention, frequent infections, and a pregnancy pattern that the authors described as "too young, too old, and too often."[33] In 1962, the President's Panel on Mental Retardation reported that the incidence of premature birth was almost three times as great among low-income mothers as compared with other groups.[34]

The desperate health needs of disadvantaged children were clearly documented in many studies; for example, one of the major programs initiated by the federal government to combat poverty was Head Start, whose purpose was to provide "children from what we have termed 'disadvantaged' homes with a cultural model which will counteract their disorganized home life and the model of dependency which would otherwise be their social inheritance."[35] Governmental officials predicted that when the first summer school Head Start program was to be initiated in 1965, of 560,000 participating children, 110,000 would be found in need of glasses, 50,000 would be found to be partially deaf, 75,000 would need basic immunizations, and 25,000 would be suffering from severe malnutrition. In a follow-up report to President Johnson, dated August 31, 1965, Sargent Shriver reported that the predictions proved to be remarkably accurate.[36] Additional experience yielded similar results. In a 5-year study of a small number of deprived children, Kugel and Parsons in 1967 found that the nutrients in food purchases by low-income families provided only 90% of the daily needed calories, 88% of calcium, and 84% of iron.[37] A few years later, a frustrated and somewhat angry Arnold B. Schaefer, physician with the U.S. Department of Health, Education, and Welfare, reported that field studies conducted in three southern states found more than 72% of 4- and 5-year-olds were below the normal growth curve, reflecting inadequate nutrition. Also, more than 92% of the children in one preschool Head Start program had vitamin A levels lower than those among children already blinded by the deficiency. "It is disgusting," he said, "in that this deficiency could be prevented at the cost of one candy bar per child per year."[38] Even the children's basic homes often posed serious health hazards, as is discussed later.

In addition to physical factors, there were many sociopsychological influences capable of producing reduced intellectual functioning. These included such diverse areas as the absence of the "hidden curriculum"; varied learning characteristics; different language factors; and a value system that influenced intellectual functioning and educational achievement within the traditional school setting.

As concerns the hidden curriculum, Radin wrote:

Mothers in middle-class families usually try to help a child solve a new problem by first explaining the entire problem and the goals to be achieved. . . . Mothers of low socio-economic status tend merely to give the children specific directions without any explanation. Again, there is a reliance on specific rules rather than principles. . . . My own research has indicated that mothers in families of low socio-economic status often do not foster the development of internal controls in their preschool children. They try to protect their children from the dangers they see in the external world and to suppress the dangers they feel are arising from within the child, such as aggressiveness and sexuality; but they do not prepare their children to cope with problems. For example, they set down specific rules for behavior, but do not explain the reasons for the rules. The child is taught to follow the orders of recognized authority not to make judgments for himself.[39]

Researchers studying the learning characteristics of disadvantaged children reported that such youngsters were often relatively slow at cognitive tasks, but not stupid; appeared to learn through physical, concrete approaches; seemed anti-intellectual, being programmatic rather than theoretically oriented; were deficient in auditory attention and interpretation skills; and read ineffectually.[40] Metfessel found disadvantaged children, especially those from various minority groups, had substantially different language characteristics that involved a distinctly different vocabulary and the use of fewer words and immature sentences to express themselves. They also tended to learn less from what they heard than did middle-class children. He also noted that such students tended to rely on inductive rather than deductive reasoning; were symbolically deprived; had poor attention spans; and, as noted previously, relied on concrete rather than abstract or insightful experiences.[41]

Kvaraceus and Miller's research results and predictions concerning changing value systems during the late fifties received confirmation and support during the sixties. These researchers distinguished between middle and lower class by referring to systems of behavior reflective of value sets. Middle-class values were defined as those consistent with "Christian-Protestant" teachings, a strong interest in education, ambition, and looking toward the future. Contrary to such values were those as-

sociated with the lower class, which tended to be concerned with: 1) getting into or out of trouble; 2) need for immediate gratification; 3) "toughness" or the physical rather than mental abilities and achievement; 4) excitement; 5) luck and fate, as opposed to planning and foresight; 6) being "macho"—a con artist is a hero; educators are effeminate; and 7) autonomy, as opposed to the need for equalized, cooperative group status.[42] These values, which became increasingly more prevalent throughout the sixties, were not conducive to learning or development, at least within the normal educational framework of the time.

In addition to such factors, it was well recognized by various developmental theorists, as exemplified by Piaget, that a child's interaction with his environment and a variety of experiences were critical to the development of intelligence. In marked contrast to this need, research demonstrated that it was not uncommon for some low-income children never to leave the block in which they lived.[43] As eventually demonstrated, many individuals living in poverty circumstances were not necessarily culturally "disadvantaged" or "deprived"; rather, they were culturally "different": They had a viable culture; a well-developed language; and definitive traditions, customs, and mores. Such differences, however, were not always compatible with formal educational expectancies.

Taking into consideration all the various possible ramifications of poverty noted, Herbert Birch and Joan Gussow developed a graphic schema for what they called the cycle of poverty—a cycle not easily broken (see Figure 2.1).

Herbert Birch

Herbert Birch (1918–1973), who contributed much both to the field of mental retardation and to the health and well-being of all children, died suddenly and unexpectedly at the zenith of his career. Holding a doctorate first in psychology and later in medicine, his knowledge was "encyclopedic, his intellect prodigious, his productivity unmatched. . . Few," eulogized Leon Eisenberg, "if any,

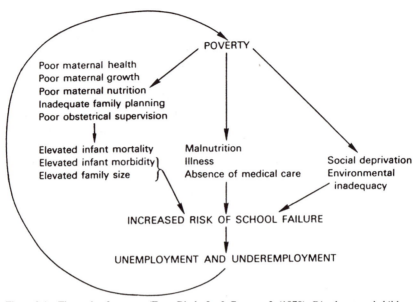

Figure 2.1   The cycle of poverty. (From Birch, J., & Gussow, J. (1970). *Disadvantaged children: Health, nutrition, and school failure* (p. 268). New York: Grune & Stratton; reprinted by permission.)

have ever so mastered the skills of epidemiology, comparative biopsychology, neurobiology, nutrition, obstetrics, pediatrics, and cognitive psychology. He fused them into weapons for social betterment."[44] At the time of his death, Birch was the principal scientist at the Rose F. Kennedy Center for Research in Mental Retardation and Human Development of the Albert Einstein College of Medicine in New York. Like Penrose, he was a humanitarian supreme, seeking through research and knowledge a better world for all humans, regardless of their status or endowments.

Summary

In the final analysis, the quarter century's experiences clearly demonstrated that the varied dynamics associated with poverty and intelligence remained poorly understood, and that it was impossible to examine scientifically all potential influences and their interacting effects in terms of a person's genotype. Thus, the notion that genetic factors play a predominant role in determining mild levels of mental retardation could be neither completely accepted nor rejected. Nevertheless, most authorities became increasingly hesitant to pre-

scribe a genetic underpinning to racial, sexual, or socioeconomic differences as they related to intellectual performance.

At the same time, there was little question that the effects of poverty—be they described

Herbert Birch

in terms of increased physical risks, inadequate learning opportunities, and/or changing value systems—were often deleterious to child development. This understanding gave rise to increasing frustration among persons proposing, implementing, or funding programs aimed at ending poverty, or at least reducing its negative impact.

Beginning in the early sixties, the federal government launched many programs and authorized massive spending to combat poverty at all levels and on all fronts. Some of the earliest legislation produced the Vocational Education Act of 1963, the Economic Opportunity Act of 1964, and the Elementary and Secondary Education Act of 1965. A few years later, through a series of amendments, Social Security provisions were expanded substantially through Medicaid and Medicare provisions. By 1982, the United States was spending approximately $125 billion a year on such programs; yet, the poverty rate remained at approximately 12%, and many authorities and taxpayers in general were asking why poverty programs appeared to be accomplishing so little. Proposed solutions were often diametrically opposed. Michael Harrington, whose earlier book, *The Other Americans,* influenced Kennedy's thinking, in 1984 called for full employment and redistribution of the wealth.[45] In opposition, and during the same year, C. Murray argued that government programs made the entire situation worse, creating an atmosphere of welfare dependency, family deterioration, and the trivialization of individual efforts.[46] A third opinion, that of Robert Samuelson, held that if poverty programs had not failed, they certainly had reached a point of stalemate, and the only answer was to ensure economic growth accompanied by greater nongovernmental incentives.[47]

Yet, much was accomplished, and despite taxpayer agitation so evident during the early eighties, many people—young and old alike—benefited in numerous ways. But, in terms of children, the situation was deteriorating rapidly. In the early sixties, tens of thousands of elderly citizens were demeaningly poor, but

a substantially enriched Social Security program elevated their living circumstances to a level of decency and respectability. Regrettably, their places were being filled by an increasing number of single parents, usually women, giving rise to the "feminization of poverty." The total number of single parents living in impoverished circumstances increased from 25% in 1960 to 50% in 1983.[48] The potential hazards for their offspring were many.

Another group that entered the poverty picture was composed of several hundred thousand mentally ill and mentally retarded persons—society's "unwanted incompetents"—who, through the process of deinstitutionalizing mental hospitals, "found themselves living in abject poverty, meaninglessly roaming the streets of our major cities."[49] In summary, while science had yet to clarify the respective roles of heredity and experience, poverty was always a threat to intellectual functioning.

PEOPLE AND THEIR ENVIRONMENT

Albert Schweitzer, servant of God, medicine, and music, once wrote, "Man can hardly even recognize the devils of his own creation . . . [he] has lost the capacity to foresee and to forestall. He will end by destroying the earth."[50] So quoted Rachel Carson, noted biologist and author, in her momentous and often disturbing book, *Silent Spring,* published in 1962. Her text, which became an immediate international best-seller, detailed the growing disastrous consequences of man's attempt to control his environment and his productivity through the use of chemical substances. Ten years later, Barry Commoner—biologist, ecologist, and educator—outlined four laws of ecology: "(1) everything is connected to everything else, (2) everything must go somewhere—matter is indestructible, (3) nature knows best, and (4) there is no such thing as a free lunch; in other words, every gain is won at some cost."[51] During the intervening years, people indeed looked about and found that the air they breathed, the food they ate, the water they drank, and the very land upon which they built their homes was often polluted and contaminated with pesticides, industrial waste, and nuclear disposal, all of which posed not only a marked threat to the quality of their environment but to their basic health and genetic heritage as well.

The direct, deadly effects of nuclear power upon life, limb, and intelligence were well documented following the dropping of two atomic bombs on Hiroshima and Nagasaki during World War II in August, 1945. The consequences of nuclear fallout, however, remained relatively undemonstrated until the late sixties when scholars began to study the intellectual performance of adolescents probably exposed to nuclear fallout years before. To illustrate, Ernest Sternglass, professor of radiological physics, and educational psychologist Steven Bell reported on the Scholastic Aptitude Test performances of adolescents who, when younger, lived in areas subject to high atmosphere or underground atomic tests. Their results showed that adolescents living in the Far West close to the Nevada, Pacific, and Siberian test sites had consistently lower aptitude scores than did students in the Midwest or East. Also, scores varied according to the years in which the tests were conducted. The researchers suggested the data substantiated their hypothesis that "radioactive iodine-131, in the milk of those exposed *in utero* or during early infancy strongly supports an ecological or medical basis for a general decline in average intellectual ability of those born during the 1950s and the early 1960s."[52]

The potential hazards of nuclear energy, however, were overshadowed by the growing dangers associated with society's increasing reliance on chemicals. "Modern living through chemistry" was not only an advertising slogan but a reality of contemporary life. The benefits were many but so were the hazards, and the list of known or suspected teratogenic agents capable of causing serious birth defects, including mental retardation, grew each year. By 1983, the list of chemicals and chemical processes with adverse reproductive effects was indeed long:

Aminopterin
Anesthetic gases
Busulfan
Carbon disulfide
DDT
1,2-Dibromo-3-chloropropane (DBCP)
Diethylstilbestrol (DES)
Diphenylhydantoin
Ethylene dibromide
Hexachlorobenzene (HCB)
Kepone
Laboratory reagents
Lead and other smelter emissions
Methotrexate
Methylmercury
Occupational exposure to pesticides
Polychlorinated biphenyls (PCBs)
Vinyl chloride
Warfarin[53]

To compound the problem, the number of women of childbearing age entering the work force, often exposing themselves to chemical hazards, increased exponentially beginning in the sixties. In 1965, 26.1 million women worked outside the house; by 1980, over 45 million women were in the work force, and it was projected that another 12.5 million would be added by 1990.[54] Nor did any industry appear to be free from potential danger. Even persons working in high-tech fields were confronted daily with chemical exposure that could result in reproductive problems, including such simple items as circuit solders that contain lead, cadmium, and zinc.[55]

Some of the substances listed attack the fetus in a most circuitous way. Methylmercury was an outstanding example of this phemonenon. Mercury, which was used in a wide variety of products such as pesticides, thermostats, plastics, paper, clothing, camera film, explosives, batteries, and cardiac pacemakers, was long recognized for its deleterious effects on intellectual functioning. Lewis Carroll's famous character, the Mad Hatter of *Alice in Wonderland,* was based on fact rather than fancy. In Carroll's day, mercury was an important ingredient in treating pelts to be used for hats, and exposed hatmakers soon became afflicted with incoherent speech and various forms of spasticity. The polluting effects of mercury byproducts and mercury's amalgamation with different types of metals was brought to the attention of the world following the tragic episode involving the disposal practices of chemical plants in Minamata, Japan. The factories discharged lethal methylmercury into the city's bay, which was then transferred through the natural food chain from fish to mother to fetus. The results were disastrous, not only in terms of death but in terms of severe mental retardation, blindness, and spasticity among newborn infants. Even when the pregnant mother did not personally suffer from eating the contaminated fish, the methylmercury passed into her bloodstream, and worked its way through the placenta to wreak havoc and destruction on the unborn child.[56]

Another metal that received considerable attention not only in the United States but throughout the world was lead. Known and used by man since at least 3,000 B.C., lead was found in innumerable metal products, batteries, pigments, gasolines, and in combination with a wide range of other chemical compounds. In 1960 alone, over 1 million tons of lead were used in the United States.[57] During the sixties, the neurologically damaging qualities of lead poisoning among young children were fully recognized. Accessibility to lead-based items capable of producing neurological harm was particularly prevalent in poverty areas where lead was often discovered in eroded water pipes, cheap pottery glazing, and, especially, household paint.[58] One report estimated that at least 25% of children living in deteriorated housing absorbed potentially dangerous quantities of lead and that 5% had clinical symptoms of lead intoxication.[59] Another report indicated that as many as a quarter million children in the United States may have been victims of lead poisoning by 1969, and as many as 25% suffered brain damage.[60] In 1971, the Surgeon General of the U.S. Public Health Service gave screening for lead intoxication among children a high priority, and lead was banned from use in common house-

hold paints, varnishes, and other finishes. Yet, even when lead paint was scraped from older houses, years of accumulation persisted as residual dust and the level of risk, though not nearly as high as before, still remained.[61] Though by no means conclusive as to etiological relationship, Marlowe and colleagues reported in 1983 that mentally retarded and borderline public school students from the Upper Cumberland Region of Tennessee had higher blood levels of lead and cadmium than did their normal peers.[62]

The federal government launched a campaign to reduce as much as possible the lead content in gasoline. Even though the exact effects of atmospheric lead pollution on intellectual functioning were not quantified, few knowledgeable persons doubted that such damage did exist and the potential hazard was again great.

Not all dangerous products were the result of nuclear or industrial waste; many were found in relatively small amounts in everyday items. Ethylene dibromide (EDB), a known chemical substance capable of producing congenital defects and possible brain injury, was a common compound used in many food items such as pancake mixes, breads, muffin mixes, and breakfast cereals. In 1984, all such products were removed from stores and the future use of EDB was banned.

To aggravate an already difficult problem, researchers discovered that many chemical compounds, though no longer produced or used, had lingering and often deleterious effects. Polychlorinated biphenyls (PCBs), one of the most dangerous pesticides ever developed, is an outstanding example. Though the manufacturing of PCBs was halted in 1979, a study reported in 1984 demonstrated that women consuming no more than 2 or 3 meals of Lake Michigan fish per month had an increased risk of premature births and youngsters with smaller than normal head circumferences.[63]

Prematurity or low birth weight, regardless of cause, was a constant concern to all interested in healthy babies. As discovered in a national collaborative study during the late fifties and early sixties, "There is an inverse relationship between birth weight and neurological defects. The lower the birth weight the greater the proportion of children with neurological abnormalities. Children below 2,500 grams show a three-fold increase in neurological abnormalities (5 percent) when compared to children weighing in excess of 2,500 grams (1.5 percent). In surviving very small prematures (below 1,000 grams), a 25–30 percent abnormality rate is observed. Between 1,000 and 2,000 grams, still 10 percent of the prematures are neurologically abnormal whereas in prematures weighing 2,000 to 2,500 grams, about 4.5 percent revealed these abnormal findings.''[64] Premature youngsters are particularly susceptible to a wide range of troubling conditions including hypoxia, intracranial hemorrhage, cerebral palsy, and lethal malformations. The soft bones of the skull are less able to protect the immature brain from compression of the head that occurs during labor and delivery, and the entire respiratory system is often seriously deficient.

Of all chemical substances suspected to cause birth defects, none was more thoroughly examined or contested than the dioxin ''Agent Orange'' used as a defoliant compound during the Vietnam War. From 1962 to 1971, the U.S. Air Force dropped about 19 million gallons of different herbicides in South Vietnam, most containing TCDD, a dioxin that is one of the most toxic substances known to man. In 1971, the use of dioxin was discontinued following reports of increased miscarriages among Vietnamese women. American veterans, however, claimed that exposure to, and in many cases being doused with, the herbicide resulted in an increased incidence of cancer, deformed children, stillbirths, miscarriages, loss of sex drive, low sperm counts, and changes in personality.[65]

While some, but not all, animal studies found a greater frequency of birth defects, and diseases of the nervous system, liver, kidney, and bladder following exposure, results among human victims were less convincing.[66] The single largest study, which was conducted by the Air Force, examined 1,269 pilots and crew members who sprayed the herbicide and were, in the judgment of the researchers, far more exposed to the substance than the thousands of ground troops who may have been sprayed. The researchers concluded, ''The study has disclosed numerous medical findings, mostly of a minor or undetermined nature, that require detailed followup. In full context, the baseline study results should be viewed as reassuring . . . at this time.''[67] These results were consistent with those previously reported involving a study of 26 dioxin-contaminated sites in the state of Missouri: only minor defects were found. Despite such results, veterans, with the support of many within and without the scientific community, remained unconvinced.[68]

Chemical hazards were not limited only to those associated with commercial or industrial activity. Many therapeutic medications were found to be equally dangerous when introduced inappropriately or taken during pregnancy. The enormous polypharmacy of contemporary society posed many hazards, and the list of potentially dangerous maternal medications developed over the quarter century was long and became longer every year:

Amethopterin
Aminopterin
Antihistamines
Bendectin
Busulfan
Chlorambucil
Cortisone
Lithium carbonate
Meprobamate
Novobiocin
Phenobarbital (excessive amounts)
Phenothiazines
Prednisone
Propylthiouracil
Salicylates (large amounts)
Sulfonamides
Sulfonylurea derivatives[69]

By the eighties, most physicians were extremely cautious in prescribing medications during or even shortly before a planned pregnancy since their effects were uncertain. As explained by Rosen and Schimmel, pediatricians with the College of Physicians and Surgeons of Columbia University in 1983, ''Many physiologic changes occur during pregnancy, including changes in total fluid volume and blood flow, renal function, and in hepatobiliary structure and function. All of these changes modify drug distribution, metabolism, and elimination, yet very little is known about drug kinetics during pregnancy."[70] Similarly, fetal drug distribution "depends on several factors, including fetal circulation, permeability of specific membranes, selective tissue uptake, protein binding, and fetal drug metabolism."[71] They concluded that although "drug usage in pregnancy is common, knowledge of perinatal clinical pharmacology is limited. Maternal drug usage affects not only the mother but fetus and neonate."[72] In the final analysis, Rosen and Schimmel supported the judgment rendered in the early sixties by Joseph Rossi of Yale University that "the pregnant mother preferably should receive no drugs at all during her pregnancy and if vitally necessary only those that have been used for many years without ill effects should be given."[73]

Once again, as with other chemical families discussed, relatively minor medications seemingly unrelated to any possible birth defect were found to be teratogenic. Accutane, an acne treatment, was discovered to trigger abortions and generate birth defects. Subsequently, on March 29, 1984, the U.S. Food and Drug Administration warned blood banks not to accept blood donations from Accutane users and called for pregnancy tests to be administered to women 2 weeks before using the substance.[74]

From the preceding precursory review of the many dangers generated or realized over the quarter century, there seemed little question that an evolving society and all its needs were creating an increasingly difficult environment in which to reproduce and rear healthy children. Every day, and regardless of intent, new substances were created, consumed, or absorbed that could adversely affect the unborn child, mentally and physically.

PEOPLE AND THEIR HABITS

In addition to the many elements over which individuals had little or no control, which in-

cluded most of the items previously discussed, people were often victims of their own habits. Unfortunately, the years proved that some activities could be deleterious to the health and well-being of the child-bearing mother and her infant. This was particularly true as concerns sexual relations that could lead to venereal disease, drug usage, alcohol, and smoking.

Venereal Diseases

During the forties and fifties, venereal disease was considered by many to be an experience of the past. Relatively strict sexual mores accompanied by the then-effectiveness of penicillin and other "miracle" drugs had nearly eliminated the problem of syphilis in the United States; however, the markedly liberalized attitudes towards sexual conduct introduced during the sixties saw a concomitant and dramatic rise in the reported cases of gonorrhea and syphilis. In the words of Norman Woody and his medical colleagues, writing in 1964, "A laid ghost walks."[75] This was in response to their finding that after 6 years and over 10,000 live births annually, no signs of congenital syphilis were evident in their hospital until 1963 when 7 newborns were so infected. The trend continued: the U.S. Centers for Disease Control, for example, stated that during 1981, over 1 million cases of gonorrhea and 33,000 cases of syphilis were reported. The latter disease was increasing at a rate of 10% a year.[76] The damage caused by such diseases to the fetus or newborn was well recognized before 1960.

In addition to the age-old problems of syphilis and gonorrhea, the sixties, seventies, and eighties saw a dramatic rise in a venereal disease which, though existing from the dawn of man, had never previously plagued society in general: herpes simplex, type II. An infected mother was found to have an increased probability of having a mentally affected newborn if during the vaginal birth process she underwent an infectious attack. It was estimated that by the eighties, as many as 500,000 new cases of herpes type II infections would occur annually.[77] To prevent mental retardation, a cesarean birth process was initiated when there was reason to suspect the mother had an active infection and when the child was believed to be at increased risk. Infants born with the infection were amenable to treatment with antiviral agents that became available during the late seventies. Yet, while this treatment resulted in a significant drop in the mortality rate from 70% to 38%, half the surviving youngsters remained seriously disabled.[78]

Although a simple blood test could determine if a women had been infected, all too often women were totally unaware of their condition. To compound the problem, the disease could lie dormant for years.[79]

In addition to contracting the infection during the birth process, some infants were known to have acquired the infection shortly after birth, perhaps through contact with cold sores; 20% of facial infections were traceable to herpes type II virus rather than the more common herpes type I. In 1982, the Food and Drug Administration approved a genital herpes drug that provided some relief of symptoms but offered no cure.[80]

Mind-Altering Drugs

Throughout the course of history, persons have used mind-altering drugs for a host of reasons. Rarely, however, were drugs or a drug-related culture accepted and enthusiasticly supported by so many people than in the sixties, which started a trend that evolved into massive drug abuse by millions of people—young and old, rich and poor. The great alienation movement among the young during that decade combined with the naivete of users and the foolishness of some university professors created a cycle of drug consumption that had not completed its course by 1985. For some, drugs were used to relieve problems and anxieties; for others, it provided an escape; for a few, such as Timothy Leary, psychologist and then-lecturer with Harvard University, "these wondrous plants and drugs could free man's consciousness and bring about a new conception of man, his psychology and philosophy."[81] One of the earliest and certainly most dangerous substances to be used was LSD (lysergic acid diethylamide), touted by Leary as a "sacramental drug" for

the new religious experience.[82] LSD had tremendously varying effects: some consumers experienced beautiful visions while others— too many others—found that the "love ecstasy potion" resulted only in sheer terror, an effect that could last weeks or months after a single dose and could recur after long periods of delay or dormancy. Resultant chromosomal damage was demonstrated. Even the most ardent believer in the "miracle" of hallucinogenic drugs moved away from LSD.

Women who turned to other hard drugs, such as heroin, once again threatened the lives and well-being of their unborn children.[83] Many, however, preferred one or more of a wide range of "soft" drugs, primarily marijuana. From 1972 to 1982, the percentage of young adults in their prime childbearing years who had at least tried marijuana increased from 48% to 64%.[84] By 1985, the use of marijuana was epidemic, and though research data had not yielded any definitive information concerning genetic disturbances or any identifiable clinical entity, pregnant women were cautioned against its use for several reasons. First, the most active ingredients, tetrahydrocannabinol and carbon monoxide, easily cross the placenta and may have a depressant effect on the fetal central nervous system.[85] Second, an increased frequency of labor and delivery complications were observed.[86]

During the early eighties, cocaine became a popular substance, and experiments conducted at Northwestern University found disturbing patterns; that is, spontaneous abortions, complicated deliveries, irritable infants, and developmental delays. In the opinion of medical researcher Ira Chasnoff of Northwestern University, cocaine could well represent the worst known drug to be taken during pregnancy.[87]

Unfortunately, and despite all warnings, the House of Representatives Select Committee on Narcotics indicated that the highest incidence of drug abuse occurred during 1984, and there was no indication that the yearly increase in substance abuse would abate in the near future.[88] Often compounding the problem of drug usage were a series of correlated practices that posed an increased threat to the unborn or young child, including: inadequate maternal nutrition; absence of adequate prenatal medical attention; high maternal consumption of tobacco and alcohol; and following birth, inadequate parenting.[89] With or without drug involvement, alcohol, cigarettes, and even caffeine were viewed with increasing suspicion.

Alcohol

The question of alcohol and its potential effects on an unborn child have been debated throughout the course of history. During the advent of our Western culture and civilization, Plato observed, "It is not right that procreation should be the work of bodies dissolved by excess wine, but rather that the embryo should be compacted firmly, steadily and quietly in the womb."[90] Throughout the years, some persons maintained that alcohol could have very marked and undesirable effects on the developing fetus, while others contended that since there were so many alcoholics and so few mentally retarded persons, the two could not be related. As late as the forties and fifties, the U.S. government released a series of publications assuring the public there was no known fetal damage resulting from maternal intoxication or alcoholism.[91] This judgment probably reflected the fact that the alcohol research examined was concerned with genetic defects.

During the fifties, several French researchers began to study the characteristics of offspring born to alcoholic mothers, noting a number of features that ultimately would be associated with the fetal alcohol syndrome. In 1957, French medical student J. Rouqette devoted his doctoral dissertation to this area, reporting that alcohol could be devastating. Since his thesis was not published in a professional journal, it failed to receive much attention.[92] A decade later, Lemoine and his colleagues published similar findings, outlining the clustering of characteristics that again, in a few years, would be well recognized and considered indicative of the fetal alcohol syndrome.[93] In the United States, Ulleland published nearly identical results to those of his

French colleagues, but the *tour de force* was the research paper identifying and labeling the fetal alcohol syndrome, published by K. Jones and D. Smith in 1973.[94] From that date on, hundreds of research articles appeared reconfirming the impact of alcohol, observing that because of alcohol's solubility in water and fat, it readily diffuses across all cell membranes and is distributed equally throughout all body tissues in proportion to their water content. The central nervous system was particularly vulnerable.

Characteristics associated with the fetal alcohol syndrome (FAS) were reported to include: growth retardation; microcephaly; facial anomalies, such as short palpebral fissures (eye slits), short upturned noses, low nasal bridges, indistinct philtrums (the groove between the nose and mouth), thin upper lips, underdeveloped jaws, and lowset unparallel ears; organ disorders such as cardiac and urogenital defects; limb and joint anomalies; subnormal intelligence; and hyperactivity.[95] Prematurity, low birth weight, and withdrawal symptoms also were observed.[96] In addition to the fetal alcohol syndrome per se, other children who might not have the total array of identified characteristics were included under the broader category of "fetal alcohol effects" (FAE).

The incidence of FAS among all live births was found to vary: 0.4 per 1,000 in Cleveland; 1.3 per 1,000 in the Seattle area; and 3.1 per 1,000 in Boston.[97] Among "hard drinkers," usually defined as women who had two or more drinks a day, research indicated that 25 per 1,000 births would be FAS and 171 per 1,000 births would be FAE.[98] It was further estimated that approximately 9% of pregnant women were "hard drinkers," again referring to two or more drinks per day. This, in turn, implied that in 1979 alone, 312,000 infants were exposed to alcohol *in utero* on a daily basis.[99]

In 1980, Sokol and colleagues reported a 5% incidence of FAS among newborns of 204 alcoholic mothers. They were cautious in appraising the role of alcohol, since, as with drug users, there were a number of associated risk factors, including general maternal health

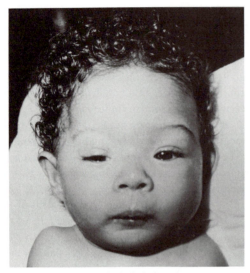

Infant with fetal alcohol syndrome

(e.g., general liver function and kidney disorders), altered nutrition, other drug use, smoking, and genotype.[100]

The effects of alcohol on intellectual functioning were found to be severe. In France, Lemoine and his coworkers reported that the average IQ of children of alcoholic mothers was 70; in Germany, Majewski and his colleagues reported an average IQ of 85; in Sweden, Olegard reported that 19% of affected youngsters had IQs below 70; and in the United States, Streissguth reported an average IQ of 65. Follow-up studies involving intellectual functioning among FAS children showed no subsequent significant increase in IQ.[101]

In 1981, the Surgeon General of the United States issued an advisory on drinking during pregnancy that read, "Each patient should be told about the risk of alcohol consumption during pregnancy and advised not to drink alcoholic beverages and to be aware of the alcoholic content of food and drugs."[102] In 1984, New York City passed an ordinance requiring the posting of a very visible sign in all bars, restaurants, and liquor stores reading: "Warning: Drinking Alcoholic Beverages During Pregnancy Can Cause Birth Defects."[103]

Some authorities believed that an occasional drink should not be harmful, and a 2-year study at Boston University found no differences between moderate drinkers and those who did not drink at all.[104] Nevertheless, and despite the fact that many alcohol-consuming mothers did not have obvious FAS or FAE children and there probably exists a genetic-environmental interaction, many physicians urged abstinence as the most prudent course to follow.

Tobacco

Smoking, which had been treated as a cancer-related health problem of national significance, was also identified as a possible cause of birth defects. Nicotine, which is in the same family as strychnine, quinine, mescaline, and such addictive pain relievers as cocaine, heroin, and codeine, has the effect of increasing the heart rate, narrowing the peripheral blood vessels, increasing the concentration of sugar in the blood, and, in general, producing high blood pressure.[105] Many believed that smoking similarly affects the fetus, not only in terms of heart rate, but in constricting blood vessels, which may limit the supply of oxygen to developing central nervous system tissue. Other evidence, suggestive in nature, indicated that fetuses of women who smoked had an increased risk for lower birth weight, decreased fetal breathing, fewer movements while *in utero,* and a significant reduction in vitamin C.[106] A higher incidence of spontaneous abortions was again observed.[107] It was estimated that 5%–15% of the infants of women who smoked may have some serious intellectual dysfunction.[108] Also, a study by the National Institute of Child Health and Development reported in 1984 indicated a much higher incidence of crib deaths (sudden infant death syndrome) among children of smoking mothers.[109]

Again, in view of the total health hazards associated with cigarettes, physicians had no difficulty whatsoever in recommending that pregnant women simply stop smoking, and once again the Surgeon General came forth requiring cigarette ads to carry the warning that "Smoking by pregnant women may result in fetal injury, premature birth, and low birth weight."[110]

Caffeine

During the quarter century, the effects of caffeine on fetal health and safety were debated at considerable length. Animal research indicated that consumption of caffeine during pregnancy resulted in reduced body, liver, and brain weight at birth.[111] Based on such findings plus the knowledge that caffeine readily crosses the placenta, in 1980, the U.S. Food and Drug Administration advised pregnant women to avoid caffeine-containing foods and drugs or to use them sparingly. Subsequent investigations among pregnant women drinking 10 or more cups of coffee per day did not support animal research. Congenital malformations were no more prevalent than normally expected.[112] Despite such findings, other researchers, as well as persons generally concerned about birth defects, encouraged the U.S. Food and Drug Administration not to withdraw their recommendation.[113] They based their request on the fact that since caffeine is common to so many products, including medications, soft drinks, candy, tea, and other food substances, it was difficult, if not impossible, to determine anyone's actual consumption. Thus, caffeine remained suspect but not confirmed.

In addition to discovering that many peoples' habits were neither as healthy nor as innocuous as previously thought, several other trends carrying implications for mental retardation became evident and were of concern. These were related to maternal age and child-rearing practices.

MATERNAL AGE

It had been long known that the healthiest childbearing years among normal women were between the ages of approximately 18 and 30. Beginning in the mid-sixties, there was an explosion in the number of births to young adolescents who, in view of changing societal expectancies and tolerances, often decided to raise their offspring. Every hour, 64

babies were born to teenage girls—for a total of 1,540 births per day. In 1980, 562,330 babies were born in the United States to teenage mothers, 50% of whom were unmarried. Nearly 10,000 of those births were to girls 14 years of age or younger. These figures represented live births only; it was estimated that at least 50% of teenage pregnancies were terminated.[114] The problem in the United States was particularly acute as the birth rate among girls 15–19 was at least 100% greater than in such countries as the Netherlands, Sweden, France, and Canada.[115]

From a physical perspective, pregnancies among young girls presented a number of problems. First, many such mothers did not receive adequate prenatal care. Only 46% of girls 12–14 years of age obtained prenatal care during the first trimester, according to a longitudinal study conducted by the Research Center and Child Welfare League of America.[116] This was double the average rate for all pregnancies. Second, the incidence of prematurity among those 12–15 years of age was approximately 16%, or again nearly double that for all women. Subsequently, many of the newborns did not go home at the time of their mother's discharge, owing to problems associated with prematurity, jaundice, and feeding difficulties. A number of studies, such as those conducted by Furstenberg in 1976 and Miller in 1984, found that infants of very young mothers had lower IQs, less advanced motor development, and lower scores on measures of school preparedness.[117] How many of these difficulties related purely to physical factors was unknown since the young mother was often confronted with innumerable and frequently insurmountable physical, psychological, and social problems.

As indicated previously, many of the young mothers kept and attempted to raise their children, but 25% were pregnant again in 1 year and 40% in 2 years, thus compounding an already difficult situation.[118] Quite often, these young girls came from homes that were economically distressed, and were simply ill prepared to fulfill the role of motherhood due to a lack of experience and/or the absence of an adequate mother model in their own lives.[119] Also, many tried to maintain a normal adolescent life socially and educationally, a task combined with mothering responsibilities that rapidly became overwhelming. "Too often," observed Auletta in 1984, "a child having a child becomes a prescription for a life of dependency and poverty."[120] As elaborated by the author, who visited several clinics intended to assist young mothers judged to be superior by the Ford Foundation:

> A visit to Lovick's "Clinic," as it's called in Houston and to the Pheonix headquarters of Via de Amistad . . . helps one empathize with how little a 15- or 17-year-old knows about parenting. Often, the child-mothers in these programs were raised by mothers who have their own demons to ward off, such as long spells of dependency on welfare that render them helpless, bouts with alcohol or drugs or mental illness, trouble with boyfriends, resentment toward their own children for robbing them of freedom. Usually, the child-mother lacks a good parenting role model as well as the kind of support system—husband, family—available to most adult American mothers.[121]

In brief, risks to both mother and child were many. In the words of one such youngster, "It is hell to be 14 and pregnant."[122]

While on the one hand there was the very young mother, on the other, there was the older primigravida, reflecting the dramatically changing role of women in contemporary American society. Many women, either out of economic necessity or a desire for self-fulfillment, entered the work force. Subsequently, many postponed childbearing until age 30 or later, a decision not without its risks.

First, research had shown that the "older" woman had more difficulties in conceiving. A Yale University study found that the average time required for women over 35 years of age to conceive lengthened from an average of 6 months for younger women to more than 2 years. Second, time alone as well as liberalized sexual practices increased the chance of various pelvic infections that scar the delicate tissues of the fallopian tubes, ovaries, and uterus.[123] This was reflected in two findings: 1) infertility rates increased 177% between

1965 and 1982, and 2) the incidence of tubal pregnancies more than doubled from 4.5 per 1,000 pregnancies in 1970 to 9.4 per 1,000 in 1978, according to the Centers for Disease Control, based on a study of the medical records of 262,000 women discharged from more than 400 hospitals after an ectopic pregnancy.[124]

Finally, and with direct reference to mental retardation, the older woman runs an increased risk of chromosomal aberrations and neurological damage. The risk of a chromosomal anomaly (usually related to meiotic error) increases from 1/1,550 live births for women under 30, to 1/700 for women 30 to 34, to 1/250 for women between 35 and 39, and 1/85 for the 40 to 42 age group, to 1/40 for women over 42.[125] In addition to chromosomal anomalies, the Collaborative Perinatal Project, a nationwide mother study involving 50,000 mothers, conducted by the U.S. government during the sixties, indicated that there was a considerable increase not only in perinatal mortality, but also in neurological abnormalities among children born to women who were 40 years of age or older. A more than twofold increase in neurological defects was found in children of older mothers.[126]

CHILD ABUSE

Another trend, and certainly one of the most tragic in this country (as well as in others of the Western world) was the unparalleled, unjustified, and unequivocal explosion in the incidence of child abuse. The first medical reference linking craniocerebral injury to child assault was published in 1860 by French physician Ambroise Tardieu, who described "thickenings of blood on the surface of the brain" in children who were victims of "abuse and maltreatment."[127] His judgment was not accepted by other noted physicians of the day who believed that such injuries and symptoms were due to infections rather than inflicted injuries. One hundred and one years later, in 1961, the American Academy of Pediatricians conducted a special symposium on child abuse and neglect, at which time Henry Kempe set forth the "battered child syndrome." A few years later, the British physician N. J. O'Doherty cautioned his fellow physicians to be alert to the fact that subdural hematomas accompanied by long-bone fractures signaled child abuse. He also was appalled at the tremendous increase in child abuse reported in his country.[128]

By 1965, a number of states had passed legislation requiring physicians and others to report any case of suspected child abuse, frequently defined as "any physical injury inflicted on a child by other than accidental means, or sexual intercourse or sexual contact . . . physical injury includes but is not limited to severe bruising, lacerations, fractured bones, burns, internal injuries or any injury constituting great bodily harm."[129] In a few years, most states added neglect to abuse. The neglected child was one "whose parent, guardian, legal custodian, or other person exercising temporary or permanent control over the child neglects, refuses, or is unable for reasons other than poverty to provide necessary care, food, clothing, medical, or dental care, or shelter so as to seriously endanger the physical health of the child."[130] The reported instances of child abuse and neglect skyrocketed, partly because of legal requirements, partly because of the increased sensitivity of those coming in contact with children, and partly because of the substantial increase in abuse per se. In Wisconsin alone, the number of reported abuse cases rose from 94 in 1964 to 9,067 in 1982. The foremost types of child abuse reported in that state were: physical neglect (30.0%); cuts / welts / bruises (29.8%); lack of supervision (23.5%); and sexual abuse (16.9%).[131]

Numerous reports of this nature ultimately raised questions about America's attitudes and feelings toward its children. In 1975, S. Boocock, a sociologist with the Russell Sage Foundation, in an address to the American Association for the Advancement of Science, reviewed the situation at that time and concluded that "The status of children in our society is highly ambiguous . . . . It does seem that there is less wanting of children in America and in the developed nations gener-

ally than in the past and that people who do want children want fewer of them."[132] Specifically, she noted:

1. Some 60,000 cases of child abuse are reported annually in the United States. This was considered to be a very conservative estimate.
2. There have been significant increases in the number of divorce cases in which *neither* parent wishes to assume custody of the children.
3. A study by the Child Welfare League estimated that in 1965 almost 1,000,000 American children under fourteen years of age were left on their own while their parents worked. Seven thousand of these were under age six. Another 1,000,000 were left in the care of older brothers and sisters under sixteen or relatives over sixty-five.
4. At recent federal and state hearings, working-class mothers testified that they had left ill preschoolers unattended in locked apartments because they feared losing their jobs if they stayed at home.
5. Children are spending most of their time alone or with other children, mostly in relatively unorganized activities such as watching television and eating snacks.[133]

By 1984, the estimate of 1 million American children under 14 years of age left alone while parents worked had increased to over 5 million children under the age of 10. At least 500,000 of the latter were preschoolers or under age 6. "Latchkey" children had become a common phenomenon, while many others were abandoned to day care centers that, in the words of Ralph Nader, America's leading consumer advocate, were often little better than "children's warehouses."[134]

With respect to mental retardation, in 1973, Brandwein estimated that permanent brain injury resulted from child abuse in as many as 170,000 cases annually. In this, his estimate may have been conservative.[135] In the same year, O'Neil and his colleagues reported that 20% of 160 abused children were mentally retarded; in 1978, Oliver found 44% of 38 abused children were mentally retarded; in 1980, Tsai and his colleagues noted that 19% of 177 battered children were mentally retarded; and, taking into consideration all passive types of abuse, Merton and Osborne reported, in 1983, that 7% of 716 abused children were suffering from mental retardation.[136] There was no question that severe mental retardation could result from such abusive practices as child beatings, arm swinging, and what became known as the "whiplash" phenomenon, brain injury due to shaking a child. As observed by Caffey in 1974, casual, habitual, manual whiplash shaking could cause mental retardation and extensive brain damage reflected in subdural hematomas and intraocular bleeding.[137] Other signs of child abuse resulting in severe brain injury included skull fractures, extra cerebral fluid collections, subdural hemorrhages, and blood clots on the brain.[138]

Some recorded cases were so severe as to result in subsequent microcephaly. In 1975, Oliver reported on three such youngsters, previously normal, who through severe child abuse became microcephalic and profoundly mentally retarded.[139] It was not only a question of whether physical abuse could result in mental retardation, it appeared from studies and interpretations by some researchers such as Morse, Sandgrund, and their colleagues, that children who are mentally retarded may also be particularly susceptible to violence.[140] Morse, for example, found that 70% of 25 children under 6 years of age from 23 families were intellectually, emotionally, socially, and motorically underdeveloped. It was contended that perhaps mental retardation and motor hyperactivity were factors that precipitated abuse. Sandgrund and her associates at the Down State Medical Center in Brooklyn agreed. They found mental retardation to be 10 times more prevalent among abused children. Both groups of researchers proposed that mentally retarded youngsters may become ready victims of abuse since they are "different" and parents often feel inadequate and frustrated in attempting to cope with them effectively. Thus, mental retardation can be a result of child abuse, a cause of child abuse, or aggravated by child abuse.

Cases of severe abuse—battering, beating, pulling, swinging, punching, burning, shaking, and sexual assault—were frequently noted in the public media; but many wondered about the more subtle effects of neglect. Alice Johnson, formerly an abused child, serving as dean emeritus and professor of English at Connecticut College, noted in 1984, "there is also a subtler kind of child abuse that can only be described as benign neglect. Children who suffer from this common garden-variety blight are never beaten, burned, or otherwise physically tortured. They are merely ignored by busy, noncaring parents who provide all the prerequisites of the good life but deny their offspring the most important and vital ingredients: love and personal attention."[141] The implications of Johnson's observations in terms of a child's total development, including intellectual functioning, remained unknown and inadequately investigated.

MALNUTRITION

In addition to those nutritional problems specifically associated with genetically based metabolic disorders, the world remained concerned about problems associated with general malnutrition among infants. Research conducted over the quarter century consistently indicated that severe dietary deficiencies, either in terms of calories (marasmus) or proteins (kwashiorkor), had negatively influenced life expectancy and total development among undernourished children.

Studies among infants and preschool children suffering from inadequate diets found reduced electroencephalogram (EEG) activity and lower developmental scores on the Bayley Scale, while autopsies of severely malnourished youngsters revealed fewer brain cells and less brain weight. An extensive study involving 129 Barbadian boys and girls age 5–11 years demonstrated that severe protein-energy malnutrition during the first year of life not only had a severe effect on intellectual development but that these effects persisted even after dietary corrections.[142] Galler found elementary school children subjected to malnutrition during the first year of life continued to perform below average on intelligence tests (50% had IQs below 90) in general academic performance.[143] The tragedy rested not only with malnutrition per se, but also with the uncontrolled population explosion in many countries unable to provide a basic, healthy diet to its children.

In view of the many environmental factors that could result in mental retardation and other birth defects, agencies and organizations concerned with healthy infants alerted millions of American women and men to the many potential hazards. The March of Dimes, for example, widely distributed the simple statement, "When you're pregnant, your baby *may* be in danger: If you don't see a doctor right away, if you don't eat enough of the right food, if you drink, if you smoke, if you take drugs, if you have VD, if you are under 18 or over 35, and if birth defects run in either family."[144]

PRIMARY PREVENTION AND TREATMENT

As evidenced by the preceding comments, medicine and its numerous contributory fields made major gains in understanding at least some forms of mental retardation. Genuine progress also was realized in a number of areas related to primary prevention and treatment; these took many forms.

GENETIC COUNSELING

Genetic counseling received new impetus for several reasons: more definitive knowledge of chromosomal anomalies and genetically related metabolic disorders; the increased number of women postponing childbirth; and advancements in scientific technology, which produced new techniques capable of providing accurate *in utero* diagnosis, especially amniocentesis and sonography, better known as ultrasound. Amniocentesis, which had been tried on several occasions during the late nineteenth century, did not become widely adopted until the late sixties and early seventies with the growing confidence that the procedure could be utilized to advantage with minimal risk to either mother or fetus. In

brief, to perform amniocentesis, a physician inserted a long needle into a pregnant woman's womb and withdrew a sample of amniotic fluid containing fetal cells and other materials. As recognized by Fuchs as early as 1960, these cells could be cultured for genetic purposes.[145] With the addition of ultrasound monitoring in the seventies, amniocentesis became increasingly safe since the physician now had visual guidance when inserting the needle. Ultrasound, which provided an actual picture of the fetus through the use of high frequency sound waves rather than radiation, was capable of noting the position, size, and structure of the fetus as well as the placenta.

Though amniocentesis could detect as many as 200 birth defects, including Down syndrome, it had several major limitations. Even though relatively safe, amniocentesis did result in an increased frequency of spontaneous abortions, estimates of which ranged from 1 per 200 to 1 per 2,000 attempts. Possible fetal damage also could occur.[146] Further, the procedure could not be performed before the sixteenth or seventeenth week of pregnancy and the culturing process usually required an additional 2–4 weeks to complete. This time factor prevented the early introduction of treatment and increased maternal risks associated with abortion.

During the mid-eighties, American physicians at several universities began to examine a technique developed during the sixties in Europe and used in France, England, and Italy. This technique, called chorionic villi sampling (CVS), was a painless procedure that could be done in the physician's office as early as the fifth week of pregnancy. In this instance, the attending physician inserted a long thin tube through the vagina into the uterus while another physician or technician closely monitored direction and progress via ultrasound. The catheter was positioned between the lining of the uterus and the chorion, a layer of tissue that surrounds the embryo during the first 2 months of life and that later develops into the placenta. The object was to collect a sample of the chorionic villi finger-like projections of tissue that transfer oxygen, nutrients, and waste between mother and embryo.[147] Even though the resulting specimen was very small in size, the chorion sample was composed of the same cells as the fetus, thus enabling a variety of genetic defects, including Down syndrome and Tay-Sachs disease, to be detected at a much earlier age; however, an increased chance of spontaneous abortion was again evident. Data compiled during the early eighties indicated that the risk was nearly double that associated with amniocentesis, but advocates of the technique believed that with further experience and refinement, spontaneous abortions could be reduced substantially. Though not widely used by 1985, it appeared that in the near future a safe prenatal diagnostic technique capable of yielding important genetic information during the first trimester was feasible.

PRENATAL TREATMENT

Over the past quarter century, there were several attempts to introduce corrective treatment *in utero*. The first of such treatments related to mental retardation involved intrauterine blood transfusions for fetuses with severe Rh disease. This technique, developed originally in New Zealand, was initially attempted in the United States at the Providence Hospital in Detroit in the early sixties. It proved dangerous, often resulting in fetal death; subsequently, it was used only in the rarest of emergencies.[148] It was soon replaced by another approach: following the typically normal first pregnancy, the mother was given an Rh vaccine within 72 hours, thus protecting her from becoming sensitive to the Rh blood factor, which would endanger future births. This procedure was repeated after each subsequent birth, miscarriage, or abortion.

On April 29, 1981, when physicians and technicians at the University Hospital in Denver implanted a miniature shunting device into the brain of the fetus with hydrocephaly, a new door to prenatal surgery was opened.[149] Postnatally, a number of surgical procedures were devised that greatly improved the outlook for physically as well as mentally af-

fected youngsters. Structural defects such as cleft lip and palate, club foot, various heart malformations, and bowel obstructions became readily amenable to advanced surgical procedures.[150]

In addition, major technological advances, often combined with highly sophisticated computer systems, opened new vistas for studying and treating brain disorders. From World War II through the sixties, the most prevalent diagnostic system for measuring central nervous system activity was the electroencephalogram, which provided an analysis of various brain waves.[151] It proved to be of value in diagnosing some forms of epilepsy and brain injury, but its results often were not reliable and many subtle brain disorders went undetected. During the seventies, a new system—computerized axial tomography (CAT) scan—was designed. The first scanner applied for clinical purposes was developed in 1972 by Godfrey N. Hounsfield, an engineer with the Electrical and Music Industries Ltd. in Middlesex, England. The Mayo Clinic purchased the first such scanner for use in the United States in 1973. The advantages of CAT scanning over other diagnostic devices intended for similar purposes were significant:

1. Speed and accuracy in making and/or confirming a diagnosis were ensured.
2. The pictures represented three dimensions, including a horizontal cross section—a view unobtainable with conventional x-ray films.
3. Serial evaluation for follow-up purposes was easily achieved.
4. The various tissues of the brain could be differentiated by density.
5. The technique was non-invasive.
6. It required approximately the same amount of radiation exposure as a standard skull series, but provided approximately 100 times more information.[152]

Through the years, the system underwent a number of modifications and improvements, and in 1982, a National Institutes of Health planning panel designated CAT scanning as the tool of choice in the primary diagnosis of brain abscesses, intracranial hemorrhage, and conditions resulting from severe head injury.[153]

In the early eighties, a new system for evaluating the central nervous system and related injuries was introduced. It possessed the positive attribute of reducing any problems associated with X rays, relying instead on natural human magnetic properties. This technique —nuclear magnetic resonance (NMR) imaging—also provided better differentiation between gray and white matter, was more capable of "seeing" through bone, and gave a better image of the spinal cord.[154]

Not only did these more sophisticated techniques enable a better understanding of the central nervous system and the location of particular brain defects or damage, they facilitated the development and advancement of stereotaxic neurosurgery. In this complicated procedure, a neurosurgeon positioned an electrode carrier, a radio frequency probe, or a needle directly into the discrete regions of the brain for biopsies, stimulation, or ablation. In 1983, knowledgeable medical persons predicted with confidence that, in the near future, stereotaxic neurosurgery would play a key role in the treatment of involuntary movement disorders due to brain trauma, intractable epilepsy, intracranial hematomas, deep brain tumors, and persistent pain.[155] The promise for some mentally retarded individuals and others with brain injury seemed great.

These technological advances in neurosurgical procedures may also hold some promise for brain tissue transplants. Animal research conducted in the early eighties indicated that transplanting cortical tissue in humans may become a reality in the future. One of the most frequently discussed studies in this area was by Donald Stein and his colleagues at the Clark University of Worcester, Massachusetts. They experimented with 21 rats from whom certain portions of the frontal cortex had been removed. To repair the damage, the researchers implanted in eight of the rats a pinhead-size lap taken from the frontal cortex of normal rat embryos. Though the treated rats did not learn as rapidly as normal, their rate of learning was significantly faster than the remaining untreated, brain-damaged rats.[156] In 1983, Richard Wyatt, pioneer in brain tissue transplantation with the National Institute of Mental Health, expressed his conviction that neurological transplants would soon cure or at least modify the effects of Parkinson's disease and some forms of blindness. One of the interesting aspects of brain tissue transplants is, for some unknown reason, the brain has less tendency to reject new tissue than do other parts of the body.[157]

NEWBORN SCREENING AND TREATMENT

Another important area of prevention involved specialized treatments for newborn infants with certain genetically determined metabolic disorders. In spite of the rarity of such conditions, interested citizens, parents, governmental representatives, and scientists combined their interests, talents, and abilities to assist those so affected. This was accomplished through the development of appropriate diagnostic measures, state legislation mandating screening of the newborn, and appropriate treatment. Though W. Centerwall developed the first newborn screening test in 1957, it was not until Richard Guthrie introduced his bacterial inhibition assay in 1963 that early diagnostic programs appeared feasible.[158] In a few years, many states passed mandatory legislation requiring newborn testing for at least phenylketonuria. Some states later added homocystinuria to the screening program since, like the preceding disorders, it was amenable to special treatment.

In the instance of hypothyroidism, the most prevalent of these conditions, the introduction of thyroid replacement therapy reduced, but did not entirely eliminate the risk of subsequent mental retardation. Without such therapy, most hypothyroid newborns would become severely mentally retarded; with such treatment, their intelligence scores tended to follow the normal distribution curve.[159] The other conditions—phenylketonuria, maple syrup urine, galactosemia, and homocystinuria—were found to respond well to dietary restrictions that limit the intake of natural substances that, in time, could produce accumulative toxic effects resulting in mental retardation and, in some instances, death. Again, however, none of these approaches was 100% effective.[160]

In addition, techniques were developed for reducing toxic substances associated with Wilson's disease (copper) and plumbism (lead). Evidence indicated that proper treatment of Wilson's disease could reverse central nervous system damage.[161] Unfortunately, the same was not true for plumbism.

While, as indicated previously, the short history of gene therapy had yet to produce any results that would directly minimize mental retardation, those discoveries and the astounding rate of progress associated with biogenetic research boded well for the future. Continued achievements could be expected since biogenetics and gene therapy had rapidly evolved into a major interest of both commercial concerns and universities. By 1983, over 200 companies and universities were actively engaged in related research areas with budgets exceeding $1 billion a year. Some advancements by the end of 1984 included the determination of the prenatal myelin protein possessing at least the potential for fetal placement to avoid degeneration of the myelin sheaths; the introduction of human growth

hormones capable of assisting victims of pituitary dwarfism; and the successful engineering of synthetic interferon and human insulin. Most promising for the field of mental retardation, C. Thomas Caskey predicted, in 1983, that within several years the enzyme vital to preventing the Lesch-Nyhan syndrome would become an effective treatment agent.[162]

IMMUNIZATION

Without question, many cases of mental retardation have been averted through the continued development and utilization of various vaccines. As shown in Table 2.4, immunization programs have had a tremendous impact on reducing the number of persons infected by historically common diseases, which often were accompanied by serious physical and/or intellectual defects.[163]

One of the most important vaccines to be developed during the latter sixties and early seventies curtailed the devastating impact of rubella, or German measles. The tragic consequences of rubella upon the human fetus were first brought to the world's attention in 1941 by the Australian ophthalmologist, Norman Gregg. His study, which followed an epidemic of German measles, not only revealed the multiple handicaps resulting from prenatal infection—congenital cataracts, heart disease, deafness, and mental retardation—but also

Table 2.4. Reduction of cases of historically common diseases in the United States due to vaccines

Disease	Number of Cases	
	In peak year (before modern vaccine)	In 1982[a] (after vaccine)
Diphtheria	206,999 (1921)	3
Measles	481,530 (1962)	1,697
Mumps	152,209 (1968)	5,196
Polio	57,879 (1952)	7
Rubella	57,686 (1969)	2,283
Smallpox	632,000[b] (1949)	0
Tetanus	601 (1948)	81
Whooping cough	265,269 (1934)	1,784

[a]Latest year for which figures are available.

[b]Worldwide figure; actual unreported cases may be 10–50 times higher.

Adapted from Ubell, 1984b.

dispelled the long-held notion that the "fetus was, with few exceptions such as syphilis, relatively invulnerable to the usual infectious agents producing illness in the mother."[164]

In the early sixties, the United States underwent a measles epidemic and the results again were tragic, because rubella has a "shotgun" effect on nervous system tissue.[165] The 1962–1964 epidemic resulted in a high rate of premature births, and according to a follow-up study by Chess and her colleagues in 1978, 72% of rubella victims studied suffered severe hearing losses, and 42% were mentally retarded.[166]

In 1969, the first measles vaccine was approved, and within a decade, 99 million doses were administered, primarily to children less than 9 years of age.[167] This approach resulted in a peculiar response: while there were marked decreases in the total number of reported cases of rubella, there was not a substantial decrease in children born with the congenital rubella syndrome. Subsequently, the immunization program was rapidly expanded to include women of childbearing age. During the seventies, several more measles vaccines were introduced.

In 1983, physicians and researchers from the University of Pennsylvania and the Merck Research Laboratory genetically engineered the first vaccine capable of successfully controlling chicken pox.[168] The virus vaccine was administered to 468 children while 446 received a placebo. Over a 9-month follow-up period, none of the vaccinated children contracted chicken pox compared with 39 cases in the control group. No serious side effects were noted; thus, another common childhood disease with implications for mental retardation may well prove preventable.

One of the most controversial, but potentially helpful vaccines in terms of both childhood mortality and mental retardation was developed to immunize against whooping cough, or pertussis. Though preliminary research indicated the vaccine would reduce the number of infected youngsters from approximately 350,000 to 34,000 cases per year and the mortality rate would drop from an estimated 457 to

44 cases, it was rejected by many parents because the vaccine was suspected of causing brain damage in rare instances.[169]

Any medical treatment that in some way invades the human system possesses some risk for some persons. Thus, one has to weigh the benefits of immunizing many children against the few that might suffer an adverse reaction. In the judgment put forth by the Centers for Disease Control in 1984, "continued use of our present vaccines, with careful attention to possible contraindications, seems the only prudent course to follow."[170]

While many states passed legislation requiring immunization of infants and preschoolers, such legislation often included a number of exemptions for reasons such as religion, health, and/or parental conviction. Subsequently, resulting rules and regulations were rarely enforced, and despite the great advances made in this critical area of prevention, periodic national and localized outbreaks of communicable diseases continued to occur.

DIETARY SUPPLEMENTS

In addition to the previously discussed conditions associated with early infant screening, a number of researchers attempted to modify mental retardation through dietary supplements. One that was considered quite successful was introduced by Scriver and colleagues in 1971 when they found that thiamine therapy in larger-than-normal doses was successful in treating maple syrup urine disease.[171]

Other scientists proposed that large doses of vitamins, minerals, and other nutrients could be successful in increasing intelligence while decreasing physical symptoms among people with Down syndrome. The first such approach during the quarter century was Turkel's "U Series," which consisted of 49 different drugs, but was not widely adopted by the medical community.[172]

Twenty years later, Harrell and her associates tested the hypothesis that mental retardation is a genetotrophic disease that requires an increased supply of one or more nutrients to modify or eliminate the condition. They selected 22 school-age mentally retarded children to participate in a study involving rather large amounts of vitamin and mineral supplements, and reported rather favorable results in terms of both elevated intelligence quotients and a reduction of physical features common to youngsters with Down syndrome.[173] Their study, however, did not satisfy basic research design requirements, and after critically reviewing the methodology and procedures, Rasmussen, for one, concluded, "Because of the many major flaws in the design, very few conclusions can be made about vitamin and mineral therapy from Dr. Harrell's study. At this time, no good scientific study has been performed proving or disproving the claim of benefits of vitamin and mineral therapy. Parents considering vitamin and mineral therapy should be aware that no scientific basis for this therapy exists."[174] Others agreed that studies relating to the effects of vitamin-mineral supplements conducted during the late seventies and early eighties demonstrated no change in IQ or adaptive behavior.[175]

Though megavitamins were of considerable interest to an exceptionally health-conscious America, their use as a treatment measure with mentally retarded persons was not widely accepted in the field. One of the reasons was that massive dosages of vitamins could produce undesirable side effects. It was found, for example, when megavitamins were used with learning disabled children and those with behavioral problems, increased amounts of vitamin A produced toxic reactions, including skin changes, pruritis, clubbing of fingers, fatigue, hypoplastic anemia, and increased intracranial pressure. Consequently, the Committee on Nutrition of the American Academy of Pediatricians issued a statement in 1976 cautioning that the use of vitamin A for psychiatric purposes was not justified. Vitamins C and D, and niacin also demonstrated adverse side effects. In 1984, Carney, following an extensive review of the literature, concluded that "though the place of megavitamin therapy (if any) in psychiatric treatment is yet

to be fully evaluated, clearly it may be dangerous."[176]

SUMMARY

The preceding review touched upon a few—only a few—of the medical and technological advances of the quarter century that had an impact upon the prevention and treatment of mental retardation. Not reviewed were research efforts in such demanding areas as cellular division and multiplication, the role of peptides, memory enhancers, growth accelerators, and eliminating the hazards of viral infections.[177] These had yet to yield great and promising results, but as history has repeatedly demonstrated, the work of yesterday often provides the answers for tomorrow.

Taken in their totality, while gains in the direct prevention and treatment of mental retardation were significant, they remained relatively few when one considers the magnitude and diversity of the problem. Yet, there was every reason to be optimistic. As expressed by Jack Stark in introducing one of the more forward-looking books of the eighties, *Curative Aspects of Mental Retardation: Biomedical and Behavioral Advances*—"It is clear that curative approaches to mental retardation will increasingly move from possibility to probability to actual treatment intervention. The vast sea of unknown in mental retardation *has* finally yielded us specific ventures in wisdom, and we have only to plumb its depths anew to reap further mental benefits for retarded persons in the near future."[178]

ISSUES IN MEDICAL TREATMENT

Two contemporary trends evolved during the seventies that had a significant impact on mental retardation: abortion and infanticide. While both had been practiced to some degree throughout the world since the dawn of the human race, changing social attitudes, advances in medical technology, and altered legal opinion all led to a marked increase in their application.

Historically, a high incidence of such practices among Western cultures have usually been associated with the declining years of a society or have at least signaled a society in deep trouble. In Greece, during the fifth century B.C., for example, both abortion and infanticide became so flagrant that one medical practitioner and teacher—Hippocrates—felt compelled to set forth a physician's oath that, in part, required:

> I will use treatment to help the sick according to my ability and judgment, but I will never use it to injure or wrong them. I will not give poison to anyone though asked to do so, nor will I suggest such a plan. Similarly, I will not give a pessary to a woman to cause abortion. But in purity and in holiness I will guard my life and my art . . . . Into whatsoever house I enter, I will do so to help the sick, keeping myself free from all intentional wrongdoing and harm. . . .[179]

ABORTION

Until recent years, abortion in the United States was legally permitted only under the most extreme circumstances when a mother's health was seriously at risk. Subsequently, a woman with an unwanted pregnancy was faced with one of three choices: 1) carry the child to term; 2) seek less-than-reputable help; or 3) if sufficiently wealthy, have an abortion in another country where such procedures were legal.

For decades, some organizations fervently fought state-imposed constraints on abortion for various reasons, including the right of a woman to control her own body. These groups found the relief they sought when, in 1973, the Supreme Court resolved *Roe* v. *Wade* by ruling unconstitutional all state laws that prohibited voluntary abortions during the first trimester and by setting limits on prohibitions during the second trimester. The final decision included what has often been cited as the "right to privacy" clause:

> The right of privacy, whether it be founded in the Fourteenth Amendment's concept of personal liberty and restrictions upon state action, as we feel it is, or, as the District Court determined,

in the Ninth Amendment's reservation of rights to the people, is broad enough to encompass a woman's decision whether or not to terminate her pregnancy.[180]

"Abortion on demand" met with mixed reactions. To some, the court's decision simply represented an overdue recognition of a woman's fundamental right. To others, it was an assault on long-valued, traditional religious teachings; or it was an attack on the very constitutional foundation of this country; or it violated deeply held personal or professional convictions; or among those who lived through or remembered well the Nazi experience, the decision was a nightmare revisited.[181]

Abortion, like infanticide, was debated, often in angry words, since the subject was not amenable to compromise. The population in general was divided on this issue, as illustrated by an Associated Press–NBC poll of 1982 that revealed that while 49% of the population sampled believed abortion was wrong, at the same time, 62% agreed that abortion should be legal.[182]

Regardless of varying philosophies and sentiments, the net effect of the court's decision was an astronomical increase in the recorded number of abortions—from 23,000 in 1969 to over 1.5 million in 1980. On the sole basis of probability, the birth of at least 2,000 infants with Down syndrome was prevented during the latter year cited. This number was deemed conservative, taking into consideration Hansen's 1978 report on the effects of New York state's liberalized abortion laws. He found that women seeking termination of pregnancy tended to be over 35 years of age and those whose pregnancies fell within the high-risk range. Consequently, there was an estimated 20% decline in the number of Down syndrome births between 1971 and 1975.[184]

Given the advancing age at childbearing among a growing number of women, combined with new prenatal diagnostic techniques, some physicians found themselves in court, being held liable for what the legal profession termed "a wrongful birth" or an "unworthy or wrongful life.''* In the 1981 case of *Speck* v. *Finegold,* for example, the physician was held financially responsible for the lifelong care of a baby girl born with neurofibromatosis following an unsuccessful abortion procedure.[185]

Medical malpractice suits involving mentally retarded and other disabled infants became prevalent. In another case, *Harbeson* v. *Parke-Davis, Inc.,* 1983, the attending physician was held responsible for a ''wrongful life,'' after failing to inform the parents of the risks of the effects of prenatal medication. The court's decision read, in part, ''The physician's negligence—his failure to adequately inform the parents of the risk—has caused the birth of a deformed child. The child argues *but for* the inadequate advice, it would not have been born to experience the pain and suffering attributable to the deformity.''[187] Settlements often ran into the millions of dollars.

Young boy with Down syndrome

INFANTICIDE

While there is little question that for years some physicians, regardless of sanction, quietly and surreptitiously permitted deformed and severely mentally retarded infants to die, the overall frequency was probably rather minimal in view of ethical and/or legal considerations. Beginning in the early seventies, however, death through the omission of treatment received increasing attention and acceptance, at least among some medical personnel and parents. Evidence offered by R. Duff and A. Campbell of the Department of Pediatrics of Yale University School of Medicine indicated that the incidence of such deaths in some medical settings was becoming more common. They reported that of 299 consecutive deaths occurring from January 1, 1970 to June 30, 1972, at the Yale–New Haven Hospital, 43 (or 14%) were related to withholding treatment.[188]

The first ''Baby Doe'' case to have some public exposure involved the prolonged death

(15 days) by starvation of an infant with Down syndrome in Johns Hopkins Hospital as reported in 1971.[189] The attending physician had deferred to the parents' wishes not to repair the infant's intestinal obstruction in the perceived interest of both the child and themselves.

In contrast, the plight of Phillip Becker in 1979 received widespread national attention and reaction. At the time of his hearing, Phillip was a 12-year-old mildly mentally retarded child with Down syndrome who had a surgically correctable coronary defect. An earlier diagnosis revealed that without surgery, the boy would die a premature death, probably before age 30. Although he had lived in various out-of-home facilities since birth, his parents vetoed the idea, citing such reasons as the possible warehousing of Phillip in an institution if he outlived them, the 5%–10% risk of surgery-related death, and the futility of extending a life ''devoid of those qualities which give it human dignity.'' Concerned over the

---

*It is interesting to note the parallel of American legal concepts with those of Hitler who termed defective infants *unlebenswert* (unworthy of life).[186]

parents' opposition, the state juvenile probation agency brought the matter before the Juvenile Court, seeking a court order authorizing the surgery over the parents' objections.
Judge Eugene M. Premo dismissed the petition, calling the proposed surgery "elective,"
rather than life-saving. "Who am I to decide
that they [the parents] can't make the right
decision," he opined. The California Court of
Appeals affirmed the lower court's decision,
noting that the parents had "a fundamental
right to control their child's upbringing."[190]
On March 31, 1980, the U.S. Supreme Court
concurred.[191]

Many knowledgeable people objected vehe-
mently to the courts' series of decisions.
George F. Will, for example, noted political
observer and commentator as well as a parent
of a boy with Down syndrome, wrote about
the case on behalf of Phillip, noting that "respect for parental sovereignty has been carried
to absurd, not to mention lethal, lengths."
Further,

> I will not speculate about the worth of those who
> presume to depreciate Phillip's worth, or about
> the quality of life in a society that, on "quality
> of life" grounds, truncates a life like Phillip's.
> But this is tiresome: just when society is begin-
> ning to acknowledge an obligation to nurture the
> significant fulfillment of even the limited poten-
> tialities of retarded citizens, the Becker case
> works to cast those citizens into legal limbo as
> less than persons with a full right to life.[192]

He ended his column with the words of an
affectionate father:

> The Down's child I know best is seven. He is
> learning to read but prefers "Happy Days," the
> Washington Bullets, and the Baltimore Orioles.
> These impeccable tastes help explain why neigh-
> borhood children treat him as what he is, like
> Phillip is: a boy.[193]

Douglas Biklen of the Center on Human
Policy at Syracuse University, also summarized the feelings of many when he entitled his
1981 review of the Becker case, "The Supreme Court v. Retarded Children."[194]
The California Association for Retarded
Citizens and an ad hoc coalition of "Friends"
of Phillip pursued the issue, and in August of

1981, Superior Court Judge William Fernandez awarded custody of Phillip Becker to
Pat and Herb Heath, a couple who had taken
an interest in him and for the last 10 years had
visited him in the facility where he lived and
had taken him to their home. In making his
decision, Judge Fernandez held Phillip's best
interests paramount to the Beckers' parental
rights. He cited the shift in California law,
which focused on the child's well-being rather
than on the historical rights of parents, noting
that the Beckers had no expectations for Phillip and that "in their view Phillip would always be a burden and of little appreciable value for the rest of his life" and that they had
refused to initiate steps to have surgery performed.[195]

Mr. and Mrs. Becker believed the court had
inappropriately removed Phillip from their
care. In an article prepared for *Newsweek,*
they described their feelings:

> In 1981, a California judge, finding no evi-
> dence of abandonment, abuse, or neglect, took
> our son, Phillip, away from us, his two teenage
> brothers, his grandparents, his uncles and his
> aunts. The judge gave Phillip, together with his
> assets, to a couple our age whom we had never
> met. The couple, who lived a few blocks from
> Phillip and were volunteers in his facility, had no
> young children of their own. They had petitioned
> the court for guardianship and persuaded the
> judge that they could make better choices for our
> son than his own family. . . .
> Many years ago we read in "1984" about the
> coming of "Big Brother." We learned how pub-
> lic leaders, judges, and committees would de-
> cide what was best for us. We were told of a time
> when people would no longer have the right to
> privacy or to decide what was best for them-
> selves and their families. That time has come—
> these rights have been taken from us.[196]

As pointed out by Herbert Grossman, however, writing on behalf of the American Association on Mental Deficiency, "The Court of
Appeals decision in the Becker case upholds
the right of a mentally retarded child to essential medical care and habilitation. Rather than
terminating the parental rights of the Beckers,
the Court made only a limited award of custody to the substitute parents. Due to the very
special circumstances of that case, this in no

way threatens the traditional autonomy accorded families whose actions are not detrimental to a child."[197]

In 1982, another "Baby Doe" case brought not only immediate national coverage but a definitive response by President Reagan and the Congress of the United States. In brief, the parents of a 5-day-old boy born with Down syndrome and internal disorders were granted their wish to withhold life-sustaining treatment, including food and water. In spite of numerous calls from families around the United States and Canada willing to accept the Down syndrome infant into their home, the Indiana Supreme Court, after holding an emergency hearing on the fate of the Bloomington baby, decided three to one not to order medical aid or to provide the infant with food and water. Justice Roger O. DeBruler, the lone dissenter, said he was concerned about judges second-guessing doctors on medical matters. It "seems almost preposterous that courts . . . should be given that kind of authority," he noted.[198] Though Baby Doe died shortly thereafter, the case was pursued to the Supreme Court, which, on November 7, 1983, refused to consider the matter.

As indicated, the Indiana court decision spurred considerable controversy and reaction. Frank E. Ball, executive director of the Indiana Association for Retarded Citizens, observed in 1982: "I cannot feel that the parents made this decision on their own, without some suggestion coming from medical people, people they felt they had to respect. The Indiana Supreme Court also dealt shabbily with the issue of the child's rights and upheld the parents. The parents, however, were simply not given enough options. . . . Baby Doe was not an unwanted child. Many offered to adopt him, but their efforts were never integrated into the process of deciding the fate of this innocent child. The parents, too are 'victims' in this instance . . . . Our system failed, and *that* has to be corrected."[199]

The Association for Retarded Citizens of the United States also responded, passing a resolution on April 30, 1982, reaffirming its 1973 position condemning practices of withholding treatment, which, in part, read:

WHEREAS, the Association for Retarded Citizens of the United States is gravely concerned that the practice of withholding medical treatment from persons—solely on the basis of diagnosis or prognosis of mental retardation—is increasing in this country at an alarming rate, THEREFORE BE IT RESOLVED THAT the Association for Retarded Citizens of the United States reaffirms the position it took in 1973 condemning such practices, AND FURTHERMORE does not support the right of physicians to recommend nor [sic] the right of parents to agree to the withholding of medical treatment where the only basis for such a decision is the diagnosis or prognosis of mental retardation. FURTHERMORE, it is the position of the Association for Retarded Citizens of the United States that counseling by a physician regarding the "quality of life" for an individual with mental retardation should never extend beyond the physician's medical knowledge of the condition.[200]

The Association sent its resolution to various medical associations and societies across the nation.

Once again George Will picked up his pen in defense of mentally retarded youngsters:

An Orwellian euphemism—"treatment to do nothing"—was concocted for this refusal of potentially lifesaving treatment. Indiana courts refused to order surgery. The baby's death was thus the result of premeditated action, in the hospital and in court.

Such killings can no longer be considered aberrations, or culturally incongruous. They are part of a social program to serve the convenience of adults by authorizing them to destroy inconvenient young life. The parents' legal arguments, conducted in private, reportedly emphasized freedom of choice. There is no reason to doubt that if the baby had not had Down's syndrome the operation would have been ordered without hesitation by the parents or, if not by them, the courts. Therefore the baby was killed because he was retarded.

Indeed, the parents' lawyer implied as much when, justifying the starvation, he emphasized that, even if successful, the surgery would not have corrected the retardation; that is, the Down's syndrome was sufficient reason for starving the infant. But the broader message of this case is that being an unwanted baby is a capital offense.[201]

An analyst for the American Bar Association's Commission on the Mentally Disabled concluded:

No one, not even parents, should be able to substitute their preferences for the preferences of their child in a matter as fundamental as life or death, particularly when parental interests do not necessarily coincide with the child's interests. The parents may sincerely believe that the best interests of their child will be served by discontinuing essential medical care or they may be more concerned with the trauma associated with raising a disabled child. In either event, the interests of the baby are not being well-served. The best interests of the child cannot possibly be determined without knowing the infant's potential for development; even if the potential were known, it is doubtful that such information would dictate withdrawing treatment. The only possible exceptions would seem to be where the child is suffering profound pain or is without consciousness. In such instances, a judicial decision should be made, based exclusively on the infant's point of view. If this had been done in Indiana, Baby Doe would not have died of starvation.

The convenience of the parents and society are interests that should be considered, but only secondarily in the context of allocating responsibilities for raising the child. Convenience should not be weighed against the baby's existence. . . .[202]

President Reagan was also incensed, contending that the decision not to treat Baby Doe represented a judgment "that retardation was the equivalent of a crime deserving the death penalty." "We cannot," he wrote, "survive as a free nation when some men decide that others are not fit to live and should be abandoned to abortion or infanticide."[203] On April 30, 1982, he sent a memorandum to the Attorney General of the United States and to the Secretary of Health and Human Services instructing their intervention in protecting newborn handicapped children. The President's memo contained language strongly supporting federal laws prohibiting discrimination against handicapped infants.

A bill was introduced in the House on May 26, 1983 that gave major authority to the National Center on Child Abuse and Neglect to investigate such cases and conduct a nationwide study on the issue. Also, a concurrent resolution was introduced on May 12 that stated an infant has the right to live and the right to medical treatment regardless of his or her handicap.[204]

During the same month, and in response to President Reagan's expressed desire to protect the potentially mentally retarded newborn, the following notice was distributed to approximately 7,000 hospitals by the Department of Health and Human Services.

Under section 504, it is unlawful for a recipient of federal financial assistance to withhold from a handicapped infant nutritional sustenance or medical or surgical treatment required to correct a life-threatening condition if: (1) the withholding is based on the fact that the infant is handicapped; (2) the handicap does not render the treatment or nutritional sustenance medically contraindicated.[205]

On March 7, 1983, the Department issued the following interim rule:

. . . each recipient that provides covered health care services to infants shall post and keep posted in a conspicuous place in each delivery ward, each maternity ward, each pediatric ward, and each nursery, including intensive care nursery, the following notice:
DISCRIMINATORY FAILURE TO FEED AND CARE FOR HANDICAPPED INFANTS IN THIS FACILITY IS PROHIBITED BY FEDERAL LAW.
Section 504 of the Rehabilitation Act of 1973 states that no otherwise qualified handicapped individual shall, solely by reason of handicap, be excluded from participation in, be denied the benefits of, or be subjected to discrimination under any program or activity receiving federal financial assistance.
Any person having knowledge that a handicapped infant is being discriminatorily denied food or customary medical care should immediately contact: Handicapped Infant Hotline, U.S. Department of Health and Human Services, Washington, DC.[206]

These rules were not well received by some medical practitioners and were appealed by the

American Academy of Pediatrics, the National Association of Children's Hospitals, and the Children's Hospital National Medical Center in Washington, D.C. On April 14, 1983, Judge Gerhard A. Gesell declared the rule invalid because it was "arbitrary and capricious and promulgated in violation of the Administrative Procedure Act." The judge, son of famed developmentalist Arnold Gesell, who frequently contributed to the field of mental retardation, did note, however, "Given the language of the statute and its similarity to other civil rights statutes which have been broadly read, it cannot be said that Section 504 does not authorize some regulation of the provision of some types of medical care to handicapped newborns."[207]

In view of the court's decision, the Secretary of the Department of Health and Human Services, on April 27, declared the original regulations to be invalid, and during the summer of 1983, issued new proposed rules.[208] While posting and the hotline were retained, the original commitment to protecting all new births was modified:

> The Secretary does not interpret Section 504 to apply to any case in which care or treatment is withheld on the basis of legitimate medical judgment. If a particular form of treatment is of dubious medical benefit to the patient or if the patient could not long survive even with the treatment, reasonable medical judgment could withhold the treatment and Section 504 does not require that the treatment be given. Section 504 does not compel medical personnel to attempt to perform impossible or futile acts or therapies. Thus, Section 504 does not require the imposition of futile therapies which merely temporarily prolong the process of dying of an infant born terminally ill.[209]

The American Association on Mental Deficiency responded favorably to the new rules when, in the summer of 1983, it not only reconfirmed its rights statement of 1973 but relayed its support of the Department's actions to the U.S. Office of Civil Rights:

> The existence of mental retardation is no justification for the termination of the life of any human being or for permitting such a life to be terminated either directly or through the withholding of life sustaining procedures.[210]

Further:

> We believe that the Association's and the Department's policies are mutually similar in two important respects. First, each policy affirms that an infant's disability (such as diagnosed for possible mental retardation) does not justify the termination of its life directly or through withholding life-sustaining procedures. Both policies, then, rest clearly on anti-discrimination grounds. Second, each policy affirms that treatment of infants who have been or may be diagnosed as disabled should be at least equal to the treatment of infants who have not been diagnosed as disabled. Both policies, then, rest on equal protection grounds.
>
> The Association believes it has a special obligation to point out that advances in the technology and methodology of specialized education, allied health, rehabilitation, and other disciplines, have developed so significantly since 1973–75, when the Association's position was adopted, that nowadays the lives of all disabled persons, particularly those with severe to profound disabilities, may be enhanced significantly, and made more meaningful and useful to them and others. Early intervention, early childhood education for the handicapped, special education with related services, and rehabilitation, among other disciplines, has [sic] made the state of art such that nowadays there is even more reason than in 1973–75 to adopt an anti-discrimination posture concerning medical treatment of disabled infants.[211]

Despite the position of the American Association on Mental Deficiency, when the Secretary of the Department of Health and Human Services called for comments, those groups against the original version re-expressed their opposition, and once again the regulations were modified; but the government's authority to have immediate access to hospital records and to pursue subsequent legal action, when indicated, was maintained. This did little to mollify those in the medical community who did not want any federal involvement whatsoever.

Once again, opponents of the regulations received support from both a state and lower federal court when ruling in a New York "Baby Jane Doe" case that federal representatives did not have access to hospital records when parents refused their release.[212] In response to these decisions plus the continuous objections from the medical community, the newly appointed Secretary of the Department of Health and Human Services, Otis R. Bowen, pursued the matter to the Supreme Court, which, in 1984, agreed to hear opposing arguments.*

While many professionals and citizens discussed and occasionally argued the merits of federal involvement and while attorneys were compiling their legal briefs in preparation for the Supreme Court hearing, Congress significantly strengthened its child abuse laws by including a number of measures to protect disabled newborns under PL 98-457, Child Abuse Amendments of 1984.[214] The Amendments and related regulations required state child abuse agencies receiving federal funds to establish procedures that would provide for the coordination and consultation between the state's child protective agency and individuals designated by appropriate health care facilities; assure prompt notification by hospital personnel in cases involving suspected medical neglect; and establish the authority, under state law, for the state child protective agency to pursue legal remedies necessary to prevent the withholding of medically indicated treatment from disabled infants with life-threatening conditions.[215]

The term "withholding of medically indicated treatment" was defined as "the failure to respond to the infant's life-threatening conditions by providing treatment (including appropriate nutrition, hydration and medication) which, in the treating physician's (or physicians') reasonable medical judgement [sic] will most likely be effective in ameliorating or correcting such conditions . . . "[216]

The Amendments also recommended but did not require that each hospital create a review committee to educate hospital personnel and families of disabled infants with life-threatening conditions, recommend hospital-wide policies and guidelines concerning the withholding of medically indicated treatment from such disabled infants, and offer counsel and review in cases involving disabled infants with life-threatening conditions.[217] Emphasis was placed on the committee's role in policy development, case review, and counseling. In essence, Congress shifted primary protective responsibility from federal to state agencies.

While this placated the medical community somewhat, others remained skeptical, and with some justification. Ten years prior to the government's issuing its final regulations, a small group of physicians, attorneys, and others interested in this complex area of decision making met in Sonoma, California, where one physician was noted to observe:

> I can persuade 99 percent of parents to my way of thinking if I really work at it, even if I am 100 percent wrong. If I tell them in such a way that I appear concerned and that I am knowledgeable and that I have their interest at heart and the interest of their . . . newborn baby, there is no question in my mind that they will let me "cut off the infant's head." I think informed consent is an absolute farce legalistically, morally, ethically. . . .[218]

Another physician, commenting on the committee approach, stated: "Typically, committee members are socially elite persons, therefore they are distant from the lives of most people. . . ." The same person also contended that committees of this nature were "very close to the German model in Nazi times. . . ."[219]

The "committee approach" received national attention in 1984 when it became evident that some hospitals were making life-determining decisions affecting disabled or

---

*The Supreme Court reached its decision on June 9, 1986, which, in essence, declared that the Department's interjection of the federal government into medical and treatment decisions made by hospitals and parents was not authorized under Section 504 of the 1973 Rehabilitation Act: ". . . nothing in the statute authorizes the Secretary to dispense with the law's focus on discrimination and instead to employ federal resources to save the lives of handicapped children newborns, without regard to whether they are victims of discrimination by recipients of federal funds or not. Section 504 does not authorize the Secretary to give unsolicited advice either to parents, to hospitals, or to state officials who are faced with difficult treatment decisions concerning handicapped children."[213] This decision did not negate the provision of PL 98-457.

handicapped infants on factors other than the baby's condition. Apparently some hospitals had adopted a formula identical or similar to that proposed by A. Shaw: $QL = NE \times (H + S)$, where QL was quality of life, NE was the infant's natural endowment, H was the contribution from home and family, and S was the contribution from society.[220] Thus, disabled infants with similar difficulties were treated differently, depending upon the committee's perception of parental adequacy and/or available community services and support.[221]

Be it a single physician or committee, in 1983, H. Rutherford Turnbull, parent, attorney, and faculty member of the University of Kansas, questioned a key assumption associated with the physician-parent decision-making process that parents would withdraw the infant from that hospital's care entirely if they and the staff disagreed about a no-treatment situation. "Much," he stated, "has been written about both the negative and positive aspects of handicapped children within families. The problem is that the negative tends to be more emphasized by physicians than the positive . . . and parents of newborns are likely to rely on physicians and medical staff for advice concerning those effects. Additionally, there are no data that parents will discharge their children from care in any case where physicians recommend nontreatment."[222]

Others felt that the entire process failed to consider sufficiently the interest of the child as an individual and that, in truth, it was veering too close to the policy of Germany's Director of Public Health during the Nazi years: "The life of an individual has meaning only in the light . . . of his meaning to this family and to his national state."[223]

Attitutes Toward Infanticide

As indicated, both the medical community and the public in general were divided over this issue. On the one hand:

> I went into medicine to do two things: to save lives and alleviate suffering. But I do not interpret that to mean that I alleviate the suffering

of the parents of my patient by disposing of my patient. (Dr. C. Everett Koop, United States Surgeon General)[224]

> The whole history of medicine is at hand to answer any . . . death-doctor. Those who delivered humanity from plague and rabies were not those who burned the plague-striken alive in their houses or suffocated rabid patients between two mattresses. . . . Victory against Down's syndrome—i.e., curing children of the ill-effect of their genetic overdose—may not be too far off, if only the disease is attacked, not the babies. (Dr. Jerome Lejeune, discoverer of trisomy 21)[225]

> We cannot destroy life. We cannot regard the hydrocephalic child as a nonperson and accept the responsibility for disposing of it like a sick animal. If there are those in society who think this step would be good, let them work for a totalitarian form of government where, beginning with the infirm and the incompetent and ending with the intellectually dissident, nonpersons are disposed of day and night by those in power. (Dr. J. Engelbert Dunphy, former president of the American College of Surgeons)[226]

> There is a haunting, forty-year-old precedent for a final solution to the Baby Does who come into the world (J. K., M.D.)[227]

On the other hand:

> . . . no newborn infant should be declared human until it has passed tests regarding its genetic endowment and . . . if it fails these tests, it forfeits the right to live. (Francis Crick, 1962 Nobel laureate)[228]

> Nature has its laws and we should observe them. Maybe we shouldn't try to rescue those whom nature or God has created so imperfectly. (Raymond Duff, M.D., professor of pediatrics, Yale University)[229]

Studies also confirmed the division among pediatricians and pediatric surgeons. Two of these, reported in 1977, indicated that approximately 55% of the pediatricians sampled would acquiesce to the parents' decision not to authorize corrective surgery if the infant also had Down syndrome.[230] According to one of these studies, 62% of all respondents would acquiesce even when believing that Down syndrome children are capable of being useful and bringing love and happiness into the home.[231]

As regards the public in general, feelings were equally mixed:

It is sickening to see the federal bureaucracy enter the case of Baby Jane Doe, who was born with serious handicaps. . . . (W.K.)[232]

Handicapped people have as much right to live and receive appropriate medical treatment as anyone else. The Reagan Administration is not "forcing hospitals to do whatever is necessary to prolong life." The Government is only ensuring that the handicapped receive fair and equal treatment. (M.M.)[233]

I personally feel that [Baby Jane Doe] does have the right to life, but the parents shouldn't keep the baby because they don't want her to have the operation. The baby should be adopted and taken care of by parents who want it and will love it. If the natural parents will be suffering while the baby is alive, they shouldn't take care of it. Every life has a right to live. (J.M.)[234]

A 1983 Gallup poll of 1,540 adults living in more than 300 localities clearly illustrated the division. The question and key findings are presented in Table 2.5.[235]

Table 2.5. Results of a 1983 Gallup poll of 1,540 adults living in more than 300 localities

Question

"When a badly deformed baby who could live only a few years was born in a Midwest city, the parents asked the doctors not to keep the baby alive. Would you take the same position as the parents did, or not?"

	Yes	No	No opinion
National	43%	40%	17%
Men	45%	37%	18%
Women	41%	43%	16%
Whites	45%	38%	17%
Blacks	28%	59%	13%
Married	43%	41%	16%
Single	52%	34%	14%
College education	54%	33%	13%
High school	38%	43%	19%
Grade school	42%	42%	16%
Protestants	43%	38%	19%
Catholics	40%	47%	13%

Source: MR right-to-life poll. (1983). *Superintendent's Digest, 2,* 28; reprinted by permission.

As regards the affected, there appeared to be little argument:

Mr. C. refers to the baby's life as one "barren of joy." When will people who are perfectly intelligent, clear-headed and well-educated stop assuming that one must be healthy, handsome and preferably wealthy to be human and happy? I am not healthy (I have cerebral palsy), not handsome and, as a Federal GS-5 clerk, will probably never be wealthy.

My childhood and adolescence were spent in more than a decade of operations and therapy. Yet I am quite sane and quite firm when I state that I would not exchange my handicapped body for that of the most muscular Redskins players, for through it I have learned more in the 30 years of my life than some people learn in a century. I am not afraid to suffer, and I am not afraid to help those who now suffer. (P.G.)[236]

Due to severe brain damage incurred at birth, I am unable to dress myself, toilet myself, or write; my secretary is typing this letter. Many thousands of dollars had to be spent on my rehabilitation and education in order for me to reach my present professional status as Counseling Psychologist. My parents were also told 35 years ago that there was little or no hope of achieving meaningful "humanhood" for their daughter.

Have I reached "humanhood"? Compared with Doctors D. and C., I believe I have surpassed it!

Instead of changing the law to make it legal to weed out us "vegetables," let us change the laws so that we may receive quality in medical care, education, and freedom to live as full and productive lives as our potentials allow. (S.D.)[237]

When I was born the doctors didn't give me six months to live. My mother told them that she could keep me alive, but they didn't believe it. It took a hell of a lot of work, but she showed with love and determination that she could be the mother to a handicapped child. I don't know for a fact what I had, but they thought it was severe retardation and cerebral palsy. They thought I would never walk. I still have seizures. Maybe that has something to do with it too. . . .

The doctors told my mother that I would be a burden to her.

What is retardation? It's hard to say. I guess it's having problems thinking. Some people think that you can tell if a person is retarded by looking at them. If you think that way you don't give people the benefit of the doubt. You judge a person by how they look or how they talk or what the tests show, but you can never really tell what is inside the person.

Take a couple of friends of mine, Tommy McC. and PJ. Tommy was a guy who was really nice to be with. You could sit down with him and have a nice conversation and enjoy yourself. He was a mongoloid. The trouble was people couldn't see beyond that. If he didn't look that way it would have been different, but there he was locked into what the other people thought he was. Now PJ was really something else. I've watched that guy and I can see in his eyes that he is aware. He doesn't know what's going on. He can only crawl and he doesn't talk, but you don't know what's inside. When I was with him and I touched him, I know that he knows.

I don't know. Maybe I used to be retarded. That's what they said anyway. I wish they could see me now. I wonder what they'd say if they could see me holding down a regular job and doing all kinds of things. I bet they wouldn't believe it. (E.M.)[238]

In the final analysis, the situation was most difficult, and while the ultimate impact of the new directions would not be assessed for many years to come, there was no question that the courts had rendered decisions unique to the history of this country. While acceptable to many, others wondered about their compatibility with Thomas Jefferson's belief that, ''Whatever be the degree of talents, it is no measure of their rights.''[239]

Chapter

3

LEARNING, MENTAL ILLNESS, AND NORM-VIOLATING BEHAVIOR

WHILE MEDICAL SCIENCE made numerous advances in treating those who were mentally retarded, including substantially increasing the life expectancy of the more severely affected, ultimately the success of each individual would be contingent upon their skills and personal-social behavior. Thus, the need for sound research in these behavioral areas became increasingly apparent, as recognized by the President's Panel on Mental Retardation in 1962; for a few years, such research was substantially supported by the federal government with promising results.[1]

LEARNING RESEARCH

Contemporary research into the learning characteristics of persons who were mentally retarded had its origins in the fifties. This resulted from a significant amount of university activity, usually federally funded. In 1952, the Institute for Research on Exceptional Children was established at the University of Illinois in Urbana; in 1954, the George Peabody College for Teachers received a large training-research grant; in 1953, the Association for Retarded Children laid down the foundations for its research program; in 1955, the American Association on Mental Deficiency received federal funding; and in 1958, the Southern Regional Education Board formed a panel on mental retardation to approach the problems associated with training and research. Though these were the major centers for much of the research activity during those years, other universities and institutions were funded for similar purposes. Those were exciting days for researchers and graduate students alike, with the result that many areas and topics were explored; yet, by 1960, much of the effort was episodic in nature, lacking what some would call the critical "second effort."[2] While over the quarter century enthusiasm for research did not abate, many of the studies continued to represent the single, dissertation-type investigation, and the field was plagued with a substantial turnover in research personnel. A few researchers, however, remained active throughout the period, concentrated on relatively limited areas of inquiry, and subsequently, generated useful data and hypotheses.

This does not mean to imply that the research trends or practices of the fifties remained unaltered. On the contrary, they underwent several dramatic changes in terms of both learning theories and the level of retardation among subjects. In order to understand, at least in very general terms, the altered course of research activity, one needs to focus on two broad categories of inquiry: 1) learning and memory and 2) operant conditioning and behavior modification.

LEARNING AND MEMORY

With substantial federal funding to universities and other agencies that provided both research and training, interested scholars during the sixties and early seventies were in an excellent position to study a wide range of learning phenomena, often employing an equally wide range of paradigms. Though it is impossible to review even briefly the tremendous amount of research conducted over the quarter century, one can gain a flavor of the investigative situation by examining one of the questions most frequently asked, "Do persons who are mildly mentally retarded learn differently than those who are not?" While no firm answer to this question was reached, significant research was conducted, which at least gave the question meaning and substance. In essence, two general points of view emerged: 1) differences were attributed to motivational factors and 2) differences were due to peculiar deficits.

Edward Zigler of Yale University, utilizing his research data, advocated a developmental approach to understanding the learning characteristics of the largest group of mentally retarded persons etiologically identified as cultural-familial; that is, those with mild degrees of intellectual impairment without any known central nervous system abnormality or damage. This approach, which he summarized succinctly in 1982, held:

. . . the familially retarded person is viewed as a normal individual in the sense that he falls within the normal distribution of intelligence dictated by the gene pool. He or she is normal in exactly the same sense that a person who is in the lower third percentile of height is considered to be normal. This person will be called "short" but will not be seen as being abnormal. As a consequence of the developmental theorists' view of a familially retarded person as a normal individual, these theorists predict that the performance of this retarded person and a nonretarded person of equivalent developmental level (most typically defined by mental age [MA] on an IQ test) on a cognitive task should be exactly the same.[3]

This position evolved from many years of research that, in the early days, related to Kurt Lewin's field theory developed during the thirties and presented in two texts: *A Dynamic Theory of Personality,* 1935; and *Principles of Topological Psychology,* 1936.[4] A unique attribute of Lewin's theory was his employment of topographical concepts to represent psychological reality. In simplistic terms, his theory set forth the proposition that each individual has a personal life space surrounded by a psychological environment. Both the person's life space as well as his psychological environment are divided into many regions. As concerns mentally retarded persons, Lewin postulated that their life space and psychological environment had fewer subsections or regions than normal, and that the associated theoretical boundaries were rigid rather than fluid. Because of rigidity, mentally retarded persons would not be able to utilize their existing intellectual resources and knowledge with the same degree of facility as their normal peers, nor would they gain as much from the psychological environment. In 1936, Lewin explicitly stated, "the major dynamic difference between a feeble-minded and a normal child of the same degree of differentiation to consist in a greater stiffness, a smaller capacity for dynamic rearrangement in the psychical systems of the former."[5]

During the forties, Lewin's field theory, with its implications concerning mental retardation, attracted the attention of Jacob Kounin. His research over that decade tended to support Lewin's premise that when the mental age is held constant "the older and/or more feeble-minded an individual is, the more will his behaviors be characterized by dynamic rigidity; that is, greater rigidity in the boundaries between regions."[6] Zigler, however, picked up on a hypothesis originally advanced by Lewin but later abandoned to the effect that perhaps rigidity reflected more on the individual's motivation than on any inherent limitations. By 1977, Zigler and Balla were able to demonstrate that socially deprived mentally retarded persons had a heightened motivation to interact with a supportive adult, had an increased responsiveness to social reinforcement, and were more sensitive to cues provided by an adult. Paradoxically, while youngsters sought the approval of a supportive adult, as they grew older they became increasingly reluctant and wary to do so. Such results, according to Zigler, supported the contention that nonorganically involved mentally retarded youngsters would perform the same as their normal counterparts of similar mental age if all positive motivational factors were in place.[7]

Other researchers, with equally strong theoretical bases and research findings took issue with this hypothesis. These scientists Zigler labeled "difference theorists," meaning those who maintained "that retarded and nonretarded persons even of equivalent developmental levels should differ in cognitive performance because of intrinsic differences over and above intellectual slowness."[8] A number of researchers qualified as "difference theorists," though none would deny the importance of motivation nor, in many instances, the possible validity of Zigler's hypothesis; but their work demonstrated to their satisfaction that mildly mentally retarded persons did have peculiar learning deficits.

Among the more notable difference theorists was Norman Ellis of the University of Alabama, whose work involved the stimulus trace theory that he introduced in the early sixties.[9] This theory held that the memory stimulus trace is shortened and the intensity of the stimulus is diminished among mentally retarded individuals. Thus, behavior involving short-term memory, which is critical to much learning, would be impaired. In his early writings, Ellis also suggested a possible neurological basis for his stimulus trace hypothesis: "A deficiency of available reverberator circuits was suggested as a possible neurophysiological substrate underlying individual capacity differences. Consequently, a learning deficit in subnormal organisms could be attributed to noncontinuity between items to be associated."[10] Though the neurological basis for the stimulus trace theory was set aside, years of research tended to support the deficit notion.

A number of other well-known and highly respected researchers also suggested deficits. Alexander Luria, for example, believed that mentally retarded individuals suffered a major defect in their ability to utilize effectively their verbal system to mediate and regulate behavior.[11] David Zeaman and Betty House noted severe attending problems.[12]

Alexander Luria

Though it is beyond the purview of this historical review to consider in depth the work of any given individual, one of the most remarkable contributors to the field was Alexander Ramonovich Luria (1902–1977). For more than 5 decades, Luria, psychologist, physician, and defectologist, sought to develop a greater understanding of human higher thought processes. In his many years as professor of psychology and director of the Neuropsychological Laboratory at Moscow University, U.S.S.R., he conducted research in many areas, including culture and thought, mental development among children, mental retardation, and the neurological aspects of behavior. One of his many contributions was *The Mentally Retarded Child,* published in 1963. Described as a man "always in a hurry" with an enormous appetite for research, Luria strongly believed that psychology should have relevance to the building of a better society. In the

Alexander Luria

words of Michael Cole, Luria's work was "a monument to the intellectual and humanistic traditions that represent the best of the human culture he labored to understand and improve."[13]

Other Research

Though, as indicated, the motivational-deficit controversy was not resolved, research over the quarter century clearly demonstrated that the learning behavior of mentally retarded persons was extremely complex and often difficult to study. Even the "simplest" of learning phenomena often proved frustratingly complicated. Zeaman and House, in a moment of delightful introspection and assessment, acknowledged:

> It has often seemed to us during our 25 years of investigation that we should be closer to achieving our programmatic goals; and it may have appeared to others that we have spent more effort in developing an adequate theory of "simple" discriminative learning than in relating intelligence to discriminative performance. To these *others*, we answer that simple discriminative learning has turned out to be surprisingly complex and that an adequate theory is necessary for our programmatic goals. It makes little sense to us to report endless correlations of intelligence

and performance on tasks that are weakly analyzed theoretically, for that is precisely where we *began*. Our own impatience with the slowness of it all can be attributed to the fact that when we were younger, we thought psychology was easier than it is.[14]

In addition to those researchers who tended to concentrate on relatively discrete functions, there were cognitive theorists who began with complex rather than simple behaviors. Throughout the years, a few such researchers pursued their efforts to generate relatively complex models of learning that encompassed such components as sensory inputs, motivation, memory, strategies, and the internal processes of integration. Though behavior modification received primary attention and visibility during the seventies, cognitive psychologists were successful in generating meaningful models of learning with strong teaching implications. Earl Butterfield of the University of Washington, cognitive theorist with a long-standing interest in mental retardation, felt comfortable in reporting in 1983 that he was "optimistic for the heady possibilities that behavioral science is on the threshold of delivering ways to improve thinking to the extent that we will be able to claim cures for cognitive defects that lead to mental retardation."[15] Part of his optimism reflected on the growing interest of experimental psychologists in general to focus on individual differences and broader cognitive processes.

Beginning with the late sixties and accelerating rapidly in the seventies, two significant changes greatly altered the course of research in the field of mental retardation. First, attention was redirected from the mildly and moderately mentally retarded person to the more severely and profoundly affected. Second, many psychologists with research interests concentrated on operant conditioning and behavior modification.

These trends were acknowledged in 1979 by a concerned H. Carl Haywood, then-editor of the *American Journal of Mental Deficiency,* who asked, "What happened to mild and moderate mental retardation?" From 1969 to 1973, he noted, most of the research articles published in the *Journal* were concerned with mild and moderate degrees of mental retardation. From 1974 to 1978, the majority of papers were devoted to persons with severe and profound degrees of mental retardation. While it was important to study the behavior of the more severely affected, at the same time, Haywood urged his colleagues to "rediscover mild and moderate mental retardation and invest in those levels renewed research interest and the necessary public support to sustain good research and a full slate of high-quality services."[16] Despite Haywood's urgings, behavior modification studies involving primarily the more severely affected persons continued to be most prevalent.

OPERANT CONDITIONING AND BEHAVIOR MODIFICATION

Operant conditioning, at least in its non-theoretical, nonstructured form, has been applied since the dawn of man when the first mother or father by smile, pat, grunt, grimace, or clout informed their offspring whether their behavior was approved. The scientific foundations of operant conditioning, however, date back only to the late 19th century and the work of three Russian scientists.

First was Ivan M. Sechenov (1829–1905), a physician who maintained a lifelong interest in psychology. He set forth a number of hypotheses about the nervous system and learning, strongly urging that the objective methods of physiology be applied to the study of psychology. His work, in turn, greatly influenced Ivan P. Pavlov (1849–1936), probably the early Russian learning researcher best known in the United States. His famous dog studies clearly demonstrated that a response could be conditioned to a known stimuli. In this instance, the dog was conditioned to salivate at the sound of a bell originally paired with the sight of food. Though Pavlov's work concentrated on stimulus properties, in contrast to operant conditioning, which places its emphasis on the response, he nevertheless set forth with scientific verification the possibility of what became known as classical conditioning.* At the same time, he won a Nobel Prize in 1904 for his scientific contributions on the subject of digestion.

Pavlov's work was expanded by Vladimir M. Bechterev (1857–1927), physiologist, neurologist, and psychiatrist, who held a faculty appointment in Mental and Nervous Diseases at the Military Medical Academy of Saint Petersburg. Bechterev was interested in conditioning not only from a methodological perspective but also in terms of extending conditioning experiments to many problems of psychology with the intent "to replace psychology with a scientific discipline called 'reflexology.' "[17]

In the United States, the first major attempt at behaviorism was by John B. Watson (1878–1958), a former student of John Dewey. Watson's bold statements concerning behaviorism are known by every student of psychology. For example, in his very first public statement in 1913, he declared:

> Psychology as the behaviorist views it is a purely objective experimental branch of natural science. Its theoretical goal is the prediction and control of behavior. Introspection forms no essential part of its methods, nor is the scientific value of its data dependent upon the readiness with which they lend themselves to interpretation in terms of consciousness. The behaviorist, in his efforts to get a unitary scheme of animal response, recognizes the dividing line between man and brute. The behavior of man, with all of its refinement and complexity, forms only a part of the behaviorist's total scheme of investigation.[19]

In 1924, following further thought and research, he confidently proclaimed, "Give me a dozen healthy infants, well-formed, and my own specified world to being them up in and I'll guarantee to take anyone at random and train him to become any type of specialist I might select—doctor, lawyer, artist, mer-

---

*With the exception of the highly respected work of Leonard Ross of the University of Wisconsin–Madison, classical conditioning research did not attract much interest in the field of mental retardation.[18]

chant—chief and, yes, even beggar-man and thief, regardless of his talents, pensions, tendencies, abilities, vocations, and race of his ancestors."[20]

Though Watson's exciting pronouncements and his famous research study of conditioning a young boy to fear furry animals were important, it was the theoretical work of Edward L. Thorndike (1874–1949) that really set the pattern for future American research and conditioning. Thorndike first published his concept of "connectionism" in *Animal Intelligence,* in 1898. In subsequent writings, he set forth several of the fundamental principles that would become indigenous to operant conditioning and behavior modification as it is known today. First was his law of effect, which referred to the notion that a connection (the association between sense impressions and impulses to action) would be strengthened or weakened as a result of its consequences. Second, he predated the operationalists' position by many years when he wrote in 1913, "By a satisfying state of affairs is meant one which the animal does nothing to avoid, often doing things which maintain or renew it. By an annoying state of affairs is meant one which the animal does nothing to preserve, often doing things which put an end to it."[21]

Though these principles were based on animal research, Thorndike was tremendously interested in children, their learning and education. It was that influence that motivated his investigating the various effects of praise and punishment. Originally, he believed that praise and punishment were of equal power but further research indicated that punishment was not. Subsequently, in one of those rare moments of public professional integrity, he confronted his audience with a simple statement "I was wrong." Further research by other scientists, however, indicated that his original thinking was at least partially correct.

Thorndike's research and notions of reinforcement as well as other dimensions of his theory were further investigated by other researchers who, in turn, would generate their own theories, including Edwin R. Guthrie and contiguous conditioning, Edward C. Tolman

and purposive behaviorism, Clark L. Hall and the hypthetico-deductive theory, and O. Hobart Mowrer with his two-factor theory.[22] But the concept that won the day and laid down the foundation for many of the practices to be adopted in the field of mental retardation was the operant conditioning theory of B.F. Skinner.

B. (Burrhus) F. (Frederic) Skinner

Born in Susquehanna, Pennsylvania, in 1904, B.F. Skinner was raised in a family environment that placed numerous strictures on his behavior, a factor that may well have influenced the development of his highly regimented, disciplined personal life-style. He received his bachelor's degree from Hamilton College in Clinton, New York, in 1926 and his advanced degrees from Harvard University in 1930 and 1931. Between the time of receiving his Ph.D. until his appointment at Harvard University as a William James Lecturer in 1947, he was affiliated with a number of universities and colleges. In 1948, he joined Harvard's department of psychology, a position he filled on a full-time basis until 1974, when he "retired," assuming the position of professor emeritus. After his retirement, he produced eight books, including three devoted to his life and work, and one on aging, *Enjoy Old Age,* co-authored with psychologist M.E. Vaughn.[23]

In 1938, Skinner set forth his principles of operant conditioning in a book entitled, *Behavior of Organisms.*[24] Since that date, both he and his theory have remained somewhat in the center of an ongoing controversy. He was even introduced on one occasion with the words, "Here is the devil."[25] Many disagreed vociferously with Skinner's position that the science of behavior was based solely on the role of the environment and its rewards, rather than on individual thought and self-determination. Emotional attributes, such as love, fear, and feelings, were, in his words, simply "collateral products" of people's genetic and environmental histories and, in terms of scientific research and theory development they proved to be "fascinating attractions along the path of dalliance."[26] Others raised serious ethical questions as to the right of society, through the principles of operant conditioning, to manipulate externally the lives of others. In contrast, Skinner, being highly influenced by the writings of Bacon, envisioned a utopian society based on his principles, one that would be free from aversive stimulation.[27]

Being a theorist by thought and a tinkerer by disposition, Skinner designed several implements to augment his learning theory. One, which created quite a stir at the time though it did no apparent disservice to those it affected, was the development of what was to be labeled, much to his chagrin, the "Skinner Box." This was an enclosed, sound-proof, and temperature-controlled environment in which his youngest daughter, Deborah, was raised for 2½ years. Less controversial was his exasperation at the quality of her elementary school instruction, in response to which he applied his behavioralistic principles and designed one of the first teaching machines.[28]

Despite his numerous critics and the various debates concerning behaviorism as a theory and as a science, in the final analysis, his principles were adopted by many. Perhaps no theory to date has ever been applied to so many people in so many different situations. Personal recognition came in many forms, including honorary degrees from 15 colleges and universities, the National Medal of Science, the Gold Medal of the American Psychological Foundation, as well as awards by the Joseph P. Kennedy, Jr. Foundation for Mental Retardation and the Association for Retarded Citizens of the United States.

Throughout the course of his professional life, Skinner wrote many papers and books concerning the science of behaviorism, each avoiding the inclusion of hypothetical constructs, such as emotions. Reflecting upon his own three-volume autobiography, in which he maintained the posture of viewing his life as a case history, he noted, "If I am right about human behavior, I have written the autobiography of a nonperson."[29]

B.F. Skinner

Principles of Operant Conditioning

The fundamental principles of operant conditioning were, as indicated previously, set forth by Skinner in his publication of 1938. In essence, behavior that is positively reinforced will tend to be repeated; conversely, behavior that is ignored, negatively reinforced, or punished will tend to extinguish. The concept, simple in expression, proved extremely complex in reality and scientific investigation. In the course of human development, which behaviors are reinforced and/or which reinforcers are of significance under which circumstances was extremely difficult to determine. Further, in application, one was confronted with the major task of consistently and immediately reinforcing (positively or negatively) behavior desired to be repeated or extinguished. Consistency, especially in nonclinical settings, was extremely difficult, if not impossible, to maintain.

Skinner's theory of operant conditioning was initially based on innumerable animal studies, but by the mid-fifties, his principles began to be applied with human subjects, gradually acquiring the clinical label of behavior modification. And it soon became evident that the principles of operant conditioning applied to human subjects could be used, misused, and abused.

Sidney Bijou

Among the first researchers to examine Skinner's principles in terms of human development, including that of persons who were mentally retarded, was Sidney Bijou, whose work throughout the years exemplified the very finest manner in which behavior modification could be applied in both theory and practice. Bijou, who had trained with Kenneth Spence at the University of Iowa, where he received his doctorate in 1941, was originally steeped in the psychological tenets of Hull and Spence. Following his appointment to Indiana University in 1946, where he worked with Skinner, Bijou, somewhat disenchanted with the large number of hypothetical constructs set forth by Hull and Spence, began to pursue the experimental analysis of behavior. In 1948, he left Indiana to take a position at the University of Washington, which included the directorship of the University's Institute of Child Development. It was here that he continued his exceptional research with children and turned his attention to mental retardation, which he conceptualized as "developmental retardation." In the early sixties, he set forth the challenge of behaviorism and mental retardation research:

Instead of viewing the cause of psychological retardation as being a theoretical construct such as mentality, or as a biological phenomenon such as impairment of the brain, it is suggested that it be conceived as generated by adverse histories or simply as failures of coordinations of stimulus and response functions. This position suggests a search for the specific conditions of which limited repertoires may be a function. The search may be directed, as it would in studying normal and accelerated development, toward analyzing organismic variables—the role of the hereditary process and the environmental events influencing consequent organismic variables— and the life history of the total organism interact-

ing with environmental events from the time of fertilization. A functional analysis suggests a search into interactions conceptualized as intermittent reinforcement and extinction, inadequate reinforcement history, severe punishment, and other factors, such as extreme satiation and deprivations, and emotional operations.[30]

After more than 2 decades of research with children, parents, and teachers, in 1983, Bijou, now adjunct professor of psychology and special education at the University of Arizona in Tucson, concluded that his efforts, as well as those of others, held great promise for preventing mild and moderate degrees of mental or developmental retardation where organic or biomedical involvement was not evident. Specifically, he proposed that "a strategy for preventing mild and moderate retardation in young children, from a behavioral analyst point of view, involves modifying through systematic training the behavior of parents and teachers in order to provide children with more and new opportunities and incentives for intellectual and academic achievement."[31] He hoped that through continued behavioral analysis of preschool children and the development of the direct and structured models for comprehensive educational intervention with

Sidney Bijou

the disadvantaged, by the time youngsters had completed the fourth grade, they would be "able to demonstrate on objective tests intellectual, personal, and academic competencies within the normal range of development."[32]

While not all answers were in and many youngsters still failed to attain the desired levels of performance, Bijou remained optimistic and confident in the advantages of behavioral analysis. Even if his proposed strategies failed to satisfy his ultimate goals, the outcome alone could not "help but enrich the lives of the children and strengthen their functioning in society."[33]

Further Research and Application

As indicated, research of the nature just described was productive in improving the performance and functional levels of many mildly and moderately retarded youngsters, and, at the same time, held great promise for the future. Skinner's principles, however, also played a vital role in enabling persons interested in assisting more severely disabled mentally retarded individuals develop techniques capable of facilitating development. For too many years, most severely and profoundly mentally retarded youngsters were committed to institutions where their lives were often void of programming short of basic custodial care, which frequently was of dubious quality. But by the sixties, advances in medical science had assured many such children a significantly improved life expectancy and had stimulated many to improve the quality of that life within the home, community, and institution, often relying on behavior modification.

The quality of research varied immensely, and the results were often equivocal, claimed only partial success, and usually failed to determine if the acquired behavior persisted beyond the training program. In 1979, Whitman and Scibak examined several hundred articles on the application of behavior modification techniques with persons who were mentally retarded and concluded that behavior modification techniques were being applied pervasively and played an instrumental role in facilitating training programs for more se-

verely affected individuals, primarily in such nonintellectual areas as basic self-care skills. In summarizing their evaluation of the literature, however, the authors noted a number of limitations, including the lack of empirical validation, the absence of any discussion of behaviors generalized or not generalized to other settings, and the failure to identify adequately the characteristics of individuals with whom a given procedure had been successfully introduced. They were also critical of the often inadequate procedural descriptions that precluded their replication in other clinical or research situations.[34] Their conclusions were similar to those reported by other knowledgeable reviewers.[35]

Throughout the sixties, many books and hundreds of articles about operant conditioning and the broader techniques encompassed under behavior modification were published, ranging in topic from simple toilet training to the treatment of problems among autistic mentally retarded persons. Yet, perhaps the most significant early book in terms of actual utilization was *Teaching the Mentally Retarded*, published by the Southern Regional Education Board in 1965.[36] Addressed primarily to direct care personnel, the text set forth a positive, encouraging philosophy toward programming for more severely and profoundly mentally retarded persons. It also presented in clear, understandable terms for the relatively uninitiated the basic principles of behavior modification and their actual application in training situations. The quality of the publication was exceptional, and it soon found its way into many homes, clinics, and institutions.

The preceding comments referred primarily to the use of positive reinforcement techniques in facilitating the acquisition of basic skills; however, with the advent of operant conditioning and its implications for managing difficult-to-control behavior, many clinicians (as well as parents and administrators) hoped they now could successfully attack some of the most disturbing and life-threatening behaviors common to approximately 10% of mentally retarded persons, including self-injurious behavior.[37] As succinctly and sensitively expressed by Baumeister and Rollings, "perhaps the most distressing and bizarre of all the behavioral aberrations that people exhibit are those repetitive or stereotyped acts that produce self-inflicted injuries. There are probably few among us, even those whose clinical experiences have inured us to most of the frailties of mankind, who do not experience a quickened sense of anguish upon witnessing a child beat and brutalize himself."[38] Also of concern were the less threatening but equally undesirable, noninjurious stereotypic behaviors, such as constant body rocking.

Throughout the years, knowledgeable persons reviewing relevant research usually came to the conclusion that some techniques worked with some problems for some period of time with some individuals in some settings when administered by some researchers.[39] Some of the techniques found to be successful, at least occasionally, were satiation, isolation, timeout, physical restraint, electric stimulation, and over-correction. Of the various techniques used, the one that seemed most effective in terms of modifying self-injurious behavior and anti-social conduct involved "alternative reinforcement procedures."[40] This multiple approach required ignoring or, under some circumstances, punishing the undesirable behavior, accompanied by positively reinforcing desirable behavior.

From a research perspective, many of the aforementioned studies again failed to adhere to the most rudimentary scientific requirements. To illustrate, of 500 studies examined by Schroeder and his colleagues in 1979, at least two-thirds consisted of "case demonstrations with inadequate experimental design."[41] In the final analysis, reviewers of related literature cited the same problems as mentioned before concerning characteristics of residents treated, generalization, durability of results, and symptom substitution. As summarized by Schroeder and associates in 1979, "The major effects that have been shown appear to be more related to the setting in which the intervention was performed and the type of intervention rather than on type of subjects used or the specific problems they exhibited. Neither taxonomic subsets of retarded persons [n]or etiological characteristics can be related to treatment selection or prognosis at this time, although there is considerable research interest in this area. . . . Some pervasive issues make comparison of the effectiveness of different intervention procedures difficult: lack of appropriate technology for programming generalization . . . lack of efficient experimental comparison designs; ambiguities in the interpretation of statistical and clinical significance of treatment effects; and lack of analysis of covariation among target and collateral behaviors."[42]

Looking at the overall direction of research with subjects who were mentally retarded, knowledgeable scientists, while recognizing that the sixties and early seventies had been particularly exciting years and that numerous gains had been made, found considerable room for improvement. In addition to the usual evaluatory comments related to design and technology, two major shortcomings were evident. First, many believed that too much emphasis was placed on small, discreet behaviors—"It has been said that the brain is the most complex system in the known universe. By looking at our experiments as isolated bits of behavior, we cannot appreciably advance our understanding of this complex system."[43] Second, it was generally conceded that all too often results obtained in the clinic or experimental setting were not generalizable to life in general. As stated by Brooks and Baumeister in 1977, "Despite considerable experimental effort, laboratory research concerning learning, memory, and cognition, more generally, has not produced a very remarkable increase in our understanding of mental retardation."[44] They offered several suggestions for remediating related theoretical and methodological problems, "namely, elaborating causal relationships in the theory, selecting subjects on more meaningful, valid grounds than the IQ score, employing tasks with demonstrated validity with respect to the theoretical construct, and defining constructs according to ecologically real factors in the lives of retarded people.''[45] Haywood, in concurring with his colleagues, noted:

> Psychology generally is not blessed with any great abundance of rich theories of learning. The psychology of mental retardation is even more poverty stricken in this area. We need basic research on the fundamental mechanisms by which human beings learn. We need somewhat more complex research on the interactions among learning strategies, personal characteristics of individuals, types of material to be learned, settings for learning, and incentive conditions. We need continuing research and technological development to find out how teachers can mix persons, methods, teachers, settings, and subject matter to maximize the learning of retarded persons.[46]

In brief, by the eighties, much research had been conducted; much was productive; much was found wanting. Most authorities had come to recognize the tremendous need to implement long-term research projects investigating increasingly complex behaviors in a variety of settings under varying circumstances, but they were confronted with two new difficulties: increased constraints accompanied by decreased funding.

ETHICAL ISSUES

The growing recognition and acceptance of human rights plus some questionable medical and behavioral research practices involving mentally retarded subjects, especially in a few institutional settings, resulted in the development of rigid federal standards during the latter seventies. However, ethical concerns about research with mentally retarded subjects was not solely a product of that decade. In 1962, the American Association on Mental Deficiency held a 2-day seminar with a select group of distinguished scientists and theologians ''to develop guidelines and bring together some of the accepted principles by which research, requiring the use of human subjects, could be conducted in an acceptable manner in a public institution for the mentally retarded.''[47]

Considered were various moral aspects of research as reflected in theological statements; hospital and military codes; legal interpretations to date; and the all-important code of ethics resulting from the Nuremberg trials, which addressed the inhuman indignities and atrocities associated with experiments conducted on concentration camp victims during World War II. The latter stipulated:

1. The voluntary consent of the human subject is absolutely essential. The duty and responsibility for ascertaining the quality of the consent rests upon each individual who initiates, directs, or engages in the experiment.
2. The experiment should be such as to yield fruitful results for the good of society, unprocurable by other methods or means of study, and not random and unnecessary in nature.
3. The experiment should be so designed and based on the result of animal experimentation and a knowledge of the natural history of the disease or other problem under study that the anticipated results would justify the performance of the experiment.
4. The experiment should be so conducted as to avoid all unnecessary physical and mental suffering and injury.
5. No experiment should be conducted where there is a priori reason to believe that death or disabling injury will occur; except, perhaps, in those experiments where the experimental physicians will also serve as subjects.
6. The degree of risk to be taken should never exceed that determined by the humanitarian importance of the problem to be solved by the experiment.
7. Proper preparations should be made and adequate facilities provided to protect the experimental subject against even remote possibilities of injury, disability, or death.
8. The experiment should be conducted only by scientifically qualified persons.
9. During the course of the experiment, the human subject should be at liberty to bring the experiment to an end if he has reached the physical or mental state where continuation of the experiment seems to him to be impossible.
10. During the course of the experiment, the scientist in charge must be prepared to terminate the experiment at any stage, if he has probable cause to believe, in the exercise of good faith, superior skill, and careful judgment required of him, that a continuation of the experiment is likely to

result in injury, disability, or death to the experimental subject.[48]

The Association's seminar produced 13 guidelines for conducting research in public institutions for mentally retarded persons:

1. No research project will be instituted involving the . . . use of human subjects without being cleared by the administrative head and/or the research director.
2. All new projects will be referred to the research review committee. The committee will advise the research director and/or the administrator as to the merits of the proposal, and will recommend its approval—approval with specific qualifications or disapproval. In all instances, the committee will give the reasons for its actions. This committee will operate under the administrative fiat to facilitate research.
3. The research project must be of a nature that will be profitable for society in general, or a specific segment of that society. It cannot be random or unnecessary in nature. It should be of a nature that is not economical or [is] difficult to obtain by other methods of study.
4. No research project utilizing the . . . use of human subjects can be initiated unless the methods used are acceptable and standard research procedures. When possible, such studies should be based upon the results of animal experimentation, a knowledge of the natural history of the disorder, and a careful perusal and evaluation of previous relevant experimentations.
5. The degree of risk to the subject must be evaluated by the research review committee and cannot be based solely upon the singular appraisal of the principle investigator.
6. There will be no unnecessary physical or mental insult. The concept of repairability must be completely investigated and provided for before any project is undertaken.
7. Adequate provisions will be made to protect the research subject against a remote possibility of injury. This will include necessary evaluative and follow-up procedures.
8. No research project will be conducted by other than properly qualified research personnel who have been so certified by the research director.
9. Voluntary consent will be obtained either from the research subject himself or, in the case of a minor or incompetent, from a properly qualified representative of the patient. In the case of certain types of behavioral and biological studies where knowledge of the outcome or consequence of the studies may bias or predetermine the outcome, the presumption of consent can be made by the research committee, utilizing the concept of the "prudent man." In any event, consent will be based upon a full knowledge of the possible consequences of the research project, the importance of the project, and the nature of the project.
10. Consent can be withdrawn at any time during the course of the experiment by the subject or his representative, and the research study terminated for that particular patient.
11. Prior to the inception of any research project, it is the responsibility of the investigator to show that provisions have been made for adequate consultation in relevant fields outside that of the competency of the principle investigator but within the scope of the particular investigation. Provisions must be made for evaluating the long-term effect of psychological or chemotherapeutic studies.
12. It must be shown that the subjects are selected not because they (1) are logical subjects due to the nature of the research design, (2) are in a position to benefit most from the results of the study, or (3) provide a natural control or natural experimental group.
13. Progress reports on all . . . human experiments will be regularly submitted to the administrative authorities. Unanticipated problems must be promptly discussed with the research review committee.

    The administrator, in cooperation with research personnel, will clearly state how patient records and photographs of research subjects will be used in the research and in publications for research findings.[49]

The question of research practices in institutional settings arose more formally in 1972 in the landmark federal court case *Wyatt v. Stickney,* where the following decision was rendered:

Residents shall have a right not to be subjected to experimental research without the express and informed consent of the resident, if the resident is able to give such consent, and of his guardian or next of kin, after opportunities for consultation with independent specialists and with legal counsel. Such proposed research shall first have been reviewed and approved by the institution's Human Rights Committee before such consent shall be sought . . . .[50]

Over the next few years, the federal government issued a series of related regulations that adopted most of the principles cited in the seminar guidelines, defined in *Wyatt* v. *Stickney* and recommended by a special presidential commission in 1981.[51] While such regulations did not preclude research with mentally retarded subjects, stringent requirements and protocols rendered it increasingly difficult to obtain clearance(s), especially when one wished to involve a relatively large subject sample selected at random for a long-term study.

DIMINISHING RESOURCES

By the mid-seventies, it also was obvious that funding of research involving mentally retarded persons was rapidly decreasing: "We are currently experiencing a crisis in mental retardation research," decried Zigler in 1978.[52] "The events of the near future will determine whether our nation continues its records of research accomplishment in the mental retardation field or whether, as appears more likely to the observer, the research effort will be stopped in its tracks and the research edifice that has taken 20 years to build will be severely weakened."[53] Zigler noted both the diminishing support of the National Institute of Child Health and Human Development and the reduction in research activity by the Association for Retarded Citizens of the United States, whose funding had dropped from $134,000 in 1965 to $74,000 in 1975. Further, the National Institutes of Health was devoting only 1.6% of its $3 billion budget to all behavior science research.

The situation continued to deteriorate. In 1982, Baumeister and Berkson pointed out with fiscal clarity the continued loss in interest of the National Institute of Child Health and Human Development, the federal agency with an explicit legislative mandate to fund mental retardation research.[54] The core support for

the mental retardation centers between 1972 and 1981, for example, increased only 13%, compared to a consumer price index rise of 117%. A number of reasons for the decline were advanced: mental retardation had its "day" during the sixties and early seventies, entitlement programs and military spending were consuming most of the federal government's fiscal resources, and research in the field had failed to have an impact on public policy.[55]

McClelland, an active researcher in the field of mental retardation, held as early as 1978 that the "American public has come to question whether psychological knowledge can be used to improve the human condition. The main reason for this disillusionment is that in the 1960s we set grandiose goals for ourselves to transform society in a hurry, applied massive doses of inappropriate behavioral technology and, by and large, failed to reach these goals."[56] The problem was by no means limited to research with mentally retarded persons; all social and behavioral scientists were dismayed. As expressed by Frank Farley, educational psychologist with the University of Wisconsin–Madison and one of the founders of the Federation of Behavioral, Psychological, and Cognitive Sciences, "The social sciences have had a bad public rap through pop psych, tabloid coverage, Golden Fleece Awards, and so forth. As a consequence, we have had difficulties obtaining funding and having our work treated seriously by those outside the field."[57]

Whatever the reason(s), federal support for critically needed behavioral research with mentally retarded persons continued to dwindle daily—just when it was needed the most.

MENTAL RETARDATION AND MENTAL ILLNESS

For generations, professionals from various fields debated whether mentally retarded persons could become emotionally disturbed or mentally ill. Some contended that mentally retarded persons were by the very nature of their limitations particularly susceptible to emotional disorders; others argued, with equal vigor, that such aberrations were indicative of and inextricably bound with mental retardation.[58] In reality, and with the exception of such individuals as Leo Kanner and Howard Potter, few psychiatrists took an active interest in the emotional and mental health of intellectually limited persons and few medical schools offered any training—a circumstance that had not been rectified by 1985.

In the early sixties, Beier and Heber reviewed the literature in this vital area of human development and both found it to be relatively meager.[59] Nonetheless, Beier felt there was sufficient evidence to warrant a tentative conclusion:

> Taking an overview of general studies of the incidence of psychoses in mental retardates, schizophrenia and psychotic episodes of excitement are most frequently associated with mental retardation, at least in the literature. Most of the observers also concluded that, although any of the psychoses may occur with mental retardation, it appears that true depressive psychoses among the mentally retarded are rare. It seems evident, too, that all psychoses become better differentiated or more clearly defined among the mentally retarded as the intellectual level increases and as the retardate becomes older. There is, however, a paucity of literature on the association of the non-schizophrenic psychoses and retardation, and a majority of the articles are case studies from which few general inferences could be drawn . . . . Inconsistencies appear in the data gathered about the association of schizophrenia and mental retardation, and many of the inconsistencies are due to differences in the populations studied. The statistics from such varied groups cannot be accepted as having any absolute value, nor is it possible to make inferences from the characteristics of institutionalized populations about the general population of retardates.[60]

Heber determined that schizophrenia appeared to be a particularly frequent form of psychosis among institutionalized retardates:

> There is a general disagreement as to whether the conditions are usually coincidental, a product of a common etiology, or whether some condition occurs secondary to the other; and the prognosis in cases involving both conditions is rather un-

favorable, particularly where infantile autism is involved.[61]

The importance of emotional illness to mental retardation was recognized in the American Association on Mental Deficiency's 1961 nomenclature. First, it made specific reference to mental retardation as a result of, or at least associated with, several emotional disorders:

> *Psychogenic mental retardation associated with emotional disturbance.*
>
> This category is for the classification of cases of mental retardation associated with a history of a prolonged period of emotional disturbance (neurotic disorder) dating from an early age. It is believed that the emotional disturbance must be extremely severe in order to have any causal relationship to the mental retardation.
>
> *Mental retardation associated with psychotic (or major personality) disorder.*
>
> Cases of mental retardation associated with psychotic or major personality disorders such as autism or childhood schizophrenia, where there is no reasonable evidence of cerebral pathology, are to be classified in this category.[62]

Second, personal-social factors were also taken into consideration as supplementary codes to the behavioral aspects of mental retardation:

> *Impairment in interpersonal relations.*
>
> This category is intended to reflect deficiencies in interpersonal skills. The individual with an impairment in interpersonal relations does not relate adequately to peers and/or authority figures and may demonstrate an inability to recognize the needs of other persons in interpersonal interactions.
>
> *Impairment in cultural conformity.*
>
> Deficiencies in this category reflect one or more of the following: behavior which does not conform to social mores, behavior which does not meet standards of dependability, reliability, and trustworthiness; behavior which is persistently asocial, anti-social, and/or excessively hostile.
>
> *Impairment in responsiveness.*
>
> Impaired or deficient responsiveness is characterized by an inability to delay gratification of needs and a lack of long-range goal striving or persistence with response only to short-term goals. Those individuals who respond only to biophysical stimuli of comfort or discomfort would be classified at one extreme of the dimen-

sion of behavioral responsivity. Individuals classified at the other extreme would be characterized by responsiveness to abstract or very symbolic rewards.[63]

While these were not sophisticated dimensions of classifying or identifying the host of psychiatric problems confronting many mentally retarded persons, they did, nevertheless, signal a heightened sensitivity to emotional and sociopersonal factors that might affect both level of intellectual functioning and adaptive behavior.

PREVALENCE

Subsequent research in this area clearly established that mentally retarded persons at all levels of intellectual functioning were susceptible to a wide range of emotional disorders, including those of a most severe nature. In 1962, for example, Chess sampled mentally retarded youngsters from public school special classes and found that of 52 students, only 21 (40%) revealed no psychiatric disorder. Eighteen were judged to have a reactive behavior disorder; 1 was deemed to have a neurotic behavior disorder; 11 were grouped under cerebral dysfunction, which included both a neurological history and behavioral symptoms; and 1 was deemed psychotic. Under psychosis, Chess included such characteristics as thought disorder, affective deviance, speech and mobility aberration, and difficulties in peer relationships other than that which might be accounted for by mental retardation per se.[64]

Menolascino's report of 1969 reconfirmed that persons who were mentally retarded could present a wide range of complex (and often perplexing) clinical findings. Of 256 emotionally disturbed mentally retarded youngsters, 134 were classified as having a severe behavioral reaction; 43 had psychotic reactions; 8 reflected functional psychosis; 4 had personality disorders; 58 presented adjustment reaction problems; and 15 were troubled youngsters with nonspecified psychiatric disorders. Several of the children fell into more than one category.[65]

Several years later, Bernstein and Rice reported on 300 consultations by psychiatrists involving mentally retarded individuals from the community as well as from a public residential facility. Again, they found a wide range of psychiatric disorders, including anxiety neurosis, schizophrenic reactions, schizoid personality, toxic psychosis, neurotic depression, obsessive-compulsive, adjustment reaction, passive-aggressive personality, hysterical neurosis, antisocial personality, inadequate personality, sexual deviation, and withdrawal reaction.[66]

In 1975, Philips and Williams reported on 100 mentally retarded children referred to a special clinic setting. Again, many of the youngsters (87%) had some form of emotional disturbance: 38 children were considered psychotically disturbed while 49 others had symptoms of "characterologic, neurotic, behavioral, or situational disorders." Of importance, the authors concluded that there was "no evidence that the mentally retarded children exhibited symptoms that fit into a special category related to their retardation."[67]

These studies typified much of the psychiatric-oriented research in this area. Though the reported frequency of emotional disturbance was rather high, the very nature of the populations sampled would tend to produce that result. In reality, the prevalence of emotional disorders among mentally retarded persons in general remained unknown. Yet, most authorities contended that it equalled and probably exceeded the occurrence of such problems among normal individuals.

INFANTILE AUTISM

One psychiatric category that continued to receive considerable attention since conceptually introduced by Leo Kanner in 1943 was infantile autism. Kanner, who at that time was the director of Children's Psychiatry Services at Johns Hopkins Hospital, summarized his research with 39 such children with the following observations:

The common denominator in all these patients is a disability to relate themselves in the ordinary way to people and situations from the beginning of life. Their parents referred to them as always having been "self-sufficient," "like in a shell," "happiest when left alone," "acting as if people weren't there," "giving the impression of silent wisdom." The case histories indicate invariably the presence from the start of extreme autistic aloneness which, whenever possible, shuts out anything that comes to the child from the outside. Almost every mother recalled her astonishment at the child's failure to assume the usual anticipatory posture preparatory to being picked up. This kind of adjustment occurs universally at four months of age.

Nearly two-thirds of the children acquired the ability to speak, while the others remained mute. But language, even when present, did not, over a period of years, serve to convey meaning to others. Naming presented no difficulty; even long and unusual words were retained with remarkable facility. An excellent rote memory for poems, songs, lists of presidents, and the like make the parents at first think of the children proudly as child prodigies. . . .

The child's behavior is governed by an anxiously obsessive desire for the maintenance of sameness that nobody but the child himself may disrupt on rare occasions. Changes of routine, of furniture arrangement, of a pattern, of the order in which everyday acts are carried out can drive him to despair. . . .

Every one of the children has a good relation to objects; he is interested in them; he can play with them happily for hours. He can be fond of them, or get angry at them if, for instance, he cannot fit them into a certain space. . . .

The children's relation to people is altogether different. Every one of them upon entering the office immediately went after blocks, toys, or other objects without paying the least attention to the persons present. It would be wrong to say that they were not aware of the presence of persons. But the people, as long as they left the child alone, figured in about the same manner as did the desk, the bookshelf, or the filing cabinet. . . .

Even though most of these children were at one time or another looked upon as feeble-minded, they are all unquestionably endowed with good cognitive potentialities.[68]

Over the years, Kanner's notion of autism underwent considerable transformation and came to encompass more and more mentally retarded youngsters, based primarily on age of onset, behavior, and the absence of charac-

teristics associated with schizophrenia. According to the 1982 diagnostic criteria of the American Psychiatric Association, the essential features of infantile autism included:

A. Onset before 30 months.
B. Pervasive lack of responsiveness to other people (autism).
C. Gross deficits in language development.
D. If speech is present, peculiar speech patterns such as immediate and delayed echolalia, metaphorical language, pronominal reversal.
E. Bizarre responses to various aspects of the environment, e.g., resistance to change, peculiar interest in or attachments to animate or inanimate objects.
F. Absence of delusions, hallucinations, loosening of associations, and incoherence as in Schizophrenia.[69]

In noting the significance of infantile autism as a major psychiatric disorder among mentally retarded children, Grossman, in the 1983 edition of *Classification in Mental Retardation,* wrote:

Infantile autism is characterized by a failure to develop interpersonal relationships, a receptive and expressive language abnormality, cognitive deficits, and ritualistic and compulsive behavior, beginning before the age of about 13 months. The syndrome is rare in the general population. Most children diagnosed as having infantile autism have IQs below 50, but some, perhaps 25 to 30 percent, have IQs as high as 70. Autistic children also show an extreme variability in intellectual functioning, with poor performance on verbal tasks but sometimes good and even superior performance in motor ability. Infantile autism is also more common among boys.[70]

While there was considerable agreement between the American Association on Mental Deficiency concept of autism and that of the American Psychiatric Association, alternative views existed. Some authorities maintained Kanner's original notion of infantile autism, labeling it "Kanner's syndrome" or "Kanner's autism." Others proposed various autistic syndromes. In 1976, Coleman, for example, based on a study conducted by the Children's Brain Research Clinic of Washington, D.C., with 78 autistic children and an equal number of controls, set forth three autistic syndromes: 1) familial autism, 2) purine autism, and 3) celiac autism. The latter two syndromes were suspected to be of biochemical origin or influence.[71]

Regardless of the nature of the specific autistic classification system used, the majority of autistic individuals were considered to be mentally retarded. Regrettably, autistic children also proved difficult to live with, to nurture, and to treat.

Psychiatric coding or labeling of persons, especially those of a younger age who happened to be mentally retarded, was never an easy task and was frequently subject to error for a wide range of reasons. As Philips and Williams noted in 1975, "Accurate diagnosis according to [psychiatric] category is difficult to obtain in children; in those with mental retardation that process of diagnosis is even more complicated. Children tend to overlap categories and differences between the personality diagnostic categories. such as neurotic and characterological disorders, are arbitrarily defined."[72] Others, even as late as 1982, continued to report on the phenomenon of "diagnostic overshadowing"; that is, once an examiner was given information that a person was mentally retarded, there was a tendency not to consider aberrant behavior reflective of emotional disturbance.[73]

Another diagnostic problem involved the failure to view clients in their entirety. As discussed by Menolascino and Bernstein as early as 1970, any major psychiatric labeling required an understanding of the individual's functioning in all areas, including development as a psychobiological organism, the total life situation, the impact of handicapping conditions, the family's response, and community attitudes.[74]

In the final analysis, since there was always the question of categories used; criteria selected; single versus collective judgment; and different professional experiences, perspectives, and biases, many individuals were classified as mentally ill at one time and mentally retarded at another.[75] In other words, one person's psychotic episode was another's developmental problem.

RESEARCH ACTIVITY

The question of emotional or behavioral difficulties did not fall solely within the purview of the psychiatric community, however. In fact, it attracted considerably more attention from psychologists, much to the disappointment of Howard Potter. In 1927, while clinical director at the Letchworth Village in New York, he wrote an oft-quoted allegorical piece concerning the relationship of mental retardation to the interests and endeavors of psychiatry and psychology:

Some years ago Dr. Salmon wrote a little allegory entitled "A Modern Fairy Tale." In it he drew a picture of Psychiatry as the Cinderella living in the "House of the Medical Sciences" with her two step-sisters Medicine and Surgery. He related her hardships. How she had to work in the kitchen with worn-out tools and wore cast-off clothing. How she was looked down upon by her step-sisters, Medicine and Surgery, and all the cruel slights she endured at their hands. To make a long story short, she finally came into her own at a function to celebrate the victory of the Great War because the Prince of Public Favor found that a belt on which was inscribed "USEFULNESS" fitted her to a nicety. And we assume she married the Prince of Public Favor and lived happily ever afterwards.

We might go on, however, and tell a little more about her. Gossip has it that she was married once before and had a child who was not, it seemed, "all there." She felt that this child was a terrible disgrace to her and although she did not entirely disown it, she boarded it out with a family of Psychologists. The Psychologists, strange as it may seem, actually loved this child and saw in her all sorts of good qualities. They found that this child, whom they called Mental Deficiency, could tell them some things which would be useful in caring for and bringing up and teaching other children who were not so unfortunate.

In the meantime, Psychiatry had become the mother of two very beautiful children, Mental Hygiene and Psycho-analysis. She idolized these two children and almost forgot her other poor unfortunate child, Mental Deficiency, whom she had boarded out with the Psychologists. Now and then, however, she had periods of remorse and would invite Mental Deficiency to attend some of the parties given for her children, Mental Hygiene and Psycho-analysis. Mental Deficiency was supposed to be very still, however, and not speak unless spoken to and, as you might expect, she was not spoken to very often.

As time went on and as Psycho-analysis and Mental Hygiene grew to maturity, Mental Hygiene began to grow a little curious about this awful step-sister, Mental Deficiency, who was not referred to when fine company was about. Mental Hygiene, when her mother was away, would slip around to the house of the Psychologists, squeeze in the back door, and visit her unfortunate step-sister. She saw how the Psychologist family loved her and really how attractive she was when she came to know her better. Mental Hygiene noticed, however, that although the Psychologist family was very kind and good to Mental Deficiency that nevertheless she did not seem exactly well. So whenever she got a chance she would sneak such of her friends as Endocrinology, Neurology and Biochemistry in through the back door. They all agreed that Mental Deficiency did need a little better care and would get along much better if her own mother would only pay a little more attention to her. On one or two occasions Mental Hygiene even induced her sister, Psycho-analysis, to go with her to see Mental Deficiency, although she knew that her mother would be very angry if she found out . . . .

The moral here is plain. Mental Deficiency does need the wholehearted interest of the psychiatric group, which in the past has been sadly lacking. The few psychiatrists laboring with this problem deserve the support of their brethren in the field of mental disease.[76]

Thirty-seven years later, in 1964, Potter, now emeritus professor of psychiatry at the State University of New York, once again complained about this situation in fewer words but with equal fervor:

In reviewing the literature, it again is obvious that child psychiatry has been especially remiss in meeting its responsibilities to the intellectually handicapped child. With remarkably myopic vision, the intrapsychic aspects of adaptive problems of these children have been ignored. Little or no thought has been given to psychogenic causology in mental retardation. Child psychiatrists and psychoanalysts preoccupied with ego development have ignored an area of human pathology or deviation which might well be a rewarding area of investigation.[77]

Potter was right: psychiatry had, by and large, abrogated its responsibility for the emotionally troubled mentally retarded person; but then, neither did psychology advance a theory of personality development among such affected individuals. Psychologists, with the exception of a brief flirtation with self-concept and anxiety, tended to concentrate on managing or modifying discrete behaviors.

As concerns self-concept, there were few who did not believe this to be an essential component to the development of mentally retarded persons and their ability to cope with the successes and stresses of life: "What a person does and how he behaves are determined by the concept he has of himself and his abilities."[78] Its importance was well expressed by Henry Cobb in an address to the International League of Societies for the Mentally Handicapped in 1966:

The perception and evaluation of himself by the retarded person is of crucial importance in his adaptation to adult life. The frequently held assumption that the retarded, because of his limited intellectual ability, does not develop a "self-concept" is far from true . . . . The retarded person does . . . develop a complex set of self-referent perceptions, attitudes, and behaviors which permeate and profoundly affect the relationships which he sustains to the world around him.

As with those of normal intelligence, the self-attitudes of the retarded are the product of experiences sustained in the developmental years . . . . In the case of retarded children, many essential components of this (developmental) process are modified: The developmental stages of maturation tend to be delayed, but not uniformly for all functions; the efforts to cope with the environment are more limited by intellectual and often motoric disabilities . . . .

. . . such stresses can be reduced if the experiences of childhood have yielded a realistic and satisfying self-image and if the transitional period of adolescence is carefully managed to assure a proper balance of responsible achievement within the limits of necessary dependency.[79]

While a person's self-concept was easily understood in its broadest context, it proved extremely difficult to define operationally and subsequently, to measure with precision or agreement. Nevertheless, in the early sixties, a number of self-concept tests were developed, many of which were intended primarily for use with mentally retarded persons: the Laurelton Self-Attitude Scale, 1961; The Way I Feel About Myself, 1964; the Illinois Index of Self-

Derogation, 1964; and the Tennessee Self-Concept Scale, 1965. These were used in addition to such popular standardized measurements as the California Test of Personality.[80]

In view of definitional difficulties and the wide variety of tests developed, the research that was conducted produced conflicting results. Some investigators found a high correlation between level of intelligence and degree of self-concept; girls had a better self-image than boys; and mentally retarded persons in segregated classes or institutions had a poorer self-image than those in regular classes or in the community.[81] Also, the culturally disadvantaged, mentally retarded person had a weaker self-image than did those from middle-class settings.[82] Others, in contrast, either found no significant differences in these areas or contrasting results.[83]

One group of researchers, including Zigler and his colleagues, proposed that not only did a person's self-concept involve life's experiences, it also reflected a developmental dimension.[84] To assess such developmental implications, investigators obtained an appraisal from mentally retarded subjects as to their current self-image, their ideal self-image (or the way they would really like to be), and noted the differences between the two. It was argued, based on research with emotionally disturbed children and adolescents, that as the youngsters matured, the disparity between actual and ideal images would increase. The few studies conducted in this area with mentally retarded subjects, however, failed to support the discrepancy theory. Kniss and his associates, for example, found that ideal self-attitudes were independent of the effects of age, as well as the length of institutionalization or intelligence. McAfee and Cleland also found no significant differences between the discrepancy scores of mentally retarded subjects who were considered to be well-adjusted as compared to those who were considered to be maladjusted.[85]

Though the data were scanty, there was little doubt that mentally retarded persons did develop a self-concept beginning at an early age, and that such self-concepts were influenced by a wide range of factors such as success/failure patterns, parental support, and sociocultural experiences. Beyond that, research did not produce a clear picture of the self-concept among mentally retarded persons, its development, or its effect upon social interaction or achievement.

Anxiety, a corollary of self-concept, was also investigated. though not thoroughly. Nevertheless, the available research evidence suggested that mentally retarded persons tended to be anxious, at least in testing situations, and that disadvantaged mentally retarded youngsters appeared more anxious than their peers from the middle-class environments.[86]

One component associated with both anxiety and self-concept was failure. Unfortunately, this area again was not explored beyond a few studies that suggested some degree of failure might motivate mentally retarded persons to persist in a given effort.[87] How much failure, however, is desirable under which circumstances and how much would prove self-defeating was not examined, nor was the individual's self-perception of failure assessed.

Regrettably, despite its importance, research in these critical areas was not pursued vigorously. As late as 1979, Balla and Zigler commented, "In view of the central role of the self-concept construct in general personality theory, it is somewhat surprising that there has not been more work on this issue in the mental retardation literature."[88]

TREATMENT

With the growing acceptance of mental illness and emotional problems among mentally retarded persons, both clinicians and researchers sought new avenues to treat related disorders, and a number of psychotherapeutic approaches proved effective, including: implosive therapy, film therapy, direct learning therapy, action therapy, music therapy, play therapy, art therapy, shadow therapy, and videotape and live modeling.[89] Such techniques were successful with children, adolescents, and adults.[90] Further, both group and individual therapy appeared effective. Working through young children's problems via parent and family counseling also proved beneficial.[91]

Yet, again reminiscent of the fifties, little effort was expended to pursue these procedures on a broad scale. Rather, professionals from many fields tended to rely too frequently on medication and/or aversive techniques associated with behavior modification.

Psychopharmacology

Several classes of drugs were prescribed for persons who were mentally retarded. Some, especially the antiepileptics, proved of immeasurable value in eliminating or significantly reducing the frequency and severity of epileptic seizures among most (but not all) affected persons. With the exception of questions relating to the interaction of such substances with other forms of medications, no one argued against their use for this purpose.

Problems and controversies surrounding medication primarily involved the introduction of tranquilizers, both major (the neuroleptics) and minor (anxiolytics). A number of reports during the sixties were most encouraging in terms of the effectiveness of such major tranquilizers as thioridazine, haloperidol, and chlorpromazine in reducing aggressive, impulsive, hyperactive, and stereotypic behavior.[92]

These favorable reports concerning neuroleptic drugs combined with a perceived need to reduce aggressiveness among mentally retarded persons, espeically in residential settings, all too often resulted in the indiscriminate, wholesale use of drugs in some facilities. It soon became apparent to many that drugs were being used in lieu of programming and were being introduced primarily in the interests of staff and administration, rather than those of the individual resident. This became most evident during the investigation associated with *Wyatt* v. *Stickney,* 1972. The court's findings were reflected in its final orders concerning medication:

a.   No medication shall be administered unless at the written order of a physician.

b.   Notation of each individual's medication shall be kept in his medical records . . . . At least weekly the attending physician shall review the drug regimen of each resident under his care. All prescriptions shall be written with a termination date, which shall not exceed 30 days.

c.   Residents shall have a right to be free from unnecessary or excessive medication. The resident's records shall state the effects of psychoactive medication on the resident. When dosages of such are changed or other psychoactive medications are prescribed, a notation shall be made in the resident's record concerning the effect of the new medication or new dosages and the behavior changes, if any, which occur.

d.   Medication shall not be used as punishment, for the convenience of staff, as a substitute for program, or in quantities that interfere with the resident's habilitation program.[93]

Subsequent cases involving institutional practices tended to add standards to those just cited. Of particular interest were the regulations set forth by Judge Gigonux in a 1978 consent decree involving the state of Maine:[94]

1.   There will be monthly reviews of the number of residents receiving tranquilizers, phenothiazines, and antiepileptics.

2.   Pharmacotherapeutic agents shall only be used as part of an individualized habilitation plan.

3.   There will be a statement explaining reasons for the choice of a given medication, including a balancing of expected therapeutic effects and potential adverse effects.

4.   There will be a statement of why non-pharmacotherapeutic treatments are inappropriate or inadequate.

5.   There will be an explanation to the residents and advocate, in lay terms, giving the reasons for pharmacotherapy, its possible benefits, and its possible adverse consequences.

6.   There will be careful monitoring of progress and side effects.

7.   There will be evaluations of pharmacotherapeutic effects on educational and habilitative performance.[95]

Other reports of abusive drug practices, primarily in institutions, appeared, and beginning in the seventies, more sophisticated, well-trained researchers, such as Robert Sprague of the University of Illinois and Stephen Breuning of the University of Pittsburgh School of Medicine, began to re-examine some of the earlier studies favoring the use of tranquilizers. It was soon discovered that many of the research protocols contained methodological errors sufficiently severe to challenge the validity of the results and related interpretations.[96]

New research conducted in the United States and elsewhere also indicated that neuroleptic drugs posed the threat of dulling cognitive functions.[97] Behavior modification approaches were often found to accomplish the same goals without any adverse side effects.[98] Finally, it became increasingly apparent by the late seventies that neuroleptic medications, which often were administered along with other drugs. could produce severe, long-lasting, and devastating physical effects, even following cessation of treatment, including a combination of abnormal and voluntary movements affecting the face, mouth, tongue, limbs, and trunk. Specific reactions could include tics, grimacing, blinking, lip smacking, chewing, tongue thrusting, and writhing movements of the arms and legs.[99] Such drug-related behaviorisms were labeled as tardive dyskinesia, a condition that received considerable attention beginning in 1980, when, in *Clites* v. *Iowa,* it was concluded that Timothy Clites, an institutional resident, suffered from this disorder and was awarded a damage settlement of $760,165.[100] In the judge's words:

> . . . major tranquilizers were given for the convenience of staff and not as part of a therapeutic program . . . . Tim did not receive the standard of medical care that was acceptable as reasonable medical practice . . . the Court finds that Tim has T.D. (tardive dyskinesia), the drugs caused it, and it is permanent.[101]

In response to these circumstances and controversy surrounding the psychopharmacological approach to managing behavior plus the growing evidence of adverse side effects, a number of agencies instituted "drug holidays"; that is, the withdrawal of psychotropic medication from individuals so treated. The results were mixed. Heistad and associates, in 1982, in specific response to a court order, removed a number of residents from thioridazine; and while many behaviors showed no change or actually improved, most individuals needed to have their drug regimen reintroduced.[102] A 1984 "drug holiday" study reported from the O'Berry Center for mentally retarded persons in Goldsboro, North Carolina, found similar results: of 72 residents receiving antipsychotic medication, 33 remained drug free for at least a year, but the remainder were restarted on psychotherapeutic medication, though in most instances, either a lower dose of the same medication or a different antipsychotic medication was prescribed.[103]

By 1984, strict standards concerning medications, their prescription, the identification of specific behavior(s) to be altered, and monitoring procedures were carefully delineated in nearly all related federal and state regulations as well as in the standards of various accrediting bodies. While such rules and expectations reduced the risk of gross error, the physician remained faced with a most difficult task, requiring the most sagacious clinical judgment in prescribing these potentially helpful drugs for several reasons. First, despite their historical use, no standard dosages for mentally retarded persons were developed, nor did accompanying pharmaceutical data provide for the biochemical anomalies or disbalances evidenced in some individuals. Compounding the problem was that no one knew with certainty which physiological or biochemical changes triggered or were associated with aggressive or self-injurious behavior nor was the biochemical reaction of the human body to many of the medications fully appreciated. Thus, physicians had to rely on their clinical judgment and a trial-and-error approach.

Though the preceding review evolved primarily around the institutional setting where studies indicated that as many as 55% of the residents were on neuroleptic drugs, the problem was by no means exclusive to that population.[104] In 1982, a study by Davis and colleagues, for example, found that of 3,500 randomly selected mentally retarded persons living in community foster or group homes, 58% were receiving some form of neuroleptic drug—thioridazine, chlorpromazine, haloperidol, or a combination thereof.[105] Subsequently, some believed problems surrounding the use of medications might become increasingly evident in the community where their use was not under heavy surveillance or governed by strict regulations. In essence, while psychotropic medications proved effective and worthwhile in some cases, they also posed innumerable human hazards.

Behavior Modification

By the mid-seventies, there was obvious agreement among many with the position of Simmons, a psychiatrist, and his colleagues that "the various problems of the retarded as a group are perhaps most effectively managed using techniques based upon learning principles, in particular those of operant learning conditions . . . ."[106] However, the application of aversive techniques, which were commonly employed to manage behavior, especially in some institutional settings, became a major social issue during the seventies, once again reflecting a growing recognition of individual rights. Various investigations found that less-than-knowledgeable persons were indiscriminately using aversive stimulation, including prolonged, unsupervised isolation; electrical stimulation by cattle prods; unwarranted, uncomfortable satiation; and a wide range of physical restraints. Like psychotropic medication, such techniques were all too often introduced in the interest of employees and in lieu of adequate programming. With the exception of perhaps over-heralding the success of their techniques, this was not the responsibility of researchers.

The courts took a dim view of such practices for a variety of reasons, including the absence of informed consent. As Schroeder and his colleagues acknowledged in their review of the literature, "If behavior management were only used for those who asked for it, most of the research reported in this paper could not have been done."[107]

Judge Johnson, in the famous landmark case involving an institutional setting, *Wyatt v. Stickney,* declared:

> Behavior modification programs involving the use of noxious or aversive stimuli shall be reviewed and approved by the institution's Human Rights Committee and shall be conducted only with the express and informed consent of the affected resident, if the resident is able to give such consent, and of his guardian or next of kin, after opportunities for consultation with independent specialists and with legal counsel. Such behavior modification programs shall be conducted only under the supervision of and in the presence of a Qualified Mental Retardation Professional who has had proper training in such techniques.
>
> Electric shock devices shall be considered a research technique for the purpose of these standards. Such devices shall only be used in extraordinary circumstances to prevent self-mutilation leading to repeated and possibly permanent physical damage to the resident, and only after alternative techniques have failed. The use of such devices shall be . . . used only under the direct and specific order of the superintendent.
>
> Physical restraint shall be employed only when absolutely necessary to protect the resident from injury to himself or to prevent injury to others. Restraint shall not be employed as punishment, for the convenience of staff, or as a substitute for programs. Such restraints shall be applied only if alternative techniques have failed and only if such restraint imposes the least possible restriction consistent with its purpose:
>
> a. Only Qualified Mental Retardation Professionals may authorize the use of restraints. Such restraints shall be applied only if alternative techniques have failed and only if such restraint imposes the least possible restriction consistent with its purpose.
>
> (1) Orders for restraints by the Qualified Mental Retardation Professionals should be in writing and shall not be in force for longer than 12 hours.
>
> (2) A resident placed in restraint shall be checked at least every thirty minutes by staff trained in the use of restraints, and a record of such checks shall be kept.
>
> (3) Mechanical restraints shall be de-

signed and used so as not to cause physical injury to the resident, and so as to cause the least possible discomfort.

(4) Opportunity for motion and exercise shall be provided for a period of not less than ten minutes during each two hours in which restraint is employed.

(5) Daily reports shall be made to the superintendent by those Qualified Mental Retardation Professionals ordering the use of restraints summarizing all such uses of restraint, the types used, the duration, and the reasons therefor.

b. The institution shall cause a written statement of this policy to be posted in each living unit and circulated to all staff members.[108]

This decision soon found its way into various federal regulations and all states ultimately adopted similar positions. In fact, some states simply forbad the use of aversive conditioning under any circumstances. This, in turn, raised concern among those who believed that in extreme cases of dangerous or life-threatening behavior, severe aversive stimulation was warranted. In 1974, Phil Roos—psychologist, former institution administrator, and at that time, the executive director of the Association for Retarded Citizens of the United States—set forth the thinking of some psychologists, a few administrators, and still fewer advocates:

It can be argued . . . that elimination of severe self-abusive behavior warrants the use of painful stimuli, since the damage to the subject is relatively milder and of much shorter duration . . . . Much human learning is the result of aversive conditioning occurring in the "natural" course of events. Fire burns, falling hurts, provoked dogs bite, and when treated with obvious hostility people retaliate in kind. The folkways in many of our subcultures advocate an approach to education and socialization based on letting a child "take his lumps," that is, letting painful consequences modify his behavior.

Many of our social systems and institutions likewise incorporate the use of aversive consequences. Parents typically rely on punishment (physical and/or psychological), time-out (e.g., locking the child in his room or prohibiting him from playing with peers), and cost-contingency (e.g., explicit or implicit withdrawal of love or

withholding the child's allowance) as effective means of shaping their child's behavior. The enforcement of laws is based almost exclusively on a complex set of aversive consequences, including cost-contingency (fines), time-out (imprisonment), and punishment (social condemnation, capital punishment).

Many of our specialized "therapeutic" techniques also rely on aversive consequences, although their aversive characteristics are usually implicit rather than explicit. For example, the use of Antabuse in the treatment of alcoholism is predicated on aversive conditioning—drinking alcohol while undergoing this form of "treatment" precipitates a highly aversive reaction. The relationship between specific behavior and aversive consequences is not always so apparent, but it is real nonetheless. Institutionalization follows certain forms of culturally condemned behavior, electroconvulsive shock follows depressive behavior, and lobotomy follows "uncontrollable psychotic episodes." Even the manipulation of the "therapeutic milieu" or of the "psychotherapeutic relationship" often involves aversive consequences predicated on behaviors which have been selected for deceleration.[109]

Regardless of such arguments, constraints on the use of aversive stimulation remained numerous, leading Marilyn Whiteside, a practicing psychologist with mentally retarded persons, to write a letter of protest that appeared in *Newsweek* in 1983. Her arguments were prefaced with several case reports involving severe, dangerous, and difficult-to-manage behaviors. For example:

He was 25 and severely retarded. And after his favorite attendant left, he became self-abusive. He beat his fists against the side of his head until a football helmet had to be ordered for his protection. Then he clawed at his face and gouged out one of his eyes.

The institution psychologists began a behavior program that had mildly aversive consequences: they squirted warm water in his face each time he engaged in self-abuse. When that didn't work, they requested permission to use an electric prod. The Human Rights Committee vetoed this "excessive and inhumane form of correction" because, after all, the young man was retarded, not criminal.

Since nothing effective could be done that abridged the rights and negated the dignity of the developmentally disabled patient, he was verbally reprimanded for his behavior—and allowed to push his thumb through his remaining eye. He is now blind, of course, but he has his rights and presumably his dignity.[110]

Then she again raised the problematic issues of individual rights, governmental control, and professional integrity:

> Clearly, our society has become almost hysterical about the issue of human rights . . . . The pendulum has swung as far as it has because we feel guilty—and, of course, we have a lot to feel guilty about. In an earlier era, abuse of the vulnerable was relatively common because we believed in the infallibility of certain types of authority and because of the way we perceived some segments of our population. Now the name of the game is open vilification of authority figures, with our charity reserved for the *potentially* abused. The collective stand is that everyone, regardless of age, intellectual capabilities, and emotional maturity and health, is entitled to evade the normal consequences of unwise behavior—everyone, that is, except the professionals.
>
> Each year, state and federal governments amplify their monitoring of professions and institutions, demanding hard evidence that the treatment of clients conforms to a plethora of regulations. The catch is that treatment programs secured with red tape—programs that cannot be implemented until a dozen forms have been filled out in triplicate and approved by as many supervisors—are often too weak. Professionals complain, validly, that they can no longer give their clients adequate care because they must spend much of their time justifying that care. The onerous task: to find an effective way to be helpful that is, at the same time, innocuous enough to pass government inspection . . . . There is no pat answer to this burdensome problem, because there is no way of escaping the phenomenon of human nature. But if we do not find a solution more realistic than what we have now, we are going to be riding the pendulum when it swings into outer space. Competent professionals will leave their fields of expertise because they will not be able to tolerate the barriers to their performance and, no doubt about it, they will be replaced by people with bureaucratic mentalities, people who won't mind the red tape because it will excuse them from having direct contact with the clients.
>
> Too often, regulations and paper shuffling are substitutes for the more arduous task of caring.[111]

In contrast, H. Carl Haywood, who had examined the same situation in 1977, placed the problem in a different perspective, declaring

that research was desperately needed to "investigate how stereotyped and self-injurious behavior can be replaced by more personally satisfying behavior without the use of aversive stimulation."[112] Others felt the same way, and soon new techniques, often combining the best of operant conditioning with cognitive considerations, were created and found to be at least equally efficacious. Two such programs were "gentle teaching" advocated by John McGee and Frank Menolascino of the Nebraska Psychiatric Institute of the University of Nebraska and the cognitive-behavioral system developed by William Gardner of the University of Wisconsin–Madison.

Briefly, the gentle teaching approach emphasized a positive "bonding" relationship between staff and client and ignoring a wide range of inappropriate behaviors while, at the same time, constantly redirecting the person to the task to be completed and rewarded. This nonpunishment technique, which reportedly worked well with even severe behavioral problems among profoundly mentally retarded persons, concentrated attention on appropriate rather than inappropriate behaviors.[113]

The cognitive-behavioral approach advanced by Gardner included two basic phases: a multidimensional behavioral assessment to discover why aggressive behavior was occurring by examining the individual's behavioral history as well as possible external and internal contributory conditions. Given this information, or at least an "exploratory hunch," the approach emphasized the teaching of self-management skills, relying on success and the positive reinforcement of preferred behavioral alternatives.[114] Approaches such as these offered great promise for the future.

NORM-VIOLATING BEHAVIOR

With the exception of a brief flurry of activity during the early seventies, the mentally retarded offender did not receive considerable or even consistent attention. Though few knowledgeable persons still held that mentally retarded individuals were innately criminal or that they remained a constant threat to the safety and well-being of the community and nation, little further understanding of their motivation was acquired.

Estimates of their prevalence among incarcerated populations varied widely. Thirty-nine percent of the prison population was judged to be mentally retarded in one interview study conducted in Georgia in 1973.[115] Louisiana, in 1980, reported a similarly high figure of 35.4%.[116] Others reported less: 9.5%, according to a national study of major penal and correctional facilities conducted by Brown and Courtless in 1971; 9.5% in Maine, 1979; 8% in South Carolina, 1973; 10% in Texas, 1973; 5.2% in Kentucky, 1975; and 3% in Iowa, 1977—different criteria, different measures, different results.[117] In the final analysis, most authorities simply adopted a 10% estimate.

Studies reporting juvenile delinquency statistics again revealed marked divergence— only 3.9%, according to Levy, in 1967; only 4.0%, by Olczak and Stott, in 1976.[118] In contrast, Dennis conservatively estimated that 9% of the delinquent group studied was mentally retarded while Haskins and Friel found 12.9% of male and 16.6% of female delinquent offenders were mentally retarded.[119] Again, the 10% estimate was generally adopted.

Such discrepancies could be attributed to a number of factors. First, many correctional facilities either used group tests or short versions of standardized intelligence tests, which may have tended to overestimate the occurrence of mental retardation.[120] Second, many of the reporting agencies did not use an IQ of 69 or 70 as the cut-off point, or use any measure of adaptive behavior. Finally, several studies revealed that the majority of mentally retarded prisoners were black or Mexican-American, which again raised the question of test appropriateness.[121]

Regardless of the exact percentage cited, two conclusions were drawn: 1) mentally retarded persons were disproportionately represented in an incarcerated population, and 2) even the more severely mentally retarded adolescent and adult may find themselves in a penal facility. Assuming the 10% estimate to be reasonably accurate, then, in 1981, according to national statistics, there were approximately 30,000 mentally retarded adults in federal and state prisons (excluding jails) and over 7,000 mentally retarded juveniles in custody of a public or private facility.[122]

One final comment concerning prevalence estimates: though it was generally accepted that 10% of persons in prisons or similar correctional facilities were mentally retarded, that did not imply that 10% of mentally retarded persons in general commit crimes or, in some other way, seriously offend society's legal norms. There were no accurate figures concerning the frequency of criminal actions among the mentally retarded population as a whole.

One less-than-desirable, but almost constant finding of studies involving mentally retarded offenders was that their crimes were serious and tended to involve acts against people rather than property. Kentucky, for example, reported a 63.1% rate of crimes against people as opposed to only 36.9% against property.[123] Brown and Courtless noted that 57% of mentally retarded offenders had committed a person crime as compared to only 27% among prisoners of normal intelligence.[124] They also found a 15.4% homicide rate among mentally retarded criminals as compared to 5.1% among their normal counterparts. Ellis and Brancale's analysis revealed that sex crimes were twice as common among mentally retarded than normal offenders.[125] Similar results were recorded by Rockoff and Hofmann.[126]

More extensive comparisons by several states reconfirmed such findings concerning both adult offenders[127] and juvenile delinquents[128] (see Table 3.1). Again, the figures cited only reflected upon an incarcerated population and not mentally retarded persons in general; however, it was statistics such as these that led both Sussman in 1974 and Biklen in 1977 to be visibly concerned about the effects of intelligence testing among mentally retarded offenders.[129] Were such tests misleading? Did they negatively affect the of-

Table 3.1.   Percentages of mentally retarded and
non–mentally retarded criminal offenders

Concerning adult offenders[a]:

Offense	Mentally retarded offenders	Non–mentally retarded offenders
Murder	19.7%	7.9%
Manslaughter	10.7%	9.8%
Rape/sex crimes	13.0%	8.0%
Armed robbery	7.4%	15.7%
Assault	12.3%	6.2%
House breaking/ burglary	21.3%	19.7%
Forgery/fraud	3.3%	8.6%
Robbery/larceny	10.7%	11.7%
Drug offenses	0.0%	6.7%
Miscellaneous property crimes	1.6%	5.7%

Concerning juvenile delinquents[b]:

Offense	Mentally retarded offenders	Non–mentally retarded offenders
Homicide	2.1%	1.2%
Crimes against persons	20.0%	20.5%
Theft and related	17.1%	19.5%
Forgery and related	0.0%	1.1%
Property damage	23.6%	24.7%
Crimes against family	0.0%	0.0%
Sex offenses	1.4%	1.5%
Drug/liquor law	2.9%	2.6%
Other felonies	2.1%	4.2%
Juvenile/minor misdemeanors	22.9%	19.6%
Other offenses	7.9%	5.0%

[a]Adapted from Cull, Reuthebuck, and Pape (1975, p. A-107).

[b]Adapted from *Services for developmentally disabled delinquents and offenders* (1977, p. 10).

fender's sentencing and treatment? Did they add to the myth that mentally retarded persons were prone to crime?

The major question concerning crime and mental retardation was, however, simple: "What, if any, was the relationship?" Again there was a wide divergence of opinion and little surety. While mental retardation per se did not directly imply criminality, it could, in the minds of some authorities, have its influence:

1. Mentally retarded persons have difficulty in controlling aggressive impulses.[130]
2. Mentally retarded persons fail to appreciate the consequences of their acts.[131]

The notion of impulsiveness received inferred support from several psychiatrically oriented studies that compared the behavior of mentally retarded offenders with that of their normal peer population.[132] However, no comparisons were made with nonoffending mentally retarded persons.

Family neglect or indifference, improper home training, and/or inadequate supervision were cited by many as primary influences in the development of delinquent behavior among mentally retarded youth.[133] Other occasionally advanced explanations included: 1) prior negative expectancies of their own behavior; 2) language difficulties; 3) poor educational history, including the absence of special classes; 4) striking out against society in frustration emanating from limitations and feelings of rejection; and 5) poverty.[134] Miles Santamour, whose interest in the mentally retarded offender persisted throughout the quarter century under consideration in this book, offered the single most comprehensive listing, divided into five general classifications: "a misunderstanding of how to use institutions in society to attain desired goals in a legally sanctioned fashion, a striking out against society in frustration stemming from one's own limitations or feelings of rejection, mental illness causing irrational criminal behavior, social pathology or criminal behavior based upon a calculated disregard for other people's rights, and naiveté or an inability to appreciate the consequences of one's behavior."[135]

Regardless of the many reasons set forth, there was little to distinguish between mentally retarded offenders, mentally retarded nonoffenders, normal offenders, and/or normal nonoffenders. The few comparative studies available seemed to indicate that no significant differences actually existed. Sternlicht, for example, could find no appreciable discrepancies between delinquent and nondelinquent mentally retarded persons in an institutional setting, nor could MacEachron between mildly mentally retarded offenders and those of borderline ability.[136]

In 1964, Delton Beier summarized a number of studies about mental retardation and crime to that date, and concluded:

> At the present time, only one conclusion regarding the association of mental retardation with delinquency and criminality seems justifiable. The mentally retarded are as capable of delinquent criminal acts as are their intellectually normal brethren; however, factors other than intellectual ones appear to be more important in the etiology of such behavior, and these factors are those commonly cited as important to the development of delinquent and criminal behavior in the general population.[137]

The same conclusion could be made 2 decades later.

RESEARCH SUPPORT

Regardless of the nature of the research conducted, such activities received considerable support, financially and professionally, during the sixties and early seventies. First, considerable federal funding was available since research into the prevention and treatment of mental retardation had high federal visibility and priority. Second, in order to assist the government implement the strong research recommendations put forth by the original President's Panel on Mental Retardation in 1963, President Kennedy signed into law PL 88-164, the Mental Retardation Facilities and Community Mental Health Centers Construction Act, which had several major impacts on research related to mental retardation.

PL 88-164 authorized the establishment of 13 mental retardation research centers to "investigate mental retardation and related aspects of human development." These centers, with one exception—the Eunice Kennedy Shriver Center located on the grounds of the W. E. Fernald State School, Waltham, Massachusetts—were associated with major universities in California, Colorado, Illinois,

Kansas, Massachusetts, New York, North Carolina, Ohio, Tennessee, Washington, and Wisconsin. Over the years, thousands of articles were produced by these centers, ranging in theme from polydactyly in Down syndrome to effects of concept familiarization versus stimulus enhancement on verbal abstracting in institutionalized mentally retarded delinquent boys; from synapse elimination and plasticity in the developing human cerebral cortex to behaving appropriately in new situations.[139] Public Law 88-164 also led to the development of university affiliated facilities (UAFs), which are discussed in greater detail in a subsequent chapter of this book.[140] Though the primary purpose of these centers was to foster interdisciplinary training, they also had a research role; but, in contrast to the mental retardation research centers, the university affiliated facilities were to concentrate on applied as opposed to "pure" research into related disorders and the efficacy of prevention, treatment, and remedial strategies.[141]

Third, researchers found ever-expanding opportunities for publication. In 1959, William Sloan, administrator and psychologist, assumed editorship of the *American Journal of Mental Deficiency,* transforming it from a general publication to a highly respected research journal. In order to compensate for this transition, the American Association on Mental Deficiency expanded its in-house newsletter to a full-fledged journal, *Mental Retardation,* which also published research. Similarly, the Council for Exceptional Children expanded its publications to include *Education and Training of the Mentally Retarded,* beginning in 1966. In 1974, the American Association for the Education of the Severely/Profoundly Handicapped, the purposes of which are discussed later, was formed, and in 1975, it launched its publication, *Review: The American Association for the Education of the Severely/Profoundly Handicapped,* which concentrated on research affecting that subpopulation. In addition, with national visibility, federal funding, and the rapid expansion of training programs, many publishers became interested in the field and, in stark contrast to earlier years,

hundreds of well-written books on mental retardation appeared.

Because of the rapid proliferation of articles
plus the expanding number of journals, it became impossible for interested persons to
monitor all the activity in the field. Fortunately
for persons interested in mental retardation in
general as well as those concerned primarily
with learning and personality development,
Norman Ellis of the University of Alabama,
one of the country's prime researchers, successfully undertook responsibility for the
rather demanding task of editing a series of
books intended to "provide a ready source of
current information on research and theory development in the field."[142] This series publication, *International Review of Research in
Mental Retardation,* has appeared regularly
since its inception in 1966. In addition to editing this series, Ellis also conducted a number of
spring conferences held at Gatlinburg, Tennessee, and edited two substantial volumes devoted to reviewing and integrating developmental and behavioral research: *Handbook on
Mental Deficiency,* 1963, and *A Handbook on
Mental Deficiency, Psychological Theory and
Research,* 1979.[143]

Fourth, scientists (and practitioners)
throughout the world had an opportunity to
meet every 3 years to share their research,
hypotheses, and speculations, beginning in
1960. During that year, an international conference on the scientific study of mental retardation was held in London, England, in obser-
vance of the World Mental Health Year. The
original meeting was sponsored by the American Association on Mental Deficiency, the
Royal Medico-Psychological Association, the
Royal Society of Medicine, and the British
Psychological Society, in cooperation with the
National (British) Association for Mental
Health.[144]

Three years later, in Copenhagen, Denmark,
the organization was duly formalized, becoming the International Association for the Scientific Study of Mental Deficiency. Harvey A.
Stevens of the United States, well-known educator and administrator, served as its first president. Several years later, in 1968, he received

Harvey Stevens

the Joseph P. Kennedy, Jr. Award for outstanding leadership. The International Association convened every three years in a different country: Montpellier, France (1967); Warsaw, Poland (1970); The Hague, the Netherlands (1973); Washington, D.C. (1976); Jerusalem, Israel (1979); Toronto, Canada (1982);
New Dehli, India (1985).[145]

Finally, a prestigious awards program was
initiated by the Joseph P. Kennedy, Jr., Foundation. This foundation, established in 1946
to foster programs of care, training, and treatment of mentally retarded persons and to promote research, presented its first set of awards
for outstanding work in the field on December
6, 1962. The first recipients were:

1. The National Association for Retarded
    Children "for its outstanding role in
    awakening the nation to the problems of
    mental retardation and for proving,
    through a diversity of means that the re-
    tarded can be helped."

2. Samuel A. Kirk, director of the Institute
    for Research on Exceptional Children at
    the University of Illinois, for his untiring
    efforts pertaining to the early education of
    retarded children.

3. Ivar Asbjorn Følling, retired chief of the
    University Hospital Clinical Laboratory
    at Oslo, Norway, "for bringing on the
    new awareness of inborn errors of metab-

The Seraphim of Raphael, awarded by the Joseph P. Kennedy, Jr. Foundation

5. Joe Hin Tijo, a Dutch-Indonesian visiting scientist of the National Institutes of Health in Bethesda, Maryland, for his discovery of the exact number of chromosomes in man.

6. Jerome Lejeune, director of the Department of Genetics at the University of Paris, for his discovery of chromosomal abnormalities associated with Down syndrome.[146]

The awards, which were given on five occasions, represented a unique contribution to the field and to those who served it so well. At the awards ceremony held in 1971, recipients included Elizabeth Boggs and George Tarjan for their leadership, Herbert Birch for science, and Mother Theresa who, in 1979, also received the Nobel Prize for Peace for her untiring efforts on behalf of those who live in the most dire circumstances associated with abject poverty.[147]

olism through his discovery of phenylketonuria."

4. Murray L. Barr, head of the Department of Microscopic Anatomy of the University of Ontario, for his discovery of sex chromatin.

The sixties and early seventies were indeed the glorious years for the field of mental retardation as they related to visibility, research support, and recognition. Regrettably, those years were too few in number.

Part
II

SOCIAL CARE
AND TREATMENT

Chapter

4

NEW FOUNDATIONS

THROUGHOUT THE TWENTIETH century, slow but steady progress had been made in providing services for mentally retarded persons and their families under various auspices, but the election of John F. Kennedy as the 35th President of the United States in 1960 signaled a new era for those who were disabled and disadvantaged. One of Kennedy's primary humanitarian interests, due perhaps to his experiences with his mentally retarded sister, was to improve the quality of life for both mentally retarded and mentally ill persons. In order to meet the needs of the former, he first appointed a special President's Panel on Mental Retardation on October 11, 1961, prefacing its charge with the following words:

> Both wisdom and humanity dictate a deep interest in the physically handicapped, the mentally ill, and the mentally retarded. Yet, although we have made considerable progress in the treatment of physical handicaps, although we have attacked on a broad front the problems of mental illness, although we have made great strides in the battle against disease, we as a Nation have too long postponed an intensive search for solutions to the problems of the mentally retarded. That failure should be corrected.[1]

The Panel, chaired by Leonard Mayo, called upon the best minds from nearly every field having an impact on mental retardation and implemented its responsibilities through special task forces and advisors; public hearings; visits to special programs in England, the Soviet Union, and several Scandinavian countries as well as the United States; and a review of the literature and existing research.* Despite all its activity, the Panel completed its report early, submitting to the President 112 recommendations under eight headings:

> *Research* in the causes of retardation and in methods of care, rehabilitation, and learning.
> *Preventive health measures* including (a) a greatly strengthened program of maternal and infant care directed first at the centers of population where prematurity and rate of "damaged" children are high; (b) protection against such known hazards to pregnancy as radiation and harmful drugs; and (c) extended diagnostic and screening services.
> *Strengthened educational programs generally,* and extensive and enriched programs of special education in public and private schools closely coordinated with vocational guidance, vocational rehabilitation, and specific training preparation for employment; education for the adult mentally retarded, and workshops geared to their needs.
> *More comprehensive and improved clinical and social services.*
> *Improved methods and facilities for care,* with

---

*Members of the original panel included: Leonard W. Mayo, chairman; George Tarjan, vice-chairman; David L. Bazelon; Elmer H. Behrmann; Elizabeth M. Boggs; Robert E. Cooke; Leonard S. Cottrell, Jr.; Edward Davens; Lloyd M. Dunn; Louis M. Hellman; Herman E. Hilleboe; Nicholas Hobbs; William P. Hurder; Seymour S. Kety; Joshua Lederberg; Reginald S. Lourie; Oliver H. Lowry; Horace W. Magoun; Darrel J. Mase; F. Ray Power; Anne M. Ritter; and Wendell M. Stanley.[2]

emphasis on the home and the development of a wide range of local and community facilities.

A new legal, as well as social, concept of the retarded, including protection of their civil rights; life guardianship provisions when needed; an enlightened attitude on the part of the law and the courts; and clarification of the theory of responsibility in criminal acts.

Helping overcome the serious problems of manpower as they affect the field of science and every type of service, through extended support, and increased opportunities for students to observe and learn the nature of mental retardation.

Programs of education and information to increase public awareness of the problem of mental retardation.[3]

Historically, many efforts of this nature had been prepared, submitted, filed away, and ignored, never to be seen or heard of again. This was not the case with the Panel's report entitled, "*A Proposed Program for National Action to Combat Mental Retardation.*" Less than 4 months following receipt and review of the recommendations, President Kennedy addressed the Congress of the United States on February 5, 1963, clearly outlining the challenge:

We as a Nation have long neglected the mentally ill and the mentally retarded. This neglect must end, if our Nation is to live up to its own standards of compassion and dignity and achieve the maximum use of its manpower.

This tradition of neglect must be replaced by forceful and far-reaching programs carried out at all levels of government, by private individuals and by State and local agencies in every part of the Union.

We must act—

to bestow the full benefits of our society on those who suffer from mental disabilities;

to prevent the occurrence of mental illness and mental retardation wherever and whenever possible;

to provide for early diagnosis and continuous and comprehensive care, in the community, of those suffering from these disorders;

to stimulate improvements in the level of care given the mentally disabled in our State and private institutions, and to reorient those programs to a community-centered approach;

to reduce, over a number of years, and by hundreds of thousands, the persons confined to these institutions;

to retain in and return to the community the mentally ill and mentally retarded, and there to restore and revitalize their lives through better health programs and strengthened educational and rehabilitation services; and

to reinforce the will and capacity of our communities to meet these problems, in order that the communities, in turn, can reinforce the will and capacity of individuals and individual families.

We must promote—to the best of our ability and by all possible and appropriate means—the mental and physical health of all our citizens.[4]

One year following the Panel's report and shortly before John Kennedy's cruel and un-

President John F. Kennedy and the President's Panel on Mental Retardation

timely death, Congress passed far-reaching legislation consistent with the President's intent and the Panel's recommendations: PL 88-156, the Maternal and Child Health and Mental Retardation Planning Amendments of 1963, and PL 88-164, the Mental Retardation Facilities and Community Mental Health Centers Construction Act of 1963. They provided for:

1. Increases in maternal and child health and crippled children's services.
2. Funds for maternity and infant care.
3. Funds for special research projects.
4. State grants to the States to assist in planning state and comprehensive services.
5. Construction of research centers to develop new knowledge for preventing and combating mental retardation.
6. Construction of university affiliated clinical facilities.
7. Construction of community facilities to provide an array of services for those who were mentally retarded and their families.
8. Funds for the training of teachers of mentally retarded students as well as other handicapped children.
9. Funds for research or demonstration projects relating to the education of mentally retarded children.[5]

Over the next 20 years, Congress passed 116 acts or amendments thereof that provided support for mentally retarded persons and their families in the areas of education; employment; health; housing; income maintenance; nutrition; rights; social services, including Social Security benefits; transportation; and vocational rehabilitation.[6] The rate at which these programs grew, plus their comprehensive nature, produced the undesirable situation where, by 1976, 135 special funding programs were administered by 11 different federal agencies, creating considerable confusion among potential applicants and some degree of interagency rivalry.[7] Adding to the frustrations of the day was the fact that basic financial assistance programs, which historically had evolved at the discretion of the states, included over 1,100 state and local

welfare jurisdictions, each of which set their own eligibility criteria, funding schedules, and procedures.[8] The latter situation gradually improved as the federal government set forth its policies for participation; however, continuous amending of federal legislation to reach more disabled persons, or to correct inadequacies, or in response to federal court decisions, combined with perpetually bureaucratically modified regulations, sustained a relatively high level of confusion and uncertainty. In the words of one astute Washington observer, federal programs came to represent a "psychodelic labyrinth . . . constantly squirming and changing with the convolutions of Congress and the regulation writers."[9] To the service provider the system could be a nightmare, leading one experienced entrepreneur to remark in 1981, "I feel real sorry for new providers trying to figure it all out. They probably won't."[10]

Despite the chaos and confusion, however, thousands of mentally retarded persons did benefit from new or expanded programs. During the 1980–1981 fiscal year, 852,000 mentally retarded children were enrolled in some form of special education programs; 165,500 mentally retarded young adults received vocational rehabilitation services; and 640,000 mentally retarded persons received some form of support or assistance through Social Security legislation, including approximately 130,000 mentally retarded residents in institutional settings.[11]

Special programs cost money, and public commitment was great, especially during the sixties and early seventies. Both federal and state governments dramatically increased their financial support. In 1960, the federal government contributed less than $5 million, most of which was earmarked for research or training.[12] At that time, the major fiscal responsibility fell to the states, whose primary obligation consisted of spending approximately $350 million for publicly sponsored institutional programs.[13] That situation changed substantially. During 1981, the federal government spent over $5 billion on special programs while the states contributed over $6 billion. The direction of such funding also shifted from institutional to community programs. In contrast with the early sixties, when all but a few dollars were spent on institutional programming, during 1981, half of all expenditures were devoted to community services, including special education.[14] This fiscal accounting did not include large amounts of money provided by private sources nor did it include federal funds available to mentally retarded persons through noncategorical programs, such as Head Start, nor did it consider state funds for general welfare programs, such as Aid to Dependent Children.

The Planning Years

One of the key accomplishments of the President's Panel was the development of a schema outlining a community-based array of services for mentally retarded persons from infancy to old age (see Table 4.1).[15] The Panel called upon nearly every agency, private and public, generic and specialized, to participate in fulfilling the needs of those who were mentally retarded, consistent with the requirements of the proposed model.

The next step in the process was for each state to examine its individual needs and resources in terms of the guidelines and recommendations set forth by the Panel. To this end, PL 88-156 provided funds to states to prepare their own plans of action. Most states followed the format set by the President's Panel, establishing various task forces to examine community services; educational programs; residential facilities; manpower needs; prevention; public and professional awareness; vocational rehabilitation; state laws and legislation, current and needed; research; and administration, interagency collaboration, and finance.[16]

Though final publications ranged in size from a 50-page single document to a 10-volume set, each clearly acknowledged the complexity of the problem; the tremendous unmet need; a mammoth shortage of trained personnel; and the nearly overwhelming challenge to garner the resources, fiscal and service, necessary to implementing a comprehensive program.

As regards need, one state reported that of an estimated 4,200 mentally retarded preschoolers, 3,268 were unserved; of 37,950 school-age youngsters, 20,301 were unserved, and only 13,572 were in any public school program. Of 54,430 adults, 53,416 were unserved.[17] This finding was by no means unique, thus typifying the extent of the problem throughout the country at that time.

In terms of programs required to meet the needs of the vast number of unserved mentally retarded persons and their families, many new services had to be developed. To illustrate: for Los Angeles County, with a population of approximately 7 million, Ivy Mooring, director of the Mental Retardation Joint Agencies Project, indicated, in 1964, that preschool or nursery school programs specifically designed for culturally deprived children needed to be provided as did day care and short-term residential facilities for severely mentally retarded children and adults. Financial assistance for marginal-income families with mentally retarded youngsters was also deemed essential. Other programs needed to be expanded to accommodate those who were mentally retarded, such as casefinding and diagnosis for preschool children; clinical services for adolescents and adults; public health nursing; foster care; classes for primary school–age children; coordinated planning of occupational training and work experience programs by public school districts and the State Department of Rehabilitation; and adult education programs.[18]

Having identified some of the service categories essential to comprehensive programming, Mooring then set forth a number of steps that would have to be undertaken, including: reviewing existing state financial provisions for special programs to determine what additional funds would be required to provide adequate physical facilities and professional staff; continuing community financial support of voluntary agencies and parent groups; removing restrictive eligibility re-

Table 4.1.   Array of services*

Life stage	Components of special need						
	Physical & mental health	Shelter nurture protection	Intellectual development	Social development	Recreation	Work	Economic security
Infant	Specialized medical follow-up; Special diets, drugs or surgery; Home nursing	Residential nursery; Child welfare services	Sensory stimulation	Home training; Environmental enrichment			
Toddler	Correction of physical defects; Physical therapy	Foster care; Trained baby sitter	Nursery school				
Child	Psychiatric care; Dental care	Homemaker service; Day care; Religious education	Special classes—educable; Special classes—trainable; Classes for slow learners; Short stay home; Boarding school	Work-school programs; Speech training	Scouting; Swimming; Day camps; Residential camps	Playground programs	
Youth	Psychotherapy		Occupational training	Youth groups; Social clubs			
Young adult	Facilities for retarded in conflict	Half-way house; Guardianship of person; Long-term residential care	Vocational counseling—Personal adjustment training	Marriage counseling		Selective job placement; Sheltered employment; Total disability assistance	Health insurance
Adult	Group homes		Evening school	Social supervision; Evening recreation	Bowling	Sheltered workshops; Guardianship of property	Life annuity or trust; "Disabled child's" benefits
Older adult	Medical attention to chronic conditions	Boarding homes				Old age assistance	OASI benefits

*Not included are diagnostic and evaluation services, or services to the family; the array is set forth in an irregular pattern in order to represent the overlapping areas of need and the interdigitation of services. Duration of services along the life span has not been indicated here.
Source: President's Panel on Mental Retardation. 1962. p. 76.

quirements so that existing services would be
available to all; developing more and varied
educational materials; and establishing specialized diagnostic and treatment services in
neglected areas of Los Angeles County. In
addition, it was recommended that approximately 14 mental retardation information and
referral centers be established and that a single
agency be created to provide ongoing services
to mentally retarded persons and their families.[19] At the time of Mooring's report, as well
as those of the states, extremely limited resources, both human and financial, rendered
even such relatively modest proposals as unre-
alistic and unattainable in the eyes of many.

Those who participated in the early planning process often found themselves enmeshed in difficult and controversial subjects,
such as: defining mental retardation, estimating the number in need, determining who
should be responsible for implementing resultant recommendations, discovering how to encourage and facilitate legislative support, and
deciding how to maintain visibility and interest in mental retardation and the various
findings once the reports had been completed
and submitted to the respective governors.
Curiously, as reported by Leo Lippman, based
on his experiences in the development of California's state plan, while most state bureau-
cracies were normally more than anxious to
extend their scope of authority, they did not
wish to become more involved with those who
were mentally retarded.[20]

As indicated, state planning reports did not
yield an immediate response in terms of greatly expanded spending or an all-out attack on
the problem. The country, let alone the single
state, was not prepared for such action: the
broad social commitment that would be evident in a few years was absent at that time.
Nevertheless, the activity not only sensitized
many people previously unaware as to the
challenge of mental retardation but also set
forth a paradigm that would be repeated in the
future—direct federal participation, comprehensive planning, and inclusion of people
with varying backgrounds, experiences, and
interests in the entire process.

EXTENDED PLANNING AND MONITORING

The original President's Panel completed its
deliberations and submitted its report in a little
over a year, and, consistent with its charge,
ceased to exist. Nevertheless, the importance
of its work did not go unnoticed by President
Johnson, who, on May 11, 1966, established
a standing President's Committee on Mental
Retardation for the overall purpose of melding
a "representative alliance of government and
private citizens that would act as the 'watch-
man at the gates.'" Specifically, President
Johnson's executive order set forth the following expectancies:

> The Committee shall provide such advice and
> assistance in the area of mental retardation as the
> President may from time to time request, includ-
> ing assistance with respect to:
>> evaluation of the adequacy of the na-
>> tional effort to combat mental retarda-
>> tion;
>> coordination of activities of Federal
>> agencies in the mental retardation field;
>> provision of adequate liaison between
>> such Federal activities and related ac-
>> tivities of State and local governments,
>> foundations, and other private organiza-
>> tions; and
>> development of such information de-
>> signed for dissemination to the general
>> public, as will tend to reduce the inci-
>> dence of mental retardation and amelio-
>> rate its effects.
>
> The Committee shall mobilize support for
> mental retardation activities by meeting with,
> and providing information for, appropriate pro-
> fessional organizations and groups broadly rep-
> resentative of the general public.
>
> The Committee shall make such reports or
> recommendations to the President concerning
> mental retardation as he may require or the Com-
> mittee may deem appropriate. Such reports shall
> be made at least once annually.[21]

The Committee consisted of 21 citizen
members appointed by the President for stag-
gered 3-year terms. The Secretary of Health,
Education, and Welfare was named chairperson with the Secretary of Labor and the Director of the Office of Economic Opportunity
serving as *ex officio* members.[22] In 1974, President Nixon expanded the *ex officio* mem-

bership to include the Attorney General; the Secretary of Housing and Urban Development; and the Director of ACTION, the national volunteer program.[23]

Though the Committee was reappointed by every president since Johnson, its major impact occurred during its early years of existence. During the sixties and early seventies, the Committee closely monitored the country's progress in meeting the challenge of mental retardation, examined many areas of concern, and advanced a series of recommendations to further the prevention of mental retardation and/or to enrich or expand current services.[24]

THE DEVELOPMENTAL DISABILITIES SERVICES ACT

While the President's Committee accomplished much, the need for extended monitoring on both the federal and state levels became increasingly evident, and, in 1970, PL 91–517, the Developmental Disabilities Services and Facilities Construction Act was federally authorized. Congress expressly intended this Act to "assist States to assure that persons with developmental disabilities receive the care, treatment, and other services necessary to enable them to achieve their maximum potential through a system which coordinates, monitors, plans, and evaluates those services and which ensures the protection of the legal and human rights of persons with developmental disabilities."[25]

In brief, this Act required each state to create a Council on Developmental Disabilities to serve in a planning-advisory capacity and to develop a new state plan. In addition, the Council was to remain relatively free from entanglement with the ongoing problems and struggles inherent to any bureaucratic structure. Subsequently, a number of organizational patterns were developed by the states with the single ingredient that, in some fashion, the Council would have direct access to the governor and appropriate federal representatives. The addition of the latter requirement generated some anxiety and ire on the part of existing state agencies that by state law or regulation had direct responsibility for planning, implementing, and monitoring programs for developmentally disabled individuals. Thus, all concerned were confronted with the most difficult task of not only planning comprehensive services but also reaching common agreement and rapport. In reviewing the new Act and its early implementation, Donald Stedman of the University of North Carolina at Chapel Hill observed that successful developmental disability programs appeared to depend on:

1. An effective internal council operation acting upon clear goals and objectives with sufficient staff to implement operational strategies;
2. Adequate communication linkages between the council and other structures in the state and region, particularly the administering and implementing state agencies designated by the governor;
3. Good organizational placement of the council, the implementing state agency, and the positional relationship between the two, as they have an effect on the extent to which the council can engage in adequate information gathering, planning and strategy development, follow-through on recommendations, and adequate monitoring and evaluation of implemented service programs.[26]

It should be noted that this Act, which over the years had a significant impact on programming for developmentally disabled persons, did not come into existence without considerable difficulty. Though a number of organizations supported its intent and its de-emphasis upon any one category of disability, namely mental retardation, administrative representatives of President Nixon were less enthusiastic. Nevertheless, the Bill was passed and signed into law by the President on October 30, 1970.[27] Though the Act was questioned by several subsequent presidents, it both survived and remained in full force.

The initial Developmental Disabilities Act:

Defined developmental disability as a disability attributable to mental retardation, cerebral palsy, epilepsy, or other neurologically handicapping condition found to be related to mental retardation or requiring treatment similar to that for mentally retarded individuals.

Set criteria for disability as a condition originating before the age of 18, continuing or expected to continue indefinitely, and constituting a substantial handicap.

Required each state to submit a plan to the Department of Health, Education, and Welfare in order to be eligible for its formula grant allocation.

Mandated that state plans describe other federal-state programs providing services for developmentally disabled persons, such as: vocational rehabilitation, public assistance, social services, crippled children's services, education for the handicapped, medical assistance, maternal and child health, comprehensive health planning, and mental health programs. Services for developmentally disabled persons were to include diagnosis, evaluation, treatment, personal care, day care, domiciliary care, special living arrangements, training, education, sheltered employment, recreation, counseling, protective and other social or socio-legal service, information, follow-along, and transportation.

Required state councils to include representatives of each of the principal state agencies and of local agencies and non-governmental organizations and groups concerned with services for persons with developmental disabilities and representatives of consumers (at least one-third were to be consumers); authorized the Secretary of Health Education and Welfare to set aside up to 10% of the amount appropriated for projects of national significance; established a National Advisory Council of 20 members; assumed responsibility for university affiliated programs; and authorized progressive funding from $60 million in FY 1971 to $130 million in FY 1973.[28]

Subsequent amendments to the Act diminished neither the state council's authority nor its duties. Though never abundantly, or, in the minds of many, adequately funded, the council did support small demonstration and tech-

nical assistance projects, and of increasing import over the years, was given the authority to assure adequate advocacy services. In 1977, for example, the federal government proclaimed that the "mission of the Developmental Disabilities Office, working through State DD councils and agencies, is to improve services through the development of comprehensive State plans and to provide for a system of advocacy and protection of individual rights for persons with developmental disabilities."[29]

GUIDING CONCEPTS AND PRINCIPLES

The spectrum of services outlined by the President's Panel was substantially augmented during the late sixties and early seventies by four interrelated, but not identical principles of programming: normalization, the developmental model, the least restrictive alternative, and mainstreaming. These, in turn, were reinforced by general declarations of rights and specific court decisions.

NORMALIZATION

No single categorical principle has ever had a greater impact on services for mentally retarded persons than that of normalization. Though various aspects of the concept had been long recognized, they were never formulated into a theory of service nor did they play such a dynamic role in the philosophy, design, implementation, and evaluation of programmatic efforts.

The principle had its origin in the legislative activity of the Danish government when, on June 5, 1959, it passed "An Act concerning Care of the Mentally Retarded and other Exceptionally Retarded Persons." The purpose of the Act and its related services was to "normalize" the lives of those who were mentally retarded. As explained in 1969 by Niels Erk Bank-Mikkelsen, Director of the Danish Service for the Mentally Retarded:

The purpose of a modern service for the mentally retarded is to "normalize" their lives. For children, normalization means living in their natural surroundings, playing, going to kindergartens, and schools, etc. Adults must have the right to leave the home of their parents, to be trained and taught, and to pursue employment. Children as well as adults need leisure time and recreation as part of a normal life. We are trying to integrate the retarded into the community in the best possible way. We help them in making use of their abilities, no matter how limited these may be. The mentally retarded have, along with other human beings, a basic right to receive the most adequate treatment, training, and rehabilitation available, and to be approached in an ethical fashion.

To provide the retarded with normal life conditions does not mean that we are oblivious of our duties to offer special care and support. We simply accept them as they are, with their handicaps, and teach them to live with their handicaps. Whatever services and facilities are open to all other citizens must, in principle, also be available to the mentally retarded.[30]

The idea spread rapidly to other Scandinavian countries, and was introduced to the United States by Bank-Mikkelsen and Bengt Nirje in 1969 during an outstanding conference sponsored by the President's Committee on Mental Retardation. The purpose of the conference, and its resulting publication, *Changing Patterns in Residential Services for the Mentally Retarded,* was to present a "group of papers as a contribution to the careful study and imaginative, people-related thinking and planning which must underlie improvement in services to the nation's millions of mentally retarded persons."[31] Bengt Nirje, then secretary general [i.e., executive director] of the Swedish Parents Association for Mentally Retarded Children, defined normalization as "making available to the mentally retarded patterns and conditions of everyday life which are as close as possible to the norms and patterns of the mainstream of society."[32] Further, he wrote:

1. Normalization means a normal rhythm of the day for the retarded.
2. Normalization implies a normal routine of life, i.e., not always structured.
3. Normalization means to experience the normal rhythm of the year with holidays and family days of personal significance.
4. Normalization means an opportunity to undergo normal developmental experiences of the life cycle, i.e., experiences and opportunities should be consistent with the appropriate life cycle whenever possible; adjustments and special provisions should be made for the mentally retarded adult and elderly.
5. Normalization means that the choices, wishes, and desires of the mentally retarded themselves have to be taken into consideration as frequently as possible and respected.
6. Normalization means living in a bisexual [i.e., among men and women] world.
7. Normalization means normal economic standards for the mentally retarded.
8. Normalization means that the standards of the physical facility should be the same as those regularly applied in society to the same kind of facilities for ordinary citizens.[33]

At this stage in its development, the normalization principle basically reflected a lifestyle, one diametrically opposed to many prevailing institutional (and community) practices. The highly influential International League of Societies for the Mentally Handicapped endorsed the Scandinavian philosophy in 1971 as representing "a sound basis for programming which, by paralleling the normal patterns of the culture and drawing the retarded into the mainstream of society, aims at maximizing his human qualities, as defined by his particular culture. Retarded children and adults should, therefore, be helped to live as normal a life as possible. The structuring of routines, the form of life, and the nature of the physical environment should approximate the normal cultural pattern as much as possible."[34]

The International League of Societies for the Mentally Handicapped, which was launched in conjunction with the World Mental Health Year of 1960, included representatives of various parent organizations, professional groups, and other individuals "anxious to advance the interests of the mentally handicapped without regard to nationality, race, or creed."[35] The intent of the League was to improve the quality of services through the interchange of experts and information on the development of services for mentally retarded persons; the exchange of workers in the field between one country and another; and the comparative study of legislation in member countries. Within a few years following its inception, the organization included 35 national members as well as individual members in 43 countries. Its deliberations were distributed not only to member associations but also to worldwide organizations concerned with mentally retarded persons and to various agencies of the United Nations.[36] In essence, its voice was truly heard around the world.

Even though by later standards the original normalization principle was relatively modest in intent and scope, it was conservatively accepted, when not actually rejected, by some American superintendents. In 1973, Warren and Jones conducted a survey among superintendents attending that year's annual convention of the American Association on Mental Deficiency. Thirty-nine administrators of public residential facilities and 25 administrators of private facilities responded. The results revealed that only 18 (46.2%) of the public administrators held a very positive attitude toward normalization. The remaining 21 public superintendents (53.8%) were either neutral or negative in their attitude. Yet, 58% indicated that the normalization principle had a good chance of being realized in the near future. The results were similar among administrators of private residential facilities; that is, 37.5% were very positive and 62.5% were neutral or negative. Again, however, 62% indicated that they believed the goal of normalization could be attained in a reasonable period of time. The authors concluded, despite the small sample, there appeared to be a lack of unanimity among administrators concerning their attitudes toward normalization, and "if pressure to pursue a normalization policy continues to grow, it would be advisable to explore in depth reasons for resistance among administrators and means of meeting the objections which they raise."[37]

Normalization Redefined

No vital doctrine such as normalization, however, remains static. In 1972, Wolfensberger significantly expanded its ideology when he redefined the principle as the "utilization of means which are as culturally normal as possible, in order to establish and maintain personal behaviors and characteristics which are as culturally normative as possible."[38] Further, normalization implied "that as much as possible, human management means should be typical of our own culture; and that a (potentially) deviant person should be enabled to emit behaviors and an appearance appropriate (normative) within that culture for persons of similar characteristics, such as age and sex."[39]

Over the next several years, Wolfensberger slightly modified his original definition, primarily for purposes of clarity: "Utilization of means which are as culturally normative as possible, in order to establish, enable, or support behaviors, appearances, and interpretations which are as culturally normative as possible."[40] Less formal and more expansive was his alternative explanation:

> Culturally normative means (familiar, valued techniques, tools, methods), in order to enable persons life conditions (income, housing, health services, etc.) which are at least as good as that of average citizens, and to as much as possible enhance or support their behavior (skills, competencies, etc.), appearances (clothes, grooming, etc.), experiences (adjustments, feelings, etc.), and status and reputation (labels, attitudes of others, etc.).[41]

For normalization to be realized fully, people who are mentally retarded must not only live in a typical community setting, they must be in a position to interact freely with others in their environs:

> For a (deviant) person, integration is achieved when he lives in a culturally normative community setting in ordinary community housing, can move and communicate in ways typical for his age, and is able to utilize, in typical ways, typical community resources; developmental, social, recreational, and religious facilities; hospitals and clinics; the post offices; stores and restaurants; job placements; and so on.
>
> Ultimately, integration is only meaningful if it is social integration; i.e., if it involves social interaction and acceptance, and not merely physical presence. However, social integration can only be attained if certain preconditions exist,

among these being physical integration, although physical integration by itself will not guarantee social integration.[42]

Wolfensberger's theory varied significantly from the early Scandinavian concept. Attention was now devoted to the behavior of mentally retarded persons as well as their general life-style and physical environment. In other words, what previously had been a means or a process, now became a goal; that is, to normalize to the greatest extent possible the conduct of socially perceived "deviant" mentally retarded people.

In 1983, Wolfsenberger once again attempted to clarify the concept of normalization, this time adopting the term "social role valorization," from the French *valorisation sociale*. While this did not negate the dual concept of eliminating or modifying individual behavior that might be viewed as deviant or encouraging society to change its attitudes, the new label, in his judgment, possessed several advantages. First, it avoided the incidental interpretations that attached themselves to the word "normalization," and second, it placed an emphasis on valuing those who, for one reason or another—mental retardation, physical handicap, or advanced age—did not participate fully and richly in the mainstream of society.[43] Despite its attractive features, it would take time for "social role valorization" to replace "normalization" in popular usage.

In his first extended and widely read text, *The Principle of Normalization in Human Services,* published in 1972, Wolfensberger wrote, "I firmly believe that the normalization principle, simple and uncomplicated as it is, is the human management principle that is most consistent with our socio-political ideals and current psycho-social theory and research on deviancy, role performance, and other social processes. I further believe that the normalization principle is so self-evidently valid as well as 'right' that it may well become universally accepted in all areas of human management."[44]

While normalization became generally accepted, at least in broad concept, it proved to be neither "simple" nor "uncomplicated," as Wolfensberger readily acknowledged when responding to those annoying, "misguided," and "numerous trivial" one- and two-page critiques: "One remarkable thing about the majority of published critiques of the normalization principle is that they consist of extremely short articles that attempt to resolve an issue that is derived from an incredibly complex theoretical system by means of very brief and superficial points of analysis."[45]

The major problem, in the eyes of many, rested with the implication, denied by Wolfensberger, that the theory required mentally retarded people to be normal. "A retarded person," wrote Fram in 1974 "should [not] be refused the right to be retarded."[46] "It is normal to be different," proclaimed Gunnar Dybwad.[47] "Normalization," observed Norman Ellis in 1979, "as a guiding principle, reminds us that retarded people are human beings and should be treated like the rest of us; as such it probably has some value. But, it can be, and often is, a dangerous notion. Retarded persons are not normal, but handicapped, and allowance must be made for them in our society."[48]

Others, such as Thorne, challenged the notion that normal means rather than specialized techniques were appropriate to meet the developmental needs of mentally retarded persons.[49] Still others, as exemplified by Charlotte Schwartz, believed that normalization "placed an undue burden upon the retardate's psychic structure by exposing him to constant and repeated frustrations of enormous magnitude in the everyday world, and that these external pressures are handled primarily by the pervasive use of primitive defense mechanisms. These mechanisms ultimately do not protect the individual from pathological processes."[50]

While one can ignore, occasionally with a sense of relief, the inevitable polemics of the professional community over every nuance of a theory, one cannot ignore the judgment of the consumer. At a National Conference on Normalization and Contemporary Practice in Mental Retardation held in 1980, representatives of the People First International, an organization of disabled persons, noted:

> Normalization has not adequately met the social needs of the consumer [i.e., disabled person]. Consumers find special and important meaning in their relationships with each other. They need each other. Consumers don't like to be lonely or isolated in the institution or the community.[51]

Further,

> normalization has not encouraged or given consumers access to peer support systems, peer relationships, peer decision making, peer culture or peer history. The roles of the institution aides have been replaced by the roles of the group home staff. So dependence on others is still essential to the survival of the consumer.[52]

Finally,

> consumers need a group identity. They need a culture, a history and their own heroes. They need each other so that they're able to develop what the rest of society has. Think of yourselves. You all come from someplace. You all belong to groups. Groups give a special meaning and identity. Without developing a history, the consumer will have no identity. Without a background, a group identity and a culture, it is almost impossible for the consumer to have input about where they are going.[53]

As evidenced by the comments, developmentally disabled individuals, including those who were mentally retarded, viewed themselves as any other minority group seeking their own identity, history, and culture. Their approach and thinking was entirely consistent with the traditions of the United States. Though it obviously was not the intent of either Wolfensberger or the normalization theory to promote social isolation, the consumers did express a most legitimate concern.

From Principle to Practice

To augment the theory, in 1973, Wolfensberger and Linda Glenn developed a procedure for its quantitative evaluation, *Program Analysis of Service Systems* (PASS). The quaternary purpose of PASS was to: "(1) establish a standard of normalizing human management agency performance; (2) provide an objective means of assessing (either by internal or external evaluation) the quality of a human service,

thereby to be able to assess quality change over time; compare the performance of different services; (3) provide a rational means for allocating limited funds on a competitive basis; (4) function as a teaching tool in disseminating the normalization principle."[54]

In essence, the PASS system was based on rating 41 items collated under two generic categories—ideology and administration. Ideology included such aspects as physical and social integration, ages and culture-appropriate activities and structures, specialization, developmental orientation, the quality of the physical setting, utilization of generic services, consumer and public participation, ties to academia, and innovativeness. Administration included manpower considerations and operational effectiveness. A supplemental device entitled FUNDET also could be applied. FUNDET, an acronym for funding determination, was intended to assist the administrator and staff in setting fiscally related program priorities.

Ten years later, Wolfensberger and Susan Thomas added another dimension to the assessment process: *PASSING: Program Analysis of Service Systems' Implementation of Normalization Goals.*[55] PASSING was designed for the specific purpose of evaluating the quality rather than the quantity of human services according to the principles of normalization. To accomplish this task, a 42-item rating system took into consideration the physical setting of service; service-structured groupings and relationships among people; service-structured activities and other uses among people; service-structured activities, and other uses of time; and language, symbols, and images. These, in turn, were rated against program elements related previously to client social image enhancement and program elements related primarily to client competency enhancement.[56]

Using these tools, researchers soon discovered that the transition from principle to practice proved extremely difficult. To illustrate, in 1980, Flynn and Nitsch reported an analysis of 256 PASS evaluations, including those for 118 community residential services and 18 institutional programs. The results revealed a mean score for community residential services of 49.91, barely meeting the 50% level or that considered "minimally acceptable." Not surprisingly, institutional programs fared poorly, scoring a mean of only 28.12, far below the minimally accepted level, and farther yet from the 85% "expected" level of service quality. Thus, the authors concluded, "This principle has been met with widespread intellectual, judicial, and legislative approval, on the one hand. On the other, implementation has frequently been sporadic and superficial, and, indeed, in many jurisdictions it can be said to have scarcely begun."[57]

Despite the disagreements and challenges, normalization became the cornerstone of positive, contemporary programming, a tribute to the humanitarianism, scholarly talent, and persistence of its author.

Wolf Wolfensberger

Wolf Wolfensberger

In a day when group thinking and collective, often anonymous decision-making were common, it was rare for any one individual to have substantial influence on any field. Wolf Wolfensberger was a remarkable exception to this rule.

Born in Germany in 1934, Wolfensberger lived through the rise and fall of the Third Reich and the crushing aftermath of World War II. In 1950, he emigrated to the United States, becoming a naturalized citizen.

His formal education included a doctorate in psychology and special education from the George Peabody College (1962) and a postdoctoral research fellowship in training at the Maudsley Hospital in London (1962–1963). Much of his early work experiences were in various institutional settings, including the Muscatatuck State School, Indiana; the Greene Valley Hospital and School, Tennessee; and the Plymouth State Hospital and Training School, Michigan. His responsibilities ranged from serving as clinical psychologist to director of research.

In 1964, Wolfensberger joined the staff at the Nebraska Psychiatric Institute of the University of Nebraska Medical Center, where he was an associate professor and a full-time researcher in mental retardation. During the early seventies, he was a visiting scholar to the National Institute on Mental Retardation in Toronto, Canada, and it was there that he received the opportunity and support to publish his most significant work on normalization in 1972. His second major contribution, prepared with Helen Zauha, appeared the following year: *Citizens Advocacy and Protective Services for the Impaired and Handicapped.*[58]

Subsequently, he served as director of the Training Institute for Human Service Planning, Leadership, and Change Agentry and as a professor in the Division of Special Education and Rehabilitation, Syracuse University. Here he expanded his theories and espoused their value to many groups throughout the country.

Wolfensberger's work was internationally recognized and frequently awarded. R. Vince Gillis, in preparing the testimonial statement for the American Association on Mental Deficiency's 1978 Leadership Award, summarized Wolfensberger's contributions succinctly: "He's been in the forefront in helping to turn the tide in the approaches being attempted as responses to the deinstitutionalization movement. He has insisted on the 'humanizing' of programs and services in order that mentally retarded persons might develop and benefit from participation in the mainstream of society and community life."[59]

THE DEVELOPMENTAL MODEL

The International League of Societies for the Mentally Handicapped was one of the first groups to proclaim that the most appropriate approach to mental retardation programming was the developmental model "according to which retarded children and adults are considered capable of growth, learning, and development. Each individual has potential for some progress, no matter how severely impaired he might be. The basic goal of programming for retarded individuals consists of maximizing their human qualities."[60] The underlying concept of the developmental model required each mentally retarded person to be considered a total human being capable of growth and development.

The developmental model was accepted by nearly all organizations interested in and/or serving mentally retarded and other developmentally disabled persons. For example, the Association for Retarded Citizens of the United States published several documents supporting the developmental model and its emphasis on facilitating each resident's degree of independence and control over his or her environment.[61]

The developmental model was offered in contradiction to the medical model, which some persons and groups contended represented the major mode of residential treatment in the United States. Though there were numerous variations of the medical model, primary aspects that were severely criticized by professionals as well as by the International League of Societies for the Mentally Handicapped and the President's Committee on Mental Retardation included:

1. The overriding concept that mental retardation was an "illness" or "disease" with the subsequent tendency to treat developmentally disabled individuals as "sick" persons

2. The emphasis on medical treatment to the neglect of the residents' total developmental needs

3. The pronounced tendency to foster dependence among residents as a result of the "healer-patient" relationship, plus an almost abnormal fear that a resident may hurt himself or herself or come into contact with a communicable disease

4. The frequent prognosis that the resident was so retarded that only custodial or skilled nursing care was required, which readily became a self-fulfilling prophecy

5. That administration, physical environment, and programming (usually identified as "treatment") was developed along hospital lines rather than those of a home or total habilitation center

6. The notion that all programming was to be delivered by medical personnel (e.g., physicians and nurses, with occasional consultation from a behaviorally trained person)[62]

Though the medical model had been in effect in some residential facilities and probably influenced programming for more severely affected persons, the major tenets of the developmental model, were, in fact, promoted by most superintendents and residential staff for many years. Unfortunately, most appeals for staff and environmental changes critical to meet the total developmental needs of more seriously affected persons fell on deaf ears.

THE LEAST RESTRICTIVE ALTERNATIVE

In contrast to the theory of normalization, the "least restrictive alternative" had its roots in law. As a legal doctrine, it was noted as early as 1819 when, in *McCulloch* v. *Maryland*, Chief Justice Marshall "indicated that regulation affecting citizens of the state should be both 'appropriate' and 'plainly adapted' to the end sought to be achieved."[63] In 1960, the Supreme Court, in *Shelton* v. *Tucker,* firmly recommitted the nation to this principle when it stated:

> In a series of decisions this Court has held that, even though the governmental purpose be legitimate and substantial, that purpose cannot be pursued by means that broadly stifle fundamental personal liberties when the end can be more narrowly achieved. The breadth of the legislative abridgement must be viewed in the light of less drastic means for achieving the same basic purpose.[64]

As evidenced by this proclamation, the least restrictive alternative primarily referred to a state's right to infringe upon an individual's freedom. In other words, if the state or its representatives felt that a person's liberty must be restricted in some manner, the means by which such restrictions were to be realized should, in the words of Robert Burgdorf, "be no nastier than they absolutely have to be."[65]

This principle as regards mentally retarded people was first cited in 1972, in *Wyatt* v. *Stickney.* It subsequently was applied in other court cases with an increasing number of ramifications. By 1985, the least restrictive alternative automatically involved:

1. Equal protection under the law
2. Due process and related hearings
3. Right to treatment and habilitation based on an individual plan
4. Informed consent by the person or guardian, if necessary
5. The right to deny as well as to accept treatment
6. The right to receive programming in the least personally restrictive setting or environment[66]

The relationship between the least restrictive alternative and normalization was exemplified by Judge Broderick's decision in *Halderman* v. *Pennhurst State School and Hospital* (1978), when one of the key issues of the hearings as well as the ultimate decision was whether Pennhurst (and, by implication, other institutions as well) could ever be appropriate. Judge Broderick concluded that the institution could not be since "the retarded at Pennhurst [were] not receiving minimally adequate habilitation [and] such minimally adequate habilitation cannot be provided at Pennhurst because it does not provide an atmosphere conducive to normalization, which the experts all agree is vital to the minimally adequate habilitation of the retarded . . . ."[67]

MAINSTREAMING

Mainstreaming, which is discussed in greater detail in this volume when special education is considered, broadly involved the placement and integration of mentally retarded and other disabled children in regular classes to the greatest extent possible. While this readily met the criteria of the least restrictive alternative, it was not synonymous with normalization, as Wolfensberger expressed on a number of occasions: "*Mainstreaming* is a term without rigorous common definition and, indeed, is commonly a code word for dumping and perversion," and "too often, the term *mainstreaming* is utilized for what normalization parlance might merely call physical integration."[68] Normalization, as demonstrated previously, was difficult to attain regardless of the physical setting.

Taken in their totality, the principles and theories associated with normalization, the developmental model, the least restrictive alternative, and mainstreaming implied that each mentally retarded person should live in an open society, if at all possible, and that any environment in which the individual resided should provide as normal a way of life as the individual is capable of handling effectively. They also mandated that every effort be made to assist the mentally retarded child or adult, regardless of degree of retardation or accompanying handicaps, to attain a maximum level of independence and the highest degree of societal integration feasible.

Rights of Mentally Retarded Persons

Paralleling the development of new programmatic philosophies and principles was the growing awareness among many people and organizations to the rights of mentally retarded persons. In 1968, Henry Cobb, of the United States, served as president of the International League of Societies for the Mentally Handicapped. In his opening address to that year's annual conference, the theme of which was "From Charity to Rights," he stated:

> We are met here to reaffirm the fundamental right of the mentally retarded to a life of decency and dignity. In this affirmation we are not speaking as citizens of any country, though we come from many countries; we are not speaking as adherents to any faith or creed, though we hold many faiths and creeds; we are not speaking in the terms of our own language, though we speak in many tongues. We are making an affirmation that transcends all nationalities, all races, all creeds, and faiths, and tongues.[69]

On October 24, 1968, the International League adopted its Declaration of General and Special Rights of the Mentally Retarded based on the universal declaration of all human rights of the United Nations. In 1971, the United Nations General Assembly, in turn, adopted the special declaration as written, thus giving in increased visibility and status. The Declaration's seven articles, which were universally accepted throughout the world, decreed:

Article I
The mentally retarded person has the same basic rights as other citizens of the same country and same age.

Article II
The mentally retarded person has a right to proper medical care and physical restoration and to such education, training, habilitation, and guidance as will enable him to develop his ability and potential to the fullest possible extent, no matter how severe his degree of disability. No mentally handicapped person should be deprived of such services by reason of the costs involved.

Article III
The mentally retarded person has a right to economic security and to a decent standard of living. He has a right to productive work or to other meaningful occupation.

Article IV
The mentally retarded person has a right to live with his own family or with foster parents, to participate in all aspects of community life, and to be provided with appropriate leisure time activities. If care in an institution becomes necessary, it should be in surroundings and other circumstances as close to normal living as possible.

Article V
The mentally retarded person has a right to a qualified guardian when this is required to protect his personal well-being and interest. No person rendering direct services to the mentally retarded should also serve as his guardian.

Article VI
The mentally retarded person has a right to protection from exploitation, abuse and degrading treatment. If accused, he has a right to a fair trial with full recognition being given to his degree of responsibility.

Article VII
Some mentally retarded persons may be unable, due to the severity of their handicap, to exercise for themselves all of their rights in a meaningful way. For others, modification of some or all of these rights is appropriate. The procedure used for modification or denial of rights must contain proper legal safeguards against every form of abuse, must be based on an evaluation of the social capability of the mentally retarded person by qualified experts, and must be subject to periodic reviews and to the right of appeal to higher authorities.[70]

In 1973, the American Association on Mental Deficiency issued a series of basic rights statements. Accordingly, specific rights of mentally retarded persons included, but were not limited to:

1. The right to freedom of choice within the individual's capacity to make decisions and within the limitations imposed on all persons.
2. The right to live in the least restrictive individually appropriate environment.
3. The right to gainful employment, and to a fair day's pay for a fair day's labor.
4. The right to be part of a family.
5. The right to marry and have a family of his or her own.
6. The right to freedom of movement, hence not to be interned without just cause and due process of law, including the right not to be

permanently deprived of liberty by institutionalization in lieu of imprisonment.

7. The right to speak openly and fully without fear of undue punishment, to privacy, to the practice of a religion (or the practice of no religion), and to interact with peers.[71]

The Association added specific extensions of the basic rights in view of the special needs of mentally retarded persons:

1. The right to a publicly supported and administered comprehensive and integrated set of habilitative programs and services designed to minimize handicap or handicaps.
2. The right to a publicly supported and administered program of training and education including, but not restricted to, basic academic and interpersonal skills.
3. The right, beyond those implicit in the right to education described above, to a publicly administered and supported program of training toward the goal of maximum gainful employment insofar as the individual is capable.
4. The right to protection against exploitation, demeaning treatment or abuse.
5. The right, when participating in research, to be safeguarded from violations of human dignity and to be protected from physical and psychological harm.
6. The right for retarded individuals who may not be able to act effectively in their own behalf to have a responsible impartial guardian or advocate appointed by the society to protect and effect the exercise and enjoyment of these foregoing rights insofar as this guardian, in accordance with responsible professional opinion, determines that the retarded citizen is able to enjoy and exercise these rights.[72]

Other organizations, not concerned exclusively with developmentally disabled persons released rights statements. For example, the Joint Commission on Mental Health of Children issued the following in 1970:

All children have:
The right to be wanted.
The right to live in a healthy environment.
The right to satisfaction of basic needs.
The right to continuous loving care.
The right to acquire the intellectual and emotional skills necessary to achieve individual aspirations and to cope effectively in our society.[73]

With regard to exceptional children and youth, the Commission stated they also had the "right to receive care and treatment through facilities which are appropriate to their needs and which keep them as closely as possible within their normal social setting."[74]

Statements such as these simply reconfirmed the fact that mentally retarded and other disabled persons were first and foremost human beings with inherent rights. While they did much to institute reforms and to sensitize both the public and professional community as to a critical area of unmet need, they lacked the authority of judicial and legislative sanction.

This situation changed dramatically during the seventies: state and federal legislators, often interacting with or responding to federal court decisions, took an increasing interest in developmentally disabled persons, attempting to assure both recognition of their rights and the perpetuation of appropriate services. By the mid-seventies, most states had adopted some statutory language outlining the rights of mentally retarded persons receiving state support. Florida passed the first such legislation in 1975 "with the unequivocal intent . . . to guarantee individual dignity, liberty, pursuit of happiness, and the protection of the civil and legal rights of mentally retarded persons."[75] The bill specifically stated that all clients, either in the community or in a public residential facility, of the Division of Retardation shall have:

The right to religious freedom;
The right to dignity, privacy and humane care;
The right to an individual program;
The right to unrestricted communication;
The right to own property, especially clothing;
The right to receive education and training;
The right to recreation and good physical fitness;
The right to receive prompt and appropriate medical treatment;
The right to be free from physical restraint.[76]

Federal programs for those who were mentally retarded also included rights statements as exemplified by the Rights of the Developmentally Disabled section added to the Developmental Disabilities Act in 1975:

(1) Persons with developmental disabilities have a right to appropriate treatment, services, and habilitation for such disabilities.

(2) The treatment, services, and habilitation for a person with developmental disabilities should be designed to maximize the developmental potential of the person and should be provided in the setting that is least restrictive of the person's personal liberty.

(3) The Federal Government and the States both have an obligation to assure that public funds are not provided to any institutional or other residential program for persons with developmental disabilities that—

   (A) does not provide treatment, services, and habilitation which is appropriate to the needs of such persons; or

   (B) does not meet the following minimum standards;

      (i) Provision of a nourishing, well-balanced daily diet to the persons with developmental disabilities being served by the program.

      (ii) Provision to such persons of appropriate and sufficient medical and dental services.

      (iii) Prohibition of the use of physical restraint on such persons unless absolutely necessary and prohibition of the use of such restraint as a punishment or as a substitute for a habilitation program.[77]

The civil rights movement, the Vietnam War experience, declaration-of-special-rights statements, highly active parent and professional groups, as well as a receptive public and political system all contributed to this change. In doing so, they gave evidence to legal historian L. Friedman's observation that "as long as the country endures, so will its system of law, co-extensive with society, reflecting its wishes and needs . . . . The law is a mirror held up against life."[78]

The federal courts and the U.S. Congress played the predominant role in initiating reform. Through a complex series of legislative and court decisions, the rights of mentally retarded persons involving education, community placement, institutionalization, vocational opportunities, self-determination, and freedom from discrimination were all affected. Some of these are reviewed in subsequent discussions; however, two pieces of

federal legislation affected all areas. First was the Civil Rights Act of 1964, previously presented. Second was Section 504 of the Rehabilitation Act of 1973 (PL 93-112), which read:

> No otherwise qualified handicapped individual in the United States . . . shall, solely by reason of his handicap, be excluded from the participation in, be denied the benefits of, or be subjected to discrimination under any program or activity receiving Federal financial assistance or under any program or activity conducted by any Executive agency or by the United States Postal Service.[79]

Since few programs for those who were mentally retarded did not involve some form of federal assistance, Section 504, the Civil Rights Act, and other congressional acts provided the federal courts with broadly based doctrines upon which to render decisions that often reflected the courts' intent to promote social change through law. Such actions were not always well received by either administrators in the field of mental retardation or state-elected officials who believed the federal courts, and on occasion, Congress itself, was intruding on local prerogatives. Legal scholars were also among those who expressed concern. Thomas Erlich, for example, a former dean of the Stanford Law School, complained, "More and more, legal pollution is clogging the everyday affairs of all of us. Thickening layers of legalism seem to surround our lives. We have far too many laws, we rely too heavily on law as an instrument of social change, we depend too much on courts, legislatures, and administrative agencies to resolve our woes."[80] Similarly, Laurence Silberman, a former Deputy Attorney General of the United States, argued that "the growing use of the legal process eventually erodes the vigor of other governmental institutions directly responsive to the populace, and thereby the health of democracy itself."[81]

In the final analysis, and setting aside all doubts and contrary opinions, a new day had arrived. In the strident words of Thomas Gilhool, in 1973, a legal activist on behalf of those who were mentally retarded, "The language has changed. It is no longer the language of favor or benefit. It is no longer the fact that what comes to the retarded child and his family comes out of the good will and graciousness of others. It is now the language of rights. What comes, comes as a right. It is really not the language of love and kindness but of justice."[82]

By 1983, the list of rights defined for mentally retarded and other developmentally disabled persons had grown long in length and powerful in implication, as evidenced by the "exemplary" compilation provided by the United States Commission on Civil Rights (see Table 4.2).[83]

Table 4.2. List of rights for mentally retarded and other developmentally disabled persons compiled by the United States Commission on Civil Rights

I. Education: Major types or areas of discrimination
   1. Exclusion
   2. Inappropriate programs and placements
   3. Nonidentification
   4. Misclassification of racial and ethnic minorities
   5. Absence of procedural protections
   6. Noneducation of institution residents
   7. Segregation (nonmainstreaming) of handicapped pupils
   8. Dealing with handicaps as disciplinary problems
   9. Lack of parental and student knowledge of educational rights

II. Employment: Major types or areas of discrimination
   1. Pre-employment inquiries
   2. Hiring criteria
   3. Lack of outreach (affirmative action)
   4. Promotions
   5. Employment benefits and insurance
   6. Termination
   7. Working conditions

(continued)

Table 4.2. *(continued)*

   8. Employer and fellow employee attitudes
   9. Institutional peonage (nontherapeutic work programs)
   10. Below-standard wages
   11. Sheltered workshops
   12. Vocational rehabilitation programs
   13. Worker's compensation

III. Accessibility of buildings and thoroughfares: Major types or areas of discrimination
   1. Types of barriers
      a. Entrances
      b. Stairs
      c. Curbs
      d. Elevators
      e. Toilet facilities
      f. Signals and warning devices
      g. Telephones
      h. Water fountains
      i. Carpeting
      j. Doorways and doors
      k. Steep, long, or dangerous ramps
      l. Absence of handrails
      m. Parking areas
   2. Where barriers occur
      a. Governmental buildings
      b. Schools
      c. Stores, shops, shopping centers, and other commercial establishments
      d. Hotels, recreational facilities, and parks
      e. Public housing
      f. Private homes
      g. Sidewalks and streets
      h. Public monuments

IV. Transportation: Major types or areas of discrimination (both physical barriers and rules, policies, and practices)
   1. Public transit systems
      a. Inaccessible buses
      b. Inaccessible trains, trolleys, and subway vehicles
      c. Inaccessible ferries
      d. Inaccessible terminals

(continued)

Table 4.2. (*continued*)

2. Bus companies
3. Trains
4. Airlines
5. Taxis and limousine services
6. Rental cars
7. Ships and boats
8. Private vehicles
   a. Adaptations
   b. Licensing requirements

V. Competency and guardianship:
Major types or areas of discrimination
1. Overly intrusive guardianship procedures (all-or-nothing approach)
2. Absence of adequate procedural protections
3. Improper persons or agencies as guardians; conflicts of interest
4. Problems with institutional and public guardianship

VI. Institutions and residential confinement:
Major types or areas of discrimination
1. Large-scale institutions
2. Commitment procedures
   a. Standards for involuntary commitment
   b. Procedural prerequisites
3. Conditions in institutions
4. Lack of treatment and habilitation programs
5. Abuse and neglect of residents
6. Denormalization
7. Absence of community alternatives
8. Continuation of construction and expansion of large institutions

VII. Housing: Major types or areas of discrimination
1. Denial of access to public housing
2. Zoning obstacles
3. Restrictive covenants
4. Lack of accessible housing
5. Overly protective fire codes and other regulations
6. Lack of group homes, cluster homes, cooperative living arrangements, and other residential alternatives for handicapped people

(*continued*)

Table 4.2. (*continued*)

VIII. Medical services: Major types or areas of discrimination
1. Denial of lifesaving medical treatment to handicapped infants
2. Problems with informed consent for medical treatment for handicapped persons
3. Electroconvulsive therapy
4. Psychosurgery
5. Psychotropic drugs
6. Access to medical records
7. Consent to medical treatment of institutionalized persons
8. Organ donations from handicapped children
9. Discriminatory policies of hospitals and doctors
10. Medical experimentation

IX. Sexual, marital, and parental rights:
Major types or areas of discrimination
1. Involuntary sterilization
2. Sexual segregation of institution residents
3. Restriction of sexual practices of persons in residential programs
4. Denial of access to contraception
5. Restriction of access to information about sexuality, reproduction, and contraception
6. Legal restrictions on marriages by handicapped people
7. Refusal to permit cohabitation of married couples in residential institutions
8. Removal of children and termination of parental rights of handicapped parents
9. Awarding custody of children to nonhandicapped party in divorce proceedings
10. Denial of adoption rights to handicapped individuals

X. Contracts, ownership, and transfer of property: Major types or areas of discrimination
1. Legal restrictions on contractual capacity
2. Legal restrictions on testamentary capacity
3. Practical difficulties of some

(*continued*)

Table 4.2.   (*continued*)

  physically handicapped persons in making a will or entering into a contract

 4. Representative payees

 5. Denial of personal possessions to institution residents

XI. Voting and holding public office: Major types or areas of discrimination

 1. State laws restricting voting rights of mentally handicapped persons

 2. Denial of opportunity for institution residents to vote

 3. Architectural barriers at polling places

 4. Absence of assistance in ballot marking

 5. Inequity of absentee ballots

 6. Restrictions on rights of handicapped persons to hold public office

XII. Licenses: Major types or areas of discrimination

 1. Restrictions on driver's licenses

  a. Vision

  b. Hearing

  c. Epilepsy

  d. Orthopedic handicaps

  e. Other conditions

 2. Restrictions on hunting and fishing licenses

 3. Other types of licenses

XIII. Insurance: Major types or areas of discrimination

 1. Restrictions on availability to handicapped persons of:

  a. Life insurance

  b. Health and accident insurance

  c. Automobile insurance

  d. Disability insurance

  e. Worker's compensation

  f. Other

 2. Availability of, and need for, actuarial data

XIV. Immigration: Major types or areas of discrimination

 1. Exclusion of handicapped aliens (even children of qualified immigrants)

Table 4.2.   (*continued*)

 2. Congressional standards for admission to U.S.

XV. Personal privacy: Major types or areas of discrimination

 1. Nude or other embarassing photos of institution residents

 2. Publication of information, including identity of handicapped persons, without permission

XVI. Recreational and athletic programs: Major types or areas of discrimination

 1. Denial of access to varsity sports teams

 2. Denial of access to intramural sports programs

 3. Denial of access to professional and semiprofessional teams

 4. Inaccessible recreation facilities and programs

 5. Absence of athletic and recreational opportunities for handicapped persons comparable to those available to nonhandicapped individuals

XVII. Criminal justice system: Major types or areas of discrimination

 1. Disproportionate number of mentally retarded people in prisons and juvenile facilities

 2. Improper handling of and communication with handicapped persons by law enforcement personnel

 3. Insufficient availability of interpreters

 4. Application of insanity defense

 5. Application of incompetency to stand trial

 6. Inadequate treatment and rehabilitation programs in penal and juvenile facilities

 7. Inadequate ability to deal with physically handicapped accused persons and convicts (e.g., accessible jail cells and toilet facilities)

 8. Abuse of handicapped persons by other inmates

XVIII. Consumer protection: Major types or areas of discrimination

 1. Defective wheelchairs, prosthetic

(*continued*)   (*continued*)

Table 4.2.   (*continued*)

         devices, canes, glasses, hearing
         aids, etc.
      2. Fraudulent schemes targeted at
         handicapped persons
XIX. Serving on juries: Major
      types or areas of discrimination
      1. Disqualification of many handi-
         capped persons from jury service
      2. Absence of accommodations to
         permit handicapped persons to
         serve as jurors
XX.   Access to mass media:
      Major types or areas of discrimination
      1. Insufficient captioning of televi-
         sion programs
      2. Insufficient availability of braille
         and tape-recorded versions of
         publications
      3. Insufficient availability of radio
         information in visual form (news,
         sports, weather, upcoming events,
         public information, etc.)
XXI. Participation in military:
      Major types of discrimination
      1. Explicit ineligibility of handi-
         capped persons for induction into
         military service

From *Accommodating the spectrum of individual abilities* (1983, pp. 86–88).

ADVOCACY

Rights exist only to the degree they can be exercised. Thus, it was imperative that a series of protective measures be introduced to augment the numerous positive philosophical and legal attitudinal changes that occurred throughout the years, especially during the seventies. This resulted in the development of new and often powerful advocacy systems.

Advocacy per se, however, was not a new phenomenon in the field of mental retardation, being well practiced by Samuel Gridley Howe and other persons in the nineteenth century who actively urged the development of humane services for those who were mentally retarded. During the twentieth century, professional organizations, such as the American Association on Mental Deficiency and the Council for Exceptional Children, frequently and fervently advocated for many social and educational reforms for mentally retarded persons. None, however, was as legislatively active as the Association for Retarded Citizens of the United States. Officially organized in 1950 as the Association for Retarded Children, throughout the years it and its various affiliated local groups assumed many responsibilities, ranging from parent support and education to establishing preschool and recreational programs, from monitoring services to promoting and conducting research, and from public education to lobbying.[84] Though generally successful in its many pursuits, over time, the Association's continuous leadership in program direction and ability to gain legislative support for its goals and ideals proved of greatest benefit to the largest number of mentally retarded persons and their families.

Advocating for appropriate services and programs, as well as the full recognition of rights, was not limited to organizations and groups. Many individuals, working within or without an organizational structure, fervently sought change, occasionally taking positions contrary to those supported by their professional colleagues.

Among these was Elizabeth Boggs, parent, scholar, a founder and first woman president of the Association for Retarded Citizens of the United States (1958), and a person of exceptional talents. Giving up a promising career in applied mathematics to become a full-time volunteer advocate, she rapidly became the most knowledgeable lay person about legislation and its related processes and served on numerous federal, state, and parent committees, including the original President's Panel on Mental Retardation.[85] Throughout the years, she worked with many groups and organizations promoting a greater understanding of and more positive legislation for mentally retarded or otherwise developmentally disabled persons and their families.

Another prominent person was Burton Blatt (1927–1985), special class teacher, professor, and ultimately dean of the School of Education at Syracuse University at New York. He

Elizabeth Boggs

The husband and wife team of Gunnar and Rosemary Dybwad advocated for mentally retarded persons throughout the world. Trained in law in Germany and later in social work in the United States, Gunnar Dybwad's early experiences were in the fields of correction, delinquency, and child welfare. In 1957, he turned his attention to the field of mental retardation when he became the executive director of the Association for Retarded Citizens of the United States. From that day forward he was one of the country's foremost critics of institutions and dehumanizing practices wherever they existed. In later years as a professor of human development at the Florence Heller Graduate School for Advanced Studies in Social Welfare at Brandeis University, Massachusetts, he dreamed of the day when all mentally retarded persons would live in an accepting community.[89]

Rosemary Dybwad, who received a doctorate in sociology from the University of Hamburg, Germany, also spent her early professional years in the area of corrections and juvenile delinquency. Beginning in 1958, however, she devoted herself full time to exploring and supporting international developments in the field of mental retardation, and, in particular, the role of voluntary organizations. Her activities were many, including co-

was a man with a passion for people and for writing.[87] Throughout his career and in his many publications, he constantly strove to better the lives of those with special needs, being a firm advocate for mainstreaming, deinstitutionalization, normalization, and true societal integration.[86] In the experience of his friends and colleagues, he was always true to his admonition, "to observe sorrow untouched is to cause it to continue."[88]

Burton Blatt

Rosemary and Gunnar Dybwad

directing with her husband the Mental Retardation Project of the International Union for Child Welfare, Geneva, Switzerland, and serving as a board member and vice-president of the International League of Societies for the Mentally Handicapped. In subsequent years, she was a senior research associate at the Florence Heller Graduate School, Brandeis University, at which time she also served on the Massachusetts Developmental Disabilities Council and as consultant on International Affairs to the President's Committee on Mental Retardation.

Together, Rosemary and Gunnar received many awards from such organizations as the American Association on Mental Deficiency, the International League of Societies for the Mentally Handicapped, and the President's Committee on Mental Retardation.

Herschel W. Nisonger (1890–1969) rendered many valuable services to the field of mental retardation even though most of his activity occurred following his retirement in 1960 as director of the Bureau of Education Research and Service and as professor of adult education at Ohio State University. As director of the American Association on Mental Deficiency's Research Project on Technical Planning, though unknown to most in the

field, he guided and directed the development of the first nomenclature on mental retardation, the first international communication system on mental retardation, the first standards for evaluating institutional services, and the first standards for community programming. Throughout his life and professional career he was known as a "kind, wise, and modest man, a pioneer . . . a catalyst."[90]

David Rosen was yet another leading advocate in the field. Social worker by training and early experience, followed by years as an institution superintendent, Rosen persisted in his efforts to keep people out of institutions and return as many as possible to the community. In doing so, while director of the Mac-Comb-Oakland Regional Center, he set forth a model of community programming that would be emulated throughout the country. In the words of his successor at the Regional Center, Rosen "displayed a sense of urgency in embracing the problems of mentally retarded citizens. He refuses to sit in contemplative silence and parry from a distance whenever controversy involves consumers being freed from our traditions."[91]

These efforts, as well as those by hundreds of other equally dedicated people, however, tended to represent the broad interests of men-

Herschel W. Nisonger

David Rosen

tally retarded persons collectively. The new laws called for greater representation of mentally retarded persons as individuals. Thus, as indicated, new schema were developed.

SELF-ADVOCACY

Of prime import, schools, parent organizations, and other groups working with more mildly affected persons initiated training programs in self-advocacy with the result that many such individuals developed the ability to represent their own interests and rights, or at least knew what resources could be of assistance. Given the opportunity, many mentally retarded persons proved quite capable of expressing their needs and desires most adequately.

Equally important, developmentally disabled persons, including those who were mentally retarded, formed their own advocacy groups, enabling them not only to share their experiences and concerns but also to speak out with a common voice. In 1974, the People's First International was established in the State of Oregon. This organization, whose primary membership consisted of mentally retarded persons, soon saw chapters started in a number of cities and towns throughout the country. Identifying themselves as "consumers," they demanded input into decisions affecting their lives. As noted previously, the members addressed their interests in the same manner as any minority group believing its rights and privileges were ignored and/or violated by society at large. On occasion, the International simply brushed aside the good intentions and cherished beliefs of the professional/parent community, as in their judgment of normalization and placement separation described earlier. They were also quite vocal about perceived inadequacies concerning professional ideas of programming and procedures used.[92] This was hardly the position that many professional and lay persons had anticipated.

Another group of developmentally disabled persons, which included those who were mentally retarded, was United Together, the goals of which were similar to those of People's First International:

1. Helping ourselves
2. Not letting other people do work for us that we can do
3. Serving on boards of directors and committees everywhere so we can better help handicapped people
4. Becoming a part of politics and working to change legislation that needs changing
5. Choosing our own helpers
6. Closing all institutions
7. Designing more community living situations
8. Getting more jobs for handicapped people
9. Getting equal pay for equal work[93]

In the fall of 1981, United Together held its first conference in Arlington, Virginia, at which time a leading U.S. senator, Robert Dole, addressed the 75 participants and requested that they prepare a list of recommendations they would like to see considered by Congress. They did, citing a number of items, including:

1. Section 504 of the Rehabilitation Act must *not* be watered down.
2. There should be at least a minimum wage that all disabled people earn in sheltered workshops—regardless of disability.
3. We need to strengthen federal programs designed to increase housing options for handicapped people.
4. We need more exploration into targeted tax incentives for the removal of architectural barriers, increasing housing, [improving] public transportation, and modification for job sites.
5. We need to get more of the higher functioning people out of institutions and into group homes or other forms of housing assistance . . . . This is particularly important in large urban areas where a lot of institutions just dump their residents into welfare hotels. Deinstitutionalization needs to be done in a *positive* way.
6. There need to be tougher penalties for people who vandalize group homes.
7. Pressure needs to be brought to bear on the U.S. Census Bureau to do a comprehensive demographic study on the disabled population in this country. This does not currently

exist, so we don't know where all disabled people are.

8. We need a commitment that the federal government will stay in the business of providing programs for disabled people so we don't have to fight for the same things year after year.

9. Make sure that disabled people are truly involved in the policy making of all programs that affect their lives.

A national survey of self-advocacy groups, reported in 1984, revealed that there were over 100 such programs engaging the active participation of at least 5,000 persons who were mentally retarded. Of the groups surveyed, 67% actively promoted individual self-advocacy, while 13% emphasized group advocacy. In addition, these organizations also worked to facilitate greater self-confidence, more active community integration, and closer social relationships.[95]

Several state parent associations also created a subdivision for self-advocacy. This once again enabled mentally retarded persons to have a voice not only in their own affairs but in those of their parents' organization as well.

CITIZEN ADVOCACY

Not all mentally retarded persons, however, had access to these organizations nor, in some cases, did they possess the ability either to participate or to represent independently their own interests and needs. For these, a number of alternative solutions were proposed and implemented. The most important was the "citizen advocate," who was defined as a "mature, competent citizen volunteer representing, as if they were his own, the interests of another citizen who is impaired in his instrumental competency, or who has major expressive needs which are unmet and which are likely to remain unmet without special intervention."[96] "Instrumental competency" referred to problems arising from daily living, such as obtaining a job or raising children; "major expressive needs" referred to the "exchange of affection that meet deep-seated needs and that often make instrumental de-

mands meaningful or bearable."[97] As conceptualized, citizen advocacy could fulfill both "formal" roles, such as adopted parenthood or guardianship, and "informal" roles, such as being a friend and a guide. The latter approach was most common. When, for example, citizen advocacy programs were initiated in Ohio in 1974, the guidelines provided that lay or citizen advocates would:

1. Be a friend.
2. Know the client's personal needs and wishes, his program needs, and his program prescription.
3. Know community resources.
4. Raise questions concerning the appropriateness of the client's program.
5. Keep in touch with the client's professional helpers.
6. Be acquainted with the client's neighbors, landlady, shopkeepers, and policemen in the area.
7. Keep promises made to the client.
8. Keep commitments . . . .
9. Attend training and refresher sessions.[98]

Heavily sponsored by the Association for Retarded Citizens of the United States and its various state and local affiliates, citizen advocacy programs rapidly appeared throughout the country. With federal financial assistance, the Association also established a National Citizen Advocacy Office that prepared and distributed guidelines for recruiting, screening, and training volunteer advocates.[99]

Studies of citizen advocacy programs reported favorable results. Danker-Brown and associates found such groups successfully fulfilling a number of roles:

Defender Roles
  Correcting a situation in which the protégé is being abused or exploited.
  Educating the protégé about his legal rights.
  Educating service agencies working with the protégé about his needs.
  Getting the protégé into a program or receiving services which he needs.
  Intervening with an agency to improve services to the protégé when they are deficient.
  Educating citizens about the developmentally disabled.
Instrumental Roles
  Teaching the protégé new home management skills.

Helping the protégé manage his money.

Helping the protégé manage homemaking and other daily tasks.

Giving the protégé a ride when he needs transportation.

Teaching the protégé to use transportation and to get around.

Teaching the protégé about good nutrition.

Teaching the protégé good hygiene and grooming habits.

Counseling the protégé on interpersonal relationships.

Counseling and educating the protégé about sex.

Helping the protégé find jobs or adjust to work.

Giving the protégé information about the community and its resources.

Helping the protégé make decisions.

Showing the protégé ways to use his free time for recreation.

Taking the protégé to places in the community he should get to know.

Expressive Roles

Being a good listener when the protégé wants to talk.

Providing emotional support during a crisis or time of depression.

Helping the protégé make new friends.

Encouraging others (family, neighbors, etc.) to provide more emotional support to the protégé.

Providing chances for the protégé to go out and have a good time.[100]

In time, advocates, who tended to be young, well-educated adult women, served as "watchdogs" over both rights recognition and programming. This was particularly apparent with the spread of advocacy into institutional settings.[101]

These programs all satisfied one essential component of the citizen advocacy model in that they were not operated by agencies or professionals acting in professional roles.[102] This does not mean, however, that the professional community abandoned any responsibility for advocating on behalf of mentally retarded persons. Quite the contrary, a number of professional groups by both policy and practice assumed that role, including educators, social workers, and physicians.[103]

While there was no question that citizen advocacy programs were highly successful in many ways, a status review by Wolfensberger in 1983 produced some notable exceptions. Citizen advocacy programs, for example, reportedly were concerned primarily with expressive activities among the more mildly affected, neglecting the potentially less demanding, but equally critical instrumental services for the more severely affected, such as guardianship. Quoting a 1977 study by the Association for Retarded Citizens of the United States, Wolfensberger reported that very few severely and profoundly mentally retarded individuals were receiving any form of advocacy services. The failure to extend citizen advocacy programs into guardianship areas for such persons hurt efforts to assure aging parents that such services would be available for their offspring when needed. Wolfensberger contended that one of the major reasons for this vital programmatic shortcoming was that most citizen advocates had difficulty with or little enthusiasm for working with individuals for whom a reciprocating relationship could not be established. He strongly urged advocacy groups to reach out and provide services in these neglected areas.[104]

LEGAL ADVOCACY

While self-advocacy and citizen advocacy programs had their roles, and as important as their activities were, there were times when rights could only be defined, defended, or fulfilled through formal court action, and, as noted, the courts played an unparalleled role in this area with increasing frequency beginning in the early seventies. While the original President's Panel on Mental Retardation was sensitive to the many issues involving the rights of mentally retarded persons and the responsibilities of the legal system, the *tour de force* was the federal court case, *Wyatt v. Stickney*, in 1972. This case gave great visibility to the potential impact of the legal system, especially the federal courts, in improving the lives of mentally retarded persons. In response, a number of legal organizations were established for the purpose of pursuing litigation in the area of rights not only for those who were mentally retarded but for those who were mentally ill or otherwise handicapped as well. The first of these, the National Center for Law and the Handicapped, founded in July of 1972, was funded by the Bureau of Education for the Handicapped, Office of Education, and by the Division of Developmental Disabilities of the U.S. Department of Health, Education, and Welfare. The Center's purpose was "to protect and insure equal protection under the law for all handicapped individuals in our country through provision of legal assistance, legal and social science research activities, and programs and processes of public education and professional awareness. Assistance for disabled individuals is provided through direct legal intervention in selected cases and, indirectly, through consultation with attorneys, organizations, and individuals considering or involved in litigation."[105] While representatives of the Center occasionally served in court cases as counsel and co-counsel, their primary role was that of *amicus curiae,* or friend of the court. Additionally, they provided assistance to various attorneys and legislators through consultation, briefs, and brief preparation.

During the same year, Bruce Ennis, who played an important legal role in several cases involving public institutions, established the National Council on the Rights of the Mentally Impaired, which was co-sponsored by the American Civil Liberties Union, the American Ortho-Psychiatric Association, and the Center on Law and Social Policy.[106] One of the major purposes of the Council was to prepare model complaints, briefs, and pretrial interrogatories, as well as listing pertinent questions to be asked under oath of mental health officials. These were sent to ACLU affiliate lawyers throughout the country who might become active in court actions involving the rights of persons who were mentally retarded. Thus, it was quite evident that early litigation both increased sensitivity to the rights of mentally retarded persons and aroused awareness of attorneys to a new area of sociolegal activism.

In order to monitor the hundreds of legal cases that were generated during the seventies

and early eighties, the National Center for Law and the Handicapped started publishing *Amicus Curiae* in 1972.[107] A few years later, in 1976, the American Bar Association released a similar publication, the *Mental Disability Law Reporter.* Even these journals, however, had difficulty in keeping track of all the cases, for litigation rapidly became a way of life.

STATE ADVOCACY

Prior to the sixties, few states had any laws intended to protect the rights of mentally retarded persons. During the late sixties and early seventies, several states introduced such legislation.[108] Two well-recognized programs at that time were those of Ohio and New Jersey. Ohio's protective service system, which resulted from state legislation in 1971, included "those services undertaken by a legally authorized and accountable agency on behalf of clients who needed help in managing their affairs. Such services could be social or legal in nature and could involve counseling, monitoring follow-along program auditing, advocacy, legal intervention, trusteeship, guardianship, and protectorship."[109] Further,

1. The Director of the Division of Mental Retardation and Developmental Disabilities could accept public guardianship of the person.
2. Before entering the system, each client had to have a comprehensive evaluation.
3. The protective service agency could provide protectorship, trusteeship, and guardianship.
4. The state could provide protective services itself or could make contract for such services.
5. The Division had to provide in writing, at least once a year, a review of the physical, mental, and social condition of individuals for whom it was acting as a guardian, trustee, or protector.[110]

Persons who were mentally retarded could get into the protective system in a variety of ways, including voluntary admission on the part of the affected individual, by parental request, by public or voluntary agency referral, by protective service worker recommendation, or by court appointment.

Duties associated with the protective service system were comprehensive, including outreach, counseling, needs appraisal, referral for service and coordination with case managers and other agencies, follow-up and follow-along, monitoring, program auditing, advocacy for rights, legal intervention, and guardianship. The protective services worker was expected to be in a position to respond to any client need on a 24-hour-a-day basis.

New Jersey's program for adults who were mentally retarded was of longer standing and intended only for those whose "reduction of social competence [was] so marked that persistent social dependency requiring guardianship of the person shall have been demonstrated or anticipated."[111] Beginning in 1965, the Division of Mental Retardation Services had legal authorization to assume guardianship responsibilities and was to "perform such services for the mentally deficient adult as he may require, which otherwise would be rendered by [the] guardian of his person."[112]

State agency programs, however, were often criticized in terms of both principle and practice. Minnesota, for example, had had protective provisions in place for many years, including the right to a judicial hearing prior to institutionalization. Levy described his experiences with that system in 1965:

> The appointment of a guardian *ad litem* has been standard since the Minnesota Supreme Court recognized in the Wretlind case that the subject's interests and those of the petitioner (either his parents or the welfare department) may be adverse. In Hennepin County the guardian is appointed from a group of lawyers whose names are provided by the Bar Association. In Ramsey County, one attorney acts as guardian in all cases. The case workers are not sympathetic to the guardian's role and seem to believe that his presence deters parents' petitions. In fact, guardians have not often disturbed the placidity of commitment procedures. Many attorneys believe that the guardian serves no real function. In a recent session in Hennepin County, during which 13 persons were committed, the guardian

asked only two questions. In one case, he asked the age of the petitioning father. In another . . . the guardian asked the parents whether they understood the petition and wanted state guardianship . . . . Only one of the Hennepin County guardians *ad litem*, of those interviewed, seemed to understand his role. He stated that he customarily opposed commitment unless the retardate needed treatment which could not be obtained without guardianship. But this attorney lacked basic information about the retardation program: He believed that casework services, foster care, and institutionalization could be obtained only after guardianship was established; and he had been informed that priority for institutional care was based solely on a 'waiting list.' In short, the guardian *ad litem* had not usually precluded necessary or improper commitments.[113]

Such practices were soundly condemned during the later sixties and early seventies. For example, R.C. Allen of the Institute of Law, Psychiatry, and Criminology of the George Washington University, and one of first legal spokespersons on behalf of mentally retarded persons wrote "protective services do not protect when legal proceedings become routinized and pro forma, and when decision-makers lose sight of both the nature of the services available and the needs of the people to be served."[114]

While few in the total field of mental retardation were aware of such abuses, many contended that state programs could not avoid problems of vested interest; that is, caseworkers or guardians, being state employees, would naturally feel somewhat obligated to respond to the needs of the state rather than those of their clients in conflict situations. As observed by one critic:

> However well-intentioned, protective services (and particularly public guardianship laws and practices) have suffered from a number of major shortcomings. Among these are the unavailability or impracticality of many protective arrangements, the dull rigidity in which they are administered, the fact that conflicts of interest are built into the very structure and functioning of protective service agency personnel, the fact that agencies—again because of their very nature—can rarely provide the sustained individual relationships that many clients need, and the inability of protective services to match protected measures to protective needs. Characteristically,

a person who needed protection received either too much or too little.[115]

Given these circumstances, it was not surprising when, in 1975, the federal government amended the Developmental Disabilities Act, requiring participating states to establish within 2 years a system to protect and advocate the rights of persons with developmental disabilities and that "such system will (A) have the authority to pursue legal, administrative, and other appropriate remedies to insure the protection of the rights of such persons who are receiving treatment, services, or habilitation within the State and (B) be independent of any State agency which provides treatment, services, or habilitation to persons with developmental disabilities."[116]

One final area of legal advocacy with implications for state and local practices was the need for those mentally retarded persons who were unable to represent themselves adequately to have a legally appointed guardian. This was deemed important not only because of the new and numerous legal ramifications concerning one's rights but also because guardianship laws themselves changed dramatically and positively, again beginning in the late sixties and early seventies. Until that time, mentally retarded persons judged legally incompetent lost all rights indiscriminately. This included

> making a will; making a contract, deed, sale; being responsible for criminal acts; standing trial for a criminal charge; being punished for criminal acts; being married; being divorced; adopting a child; being a fit parent; suing and being sued; receiving property; holding property; being committed to a mental institution; being discharged from a mental institution; being fit for military service; operating a vehicle; giving a valid consent; giving a binding release or waiver; voting;

being a witness; and receiving compensation for inability to work as a result of an injury.[117]

Laws relating to incompetency were revised so as to deny only those rights and activities that the individual, following thorough evaluation, obviously could not perform. To illustrate, the statutes of the state of Wisconsin were revised in 1974 to read:

> Any finding of limited incompetency shall specifically state which legal rights the person is incompetent to exercise. Guardianship of the person shall be limited in accordance with the order of the court accompanying the finding of incompetence. No person determined to be incompetent in accordance with this subchapter shall be deprived of any legal rights, including the right to vote, to marry, to obtain a motor vehicle operator's license, to testify in any judicial or administrative proceedings, to make a will, to hold or convey property, and to contract except upon specific finding of the court. Such findings must be based on clear and convincing evidence of the need for such limitations.

Similar laws were adopted by other states, leading to the active recruitment of guardians, especially for individuals living in residential facilities. One of the major unresolved problems, however, was locating a sufficient number of guardians to fulfill such a role.[118]

With all the new trends, ideas, and laws, plus experience in implementing comprehensive services, the original schema presented by the President's Panel in 1962 required considerable expansion and redefinition by the mid seventies, as illustrated by the outline developed in Minnesota (see Table 4.3).[119]

The list was ever evolving. In a few years, case management, a greater emphasis on those with emotional problems, and providing more adequately for elderly mentally retarded persons would be added. In turn, maintaining quality services in all these areas became increasingly difficult and often expensive.

Table 4.3. Outline of areas of services to mentally retarded or otherwise developmentally disabled individuals, as developed by the state of Minnesota

I. Advocacy
   A. Architectural barrier removal
   B. Employment advocates
   C. Legal advocates
      1. Child abuse
      2. Civil rights
      3. Confidentiality (maintaining privacy)
      4. Guardianship
      5. Marriage
      6. Police protection
      7. Prison reform for developmentally disabled persons
      8. Service receipt on follow-up
      9. Treatment versus nontreatment
      10. Wills and trusts
   D. Legislative advocates

II. Community education about developmental disabilities
   A. Clergy
   B. General public
   C. Law enforcement officers
   D. Medical personnel
   E. Peer group education
   F. Residential program providers
   G. Social workers
   H. Teachers

III. Education of developmentally disabled individuals
   A. Behavior modification therapy
   B. Driver's training
   C. Health
   D. Homebound
   E. Infant stimulation
   F. Referral
   G. Special class programs
   H. Special school programs
   I. Vocational

IV. Health of developmentally disabled individuals
   A. Dental care
   B. Drug counseling
   C. Family planning
   D. Genetic counseling
   E. Health screening
   F. Hearing prosthetics
   G. Hospital care
   H. Immunization
   I. Medical care
   J. Medications
   K. Motor prosthetics (braces, etc.)
   L. Nutritional counseling
   M. Optical prosthetics
   N. Psychiatric care
   O. Psychological testing
   P. Routine physical examinations
   Q. Specialized equipment
   R. Speech and hearing therapy

V. Parent support
   A. Crisis assistance
   B. Family planning
   C. Genetic counseling
   D. Homemaker services
   E. Medical support
   F. Parent education programs
   G. Respite care (short-term)
      1. Weekend and vacation relief
      2. Crisis relief
   H. Sibling counseling
   I. Special funding
      1. Home care
      2. Transportation
      3. Special diets
      4. Babysitting and day nurseries

VI. Recreation
   A. Friendship-enabling services
   B. Programs for developmentally disabled young adults
   C. Programs for individuals having severe physical disabilities

VII. Religious programs
   A. Parent counseling
   B. Religious classes

VIII. Residential program support
   A. Construction
   B. Consultants/specialists
   C. Licensing
   D. Monitoring

(*continued*)

Table 4.3.   (*continued*)

E. Operating costs	E. To jobs
F. Special diets	F. To schools
G. Special meal programs (e.g., meals-on-wheels)	X. Vocational
H. Staff training	A. Job counseling and placement
	B. Occupational therapy
IX. Transportation	C. Retirement counseling
A. For appointments	D. Sheltered employment
B. For emergency care	E. Skills assessment
C. For recreation	F. Work evaluation
D. To activities	G. Work training

Adapted from Minnesota State Planning Agency (1975, p. 25).

Chapter

5

CHILDHOOD AND ADOLESCENCE

CHANGING PERSPECTIVES AND PROGRAMS

WITH THE EXCEPTION of institutions, prior to the seventies, the public schools were often the sole provider of special services. This changed substantially during the 25 years under consideration as meeting the needs of mentally retarded persons from birth to death gradually became a recognized and accepted responsibility of many practitioners and agencies. Though a primary emphasis remained on formal educational experiences during the formative years, meeting the care, treatment, and training needs of the infant and preschooler also became challenges of national significance.

SERVICES FOR INFANTS AND PRESCHOOLERS

One of the great urgencies of the sixties was to attack the problem of mental retardation as soon as possible in hopes of eliminating or at least modifying any potential intellectual deficits or other possible handicapping conditions. This effort took many forms; some, as already noted, aimed at correcting biochemical imbalances to reduce any adverse effects. Proper prenatal care received increased emphasis, and gains in medical knowledge concerning both the physical and psychological aspects of prematurity, combined with specialized treatment and parental training, greatly increased the probability of a premature infant living a full, normal life. Research demonstrated that with proper monitoring and intensive care in the hospital, attention to psychodevelopmental factors in the intensive care unit, combined with family participation and counseling, as well as specialized home training programs, 90% of premature infants would approach normality.[1]

The entire movement toward providing comprehensive assistance to infants at risk received great attention from the medical community, which was most appropriate since most clinical forms of mental retardation were diagnosed at the time of birth or shortly thereafter, and usually in a hospital setting.[2] Fortunately, most large hospitals over the years expanded their historically limited medical services to include a wider range of professionals with varying backgrounds and skills to work with parents in providing appropriate physical and developmental care. The importance of such services skillfully and sensitively proffered soon proved of inestimable value. One study, for example, based on interviews with hundreds of parents of newborn infants with Down syndrome consistently found parents desperately seeking emotional support, information, and guidance from those around them in order to understand and accept their new child. The behavior and expressed attitudes of hospital personnel were most influential.[3]

The significance of physicians in working closely with mentally retarded children and their families was readily acknowledged at a special conference sponsored by the American Medical Association in 1964, the purpose of which was to draw together some of the best medical minds in the country to formulate guidelines to aid the practicing physician in the prevention, diagnosis, and treatment of mental retardation. The role of the physician was viewed as all encompassing:

> In the management of mental retardation, the physician occupies a unique position. In contrast to others with more peripheral and transitory roles, he is the only professional person who will maintain a continuous professional relationship with child and family during the individual's total life span.
>
> He may be dealing with a child now; ultimately he will be dealing with an adult. Good management, therefore, requires the development of a total life plan for each individual, insuring continuous care and enabling the retardate to achieve his maximum potential. It is the responsibility of the physician—consulting with the family and professional colleagues—to devise this life plan and to mobilize the resources of the individual, the family, and the community to put it into effect.[4]

It was not unusual during the sixties and early seventies for nearly all professional groups to define for themselves a new or at least revitalized concept of their responsibilities for mentally retarded persons and their families. In most instances, such roles were set forth in broad, all inclusive terms; however, the transition from philosophical commitment to practice remained difficult and nearly impossible in some cases. This was particu-

larly true of the medical profession for several reasons. First, medical curricula were already replete with content and little room was found (or made) for the subject of mental retardation. While, throughout the years, some universities did attempt to offer an occasional experience in the area, many physicians continued to lack even a rudimentary knowledge of mental retardation and all that it entails.[5] Regrettably, this all too often left the physician in the awkward position of rendering judgments and giving advice based on a paucity of knowledge and information.[6] Second, physicians did not hold a common view as to the value of persons who happen to be mentally retarded, as exemplified by the "Baby Doe" controversy. The combination of inadequate preparation and ambivalent feelings remained a major problem to the medical profession, as highlighted by a parent survey conducted by the President's Committee on Mental Retardation in the early eighties. One of the parents' most common complaints was that physicians, the "trusted family advisor," often were insensitive and not well informed about mental retardation, service options, and advances in programming.[7] It may well have been for such reasons that Derek Bok, president of Harvard University, stated in 1984 that schools of medicine offer "an education too narrow to prepare [physicians] for the challenges that await them in their working lives." He believed courses dealing with ethics and psychology, among others, needed to be strengthened considerably.[8]

This does not mean, however, that no gains were realized. Quite the contrary, many physicians and medical facilities rose to meet the challenges of mental retardation with often promising results, and the counseling situation did improve, as demonstrated in at least one study. Zorzi and associates, in a survey of parents of children with Down syndrome, found that such services offered in the later seventies were much superior to those of earlier years. Counseling now included not only genetic aspects but also practical information on care, education, and expectations, as well as on emotional and psychological development, the latter of which parents valued more than the genetic/medical aspects.[9]

In addition to expanding hospital programs, a number of physicians and related professionals interested in youngsters who were mentally retarded developed innovative approaches to meeting their needs. New clinics were established, and existing ones generated enriched programs to include at least an interdisciplinary approach to diagnosis and service.[10] In sparsely populated areas, highly specialized hospital services were created. During the mid-sixties, for example, the Children's Hospital in Denver, Colorado, established a Newborn Center for Infants at Risk, which, by 1985, served over 200 hospitals within an area of 500,000 miles.[11]

Infant services took many forms, ranging from the advice of the family pediatrician to highly specialized university programs, such as those established during the seventies at George Peabody College at Vanderbilt University, Tennessee; the University of Washington, Seattle; and the University of California at Los Angeles.[12] Parent groups and eleemosynary agencies sponsored small day care programs for infants, occasionally receiving some support from local governments; federal funds for such purposes were extremely limited. A number of agencies also provided parents with home trainers and/or public health nurses.[13]

Most programs for infants, whether offered at home or in another setting, stressed parent-child interaction; basic health care; physical and/or occupational therapy; and perceptual, communication, and socialization activities. Of these areas, parent-infant relations were critical. Without assistance and support, many parents had a tendency to withdraw from their mentally retarded youngster, which, in turn, could exacerbate any existing feelings of guilt and anxiety.[14]

The value of such services was summarized by Denhoff in 1981 in a presentation requested by the Committee on Children with Handicaps of the American Academy of Pediatrics: "(1) They provide the infant and his/her parents with opportunities for both to develop to full potential. (2) Strengthening of the natural interactions between infants and parents that these programs provide is fundamental to good family development. (3) Various and numerous problems that produce parent guilt, anger, and frustration are lessened in a supportive milieu. (4) Constant reinforcement between infant and parents . . . may lay the groundwork for the eventual emergence of positive developmental patterns."[15]

Since infant training/therapeutic programs, however, were not mandated by either state or federal legislation, they often remained few and far between and were frequent victims of unreliable financial support. Thus, one of the critical persistent problems of the period was providing adequately for the youngest in need.

UNIVERSITY AFFILIATED PROGRAMS

One key educational force in facilitating the interdisciplinary approach in the clinical setting and in promoting increased knowledge of mental retardation and related practices was the University Affiliated Program, the establishment of which was a direct outcome of the recommendations of the original President's Panel. The Panel had reacted to the fact that, in 1962, there were only 97 special clinics available to mentally retarded persons and their families in the United States, the service quality of which often suffered from the absence of adequately trained personnel and contributions from allied fields.[16]

The Panel was also concerned with the lack of what was termed a "continuum of care," which described the selection, blending, and use, in proper sequence and relationship, of the medical, educational, and social services required by mentally retarded persons to minimize their disability at every point in their lifespan. Thus, "care" was used in its broadest sense and the word "continuum" underscored the many transitions and liaisons, within and among various services and professions, by which the community attempted to secure the kind and variety of help and accommodation needed by mentally retarded persons. The Panel held that a functional "continuum of care" would permit the fluidity of movement of individuals from one type of service to another while maintaining a sharp focus on their unique requirements.[17]

By 1981, 43 university affiliated programs were in place in 30 states and thousands of professionals, paraprofessionals, parents, and volunteers had been trained in the interdisciplinary approach and the importance of a continuum of care.[18] Such education often occurred in settings that also provided models of both practice and management. Over the years, these programs aided greatly in overcoming a critical shortage of appropriately trained people to serve not only in clinics but in a wide variety of settings. Subsequently, they additionally served as agents of change.[19]

PRESCHOOL TRAINING

The sense of urgency manifested during the sixties was not restricted solely to infants. Rather, there was equal concern for implementing a wide range of preschool programs for high-risk children, or those without any known or suspected prenatal or biological cause that might impede development. Impetus for such action emanated from several sources. First, numerous psychological studies and theories relating to intellectual development stressed the importance of early experiences: "In terms of intelligence measured at 17," wrote noted psychologist Benjamin Bloom in 1964, "about 50% of the development takes place between conception and age 4."[20]

Other research conducted during the fifties led psychologists and educators to be exuberantly enthusiastic over newly discovered procedures and techniques. Following a 1959 conference sponsored by the National Academy of Sciences in which some 35 renowned scientists, scholars, and educators met to discuss the improvement of education, Jerome Brunner set forth the oft-quoted pronouncement, "Any subject can be taught effectively in some intellectually honest form to any child at any stage of development."[21]

The combination of scientific judgments and a growing concern for both mentally retarded and poor youngsters on the part of the federal government resulted in what was to become a massive attempt at improving the lives and abilities of millions of preschool children. The entire effort, however, started in relatively modest terms.

During the early sixties, a few preschool programs were funded by the Social and Rehabilitation Service of the U.S. Department of Health, Education, and Welfare. One such effort—The Milwaukee Project—lent support to those who contended that early training experiences would significantly influence intellectual functioning. The intent of this project, unlike others that would be funded, was not to enhance intelligence, but rather to reduce the often noted measured losses among children from settings of poverty. As initially conceived by Rick Heber of the University of Wisconsin, the program focused on the daily training of infants who had no significant birth injuries and whose mothers' IQ was less than 75. A major component of this program, in addition to the individually prescribed infant training, was the rather unique emphasis upon assisting the mother to influence the environment she created and controlled. In brief, mothers were offered vocational training and placement opportunities as well as training in homemaking and baby-tending skills.[22]

Early results indicated that the experimental group of 40 children attained relatively higher intelligence scores than did their matched counterparts; most fell within the range of normal expectancy, and language skills were markedly improved. These findings were reported by Stephen P. Strickland in an article prepared for *American Education,* which also quoted Heber as saying:

We have seen a capacity for learning on the part of extremely young children that previously I would not have believed possible. While the results are by no means fully conclusive and must continue to be tested, the least that I am willing to say is that it is difficult to conceive of the children in the experimental program ever falling back to the level of their age peers in the language control group.[23]

The article and Heber's comments, which were soon reported in several major national publications, including the *Washington Post,* raised great expectations.[24] A number of researchers, however, questioned Heber's declarations and urged him to release his data for scrutiny by others. The data, however, did not come forth; subsequently, the study lived under a cloud of suspicion and skepticism until the early eighties when Howard Garber, Heber's collaborator, published the results of his follow-up efforts.

For 10 years, Garber was able to re-examine the performance of 80% of the initial sample with the finding that original intelligence test scores remained constant over time, and even siblings of the experimental group revealed higher-than-expected intelligence test results. It was hypothesized that the training proffered to mother and child also influenced the functioning of other children in the family. Regrettably, as was so often the case with such studies, while measured intelligence remained high, school achievement, by the fourth grade, approximated that of other disadvantaged students. The adequacy of public school programs for disadvantaged students was again questioned.[25]

Head Start and
Early Childhood Special Education

In terms of sheer numbers served, Head Start represented the largest single effort of the federal government to promote preschool training. Born in 1964 as one small phase of President Johnson's War on Poverty, Head Start was originally intended as a summer enrichment program for 25,000 poor children at a cost of $10 million, and, as explained by Edward Zigler many years later, expectancies ran high:

In reaction to the Gesellians and other proponents of fixed IQ, J. McV. Hunt, Benjamin Bloom, and others constructed for us a theoretical view that conceptualized the young child

as possessing an almost unlimited degree of plasticity. Joe Hunt continued to assert that the norm of reaction for intelligence was 70 IQ points . . . and that relatively short-term intervention efforts could result in IQ gains of 49 or 63 points. With such environmental sugarplums dancing in our heads, we actually thought we could compensate for the effects of several years of impoverishment as well as inoculate the child against the future ravages of such impoverishment, all by providing a six- or eight-week summer Head Start Experience.[26]

Within a year, the program was serving over 500,000 children at a cost of $96 million and by 1984, the budget exceeded $1 billon annually.[27] Regardless of later assessments, there was little question that many in both the professional and political community thought that through such programs, intelligence, rates of development, and academic achievement would be accelerated, approximating normality. Many also believed, or at least hoped, that ultimately such experiences would be instrumental in breaking the cycle of poverty previously mentioned.

Head Start programs rapidly appeared throughout the country and were operated by various agencies—community action groups (65%), local public schools (10%), and private agencies (25%).[28] Not surprisingly, the program offerings varied markedly in terms of structure, approach, curriculum, and overall quality, but all centers elicited the participation of parents, especially mothers, many of whom became employees. In addition to providing educational experiences, the children's nutritional status was improved, and medical and dental services were provided.

The high hopes initially associated with these programs, however, were soon dashed with the release of the Coleman report in 1966, which stated that for most of the 570,000 students included in the study, preschool experiences had little effect on achievement.[29] Other reports with similar findings soon appeared, indicating either no significant gains or that any increments noted were transitory in nature.[30]

Opponents to federal programs considered wasteful and skeptics in general soon spoke

out. Roger Freeman, for example, in an editorial prepared for *The Wall Street Journal* in
1968, wrote:

> It has long been known that education, in-
> come, and employment status are closely interre-
> lated. If inadequate education is indeed the ma-
> jor cause of poverty, the solution to a vital
> problem seems clear: Give more education to
> school children who lag significantly in essential
> skills and knowledge and, above all, give them a
> better education. That's what the American peo-
> ple have been trying to do on a massive scale for
> some years.
>
> But ever since researchers and administrators
> began measuring the basic skills of children par-
> ticipating in the new programs, they have found
> disconcertingly few signs of pupil progress. Are
> we again, as we have so often in the past, chas-
> ing the end of the rainbow? Is there no cure for
> our educational ills, or have we simply not hit
> upon the cure?
>
> Financial starvation of education has often
> been blamed for shortcomings in the quality of
> American education. But the record of school
> support by the American people is truly magnifi-
> cent. While business and other private invest-
> ment and personal consumption approximately
> tripled over the past 20 years, spending for all
> education multiplied nearly eight times, to an
> estimated $52 billion in 1967–68, making edu-
> cation America's most ebullient growth indus-
> try. In the past four years, Congress has passed
> 40 major education laws and boosted annual
> Federal spending for education from $375 mil-
> lion 10 years ago—and less than a billion as
> recently as 1963—to more than $4 billion in
> fiscal 1968.
>
> [Following a review of failed compensatory
> programs, he addressed Head Start:] Project
> Head Start, which aims to help pre-school chil-
> dren from poor families overcome their environ-
> mental handicaps and to equal middle-class chil-
> dren in learning readiness on entering school,
> was easily the most enthusiastically received of
> all "war on poverty" programs. Initial Head
> Start results were encouraging and, in some
> cases, suggested an average gain of 8 to 10
> points on the I.Q. scale on verbal tests. But it
> soon became apparent that the gain was only
> temporary and disappeared within a few months.
>
> The poor results of Head Start apparently did
> not cause its sponsors to have second thoughts
> about the program's effectiveness. Rather, they
> prevailed on Congress to extend Head Start up-
> ward to grade schools by the Follow-Through
> program.

> The U.S. Commission on Civil Rights sur-
> veyed compensatory educational programs na-
> tionwide and found that "none of the programs
> appear to have raised significantly the achieve-
> ment of participating pupils, as a group, within
> the period evaluated by the Commission. . . ."
>
> [After commenting on the Coleman report and
> other data, he concluded:] It may well be that
> present programs seemingly based on the as-
> sumption that all children are possessed of the
> same—or at least an average—ability must run
> their course until the frustration and conflicts
> they create become unbearable and the waste of
> scarce resources too costly. Our emotional need
> to believe that all children can be made equal is
> too deep, and our national idealization of the
> average man too entrenched, to be quickly re-
> placed by an acceptance of the notion that the
> range of educational and occupational offerings
> must be kept as wide as the range of human
> abilities. But until this awareness dawns, we
> shall not do justice to children poorly endowed
> by nature or to those who are highly gifted.[31]

The rash of negative reports even took their
toll on the program's most ardent supporters,
as evidenced by the comments of Eveline Omwake, President of the National Association
for the Education of Young Children:

> At the close of 1968, after three years of a grand
> effort, we have to face the reality that the once
> promising Head Start project has already begun
> to go down-hill . . . negative effects are by now
> clearly observable. . . . One can speculate that
> with the anticipated budget cuts, with the con-
> tinued push to involve nonprofessionals in place
> of professionals and to appoint sketchily pre-
> pared nonprofessionals to positions of authority,
> Head Start programs may contain little else than
> the children enrolled, angry, frustrated, tired
> adults, broken crayons, incomplete puzzles, torn
> books, and diluted paints left over from the hal-
> cyon days of early Head Start. . . . The (federal
> agencies) muffed it when they began to exploit
> the children's programs to bolster the econ-
> omy.[32]

In 1968, in partial response to the repeatedly reported failures of Head Start, Congress
authorized a special 3-year program to develop, implement, and evaluate special training
systems for preschool youngsters. This legislation, officially titled the Handicapped Children's Early Education Assistance Act (PL
90-538), but better known as "First Chance,"

was administered by the Bureau of Education for the Handicapped, which, over the next few years, financed approximately 200 such programs. Again, approaches and theories varied widely, with no one single model or technique proving superior.[33]

Despite differences in structure and approach, there were remarkable similarities in terms of general goals, as exemplified by those of Project Memphis. As regards students, the purposes were:

1. To increase functioning in deficient or lagging developmental areas such that:
   a. the child becomes a less dependent individual
   b. institutionalization is voided
   c. legal adoption or return to the natural home is more easily facilitated
   d. regular class placement and learning is facilitated when the child enrolls in school
2. To enhance the level of functioning in already normal development such that:
   a. greater self-sufficiency is developed in the child
   b. more healthy and constructive modes of interaction with others are developed in the child
   c. greater opportunities for enhanced school learning and adult adaptiveness are provided the child[34]

To realize such goals, most programs emphasized the development of personal-social, gross motor, fine motor, language, and perceptual-cognitive skills.[35]

As indicated, preschool programs also placed considerable emphasis upon parent training. Again, referring to the policies of Project Memphis, "a training program for parents of exceptional children may have as its general goals the following":

1. To increase the parents' knowledge and understanding of the human development process
2. To increase the parents' knowledge and understanding of exceptionality and handicapping conditions
3. To increase the parents' knowledge and understanding of desirable child-rearing practices
4. To increase the parents' acceptance of their own handicapped child as well as handicapped children in general
5. To enhance the child care-effecting techniques of the parents
6. To enhance the child-teaching techniques of the parents[36]

Many programs also made a concerted effort to integrate developmentally disabled children, including those who were mentally retarded, with their normal peers. Results in this area tended to be positive:

The integration of delayed and nondelayed children into the same program produced an unexpected outcome. Not only did the children have the opportunity to explore and learn about each other but also the parents of nondelayed youngsters had the chance to interact closely with parents of children who had moderate to severe problems. This interaction has the potential of being an enlightening experience for parents. An often heard comment by mothers in the project as they entered their children in the program was that they had a real fear of or great uncertainty about handicapped children. Their experiences in the project quickly changed fear to calm once they realized that handicapped children, first of all, are children. The close interaction between parents allowed for communication which we believe has been important in terms of educating a wide variety of people about developmental disabilities.[37]

In 1970, Head Start also introduced a series of changes intended to increase its effectiveness. Home visitations, bilingual/multicultural program components were added, and staff training was formalized, producing a Child Development Associate Certificate.

Despite these supplemental efforts, research continued to question the effectiveness of these programs. In 1974, Bronfenbrenner again concluded, "the substantial gains achieved in the first year of group intervention programs tend to wash out once the program is discontinued."[38] Nevertheless, preschool projects remained popular and lived a politically "charmed life," since, in the words of one observer, they were "able to deliver something to just about everyone."[39]

In 1972, the federal government added the requirement that not less than 10% of the total number of enrollment opportunities in Head Start programs was to be made available for children diagnosed with a handicap. During 1975, that goal was reached—10.4% of the enrollees were handicapped.[40] Though the established quota was met, many developmentally disabled children still did not participate: of the estimated 190,000 preschool eligible handicapped children, 36,133 were known to be enrolled. Of these, only 2,399 (6.6%) were mentally retarded.[41]

An increase in the participation of mentally retarded preschoolers occurred in 1975 with the passage of PL 94-142, the Education for All Handicapped Children Act, which provided:

a free appropriate public education will be available for all handicapped children between . . . the ages of three and twenty one within the State not later than September 1, 1980, except that with respect to handicapped children aged three to five . . . the requirements of this clause shall not be applied in any State if the application of such requirements would be inconsistent with State law or practice, or the order of any court, respecting public education within such age groups in the State. . . .[42]

Given the optional nature of the 3–5 provision, some states responded well, others did not. By 1985, less than 20 states had sponsored services for that group.[43]

Assessments of preschool programs during the eighties continued to yield mixed results. Persons looking for hard evidence that such experiences permanently and significantly increased intellectual functioning were disappointed and would continue to raise questions concerning related costs. In 1983, for example, Mullen and Sumner, after reviewing 47 research articles on compensatory education, concluded that actual gains were rather minimal and doubted they justified the dollars expended.[44]

The research did, however, demonstrate that preschool programs, be they Head Start or others, tended to increase school attendance, reduce special class placement or grade retention, increase postschool employment, positively affect delinquency and arrest rates, and lower the tendency to seek welfare assistance.[45] Stickney and Plunkett, following a review of high school graduates who had attended the Perry Preschool Projects, observed:

Federal compensatory programs . . . may have fallen short of their lofty goals of equalizing IQ and achievement, but recent research suggests that they *are* making a difference. If the total environment is largely responsible for class-related differences in achievement, substantial reductions in such academic inequalities will ultimately require substantial reductions in environmental inequality. In the meantime, [such programs] are our most important egalitarian efforts.[46]

An evaluation of Colorado's preschool educational program for developmentally disabled children commissioned by the General Assembly yielded similar positive results:

If some handicapped children are not helped at an early age their handicaps may become compounded and produce the need for more intensive services.

Early childhood programs positively influence development and this positive impact significantly affects later development and performance.

Early special education can reduce the effects of a handicapping condition and result in higher scholastic achievement.

Early childhood programs can reduce the need for lengthy and costly special education services at a later time.

Early education is effective for all types and levels of handicapping conditions. Substantial gains have been documented for mild, moderate and severely handicapped children.

Early education reaps immediate and long-term gains for handicapped children, their families and society. Delaying is costly to everyone.[47]

One group of youngsters who often made remarkable gains were those with Down syndrome. For years, such children automatically were assumed to be severely mentally retarded, never capable of any form of self-sufficiency, and frequently recommended for institutionalization. A number of reports, often based on preschool training, demonstrated that the above notions were clearly inaccurate. Many children with Down syndrome were not severely retarded; they could acquire many skills, including academic; and, with rare exception, did they actually require institutionalization.[48]

In essence, though preschool programs failed to produce the changes in intelligence and academic performance anticipated by many in the early sixties, they enhanced motivation, increased the probability of mainstreaming, and provided greater attention to basic health care needs. Such programs also fostered understanding by parents, enabling them to interact more meaningfully in a positive manner with their children, and, at the same time, often offered them well-deserved and needed respite from trying to attend their youngster alone in the home setting. Further, since many of these programs accepted severely and profoundly mentally retarded infants and preschoolers, institutionalization was often averted. Though these programs did indeed live a ''charmed life,'' finances permitting, there appeared to be no serious question as to their continuation. However, significantly improving intellectual functioning among all disadvantaged children as the result of preschool experiences remained an unanswered challenge.

THE FORMAL SCHOOL
YEARS AND SPECIAL EDUCATION

Historically, the field of education was most closely involved with the largest number of young people who were mentally retarded and was often most sensitive to both their progress and problems. It was not surprising, therefore, that educators were among the first to anticipate the many changes that occurred during the late sixties and seventies. One such educator, characterized as a ''humanitarian'' and a ''dynamic, effective leader'' by Samuel Kirk, was Ray Graham, who, in a paper published shortly after his death in 1961, commented:

> It is not an opportunity for a child to learn to adjust to all the complexities of the society in which he must live if we isolate and segregate him by placing him only with the handicapped of his own type. . . .
> The rapid growth of special education programs has often resulted in a growing apart instead of together with the total education framework. Special education developed because regular educators were concerned about children with problems. And they asked for those special facilities to be furnished to supplement their regular facilities. Too often we find them operating entirely unrelated to each other. This leads to misunderstandings and poor functioning. We should probably return frequently in our thinking to the original premise that ''special education has no justification to existence except as special facilities not available in the regular school are needed.''
> Special education needs status. Status comes only from understanding and acceptance. It is easy to set up special services that are so separate in administration, in housing, and in program that it soon becomes a school within a school. No child should be in a special class if he can be fairly and adequately served in a regular class. He should be returned to that regular class for any part of the program where he can adjust to it. Special education should never become possessive of these children, nor should regular education ever totally release them.[50]

Graham's position well reflected his personal and professional creed. ''This,'' he wrote, ''I do believe'':

Every child is important.
Every child is basically a normal child and that even the so-called handicapped child is rather a normal child with a handicap.
Public education can and should render a service to all children including those with handicaps.
The basic consideration is not the lowness of the child but rather the highness of our ability to help him.
Special education is a part of and not apart from regular education.
Every child is entitled to a program of education wherein he can experience success.

In education it is not as important what we do for the child as it is what we do to him.

Laws do not so much give schools the authority to serve children as it [sic] does give opportunity.

Our success in special education should be measured not in the numbers we have served, but in the degree of our success with the most difficult ones.

No reward in life surpasses that spiritual reward of helping the child to overcome his handicap by adjusting to it.[51]

It was sentiments such as these combined with a cheerful, supportive personality that made Ray Graham not only one of the most respected but also one of the personally admired professionals of his day.

Similarly, in the early sixties, Edgar Doll, psychologist, educator, and historian, predicted:

Public school education will expand its provision for all categories of retardation. Heterogeneous grouping will replace homogeneous classes. Curricula will be more clearly related to personal needs than to category stereotypes. Psychological evaluation will be in terms of descriptive inventories rather than diagnostic categories or IQ scores.

Parent consultations will be integral with evaluations, placements and programs. Family concerns will increasingly be essential components of the total programs.

The spurious and invidious distinctions of "trainable" versus "educable" will be discarded. The formula will be, "The trail is for all"—each according to his needs in relation to his abilities and limitations. Teaching will undergo radical changes due to programmed instruction, machine teaching, and maturationally designed curricula. More use will be made of education as therapy. Classrooms will be structured for supportive education. New theories of learning will require new concepts of training and education.[52]

In a few years, many of these ideas would find their full expression in the Education for All Handicapped Children Act of 1975.

PL 94-142 AND ITS ANTECEDENTS

When Congress passed and President Ford signed, with considerable reservation, the Education for All Handicapped Children Act of 1975, the entire educational world for mentally retarded and other disabled youngsters changed dramatically. No longer was any school-age child who was mentally retarded, regardless of level of retardation, to be denied a "free appropriate public education."[53]

The very dimensions of what constituted special education, as well as the public schools' responsibilities, expanded substantially with the new requirement for "related services," which by definition included "transportation, and such developmental, corrective, and other supportive services (including speech pathology and audiology, psychological services, physical and occupational therapy, recreation and medical and counseling services, except that such medical services shall be for diagnostic and evaluation purposes only) as may be required to assist a handicapped child to benefit from special education, and includes the early identification and assessment of handicapping conditions in children."[54]

The "least restrictive environment" was a cardinal principle of the law inasmuch as each state was to establish "procedures to assure that, to the maximum extent appropriate,

Ray Graham

handicapped children, including children in public or private institutions or other care facilities are educated with children who are not handicapped, and that special classes, separate schooling, or other removal of handicapped children from the regular educational environment occurs only when the nature or severity of the handicap is such that education in regular classes with the use of supplementary aides and services cannot be achieved satisfactorily. . . ."[55]

Other critical components of the new legislation included individually designed educational programs; the right of parents or guardians to participate in the evaluation, planning, and decision-making process; and the obligation to guarantee due process and confidentiality. (The regulations, in terms of intellectual assessment, were previously reviewed.)

This omnipotent Act was not, however, the result of any one person's sudden insight into the dynamics of educating mentally retarded youngsters; rather, it reflected the changing attitudes and philosophies of persons and agencies often representing diverse fields of endeavor and special interests. In brief, it was the "offspring" of many "mothers," not all of whom consistently agreed with each other. Further, many of the historical forces that led to PL 94-142 and its provisions were quite evident during the sixties, but were then addressed to the notion of mainstreaming.

The Quest for Mainstreaming

Mainstreaming, as already noted, had its origins in the normalization principle and early rights statements, but in the United States, it rapidly acquired a dual interpretation. In addition to the original broad intent of mentally retarded persons engaging and interacting with society as a whole, the concept found particular favor with educators who, under the rubric of mainstreaming, advocated for the maximum integration of exceptional students with their normal peers in the regular classroom.

Propelling this movement were a number of factors, as summarized by Phil Roos, then with the Association of Retarded Citizens of the United States, and Jack Birch of the University of Pittsburgh. Roos's 1970 listing placed primary emphasis on the potential benefits for individuals affected—mainstreaming:

1. Harmonizes with the principle of normalization by including the retarded in the mainstream of life
2. Encourages the use of generic services
3. Facilitates generalizing from the classroom situation to other situations
4. Improves students' self-image by not stigmatizing them as being "special" or "different"
5. Minimizes the danger of self-fulfilling prophecies derived from labeling and segregating students into classes with limited goals
6. Is less expensive than specialized services and generally allows for wider geographical distribution of services and thus greater accessibility[56]

Roos also summarized the commonly held reservations about mainstreaming. The special class:

1. Facilitates homogeneous groupings of students with similar disabilities and needs
2. Allows development of specialized staffs and resources
3. Offers opportunities for training special personnel
4. Facilitates individualizing special programs
5. Increases visibility
6. Allows development of supportive services and programs
7. Improves students' self-esteem by decreasing the frequency of failure experiences[57]

In a few years, however, a number of forces merged to render mainstreaming increasingly attractive. These, according to Birch in 1974, included:

1. The capacity to deliver special education anywhere had improved.

2. Parental concerns were being expressed more directly and forcefully.
3. Rejection of the labeling of children was growing.
4. Court actions had accelerated changes in special education procedures.
5. The fairness and accuracy of psychological testing was questioned.
6. Too many children were classified psychometrically as mentally retarded.
7. Civil rights actions against segregation uncovered questionable special education placement practices.
8. Nonhandicapped children were deprived if they were not allowed to associate with handicapped children.
9. The effectiveness of conventional special education was questioned.
10. Financial considerations foster mainstreaming (i.e., it costs less).
11. American philosophical foundations encourage diversity in the same educational setting.[58]

"Although," Birch concluded, "no one of the 11 listed elements is probably solely responsible for change in any one school system, taken together in various combinations and weights they have motivated a discernable and growing trend toward the integration of special education and regular classes."[59] In view of their importance, however, several of the stated reasons should be examined separately.

Special versus Regular Class Placement

One of the most frequently posed questions throughout the fifties was, "What is special about special education?" Or, in other words, "Were special classes justifiable?" Responses to this oft-discussed and debated topic tended to fall into one of two categories, either the educational or the socioemotional. Persons viewing segregation in terms of learning experiences tended to favor the special class. Kirk, for example, enumerated five positive attributes of special education: 1) modified or special academic materials, 2) clinical teaching procedures based on technical diagnosis, 3)

systematic approaches, 4) individualized instruction, and 5) intensification of parent education.[60]

In contrast, Tenny observed, the "segregated nature of our special education programs have prevented the non-handicapped majority from intimate social contact with the handicapped in school and probably also discourages out-of-school contacts. Understanding and acceptance come about most readily through individual acquaintance; therefore, segregation should be eliminated wherever possible."[61]

This controversy, which centered primarily around the educable mentally retarded student, continued unabated during the sixties, but with added dimensions. In 1962, G. Orville Johnson, highly respected professor of special education at Syracuse University, New York, reviewed the research literature on the efficacy of special education and discovered a paradox:

> From the studies cited, there is almost universal agreement that the mentally handicapped children enrolled in special classes achieve, academically, significantly less than similar children who remain in the regular grades. In the area of motor or manual skills, there appears to be no difference in their development. The results related to personal and social development are not in complete agreement. If the special class groups have any advantage over the regular class groups, it appears to be slight and probably not particularly meaningful. This latter finding comes despite the overwhelming evidence of lack of peers' acceptance of the mentally handicapped in the regular classroom. The only area in which the special class has demonstrated superiority of any significance is in peer acceptance. The mentally handicapped children are more accepted by their mentally handicapped peers in a special class.[62]

Thus, the paradox:

> It is indeed paradoxical that mentally handicapped children having teachers especially trained, having more money (per capita) spent on their education, and being enrolled in classes with fewer children and a program designed to provide for their unique needs, should be accomplishing the objectives of their education at the same or at a lower level than similar mentally handicapped children who have not had these

advantages and have been forced to remain in the regular grades.[63]

Johnson did not encourage the abandonment of special classes; however, he recommended greater emphasis be placed on each student's need to learn and, at the same time, questioned the adequacy of teacher preparation:

> During the past three decades the general orientation of teacher preparation programs for the mentally handicapped has been (a) an emphasis upon disability rather than ability and (b) the necessity for establishing a "good" mental hygiene situation for the children where they can develop into emotionally healthy individuals. Thus, the pressures for learning and achievement have often been largely removed so that the child has no need to progress.[64]

In the same year, the ever-perceptive Maynard Reynolds, professor of educational psychology with the University of Minnesota, proposed a scheme that, in a decade, would be widely adopted as a "continuum of least restrictive" settings. Underlying his proposal, which was intended for a variety of developmentally disabled persons, was the conviction that when "a special placement is necessary to provide care or education, it should be no more 'special' than necessary" to avoid unwarranted separation or segregation.[65] The model also reflected Reynolds's perpetual concern for "default" students or those who were simply transferred to special classes because they had been rejected everywhere else. His scheme required careful evaluation and placement in a program closest to normal given the individual's actual needs (see Figure 5.1).[66]

The most forceful and direct criticism of special classes, however, appeared in 1968 under the authorship of Lloyd Dunn, then director of the Institute on Mental Retardation and Intellectual Development at George Peabody College for Teachers, Tennessee. His presentation not only assessed special classes, the evaluation process, and regular education in highly negative terms, it also, unbeknownst to most, portended the future.

Basic to Dunn's disagreement with existing educational practices was the unwarranted classification of many elementary school children as mildly mentally retarded who, in his judgment, were really "socioculturally deprived children with mild learning problems who have been labeled educable mentally retarded."[67] He did not intend to argue against special education programs "for the moderately and severely retarded, for other types of more handicapped children, or for the multiply handicapped," nor was any attempt made to "suggest an adequate high school environment for adolescents still functioning as slow learners."[68]

Dunn's position that "we must stop labelling . . . deprived children as mentally retarded" and "stop segregating them by placing them into our special programs" was predicated on a number of assumptions, including:

1. Most students were placed in classes for educable or mildly mentally retarded youngsters to relieve pressures on the regular classroom teacher.

2. Special class educators were ill prepared

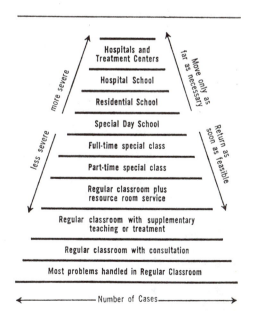

Figure 5.1   Continuum of special education programs. (From; Reynolds, M. [1962]. A framework for considering some issues in special education. *Exceptional Children,* 28, 368; reprinted by permission.)

for and ineffective in educating such chil-
. dren.
3. The diagnostic process, conducted either
    by a psychologist or a team, failed to look
    at the "complete child" but merely la-
    beled him mentally retarded.[69]

In addition to these undesirable aspects of
special education, Dunn also emphasized the
sociopersonal damage that resulted from such
practices. Like Birch, he had considerable
(perhaps exceptional) faith in the current ability of regular school programs to accommodate individual differences, noting recent
changes in school organization, curricula,
professional personnel, and the introduction
of computerized equipment and programmed
instruction.

Finally, he brought to the attention of many
special educators the 1967 decision of Judge
Wright in *Hobson* v. *Hansen*.[70] Accordingly,
the track system of the District of Columbia's
school system had to be abolished since it
"discriminated against the socially and/or
economically disadvantaged" and therefore
violated "the Fifth Amendment of the Constitution of the United States."[71]

Dunn summarized his position and arguments in cogent terms:

The conscience of special educators needs to rub
up against morality. In large measure, we have
been at the mercy of the general education establishment in that we accept problem pupils who
have been referred out of the regular grades. In
this way, we contribute to the delinquency of the
general educations since we remove the pupils
that are problems for them and thus reduce their
need to deal with individual differences. The *en-
tente* of mutual delusion between general and
special education that special class placement
will be advantageous to slow learning children of
poor parents can no longer be tolerated. We must
face the reality—we are asked to take children
others cannot teach, and a large percentage of
these are from ethnically and/or economically
disadvantaged backgrounds. Thus much of special education will continue to be a sham of
dreams unless we immerse ourselves into the
total environment of our children from inadequate homes and backgrounds and insist on a
comprehensive ecological push—with a quality
educational program as part of it. This is hardly
compatible with our prevalent practice of expe-

diency in which we employ many untrained and
less than master teachers to increase the number
of special day classes in response to the pressures of waiting lists. Because of these pressures
from the school system, we have been guilty of
fostering quantity with little regard for quality of
special education instruction. Our first responsibility is to have an abiding commitment to the
less fortunate children we aim to serve. Our
honor, integrity, and honesty should no longer
be subverted and rationalized by what we hope
and may believe we are doing for these children—hopes and beliefs which have little basis
in reality.[72]

Reactions to Dunn's critique were mixed,
but rarely mild, ranging from enthusiastic acceptance to consternation and anger. Few
papers to that time had generated as much
controversy or so seriously challenged the ideology, programs, and practices of a given
profession.

Many wondered, however, as to the accuracy and adequacy of the cited efficacy
studies that had been reviewed by Johnson,
Dunn, and others. Did, for example, achievement test studies accurately reflect upon the
purposes of special education? Johnson referred to this question when asking: Could the
objectives of education listed below "be realized to a greater degree in the special class or
in the regular class?"

The general objectives of personal, social, and
economic development and adjustment are fairly
universally accepted as realistic and practical for
the mentally handicapped. That is, education can
and should promote their personal adjustment so
that they will be capable of solving problems and
facing frustrations with emotions they can understand and effectively control. They should be
taught social skills and be able to handle situations involving interpersonal relationships in an
acceptable manner. They should learn the basic
skills, attitudes, and concepts required to earn a
living, spend their money, and take care of their
economic needs independently.[73]

Further, as regards achievement studies per
se, were initial learning levels equated? Were
the curricula identical? Were similar instructional techniques applied? Was the emphasis
the same? Were the differences observed of
practical as well as statistical significance?
Was it not often the more difficult-to-manage,

disruptive, and educationally lagging mildly mentally retarded person who ended up in the special class? Were any of these factors considered in either design or interpretation? Usually they were not.

In another provocative article published in 1967, James Gallagher offered the "unthinkable thought" that "maybe special classes for mentally retarded [students] really don't help them very much in preparation for life in modern society."[74] "Is it possible," he queried, "that all of the millions of dollars that we placed into evaluation of special programs for various kinds of exceptional children were wasted and that, in fact, the wrong approach to the problem was used?"[75]

In self-response, he wrote, "as well you know, one of the most popular research designs is to take a group of exceptional children—it doesn't matter whether we choose mentally retarded children, emotionally disturbed children, children who have severe hearing impairment, or children with articulation problems—and compared their performance with a control group of children who have similar problems but who are not in the special program. We should seriously consider whether or not we should pursue any more of that kind of research. The reason for abandoning this design is not that we are getting discouraging results, which we are, but rather because we cannot really evaluate the results at all. Is the program for the EMH in Crossroads Junction the same as the program in Big Town? Is the one in Big Town the same as the one in Main Street? Indeed, is there such an animal as a special class program or curriculum?"[76]

In elaboration, he called upon his own experience involving an experiment with teaching a single subject (photosynthesis) in six junior high school classes of high ability students using a single instructional version with accompanying materials. The results were variable because each teacher, given the same topic, outline, and materials, still approached the subject differently in terms of emphasis and time. Thus, Gallagher concluded, ". . . if we can get substantial differences between teachers who had so much in common, just think of what the differences might be if we analyzed different classrooms of educably retarded children in which the curriculum was not the same. How can we then bunch all of these classes together and run an ability grouping study or test the effectiveness of special classes? The answers are clear. We cannot."[77]

Others also raised questions:

I suspect that the scientific evidence used in support of mainstreaming, for example, probably satisfied a greater philosophical than scientific intent since most of the research cited was inadequate and none was intended primarily to estimate the feasibility of mainstreaming. What the research demonstrated was that some children did better in special classes while others did better in regular classes; unfortunately, as is often the case, the real question was not answered— "Who did best under what circumstances in which setting?" The literature cited concerning mainstreaming tended to ignore those research studies in which special class students demonstrated greater verbal fluency, more effective interaction with peers and adults, and more creativity. Studies that indicated special class students enjoyed their program, their classmates, and their teachers, even though adolescents were somewhat worried about the segregation phenomenon, were not cited at all. Of greater concern, however, is the fact that a decision was made affecting tens of thousands of school-age children seven or eight years ago and to date no comprehensive study of the effects of mainstreaming has been conducted. . . .

The above comments are not intended as criticism of mainstreaming per se, but simply to point out our desperate need for substantial research . . . to support, reject, or modify decisions made primarily on the basis of philosophical premises or quasi-scientific assumptions. Let us always approach mental retardation from the perspective of uncertainty and curiosity rather than conviction, for what we do not know far exceeds what we do.[78]

Regardless of the merits of the debate or the various positions held, failure of special classes to demonstrate clear superiority over regular class placement contributed greatly to the mainstreaming movement.

The Courts and Special Education

One can predict with reasonable assurance that political and legal historians of the future will look back at this century and declare the Supreme Court's 1954 decision in *Brown* v. *The Board of Education* to be of singular importance not only in ending racial discrimination in the United States, but also in influencing significantly the future course of special education. The long-held opinion and practice that "separate but equal" was acceptable was soundly declared unconstitutional. At the time of that declaration, few people, if any, suspected it would be used to advance the cause of mentally retarded children, even though the Court clearly stipulated:

> In these days, it is doubtful that any child may reasonably be expected to succeed in life if he is denied the opportunity of an education. Such an opportunity, where the state has undertaken to provide it, is a right which must be made available to all on equal terms.[79]

It was the *Brown* decision that was called upon in 1969 by a Utah court when reaching its decision in the first contemporary right-to-education suit involving students who were mentally retarded:*

> Today it is doubtful that any child may reasonably be expected to succeed in life if he is denied the right and opportunity of an education. In the instant case the segregation of the plaintiff children from the public school system has detrimental effects upon the children as well as their parents. The impact is greater when it has the apparent sanction of the law for the policy of placing these children under the Department of Welfare and segregating them from the educational system can be and probably is usually interpreted as denoting their inferiority, unusualness, uselessness, and incompetency. A sense of inferiority and not belonging affects the motivation of a child to learn. Segregation, even though perhaps well intentioned, under the apparent sanction of law and state authority has a tendency to retard the educational and mental development of the children.[80]

Though the Utah judgment was important, its significance in the history of court decisions was overshadowed by two other landmark cases, the first of which was the *Pennsylvania Association for Retarded Children et al.* v. *Commonwealth of Pennsylvania et al.*, 1971.[81] In this instance, the state Association had identified 14 mentally retarded children who were not receiving active treatment and went to court not only on behalf of those identified but also on behalf of all other children similarly situated. Defendants included the Commonwealth of Pennsylvania, the Secretary of the Department of Education, the State Board of Education, the Secretary of the Department of Public Welfare, certain school districts and intermediate units in the Commonwealth, their officers, employees, agents, and successors—no one was omitted.

In 1971, representatives of both the parties mutually agreed to a plan of correction, which subsequently was reviewed and approved by a three-man federal court. The resultant consent decree read, in part:

> . . . expert testimony in this action indicates that all mentally retarded persons are capable of benefiting from the program of education and training; the greatest number of retarded persons, given such education and training, are capable of achieving self-sufficiency, and the remaining few, with such education and training, are capable of achieving some degree of self-care; that the earlier such education and training begins, the more thoroughly and the more efficiently the mentally retarded person will benefit from it; and, whether begun early or not, that a mentally retarded person can benefit at any point in his life and development from the program of education and training. . . . It is the Commonwealth's obligation to place each mentally retarded child in a free, public program of education and training appropriate to the child's capacity within the context of a presumption that, among the alternative programs of education and training required by statute to be available, placement in a regular public school class is preferable to placement in a special public school class, and placement in a special public school class is preferable to placement in any other type of program of education and training.[83]

---

*Though the courts played an unparalleled role in setting forth the rights of mentally retarded citizens during the seventies, they had been called upon for many years to assure access to a free public education. Historically, however, they had consistently upheld the authority of the local school board to exclude mentally retarded or other handicapped students.[82] What changed was both judicial attitudes and the courts' willingness to address broad social issues.

The decree also focused on the rights of due process, specifically stating that mentally retarded children were not to be denied admission to a public school program or have their educational status changed without proper notification and the opportunity for a due process hearing. Due process requirements were outlined in detail, beginning with provisions to ensure notification of parents that their child was being considered for a change in educational status and ending with detailed provisions for a formal due process hearing, including representation by legal counsel; the right to examine the child's record before the hearing; the right to present evidence of one's own and to cross-examine other witnesses; the right to independent medical, psychological and educational evaluation; the right to a transcribed record of the hearing; and the right to a recorded decision.

Finally, defendants were specifically instructed to refrain from applying any section of the school code to deny any mentally retarded child access to a free public program of education and training. This also would be in violation of the equal protection clause of the Fourteenth Amendment.

The second landmark case was *Mills* v. *The Board of Education,* 1972.[84] This class action suit brought against the District of Columbia broadened the Pennsylvania decision by expanding the eligible class members to all children suffering from or alleged to be suffering from mental, behavioral, emotional, or physical handicaps or deficiencies. In August, 1972, Joseph C. Waddy, the presiding federal court judge, held that the due process clause of the Constitution demanded:

> No child eligible for a publicly supported education in the District of Columbia public schools shall be excluded from a regular public school assignment by rule, policy, or practice of the Board or its agents unless such child is provided: (a) adequate alternative educational services suited to the child's needs, which may include special education or tuition grants; and (b) a constitutionally adequate prior hearing and periodic review of his status, progress, and the adequacy of any educational alternative.
>
> Defendants and those working with them shall

be enjoined from taking any actions which would exclude plaintiffs and members of their class from a regular public school assignment without providing them with alternatives at public expense and a constitutionally adequate hearing.

> The District of Columbia shall provide to each child of school age a free and suitable publicly supported education regardless of the degree of the child's mental, physical, or emotional disability or impairment. Insufficient resources may not be a basis for exclusion.
>
> Defendants may not suspend a child from public schools for disciplinary reasons for more than two days without a hearing and without providing for his education during the period of suspension.[85]

The judgment again set forth elaborate notice and hearing procedures relating to placement, disciplinary actions, and transfers. Participation in a regular classroom situation with appropriate ancillary services was declared preferable to enrollment in a special class.

To the complaint that the school district could not financially support such a program, Judge Waddy responded: ''If sufficient funds are not available to finance all of the services and programs that are needed and desirable in the system, then the available funds must be expended equitably in such a manner that no child is entirely excluded from a publicly supported education consistent with his needs and ability to benefit therefrom. The inadequacies of the District of Columbia Public School System, whether occasioned by insufficient funding or administrative inefficiency, certainly cannot be permitted to bear more heavily on the 'exceptional' or handicapped child than on the normal child.''[86]

Though these two federal court cases greatly influenced the final provisions of PL 94-142, they by no means represented the entire scope of legal activity during the early seventies. Individually and collectively, parents throughout the country—tired, frustrated, and furious over the unresponsiveness of local and state governmental agencies to the needs of their children—addressed their concerns and grievances to the court system. Local school systems and/or state departments of education across the country were involved in uncomfortable and often disquieting litigation: Arizona, Delaware, Indiana, Louisiana, Michigan, Mississippi, New Hampshire, North Dakota, Ohio, Rhode Island, Tennessee, and Wisconsin.[87]

Additional Factors

Though not mentioned by Birch, several other major influences were at work directly or indirectly in promoting a comprehensive education bill for those who were mentally retarded. Various federal agencies and advisory committees urged the creation of such a law. The 1973 annual report of the National Advisory Committee on Handicapped Children, for example, included the statement, "We reaffirm the right under the U.S. Constitution of *all* handicapped children to a tax-supported and appropriate education regardless of their physical or mental capabilities."[88]

By 1975, a number of states had already passed comprehensive educational laws for the mentally retarded, including Massachusetts (1972), whose statute served as the model for PL 94-142; North Dakota (1973); and Michigan (1973).[89] Unfortunately, however, many leaped into mainstreaming without adequate forethought, preparation, or supportive services. The results were often disastrous. Burton Blatt was troubled:

> The great majority who have been identified as retarded, have been put in segregated classes. There are others who are identified as retarded who are now supposedly mainstreamed but they're not. They're dumped back in regular classrooms, ordinary classrooms, without any special help.[90]

Wolf Wolfensberger was "scandalized":

> I think we are going to have a catastrophe on our hands because of the mindlessness in which the term "mainstreaming" is used. Mainstreaming does not necessarily have anything to do with normalization. I think the term "mainstreaming" symptomatizes a lack of understanding because the very term itself implies that someone is inserted into the mainstream. Normalization says that people should be integrated "as much as possible," and that integration should be adaptive and successful.
>
> You see there are two distinguishing marks

here, two distinguishing characteristics. First, that integration is "as much as possible," and not every person can be fully integrated, or not so at all times, or in all endeavors. Mainstreaming is either all or nothing. Either you're segregated or "mainstreamed." Normalization sees a continuum.
>
> Secondly, if integration is not successful, it really isn't integration. It's dumping.[91]

Finally, there was Congress itself. Beginning in the mid-fifties and continuing through the sixties and early seventies, Congress passed or amended existing legislation that incrementally expanded educational benefits for mentally retarded youngsters.

Federal interest in financing supportive educational services to mentally retarded persons (categorically identified) had its inception during President Eisenhower's administration, when three major pieces of legislation, two of which pertained to mental retardation, were passed and signed into law. One was PL 83-531, the Cooperative Research Act, 1954, which due to congressional reluctance was not funded until 1957. Of $1 million finally appropriated, $675,000 were devoted to research related to the education of mentally retarded persons.[92] In 1958, PL 85-926, the Training of Professional Personnel Act, was approved. This Act encouraged expansion of teaching in the education of mentally retarded children through grants to institutions of higher learning and to state educational agencies. According to Edwin Martin, Jr., who served in a variety of key federal administrative positions, this law was directed "primarily at training professional personnel who would, in turn, train teachers to work with mentally retarded children," and was, in his judgment, "perhaps the most significant of the early legislative accomplishments."[93] The remaining act, PL 85-905, the Captioned Films for the Deaf Act, which was signed into law on September 2, 1958, established a loan service of captioned films to provide cultural enrichment and recreation for persons with severe hearing impairment.

During the sixties, both Presidents Kennedy and Johnson markedly expanded federal participation. As acknowledged previously, in

1963, President Kennedy signed into law PL 88-164, the Mental Retardation Facilities and Community Mental Health Centers Construction Act, which combined "earlier training authorities for professional personnel in the areas of retardation and deafness, and authorized grants to institutions of higher education and to state education agencies. Under the new definitions of this section, personnel could be trained to provide special education, speech correction, and related services to handicapped children, i.e., 'mentally retarded, hard of hearing, deaf, speech impaired, visually handicapped, seriously emotionally disturbed, crippled or other health impaired children, who by reason thereof, require special education.' "[94] It also authorized the Commissioner of Education to provide "grants for research and demonstration projects relating to education for handicapped children to States, State or local educational agencies, public and nonprofit institutions of higher learning, and other public or nonprofit educational or research agencies and organizations."[95]

President Kennedy also signaled his intense interest in this legislation and developmentally disabled persons by creating the Division of Handicapped Children and Youth within the U.S. Office of Education, the highest administrative status mental retardation had ever attained in the federal government. To establish and direct this program, the President called upon the services of Samuel Kirk, who took a leave of absence from his position at the University of Illinois, and served as director for one year, succeeded shortly thereafter by Morvin Wirtz.

With the passage of PL 89-10, the Elementary and Secondary Education Act of 1965, the Division was dissolved. As humorously noted by Representative Hugh Carey of Brooklyn, New York, in an address to the 1966 convention of the Council for Exceptional Children, it was a "case of separation of Kirk and State."[96] Though short-lived (18 months), the Division accomplished much in facilitating new programs and bringing to the attention of many citizens, in and out of government, the abilities and needs of mentally retarded and other disabled persons.

Samuel A. Kirk

Of the many fine people who crossed the stage of special education during the period under review, few served with more distinction and dedication than Samuel Kirk. Born in Rugby, North Dakota, he earned his bachelor's and master's degrees in psychology from the University of Chicago and his doctorate in physiological and clinical psychology from the University of Michigan. Following receipt of the latter degree, he assumed responsibility for directing the Division of Education for Exceptional Children at the University of Wisconsin–Milwaukee, and soon established a program of national renown. His early text, coauthored with G. Orville Johnson, *Educating the Retarded Child*,[97] became a classroom standard for teacher preparation throughout the country for many years. From 1962 to 1967, he directed the Institute for Research on Exceptional Children, where once again he established an outstanding program. His interests were many, including special education, language, measurement, and preschool training. He received numerous awards, including that of the Joseph P. Kennedy, Jr. Foundation in 1962 for "his vision, dedication, and outstanding service in mental retardation. . . . Psychologist as well as educator, 'Sam' Kirk's contributions represent a lifetime investment in scientific research and project development. A prolific and lucid writer, his contributions to the literature on special education have found their way to teachers in virtually every language and every country. Classes for the retarded in every corner of the world bear his mark. There is scarcely a university or school concerned with special education which does not have on its faculty a 'Kirk-trained' or inspired teacher."[98] That judgment held true throughout his career, which, in 1984, included serving as professor of special education at the University of Arizona and as professor emeritus at the University of Illinois.

Samuel A. Kirk

The Elementary and
Secondary Education Act

The hallmark of federal legislative activity during the sixties was PL 89-10, the Elementary and Secondary Education Act of 1965, which provided for a wide range of youngsters with differing educational needs and authorized an initial budget of $1.3 billion. As described by Edwin W. Martin, Jr.:

Of the many programs developed and approved by the Congress and the Administration—programs aimed at the cities, at the aged ("medicare"), etc.—none outranked in brilliance The Elementary and Secondary Education Act of 1965, PL 89-10. Its final passage, with its programs of assistance to children in disadvantaged areas (including handicapped children), new instructional materials, centers for innovation and research, and support for strengthening state educational agencies, was precedent shattering not only in its educational implications, but also in the brilliance of its legislative drafting and strategy which succeeded in overcoming the traditional barriers to federal aid to education.[99]

In 1965, the Elementary and Secondary Education Act was amended to provide funds for the education of mentally retarded and other handicapped youth in institutional settings. This broad-based funding program enabled residential facilities to obtain additional teachers, supplemental personnel, and sorely needed equipment. For many residents, custodial care was replaced by education.

The following year, the Elementary and Secondary Education Act was again amended. The new version not only established a program of grants to the states for the initiation, expansion, and improvement of programs for educating handicapped youngsters from preschool through secondary school age, it also called for the appointment of a national advisory committee to the Commissioner of Education and creation of a bureau within the U.S. Office of Education to provide coordination of and direction to federal programs for the handicapped child.

The latter proposal brought forth some resistance from the White House for several reasons: "(1) its statutory nature overruled a usual prerogative of the Executive Branch to plan its own administrative structure; (2) it could possibly set a precedent for the establishment of bureaus for other special interest or minority groups within education; and (3) it would take the research in education of the handicapped program out of the Bureau of Research, thereby undoing the organizational pattern of the Office of Education in which all research activities were under this one structure."[100]

Despite such reservations, the amendment was signed into law, and a Bureau of Education for the Handicapped was established, initially under the leadership of James Gallagher. Similarly, on January 12, 1967, a National Advisory Committee of twelve members was appointed to the U.S. Office of Education to "review the administration of this act . . . and other provisions of law administered by the Commissioner with respect to handicapped children, including their effect in improving the educational attainment of such children and make recommendations for the improvement of such administration . . . . The Advisory Committee shall from time to time make such recommendations as it may deem appropriate to the Commissioner [who] shall transmit such report, comments, and recommendations to the Congress . . . ." Samuel A. Kirk was once again called upon to serve as chairperson of this Committee.[101]

In 1967, the administration took the initiative to expand substantially the provisions of the Elementary and Secondary School Act to include funds for:

1. Creating regional resource centers
2. Disseminating information on mental retardation and new recruiting systems for professional personnel
3. Expanding media programs originally intended for the deaf to all handicapped children
4. Designing and implementing new educational programs
5. Increasing financial assistance for educational programs
6. Encouraging more training and research[102]

Considering the tremendous expansion of federal activity on behalf of mentally retarded and other disabled and disadvantaged children, it is little wonder that Kirk could observe in 1968, "Concern for the education of handicapped children has acquired a broad base in American society. It is the concern not only of parents and teachers, but of state and local governments. It now has become the concern of governmental officials at the highest level—the President and members of the Congress of the United States. This is reflected in recent federal acts and appropriations for research, training, and services for handicapped children."[103] In 1969, federal legislation was once again amended to expand educational programs for developmentally disabled persons.

Thus, Congress and the administration had gradually but undauntedly paved the way for PL 94-142, which was passed and approved in 1975 for nine specific reasons:

1. There were more than eight million handicapped children in the United States at that time.
2. The special educational needs of such children were not being fully met.
3. More than half of the handicapped children in the United States did not receive appropriate educational services that would enable them to have full equality of opportunity.
4. One million of the handicapped children in the United States were excluded entirely from the public school system and would not go through the educational process with their peers.
5. There were many handicapped children throughout the United States participating in regular school programs whose handicaps prevented them from having a successful educational experience because their handicaps were undetected.
6. Because of the lack of adequate services within the public school system, families were often forced to find services outside the public school system, often at great distance from their residence and at their own expense.
7. Developments in the training of teachers and in diagnostic and instructional procedures and methods had advanced to the point that, given appropriate funding, state and local educational agencies could and would provide effective special education and related services to meet the needs of handicapped children.
8. State and local educational agencies had a responsibility to provide education for all handicapped children, but present financial resources were inadequate to meet the special educational needs of handicapped children.
9. It was in the national interest that the federal government assist state and local efforts to provide programs to meet the educational needs of handicapped children in order to assure equivocal protection of the law.[104]

PL 94-142: IMPACT, PROGRESS, AND PROBLEMS

With the passage of PL 94-142, education for mentally retarded youth and other developmentally disabled children and adolescents underwent a transformation few believed possible. All states complied, which was in marked contrast to 1960 when only 16 states had mandatory education laws for the educable mentally retarded students and 13 for trainable mentally retarded students, and when severely and profoundly mentally retarded youngsters with their multiple handicaps and lack of toilet training skills were simply labeled "untrainable" and with rare exception were excluded from public schools.[105] "The public schools," observed Tisdall and Moss in 1962, "cannot provide services for the very young, to those who are behavior problems, to the non–toilet trained or the adult."[106] Such was the prevailing attitude of the day.

Thus, the first significant trend associated with PL 94-142 was the dramatic increase in the number of disabled students served. One indicator, important to both special educators and civil rights advocates, was the school enrollment figures, which for all developmentally disabled youngsters grew from 818,809 in 1958 to 4,298,308 in 1982.[107] As regards those who were mentally retarded, the number grew from 213,402 to 853,973 during the same time interval.[108] During 1982, the federal government estimated that over 90% of exceptional children were receiving an appropriate education. This was in marked contrast with the early sixties when less than 25% were served.[109]

This should not, however, be interpreted as meaning that no progress had been made prior to 1975. Quite the contrary—the total mentally retarded school population considered to be appropriately served rose from just under 300,000 in 1958 to 703,800 in 1969.[110] The trainable population alone grew from 17,000 in 1958 to over 89,000 in 1967.[111] As concerns the latter, however, until 1975, such admissions were governed by rather strict criteria:

1. The age of admission for trainable retarded children in the public school classes is generally the same as for other children. In most instances, this age is 6.
2. The objective criterion which appears to be the most valid for admission is the IQ based on individual psychometric tests administered by a psychologist trained and experienced in the diagnosis of mental retardation.

The usual IQ range for these classes is between 30 or 35 and 50 or 55.
3. Most children admitted into the classes are required to have a medical examination to determine their physical ability to participate in the program.
4. Not all children with IQs between 35 and 50 are admitted. Other criteria include ability to get along in the class and a minimum ability to take care of their needs, such as toileting, partial dressing, and so forth. Schools tend to exclude children who are a danger to themselves or others and those whose behavior is likely to disrupt the classroom program.
5. Children admitted to these classes must have some minimum communication ability in the form of either speech or gestures. Most trainable children above the age of 6 with IQs over 30 have these abilities.[112]

Despite such gains, approximately 4 million developmentally disabled children in 1975 were not being provided an appropriate education, and over 1 million, many of whom were mentally retarded, remained excluded entirely from the public school system.[113] Providing for this neglected population left quite a problem for many states, especially larger ones such as California and Ohio, which were each estimated to have up to a quarter million unserved school-age children.[114]

Regardless of the potential positive impact on developmentally disabled youngsters, not all professionals welcomed the passage of PL 94-142. One professor labeled PL 94-142 as education's "Three Mile Island," declaring the bill to be "an ill-conceived law embodying a 'Pollyana-Horatio Alger–like euphoria contrary to fact perception of reality.'"*[115] Further, in his judgment, it threatened "the education of an entire generation of handicapped youth and squanders the limited educational funds available in our country for both disabled and regular children"; and it "raised Constitutional, economic, and moral issues at the heart of this nation, currently and in the future."[116] Part of this observation re-

---

*Three Mile Island" refers to the first major nuclear power plant accident in the U.S., which occurred in 1979. It resulted in a panic reaction and caused many to question the future use of that energy resource.

flected the author's explicit concern over federal control: "Can the federal government tell local school districts how to spend their own educational dollars and remain consistent with the Constitution?"[117] Federal dominance over what historically had been clearly a state right bothered many persons.[118] Nevertheless, both the federal government and various state and federal courts held firm.

While supportive of the Act's intentions, many people were anxious about its implementation, especially as it related to the procurement of needed resources and the capabilities of local schools to integrate mentally retarded and other disabled students with their normal peers. This was exemplified by the initial position of the National Education Association, the country's largest teachers' union. In testifying before a congressional subcommittee in 1976, the Association's representative, James A. Harris, forcefully stated that the union would support "mainstreaming handicapped students only when":

> It provides a favorable learning experience for handicapped and for regular students.
> Regular and special teachers and administrators share equally in its planning and implementation.
> Appropriate instructional materials, supportive services, and pupil personnel services are provided for the teacher and the handicapped student.
> Modifications are made in class size, scheduling, and curriculum design to accommodate the shifting demands that mainstreaming creates.
> There is a systematic evaluation and reporting of program developments.
> Adequate additional funding and resources are provided for mainstreaming and are used exclusively for that purpose.[119]

Harris also recommended that teacher corps be created to assist in preparing teachers to work with developmentally disabled persons; the National Institute of Education should conduct studies on promising teaching practices for educationally handicapped persons and widely disseminate its findings; training programs should be developed for regular teachers; state and local educational agencies should be accountable for delivering needed services, and providing safeguards for identi-

fication, evaluation, and placement of disabled children, as well as assuring due process procedures. Some of these proposals were met; most were not.

Despite these concerns and reservations, mainstreaming began in earnest following the passage of PL 94-142. A number of approaches were used in attempting to integrate mentally retarded youngsters with their regular class peers. Many adopted the previously presented model of Maynard Reynolds that established a sequence of placements: regular classroom with specialist consultation; regular classroom with itinerant teachers; regular classroom plus resource rooms; part-time special class; full-time special class; special day school; and a residential institution.[120] One early study of California schools reported three common approaches: 1) programmed partial integration, with all mentally retarded students being assigned to a special class and participating in other regular programs; 2) the combination class, with all mentally retarded students in a regular classroom all day with supplemental aids and materials provided; and 3) the introduction of the resource center.[121]

Of all the problems associated with PL 94-142, those related to mainstreaming were most evident. First, no one was sure what mainstreaming actually entailed, and subsequently, how or when it would be realized. A number of definitions were advanced. One required that a child be in a regular class for 50% or more of his school days.[122] Another stated:

> Mainstreaming refers to the temporal, instructional, and social integration of eligible exceptional children with normal peers based on an ongoing, individually determined, educational planning and programming process and requires clarification of responsibility among regular and special educational administrative, instructional, and supportive personnel.[123]

Still another defined mainstreaming as

> . . . a philosophy or principle of educational service delivery which is implemented by providing a variety of classroom and instructional alternatives that are appropriate to the individual educational plan for each student and allows maximal temporal, social and instructional interaction among mentally retarded and non-re-

tarded students in the normal course of the school day.[124]

The Council for Exceptional Children defined mainstreaming through the dual process of inclusion and exclusion:

Mainstreaming Is:
—providing the most appropriate education for each child in the least restrictive setting.
—looking at the educational needs of children instead of clinical or diagnostic labels such as mentally handicapped, learning disabled, physically handicapped, hearing impaired, or gifted.
—looking for and creating alternatives that will help general educators serve children with learning or adjustment problems in the regular setting. Some approaches being used to help achieve this are consulting teachers, methods and materials specialists, itinerant teachers, and resource room teachers.
—uniting the skills of general education and special education so all children may have equal educational opportunity.
Mainstreaming Is Not:
—wholesale return of all exceptional children in special classes to regular classes.
—permitting children with special needs to remain in regular classrooms without the support services they need.
—ignoring the need of some children for a more specialized program than can be provided in the general education program.
—less costly than serving children in special self-contained classrooms.[125]

The Association for Retarded Citizens of the United States, having examined the various concepts, concluded: "Mainstreaming has been defined in many different ways, and sometimes the philosophy of mainstreaming is confused with techniques used to implement the principle. Some educators say that mainstreaming simply means the elimination of categorical labels and the mass integration of mentally retarded students into school classes with their nonretarded peers. Others believe that it means the physical placement of self-contained special classes in the same school building with non-retarded students. For others, mainstreaming refers to the assignment of retarded students to a regular class teacher who, in turn, receives diagnostic, curricular and instructional help from a resource or itin-

erant teacher. Still another view is that mainstreaming represents an educational model which encompasses a continuum of education programs ranging from self-contained classes to regular class placement for those students who require little or no special assistance."[126] In the final analysis, there was little common agreement except that, in some manner, mentally retarded youngsters were to be integrated with their peers in as normal an educational environment as possible.

Regardless of definitional difficulties, many persons in the professional, legal, or parent community believed in the basic tenets of mainstreaming. Interestingly, on that rare occasion when the opinion of those who had been or would be affected by such decisions was sought, the results were not so certain. In a study by Gan and colleagues in 1977, for example, 60% of the sample of mentally retarded individuals disagreed with the statement, "The mentally retarded should not be in a special class in school."[127] Of the remaining 40%, only 21% agreed; 19% were uncertain.

Problems in Implementation

Though mainstreaming would improve significantly following the passage of PL 94-142, its course was not always smooth. Sincere doubts continued to exist relating to both attitudes and preparation of regular classroom teachers.[128] "To take a child out of a self-contained special class and place him in the mainstream is not an educational service," observed Horn in 1976, "It is merely an administrative exercise in geography."[129] He was, of course, referring to such placements without due preparation and adequate support.

Even with experience, and when believing mainstreaming to be beneficial for mentally retarded students, many teachers remained unreceptive to the idea.[130] Following several years of mainstreaming in Massachusetts, one study reported that teachers felt there were not enough hours to do all that was required; time spent with average children was reduced; there were too many discipline-related problems; and average children resented having their lesson plans modified to meet the needs of the slower learner.[131]

Seven years later, in 1983, a similar survey conducted in Virginia revealed that 79% of the teachers sampled still contended that the practice had a negative effect on their classes.[132] According to another study of 200 classroom teachers, most of them veteran educators experienced in mainstreaming, only 38% supported the practice. The majority, in this case, felt that mentally retarded students simply could not master the regular classroom curriculum.[133]

The preponderance of negative reports, especially during the early years following passage of PL 94-142, may well have reflected the frustrations shared by all. Several investigations found that the additional mandated responsibilities for mentally retarded students, interdisciplinary planning, greatly increased paperwork, unclear role expectations, the new role and authority of parents, and the absence of training and support produced considerable stress and "burnout."[134] Yet, studies during the late seventies and early eighties frequently reported that the climate for accepting mainstreaming had changed very little.[135] In fact, several reports indicated integration led to more disfavorable attitudes.[136]

Teacher attitudes were not the only ones examined; a number of investigators attempted to ascertain administrators' sentiments as well. Again, the reports were not particularly encouraging. To illustrate, in 1980, well after the passage of PL 94-142, a study of elementary and secondary school principals found that only 46.4% believed successful integration was possible with mildly mentally retarded students; 24.9% with trainable youngsters; and 3.8% with more severely affected students.[137] This did not bode well for mentally retarded students, since a number of studies also indicated the further one was removed from the actual classroom setting, the more positive would be the response to mainstreaming.[138] In the words of one team of investigators, "Those staff members who were more distant from the students (central administration) were most positive toward integration, while those closest (teachers) had a greater incidence of negative feelings."[139]

The historical question concerning the effect of professional labeling upon student acceptance and teacher expectations, despite innumerable studies, remained without firm resolution. As concerns the educational setting, research indicated that the import of labeling and acceptance depended on many factors, including the mentally retarded student's social behavior, skills and competence, physical appearance, age, sex, socioeconomic status, and race. Normal peers' reactions reflected upon their upbringing, contact with mentally retarded people, sex, race, degree of personal security, age, and understanding. Teachers' reactions involved many of the same factors as their normal students.[140]

In brief, while research demonstrated that teacher expectancies, especially first impressions, could be influenced by labeling, there was no documentation to indicate that learning or performance of the students was significantly or lastingly affected.[141] Safer, in her 1980 review of the literature, concluded that "it would seem that teacher expectancies for the handicapped, particularly the retarded, may be said to be biased in the sense that they are inappropriately low. There is no evidence, however, that teacher expectancies for handicapped students are so biased that they preclude the teacher's perceiving the progress or achievement the child does make."[142]

Regrettably, as Wolfensberger feared, mere physical integration—be it regular classroom or resource center—did not ensure genuine social acceptance.[143] Whether professionally labeled or not, even preschool children readily recognized the occurrence of exceptionality, including mental retardation.[144] Also, it appeared that a positive teacher attitude did not necessarily influence that of the students.[145]

Subsequently, many youngsters and adolescents who were mentally retarded continued to experience the disappointment and hurt so aptly expressed by a mainstreamed 16-year-old high school sophomore in a letter that originally appeared in her high school newspaper:

Handicapped kids are not vegetables and not trash. We're human just like you. And all we're asking is that you take a look at us and change your opinion about us. Give us a chance to be like you in some ways. What I mean is, give us a chance, please. And if people don't get this through their thick heads, then they're worse off than we are.

Do you know what it's like being different from other kids? I have some friends like me, too. We are in a different special class. Some of them are slow learners like me. And it's a shame how the other kids treat us because we're different from them.

My father has always told me, ''Don't worry about being different.'' But sometimes I do because people are cruel in their ways and they hurt our feelings. They walk away and laugh at us behind our backs. They don't know we know. But we know.

Well I said what I had to say, so please help me and help them. If you have a handicapped person come looking for a job, open your heart, and take an interest in him.[146]

Rather than accept that state of affairs, special educators sought supplemental ways to encourage real participation and friendships, including cooperative, goal-oriented games; bowling; swimming; gardening; creative work projects; joint play sessions; and human difference training.[147] Whatever gains were made, however, often disappeared following the special effort.[148]

As evident, attitudes required changing and new approaches needed to be introduced to facilitate social integration, especially among severely affected, less physically attractive youngsters. To this end, special educators were innovative and persistent. A number of suggestions were set forth:

1. Prior to the school year, employ a faculty member and/or consultant whose major responsibility is the integration of severely handicapped students.
2. Present inservice training sessions to special and regular education faculty to explain integration efforts.
3. Arrange special and regular school visits for faculty members.
4. Meet with school system administrators, regular education building principal(s), and classroom teachers at the integration sites.
5. Arrange for severely handicapped students to use as many school facilities as possible.
6. Conduct sessions with severely handicapped students to teach age-appropriate behavior expected in the regular school environment.
7. Involve parents in plans to integrate their severely handicapped child and present results of integration efforts to parents.
8. Provide additional support personnel at the integration sites.
9. Present sensitization sessions for students and other interested persons.
10. Locate contact person(s) within each integrated school site to facilitate integration activities.
11. Special class educators should associate with team teachers.
12. Offer a training source to special and regular educational faculty in sensitizing nonhandicapped students to handicapped peers.
13. Arrange for flexible individual programming and team teaching among special education classes.
14. Make faculty members aware of appropriate media available for sensitizing nonhandicapped students to handicapped peers.
15. Meet with special education teachers who may be sending additional handicapped students to the integrated site in the future.
16. Integrate sensitization efforts into the regular education curriculum.
17. Document integration efforts to serve as a model for future integration efforts.
18. Arrange a faculty drop-in to relate to faculty integration questions.
19. Offer an ''open door'' visitation policy for special education classroom(s).
20. Spend time in regular faculty lounge.
21. Bring special and regular education classes together for special lessons.
22. Provide copies of integration activity outlines in a systemwide central location for faculty use.
23. Provide information regarding integration efforts through schoolwide and/or systemwide newsletters.

In addition, students may (1) be involved with school jobs—handicapped; (2) participate in school activities—handicapped; (3) serve as partners or tutors of severely handicapped students—nonhandicapped; (4) write articles for the school newspaper and/or yearbook regarding integration efforts—nonhandicapped; and (5) make integration efforts a school objective—nonhandicapped.[149]

Thus, while in many situations mentally retarded students were increasingly welcomed into the educational setting, they had yet to attain the same degree of acceptance found among their normal peers or to fulfill the hopes of normalization.[150] Understandably, labeling, peer acceptance, and teacher expectancies remained an active concern, one subjected to continuous investigation and new interventions.

On one point there were conflicting data. As indicated previously, in 1982, administrators reported that 90% of all secondary handicapped students completed their high school program. Yet, high school dropout rates in the United States, especially in larger urban areas, were horrendous: Chicago, 52%; St. Louis, 52%; Detroit, 51%; New York, 49%; Baltimore, 45%; Cleveland, 40%; Philadelphia, 40%; Washington, D.C., 40%; Memphis, 39%; Milwaukee, 34%; Dallas, 33%; Houston, 33%; Phoenix, 31%; Los Angeles, 30%; and San Diego, 29%.[151]

Several special class administrators readily admitted that many in the dropout population were mentally retarded, learning disabled, and/or emotionally troubled.[152] Lee Gruenewald, director of an internationally recognized public school special education program, when addressing a conference in Paris, France, in 1979, noted:

> For the mildly handicapped, especially the learning disabled, mildly retarded, and mildly behaviorally disoriented/emotionally disturbed, the drop out rate at age sixteen greatly increases. Graduation from high school, even with resource teacher support and the availability of special education classes in the regular school, is not viewed as a valued reachable goal for some of these handicapped students.[153]

Also, it was extremely difficult for many in the secondary school system to adapt their regular curricula and approaches to include the mentally retarded student, who often lacked both interest in and skills to pursue many of the courses successfully.

Despite the gains and progress, age-old problems persisted, and once again, in 1984, James Gallagher contended that the question of who should attend regular classes as opposed to special classes remained at issue, and "from an educational perspective has yet to be resolved . . . how intense must the problem become before the major responsibility shifts from the regular education to special education? Where is the dividing line on behavior problems, learning disabilities, mental retardation, or giftedness? It is difficult to find a clear-cut division point that would assign children to one category or another."[154]

He also observed, "Certainly the most chronic problem facing the special education community is its continuing and often abrasive relationship with the regular education program. On one hand, many people in the traditional education program look on special educators as outsiders. They are often seen as the physical manifestation of the inability of the regular educator to deal with certain problems. That no one individual, however competent, should be expected to deal with the range of problems with which exceptional children confront the school is not easily understood or accepted."[155]

In a similar vein, Samuel Kirk, in the same year, offered the following assessment: "Although mainstreaming is philosophically a sound idea, our enthusiasm for it is gradually waning because we have failed to train regular teachers to teach and manage these children . . . . Our mistake, as usual, was to launch a program without adequate preparation and without really training the classroom teacher. . . . We, as yet," he continued, "have no detailed description of how mainstreaming is accomplished nor an exact distribution of responsibilities of both regular and resource teachers. Until and unless this is done, mainstreaming for the mentally retarded may falter or fail. Mainstreaming for other handicapped children is more readily accepted."[156]

The challenge was great, for the task was not easy; and federal reports indicated that, in spite of all efforts, in 1980, regular class placements remained rare with only one-third of the mentally retarded school population being served in that setting.[157] In fact, reliance on the special class or special school actually increased between 1979 and 1980, primarily in response to parental demands.[158] Further, despite all protections, parents were not uniformly satisfied. Bill Granger, father of

Alec, author of 13 books, and columnist for the *Chicago Tribune,* attacked both current practices and the federal government's possible role:

> As Jack Henneberry, a school principal in Flossmoor, Ill., wrote me: "I realize, having worked with youngsters for 32 years, that there are some who do need special help and, in some rare instances, special placement. But I also realize that since the federal special-education law, their number has increased dramatically. Every month, I ask in frustration: Why are we talking about classifying this child because he reverses his b's or because he can't write on a line or because of this or that, when in reality another year or two will take care of the problem?"
>
> Throughout our [the parents'] ordeal I have thought about all the other Alecs tested in all the other schools across the nation. Where are they? Rotting in some place where they have learned to become "special" because no one thought to take the time to give them the right diagnosis—or better yet, to forget diagnoses and teach them?
>
> How can there be such a sudden growth of children in need of special education in this country? While the public-school population was declining, the number of special-ed students grew from 3.7 million in 1977 to 4.3 million in 1984. Can the rush to label children as "special" be related to the federal monies pouring through the pipeline to the one growth area of public education?[159]

He also quoted a teacher as stating, "Special education has, today, become the dumping ground for any child who doesn't follow the norm—whatever that may be."[160] The more things change . . . .

Individualized Education Program

One critical dimension of PL 94-142 was the individualized education program (IEP), which not only required the participation of an interdisciplinary team in the decision-making process, but also provided for the active involvement of parent and student as well:

> The term "individualized education program" means a written statement for each handicapped child developed in any meeting by a representative of the local educational agency or an intermediate educational unit who shall be qualified to provide, or supervise the provision of, spe-

cially designed instruction to meet the unique needs of handicapped children, the teacher, the parents or guardian of such child, and, whenever appropriate, such child, which statement shall include (A) a statement of the present levels of educational performance of such child, (B) a statement of annual goals, including short-term instructional objectives, (C) a statement of the specific educational services to be provided to such child, and the extent to which such child will be able to participate in regular educational programs, (D) the projected date for initiation and anticipated duration of such services, and (E) appropriate objective criteria and evaluation procedures and schedules for determining, on at least an annual basis, whether instructional objectives are being achieved.[161]

Here then existed a long sought after right of parents to influence the educational programming and placement of their child. Many parents came forth; all too many did not. One of the less satisfying experiences associated with PL 94-142 was that only 50% of parents took advantage of this provision.[162] Equally discouraging were reports that less than 10% of potentially affected students were included.[163]

Joint planning by parent and professional, while successful in many instances, was not without its difficulties. Many parents found the experience frustrating and demeaning:

> They "the evaluators" think of themselves as professional and they are there to tell you about your child. And if you disagree with their professional judgement, [sic] they are not interested.[164]
>
> They listened, but they didn't listen, if you know what I mean. They listened, but they had their minds made up. The meeting is just really a pretense of listening, and then they write the plan they want.[165]
>
> After the core meeting, I thought finally they were going to give him a separate program. At the meeting, they seemed to all agree that a resource room hadn't helped him, and that he needed a full-time program. Then when we got the plan, it was the same old thing.[166]

Other reports contained similar findings: many parents found the individual program plans completed before the meeting; teachers did most of the talking; and the discussion frequently involved personal/family issues rather than educational plans and programs.[167]

In reviewing the situation, Ann and Rutherford Turnbull, special educator and attorney, respectively, called for clarity of the parents' role and valuative criteria for their participation, greater heed to parents' contributions and perhaps a revised public policy, one that would "tolerate a range of parent involvement choices and options, matched to the needs and interests of the parents."[168]

The problem was by no means one-sided. Some professionals also found the process to be exasperating:

> There isn't time to carry out this "important" function due to scheduling and numbers of children.
> It's difficult enough just getting their approval for the testing and eventual placement.
> They really don't understand what we are trying to do anyway.
> They literally hide and won't come to answer the door when I try to visit.
> I don't speak the language used in the home, and I can't communicate with them.
> They appear to fear the school and school people, and they won't come for conferences.
> They won't accept the fact that their child has problems and needs special education services.
> They may need informing and counseling, but the education of their children is my responsibility.
> The meeting I set up for the parents of my children was a flop . . . they just don't want to meet other parents and learn about our program.[169]

Others complained that the IEP was not ever shared with the regular class teacher and that frequently the regular classroom teacher did not even participate in the process.[170] Some challenged the quality of the IEPs: "the wide variance and low levels of acceptable quality cannot translate into anything but mixed messages for teacher educators."[171]

While many called for change, no one seriously recommended the abandonment of this regulation or the process. In time, it was felt both parent and professional, especially the latter, would acquire the sensitivities and skills to reach mutually agreeable conclu-

sions. At the same time, there was an inherent danger. As Horn pointed out soon after PL 94-142 became law: "Substantive due process requires that we provide what we are promising."[172] Failure to do so, as many discovered, produced parental alienation rather than heightened interest and involvement.

PL 94-142: 1984

As of the last day of 1984, the Education for All Handicapped Children Act was alive and well, though far from being fully realized. During the interceding years from the date of passage, it underwent a number of challenges, politically and legally.

In 1982, under the Omnibus Budget Reconciliation Act of 1981, the administration attempted to amend the regulations, combining special education funding programs under one title, modifying many of the requirements associated with state plans and reports, eliminating several eligible classifications, and limiting the possible participation of institutional youngsters in public school programs. Despite Secretary of Education T.R. Bell's pronouncement that the proposed changes would "satisfy the dual purpose of protecting the guarantees to a free appropriate public education for all handicapped children, while reducing fiscal and administrative burdens on State and local school systems," parents, teachers, and advocacy groups responded so negatively that the modifications were never put into force.[173]

The Supreme Court also addressed provisions of PL 94-142 on several occasions. In one instance, it upheld a lower 1981 district court decision that certain mentally retarded youngsters were entitled to more than the regular 180-day school year.[174] Though not directly related to educational provisions for those who are mentally retarded, the Supreme Court, in 1982, did place some constraint on the definition of "free, appropriate education." This decision arose from a case in which a girl who was deaf and making progress in her regular classroom but whose parents sought to have the school hire a sign language interpreter to assist her. The court concluded, "the furnishing of every special service necessary to maximize every handicapped child's potential is . . . further than Congress intended to go."[175] The implication for all developmentally disabled children was unclear, except that the court was apparently willing to set some limits on the extent of the public school's obligations.

A continual potential threat to PL 94-142 was cost; providing adequate services for mentally retarded students required considerable financial support. Comparative cost studies found special programs for educable mentally retarded students were at least twice as expensive as regular education, and classes for trainable youngsters, which included considerable transportation fees, were five times as expensive.[176] Many people questioned the cost benefits of special education for mentally retarded persons, especially for those who were more severely affected, whose contributions to the fiscal well-being of society were questionable. In a television interview, Governor Richard Lamm of Colorado openly expressed what many of his colleagues probably felt. Faced with increasing fiscal problems and no abatement in people's expectancies, he questioned the wisdom of massive spending for more severely mentally retarded persons. The interviewer's prefaced question was: "You said of retarded children, does it really make sense to spend $10,000 'educating a child to roll over.' Is it your view that there are some lives that simply aren't worth living and aren't worth saving or what?" Lamm responded:

I don't think that's my feeling at all. I think the point that I was really trying to make in the mainstreaming controversy with regard to retarded children is that there are certain children that, in fact, do not benefit from a public school experience; and yet, at great expense to society, we bring them to public school sometimes just simply to lay on the ground and try to absorb the ambiance of public schools. I think very strongly that we ought to educate even a retarded child to his highest functioning level, but frankly the idea of mainstreaming them in a school where it's often disruptive to the others' learning process I think is wrong and one that we have gone too far in.[177]

Unfortunately, no one in the country could respond to Lamm's position since one of the most regrettable (and inexcusable) educational phenomena during the seventies and early eighties was the absence of critical research.[178] All appeared to be philosophy and its correlate, the law. Unlike the fifties and sixties, when the educational and psychological communities faced the question of special class efficacy and often severely criticized such efforts, research following the passage of PL 94-142 through 1984, was, for all practical purposes, nonexistent. Yet, nearly every professional organization placed considerable emphasis upon the importance of research. The Association for Retarded Citizens of the United States in 1978, for example, specifically called for research dealing with such areas as: the acceptance or rejection of mentally retarded and other handicapped students by their peers in regular education classes; the efficacy of regular class placement for mentally retarded students with differing degrees of handicaps, ages, and backgrounds; the cost-effectiveness and cost-benefit associated with mainstreaming; and the relationship of mainstreaming to the short-term and long-term educational and life skills performance of mentally retarded persons.[179] The Association also pointed out that "early mainstreaming efforts were begun without systematic planning for evaluation and without a national evaluation component. Consequently, no unequivocal data exist to support these movements."[180] The same situation existed at the end of 1984.

Thus, PL 94-142, the most powerful educational legislation passed during the quarter century was implemented with numerous immediate gains, unanticipated problems, and a bevy of growing pains. Few doubted, however, that it would remain in effect and that the future lives of millions of developmentally disabled youngsters would not be markedly improved and enriched by its existence.

EDUCATIONAL OBJECTIVES AND PROGRAMS

Fundamental to all societally sponsored education is a set of broad, usually categorically defined goals that apply to every student, gifted, average, or slow. Throughout the years, these have been expressed in slightly different terms, but with remarkable consistency: each student should gain knowledge and understanding, skill and confidence, appropriate attitudes and interests, and effective strategies of action relative to: 1) good mental and physical health; 2) a command of the fundamental processes, such as communication skills, reading, writing, and arithmetic; 3) worthy home membership; 4) vocational preparation; 5) citizenship; 6) wise use of leisure time; and 7) character or ethical development.[181] Another set developed by the Mid-Century Committee on Outcomes in Elementary Education stated that each child should gain a firm background with respect to: 1) physical development, 2) individual social and emotional development, 3) ethical behavior and standards, 4) social relations, 5) the social world, 6) the physical world, 7) aesthetic development, 8) communications, and 9) quantitative relationships.[182] In the 1972 revision of *Educating Exceptional Children,* Samuel Kirk cited the four major objectives of education formulated by the Educational Policies Commission: "(1) self-realization, (2) human relationships, (3) economic efficiency, and (4) civic responsibility."[183] He also observed, "special education is not a total program which is entirely different from the education of the ordinary child. It refers only to those aspects of education which are unique and/or in addition to the regular program for all children."[184]

For the educable mentally retarded student, Kirk listed eight major purposes, which clustered around social competence, personal skills and occupational adequacy:

1. They should be educated to get along with their fellow men; i.e., they should develop social competence through numerous social experiences.

2. They should learn to participate in work for the purpose of earning their own living; i.e., they should develop occupational competence through efficient vocational guidance and training as a part of their school experience.

3. They should develop emotional security and independence in the school and in the home through a good mental hygiene program.

4. They should develop habits of health and sanitation through a good program of health education.

5. They should learn the minimum essentials of the tool subjects, even though their academic limits are third to fifth grade.

6. They should learn to occupy themselves in wholesome leisure time activities through an educational program that teaches them to enjoy recreational and leisure time activities.

7. They should learn to become adequate members of a family and a home through an educational program that emphasizes home membership as a function of the curriculum.

8. They should learn to become adequate members of a community through a school program that emphasizes community participation.[185]

To meet such objectives, curricula for the educable mentally retarded student usually included such areas as: 1) perceptual development, including motor, visual, and auditory skills, and such creative activities as fine arts, physical activities, practical arts, and physical education and recreation; 2) language and cognition skills; 3) academic or literary skills, including reading, arithmetic, and language arts; and 4) socialization, including self-image, social relationships, career development, and environmental awareness (e.g., home and family, communities, historical heritage, living things, earth and space, weather and seasons, machines.[186] In high school, considerable emphasis was placed on living independently, caring for one's self and family, and acquiring basic vocational understandings and skills. In more progressive school systems, educable mentally retarded adolescents also enrolled in issue courses dealing with such contemporary problems as drug and alcohol abuse as well as sexuality, marriage, and parenthood.[187] Other elective courses dealing with computers, photography, and social living were available in increasing frequency.

With the exception of a few of the latter courses that reflected modern problems, the basic curriculum for mildly retarded students did not change substantially over the years. What did change was an increased emphasis on academic skills, greater interaction with normal peers, individualized programs with specific objectives, age-appropriate activities, and the utilization of operant conditioning principles.

Objectives and curricular provisions for trainable mentally retarded youngsters, which in some school systems included those who were severely mentally retarded, tended to cluster around three primary areas: self-help, social adjustment in home and neighborhood, and economic usefulness. Curricular activities included arts and crafts, dramatization, physical development and hygiene, language, practical arts, mental development, motor development, self-help, socialization, various social studies, and music.[188] A number of programs also included elemental academics, since it had been demonstrated that some trainable youngsters, especially those with Down syndrome, could acquire some reading and arithmetic skills.[189] Secondary education included not only a continued emphasis in these areas but also focused on employability, adult living skills, and decision-making.[190] The latter three became essential components of the educational program, since moderately mentally retarded individuals were no longer considered appropriate for institutionalization following completion of their formal schooling. This alone marked an important attitudinal change during the historical period under review.

For more profoundly mentally retarded persons, who, with rare exception, were not seriously considered for public school enrollment prior to 1975, educational programming was a new experience for student, parent, teacher, and administrator alike. Educational programs for the profoundly mentally retarded student were comparatively simple in principle and context, but extremely difficult to deliver in practice. As with the more severely retarded student, programming for the profoundly mentally retarded youngster required the talents and skills of many professions, especially education, occupational therapy, and physical therapy. Rudimentary life skills centered around attending behavior; self-help; communication, verbal and nonverbal; daily social skills; and vocational skills.[191] While not all students could benefit from each of the curricular offerings, especially in regard to the vocational aspects, many could. One of the great understandings gained over the 25 year period under review was, regardless of intelligence classification, there is always a remarkable range of variance among individuals and between groups.

Individually developed programs, extremely small sequential steps, special reinforcement procedures, and the developmental model were evident in all educational programs. Also evident, even for the most profoundly mentally retarded of the school population, was a constant emphasis on normalization and the "least restrictive" environment. As stated by Lou Brown of the University of Wisconsin, one of the country's leading innovators of educational programming for severely affected persons and an adamant foe of any form of institutionalization: "Any environment that can be reasonably considered 'least restrictive' or 'most habilitative' must include opportunities for longitudinal and comprehensive interactions with nonhandicapped age peers and others; must provide the extensive range of experiences necessary to prepare for functioning in a wide variety of heterogeneous nonschool and post-school environments; must allow for constructive participation; and must offer the rich variety of sights, sounds, smells, spontaneous happenings, and general unpredictability that so characterize heterogeneous environments that are so important for maximal development and functioning."[192]

THEORIES AND PRACTICES

With the increased visibility and funding of education for mentally retarded students, special educators found an abundance of both theories and materials with which to work. Gone were the pre-sixties days when special teachers designed their own materials; spent hours cutting and pasting, tearing, and reassembling reading items; and devoted endless time to preparing materials for duplication.

Due primarily to the remarkable advances in research during the fifties and early sixties, a number of theories were put forth that increased the effectiveness with which educators could address their task. A number of the early theories placed considerable emphasis upon the relationship of sensorimotor learning and subsequent achievement, often based on some neurological premise.[193]

Neurologically Based Approaches

One such theory was put forth by highly respected, personable Newell C. Kephart. Drawing upon the neurological studies and theoretical formulations of Donald Hebb, Kephart wrote in 1971:

> The functional unit of the nervous system is the neural impulse. This impulse is a wave of negative electricity which passes without decrement from one end of a fiber process to the other.
>
> Neural fibers grow into close approximation to each other but do not make contact. Between each fiber and the next is an open space called the synapse. In order for a neural circuit to be established, the neural impulse must be transmitted across this synapse. The mechanism of synaptic transmission is a complex electrochemical process which need not concern us here.
>
> Behavior results from the operation of a neural circuit. The method of "wiring" a circuit involves a mechanism at the synapse. When an impulse is transmitted across a synapse, there develops on the tips of the fiber process of the post-synaptic neuron small tissue growths called synaptic knobs. These growths are anatomical structures which result from the transmission of the impulse. Whenever a synapse is used, one or more such knobs develop. The more frequently a synapse is used, the larger and more numerous become the knobs. When a used synapse falls into disuse for any reason the knobs decrease in size but never completely disappear.
>
> A general principle now becomes apparent: function alters structure. Since the synaptic knob is an anatomical structure, this alteration is anatomical. Since the knob is produced directly by the transmission of an impulse, the structural alteration is produced by function. Such alteration is progressive, since the knobs increase in number and size with increased use of the synapse, and it is permanent since the knobs never completely disappear thereafter . . . once the function has altered structure, this alteration influences future function. By its own activities, therefore, the nervous system patterns its own function.
>
> This patterning, however, is neither random nor haphazard. It rather tends to concentrate functionally formed circuits together and to relate new circuits to old. There are two reasons for this intensification of pattern. On the one hand, when a synapse is modified, it will tend to draw neural impulses toward itself since its threshold is lower; hence, energy will tend to flow through this lower threshold. Thus the operation of the system itself tends toward pattern. Experiences which are contiguous in space and time will tend to develop circuits having common synapses between them.
>
> In the second place, the laws of the universe will tend to dictate patterns of circuits. By virtue of these laws, the environment of the child is an organized environment. It is not random. The environment, therefore, will tend to present to the child experiences which belong together contiguously in space and time. Because of this contiguity the circuits representing these experiences will tend to have synapses in common and to form a pattern of neural activity whose commonalities represent commonalities in the surrounding environment.
>
> The patterns characteristic of reality tend to be reproduced in patterns of neural activity as a result of experience—that is, if adults do not interfere. If we put together and present to the child things which do not belong together in reality, these things get put together in the child's developing neural patterns because of their contiguity in space and time. The resulting neural patterns are often distorted or disrupted and do not conform to reality.[194]

In a manner consistent with such theories, Kephart contended that there were stages of development through which a youngster has to progress in order to assure desirable levels of intellectual and academic functioning: 1) perceptual-motor match, 2) figure-ground relationships, 3) meaningful movement control, 4) systematic exploration, 5) perceptual continuity, 6) intersensory integration, and 7) concept formation. As concerns slow learning or mental retardation:

The slow learning child is one in whom progress through these stages of development has either broken down or is noticeably delayed. If progress appears to be normal but slow in its course, the condition is usually associated with borderline mental retardation or with cultural deprivation. If the progress is disrupted in its course, the condition is usually associated with diagnosed or assumed disturbances of neurological functioning. In either event, if the delay is sufficient or if the disturbance is severe enough, mental retardation will accompany the condition.

In educating the slow learner, the problem is to determine where, in the course of development, the child has broken down and, through teaching and/or therapeutic procedures, restore the course of development. Normal classroom presentations assume certain levels of development (at least the early perceptual stage by kindergarten and the early conceptual stage by second grade). The skills and abilities characteristic of this stage are an integral part of the design of the classroom presentation. If the child has not yet achieved this level of development, he will find it impossible to participate in the classroom learning presentation or to interact, for the purpose of learning, with the materials and events included herein. Classroom activities thus become meaningless to him and the learnings which they are designed to stimulate become impossible.[195]

To assist a youngster progress through these stages in a normal or desirable manner, Kephart designed or adapted a number of activities to facilitate: perceptual-motor training, which included the utilization of walking and balance boards, the trampoline, stunts and games, and various rhythmic exercises; perceptual-motor matching tasks; correct ocular control; directionality and orientation; and form perception, including form recognition and completion as well as figure-ground relations.

The Doman-Delacato Theory

One of the more controversial neurological theories of the early sixties was advanced by Carl Delacato, Glenn Doman, and Robert Doman, an educator, a physical therapist, and a physician, respectively. The Doman-Delacato theory or method, as it was commonly identified, was based on neurological organization with the intent of affecting the central nervous system rather than any resulting peripheral symptoms.[196] As explained by Carl Delacato:

Neurological organization is that psychologically optimum condition which exists uniquely and most completely in man and is the result of a total and uninterrupted ontogenetic neural development. This development recapitulates the phylogenetic neural development of man and begins during the first trimester of gestation and ends at about six and one half years of age in normal humans. This orderly development in humans progresses vertically through the spinal cord and all other areas of the central nervous system up to the level of the cortex, as it does with all mammals. Man's final and unique developmental progression takes place at the level of the cortex and it is lateral (from left to right or from right to left).

This progression is an interdependent continuum, hence if a high level of development is unfunctioning or incomplete, such as in sleep or as the result of trauma, lower levels become operative and dominant (mid-brain sleep and high cervical pathological reflexes). If a lower level is incomplete, all succeeding higher levels are affected both in relation to their height in the central nervous system and in relation to the chronology of their development. Man's only contribution to this organizational schema is that he has added to the vertical progression, the final lateral progression at the level of the cortex. Here again, at the cortical level, the same premises apply. The final progression must become dominant and must supersede all others. Prerequisite, however, to such dominance is the adequate development of all lower levels.

In totally developed man the left or the right cortical hemisphere must become dominant, with lower prerequisite requirements met, if his organization is to be complete.[197]

Subsequently, "The basic premise of the neuropsychological approach as outlined by the author is that if man does not follow this schema he exhibits a problem of mobility or communication. To overcome such problems one evaluates the subject via the neurological schema outlined above. Those areas of neurological organization which have not been completed or are absent are overcome by *passively imposing* them upon the nervous system in those with problems of mobility and are *taught* to those with problems of speech or reading. When the neurological organization is complete the problem is overcome."[198]

Early research findings primarily by the theorists were most encouraging, even remarkable. In an early report published in the *Journal of the American Medical Association,* in 1960, the authors reported significant mobility gains among most of the 76 brain-injured children subjected to the neuropsychological approach for a period of 2 years.[199]

In his text on the diagnosis and treatment of speech and reading problems, Carl Delacato again reported a number of successful case histories. The average reading gains made, for example, by 248 children attending a 5-week summer session employing the Doman-Delacato method was 1.6 years (the range was 0 growth to 4.5 years). Over a 4-year period, 204 of 287 children were cured of strabismus. In this book, Delacato also included the research that Gayle L. Piper conducted in a high school special education class of 14 students for the 12-week period of February 1, 1962 through May 1, 1962. Among the benefits noted was an average increase of IQ scores from 72 to 86, which, in effect, meant that all but a few subjects now fell within the normal range of expectancy.

Independent studies, however, were not as supportive. In 1966, Melvyn Robbins found no evidence to support the neurological theory as it affected the intelligence, reading, or arithmetic performance of second graders.[200] A few years later, John Kershner, working with a group of trainable youngsters, did report some gains in intelligence as measured by the Peabody Picture Vocabulary Test, but found no significant improvement in perceptual skills not practiced. He also cautioned that the differences in IQ gains may have been due to factors associated with initial group variances since subjects were neither selected nor assigned at random.[201]

While the professional community retained many reservations about the Doman-Delacato method, the public media did not. Newspapers and magazines such as the *New York Times, Life,* and *The Saturday Evening Post* tended to extol the alleged virtues of the method under such headings as "Hands of Hope for New Life," "Miracle in Pennsylvania," and "Hope for Brain-Injured Children."[202]

Disputes of this nature among professionals and varying schools of thought are a relatively frequent occurrence, and occasionally one side or the other is glamorized in the public media. In the case of the Doman-Delacato approach, however, the situation was more serious. The method required the complete adherence to a prescribed, difficult-to-implement protocol that often proved physically and psychologically exhausting. It also could be expensive. To illustrate just one regimen, Doman and his colleagues outlined the following for nonwalking children:

> *Treatment Type I:* All nonwalking children were required to spend all day on the floor in the prone position and were encouraged to crawl (prone method) or creep (hand-knee method) when that level of accomplishment was possible. The only permissible exceptions were to feed, love, and treat the child. This increased the opportunity for the reproduction of the normal functional-positional situation of a healthy child during the first 13 months of life.[203]

The treatment was simple but potentially stressful. Yet, one study conducted in 1977 by persons actively engaged in the field of mental retardation reported a very low incidence of any harmful effects on the family and a low occurrence of any extravagant claims concerning ultimate outcomes. The parents could not, however, identify any real functional changes.[204]

In 1967, the Executive Boards of the American Academy of Pediatrics and the American Academy of Neurology published a statement concerning the Doman-Delacato treatment of neurologically handicapped children. They prefaced their recommendation by pointing out first, "varying degrees of progress are made in the handicapped from maturation. In addition, individual attention and care and physiotherapy techniques offer some benefits. Some of the improvements noted in Doman-Delacato treated cases may accrue from such factors."[205] Second, "physicians should be aware of the sacrifices which a family must make in order to participate in this program." Third, as "more than five years have passed since the publication of the preliminary results of the studies of the program . . . the absence of an acceptable evaluation of the program after such a period of time is of disservice to the program if, in fact, it is responsible for the successes claimed for it."[206] Finally, "individual members report that they have been informed of cases in which the Doman-Delacato program appears not to have helped the patient."[207] Thus, "the Executive Boards of the American Academy of Pediatrics and American Academy of Neurology, acting jointly, feel, therefore, that physicians should make their decisions and recommendations for management of the neurologically handicapped child on the basis that there is as yet no firm evidence substantiating the claims made for the Doman-Delacato methods and program. What is needed are well controlled studies by recognized experts."[208]

Despite this pronouncement and professional concern, many parents continued to support the Doman-Delacato method and its patterning approach. In 1980, Edward Zigler and Ellen Weintraub once again went on record indicating that the methods still lacked verification through research: "to date, no independent scientific study of the patterning treatment has been able to document the kind of dramatic gains that any parent would hope for his handicapped child." Thus, "we share the frustrations of the families of the paucity of options currently available to parents of brain-damaged children. We do not counsel abandoning hope, but neither do we suggest grasping at straws. The old saw about the cure being worse than the disease may prove sadly true for the families who try patterning."[209]

Many of these techniques, which were originally intended for those who had been classified historically as "brain-injured," were adopted by special educators, even when disagreeing with the underlying neurological constructs.[210] These included the numerous ideas and suggestions proposed by Alfred Strauss and Laura Lehtinen in the forties.[211]

Cultural/Behavioral Approaches

Another broadly based theory to receive considerable attention was culturally, rather than neurologically, oriented. Reuven Feuerstein, director of the Hadassah-Wizo-Canada Institute in Jerusalem, relying on both the research of others and his own with immigrant youngsters from nations in North Africa and other Arabic-speaking countries, held that intelligence was modifiable since it was largely governed by environmental influences: "except for the most severely affected, the retarded performer differs from normals in motivational, attitudinal, and experiential background rather than in innate capacity. Therefore, his state can be considered reversible."[212] He also contended that significant modification could occur at any age, and that the educational emphasis should be placed on learning-to-learn (the active-modificational approach) as opposed to the simple absorption of content (the passive-acceptant approach).

The manner in which the entire educative process of the retarded performer is undertaken is highly indicative of an active versus a passive approach. First, let us consider the nature of the educational investment. The passive-acceptant approach is in evidence if the educational system is based on an expectation of maximal concrete output for minimal investment, and if concrete profit and gains (in vocational areas for example) are viewed as the educative goal with retarded performers. If the goals are more oriented toward a modification of the retardate's performance in the direction of heightened intellective abilities, the active-modificational approach is operative. In this instance, the difference between the active and passive approaches lies in "how" [a subject is taught] and not necessarily "what" is taught. A given subject can be taught as an end in itself to yield a concrete dividend (passive-acceptant approach) or as the basis for generalizability and transfer of a more abstract concept (active-modificational approach).

Certain aspects of the teaching situation are also relevant. If teachers involve themselves with the creation of a program closely matching the manifest level of functioning of the retardate, if their teaching reflects an over-emphasis on the concrete and immediate, very little will be done to help the retarded individual to transcend his actual level of performance. In such teaching, the teacher, of necessity, talks down to the students and uses obvious situations in a redundant way. She will be reluctant to introduce anything which might be considered as innovative under the assumption that the retardate, being unmodifiable, will not be able to integrate it. The teaching will be content oriented; that is to say, she will stress certain subjects in the classroom which she may consider as necessary to the child's immediate adjustment rather than providing him with learning sets. Learning sets, once established, would enable the child to integrate new experiences and become enriched by them.[213]

Feuerstein expanded these basic principles and set forth extensive discussions of appropriate diagnostic techniques and educational approaches in two well-received texts, *The Dynamic Assessment of Retarded Performers*, 1979, and *Instructional Enrichment*, 1980.[214] Interestingly, and in marked contrast to American thinking, Feuerstein recommended that culturally disadvantaged youngsters live in group residential settings composed of a heterogeneous population rather than at home in order to provide an enriched environment.

In addition to the more global approaches to education, many educationally related areas or activities, ranging from art therapy to yoga, were expanded in scope, became more sophisticated in regimen, and were held to have many benefits for students who were mentally retarded.[215] To illustrate, physical education was viewed as highly significant to the total development of mentally retarded youngsters, and not simply limited to such motor aspects as coordination, strength, and speed. Bryant Cratty, of the department of physical education of the University of California–Los Angeles, who contributed a number of books in this area, outlined 11 ways in which motor activities could contribute to the overall education of mentally retarded and other developmentally disabled students:

1. Movement tasks, designed to arouse or calm, may enable a child to achieve a level of arousal appropriate to classroom tasks with which he is confronted.
2. Movement experiences help retarded children to exercise more self-control, and to focus their attention for longer periods of time on tasks at hand.
3. Lead-up activities involving hand-eye coordination tasks will enable the retardate to effectively transcribe his thoughts to paper and to draw with more facility.
4. To a large extent vocational opportunities for retarded children and young adults involve competency in motor task performance. Improvement in motor abilities appropriate to proficiencies needed in industry should increase chances of employment.
5. A retarded child may be helped to better structure space by engaging in movement tasks in which spatial concepts are inculcated.
6. Rhythmic activities may aid a retarded child to organize time, to speak, to read, and to write more efficiently.
7. Improvement of the generally low fitness levels of retardates may be achieved in well-motivated programs of physical activity.
8. Certain basic components of intellectual processes involving choicemaking, categorizing, and seriation may be "acted-out" in movement tasks.
9. Mathematics and spelling skills may be improved by engaging in movement activities.
10. The general self-concept of retardates may be improved by successful experiences in physical education activities which in turn may positively influence their level of aspiration and performance on other types of tasks to which they are exposed.
11. The motivating nature of motor activities may be utilized to improve the linguistic and verbal skills of children with learning difficulties.[216]

While each of these areas played a major role in improving the quality of educational experiences for mentally retarded pupils, the greatest gains by far were realized in the areas of language and communication. In view of the tremendous importance of language to learning, mediation, and social interaction, the theoretical models developed along with their diagnostic and remedial programs were greatly appreciated and highly influential in facilitating both verbal and nonverbal communication, even among more severely affected individuals.

During the early sixties, Kirk and McCarthy, expanding on one of Charles Osgood's generalized behavior models, generated the Illinois Test of Psycholinguistic Abilities, which was extensively used in a variety of educational settings. In essence, the diagnostic test and the associated remediation or instructional materials took into consideration six dimensions of representational thinking (auditory, visual, auditory visual, visual motor, vocal, and motor distributed according to decoding, association, and encoding) plus three dimensions of automatic-sequential functioning (auditory vocal—automatic, and auditory vocal and visual motor—sequential).[217]

Another major diagnostic-teaching language approach developed by Lloyd Dunn and his colleagues at the George Peabody College for Teachers, a major research center on mental retardation during the sixties and early seventies, was the Peabody Picture Vocabulary Test. Originally designed in 1959 and revised in 1981, it was a nonverbal multiple choice test intended to evaluate the receptive vocabulary ability of children and adults.[218] Again, related curriculum materials were developed.[219]

Richard L. Schiefelbusch

Of significance, much effort was devoted to increasing an understanding of the development of speech and communication skills among those individuals who were severely and profoundly mentally retarded. In the forefront of much that occurred in this vital field of facilitating communication among mentally retarded children was Richard L. Schiefelbusch, a University Distinguished Professor of Speech and Language, director of the Bureau of Child Research, and director of the Kansas Center for Mental Retardation and Human Development at the University of Kansas.[220] The start of his innumerable contributions in the area of speech and language began in 1958 with the Parsons Language Project, which was the first research project to study institutionalized severely retarded children and their language using behavior analysis procedures. The purpose of the project was to "develop an optimal language and communication program for mentally retarded children in an institutional setting." Its subgoals were:

1. The formulation of a set of experimental constructs relative to language and communication as features of social adequacy.
2. Diagnostic assessments of maladaptive patterns affecting language and communication.
3. The development of a battery of language and communication tests to assess verbal characteristics of institutional children and to determine gains made in the training program.
4. The development of special clinical techniques for improving the verbal behavior of mentally retarded children.
5. The development of an environmental milieu for purposes of stimulating verbal development.[221]

From this beginning, his work expanded greatly over the years and received international attention, and his theories and techniques were applied in numerous settings.[222] What once had been a neglected area was now endowed with a rich array of ideas and techniques to be utilized in perpetualizing communication skills among mentally retarded youngsters and adults.

Richard Schiefelbusch

Nonverbal Communication

To facilitate communication among those with verbal difficulties, especially more severely affected persons, nonverbal communication systems were developed or used, including sign language and communication boards.[223] In the area of communication boards, one of the most effective involved the adaptation of Bliss's semantography during the early seventies, which had its own rather unique history. Charles K. Bliss, a research chemist by training, developed his symbolic system during the forties in response to his experiences as a youth in dissent-ridden Austria and as a prisoner during the Nazi years. He was firmly convinced that words and the inability of various peoples to communicate effectively resulted in violence and war. In his 1966 text, he observed that "all languages are without logic," and "the most desperate task in the world is to expose the catastrophic falsehoods in the many words which lead to strife and war. What every boy and girl should learn in school is a simple semantics and logic in order to recognize the ambiguities, the fallacies, and the demagogies in the words which cause debates, dissension, despair, destruction and death to many millions."[224] In 1942, he began to develop a universal, symbolic language, publishing his first three-volume set in 1949. Though supported by such intellectuals as Bertrand Russell and Julian Huxley, and in spite of subsequent revisions, extensive pleadings and correspondence, his system never received the full attention or acceptance he desired.

In 1971, educators at the Ontario (Canada) Crippled Children's Center discovered what became known as Blissymbolics and adapted it for application with children with cerebral palsy.[225] The results were most gratifying, and over the next few years, the system was gradually adopted throughout the United States. Regardless of its original intent, Blissymbolics proved to offer a communication vehicle never before available to a group of youngsters in desperate need.

However, not all methods that receive considerable attention persist in practice. One such approach was the Initial Teaching Alphabet (i.t.a.), originally developed by Sir James Pitman of England during the late fifties.[226] Known as the Augmented Roman Alphabet, Pitman's intent was to provide the beginning reader with a notably simpler symbolic code. For this purpose, he introduced 44 characters, known as the i.t.a. (see Figure 5.2).[227]

Early research in both England and the United States indicated that Pitman's alphabet did facilitate reading among young mentally retarded students. In the United States, for example, Albert Mazurkiewicz found his subjects demonstrated increased ability to use word attack skills, developed fluency in oral reading, and significantly improved word recognition and auditory discrimination.[228] With the acquisition of reading skills, his seven students also showed marked improvement in self-concept and motivation for continued learning.[229] Phillip Williams, in England, reported similar results. Despite such encouraging early results, the method was not widely adopted.

Finally, two additional services became available to mentally retarded students in public schools as a consequence of PL 94-142: occupational and physical therapy. Fortunate-

Blissymbols

ſhis is printed in an augmented rœman alfabet, ſhe purpos ov whiďr is not, as miet bee suppœsd, tœ reform œur spelliŋ, but tœ imprœv ſhe lerniŋ ov reediŋ. it is intended ſhat when ſhe beginner has aďheevd ſhe iniſhial sucsess ov flœoensy in ſhis speſhially eesy form, his fuetuer progress ſhœd bee confiend tœ reediŋ in ſhe present alfabets and spelliŋs ov ſhem œnly.

Figure 5.2   A sample paragraph written using the Initial Teaching Alphabet (i.t.a.).

ly, these therapists also had a well-established theory to call upon: the neurodevelopmental treatment approach originated by England's Karl and Berta Bobath, which emphasized postural tone, reflexes and reactions, and movement patterns.[230]

Regardless of the theory applied, most teachers and many therapists adopted an approach that was identified under a number of titles, such as "Precision Teaching" or "Diagnostic Teaching." Precision Teaching was not a theory of instruction, but rather a principled approach, fundamentally based on operant conditioning. As clarified by several of its adherents, "Precision Teaching is not a way of teaching. Precision Teaching is not another method of teaching. Precision Teaching is one way to plan, use, and analyze teaching style, technique, method, or theoretical position—old or new."[231] In brief, the system called for the establishment of individualized educational goals, the determination of the student's level of readiness or current response repertoire, the designation of measurable steps to realize a goal, and the constant measurement of progress. As succinctly stated by Norris Haring, "The Precision Teaching format follows a simple pattern of pinpoint, record, change, try again."[232]

Computers

One cannot leave the area of educational methodology without some consideration of one of the greatest scientific achievements of the quarter century: the microcomputer. The original impetus for the use of computers in education, including special education, was provided by B. F. Skinner, who as previously noted, developed a teaching machine in response to his exasperation with the quality of teaching extended to his daughter. Underlying his approach was the belief, held by many, regardless of mechanical assistance, that large tasks needed to be divided into a series of smaller steps to assure control of learning behavior, prompt reinforcement, and ultimate goal realization. These sentiments were well expressed in his widely read text, *The Technology of Teaching*, published in 1968:

The whole process of becoming competent in any field must be divided into a very large number of very small steps, and reinforcement must be contingent upon the accomplishment of each step. This solution to the problem of creating a complex repertoire of behavior also solves the problem of maintaining the behavior in strength . . . . By making each successive step as small as possible, the frequency of reinforcement can be raised to a maximum, while the possible aversive consequences of being wrong are reduced to a minimum.[233]

As regards the role of the teacher:

The simple fact is that as a mere reinforcing mechanism, the teacher is out of date. This would be true even if a single teacher devoted all her time to a single child, but her inadequacy is multiplied manyfold when she must serve as a reinforcing device to many children at once. If the teacher is to take advantage of recent advances in the study of learning, she must have the help of mechanical devices.[234]

In principle, Skinner received support from many other psychologists and educators. The need for goal stipulation, and breaking a task into small sequential steps was well recognized by many in those fields concerned with learning, especially behavioral psychology.[235]

The question of computer use with mentally retarded students was visible by the early sixties. In 1960, Lawrence Stolurow of the Institute for Research on Exceptional Children at the University of Illinois in Urbana, following a description of the most rudimentary forms of computerized learning, concluded that the "teaching machine introduces into the classroom a new concept in the type of aid provided by the teacher. This is the closed-loop concept. It is implemented by a system-learner, machine and program in a closed-loop interaction which emulates tutoring . . . . The substantial gains already made through research and development efforts with teaching machines argue forcefully for the real and substantial contributions of this technology to the future of both special and general education."[236]

Computer programming for educational purposes did not become a reality during the sixties or even the early seventies for a variety of reasons: the equipment was cumbersome and inflexible, tasks that could be programmed were few in number, and costs were prohibitive. Few persons of the day, even ardent enthusiasts, could envision the tremendous impact of the microchip or that a roomful of equipment would be reduced to a hand-held computer. By the mid-eighties, computers found their way into 64,000 special education classes, primarily in those for the sensorially handicapped or learning disabled.[237]

The benefits of microcomputer-assisted instruction were consistently heralded and included such areas as drill and practice, tutorial assistance, stimulation, computer-managed instruction, problem-solving, assessment/evaluation, and data retrieval.[238] Many firmly believed that computers would play a significant role in individualized instruction and in facilitating motivation among learners.[239]

In spite of the enthusiasm and pronouncements, actual research among mentally retarded students was sparse and hardly supportive of the many alleged benefits. The few available studies demonstrated that mentally retarded youth with mental ages of approx-

imately 7 could, with the assistance of picture prompts, learn to access and terminate a microcomputer program; severely mentally retarded youngsters could advantageously participate in computer programming to facilitate matching of sizes, shapes, and colors; and computers could assist in sight-word acquisition and number conservation.[240] Yet, while computers had played an important role in facilitating mobility, positioning, and communication among the multiply handicapped, their use in terms of individualized instruction and motivation among those who were mentally retarded remained a promise to be fulfilled.[241]

Not only did educators have new theories and techniques at their disposal, they also received considerable support from a number of other resources. Beginning in the sixties, the field of mental retardation witnessed a publication explosion in terms of both new journals and books, a number of which were aimed at special education. In 1963, the American Association on Mental Deficiency initiated its second publication, *Mental Retardation*. Several years later, in 1966, the Council for Exceptional Children expanded its publication roster to include *Education and Training of the Mentally Retarded*, and, in 1968, *Teaching Exceptional Children*. Independent publications also appeared, such as *Focus on Exceptional Children*, Love Publishing Company, in 1967; and *Applied Research in Mental Retardation*, Pergamon Press, in 1980.

To assist the educator assess some of the new techniques and materials, the U.S. Office of Education, in response to one of the original President's Panel's recommendations, established 14 regional material centers housed in various university settings. These provided information, field-tested newly developed materials and techniques, established special libraries, and stimulated the continued generation of new ideas.[242]

In addition, two documentation services were established, both of which were intended to collect, abstract, collate, store, and retrieve information related to mental retardation. First was the documentation service developed during the early sixties under a federal grant to the American Association on Mental Deficiency, which produced a quarterly publication, *MR Abstracts,* that contained summaries of the world's major literature on all aspects of mental retardation. This project, like the regional resource centers, lasted until the mid-seventies. The other project, the Educational Resources Information Center, established in 1966 by the National Institute of Education of the U.S. Department of Education, attained permanency. Better known by its acronym ERIC, the center provided interested persons with ready access to educational literature by and for practitioners and scholars.

The Association for Persons with Severe Handicaps

In November 1974, a new professional organization joined the ranks of the Council for Exceptional Children and the American Association on Mental Deficiency in promoting the interests of developmentally disabled persons: the Association for Persons with Severe Handicaps, originally known as the American Association for the Education of the Severely/Profoundly Handicapped. It was primarily concerned with more severely affected persons, as defined by the Bureau of Education for the Handicapped:

> . . . those who because of the intensity of their physical, mental, or emotional problems, or a combination of such problems, need educational, social, psychological and medical services beyond those which are traditionally offered by regular and special educational programs, in order to maximize their full potential for useful and meaningful participation in society and for self-fulfillment.
> (a) The term includes those children who are classified as seriously emotionally disturbed (including children who are schizophrenic or autistic), profoundly and severely mentally retarded, and those with two or more serious handicapping conditions, such as the mentally retarded blind, and the cerebral-palsied deaf.
> (b) 'Severely handicapped children' (1) May possess severe language and/or perceptual-cognitive deprivations, and evidence abnormal behaviors such as: (i) Failure to respond to pronounced social stimuli, (ii) Self-mutilation, (iii)

Self-stimulation, (iv) Manifestation of intense and prolonged temper tantrums, and (v) The absence of rudimentary forms of verbal control, and (2) May also have extremely fragile physiological conditions.[243]

During the initial 1974 meeting in Kansas City, with 60 persons in attendance, the Association postulated its purposes:

1. To function as an advocate organization for the development and implementation of comprehensive, high quality educational services for severely and profoundly handicapped individuals from birth through early adulthood in the public school sector.
2. To serve as a separate entity in advocating
   (a) the development of relevant and efficient pre-service and in-service teacher-training programs; and
   (b) the development of highly specialized doctoral level teacher training, research, and instructional design personnel.
3. To develop, refine and disseminate inexpensive training packages, instructional programs, and materials pertinent to the educational programs for the severely and profoundly handicapped.
4. To facilitate parent involvement in all program services for the severely and profoundly handicapped.[244]

By May 1975, at which time the Association was formally incorporated, the membership had grown to well over 1,000 members and an impressive set of publications was formulated. In 1984, the Association enjoyed a membership of over 6,000.

TEACHER TRAINING

Given the increasing recognition of mentally retarded youngsters as a public school responsibility, one of the most critical problems of the sixties and early seventies was recruiting and training a sufficient number of teachers. The shortage, especially in the early sixties, was most acute: less than 500 students were graduated annually against a total need of 55,000 teachers.[245] Fortunately, by the early sixties, due to federally funded teacher training programs initiated during the preceding decade, approximately 250 colleges and universities were offering undergraduate and graduate degrees.[246] Scholarships and fellowships, as well as direct university support for special education, were available from both federal resources and numerous private organizations, including parent associations, radio stations, fraternities and sororities, and special foundations.[247] With the combination of increased interest, financial assistance, and high visibility for job placement and security, the number of trained special teachers for mentally retarded persons rapidly rose to over 6,000 graduates per year by 1976. Following that date, the number gradually diminished to only 2,128 in 1981.[248] Reasons for the decrease included a lessened need for teachers in general, confusion over the role of special educators in mainstreaming, and a general tendency for women to seek employment in occupations other than education. Also, federal support for special teacher training programs was gradually reduced over the years.

Changing attitudes or philosophies in the field of special education as well as the introduction of new populations to be served proved to be quite challenging for university personnel, and one in which a total agreement was not reached. Some authorities contended that in view of mainstreaming, special education specialties should be eliminated entirely. Others, in contrast, believed that specialties such as resource teachers, consulting teachers, and special class teachers should be emphasized, and at least courses, if not certification, should be required for teaching those who were severely and profoundly mentally retarded. In the final analysis, neither universities or colleges in their programmatic offerings nor states in their certification requirements settled on any single set of standards. While Pennsylvania, for example, established a generic special education certificate, most states continued to require certification for various special subcategories. In 1979, Thurman and Hare best illustrated the resultant quandary confronting persons responsible for teacher training:

> . . . some states . . . have initiated generic special education certification. This certificate designates an assumption that a special education teacher can instruct any type of handicapped child, with the exception of those with sensory impairment. It is naive at best and absurd at worst to believe that any teacher training program has the potential to prepare a teacher to meet the mandates suggested by a generic approach to certification. On the other hand, it is equally unreasonable to assume that all service delivery needs will be met by training teachers according to one rather specific mode, such as the resource room or consulting teacher model. It is difficult, also, to see how such models can be adjusted to meet requirements of categorical structures that are inherent in reimbursement systems as well as remaining as the predominant method of service delivery and certification.[249]

Ultimately, most teacher training programs attempted to train teachers to be able to work effectively in a variety of educational settings, and a number of new teacher training models were generated, including the clinical teaching model, the accumulative development, the consulting teacher model, diagnostic-prescriptive teaching models, the teacher catalyst model, the multimedia teaching model, the dialectic teaching system, the diagnostic approach, and the accountability model.[250]

Regardless of the specific model used or encouraged, most universities and colleges emphasized a competency-based approach, which called for a hierarchial structure of well-defined skills to be achieved, observed, and documented by knowledgeable university staff.[251] One such model proposed in 1975 included 12 related categorical goals:

1. To provide an early practicum experience for prospective special education majors.
2. To develop an awareness of one's attitudes, prejudices, feelings, and responses as they influence, and are influenced by exceptional children.
3. To introduce the social, medical, emotional, physical, and mental characteristics of the handicapped.
4. To identify the needs of exceptional children in relation to educational and social environments.
5. To identify the goals and objectives of Special Education programs for various types of handicapping conditions.
6. To become familiar with a specific area of exceptionality in general; institutionalized

facets, the goals of an institution for the handicapped.

7. To identify similarities that exist between teaching in regular education and special education.

8. To provide "hands-on" experience in a variety of settings (institutional, rural and urban) prior to receiving a degree in Special Education.

9. To provide exposure and supervised experience with children afflicted with many types of handicapping conditions prior to graduation for prospective special education personnel.

10. To become familiar with the common "core" of approaches and techniques to be utilized in the intervention process of specific deficiencies in skill areas.

11. To place the emphasis on immediate practical application of theory to practice.

12. To develop the six categories of teacher competencies in a progressional sequence which would terminate in demonstration of acquired competence for exit requirements.[252]

Over the next few years, such listings increased in length and complexity, and, though varying in detail, usually clustered around a number of relatively common categories. For example, in 1978, Haring collated 450 informational and performance competencies under nine categories that, though originally intended for severely and profoundly mentally retarded persons, were equally applicable to moderately and mildly retarded persons: 1) techniques for managing behavior problems; 2) procedures for developing teacher-made instructional materials; 3) engineering physical properties of a classroom; 4) basic principles of the acquisition of operant behavior; 5) basic principles and techniques of measurement; 6) basic principles of imitation training, generalization, discrimination, and maintenance; 7) basic principles of task analysis; 8) development and implementation of instructional programs; and 9) procedures used to develop curriculum sequences.[253]

Similarly, Stamm in 1980 identified six broad categories of abilities related to competency-based programming, which he believed were acutely absent among both regular and special class teachers:

1. Ability to individually assess and diagnose specific skill strengths and weaknesses in order to develop appropriate instructional programming.

2. Ability to discriminate between assessment for classification purposes and for instructional purposes.

3. Ability to design effective instructional programs, i.e., specify learning requirements (goals) and instructional objectives.

4. Ability to systematically analyze instructional objectives (task analysis) and specify alternative program strategies to achieve them.

5. Ability to evaluate learner outcomes.

6. Ability to work effectively with other professionals and parents (communication and consulting skills).[254]

Though competency-based models were developed by nearly every major college and university in the country, there remained one critical question: What specific competencies should be developed?[255] As expressed by Thurman and Hare in 1979, "competency-based teacher training programs are pervasive; however, the basis upon which teaching competencies are selected is rarely supported by empirical data on the behavioral outcomes in children. Competencies tend to be included because a group of experts deems them important, not because there is a demonstrated relationship between these skills and the learning process in a school setting."[256] Meyen also observed that "the state of the art, at least from my observation, is such that it is difficult to predict which child is going to respond to which methodology."[257]

Though many of the competencies recorded lacked substantial research support, they often appeared justified in terms of practical experience and obvious need. Milne, for example, surveyed teachers and administrators concerning competencies and found the following to be of most critical import: competence in learning activities, pupil self-concept, pupil self-discipline, communications development, and parent interaction domains.[258] In essence, while there was variation among the various sets of tasks introduced and criteria used, the commonalities far exceeded any differences.

In addition to the mission of the universities

and colleges to train teachers in terms of curriculum and teaching techniques, the introduction of the individualized education program, with its emphasis on parent involvement and interdisciplinary teams, required extra experience in interpersonal relations. Also, it was quite evident that many people were teaching special children, including parents, teacher aides, other mentally retarded youngsters, and normal students.[259] Thus, skills in adult training and management were needed.

In view of the close relationship between mental retardation, labeling, and socioeconomic circumstances, numerous agencies and groups, including the President's Committee on Mental Retardation, felt strongly that teacher certification should require "courses focusing on both the positive and negative impact of racial, ethnic, and economic factors on human development. Such curricula should focus on":

> Sensitivity to the hazards of cultural bias and prejudice to individual development.
> Contributory values of cultural diversity and the contribution of varied ethnic groups to the common culture of all.
> Assistance to children in examining their own attitudes toward minorities including the minority of mentally retarded children.
> Selection of textbooks and other media of instruction which appropriately and adequately reflect the realities of ethnic and individual diversity.
> Creation of learning environments which will minimize feelings of cultural exclusion and disadvantage and augment feelings of acceptance and participation.[260]

Further, as indicated by a number of professors, the teacher had to be familiar with the law, especially the provisions of PL 94-142.[261] Correspondingly, many expected teachers to acquire knowledge and skills associated with advocacy.[262]

In essence, though not all answers had been reached nor all dilemmas resolved, the role of the special educator had become increasingly complex, as did that of those responsible for their training. Unfortunately, the absence of desperately needed research rendered that task more difficult.

Chapter

6

ADULT SERVICES

THE GREAT UNMET NEED

SOCIOLOGICAL RESEARCH ONCE again demonstrated that most adults who were mentally retarded enjoyed the same satisfactions and suffered the same disappointments as their fellow citizens. They loved and lost, married and divorced, had youngsters, understood their condition, held political opinions, sought independence, looked to a better future, and, like everyone else, occasionally worried about death.[1] A few fell victim to alcoholism, and as already noted, mental retardation per se precluded neither norm-violating behavior nor mental illness.[2] Unlike their normal counterparts, however, mentally retarded adults were confronted with many problems, some associated with their intellectual limitations, others with parental or public attitudes. In general, they tended to live on the socioeconomic margin of life; they did not participate fully in civic affairs; they had limited leisure-time activities; and perhaps most unfortunate of all, they tended to be lonely.[3]

During early adulthood, many mentally retarded persons were found to seek normality through greater independence and denial of their condition, as exemplified by the works of Robert Edgerton and his colleagues, as well as Lous Heshusius, who spent approximately 200 hours visiting and interacting in a variety of ways with eight young mentally retarded adults living in a supervised group home.

Similar to Edgerton, Heshusius desired to gain more information about independence, marriage, interpersonal behavior, and intrapersonal understanding, and once again discovered that young adults fervently sought to deny the existence of mental retardation and to explore all avenues that, in their judgment, would result in a normal life:

> The data in this study may present the subjects' view of normalcy, since it seems patent that their conception of normalcy can be seen from the ways they wanted to live differently than their retarded status (which they denied) allowed them to. Since they did not want to be labeled retarded, they wished for living conditions that, from their perspective, would put them in a situation in which they would not be seen as retarded. The logic in this reasoning is as follows:
>
> > The subjects deny being retarded;
> > They know that they live and work in places where they are judged retarded;
> > They cannot specify what it means to be normal since such specification is not possible in terms of their actual living conditions and to specify normalcy in terms of anything else would be to acknowledge that they are not that;
> > Therefore, they wish for living conditions that would make them "not retarded . . . ."
>
> In sum, the conclusion seems to present itself that normalcy, as defined by what the subjects wanted to be different, meant for most living "on-my-own," coming and going without hav-

ing to account for it, and the freedom to get married and to be sexually involved. It seems interesting to note that none of the subjects ever expressed the desire to own a house, to have a lot of money, to have a well-paying or stable job or any of the more stereotypic middle class desires. The subjects who did mention money did so only out of concern to have enough to get married or to just live on.[4]

One of the critical lessons learned about adult mentally retarded persons striking out on their own was their tremendous need for some form of social support system or network, which Gail O'Connor defined as including "the emotional, informational, and material support provided by friends, relatives, neighbors, service providers, and others with whom one has an ongoing relationship, and to whom one can turn in time of need or crises."[5] The importance of such assistance was well illustrated by Edgerton's initial study in 1967, which found that the subjects' normal neighbors were often sympathetic, understanding, and supportive:

> The ex-patients usually fail in their attempts to cope with the exigencies of everyday life; it would appear that, with a few exceptions, they would not be able to maintain themselves in the outside community without the assistance of normal benefactors. They usually fail to pass as well. They are often surprisingly clever in their techniques of passing and they are always dogged in their efforts. Nonetheless, they are successful in deceiving relatively few people, and they deceive these only if the ex-patients' exposure before them is brief and superficial. The normal persons with whom these former patients regularly come into contact typically "know" that the former patients are mentally deficient. Their words in this regard permit no doubt of that. But in what I have termed a benevolent conspiracy, normal persons not only avoid humiliating these retarded persons by failing to disclose that they are aware of the source of their incompetence, but they also actually help them to pass with others who may not be aware.[6]

While, as discussed previously, the need to "pass" became less urgent as mentally retarded adults became older and assumed more normal roles and activities, an effective support system—large or small, formal or informal—remained important.[7]

Marriage and the Family

Throughout the course of history, there have always been those who have fervently sought to eliminate or at least severely control the occurrence of mental retardation for a wide range of reasons, all of which shared one common denominator—persons of limited intelligence were deemed undesirable. Prior to the sixties, two approaches aimed at reducing the number of mentally retarded persons involved sterilization and the prohibition of marriage. These were discussed by many, tried by few, and judged a failure by most; and during the period under review, they also were determined to be legally inappropriate under most circumstances.

PROHIBITION OF MARRIAGE

While as late as 1980, 33 states still maintained statutes prohibiting marriage involving mentally retarded persons, in reality, by 1960, all had abandoned any broad scale effort to implement their original intents.[8] The few cases brought before the courts during the sixties either challenging the right to marry or to have a marriage annulled on the grounds of mental retardation were not favorably received. In 1967, Judge Boslaugh, in *Homan* v. *Homan*, refused to set aside a marriage on the basis of incompetency. In rendering his decision, he noted that though the husband was mentally retarded, he had sufficient ability to transact business and the capability to enter into the marriage in 1960. Subsequently, though the marriage may "have been unwise or unfortunate," in the judge's opinion, it was not void.[9] This judgment was similar to that in *Johnson* v. *Johnson* in 1960.[10] In 1977, the Supreme Court cast a jaundiced eye on such statutes, stating, "any statutory classifications [that] significantly interfere with the exercise of the [right to marry] cannot be upheld unless it is supported by a sufficiently important state interest and is closely tailored to effectuate those interests."[11]

Though marriage of mentally retarded people was judged legally acceptable, public opinion and parent attitudes were not always as positive. In 1970, one public opinion poll found 53.9% of respondents disagreed with mentally retarded people marrying, while another, conducted during the same year, found 80% of 1,113 participants even objected to mentally retarded individuals dating those considered to be normal.[12]

Similarly, parents tended to view marriage conservatively. One study among parent members of the Association for Retarded Citizens of the United States reported that 77% opposed marriage. This rather high figure may have reflected the fact that most members of the Association had severely affected offspring.[13]

The status of marriage among mentally retarded adults was not explored extensively. What research was accomplished indicated that mentally retarded persons tended to remain together more often than their normal peers. Ruby Kennedy, in her 1966 follow-up report of her 1948 study noted that 94% of 154 adult subjects had remained married.[14] Similarly, in 1980, Crain found only one divorce among 130 subjects.[15] Such results indicated that marriages involving mentally retarded persons were relatively stable, and as observed by Edgerton and his associates, such marriages could be meaningful, fulfilling, and supportive.[16]

STERILIZATION

While marriage among mentally retarded persons appeared more acceptable than in the past, having children did not. "Marry if you like," begrudgingly conceded an aging Walter Alvarez, noted physician and popular author, "but you may not keep dumping hundreds of feebleminded children on our doorstep—most of them candidates for our poor house and county hospital."[17] Medora Bass, longtime advocate of sterilization agreed, noting that marriage without children could be more "normalizing."[18]

Though by 1960 sterilization was no longer a widespread practice, 26 states still retained

sterilization laws, 23 of which were compulsory. All provided for the sterilization of mentally retarded persons; 24 included the mentally ill; 14, epileptic persons; and 12, criminals. Usually, determination of the need for sterilization was invested with an administrative agency or person, often without recourse to objection, a guardian *ad litem,* transcripts, or judicial review.[19] Statutory reasons for sterilization ranged from the eugenic to the noneugenic; that is, from the desire to avoid the alleged transmission of defective genes to the rather liberal provision of a Wisconsin statute that simply read, "where procreation is inadvisable."[20] As with marriage prohibition, the implementation of sterilization laws had decreased significantly by 1960. In 1963, there were 467 sterilizations, as compared to 1,638 in 1943. For both years, approximately 50% of the patients were mentally retarded.[21] This decrease reflected the growing apprehension among the professional community as to the appropriateness and advisability of the procedures. Most knowledgeable persons directly involved with sterilization programs concurred with the thinking of Bernard L. Diamond, expressed in his special report to the American Psychiatric Association in the early sixties:

> Present day psychiatry, although still vitally interested in the possible genetic factors in mental illness and mental deficiency, avoids the sweeping generalizations so prevalent in the past. Genetics has evolved into a much more precise science and very significant work is being done on the inheritance of mental illness. Nevertheless, this is a field of great conflict; there has been much learned in recent years of the impact of environment on child development; of the essential role of psychodynamic factors in personality development and production of mental illness; and of the susceptibility of the child in utero to unfavorable metabolic and infectious conditions of the mother.
>
> In short, the present state of our scientific knowledge does not justify the widespread use of the sterilization procedures in mentally ill or mentally deficient persons . . . .
>
> It is sometimes proposed that sterilization is demanded, irrespective of the uncertainties of our knowledge of heredity, in that a mentally ill or feebleminded person is incapable of providing

the emotional and material environment required to raise a normal child. Perhaps this is so, but it raises issues of a sociological and political nature of a very uncertain character and it may be most dangerous to apply such sociological concepts under the guise of a genetic thesis that is far from proven and highly uncertain in its application.[22]

Though fewer in number, there were those who persisted in recommending rather large-scale sterilization programs to reduce the risk of marital failure, to offset inadequate parenting ability, and to reduce the financial burden of the welfare system. Medora Bass, who at one time served as vice-president of the Association for Voluntary Sterilization, prepared a series of articles on this subject.[23] To illustrate her position, in a paper delivered at the Annual Conference of the World Federation for Mental Health, in 1967, she warned that "social adjustment and marriage are more satisfying when there are few children or none. Retardates are generally inadequate parents. . . . There is a general feeling that the retarded regard a baby as a doll to be played with. . . . Mental retardation is the most frequent of all handicaps among children, and, you as leaders in your community, have the power to reduce this scourge, whether environmental or hereditary by 50 percent in your generation."[24]

Her last observation was based on a frequently cited study by Elizabeth and Sheldon Reed, who wrote extensively about genetic counseling and mental retardation. In 1965, they reported on a longitudinal investigation of the family histories of 289 mentally retarded persons living in an institution and concluded, in part, that mental retardation could be reduced from 25% to 50% every generation if mentally retarded persons did not reproduce, and "where the transmission of a trait is frequently from parent to offspring, sterilization will be effective and it is irrelevant whether the basis for the trait is genetic or environmental . . . ."[25]

Sterilization and the Courts

In those few instances when the question of sterilizing a mentally retarded person was ad-dressed to the courts during the sixties, judges strongly supported such actions, if for no other reason than to reduce the welfare rolls. In 1962, for example, Nora Ann, with an IQ of 36, was determined to be "feeble minded" and was ordered to submit to an operation partly because of her personal health and partly because of welfare implications: "To permit Nora Ann to have further children would result in additional burdens upon the county and state welfare departments which have already been compelled to reduce payments because of a shortage of funds. . . ."[26] The same judge later addressed an Ohio Welfare Conference appealing to the audience to start a campaign in their own communities for compulsory sterilization which, in his opinion, was "a positive action which can be taken to help reduce the ever-expanding cost of public welfare."[27]

In 1966, another Ohio probate judge issued sterilization orders for mentally retarded sisters, age 19 and 22, for the same fundamental reasons:

> Due to their physical attractiveness and considering their mental capacity and further considering the medical testimony these girls would in all probability continue to be promiscuous and likely to again become pregnant, there is still the probability that such offspring would become mentally deficient and become public charges the same as the two young mothers are at the present time. This would present an additional burden upon the mother, [and the] State and County Welfare Departments, where support payments have of necessity been reduced due to lack of funds.[28]

The extent to which the courts were ready to sterilize almost any offender to the public welfare was clearly evident in California. In 1965, for example, a young man was charged with nonsupport for his minor children and was given the choice of a jail sentence or probation with sterilization. He later regretted his decision to be sterilized and initiated litigation, requesting the Supreme Court to decide whether conditioning probation upon sterilization constituted cruel and unusual punishment. The Supreme Court refused to review the case.[29] In the same year, however, a judge of the Superior Court of California overturned a decision involving sterilization and welfare costs, noting that "if the aid to needy children provisions of our welfare statutes are not to the liking of a particular judge, he may not ignore them, or substitute a penalty of his own which is not authorized by law. It is for the people or their legislative representatives to make any change in the law that they deem desirable. . . . Judges may not ignore a law simply because they do not like it or believe in it. . . . Nor may a court act in excess of the power given under the law."[30]

The preceding cases illustrate the drift of state and local courts in rendering decisions concerning the appropriateness of sterilizing mentally retarded persons. During the early seventies, the entire issue reached national significance as the result of two cases: *Relf* v. *Weinberger,* in 1973, and the *National Welfare Rights Organization* v. *Weinberger,* in 1974.[31] The more celebrated of these was *Relf* v. *Weinberger.* In brief, the plaintiffs included five women: Katie Relf, a 17-year-old girl, who alleged that she had been injected with an experimental birth control drug; her two sisters, Minnie Lee and Mary Alice, who alleged that, in addition to the experimental drug, they were forced to undergo a sterilization operation; Mrs. D.W. and Mrs. V.W., who alleged that they had been coerced by a physician into being sterilized under threat of losing either Medicaid payments relating to delivery services or welfare aid. All plaintiffs alleged that these abuses took place pursuant to programs of the Office of Economic Opportunity and the U.S. Department of Health, Education, and Welfare. They further alleged that when sterilization was first authorized in 1971, there were no guidelines on the procedures to be followed.[32]

New Regulations and Guidelines

The judge dismissed the case because of pending rules to be released by the U.S. Department of Health, Education, and Welfare. He felt the appropriate time to raise issues about proper safeguards for sterilization would be after the new regulations had been approved. In 1974, the case was reheard with the district court declaring that relevant statutes did not authorize federal funding for the sterilization of any person who: 1) had been judicially declared mentally incompetent or 2) was, in fact, legally incompetent under the applicable state laws to informed and binding consent to such an operation because of age or mental capacity. The court permanently enjoined the Department from providing federal funds for this purpose. It also ordered the Department's regulations to be amended to state unequivocally that federal funds would not be provided for purposes of sterilizing a legally competent person without requiring such persons to be advised that no benefits provided by programs or projects receiving federal funds would be withdrawn or withheld by reason of his or her decision not to be sterilized. In April, 1974, the Department issued its new regulations:

(a) State plan requirements. A State plan under . . . the Social Security Act must provide, with respect to sterilization procedures, that all requirements of this paragraph (a) will be met.

(1) Restrictions on sterilization. (i) In addition to any other requirement of this paragraph, no nonemergency sterilization may be performed unless: (A) Such sterilization is performed pursuant to a voluntary request for such services made by the person on whom the sterilization is to be performed; and (B) such person is advised at the outset and prior to the solicitation or receipt of his or her consent to such sterilization that no benefits provided by programs or projects may be withdrawn or withheld by reason of his or her decision not to be sterilized.

(ii) No nonemergency sterilization may be performed unless legally effective informed consent is obtained from the individual on whom the sterilization is to be performed.

(iii) No nontherapeutic sterilization may be performed sooner than 72 hours following the giving of informed consent.

(2) As used in this paragraph:

(i) Informed consent means the voluntary, knowing assent from the individual on whom any sterilization is to be performed after he has been given (as evidenced by a document executed by such individual):

(A) A fair explanation of the procedures to be followed;

(B) A description of the attendant discomforts and risks;

(C) A description of the benefits to be expected;

(D) Counseling concerning appropriate alternative methods; and the effect and impact of the proposed sterilization including the fact that it must be considered to be an irreversible procedure;

(E) An offer to answer any inquiries concerning the procedures;

(F) An instruction that the individual is free to withhold or withdraw his or her consent to the procedure at any time prior to the sterilization without prejudicing his or her future care and without loss of other project or program benefits to which the patient might otherwise be entitled. The documentation referred to in this paragraph shall be provided by one of the following methods:

(1) Provision of a written consent document detailing all of the basic elements of informed consent (paragraph (a)(2)(i)(A) through (F) of this section).

(2) Provision of a short form written consent document indicating that the basic elements of informed consent have been presented orally to the patient. The short form document must be supplemented by a written summary of the oral presentation. The short form document must be signed by the patient and an auditor-witness to the oral presentation. The written summary shall be signed by the person obtaining the consent and by the auditor-witness. The auditor-witness shall be designated by the patient.

(3) Each consent document shall display the following legend printed prominently at the top:

NOTICE: Your decision at any time not to be sterilized will not result in the withdrawal or withholding of any benefits provided by programs or projects.

. . . (3) Reports. In addition to such other reports specifically required by the Secretary, the State agency shall report to the Secretary at least annually, the number and nature of the sterilizations subject to the procedures set forth in this section, and such other relevant information regarding such procedures as the Secretary may request.[33]

Later that year, the American Association on Mental Deficiency issued a related rights statement:

Mentally retarded persons have the same basic rights as other citizens. Among these are the rights in conformance with state and local law, to marry, to engage in sexual activity, to have children and to control one's own fertility by any legal means available. Since sterilization is a method of contraception available to most North American adults, this option should be open to most retarded citizens as well. However, recent reports on cases involving the sterilization of mentally retarded individuals without even the most elementary legal and procedural safeguards raise serious questions concerning the adequacy of current efforts to protect the human and Constitutional rights of such citizens. Indications that retarded persons have been involuntarily rendered incapable of procreation because of presumed social irresponsibility, real or supposed genetic defects, or as a quid pro quo for release from an institution or receipt of financial assistance and social services are deeply disturbing. . . .[34]

In a matter of weeks, the Department's revised rules were well known in both legal and medical communities with a subsequent decrease in sterilization accompanied with a greater recognition of individual rights. States with sterilization laws and the courts began to set forth new criteria for revising sterilization petitions. In a 1981 case involving a 19-year-old mildly mentally retarded female with Down syndrome, the court withheld approval of sterilization because adequate safeguards had not been observed. The court outlined its minimal expectancies:

1. Those advocating sterilization bear the heavy burden of proving by clear and convincing evidence that sterilization is in the best interests of the incompetent;

2. The incompetent must be afforded a full judicial hearing at which medical testimony is presented and the incompetent, through a guardian ad litem, is allowed to present proof and cross-examine witnesses;

3. The trial judge must be assured that a comprehensive medical, psychological, and social evaluation is made of the incompetent;

4. The trial court must determine that the individual is legally incompetent to make a decision whether to be sterilized and that this incapacity is in all likelihood permanent;

5. The incompetent must be capable of reproduction and unable to care for the offspring;

6. Sterilization must be the only practicable means of contraception;

7. The proposed operation must be the least restrictive alternative available;

8. To the extent possible, the trial court must hear testimony from the incompetent con-

cerning his or her understanding and desire, if any, for the proposed operation and its consequences; and finally

9. The court must examine the motivation behind the petition.[35]

Similarly, in 1982, for the first time in Pennsylvania judicial history, a state appeals court held that authorizing sterilization of an incompetent person should consider only the best interests of that person, not the interests or convenience of other individuals, parents, guardian, or society. Accordingly:

1. The judge must appoint an independent guardian ad litem, with due notice of proceedings to be given to all interested parties.
2. The guardian ad litem must have full opportunity to meet with the ward, present evidence and cross-examine witnesses at the hearing.
3. The court must assure itself that a comprehensive medical, psychological, and social evaluation is made of the incompetent.
4. The presiding judge must meet with the individual to obtain his own impressions of competency . . . observ(ing) the person's physical and mental condition.
5. The incompetent should be given the opportunity to express his or her own view on the subject . . . and, albeit not controlling, his or her wishes not to be sterilized must weigh heavily against authorizing the procedure.
6. The court must find that the (incompetent) individual lacks capacity to make a decision about sterilization and that the incapacity is not likely to change in the foreseeable future.
7. It must be established that sterilization is the only practicable means of contraception.[36]

In stark contrast with their judgments of the sixties, judges now became quite conservative, and, in case after case, the parents' petition was denied.[37] And, in 1981, the Supreme Court of Colorado clearly reversed the thinking of yesteryear when it wrote:

It is not the welfare of society, or the convenience or peace of mind of parents or guardians that these standards are intended to protect. The purpose of the standards is to protect the health of the minor retarded person, and to prevent that person's fundamental procreative rights from being abridged.[38]

The new rules and procedures went far in protecting the rights of institutionalized and/or legally declared incompetent mentally retarded minors. At the same time, legally competent, mildly retarded adults could voluntarily seek or approve sterilization.

Changing Attitudes

These noteworthy changes were consistent with the times and the growing recognition and acceptance of mentally retarded persons as citizens and as people with dignity, rights, and abilities. As part of the normalization movement, mentally retarded persons were encouraged and expected to integrate more fully with the mainstream of society. This, in turn, implied greater opportunity for sexual encounters and expression. Thus, sexuality among mentally retarded persons became a recognized reality among parents and professionals alike, but many parents remained or became anxious over their son's or daughter's future. A number of studies during the seventies and eighties demonstrated this persistent concern and continued interest in sterilization. While these investigations often lacked the precision and clarity of variables that one might desire, there appeared to be a relatively common consensus that approximately 60% of the parents sampled favored sterilization.[39] The fundamental concern of parents involved the ability of their offspring to manage marriage and the possibility of children. Yet, one study, reported in 1984, suggested that perhaps an attitudinal change might have been occurring. A survey of 69 parents of primarily mildly mentally retarded adolescent young women found that 54% had never thought of sterilization; 19% had considered the matter but decided against such action; while 26% were seeking sterilization.[40] Only one such operation had actually been performed.

Many within the professional community challenged the need for and desirability of sterilization among mildly mentally retarded persons. Eileen Vining and John M. Freeman, physicians with the Johns Hopkins University School of Medicine and The John F. Kennedy

Institute, simply stated that "sterilization should not be an issue within this population."[41]

From the preceding observations, it can be seen that the opinions of the courts, the parents, and the professional community were not entirely compatible. But what of the people most directly affected?; that is, the sterilized mentally retarded person. What research was available clearly indicated that sterilization of mentally retarded individuals, especially those mildly affected, represented a lifelong traumatic experience.

During the early sixties, Sabagh and Edgerton conducted a follow-up study of 110 sterilized mentally retarded residents who had been discharged from an institution between 1949 and 1958. The results substantiated that almost all the women and most men objected to being sterilized. Their testimony illustrates the long-standing impact of such an operation:

> (A woman) I love kids. Sometimes now when I baby-sit, I hold the baby up to myself and I cry and I think to myself, "Why was I ever sterilized."
>
> (A woman) Naturally, when a girl comes out of the hospital and meets a guy and gets married—well, if she is sterilized, then the guy wonders why she can't have no children. She's either got to tell the guy the truth or lie to him and say, "Well, I had an accident," or something.
>
> (A woman) Two or three times I could've got married but I didn't dare tell the man I was sterilized. How could I tell a man a thing like that?
>
> (Another woman) I was all engaged to marry a man that I really loved. He loved me too, but one day we were sitting and talking with his mother and father and they were saying how happy they would be when we were married and had children. I couldn't do it, because his parents wanted us to have children. When I heard this, I said, "No, I don't never want to get married." I almost told her (the mother) why but I just couldn't bear to tell her.
>
> Another sterilized woman lies to all her friends, telling them that she has a seventeen-year-old daughter. She says, "I feel like being in that hospital wrecked my life. They made it so I can't have kids."[42]

Sabagh and Edgerton also observed, "Women regularly explain the prominent abdominal sterilization scar to their husbands or lovers as the result of an appendectomy. 'When I first had, you know, sex with a guy after getting out (of the hospital), I could just feel him looking at my scar and wondering what it was. I was gonna cover it up, but then I thought that would look bad, so I told him it was my appendix scar. He believed me OK.' This is a nice irony, since sterilization surgery at the hospital was usually described to the patient as an appendectomy rather than what it actually was."[43]

The most famous Supreme Court decision involving sterilization was *Buck* v. *Bell* in 1927, in which Oliver Wendell Holmes rendered the oft-quoted sentiment, "Three generations of imbeciles are enough."[44] In 1981, Stephen J. Gould reported on the two Buck sisters who were the center of that controversy. Neither Carrie nor her sister, Doris, by current standards would have been considered mentally retarded. Carrie never married; but Doris did, and at age 72, she related her experiences. "They told me," she recalled, "that the operation was for an appendix and rupture." So she and her husband tried to conceive a child. They consulted physicians at three hospitals throughout her childbearing years; no one recognized that her Fallopian tubes had been severed. In 1979, Doris finally discovered the cause of her lifelong sadness. "I broke down and cried. My husband and me wanted children desperately. We were crazy about them. I never knew what they'd done to me."[45]

In summary, over the course of the 25 years under consideration, sterilization of mentally retarded persons decreased significantly as their rights were increasingly recognized, but the subject remained one of controversy among some parents and some professionals. In final analysis, the matter of sterilization raised many questions, none of which was answered satisfactorily, including: 1) Who should be sterilized, recognizing the inadequacy of intelligence tests and the lack of knowledge concerning the role of cultural aspects in familial mental retardation? 2) What constitutes reproductive fitness? 3) Are there adequate means of assessing the competency of mentally retarded persons to consent to sterilization? 4) What are the components of parenting ability and how should they be measured? 5) Should mentally retarded persons lacking parental ability be treated differently from normal persons lacking parental ability? 6) If some mentally retarded persons are inadequate parents, is that inadequacy a function of intelligence or training?[46]

Despite the importance of parenting behavior among mentally retarded persons, no relevant research conducted during the 25-year period under review could be located. Thus, there was no evidence to refute the judgment of eminent child psychiatrist and mental retardation expert Leo Kanner, who, in 1949, observed: "In my 20 years of psychiatric work with thousands of children and their parents, I have seen percentually at least as many 'intelligent' adults unfit to rear their offspring as I have seen such 'feeble-minded' adults. I have . . . and many others have . . . come to the conclusion that to a large extent independent of the IQ, fitness for parenthood is determined by emotional involvements and relationships."[47]

OCCUPATIONAL ADEQUACY

One of the greatest unmet needs of adult mentally retarded persons was employment in an open work setting. Regardless of the many gains in special education, an age-old criticism persisted—the schools were failing to provide a functional program or, in other words, too much time was devoted to academic subjects.[48] As early as 1963, Edgar Doll warned against viewing special education as a limited experience and "de-emphasizing [the students'] disabilities and peculiarities."[49] He was vitally concerned with the proper "adultation" of the special child, which he defined as "the process of becoming, or assisting someone to become, an adult, and by implication a mature, competent person who will be relatively self-sufficient and a contributing member of his family and his social community."[50]

Vocational adequacy was also a major concern of the original President's Panel on Mental Retardation. Recognizing that more than 75,000 mentally retarded youth were leaving school each year with a potential for self-support, the Panel specifically called for:

1. Vocational evaluation, counseling, and job placement
2. Training courses in appropriate vocational areas
3. Joint school-work experience programs operated cooperatively by schools and vocational rehabilitation agencies
4. Clearly defined and adequately supervised programs for on-the-job training of retarded workers
5. Employment training facilities for those who require further vocational preparation after completion of the public school program
6. Sheltered workshops for retarded workers capable of productive work in a supervised, sheltered setting
7. Vocational rehabilitation services in conjunction with residential institutions
8. Counseling services for parents to provide them with an adequate understanding of the employment potentials of their children and to provide guidance that will enable them to participate more fully in the rehabilitation process
9. Coordination of vocational counseling with the entire school program[51]

"Every effort," the Panel concluded, "must be made and all available services used, to equip and train the retarded and assist them in finding suitable employment."[52] To implement this mandate, the Panel put forth a series of recommendations:

1. Relate the education and training of mentally retarded persons to employment requirements, especially through expert evaluation and counseling.
2. Advise mentally retarded persons and their employers about the kinds of jobs they can perform and how jobs can be

redesigned so that mentally retarded persons can perform them.

3. Refer mentally retarded persons to jobs they can perform or to training opportunities.

4. Advise mentally retarded persons and their fellow workers and employers about the best ways for working together.

5. Expose mentally retarded persons to work in competitive work situations.

6. Provide mentally retarded pserons with employment in noncompetitive situations if competitive employment is not possible.[53]

Though, in one form or other, some of these proposals would be realized over the next 2 decades, major problems persisted. In 1983, the President's Committee once again complained, "Despite legislation which guarantees a free and appropriate education up to the age of 21, many mentally retarded persons leave school each year lacking even basic self-care and independent living skills."[54]

Among the first persons to respond to the original President's Panel's recommendations was President Kennedy. In 1963, he sent forth an Executive Order to heads of the federal government agencies and departments, which in part stated: "I therefore urge you to examine your operations and determine the extent to which positions in your organization may be filled by the mentally retarded without detriment to the Federal service. When appropriate positions have been identified and become available, I hope you will give full consideration to mentally retarded persons that meet the necessary performance requirements."[55]

Kennedy's order rapidly led to action, which included immediate hirings and modifications in the federal civil service procedures, when necessary. By 1967, the federal government had successfully hired and placed over 3,000 mentally retarded persons in over 60 jobs, ranging from animal caretaker to washman's helper, with a 91% success rate.[56] By 1970, the number of job classifications had grown to over 100 and less than 18% of the tasks had to be restructured. There was a sig-

nificant reduction in the high turnover rates normally associated with such jobs.[57]

Paralleling President Kennedy's efforts, Governor Nelson A. Rockefeller of New York launched a similar campaign for state employment based on three fundamental beliefs:

1. A large percentage of mentally retarded persons when properly trained, can be productively employed in selected civil service positions.

2. Employment of retarded people requires careful job selection and placement similar to that necessary for the employment of all other workers.

3. Mentally retarded persons who are adequately trained, and properly placed and supervised can provide a source of stable manpower for those jobs that usually have a high rate of turnover.[58]

New York identified over 12,000 positions that could be filled by mentally retarded persons, and active recruitment began.

During those years, school systems that emphasized vocational programming in their special classes were successful in placing students. In 1967, for example, the Special School District of St. Louis County successfully trained and placed 81% of its mildly mentally retarded graduates.[59]

Similar to public education for all mentally retarded youth, Congress attempted to expand vocational opportunities through a series of amendments to related acts. The first inclusion of mental retardation under such legislation occurred in 1953, when the Vocational Rehabilitation Act (PL 83-566) mandated state vocational agencies to subsidize vocational rehabilitation for mentally retarded persons.[60] The Act was again amended in 1963 to lower the age of eligibility and to offer greater financial assistance[61]:

Ten percentum of the sums appropriated . . . shall be used by the Commissioner to make grants to colleges and universities, and other public or nonprofit private agencies and institutions, to State boards, and with the approval of the appropriate State board, to local educational agencies, to pay part of the cost of research and training programs and of experimental, developmental, or pilot programs developed by such institutions, boards, or agencies, and designed to meet the special vocational education needs of youths, particularly youths in economically depressed communities who have academic, socioeconomic, or other handicaps that prevent them from succeeding in the regular vocational education programs . . . a special program for the testing, counseling, selection, and referral of youths, sixteen years of age or older, for occupational training and further schooling, who because of inadequate educational background and work preparation are unable to qualify for and obtain employment without such training and schooling.[62]

The most dynamic congressional moves again occurred during the early seventies with the passage of the Rehabilitation Act of 1973 (PL 93-112). This Act included the all important Section 504, encompassed the "severely handicapped," and required a total revamping of the federal-state rehabilitation program. Subsequent amendments in 1978 established a community service employment program, provided for independent living, rehabilitation services for the severely handicapped, and merged rehabilitation and developmental disability acts into one overall legislative package.[63]

Unlike PL 94-142, however, this legislative activity did not result in an explosion of national programs to increase substantially the participation of mentally retarded persons in effective vocational training, placement, and follow-up programs. This was true even though the Rehabilitation Services Administration defined "severely handicapped" as including "those whose retardation is moderate or severe."[64] The service manual excluded only those who were profoundly mentally retarded since they were "generally in institutions where they must receive continuing care and supervision, are incapable of gainful employment, and thus are not suitable candidates for vocational rehabilitation."[65]

Many parents and professionals alike were disappointed in the rehabilitation system for, in their judgment, its priorities and funding base were incompatible with the needs of tens of thousands of mentally retarded persons. And there was evidence to substantiate such allegations. In 1976, for example, the Comp-

troller General of the United States reported to Congress, "State vocational rehabilitation agencies seemed to be serving many persons who were not retarded but were apparently classified as mildly retarded because of maladaptive behavior or other problems. Certain State practices and disability classification procedures appeared to result in the lack of emphasis on or denial of vocational rehabilitation opportunities to the more severely retarded."[66]

The significance of the problem was clearly set forth in one of the period's most remarkable books, *The Economics of Mental Retardation,* published in 1973.[67] According to its author, Ronald W. Conley, an economist and director of the Division of Monitoring and Program Analysis of the Rehabilitation Services Administration of the U.S. Department of Health, Education, and Welfare, the earning losses to the country due to either below or nonexistent production among mentally retarded persons was a staggering $3.4 billion for 1970. He based his financial report on the estimate that there were over 690,000 "economically idle" mentally retarded adults of whom he contended 400,000 could be gainfully employed.

The estimated number of unemployed continued to grow over the years. In 1975, only 21% of the mildly mentally retarded population were believed fully employed.[68] In 1984, the U.S. Department of Health and Human Services estimated "there [were] approximately 3.9 million developmentally disabled persons in the United States. Of these, approximately 2 million [were] over the age of 18. More than 95,000 leave the special education system each year, having received varying levels of vocational training. However, only about five percent of these individuals find employment."[69] Again, the educational system was criticized and held at least partially responsible.

Despite such discouraging statistics and observations, some gains had been made in placing mentally retarded adolescents and adults in viable occupational settings, and unique to the period under review, the more severely affected received increased attention and training. To illustrate, one of the most notable undertakings in training and placing individuals who were mentally retarded throughout most of these years was conducted under the auspices of the Association for Retarded Citizens of the United States. Beginning in 1966, with support from the U.S. Department of Labor, the Association had enabled the training of over 35,000 mentally retarded persons by 1985 and had established a network of 18 field offices throughout the country.[70]

THE MENTALLY RETARDED WORKER

Research throughout this period continued to confirm that differences between mentally retarded and ''normal'' workers were miniscule. Primary reasons for job failure were identical: poor work attitudes and habits, inadequate motivation, and difficulty in getting along with supervisors and/or co-workers.[71]

There were, however, several interrelated characteristics that appeared more prominent among workers who were mentally retarded, especially their inability to communicate effectively, which often resulted in aggressive behavior.[72] To combat this difficulty, many programs emphasized social and work-related communication skills and introduced assertiveness training, an approach intended to enable individuals to express their concerns forthrightly but in a positive manner. Occasionally, there was the problem of physical fatigue among more severely affected persons.[73]

Like all employees, those who were mentally retarded responded well to a pleasant working environment, positive reinforcement, bonuses, self-monitoring, and job enrichment.[74] As with any worker, job satisfaction was reflected in good attendance, dependability, and general efficiency.[75] Through it all, however, many mentally retarded employees remained sensitive to and disappointed in their low occupational status and reduced earnings.[76]

Marc Gold

The preceding comments held true for those who were mildly or severely affected. Much of the credit for defining new directions for the vocational training and placement of the latter group belonged to Marc Gold (1939–1982), an enterprising young scientist and teacher, who died of cancer at the young age of 42.

Trained as a teacher of moderately retarded youngsters, Marc Gold attacked the nature of productivity among such adolescents and clearly demonstrated that they were capable of performing multi-stage, complex tasks such as assembling bicycle brake units.[77] Gold's efforts were guided by a very positive philosophy, one highly consistent with the principles of normalization. He strongly believed that one of the major problems in promoting higher levels of activity among more severely affected persons was the ''basic societal expectancies and previous experiences in the field,'' and there was considerable evidence to support his contention.[78] Alper and Retish, for example, reported in 1978 that teachers' knowledge of an individual's IQ and academic achievement resulted in the underestimation of vocational ability.[79] Also, it was repeatedly confirmed that the correlation between vocational adequacy and measured intelligence was quite limited.[80]

Gold also contended that increasing the competence level of more severely mentally retarded persons would, in turn, increase their acceptability to the public.[81] Again, his belief was confirmed by a number of studies that showed the degree of public acceptance was dependent upon the degree to which the individual could cope with his disability.[82]

Underlying Gold's entire approach was his concept of a balanced relationship between learner and trainer:

A balanced relationship is based on mutual respect of (a) personhood, (b) abilities, (c) rights, (d) time commitment, and (e) personal preferences and feelings. If mutual respect in these areas exists, benevolence, patronization, and artificial concern are excluded. This kind of mutual respect leads to the recognition that both parties have a responsibility to adapt. They must adapt to each other in terms of the learning process and the content, and they must adjust to each other in respect to their human relationship. Quite simply, the relationship between any learner and trainer should rest on the same basis as that for any sound relationship between two persons working together toward a common goal. This basis of respect and recognition allows each to be free to be himself or herself, adapting only for the sake of the relationship or the common goal. This concept is difficult to understand and observe when the learner is a person with profound learning problems, but, to me, the concept is every bit as applicable.[83]

In a few years, others demonstrated that more severely affected persons could perform numerous complex tasks, including assembling cables, chain saws, and drain valves.[84] In brief, the more severely mentally retarded worker could perform in a work setting, which many found to be more meaningful than a program based on social or recreational activities.[85]

THE SHELTERED WORKSHOP VERSUS OPEN EMPLOYMENT

As more and more mentally retarded persons finished school, greater reliance was placed on the sheltered workshop setting, the number of which increased exponentially throughout the country. Though there were variations in the general responsibilities of such workshops, they generally took one of two major roles: 1) evaluation, training or retraining, and placement; and 2) extended enrollment and reimbursement.

The need for accreditation of such facilities became increasingly evident and by the mid-seventies, such standards were developed, primarily under the auspices of the Association of Rehabilitation Centers and the National Association of Sheltered Workshops and Homebound Programs. This, in turn, resulted in the establishment of the Commission on Accreditation of Rehabilitation Facilities (CARF) whose purposes were:

Marc Gold

1. To upgrade the rehabilitation facility movement and improve the quality of services provided to the disabled and disadvantaged.
2. Through accreditation, to offer to the general public and providers, purchasers, and recipients of rehabilitation facility services a single means of identifying throughout the Nation those facilities in terms of concepts and services which are rehabilitation in nature and competent in performance.
3. To develop and maintain relevant standards which can be used by rehabilitation facilities in order to measure their level of performance and strengthen their program.
4. To provide through the accreditation process an independent, impartial, and objective system by which rehabilitation facilities can have the benefit of a total organizational review.
5. To offer to the facility, the community, and the consumers a mechanism of program accountability, and assurance of a continuing high level of performance.
6. To feed back to the facility movement information based upon aggregate findings obtained in site surveys in order to share basic data on common strengths and weaknesses of facility operations.
7. To provide within the voluntary sector an organized forum through which all involved in rehabilitation can participate in standard-setting and program improvement.[86]

Mary Switzer

Like so many vocationally oriented federal activities, this accreditation effort was strongly supported and guided by one of the federal government's most capable bureaucrats, Mary Switzer (1900–1971). Switzer, who took great pride in being a "bureaucrat," served in the federal government for over 50 years, entering federal service with the Harding administration and leaving with that of Nixon. Throughout these years, she devoted herself to promoting the well-being of all disabled persons through vocational rehabilitation and related support services. Known as one of the "radicals of Radcliffe," she pursued her dedication and responsibilities with the true spirit of a Bostonian, noting that her "intellectual activity was influenced by a basic commitment to a revolutionary point of view for accomplishing justice in the world."[87] Though the notions of "severely handicapped" and "independent living" did not appear in federal regulations until the seventies, as usual, she had laid the foundations for such significant modifications by the mid-sixties.

Sheltered Workshops and Normalization

Though sheltered workshops had provided for thousands of mentally retarded individuals, they came under increasing criticism during the late seventies and early eighties. Consistent with the principles of normalization, accompanied by the recognized vocational capabilities of mentally retarded persons, including those more severely affected, many contended that the proper occupational setting was open employment. A typical criticism was that "Mentally retarded workers in sheltered employment settings have little opportunity to realize the benefits of work—self-identity, socialization, or personal autonomy. For many mentally retarded workers, the principle benefit they derive from work is merely the opportunity to leave the isolation of their residences to socialize with other handicapped persons. The wages they receive are far below the level where they might be useful for attaining personal autonomy or community inde-

Mary Switzer

pendence or even for adequately meeting an individual's basic survival needs."[88] In stronger words:

> Such ubiquitous, unnecessarily costly, counterproductive, and antihabilitative practices as placement in sheltered environments, and maintenance in prevocational programs that in fact never lead to real work in the real world should be terminated.[89]

Once again, there was substantial evidence to indicate that perhaps too many individuals were working in a sheltered workshop when, in fact, open employment would prove more normal and probably more financially rewarding. In one of the national studies conducted by the Center for Residential and Community Services of the Department of Educational Psychology at the University of Minnesota, of 701 mentally retarded adults, 18–65 years of age, 61.4% were working in a sheltered workshop as compared to only 6.9% in open employment. Of the mildly mentally retarded group, 36.0% were in the workshop setting as compared to only 9.9% in the open job market.[90]

In fact, some authorities contended that rather than sheltered employment, mentally retarded persons should work in open settings, even without reimbursement. This led to a minor skirmish in 1984. Those who advocated for free employment in a typical job site held that the work experience along with interacting with normal adults would be socially supporting, stimulating, and instructional.[91] In essence, the latter features would be of value in and of themselves: "The hypothesis offered is that the performance of meaningful work in nonsheltered environments in exchange for something other than direct pay is inherently better than functioning in sheltered environments."[92]

This hypothesis, however, was not accepted by many, for, as expressed by G.T. Bellamy and colleagues, "Work without pay in an employer-employee relationship is illegal, and for the protection of all persons with disabilities, should remain so."[93]

In the final analysis, what most mentally retarded adults needed was an opportunity. Experience throughout the years by a number of major corporations that had hired mentally retarded workers proved that such employees were capable and dependable. Their work histories showed no greater absenteeism or work-related injuries than those of their normal co-workers. The W.T. Grant Co., as early as the sixties, encouraged their stores to seek out mentally retarded employees and reported that 77% of those hired were rated good to excellent in their job performance by their supervisors.[94] Similarly, McDonald's undertook a pilot project with the Columbus, Ohio, Program for the Mentally Retarded to determine if mentally retarded adults could be trained to fill fast-food positions and have a better longevity record than other employees. A follow-up study in 1979 revealed that the turnover rate was 41% at the end of the first year, compared to 175% among all employees. All managers who lost a mentally retarded employee requested a similar replacement. A subsequent follow-up study at 24 months showed that the net turnover among mentally retarded employees during the second year was zero.[95]

Armed with affirmative action legislation, Section 504, and various rights declarations, combined with President Reagan's emphasis on employment in the private as opposed to the public sector, federal agencies strongly encouraged nonpublic organizations to hire disabled individuals and offered tax incentives to do so. Under this program, many mentally retarded persons were hired to work in hotels, motels, utilities, manufacturing industries, hospitals and nursing homes, banks, and insurance companies.[96] Again, their job performance was rated highly:

> Food service is an industry traditionally hampered by high employee turnover. Our experience shows that handicapped employees are reliable, faithful, and long-term. (President, National Restaurant Association)[97]

> The developmentally disabled have proven themselves to be honest and dependable workers. They need the jobs we can offer and hospitals need eager and reliable employees. (President, American Hospital Association)[98]

In response to the overall vocational problem, federal agencies concerned with labor, education, and vocational rehabilitation pooled their efforts and shared a common determination to facilitate the placement of mentally retarded individuals in open, competitive employment. To accomplish this task, two techniques were introduced during the eighties: transitional programming and supported employment. Transitional employment simply provided more opportunity for those graduating from school to receive additional training, counseling, placement, and follow-up. A number of such projects proved to be highly successful. One such program, the Manpower Demonstration Research Corporation, provided transitional programming for 18- to 24-year-old mentally retarded adults and placed 42% of them in competitive employment. The major problem was to develop sufficient, appropriate jobs: of over 1,207 employers contacted over a 5-month period, only 4% were willing to provide positions for mentally retarded workers.[99] The public schools also acknowledged a greater role in this area, and in 1984, Massachusetts became the first state to extend the upper age of school eligibility from 21 to 22.[100]

The supported work program, which was a

new innovation, receiving initial official sanction in 1984, was intended primarily for the
more severely affected or multiply handicapped individual. According to those who
worked closely in the development of this
idea, supported work provided:

> a framework for developing the needed range
> of employment services and opportunities. . . .
> Supported employment is wage-generating work
> for persons normally served in day activity, de-
> velopmental achievement, and work activities
> centers. Unlike other employment programs,
> supported employment is designed to provide
> publicly-funded support throughout the period of
> employment, and is consequently intended for
> persons who can only work when such support is
> available. In federal regulations, supported em-
> ployment is defined as "paid work in a variety
> of settings, particularly regular work sites, es-
> pecially designed for handicapped individuals (i)
> for whom competitive employment at or above
> the minimum wage is unlikely; and (ii) who,
> because of their disability, need intensive, on-
> going support to perform in a work setting."

As used by the Department of Education, supported employment has three defining characteristics: (1) It is designed for persons with severe disabilities who are unserved in developing
competitive employment programs, i.e., those
individuals for whom ongoing services are now
made available in nonvocational services. (2) It
is paid work that creates the full range of employment benefits for participants. Supported
employment requires pay for work, and also includes only those settings that offer some possibility of social integration during the work day,
either with co-workers, supervisors, customers,
or others in the vicinity of the workplace. (3) It
involves ongoing, intensive support in the workplace, without which maintenance of the job
would be impossible. The quality of supported
employment options is a function of the extent to
which participants receive the full range of benefits of working, and can be assessed by wage
level, extent of actual social integration, and
security.[101]

In justifying federal support for these transitional programs, the U.S. Department of Education's Office of Special Education pointed
out that approximately 8% of the gross national product was being spent on disability
programs, with most of the money being directed toward "supporting dependence."[102]

Though not directly associated with transitional programming in an official sense, a
great opportunity for continued training and
education became available to many mentally
retarded adults throughout the country. Beginning in the late seventies, a number of junior
or community colleges as well as 4-year
schools began to offer special courses for
those who were mentally retarded. According
to the information provided by one report, the
Victor Valley Community College in Victor-
ville, California, may have been the first
school to pursue this effort. It was the only
college that listed any such offerings in a survey by Gollay in 1977.[103] In a few years,
many colleges were participating, including
all community colleges in the state of Washington.[104] Such programs were consistent
with and perhaps stimulated by the Rehabilitation Act of 1973. This Act, as amended in
1976, provided supplemental funding to post-
secondary schools to serve mentally retarded
and other disabled persons.

Many of the courses offered were intended
to facilitate the transition from adolescence
and high school to the affairs and activities of
adult living, including vocational preparation.
The results were most encouraging, not only
in terms of gaining additional knowledge but
in meeting new people as well. In the words of
several special students enrolled in the New
York State University College at Brockport:
"I've learned about a dozen different things
but what I like best of all is the college kids I
work with and all the new friends I've made."
And, "I never used to do much but watch TV,
but I take this course every semester and I
made new friends and do new things every
Thursday night."[105]

Given the full recognition of the rights and
needs of mentally retarded individuals, combined with new incentives and training concepts, the future employment of mentally retarded persons looked promising. Aiding this
effort was the fact that, according to the U.S.
Bureau of Labor Statistics, there would be a
significant increase in such job opportunities
as nurses' aides and orderlies, janitors, fast-

food workers, and kitchen helpers during the remainder of the twentieth century.[106]

SERVING THE ELDERLY

One of the most dramatic demographic occurrences in American society during the quarter century under examination was the rise in the number of senior citizens, and this was one experience that was shared with those who were mentally retarded. Though forewarned by Gunnar Dybwad in 1962 that governments and agencies should be alert to both the adult and aged mentally retarded person, nothing of significance occurred until the question of aging became a national issue.[107]

As indicated previously, the life span of mentally retarded persons, including those severely and profoundly affected, had increased appreciably over the years. Estimates of how many mentally retarded persons were considered elderly varied from 2% to over 6%, depending upon the minimum age used, which ranged from 55 to 75.[108] While estimates of this nature were important for planning purposes, Gunnar Dybwad again cautioned his colleagues not to set any arbitrary age since premature labeling of a mentally retarded person as elderly was both unwise and often unjustifiable.[109]

Little research was conducted concerning the physiological and psychological aspects of aging among the various subpopulations encompassed under the rubric of mental retardation. Though several studies did follow mentally retarded persons into their middle years, they were intended to assess the subjects' social adjustment rather than investigate any phenomena associated with aging.[110] Yet, they did not present any evidence that at least their mildly mentally retarded, middle-age subjects suffered from any unique signs of physical or psychological degeneration, but, like all people, they were found to suffer some losses in visual acuity and reaction time after age 50.[111]

The exception to the paucity of research on aging and mental retardation involved individuals with Down syndrome. Their condition was of particular interest since many scientists believed that the premature aging associated with Down syndrome could lead to a greater understanding of Alzheimer's disease.[112]

What did typify the aging mentally retarded population was a high rate of institutionalization (50%–60%) and inactivity, regardless of living environment.[113] Hauber and her colleagues, for example, discovered that over 80% of their aging sample "sat around doing nothing."[114] Another study reported that the older mentally retarded adults' activities were governed completely by the primary caregiver.[115]

Though little was actually known concerning the aging process of mentally retarded people, two things were well understood by the mid-eighties: an increasing number of mentally retarded individuals would be living longer, and regardless of the current level of knowledge, community programs and services must be put in place to ensure the older individual as normal and active a life as possible.

The few model programs implemented during the eighties clearly demonstrated that neither institutionalization nor inactivity was justifiable in most cases. Elderly people, even those leaving an institution at an advanced age, were doing well in group homes, and specially designed community services were keeping them active.[116]

As was so often true in the past, local parent associations created excellent programs. The St. Louis (Missouri) Association for Retarded Citizens established a center for older mentally retarded adults that programmatically emphasized health, medical care, and motor needs; integration into other community activities; redirected work experiences; and active leisure pursuits. Similarly, the Peoria (Illinois) Association for Retarded Citizens established a 5-day-a-week full-day program for mentally retarded persons 45–72 years of age, again highlighting developmental instruction, social and leisure activities, health and phys-

An elderly man at home

level; peer socialization opportunities; nutritional counseling and supports for persons living independently or semi-independently; counseling and life planning involvement to aid in orientation to aging; family interaction/small group and family living situations with appropriate accommodations to changing individual needs; exercise and other preventive physical activities for health maintenance; community exposure/involvement; available options for decisionmaking, re: retirement, placement; hospice care; involvement in services and activities included in the generic aging system; personal stabilization, i.e., maintenance of residential placements to minimize movement trauma; home health and homemaker services in both natural and foster family, and small group settings; adult protective services; respite care; outreach and identification to support prospective assessment of service needs.[118]

ical fitness, support services, and productive work.[117]

Such programs were essential, and most states, by the mid-eighties, were planning comprehensive services similar in nature to those outlined by the Committee on Aging and Developmental Disabilities of the state of New York, which noted, "In the broadest sense, the needs of aging and aged developmentally disabled persons are similar to those of many other developmentally disabled or elderly persons: needs for case management, services couched within a well-planned and coordinated interagency framework, services from appropriately trained staff, advocacy, adult protective services, support services, alternative living arrangements, transportation, and social, medical and recreational services. More specifically, however, special needs particular to this population can be identified which have not been adequately addressed through current service system structures. These special needs include:"

. . . access to services to meet increasing medical needs; leisure time/recreational activities appropriate to disability and aging impairment levels; access to day program services which provide skill development and interventions designed to sustain an individual's current skill

Offender Programs

The law, civil and criminal, was a key item on the agenda of the original President's Panel, for it "should be eagerly adjusted to account for the relatively new understanding of the great variety of the causes and configurations of mental retardation."[119] In its expanded report of 1963, the Task Force on Law, chaired by Judge David L. Bazelon, long noted for his activities on behalf of mentally retarded persons, set forth in few words the law's responsibility:

The possibility of doing justice, and thus fulfilling the function of the law, turns upon at least two conditions: correct appreciation of the relevant circumstances, and a suitable range of possible dispositions. Failing the first, justice is truly blind; failing the second, it is impotent. Justice is blind if it does not inquire into the significance of mental retardation as a relevant circumstance, and impotent if it has no dispositional variants suited to the conditions it finds.[120]

Many participants in the legal process as well as social observers readily concluded that, in the words of the Task Force, justice for mentally retarded persons was indeed both "blind" and "impotent." Dennis Haggerty, parent, attorney, and one of the field's early legal activists, was particularly concerned about the general failure of the legal system to recognize the special problems of the retarded defendant: "Simply put (in almost all cases) a mentally retarded suspect who has been charged with a crime cannot understand the charge, cannot tell his side of the story, and cannot help his lawyer defend him. If no one realizes he is retarded, this greatly hinders his chances for a fair trial."[121] Given these circumstances, the legal rights of the mentally retarded defendant were "often ignored, disregarded, or simply violated."[122]

Others elaborated on the problems of the mentally retarded defendant, including:

1. An adequate defense may never be formulated if the attorney relies solely on an incompetent person-to-stand-trial plea.
2. An attorney may choose to plea bargain on the client's behalf either as a matter of experience or out of fear that a trial would prove too difficult. Mentally retarded people are said to be especially susceptible to accepting agreements made through plea bargaining.
3. Mentally retarded people who have been accused of criminal acts may more readily confess to the crimes, whether or not they committed them.
4. Mentally retarded people are said to be unable, frequently, to represent their own interests in court and, therefore, are particularly vulnerable to coercion and to convictions.[123]

In 1972, Fred Krause, who admirably served for many years as the executive director of the President's Committee on Mental Retardation, summarized the situation by noting that "juvenile offenders, especially the retarded, present special problems for law enforcement agencies. Retarded juveniles alleged to have committed an offense are often faced with legal procedures which they do not understand. They go through arrest, trial and conviction, dealt with by people who have little or no understanding of their mental handicap."[124] The same applied to the adult offender according to Marsh, Friel, and Eissler in 1975.[125]

As acknowledged by Krause and others, there was question as to the knowledge and ability of judges, attorneys, and law enforcement officials to deal effectively, yet realistically, with mentally retarded persons—and

with good reason. Reichard and his associates surveyed 36 state court administrators in 1980, discovering most were not providing preservice training and/or inservice training for judges or lawyers concerning the mentally retarded defendant-offender.[126] Others reported similar findings.[127] Schilit also found that while his sample of judges, lawyers, and members of a city police department had some understanding of mental retardation, they remained "confused and uncertain about how to deal with this population in a professional manner."[128]

During the seventies, a number of groups and agencies undertook a series of projects to inform law enforcement officials as to the nature of mental retardation. To illustrate, the Tennessee Association for Retarded Citizens developed a manual entitled "The Mentally Retarded Offender and The Law Enforcement Official." Like other similar brief pamphlets prepared for such purposes, it covered in few words a basic description of mental retardation, classification of levels, causes and prevention, distinctions between mental retardation and mental illness, characteristics of the mentally retarded offender, and various agencies that might be of assistance. Though such efforts did not constitute extensive training programs, they nevertheless were reasonably successful in at least sensitizing the officer of the law or the court as to mental retardation. In many instances, the information received was not as immediately applicable as perhaps desired since mildly mentally retarded offenders were often extremely "streetwise," and the extent of their intellectual limitations was not immediately evident.[129]

MENTALLY RETARDED OFFENDERS AND THE COURTS

Numerous well-informed persons were also concerned that the rapidity of the process from booking to incarceration was so short, frequently because of easily obtained confessions, that often mentally retarded persons were denied a jury trial, which, according to the research of Gibbons and associates, might well have acted in their favor. In their study, most of the 72 male and female college students believed that mental retardation "should relieve a defendant of some culpability and, therefore, the jurors would take this into account when assigning a verdict."[130] By inference, a jury might be more kindly predisposed to the mentally retarded offender than would a judge.

To compound the problem, many courts had considerable difficulty in distinguishing between mental retardation and mental illness and, in turn, assigning respective levels of competency and responsibility, despite the famed *Durham* decision of 1954. In that instance, the U.S. Court of Appeals of the District of Columbia drew a distinction between "mental disease" and "mental defect":

> We use "disease" in the sense of a condition which is considered capable of either improving or deteriorating. We use "defect" in the sense of a condition which is not considered capable of either improving or deteriorating and which may be either congenital, or the result of injury, or the residual effect of a physical or mental disease.
>
> Whenever there is "some evidence" that the accused suffered from a disease or defective mental condition at the time the unlawful act was committed, the trial court must provide the jury with guides for determining whether the accused can be held criminally responsible.[131]

The Court's statement was intended to move beyond the legally ingrained *M'Naghten* insanity ruling, which, in essence, stated "that understanding the nature and quality of the offense and knowledge of right and wrong as to the act charged was the test to be applied."[132] The U.S. Court of Appeals was not alone in its opinion: the highest court of the state of Washington also addressed the *M'Naghten* ruling as, "archaic, inadequate and not scientific and that it should be abandoned for a more enlightened and psychiatrically-sound test."[133]

In 1972, the American Law Institute adopted a position reflective of the *Durham* decision:

> A person is not responsible for criminal conduct if at the time of such conduct, as a result of mental disease or defect, he lacked substantial capacity either to appreciate the criminality of

his conduct or to conform his conduct to the requirements of law; the terms "mental disease or defect" do not include an abnormality manifested only by repeated criminal or otherwise antisocial conduct.[134]

Old traditions, however, die hard, and jury "guidelines" were most difficult to provide. Thus, despite all good intentions, mentally retarded persons continued to be apprehended, tried, and often found guilty or innocent according to the *M'Naghten* ruling:

> 1960—A 16-year-old Virginia youth with an IQ of 58, accused of killing a man was acquitted on the ground of "feeble-mindedness." Judge Backus called upon a little used section of the Virginia Code and found that mental deficiency was an absolute ground for acquittal.[135]
>
> 1980—Eddie, a 43-year-old man with an IQ of 61, had served several prison terms for holding up donut shops after which he was always caught while he was walking down the street eating his treats. After serving several sentences for such offenses, he was released, and within a week, he was once again arrested. This time he held up a bank; police caught him standing outside on the sidewalk counting his loot. He received another three-year term in adult corrections.[136]
>
> 1980—Ron, a 33-year-old man in the mild to moderately retarded level of retardation, was serving five years in a correctional institution for holding up a bank. The police had no difficulty in apprehending the offender: he had signed his name to the hold-up note.[137]
>
> 1983—In Illinois, an 18-year-old mildly mentally retarded man with an IQ of approximately 66 was convicted of a brutal murder and received an 80-year extended prison term. The case was appealed to a federal court, with the defendant's attorney arguing that his client's limited mental capacity rendered him unable to formulate the mental state necessary to merit an extended sentence. The District Court reviewed the situation as well as the question of mental capacity and found that the lower court had considered the defendant's mental ability and had weighed the conflicting testimony on this issue. The state court's factual findings, based primarily on a clinical psychologist's testimony that the defendant could appreciate his criminality and could conform to legal requirements, were presumed to be correct.[138]

In the final analysis, there was always the question of fairness. In the words of J.J. Maloney, ex-convict and dedicated penal system reformer:

> The same crime should carry the same penalty for the rich and the poor, black and white, the educated and the ignorant. Contemporary theory, however, is going in the other direction. The way we do it now, a mildly retarded defendant from a poor family, with little education, is punished much more harshly than an honor student from a good family. The honor student is seen as a potential asset to society, the other defendant as more likely to be a lifelong liability.[139]

THE PRISON EXPERIENCE

The historical debate of the most appropriate institutional setting for the mentally retarded offender persisted throughout the period. Correctional administrators frequently contended that the prison was a totally inappropriate environment: "Mentally retarded [persons] are victimized in the traditional correctional setting." "There is a definite need for specialized remedial programs." "Incarceration should be used as a last resort." "The Department is not equipped to meet the needs of this particular group." "Resources are spread too thin—there is a definite need for a separate facility to house them." "Correctional administrators should have more access to community resources."[140] Problems of security, safety, and discipline were most frequently mentioned regarding institutional management of the mentally retarded prisoners.

Administrators of institutional programs for mentally retarded persons continued to believe that their setting was equally inappropriate, since other residents were rarely in a position to defend themselves, physically and psychologically. As one superintendent observed: "Committing those retarded offenders to my institution is like letting gangsters into a kindergarten."[141]

Researchers and social commentators tended to agree that prisons were, in fact, undesirable settings for four primary reasons:

1. Other inmates ridicule and take advantage of the mentally retarded offender.

2. Normal prisoners often vent their feelings of anger, hostility and frustration on mentally retarded persons, thus exposing them to physical brutality, rape, and extortion.

3. Correctional personnel lack the knowledge and skills to deal therapeutically with the intellectually limited prisoner.

4. Habilitation and rehabilitation programs and services were rare.[142]

Specific examples tended to support their judgments:

> The prisoners "call him names and heap verbal abuse on him. They call him stupid. Then he yells at them since he can't really talk very well, and they hit him; then he kicks them. He is gentle, but the others don't understand him, so they fight." Upon investigation, it was learned that the youth was incarcerated in a small steel cubicle that had only a bunk, toilet, and sink. His cell was like all the others on his cellblock. He remained in this cell all day except for one-half hour during which time the guards permitted him into the yard. His records revealed repeated references to his violent outbursts, but not one reference to an habilitative plan.[143]

"The World of Timothy," a specially written article published in a prison journal, described the life of one mentally retarded individual. The following excerpts illustrate his sad existence:

> Timothy waddles down the aisle and out of the dorm. No one walks with him. Prisoners don't like him. "He's a stupid, funky mother ...," they say of him. He walks down the covered concrete walkway to the messhall. The other prisoners walk in a straight line. Not Timothy. He staggers in and out of line. He doesn't really look drunk or sober. He looks as if he is trying to get his bearings, like each step is a difficult task. He's awkward and clumsy. "Man, get yore ole crazy . . . in that line 'fore that man writes ya' . . . up," the prisoner behind tells him. "You're sickening, you know that!" another voice chimes in. Timothy says nothing. He just grunts, mutters something under his breath, and keeps walking to the messhall.
>
> Once in the messhall, Timothy sits alone at his table. He doesn't see the other prisoners moving past him to take a seat elsewhere. He doesn't hear the incessant hum of clanging spoons, excited conversation, and coarse laugh-

ter. His brain cannot comprehend more than one thing at a time. He just looks at his tray. He eats steadily, gulping his food in huge bites. He spills bits of it on either his lap or the table. He doesn't care. The only true methodical thing in this world he does is eat. He eats as deliberately as a brain surgeon uses a scalpel. He doesn't care what it is; his world isn't confused by too many likes and dislikes. He simply eats whatever is put on his tray.

The prisoners return to their dormitories. They have thirty minutes before reporting to work. Some prisoners make their beds while others sweep around theirs. Not Timothy. His bed is disheveled and rumpled. One side of his bunk sags horribly from the bulk of his enormous weight. He sleeps fully clothed, at times urinating and defecating on himself during his sleep. He smells terrible. He hasn't washed his face, hands, brushed his teeth, shaved, or combed his hair.

"Make up your bed, Timothy," the guy in the next bunk tells him.

"No, I don't want to." He half-whines when refusing to do something. He continues to roll another Bugler [a cigarette].

"Look, you already got two writeups."

"I don't care. I ain't doing nothin'."

The other prisoner moved out of his bunk like an attacking leopard. With one motion, he grabbed Timothy by the hair of the head and slapped him hard across the face. The slap sounded like a .22 bullet shot in a quiet room. An animal silence struck the dorm. No one said anything. The other prisoner pushed Timothy down on the bunk and straddled him. With Timothy's arms pinioned under his knees, he repeatedly slapped him across the face, occasionally punching him with a closed fist alongside his head.

"Yeah, you gonna do something, you filthy sonuvabitch," the other prisoner said. "I'm sick of yore dumbass crap. You smell like a pig—you are a pig. All you do is waste good oxygen!"

No one made an attempt to interfere. It wasn't their business. Besides, it's not the first time Timothy has been beaten up. He's constantly punched, slapped, or abused by other prisoners, particularly when he eats sardines. When he has money, he spends most of it on sardines. He eats them straight out of the can with his fingers. He discards the empty cans under his bunk. The funk of his natural body odors and the soured sardine cans leaves the dormitory smelling like a West German cheese factory. Timothy makes it easy for the rest of the prisoners to hate him, to want to abuse him. Anytime anyone has to strike

out with frustration, he is a convenient punching bag.

Not only do the prisoners hate him, but the guards hate him as well. He doesn't follow orders too well. He certainly can't be given more than one at a time. He moves slow and slovenly. He's personally dirty and his living area is always filthy. That infuriates the guards. They're constantly giving him disciplinary reports. But it doesn't change Timothy. He continues to do as he does every day. The guards think he is stupid, always good for a good joke.

That is the nature of Timothy's prison world. It's a bleak and lonely world. A world of the unloved and misunderstood. A world where a look shatters the expectation of a moment and a curse can cut like a sharpened knife. Timothy must survive in a world where the weak either perish or serve. He is mentally deficient.[144]

Despite all arguments to the contrary, a number of prisons and institutions developed special programs for mentally retarded offenders. One penal program discussed rather frequently during the sixties involved the "Patuxent concept."

The Patuxent Institution and the Indeterminate Sentence

In order to understand the significant departure from most previous penal practices, it is necessary to return to 1951 when the legislature of the state of Maryland passed a law that, in essence, imposed upon psychiatry and its allied professions a responsibility for treating and rehabilitating a wide range of mentally disturbed and developmentally disabled offenders. The law read:

A defective delinquent shall be defined as an individual who, by the demonstration of persistent aggravated antisocial or criminal behavior, evidences a propensity to criminal activity, and who is found to have either such intellectual deficiency or emotional unbalance, or both, as to clearly demonstrate an actual danger to society so as to require such confinement and treatment, when appropriate, as may make it reasonably safe for society to terminate the confinement and treatment.[145]

In a series of articles, Harold M. Boslow, psychiatrist and director of the Patuxent Institution, Jessup, Maryland, discussed the approach and the facility.[146] First, however, he extended his interpretation of the defective delinquent as one who is "basically amoral, shares no social values with others, and is flagrantly hedonistic and opportunistic. His crimes are of impulse, sometimes of a compulsive, neurotic or prepsychotic nature, and usually involve inadequate planning at best. Defective delinquents include some organic and congenital mental defectives, epileptics, sex offenders, drug addicts, compulsory neurotic criminals such as fire setters and kleptomaniacs, and some severely amoral people who cannot be integrated into a usual prison routine."[147]

When the Patuxent Institution opened in 1955, it was under the administrative authority of the Department of Corrections; however, in 1960, the institution was removed from the Department of Corrections, granted autonomy, and assigned to a psychiatrically trained administrator. Its new goal was to rehabilitate.

Major decisions concerning the program as well as the fate of the individual prisoner were vested with six people, each representing a different professional discipline or prison service, including: psychiatry, psychology, social work, education, vocational training, inmate classifications, and security. The primary emphasis of the program, though it involved education and vocational training, was psychotherapy. To this end, various psychotherapy groups were established; in 1961, there were 16 such groups, each consisting of 8–10 "patients." One unit consisted of mentally retarded offenders.

In addition to psychotherapy and the use of positive and negative rewards, a four-tier structure was implemented. As each prisoner's behavior and conduct improved, he advanced through the four-tier structure and ultimately was paroled. The four tiers were distinguished primarily by the number of privileges permitted at each level. Such privileges included extensions past "lights out," kinds of commissary items that could be purchased, type of job, freedom of movement within the institution, and increased personal responsibility. Some programs, such as vocational

training, were initiated at the third level of the tier system. Unfortunately, mentally retarded prisoners did not readily progress through the system and subsequently did not fare as well as others. As Harold Boslow reported, "it is of some theoretical interest that those inmates who remain residents of the first or lowest tier level are characteristically younger in age, have somewhat lower IQs, are often Negroes, and typically come from homes that were broken or disorganized from infancy on and had a malignant psychological climate."[148]

Some aspects of the program earned praise, such as its emphasis on habilitation and treatment as opposed to security and restraint, and its reliance on an interdisciplinary approach to decision-making. Other aspects were negatively criticized, especially indeterminate sentencing, the limited opportunities for mentally retarded individuals within the tier system, and the failure to protect the defenseless from the aggressive.[149]

Indeterminate placements or sentences resulted in constant problems, which aggravated both jurists and professionals. Difficulties arose in two ways: first, if a defendant were found incompetent to stand trial, he or she could be remanded to a mental hospital or similar facility until "cured" and/or ready to stand trial. Second, a person, as illustrated by the Patuxent procedure, could be sentenced to a facility for an indeterminate period of time until ready to resume a nonoffensive, productive life in the community. To many individuals, this represented a violation of a person's basic rights, and though this problem was not entirely resolved, several critical court decisions were rendered that altered the course of events. Several of these decisions would be called upon during the seventies when judgments were made concerning the adequacy of institutional commitment procedures and programming in residential facilities for mentally retarded persons.

First was *Jackson* v. *Indiana,* 1972, which involved Theon Jackson, a mentally retarded deaf mute with a mental age of less than 6. Theon could not read, write, or otherwise communicate, with the exception of a limited sign language ability. At age 27, in 1968, he was charged with having committed separate robberies of two women. Acting in a manner consistent with state statutes, the original state court found that the defendant lacked comprehension sufficient to make his defense and ordered him committed to the Indiana Department of Mental Health until such time as the Department could certify to the court that the defendant was sane. Jackson's attorney filed a motion for a new trial, contending that Jackson was not insane. After several state court appeals, the U.S. Supreme Court overturned the initial decision, stating that "Indiana cannot Constitutionally commit the petitioner for an indefinite period simply on account of his incompetency to stand trial on the charges filed against him."[150] The court held that such indefinite confinement was a violation of both due process and equal protection, and that a person committed as incompetent may not be held under such a commitment more than the reasonable period of time necessary to determine whether there is a substantial probability of his attaining competency in the near future. If no such probability exists, the court held, such an individual must be either released or committed in accordance with civil procedures applicable to those not charged with crimes.

In reaching this decision, the U.S. Supreme Court referred to another landmark case, *Baxstrom* v. *Herold*, 1966. In this instance, the U.S. Supreme Court held that "equal protection does not require all persons to be dealt with identically, but it does require that a distinction made have some relevance to the purpose for which the classification is made."[151] This conclusion not only supported contemporary thinking that not all people must be treated equally, but it also emphasized that labels placed on people tend to legitimize certain behaviors toward them on the part of the state.

Soon after the *Jackson* determination, the Supreme Court rendered a decision directly involving the Patuxent Institution and its practice of indefinite stays:

> Respondent contends that petitioner has been committed merely for observation, and that a

commitment for observation need not be surrounded by the procedural safeguards (such as an adversary hearing) that are appropriate for a final determination. . . . Were the commitment for observation limited in duration to a brief period, the argument might have some force. But petitioner has been committed "for observation" for six years, and on respondent's theory of his confinement there is no reason to believe it likely that he will ever be released. A confinement that is in fact indeterminate cannot rest on procedures designed to authorize a brief period of observation.[152]

These decisions, in turn, were supported by the U.S. Supreme Court in 1966 in *United States* v. *Ewell:*[153] indefinite commitments to a mental institution violate a defendant's rights to a speedy trial, and lead to the presumption of prejudice to the defendant. *Rouse* v. *Cameron,* 1966, went one step further: even when hospitalization was involuntary, treatment rather than punishment was required. In brief, the Supreme Court frowned upon the indiscriminate use of indeterminate sentencing and declared that if one were committed to an institutional setting, even on an involuntary basis, treatment must be available.[154]

COMMUNITY SERVICES AND PROGRAMS

While the Patuxent model was not emulated by others, some states did attempt to modify prison programming. South Carolina, for example, created a special learning unit for developmentally disabled offenders at the Kirkland Correctional Facility; North Carolina set aside three separate prison facilities, known as the Sandhills Youth Complex, to meet the rehabilitative needs of mentally retarded offenders.[155] Similarly, a few public residential facilities established programs, the most notable of which was the Developmentally Disabled Offenders Unit at Camarillo State Hospital, California. This unit provided a variety of therapeutic experiences, including socialization effectiveness training, individual counseling, transactional analysis, and behavior modification. Its goal was community placement.[156]

How to offset the numerous deficiencies in the legal system observed during the early sixties challenged many a creative mind. Richard Allen, for example, professor of law in the George Washington University Graduate School of Public Law and director of the Institute of Law, Psychiatry, and Criminology, proposed an "Exceptional Offenders' Court." Partially modeled after the juvenile court, Allen sought to have a legal system perpetuated that would be sensitive to persons "inadequately equipped to meet certain responsibilities of adulthood" because of intellectual deficits and that, at the same time, would "have as a primary objective the welfare of retarded persons coming under its wardship, rather than imposing punishment for criminal offenses."[157] Further:

> The court should have broad supervisory powers over all persons properly coming under its jurisdiction, including authority to commit exceptional offenders to appropriate specialized institutions for indeterminate periods. Institutionalization should, however, be based upon a finding of dangerousness to self or to others, and such orders should be subject to periodic review. Where the offender is capable of living in society under supervision, probation should be available, making full use of group therapy, special education, and other techniques.
> The court should also have authority to confer powers of guardianship (of the person, of the estate or both) on the probation officer, where the exercise of such powers is deemed necessary or desirable. Where a guardian had previously been appointed for the exceptional offender by another court, the exceptional offenders' court should have authority to make the appointed guardian subject to its supervision, or to terminate the prior order of guardianship.[158]

While, as already noted, some of the suggestions would not be approved in light of subsequent court decisions, there was no question that Allen was seeking a substantially different approach to dealing with the mentally retarded adult offender, one that was both humane in essence and therapeutic in intent.

Such a court system, however, would also have the effect of removing a mentally retarded person from the mainstream of the legal system, and philosophically, there were those who objected. Catherine C. Morrow, director of the King County (Seattle, Washington) Legal Center spoke out against the notion of a special offenders' court for several noteworthy reasons: "I think this is a very inappropriate idea because the Constitution applies to everybody. I think that if society accuses you of a crime, you should have an open forum, you should have representation, and you should have the right to have it proven that you did it. I think so many of these things, like the special offenders' court and some (I stress "some") of the diversionary systems that have been proposed leave out that part. They assume that you probably did it. It's the same syndrome that was wrong with the juvenile court."[159]

In her statement, Morrow commented on "diversionary systems," which referred to a number of approaches intended to assist the court in meeting the needs and challenge of mentally retarded offenders. These took varied forms. In 1975, the University Affiliated Program at the Georgetown University Child Development Center established what became known as the Georgetown Adolescent Intervention Team (GAIT). Its purpose was (and remains) to "identify developmentally disabled and other handicapped young people involved with the District of Columbia Juvenile Justice System with the ultimate goal of helping to secure appropriate treatment for these individuals through a process of interdisciplinary evaluation followed by treatment plan recommendations."[160] Similarly, in 1976, a Special Offender Council, a private, nonprofit, community-based program, was organized in St. Louis, Missouri. This effort included not only the training of law enforcement, judicial, and criminal justice personnel, but also the participation in a diversionary treatment program that would act as a referral source for the St. Louis city and county adult judicial systems. The major goal of the diversionary program was to assist each client in making a successful and independent reintegration into the community.[161] The Mentally Retarded Defendant Program, established in Florida in 1977, provided the court system and the Department of Health and Rehabilitation Services with competency recommendations as well as advice on residence and treatment. This program, like the others, was successful in averting the total need for incarceration in either an institutional or prison setting. Of 39 probationers studied, 39% went into a home; 15% to a group home for mentally retarded persons; and 18% into a transitional community facility for offenders. Only 28% required some form of residential service, be it in a mental retardation facility, a mental health institution, or a state prison.[162]

Though these various groups and organizations provided the courts with a comprehensive diagnosis of an alleged offender, this did not mean that a person would be excused of committing a crime simply on the basis of intellectual limitations. This was quite obvious in several cases in which mild degrees of mental retardation, while noted, did not reduce potential culpability. In *Louisiana* v. *Brown*, 1982, the defendant was charged with first-degree murder. An effort was made to have the court declare him incompetent to stand trial for such charges on the grounds that he was mildly mentally retarded (IQ 65) and that such retardation rendered him incapable of assisting in his own defense. The court rejected the argument that mental retardation and incompetency were essentially one and the same and stated that a competency determination would have to be made in this case "with specific reference to the nature of the charge, the complexity of the case, and the grounds of the decisions with which he (the defendant) was faced."[163] In *Kansas* v. *Moss*, 1982, an appeals court upheld the conviction of a mentally retarded arsonist who claimed it was improper for the trial judge to allow into evidence a part of his confession because of his limited mental capacity. Despite the accused's low intelligence (IQ 63), the court contended that he had sufficient verbal skills to respond to the officer's questions and to waive his *Miranda* rights. The court stated that "moderate retardation and a low intelligence quotient do not of themselves vitiate

the ability to knowingly and intelligently waive Constitutional rights and make a free and voluntary confession."[164]

Model Programs

While some programs offered both diagnostic and consultancy services as well as diversionary activities, a number of programs were established primarily for the purposes of aiding the mentally retarded person on probation. One of the earliest, well-recognized efforts was initiated in 1972 in Pima County, Arizona. Experience in that program soon indicated that mentally retarded persons on parole could successfully participate in an open community but that they also presented some unusual problems. They often could not comprehend the conditions of probation or counseling instructions imparted in the typical manner. Four techniques proved of particular value: 1) environmental manipulation, 2) supportive relationships, 3) clarification, and 4) interpretation. Though categorically there was nothing unusual about this approach, it did require the strict observation and assurance that the mentally retarded probationer clearly understood what was required.[165] A program developed in Corpus Christi, Texas, yielded similar results. They again reported probation could be highly successful but that the mentally retarded participants required constant supervision and the repetition of expectations.[166]

Such programs proved critical not only because they offered alternatives for juvenile and adult offenders but because they increased the probability of a mentally retarded individual being considered for probation. Research conducted in the early sixties frequently reported that mentally retarded offenders because of poverty, educational and vocational limitations, inadequate legal counsel, and/or prevailing stereotypes were not often given the opportunity for probation.

The same held true for parole; over the years mentally retarded persons were often considered ineligible for parole. This was illustrated by a study conducted by the George Washington University in 1969, which found that the average prison stay for mentally retarded offenders was 6.9 years compared to only 3.9 years for nonretarded offenders.[167] But again, new programs could and did alter such biases. One such effort was conducted by the Office of Adult Probation and Parole in the Lancaster County Pennsylvania Court of Common Pleas. An adult probation officer and a guidance-centered case manager, each with a caseload of about 60 mentally retarded offenders, were highly successful in their efforts. Recidivism for the normal population of the paroled caseload in Lancaster County was 18%; the rate for mentally retarded offenders was only 3%. In addition to reducing recidivism among mentally retarded offenders, the program satisfied several other objectives, such as increasing the awareness of the criminal justice community as to the existence and special needs of mentally retarded offenders and increasing the use of generic community and other social services by offenders.[168]

As indicated previously, a wide range of community options were becoming available for the mentally retarded offender. One unique, experimental day program was "Our House," established during the seventies in Nashville, Tennessee. In developing this program, which was based on the principle of normalization, the designers took into consideration three demonstrated facts related to the mentally retarded offender. First, their home life had not provided the experience necessary to develop a wide repertoire of skills needed to get by socially, educationally, or vocationally. Second, outside the home, the boys had experienced failure so often that they preferred to avoid work and also felt they had no control over what happened to them. Third, being basically more alike than different from other people, they did not like to be ignored, were likely to repeat actions that "paid off," and learned from experience. It was intended that the house provide a setting where the rules were simple; the boys could learn new ways of succeeding with people, school subjects, and work tasks; and they would be provided opportunities that "offered quick wins and slow losses."[169] In addition, staff on occasion served as a buffer between the boys and the police, courts, and employers. Though the project encountered some difficulties in development and funding, after 2 years, it was concluded that most of the mentally retarded participants would attend programs in their home community and would do so without undue disturbance or disruption. In a positive setting, they not only would become increasingly competent in academic and social skills, they could also prove effective teachers and behavioral change agents for their peers.[170]

In addition to the wide range of programs developed, mentally retarded offenders were found to respond positively to a variety of therapeutic techniques. Friedman reported a highly successful instance of intensive individual psychotherapy; Scheer and Sharpe reported social group work during a special summer camping program was effective; and a number of studies reported that behavior modification programs also could be employed to advantage.[171]

Many of the programs just presented were intended to deal with an existing problem. A number of knowledgeable persons were equally concerned with developing broad-based community programs aimed at not only treatment but prevention as well. Frank Menolascino of the Department of Psychiatry at the University of Nebraska Medical Center, Omaha, outlined a rehabilitation-correctional service needs schema for mentally retarded offenders that took into consideration prevention, advocacy, and treatment:

1. PREVENTION
   A. Family and individual support of potential offender
      (1) Enhancement of home environment
      (2) Counseling; educational or vocational
      (3) School testing programs
      (4) Specialized educational and vocational program
      (5) Parent education and counseling
      (6) Consultation to public school or vocational training personnel
   B. Public and professional education
      (1) Teacher education
      (2) Inservice training

(3) Professional consultation
(4) Law enforcement training
(5) Strengthen law enforcement and community relations
(6) Encourage public participation in prevention and control

2. ADVOCACY
   A. Personal
   B. Legal
   C. Legislative
   D. Therapeutic
   E. Public information and education

3. TREATMENT
   A. Early treatment intervention
   B. Thorough evaluation and prescriptive treatment
   C. Individual and group therapy
   D. Parent and/or spouse counseling
   E. Spectrum of specialized residential services, e.g., structured-correctional hostels
   F. Follow-up supportive services to the family
   G. Continuing educational, vocational, and socialization experiences.[172]

In 1983, some of these ideas were incorporated into Nebraska's Special Offender Project, which placed an emphasis on implementing a comprehensive, community-based response to illegal, offending behavior exhibited by developmentally disabled offenders who had no historical pattern of violent behavior. Key to the approach was the development of an "Individual Justice Plan," modeled after the individualized education program in intent and formulation. Ultimately, the goal was to establish a network of community services and opportunities for nonviolent offenders, thus improving the quality of their lives, and hopefully, avoiding the need for incarceration.[173]

The emphasis on treating the mentally retarded offender had changed significantly during the seventies, reflecting a greater concern for normalization and programming in the open community. While creativity and innovative thinking were quite evident, public support and funding were not. Denkowski and associates, for example, received responses from 49 states that indicated that only 922 residential beds existed for this population on a nationwide basis and only 150 more were to

be expected by the end of 1983. Of the total number of beds, only 185 were established in the community.[174]

PROGRAMMING FOR THE EMOTIONALLY DISTURBED MENTALLY RETARDED PERSON

One of the most vexing problems of the quarter century under review was attempting to program adquately for those mentally retarded persons who were considered to be mentally ill or at least extremely difficult to manage, especially when such behaviors involved self-abusiveness or physical aggression against others or property.[175] While ameliorating such behaviors had been a primary treatment goal for decades, all too often psychologists and psychiatrists were reluctant to practice their skills with those who were mentally retarded. Recognizing the severe crisis in this area, in 1962, the original President's Panel called for a renewed campaign to reattract psychiatrists to the field.[176]

Though physicians and "alienists" played an important role in the early development of special programs for those who were mentally retarded, they began to lose interest in the field by the twenties, a loss that continued to grow throughout the "Golden Age of Child Guidance."[177] A number of reasons for this disinterest were advanced, including the belief that psychoanalytically based psychotherapy required at least normal intelligence as a prerequisite for successful treatment, the absence of appropriate professional training and experience, the supposition that brain injury precluded psychiatric treatment, an unconscious bias against such practices since the physician's role was to cure, and an acceptance of society's generally low esteem of mentally retarded persons.[178] At the same time, the vigorous rejection of the "medical model" by parent organizations and many in the professional community did little to encourage the participation of psychiatrists. This was particularly true as institutions made the transition from custodial facilities to developmental training centers.

In response to the urgings of the President's Panel, several psychiatric organizations re-examined their positions and came forth with rather grandiose statements intended to elicit greater participation of psychiatrists. In 1966, for example, the American Psychiatric Association reviewed its activities and once again supported efforts to elicit greater participation of psychiatrists, noting that "mental retardation . . . has always been viewed as an area of special interest with psychiatry," and that psychiatrists believed the mentally retarded child "stands in the same need of love, affection, security and personal significance as do all children."[179]

In 1979, the Group for the Advancement of Psychiatry noted that psychiatrists could be of particular value in treating mentally retarded persons and their families since "they were conversant with the psychobiology of human disease, with basic theories of personality development, and with the vital concepts of fixation and regression, both in individuals and their families. They are trained in crisis intervention, pharmacotherapy and psychotherapy. They can deal with maladaptions and psychoses of physical illness, organic brain syndromes, congenital defects, and dementia. The range of neurotic disorders, psychoses, and psychosomatic conditions that psychiatrists see in the general population also exist in retarded people. The psychiatrist is a physician who bridges medical and nonmedical areas in individual development and family life problems."[180]

In resolution, the Group for the Advancement of Psychiatry encouraged psychiatrists at least to assume the role of consultant to the family, home, community, and institution. They also recommended the inclusion of mental retardation in formal training programs, including specific reference to the multidisciplinary approach and working with various agencies.

Unlike the Group for the Advancement of Psychiatry, and in contradiction to the experiences of psychiatrists more familiar with mental retardation, such as Frank Menolascino and Joseph Wortis, the American Psychiatric Association called for greater leadership of the medical community, rather than relying on the multi-disciplinary or transdisciplinary approach: It is "incumbent on the American Psychiatric Association to strengthen its own leadership role in the field of mental retardation, and to work with other medical specialists and physicians generally toward more concentrated concern with retardation."[181] They also contended that "the treatment and care of the retarded can efficiently be made part of the total network of community mental health services."[182] This strong emphasis on medical dominance received further support from the National Association of State Mental Health Program Directors in 1965 when it concluded:

> The care and treatment, including education, training and habilitation of the mentally retarded needs overall socio-medical and psychiatric direction, . . . and this organization is on record as favoring the care and treatment of the mentally retarded, and the prevention of mental retardation, as part of the practice of medicine, including obstetrics, pediatrics, and neurology, all of which can best be managed and coordinated by that branch of medicine which deals with human behavior, namely psychiatry.[183]

As indicated, those more familiar with mental retardation did not support the notion that all should be vested with the psychiatrist or medical community:

> In summary, one can say that although psychiatry has an important and indeed essential contribution to make to the field of mental retardation, it cannot claim the right to control and leadership. The traditions of service in this area have not been psychiatric, the interest of psychiatrists in this field, certainly in the U.S.A., has in recent decades largely disappeared, and the technical demands of the work do not call upon the special skills or training of the psychiatrist. Other medical specialists, such as pediatricians, neurologists, physical therapists, [and] family physicians, have equal rights, and indeed any physician willing to commit his interest and learn the skills can assume leadership. Though many professions and disciplines are needed, the center of gravity of the mental retardation field should be in education, with all of the other disciplines in accessory relationship. Administrative policy based on recognition of this fact

would promote clarity and enrich services in the field.[184]

In the final analysis and regardless of the pleadings and positions of major psychiatric associations, mental retardation continued to have little appeal to all but a few psychiatrists, such as Stella Chess, Frank Menolascino, Herbert Grossman, Ludwik Sysmanki, Joseph Wortis, Norman Bernstein, and George Tarjan. In view of their interest in mental retardation, these psychiatrists often made major contributions to many areas having an impact on the field. George Tarjan's career in mental retardation is an excellent example.

GEORGE TARJAN

A native of Hungary, George Tarjan graduated from the medical school at the University of Budapest in 1935. He practiced internal medicine in that country for 3½ years before emigrating to the United States in 1939. Following a few years' experience in several institutional settings, Tarjan became the director of Clinical Services at the Pacific State Hospital in Pomona, California, where he was promoted to superintendent in 1949, a position he held for nearly 16 years, abandoning his original intention to go into private practice. During his tenure at that facility, he actively pursued with many groups and organizations the need to become interested in mental retardation as well as to recognize the importance of looking at mental retardation in a multicultural perspective. He was also instrumental in promoting one of the earliest and finest research centers, which took a critical role in the study of demographics and mental retardation. In 1965, he assumed a series of leadership positions at the University of California School of Medicine, including the directorship of the Division of Mental Retardation and Child Psychiatry in that university's Neuropsychiatric Institute. In addition to his many duties as an administrator, researcher, and educator, he served as vice-chairperson of the original President's Panel on Mental Retardation and as a member on the first President's Commit-

tee on Mental Retardation. His contributions were recognized by many organizations, including the Joseph P. Kennedy, Jr. Foundation. In 1984, he was still active, constantly promoting the welfare of those who were mentally retarded.

AN ABSENCE OF INTEREST

Psychiatrists were not the only ones to avoid practicing with persons who were mentally retarded. This apparently was the response of many, if not most, psychologists and other clinicians engaged in psychotherapy. After noting that numerous psychotherapeutic techniques had proven effective with troubled mentally retarded persons, Matson, in 1984, sadly concluded, "It is ironic . . . that the treatment of psychotherapy in these persons [i.e., mentally retarded] has not occurred more frequently in recent years. In fact, the use of psychotherapy with persons who are mentally retarded has actually decreased to the point where many clinicians interested in mental health consider treatment of those with mental retardation well outside their purview."[185] Thus, the problem of coping with and treating emotional problems among mentally retarded individuals remained the primary responsibility of parents, teachers, institu-

George Tarjan

tional aides, and the family physician, all of whom often lacked adequate understanding and training.[186]

MODEL EFFORTS

Despite the rather gloomy outlook, some progress was made. A few programs such as the Psychiatric Training Program at the Walter E. Fernald State School, with personnel from the Harvard Medical School, did offer training to psychiatrists, and included such topics as:

Modern Educational Approaches to the Educationally Handicapped
Speech Development in the Retarded
Biology of Mental Defect
Research with Neonates Observing Innate and Cultural Differences
Drugs and Learning
Social Systems in Total Institutions
Runaway Girls at Training Schools
Societal Aspects of Intellectual Defects, Stigma and Deviance
Intact Personality Development in an Institution for the Retarded
Conceptualizations of Intelligence:
    Special and General Factors
    Test Design
Operant Conditioning and Behavior Shaping with Training School Inpatients
Specific Reading Defects
Behavioral and Neurologic Examination of the Young Child
Deranged Memory and Research with Memory Enhancing Drugs
Family Diagnosis
Genetics in Retardation
Psychotherapy with Individuals
Group Therapy
Syndromes and Therapy of Minimal Brain Damage
Reaction of Mothers to Rearing Retarded Children
Psychopathology of Expression, Speech and Art
Psychosurgery of Aggressive Behavior
Drug Therapies with the Retarded
Seminars: Ego Development of the Retarded
    Early Ego Substrates—Oral Phase and Neurologic Defect
    Anal Phase and Dependency of Intellectually Handicapped
    Oedipal Phase—Individuation and Sexuality
Adolescent Development
Adult Life and Work
Aging and Senescence[187]

Also, a number of universities and hospitals established clinics for working with disturbed mentally retarded children and their families. Programs such as the Developmental Evaluation Clinic of the Children's Hospital Medical Center of Boston were highly successful and set forth good models for other facilities to emulate.[188] A number of mental hospitals established units to serve this particular population, often emphasizing outpatient treatment or an early return to the community. Institutions for mentally retarded persons gradually turned their limited resources and programming efforts to meet the needs of their disturbed residents more effectively and humanely.

Finally, and of utmost importance, during the late seventies and early eighties, communities began to establish special homes and services for the more difficult-to-manage individual.[189] Such programs, adequately staffed with well-trained persons, including expert consultation and training from psychiatrically oriented resources, proved most successful. This was aptly demonstrated by the Vineland Treatment Program in Wisconsin, which was predicated on three basic premises: 1) a small home-like environment is important, 2) treatment should be designed to give the individual as much self-control and determination as possible, and 3) each participant should have an individual plan of treatment and training. Relying on the assistance and training of staff by psychiatrists or psychologists from the local mental health clinic, a group home for six disturbed mentally retarded residents was established. Reporting on 15 participants, Luecking noted that only 2 had to be reinstitutionalized while 8 went on to live in regular group homes; the remaining 5 persons were still in the specialized home. Careful screening, training, and support of staff were believed to be key ingredients to success.[190] Other model programs were evident throughout the country—in Rhode Island, there was the Behavior Research Institute; in Kansas, the Teaching Family Model; in Illinois, the Institute for the Study of Developmental Disabilities; and in Massachusetts, the May Institute.[191]

In the final analysis, however, the few model programs available could not begin to meet the need. Subsequently, too many mentally retarded persons with behavioral problems continued to reside in an institution, mental institute, or correctional facility when a community alternative may have proven more normalizing and effective.[192] This situation was widely recognized by both community programmers and institutional administrators, and once again, beginning in the early eighties, providing for the "dually diagnosed" became a top priority.

PARENTS AND THE FAMILY

The text to this point has concentrated on mentally retarded persons and their service needs from infancy to advanced age; yet, they were also an integral part of a total family structure and some attention should be devoted to parents and siblings. Fortunately, in many respects, the situation for parents changed radically during the period under review.

In the early sixties, many of the previously held negative misconceptions concerning parents, their reactions, and abilities were summarily dismissed. No longer were parents viewed as perpetually guilt ridden, overprotective, rejecting, and, in general, unable to cope with their mentally retarded offspring. Nor were they subject to continued treatment as a "pathological client or patient."[193] Numerous laws and regulations, such as the Education for All Handicapped Children Act of 1975, legally provided parents with a clear and important decision-making role.

Common sense, the collective voice of the Association for Retarded Citizens of the United States, and research all contributed to a heightened sensitivity to the individuality of each family situation. Particularly valuable in changing attitudes among professionals were the classic studies by Bernard Farber and his colleagues, which unequivocally demonstrated that a host of factors influenced parental response, including sex of the mentally retarded person, sex of the parent, mother's

view of the child's degree of dependency, age of the child, socioeconomic status, sex of normal siblings, family tension, religion, mother and grandmother relationships, number of close friends, ethnic background, and clarity of family role expectations.[194]

This does not mean that parents of mentally retarded children did not experience stress that might be expressed in terms of shame, guilt, ambivalence, depression, sorrow, defensiveness, self-sacrifice, denial, overprotectiveness, and mourning.[195] The 1982 survey of parents conducted under the auspices of the President's Committee on Mental Retardation reconfirmed that they occasionally became overwhelmed with feelings of "disbelief, guilt, fear, anger, confusion, panic, and helplessness."[196] Such feelings and reactions were not, however, debilitating to the extent that parents could not function with genuine love and affection for their offspring or seek out the best for them.[197] In fact, research consistently demonstrated that "most families have adequate personal resources to cope with the problems of having a retarded child and are able to provide an environment for the proper development of their normal children."[198]

Perhaps James L. Paul offered the best summary of families with a mentally retarded or other developmentally disabled member:

> Each family has its own strengths and resources, hopes and dreams, problems and needs. There are big families and small ones, relatively stable and well-integrated families, and some that are chaotic and disorganized; there are families that are happy most of the time, and some that are most often unhappy and sad. There are families with normally developing, healthy children, and some with children who need special attention and care. No two families are alike. Each family, with or without a handicapped child, is unique and has its own particular needs, as well as abilities to meet those needs.
>
> There is no "typical" family of a handicapped child. Families of handicapped children have in common only the additional pressures imposed on family life by the presence of the handicapped child. The handicapped child and the family interact, each affecting the growth and development of the other. The interactive nature of child and family development exists

whether or not a handicapped child is present. If a handicapped child is present, the experiences may be qualitatively different, with different demands on the family and different opportunities for growth. . . . The impact, whether positive or negative, varies with individual families and depends on both the child and the family.[199]

The only negative research note was that better educated parents tended to reflect lower levels of acceptance.[200] Whether this related to social concerns or personal ambitions was not acertained, but the adequacy of their "education" was suspect.

Further, reactions such as anger, confusion, and helplessness often reflected what Menolascino and Egger called the "reality crisis," or that which arises from the daily practical problems and frustrations associated with raising and supporting a mentally retarded child or adult and attempting to ensure adequate services.[201] The notion of "reality crisis" was supported by a number of researchers. Unusual caregiving responsibilities, related financial difficulties, and the absence of relief from child rearing could produce considerable stress and anxiety.[202]

Additionally, as various services became available for children and adults who were mentally retarded, parents were no longer limited to the two choices of either retaining their children at home, hoping to receive some form of special education, or placing them in an institution. The combination of new programs, better counseling and training, and legal protection of rights gave parents a powerful voice in guiding the course of their child's development.

In addition to the parents, the needs of normal siblings were also recognized, and in 1967, the Association for Retarded Citizens of the United States started its Youth ARC movement, which in a decade had over 25,000 members who shared their experiences and difficulties and provided innumerable volunteer services. Throughout the years, other sibling groups were formed, for in the words of one young woman, "Sibling groups and sibling networks are very important. It's hard to relate to someone you feel can't understand."[203]

In brief, the mentally retarded person was no longer viewed as an entity separate from the family unit which, in turn, often required a comprehensive series of services, as graphically illustrated in Figure 6.1.[204]

As concerns the adequacy of services available during the early eighties, the survey of parents previously noted identified a number of unfulfilled needs, including:

Early and sensitive medical management as to diagnosis, realistic expectations as to future development, and guidance to the array of available in-the-home services in the early months and years of their child's life.

Education of physicians so that they better understand mental retardation, the need for service support to parents in dealing with the emotional stress they experience, and the responsibility of linking parents to appropriate resources.

Respite services wherein the parents can leave their child with trusted and knowledgeable caregivers so that they—the parents—can avoid the burnout which often comes from 24 hour [days], seven day weeks of work and worry. Respite care was viewed as a clear way to support the family in lieu of long-term (and costly) out-of-the-home placements.

The presence of integrated preschool and educational-development services within the mainstream of their communities. They also stressed the need for educational services which will further the social-adaptive aspects of their children's ongoing developmental needs.

The ready availability, preferably mandated by law, of programs that teach the young adult to work: from sheltered workshops, through job-stations-in-industry, to—as much as possible—independent job opportunities. If these work opportunities are not available, parents feel their son or daughter's previous educational experience, "would, for all practical purposes, have been wasted."

A wide range of residential alternatives (e.g., adoptive homes, foster homes, group homes, independent living arrangements, etc.) when the primary family is no longer capable of caring for their mentally retarded member. A minority of the parents interviewed noted that the traditional institutional setting would meet their family's needs. The majority of the parents wanted residential alternatives in the primary family's community so that the continuity of family relationships would not be adversely affected; and their son or daughter would continue to live within the mainstream of community life.[205]

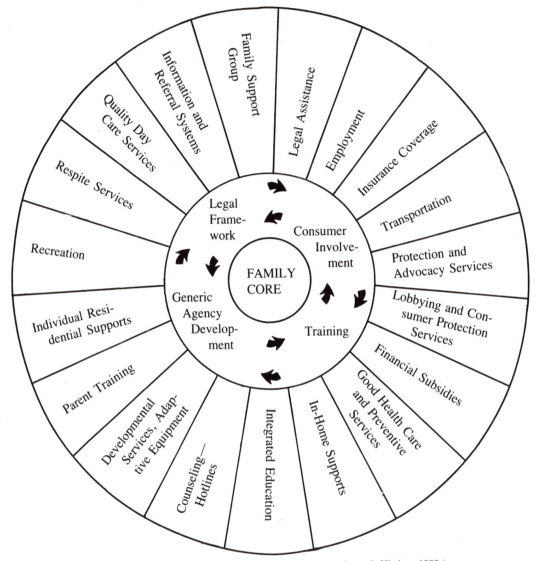

Figure 6.1   Circle of family resources. (Adapted from Loop & Hitzing, 1980.)

Thus, from the parents' perspective, there were many empty spaces in the continuum of care required by child and family. In terms of adult services, whether it be from the standpoint of the mentally retarded individual, the family, or the professional community, what gains were made over the years were extremely limited.

Chapter
7

INSTITUTIONS AND DEINSTITUTIONALIZATION

A SHIFTING EMPHASIS

B Y THE SIXTIES, it was becoming increasingly apparent to the professional community in general and to the public on occasion that too many institutions serving mentally retarded persons, at least those publicly supported, were substantially failing to meet even the most elemental human needs of the people they were intended to serve. In brief, there was a great and growing dissatisfaction with the quality of life experiences and programs proffered to tens of thousands of mentally retarded persons living in state facilities. One of the most pervasive condemnations during the sixties and early seventies related to dehumanizing conditions and the absence of individual dignity. As defined by the Association for Retarded Citizens of the United States:

DEHUMANIZATION IS:
Being treated as a prisoner—instead of as a resident.
Being called "Hey, you." Being shouted at when a normal voice would do the job.
Having only certain days for bathing and shaving.
Being behind locked doors.

Being subjected to standards set for the least capable resident.
Not being able to obtain dentures, eye glasses or hearing aids.
Being expected to "Participate," even in childish games, regardless of your feelings in the matter.
Having "State School" stamped on your clothing.
Being brought to school by a sheriff or police officer.
Having to ask for personal items.
Being treated and referred to as a diagnosis.
Having 40 room-mates.
Having mail and packages opened and censored.
Being discussed as if you were not present.
DIGNITY IS:
Privacy in dressing, in the lavatory and in the showers.
Receiving encouragement and an occasional word of praise.
Being recognized as an individual—with individual needs.
Having someone care enough to listen to you.
Having a place of your own for personal belongings.
Being able to see yourself in a full length mirror and having clothes that look [nice] and fit appropriately.

221

Being told "why" about things affecting your activities and welfare.

Being paid appropriately for work performed. Having an opportunity to contribute your ideas or suggestions.

Having money in your pocket for ordinary purchases.[1]

Nor were the residents particularly happy, as illustrated by a 1961 study conducted by Robert Jacobs, who received responses from 149 females, varying in IQ from 50 to 80 and in life ages from 14 to 32, with a minimum institutional residence of 3 months. Most of the replies were highly critical: 61% said, "institutional life made them worse;" 82% said, "they keep you too long;" 40% said, "a girl is forgotten when sent here"; and 41% said, "the attendants are just as bad as the girls." Although the chief yearning seemed to be to get out of the institution, 80% conceded that "people here did a lot of good things for the girls."[2]

EARLY ASSESSMENTS

Given these circumstances, it was not surprising that residential care received prime attention from the original President's Panel on Mental Retardation in 1962. The Panel assessed the status of residential programming in the United States in the following words:

The quality of care furnished by State institutions varies widely, but from the standpoint of well-qualified and adequate personnel and the availability and use of professional services and modern, progressive programs, the general level must be regarded as low. In large State institutions, the normal problems of administration and care are compounded by overcrowding, staff shortages, and frequently by inadequate budgets. In face of these difficulties, it is to the credit of State authorities and superintendents that there are a number of good, and a few first-rate institutions. The population of State residential facilities runs the gamut from a few hundred to more than 5,000; but on the average, each institution is caring for 350 patients over stated capacity. . . .[3]

It should be noted that the problem of overcrowding was based on the then-rated bed capacities which, by subsequent standards, often allowed little more than standing room. It was difficult for persons entering the field in the late seventies and early eighties to realize the extent of overcrowding that then existed, primarily because residential programming was inappropriately viewed as an "alternative": that is, institutions served as an educational alternative to unresponsive school systems, as an orphanage for unwanted or abandoned children thought to be mentally retarded, and as a detention home for youngsters and adults whose minor infractions normally would not have resulted in extrusion from the community. This interpretation of the role of institutions combined with political pressure in some states resulted in many mentally retarded persons being inappropriately admitted to residential facilities. This practice not only denied the rights of such individuals, even in those days, but also resulted in long waiting lists of youngsters in dire need of critical, and otherwise unavailable services, behavioral or medical. In many, if not most, instances, rated bed capacities were simply ignored. As described by an exasperated L. Klebanoff, "Officials who solemnly declare the financial inability to provide increased facilities will plead for admission of a worthy case. As the worthy cases spill over into the corridors, the already inadequate personnel-to-resident ratios become impossible and there is little the staff can do except fold laundry and keep a fire watch."[4]

Overcrowding and inadequate staffing levels were only two of the concerns expressed by the Panel. It also sought significant changes in attitudes toward residents, programming, and administrative practices:

1. Every institution, including those that care for the seriously retarded, should be basically therapeutic in character and emphasis, and closely linked to appropriate medical, educational, and welfare programs in the community.
2. Every institution has some unique quality or potential that can be developed for the benefit of the entire field. No institution should be regarded as merely "custodial"; those

caring for the profoundly retarded offer unusual opportunities for the application of new methods of treatment and care, and for research.

3. Diagnosis and evaluation should take place before admission and be followed promptly by treatment when the patient is received.

4. The institution should extend its services beyond the traditional boundaries of its own campus and reach out to assist the patient and his family before his actual admission; this facilitates visits by parents and friends after admission and is an important factor in early adjustment.

5. Flexible admission and release policies and outpatient programs similar to those of a hospital or school are essential in meeting the needs of the retarded and their families.

6. The goal of every residential program should be the elimination or amelioration of as many symptoms as possible and the achievement of independent, semidependent, or even a sheltered extramural life for every person under care in accordance with his potential. This can be accomplished only by a devoted staff with a variety of professional skills and a competent administration. Both can be rendered impotent, however, without the support and leadership of a competent and interested State department or board of trustees. Indoor and outdoor recreation; social activities; programs of physical fitness; opportunities for self-expression through music, painting, worship; and other creative outlets are essential aspects of sound institutional programs.

7. No child or adult should remain in residential care any longer than necessary. Regular and frequent reevaluations must be scheduled to reveal any possibilities that may have been developed in his community and to determine whether the individual himself has reached the point where he may profit by some other form of care.

8. If and when the child or adult is ready for return to the community, adequate resources and services for his support should be made available. It may not be wise or possible for some to return to their own families, hence the importance of developing foster or boarding home placements, or homes for small groups similar to those in several European countries.

9. Responsibility for the care of persons returned to the community should not be relinquished by the institution until assistance is assured from some other source; efforts should be made to see that community services are made available to him before he leaves. . . .[5]

The Panel also desired to add residential facilities to accommodate the more than 50,000 children and adults waiting for such services and to replace obsolete facilities for another 50,000 persons. The Panel members further recommended that future residential facilities not exceed a total rated bed capacity of 500.

According to the philosophical premises of the eighties, the Panel's position would be interpreted as extremely conservative, if not regressive; however, at that time, it represented a major step forward, frequently producing heated debate over both the need for programming for more severely affected individuals as well as the proposed size limitation of future institutions. To illustrate, as late 1958, the board of directors of the Association for Retarded Citizens of the United States adopted a progressive policy that future institutions should house no more than 1,500 persons.[6]

Often overlooked in the pursuant arguments were the Panel's subtly presented closing recommendations, based on the Scandinavian experience:

The mission to the Netherlands sponsored by the Panel made the following recommendations, among others, which are germane to the future of residential care in the United States.

1. Impetus should be given in the United States to the development of a wider range of diversified residential arrangements for those retarded persons who, for whatever reason, cannot live with their own or foster families; i.e., small units designed in program and structure to meet different needs.

2. Emphasis should be directed to the development of group homes in urban and suburban areas for small homogeneous groups of retarded persons who can use the various community opportunities for work, recreation, and education.[7]

In 1967, Lyndon Johnson's recently created standing President's Committee on Mental Retardation submitted its first report in which it assessed the situation in far less modest terms than did the original Panel, proclaiming many of the country's institutions were "plainly a disgrace to the nation and to the states that operate them. . . ."[8] The President's Committee had ample evidence to support their contention: 60% of the institutions were overcrowded; the staff:resident ratio, considering the 7-day work week, was 1:16 despite the fact that 82% of the population was moderately or more severely affected; many of the staff—direct care and professionals alike—were inadequately trained, with the latter often failing to possess even basic licensure; many trainable and educable mentally retarded youngsters were not receiving an appropriate education; there was a constant position vacancy rate of 30%; and attitudes toward residents and their programming varied significantly, not only between but among institutional administrators, professionals, and attendant personnel.[9]

Much of the problem—but certainly not all—rested with the gross underfunding of residential facilities. The per diem rate was $5.57 in 1964; even taking into consideration the then-purchasing power of the dollar, this amount was wholly inadequate.[10] For comparative purposes, the $5.57 per day rate was approximately one-half the amount devoted to tending animals in a zoo.[11]

Attempts to answer the question, "Who was responsible for the deplorable conditions found in many institutions?" resulted in considerable finger pointing, spanning a number of directions. Many individuals and organizations condemned the medical profession and its model of programming, as already reviewed. Physicians, however, were not the only culprits. In 1972, Eleanor Elkin, reflecting the position of the Association for Retarded Citizens of the United States, included:

Parents, who fear possible retaliation against their child if they speak too loudly; parents who fear their child in the institution may be forgotten as attention is drawn to community residential programs. . . .

Bureaucracy, with its power struggles and empire building. Bureaucracy, whose members must nervously defend their jobs and their territory. . . .

Civil Service regulations that protect incompetents and rigidly prevent the hiring of some desirable candidates; a reluctance to abandon outdated philosophies; and

Public belief in the necessity of mass care for retarded persons.[12]

Regardless of the reasons and responsible persons, the net effect was disastrous for many residents, especially those more severely affected who had little or no programming. Though somewhat long in text, the description of one ward (actually a 10-year-old, high-priced building) of severely and profoundly mentally retarded, ambulatory adult males by MacAndrew and Edgerton in 1964 typified the situation found in all but a few institutions at that time:

First Impressions of Ward Y
Words, however well-chosen, cannot begin adequately to convey the combined sights, sounds, and smells which initially confront and affront the outsider on his first visit. What follows is at best an approximation.

Despite the size of Ward Y, the simultaneous presence of its 82 patients evokes an immediate impression of overcrowding. Additionally, most of the patients are marked by such obvious malformations that their abnormal status appears evident at a glance. One sees heads that are too large or too small, asymmetrical faces, distorted eyes, noses, and mouths, ears that are torn or cauliflowered, and bodies that present every conceivable sign of malproportion and malfunction. Most patients are barefooted, many are without shirts and an occasional patient is—at least momentarily—naked. What clothing is worn is often grossly ill-fitting. In a word, the first impression is that of a mass—a mass of undifferentiated, disabled, frequently grotesque caricatures of human beings.

Within moments, however, the mass begins to differentiate itself and individuals take form. A blond teen-ager flits about rapidly flapping his arms in a bird-like manner, emitting bird-like peeping sounds all the while. A large Buddha-like man sits motionless in a corner, staring straight ahead. A middle-aged man limps slowly in a circle grunting, mumbling, and occasionally shaking his head violently. A shirtless patient lies quietly on a bench while a small patient circles about him furiously twirling a cloth with his left hand. A blind youngster sits quietly digging his index fingers into his eyes, twitching massively and finally resolving himself into motionless rigidity. A red-haired patient kneels and peers intently down a water drain. A portly patient sits off in a corner rocking. Another patient rocks from a position on all fours. Still another patient, lying supine, rolls first to one side then to the other. Several patients walk slowly and aimlessly around, as if in a trance, showing no recognition of anyone or anything. A microcephalic darts quickly about, grinning, drooling, and making unintelligible sounds. An early-twentyish mongol wearing an oversized cowboy hat strides about with his hands firmly grasping the toy guns in his waistband holsters. Others smile emptily, many lie quietly, still others from time to time erupt into brief frenzies of motion or sound.

A few patients approach the newcomer to say, "Daddy," or "Wanna go home," or to give their name or to offer some paradoxical phrase such as "tapioca too, ooga, ooga." One or another patient may attempt to touch, pull, or grasp the stranger, but such attempts at interaction are usually of the most fleeting duration. Others may approach and observe from a distance before moving away. Most pay no attention to a new face.

In the background, strange and wondrous sounds originate from all sides. Few words can be distinguished (although many utterances, in their inflection, resemble English speech); rather, screams, howls, grunts, and cries predominate and reverberate in a cacophony of only sometimes human noise. At the same time, loud and rhythmic music is coming out of the loudspeaker system.

There are, finally, the odors. Although many patients are not toilet trained, there is no strong fecal odor. Neither is there a distinct smell of sweat. Yet there is a peculiar smell of something indefinable. Perhaps it is a combination of institutional food and kitchen smells, soap, disinfectant, feces, urine, and the close confinement of many human bodies.

In sum, Ward Y and its inhabitants constitute a staggering visual, auditory, and olfactory assault on the presupposedly invariant character of the natural normal world of everyday life. Here, to a monumental degree, things are different.[13]

What MacAndrew and Edgerton described in words, a photographer for the *Philadelphia Inquirer* captured on film: the endless hours of meaningless meandering in an environment devoid of spirit and experience.

A few years later, in 1966, Burton Blatt, with the assistance of Fred Kaplan, a freelance photographer, compiled a photographic essay on institutions entitled, *Christmas in Purgatory*. The text and photographs, which received national attention, depicted deplorable conditions found in four institutions located in three eastern states. With typical literary flair, Blatt introduced the first chapter with a quote from Dante: "Abandon all hope,

"A World Alone," as captured by a photographer for
the *Philadelphia Inquirer*

ye who enter here.''[14] In brief, the publication confirmed Blatt's prefacing judgment that ''there is a hell on earth, and in America there is a special inferno''—the institution.[15] Yet, Blatt did end his essay by praising a positive residential setting; again, the variability among institutional services was quite evident.

In view of the preceding comments and assessments, it was not surprising that the subsequent President's Committees on Mental Retardation would continue to place a high priority on promoting the ''improvement in standards of residential service for the retarded and to develop a national policy on improved living conditions for those mentally retarded citizens who live in public and private residential facilities.''[16] To assist in realizing its intentions, the President's Committee sponsored several conferences in the late sixties and early seventies to set forth new directions for residential services. In 1969, for example, the President's Committee called together representatives from the American Association on Mental Deficiency, the International League of Societies for the Mentally Handicapped, the National Association for Retarded Citizens, and the National Association of State Coordinators of Programs for the Mentally Retarded. Of these groups, the latter was relatively new, being organized in 1963 to represent states in the development of national policies on mental retardation, and to facilitate communication among and between state directors.[17]

The results of the conference were set forth in the 1970 publication, *Residential Services for the Mentally Retarded: An Action Policy Proposal*, which emphasized maximizing human potential and independent functioning:

> The prime purpose of residential services for the mentally retarded is to protect and nurture the mental, physical, emotional, and social development of each individual requiring fulltime responsible services. Inherent in this commitment is the responsibility to provide those experiences which will enable the individual (1) to develop his physical, intellectual, and social capabilities to the fullest extent possible; (2) to develop emotional maturity commensurate with social and

intellectual growth; (3) whenever possible, to develop skills, habits, and attitudes essential for return to contemporary society; and (4) to live a personally satisfying life within the residential environment.[18]

In addition, the group addressed the need to give greater recognition to the legal rights of the individual resident; to create an atmosphere of warmth and affection, dignity, and respect; to establish greater interaction with community agencies; to eliminate any form of dehumanizing conditions; to place constraints on excessive use of physical restraints, drugs, and isolation; and to give both resident and family a greater voice in institutional programs and practices.

A few years later, in November 1973, the President's Committee called upon another group to propose policy statements regarding residential facilities. In this instance, representatives of the National Association of Superintendents of Public Residential Facilities for the Mentally Retarded were requested to set forth their thinking. This organization was also relatively new, being organized in 1970 to promote: 1) the continuous improvement of residential programs, 2) the interests of severely and profoundly mentally retarded persons, 3) the development of community services, 4) public awareness of the role and significance of residential services, and 5) to collaborate with other professional agencies and national organizations in the development and implementation of comprehensive community and residential services for mentally retarded persons.[19]

The Association prefaced its positions with the clear acceptance of the fundamental rights of the mentally retarded person outlined in the Declaration of General and Special Rights of the Mentally Retarded, previously reviewed, and the President's Committee's 1970 statement concerning the role of institutions. The Association clearly supported the recent emphasis on community programming; efforts toward deinstitutionalization and institutional reform; the utilization of residential staff services and facilities to aid in the development of community programs essential to deinstitutionalization; and "strongly encouraged the federal government to establish and maintain a constant, flexible system of financial assistance to community and residential services providing for developmentally disabled persons."[20] In essence, the Association's position statements were entirely consistent with current trends and thinking, accepting the role to provide for an increasingly smaller number of individuals who would prove to be among the most difficult to treat, program, or manage.

Both these reports, as well as other similar statements, such as those released by the Association for Retarded Citizens of the United States, were far overshadowed nationally by one of the period's most consequential and successful publications, *Changing Patterns in Residential Services for the Mentally Retarded.*[21] As noted previously, contributors to this document included not only several outstanding leaders from the United States but also N. E. Bank Mikkelsen (Denmark), Karl Grunewald (Sweden), Bengt Nirje (Sweden), David Norris (England), and Jack Tizard (England). This document represented much more than another condemnation of the current status of institutional programs in the United States. It brought to the nation's attention the normalization principle and the Scandinavian experiences in providing for a wide range of service models often based on significantly different philosophies than those held by many in the United States. Few documents of the quarter century under consideration had greater impact.

As implied, the primary mood of the country during the sixties and early seventies was one of reform—institutions simply had to provide better services for those for whom they were responsible. One step in this direction was to develop standards of care, programming, and administration.

ACCREDITATION STANDARDS

For years, the American Association on Mental Deficiency had been concerned with the conditions found in many institutions, and,

following a series of pilot efforts, published a set of standards in 1964. These dealt with such areas as management services; personnel training and staff development; physical plant; and records, reporting, and research.[22] Over the next few years, 134 state institutions were evaluated by visiting teams composed primarily of institutional professionals. While these standards were stated in relating broad guideline terms and their compliance was reviewed by colleagues, only 11% of the institutions could satisfy the requirements.[23]

This initial effort was soon followed by an extended planning process, one that called upon the participation of other concerned organizations as well as the knowledge and skills of individual professionals throughout the country. Subsequently, in 1966, the National Planning Committee on Accreditation of Residential Centers for the Retarded was created and included representation from the American Association on Mental Deficiency and four other groups interested in those who were mentally retarded: the American Psychiatric Association, the Council for Exceptional Children, the Association for Retarded Citizens of the United States, and the United Cerebral Palsy Association. Finally, the Joint Commission on Accreditation of Hospitals assumed responsibility for developing appropriate accreditation standards and procedures in 1969 with the establishment of the Accreditation Council for Facilities for the Mentally Retarded, which comprised members from the five professional organizations previously mentioned plus the American Medical Association.[24]

The resultant standards were divided into seven primary sections:

1. Administrative Policies and Practices (Philosophy, Location, and Organization; General Policies and Practices; Admission and Release; and Personnel Policies)
2. Resident Living (Staff-Resident Relationships and Activities; Food Services; Clothing; Health, Hygiene and Grooming; Grouping and Organization of Living

Units; Resident-Living Staff; and Design and Equipage of Living Units)

3. Professional and Special Programs and Services (Dental, Education, Food and Nutrition, Library, Medical, Nursing, Pharmacy, Physical and Occupational Therapy, Psychological, Recreational, Religious, Social, Speech Pathology and Audiology, Vocational Rehabilitation, and Volunteer Services)

4. Records

5. Research

6. Safety and Sanitation

7. Administrative Support Services.[25]

In 1971, the Accreditation Council approved and distributed the standards. Well-qualified, highly trained, independent professionals were hired, and institutions wishing accreditation began to apply.

The uniqueness of the Accreditation Council's approach was not in its standards, but rather in its procedures. One of the most frequent complaints about the typical licensing and accreditation process had been that only written materials, such as manuals and records, were surveyed. Rarely was there ever a check to see if the written documents actually reflected what was occurring nor was the quality of treatment assessed directly. Now, however, accreditation was based primarily on an evaluation of programs and services offered to a sample of residents, individually studied.

In 1973, the Accreditation Council developed a new set of standards for community agencies serving persons with mental retardation and other developmental disabilities. In 1978, both sets of standards, residential and community, were substantially revised and merged into *Standards for Services for Developmentally Disabled Individuals*.[26]

The impact of these standards took several forms. First, many facilities sought accreditation. Second, state and local agencies, as well as parents and parent groups, used the standards to assess the programmatic and administrative qualities of a residential facility. Third, the standards were adopted in their near

entirety by the federal government when, in 1971, Congress agreed to assume a major fiscal responsibility for institutional programs under the Medicaid provisions (Title XIX) of the Social Security Act, as is reviewed later in this chapter.

LITIGATION

The late sixties also witnessed the twilight years of a century-old tradition of local and state autonomy. Failure of the states to alter the course of institutional programming led disillusioned and often angry advocates to address their grievances to the court system.

Litigation, in turn, had its impact not only on those institutions directly affected, but also upon the development of federal regulations and state practices throughout the country. During the early seventies, most of the litigation brought against institutions involved three broad categories of concern: right to treatment, due process, and involuntary servitude.

Before considering some of the suits, however, the elemental provisions of the Fourteenth Amendment to the Constitution should be reviewed since it was crucial to many of the decisions rendered. The Fourteenth Amendment reads:

All persons born or naturalized in the United States and subject to the jurisdiction thereof, are citizens of the United States and of the State wherein they reside. No State shall make or enforce any law which shall abridge the privileges or immunities of citizens of the United States, nor shall any State deprive any person of life, liberty, or property without due proces of law; nor deny to any person within its jurisdiction to equal protection of the laws.

Two clauses contained within that Amendment were of particular import—"due process" and "equal protection." According to Schwindler, an authority on constitutional law, the fundamental objective of the due process of law "is to safeguard the individual and his well-being—i.e., his life, his independence of action, and his possessions. It is the basic standard of conduct in governments dealing with individuals, requiring that government abide by the required limits and procedures which the people have set up as guidelines to its actions. In the twentieth century it has been distinguished both as a procedural and a substantive right . . . ."[27]

The procedural dimension of the due process clause requires that safeguards be established and followed to ensure each person a fair and equitable hearing. This includes such aspects as prior notice, adequate legal representation or counsel, and trial by jury.

The substantive right (or principles of liberty) associated with the due process clause means ". . . not only has the citizen the right to be free from the mere physical restraint of the person as by incarceration, but the term is deemed to embrace the right of the citizen to be free in the enjoyment of all his faculties; to be free to enjoy them in all lawful ways; to work and live where he will; to earn his livelihood by any lawful calling; to pursue any livelihood or avocation; and for that purpose to enter into all contracts which may be proper, necessary and essential to his carrying out to a successful conclusion the purposes mentioned above."[28]

In other words, no individual can have any of his civil rights denied without the full sanction of the courts and only when all procedural safeguards have been assured. This clause was to be interpreted to mean that any mentally retarded person involuntarily committed to a residential facility must receive a full treatment program, not simply custodial care.

RIGHT TO TREATMENT

Litigation involving institutions began rather quietly when, in 1970, the guardian of Ricky Wyatt, who also was his aunt, initiated a class action suit against the Alabama Department of Mental Hygiene alleging failure of the state to provide proper treatment for mentally retarded residents in one of its facilities, the Partlow State School and Hospital.

In 1971, Judge Johnson of the District Court of the United States for the Middle District of Alabama, North Division, heard testimony from persons directly involved with the Partlow State School and from representatives of various professional organizations concerned with mentally retarded persons. His final judgment in *Wyatt* v. *Stickney* was precedent setting not only because it declared the constitutional rights of mentally retarded residents were being violated, but the final document included a 20-page appendix that defined minimum treatment standards for the state school to meet. An independent monitoring committee was created by the court to ensure the implementation of its judgment.[29]

The standards were both specific and encompassing, covering such areas as admission policies, residents right to treatment and habilitation, staffing patterns, records and review, physical plant and environment, medication, and resident labor. As concerns the right to treatment:

> Residents shall have a right to habilitation, including medical treatment, education and care, suited to their needs, regardless of age, degree of retardation, or handicapping condition.
>
> Each resident has a right to a habilitation program which will maximize his human abilities and enhance his ability to cope with his environment. The institution shall recognize that each resident, regardless of ability or status, is entitled to develop and realize his fullest potential. The institution shall implement the principle of normalization so that each resident may live as normally as possible. . . .
>
> Each resident shall have an individualized habilitation plan formulated by the institution. This plan shall be developed by appropriate Qualified Mental Retardation Professionals, and implemented as soon as possible, but no later than 14 days after the resident's admission to the institution. An interim program of habilitation based on the preadmission evaluation . . . shall commence promptly upon the resident's admission. Each individualized habilitation plan shall contain:
>
> a. a statement of the nature of the specific limitations and specific needs of the resident;
> b. a description of intermediate and long-range habilitation goals, with a projected timetable for their attainment;

c. a statement of and reasons for the plan of habilitation for achieving these intermediate and long-range goals;

d. a statement of the least restrictive setting for habilitation necessary to achieve the habilitation goals of the resident;

e. a specification of professional and staff responsibility for the resident in order to attain these habilitation goals;

f. criteria for release to less restrictive settings for habilitation including criteria for discharge and a projected date for discharge.[30]

The significance of this case was fourfold: 1) it held that mentally retarded persons had a constitutional right to appropriate habilitation and treatment; 2) it was the first such case to apply specifically to mentally retarded people; 3) it was the first case where the court set standards and established monitoring procedures; and 4) it was a class action suit.

In a subsequent class action suit, *Burnham v. Department of Public Health of the State of Georgia* (1972), an entirely different decision was reached.[31] Though the allegations were very similar to those cited in *Wyatt v. Stickney,* Judge Smith of the United States District Court for the Northern District of Georgia granted the defendants' motion to dismiss the case. While he recognized that persons in mental institutions had a moral right to treatment, he disagreed that there existed a legal mandate to provide such programming. Further, he found no legal precedent for assuming a federal constitutional right to treatment, and also contended that a federal court could not require state expenditures in an area controlled by state law. Finally, Judge Smith did not hold that federal courts had the right to establish and police individualized treatment programs since such would be beyond the capabilities of the court and should be left to the discretion of professionals.

This resulted in a judicial situation where two courts faced with almost identical suits reached diametrically opposite conclusions. The conflict could be resolved only by appeal to a higher court.

In May 1972, Governor George Wallace of the state of Alabama filed an appeal to the United States Court of Appeals, Fifth Circuit, based on the arguments put forth by Judge Smith. This case, *Wyatt v. Aderholt* (1974) consolidated the results of *Wyatt v. Stickney* and *Burnham v. Department of Public Health for the State of Georgia.*[32]

A three-judge panel of the Fifth Circuit Court of Appeals reached its decision in November, 1974. In essence, the original judgment of the Alabama suit was sustained. The Court held that mentally retarded persons had a constitutional right to treatment, federal courts could enter into cases of this nature, and the court could set standards and monitor their implementation.

The Fifth Circuit Court's decision paralleled their earlier judgment of *Donaldson v. O'Connor* (1974). Since this similar case had been appealed to the Supreme Court, those states concerned with institutions for mentally retarded persons awaited its determination. Briefly, Donaldson, an emotionally troubled person, was committed in 1957 by his father, following a hearing before a county judge, to the Florida State Hospital. Donaldson, who was released from the hospital in July, 1971, contended that the defendants confined him knowing that he was neither dangerous nor reckless and that they did not provide him with adequate treatment and therapy. For example, it was stated that the defendants had unjustifiably withheld such forms of treatment as "grounds privileges," occupational therapy, and psychiatric counseling. The jury returned a verdict in favor of the plaintiff.

As indicated, the Fifth Circuit Court upheld this decision on appeal, stating that the Fourteenth Amendment guaranteed involuntarily civilly committed mental patients a right to treatment. The court also found that the "attending physicians had acted in bad faith with respect to their treatment of the patient. . . ."[33] On June 26, 1975, the U.S. Supreme Court reached its decisions concerning *Donaldson v. O'Connor.* Contrary to the expectations of many, the Court did not deal with the question of constitutional right to treatment; rather, it emphasized due process.

In fact, as is later reviewed, the Supreme Court averted the question of constitutional right until 1982.

An interesting sidelight to the *Donaldson* case was Justice Burger's written admonition to the lower federal courts concerning the Supreme Court's role in determining what is and what is not a constitutional right:

> As the Court points out . . . , the District Court instructed the jury in part that "a person who is involuntarily civilly committed to a mental hospital does have a *constitutional* right to receive such treatment as will give him a realistic opportunity to be cured," (emphasis added) and the Court of Appeals unequivocally approved this phrase, standing alone, as a correct statement of law. The Court's opinion plainly gives no approval to that holding and makes clear that it binds neither the parties to this case nor the courts of the Fifth Circuit . . . . Moreover, in light of its importance for future litigation in this area, it should be emphasized that the Court of Appeal's analysis has no basis in the decisions of this Court.[34]

The Supreme Court's hesitancy or unwillingness to address the question of constitutional rights frustrated many in the field, and though Judge Johnson may have exceeded his authority in making certain judgments, the *Partlow* provisions stood and many other states, taking note of the case, began to alter their expectancies accordingly.

It should be noted that the opinions of Judge Johnson and the Fifth Circuit Court of Appeals supported an earlier judgment by Judge Bazelon, one of the country's first leaders in the area of right to treatment. In 1966, Judge Bazelon, in an appeal decision in the case of *Rouse* v. *Cameron* (1966), noted:

> The principle issues raised by this appeal are whether a person involuntarily committed to a mental hospital on being acquitted of an offense by reason of insanity has a right to treatment that is cognizable in habeas corpus and if so, how violation of this right may be established. The purpose of involuntary hospitalization is treatment, not punishment. The provision of commitment rests upon the supposed necessity for treatment of the mental condition which led to the acquittal by reason of insanity.[35]

Three years later, Judge Bazelon again wrote, "The most important fact of the right to treatment is not that the hospital does something for everyone, but that it does the right thing for the right patient. Because individual patients, particularly mental patients, vary so much in their needs, considerable attention must be paid to the patient as an individual."[36]

Over the years, a number of similar cases involving the adequacy of residential programming and procedures were introduced. Within a decade following the Alabama case, 29 states were embroiled in 43 suits involving institutional programs.[37]

Of the many cases, two deserve special note. The first was *New York State Association for Retarded Citizens et al.* v. *Carey et al.*, a class action suit brought against the state of New York in 1972, alleging severe violations at the Willowbrook State School and Hospital, located on Staten Island.[38] At that time, Willowbrook served a population of 5,200 and was 65% over rated bed capacity.[39] The allegations, which were quite similar to those introduced in other cases, included:

1. Most residents were confined for unspecified periods, usually until they "recovered."
2. Residents who should have been released were not.
3. No habilitation was occurring to justify the confinement of residents.
4. There were no individual habilitation plans for residents.
5. There were no periodic evaluations of residents to assess their progress and redefine goals and programs.
6. There were no educational programs provided for residents. In fact, virtually no stimulation of any kind was provided.
7. Services such as speech, occupational, and physical therapy were inadequate, if available at all.
8. The facility was overcrowded.
9. The residents had no privacy and there

was an attendant absence of regulations that protected residents from theft. In the atmosphere that prevailed, personal property was nonexistent.

10. The residents were not protected against assault and injury, either by other residents or staff.

11. Experimentation was practiced on residents.

12. Residents were not given adequate clothing.

13. The diet in the facility was inadequate and the meals were rushed.

14. The facility was dirty.

15. Toilet facilities were not adequate to accommodate the institutional population.

16. Residents were segregated from those of the opposite sex.

17. Many residents were unwarrantedly confined to beds or chairs or kept in solitary confinement.

18. Many residents were denied grounds privileges and practically none were given passes.

19. Residents were not given help in reading, writing, or posting mail.

20. There was a paucity of bilingual staff; thus non–English-speaking residents had difficulty in communicating.

21. Residents were not compensated for work performed.

22. The facility was understaffed with professionals and paraprofessionals. The absence of proper supervision contributed to the fact that some residents died of such things as aspiration of food or vomit.

23. Medical facilities were inadequate.

24. Many of the professional staff were shown to be incompetent.[40]

This case was contested vigorously by representatives of the state despite overwhelming evidence that many of the allegations were true. It was not until 1975 that a consent agreement was reached and approved by the court. The consent decree not only called for a major upgrading of the facility's programs and recognition of residents' rights, but also that it

phase down over the next 10 years to a residual population of 250.

The second suit, one that would be argued and reargued for years, involved the Pennhurst State School and Hospital, Pennsylvania. The uniqueness of this case involved Federal Judge Raymond Broderick's challenging the very existence of institutions, when, in 1978, as noted previously, he stated that institutions represented a "monumental example of the unconstitutionality with respect to the habilitation of the retarded. As such it must be expeditiously replaced with appropriate community-based mental retardation programs and facilities designed to meet the individual needs of each class member."[41] Thus, a new dimension had been added to litigation involving institutions; namely, the need for deinstitutionalization.

Judge Broderick's judgment, however, was supported by the U.S. Supreme Court neither in 1981 nor in 1982. In 1981, the Supreme Court failed to sustain his decision due to a technicality.[42] In 1982, in *Youngberg* v. *Romeo,* the Supreme Court finally addressed the question of constitutional rights, rendering an extremely conservative decision that many found disappointing. Recognizing that 33-year-old Nicholas Romeo was profoundly mentally retarded, the Court determined that he had the right to safe conditions of confinement; freedom from bodily restraints, whenever possible; and "minimally adequate training." In Romeo's case, "minimally adequate training required by the Constitution is such training as may be reasonable in light of respondent's liberty interests in safety and freedom from unreasonable restraints."[43] The Supreme Court summarized its opinion in the following words:

In deciding this case, we have weighed those post-commitment interests cognizable as liberty interests under the Due Process Clause of the Fourteenth Amendment against legitimate state interests and in light of the constraints under which most state institutions necessarily operate. We repeat that the state concedes a duty to provide adequate food, shelter, clothing and medical care. These are the essentials of the care that the state must provide. The state also has the unquestioned duty to provide reasonable safety for all residents and personnel within the institution. And it may not restrain residents except when and to the extent professional judgment deems this necessary to assure such safety or to provide needed training. In this case, therefore, the state is under a duty to provide respondent with such training as an appropriate professional would consider reasonable to ensure his safety and to facilitate his ability to function free from bodily restraints. It may well be unreasonable not to provide training when training could significantly reduce the need for restraints or the likelihood of violence.

Respondent thus enjoys constitutionally protected interests in conditions of reasonable care and safety, reasonably non-restrictive confinement conditions and such training as may be required by these interests. Such conditions of confinement would comport fully with the purpose of respondent's commitment . . . .[44]

Chief Justice Burger, who concurred with the court's judgment, added:

I agree with much of the Court's opinion. However, I would hold flatly that respondent has no constitutional right to training, or "habilitation" per se. The parties, and the Court, acknowledge that respondent cannot function outside the state institution, even with the assistance of relatives. Indeed, even now neither respondent nor his family seeks his discharge from state care. Under these circumstances, the State's provision of food, shelter, medical care, and living conditions as safe as the inherent nature of the institutional environment reasonably allows, serve to justify the State's custody of respondent. The State did not seek custody of respondent; his family understandably sought the State's aid to meet a serious need.

I agree with the Court that some amount of self-care instruction may be necessary to avoid unreasonable infringement of a mentally retarded person's interests in safety and freedom from restraint; but it seems clear to me that the Constitution does not otherwise place an affirmative duty on the State to provide any particular kind of training or habilitation—even such as might be encompassed under the essentially standardless rubric "minimally adequate training," to which the Court refers . . . .

I also point out that, under the Court's own standards, it is largely irrelevant whether respondent's experts were of the opinion that "additional training programs, including self-care programs, were needed to reduce [respondent's]

aggressive behavior," . . . a prescription far easier for "spectators" to give than for an institution to implement. The training program devised for respondent by petitioners and other professionals at Pennhurst was, according to the Court's opinion, "presumptively valid"; and "liability may be imposed only when the decision by the professional is such a substantial departure from accepted professional judgment, practice, or standards as to demonstrate that the person responsible actually did not base the decision on such a judgement [sic] . . . ." Thus, even if respondent could demonstrate that the training programs at Pennhurst were inconsistent with generally accepted or prevailing professional practice—if indeed there be such—this would not avail him so long as his training regimen was actually prescribed by the institution's professional staff.

Finally, it is worth noting that the District Court's instructions in this case were on the whole consistent with the Court's opinion today; indeed; some instructions may have been overly generous to respondent. Although the District Court erred in giving an instruction incorporating an Eighth Amendment "deliberate indifference" standard, the court also instructed, for example, that petitioners could be held liable if they "were aware of and failed to take all reasonable steps to prevent repeated attacks upon" respondent . . . . Certainly if petitioners took "*all* reasonable steps to prevent repeated attacks upon" respondent, they cannot be said to have deprived him either of reasonably safe conditions or of training necessary to achieve reasonable safety.[45]

The Supreme Court's decision was immediately translated into practice by the Civil Rights Division of the Justice Department. Accordingly, the Division had a continuing responsibility to investigate facilities to make sure residents were guaranteed a reasonably safe, unrestrained living environment. Department of Justice lawyers, however, were no longer required to ascertain whether an institution provided psychiatric care, psychological treatment, or individualized therapeutic efforts designed to enhance capacity, capability, and competence among its residents. The latter services were permissible, but the lack thereof no longer represented a constitutional violation.[46] This new interpretation by the Justice Department was devastating to persons pursuing litigation against institutions since its attorneys frequently appeared on behalf of the plaintiffs. In the final analysis, however, neither the Supreme Court's decision in *Youngberg* v. *Romeo* nor its interpretation by the Justice Department resulted in any rewriting of federal standards nor did states desist from expanding resident programs and services.

DUE PROCESS

As indicated previously, "equal protection of the laws" refers to the fact that no group of people, such as those who are mentally retarded or mentally ill, can be singled out and treated as a group. Each person has the right to have his particular case considered individually, irrespective of any commonalities he may share with other people.

Though several of the court actions involving residential programs for mentally retarded persons referred to due process and equal protection under the law, none was more specific than the *Lessard* v. *Schmidt* decision of 1972 in which the United States District Court for the Eastern Division of Wisconsin ruled that Wisconsin's civil commitment procedures were constitutionally defective.[47]* Briefly, the court found that the existing procedures:

1. Failed to require effective and timely notice of the *charges* under which a person is sought to be detained.
2. Failed to require adequate notice of all rights including the right to jury trial.
3. Permitted detention longer than forty-eight hours without a hearing on probable cause.
4. Permitted detention longer than two weeks without a full hearing on the necessity for commitment.
5. Permitted commitment based on a hearing in which the person charged with mental retardation was not represented by adversary counsel at which hearsay evidence was admitted and in which medical evidence was presented without the resident having been given the benefit of the privilege against self-incrimination.
6. Permitted commitment without proof beyond a reasonable doubt that the resident was both mentally retarded and dangerous.
7. Failed to require those seeking commitment to consider less restrictive alternatives to commitment.[49]

The net effect of this decision was that all involuntarily committed residents 18 years of age and older had to have their commitments reviewed in a formal court hearing, adhering to the principles and guarantees noted. Not only did the courts take into consideration whether placement in a residential facility was appropriate (i.e., whether the residents were dangerous to themselves or others), they also took into consideration whether less restrictive alternatives were available. Subsequently, some residents were transferred to smaller residential facilities located in their home communities.

Residents who were found not to be dangerous to either themselves or others could convert from an involuntary to a voluntary commitment. Their rights, however, had to be explained in terms they could understand, and the applicant had to agree freely to remain in the residential facility. The decision had to represent a true voluntary application. In many instances this was not possible because the applicant could not comprehend the implications of the decision, including the right to leave at any time, the nature of the treatment to be offered, and probable outcomes of such treatment. When this situation arose, the court usually ordered the residential facility to locate an alternative placement for the resident as soon as possible. Though the decision only affected residents 18 years of age and older, greater attention was paid to the "voluntariness" of all admissions.

On March 8, 1974, a three-judge federal court in Tennessee declared the admission procedures for mentally retarded persons in that state were unconstitutional.[50] Briefly, a

---

*Over the years, Alberta Lessard, the original plaintiff, a teacher and "a peppery proponent of personal freedom," became angry and "a little bit tired of people accusing [her] of causing all those suicides" among former mental hospital patients. She was no more pleased with the ultimate ruling than she was with psychiatry, a "most lucrative form of witchcraft," or the legal profession, which consisted of "lawyers [who] take money from both sides without giving you an opportunity to say anything."[48]

mentally retarded person could be admitted on the following basis:

> Application to the superintendent by the parent or guardian or person having lawful custody of a mentally retarded minor or by the guardian of a mentally retarded adult or by a mentally retarded individual eighteen (18) years of age or over on his own behalf.
>
> Application to the superintendent by the spouse, adult, or child or other close relative of the individual, or by any health or by any public welfare officer, or school official, with the consent of the individual or his parent, guardian or person having lawful custody of him, accompanied by a certificate of a licensed physician or a licensed psychologist that he has examined the individual within thirty (30) days of the date on which admission is sought and that he is of the opinion that the individual is mentally retarded and is in need of care and treatment in a hospital and school.[51]

The court rejected this approach since it violated due process under the Fourteenth Amendment. In other words, the existing procedures for both minors and adults, *voluntary* or *involuntary*, did not provide adequate legal safeguards.

In view of the court order, admission procedures for that state were revised. When parents requested admission of their child to a residential facility, the child first had to receive a comprehensive diagnosis and evaluation by qualified mental retardation professionals. If, following the evaluation, it was recommended that the child be voluntarily admitted to a residential facility, then the case had to be re-examined by an independent review board. This board comprised three persons, one of whom was to be a parent whose child was not in a residential facility and one a professional. None could be a state employee. If the review board concurred with the recommendation, the child could be admitted. If, however, the board rejected the recommendation, the child could be admitted only by court order. Following placement in a residential facility, a representative of the board was required to review the continued appropriateness of the residential placement at least annually.[52]

The Tennessee procedure provided that a mentally retarded minor "may retain private counsel of his own choice or, absent such employment, said proposed resident shall be represented at the hearing by the Citizens Advocacy Council for the Developmentally Disabled, Inc., as advocate."[53] This approach established additional guarantees that the rights of due process were recognized for all mentally retarded persons, regardless of chronological age.

The new decisions by district-level federal courts had the full support of the Supreme Court, based on its findings in *O'Connor* v. *Donaldson:*

> A finding of "mental illness" alone cannot justify a State's locking a person up against his will and keeping him indefinitely in simple custodial confinement. Assuming that that term can be given a reasonably precise content and that the "mentally ill" can be identified with reasonable accuracy, there is still no constitutional basis for confining such persons involuntarily if they are dangerous to no one and can live safely in freedom!
>
> May the State confine the mentally ill merely to ensure them a living standard superior to that they enjoy in the private community? That the State has a proper interest in providing care and assistance to the unfortunate goes without saying. *But the mere presence of mental illness does not disqualify a person from preferring his home to the comforts of an institution!* Moreover, while the State may arguably confine a person to have him from harm, incarceration is rarely if ever a necessary condition for raising the living standards of those capable of surviving safely in freedom, on their own or with the help of family or friends . . . .
>
> May the State fence in the harmless mentally ill solely to save its citizens from exposure to those whose ways are different? One might as well ask if the State, to avoid public unease, could incarcerate all who are physically unattractive or socially eccentric. *Mere public intolerance or animosity cannot constitutionally justify the deprivation of a person's physical liberty!* [54]

New statutes and procedures were soon established in all states.

"PEONAGE" OR INVOLUNTARY SERVITUDE

The question of involuntary servitude relates to the Thirteenth Amendment to the Constitution, which reads, in part: "Neither slavery nor involuntary servitude, except as a punishment for crime whereof the party will be duly convicted, shall exist within the United States, or any place subject to their jurisdiction."

Historically, many residential facilities relied heavily upon resident labor to maintain their levels of operation. During the sixties, for example, 74% of the institutions relied on resident labor.[55] Older residents commonly worked in the laundry or in food service and frequently tended younger, less capable residents. Many received little or no remuneration, and it was this form of involuntary servitude that was challenged.

In 1973, a class action suit (*Townsend* v. *Treadway*) was filed with the United States District Court for the Middle District of Tennessee, Nashville Division, alleging that the "defendants subjected the plaintiffs during their residency at the defendant institution to peonage and involuntary servitude, failed to pay them the minimum wage required by the Federal Fair Labor Standards Act, and failed to provide them state retirement benefits as required by state law, and that these failures continue to the present time."[56] In this particular case, the court denied injunctive relief on all issues. It was determined that residents were offered a range of job opportunities, could refuse all work, and that no one was ordered to work for "medical reasons." It was the opinion of the court that no proof of coercion or lack of choice was evident with regard to duties performed. Further, plaintiffs were not subject to state retirement or Social Security benefits since by state law they were not employees.

On March 13, 1973, another class action suit (*Souder* v. *Brennan*) was brought against the United States Department of Labor to compel the Department to enforce provisions of the Fair Labor Standards Act of 1966 relative to resident workers in residential facilities for both the mentally ill and the mentally retarded.[57] The American Association on Mental Deficiency, the National Association for Mental Health, and three individual plaintiffs filed the suit in the United States District

Court in Washington, D.C. Named as defendants were the Secretary of Labor and four subordinate Labor Department head administrators. On December 4, 1973, a declaratory judgment and injunction order was issued, stating: "The Secretary of Labor has a duty to implement reasonable enforcement efforts applying the minimum wage and overtime compensation provision of the Fair Labor Standards Act to patient-workers at non-Federal institutions for the residential care of the mentally ill and/or mentally retarded . . ."[58] In other words, the court held that the minimum wage, overtime, and other provisions of the Fair Labor Standards Act applied to developmentally disabled persons residing and working in a residential facility. Though this decision was subsequently overturned in *National League of Cities* v. *Usery* (1976), the message was clear: institutions could no longer rely on resident labor free of charge. Subsequent federal regulations and standards both required substantial change.[59]

PROS AND CONS OF LITIGATION

The fact that the Constitution of the United States contains provisions that could be interpreted to protect the rights of all citizens reconfirms the integrity and creative intelligence of our forefathers. That contemporary jurists utilized the Constitution to protect the rights of mentally retarded persons in residential settings and to advance a new social policy was also of considerable merit. Many persons, however, regretted that the courts had to be called upon to ensure that the rights and programmatic needs of mentally retarded persons were being honored.

The positive aspects of litigation, especially in principle, were many. As stated previously, it was one of the few avenues left to concerned parents, guardians, professionals, and interested citizens in general that could influence state practices. Even the threat or potential threat of litigation often produced changes in both residential and community programming.

Litigation and its attending publicity also

brought the plight of mentally retarded persons in some residential facilities to the public's attention. That, in turn, had its effect; various federal regulations were written or modified in response to court judgments. This was especially true as regards admissions, length of stay, and quality of services.

Writing in 1975, Turnbull noted that litigation also increased the awareness of the legal profession to the needs of mentally retarded persons, especially those living in a residential facility.[60] This was important. No person, for example, was ever involuntarily committed to an institution by a governor, a legislator, a director of a department of mental hygiene, or a superintendent. They were committed through the legal process; and historically, as already presented, that procedure often failed to recognize the dignity and rights of mentally retarded persons. In essence, the legal profession needed to become more knowledgeable about and sensitive to the needs and rights of mentally retarded persons as well as programming and alternatives to institutional placement.

There were some negative aspects associated with litigation. In some cases, it was impossible to comply with the court's judgment within the time allotted. For example, Judge Johnson, in an interim order issued in 1972, required:

> . . . within 15 days defendants shall completely eliminate all fire and safety hazards; that within 15 days they will engage a team of physicians to examine every resident . . . currently receiving anticonvulsants and/or behavior modifying drugs; within 10 days . . . defendants shall engage a team of physicians to conduct a program of appropriate immunization for all residents; and within 30 days . . . defendants shall employ 300 additional resident care workers, including professionals of the various disciplines . . . .[61]

This requirement simply could not be met. As again observed by Turnbull, a judgment of this nature was not only administratively difficult to comply with but would be expensive to satisfy and perhaps not prove productive, especially when it demanded instant changes rather than well-planned and systematic changes accomplished with reasonable speed.[62]

There were also other administrative difficulties. Most court cases required several years to resolve, and during this interval, the residential facility was under constant scrutiny, reporting, and stress. Usually, public statements such as newspaper articles concentrated on the negative aspects of the situation to the complete neglect of any positive features. This, in turn, had a marked demoralizing effect on staff, which soon became apparent in programming. Further, because of the constant legal overtones to the investigation and proceedings, staff became hesitant to interact with residents or to prescribe any treatments for fear of being sued.[63]

In time, however, court decisions became more realistic in terms of feasible implementation and the court's role in setting forth new social policies became increasingly accepted, if not always appreciated. Time also demonstrated the limitations of litigation. While the courts could render decisions and set forth new directions, they lacked both the authority and the resources to ensure compliance. That authority rested with state government, which often did not or could not comply with court mandates. Subsequently, many of the facilities involved in early litigation, including the Partlow State School and Willowbrook, failed to improve as rapidly as jurists and attorneys had anticipated.[64] The situation involving Willowbrook, which was by no means atypical, was well described by Christopher Hansen of the Mental Health Law Project. In 1977, 5 years after litigation was instituted and 2 years following the consent decree, the residents' circumstances had not improved appreciably:

> Despite all of this energy, time, and expense, life has not changed significantly for most of the 5,200 plaintiffs. Willowbrook is much less crowded and there are more staff. However, very few residents have been transferred to community facilities. Most have been transferred to other large state institutions which are, at best, marginally better than Willowbrook.
>
> Not all residents receive six hours of programming per day and some still receive no programming at all. The wards are cleaner, but few have been partitioned and most look exactly like they

did in 1972. State officials have plans to improve conditions for Willowbrook's residents.[65]

As concerns the limitations of the court, Hansen explained:

> There are inherent limitations on the degree of social change which can be accomplished through litigation. So far, lawyers have shown an ability to highlight problem areas, to focus professional and public attention, and even to assist in setting professional standards. There are, however, no really effective means for lawyers to force recalcitrant or incompetent state officials to obey a court order such as the Willowbrook Consent Judgment. The only apparent recourse for the lawyers, faced as in Willowbrook with massive noncompliance, is to seek to have the state officials held in contempt. Even if the court does find them in contempt, it is limited in what it can do. It can fine state officials, taking away money which should be used to implement change. It can, though rarely ever would, imprison state officials. Or, it could appoint a master who would be given the power to take over the administration of Willowbrook. Naturally, federal judges are reluctant to become involved in the daily administration of institutions such as Willowbrook. And, the administrative problems would be even more difficult for an outside master, confronting a hostile bureaucracy.[66]

During the same year, Frederick Grunberg, former Deputy Commissioner of Mental Retardation for New York, added:

> . . . a court can make an individual or an organization take specific remedial actions under threat of sanctions for noncompliance, but it cannot order an organization such as a bureaucracy to become "competent" at changing a system on a grand scale within a limited time span. The task defined in the Consent Decree requires the solution of a very large, complex, and difficult system problem, which has not yet been accomplished anywhere, and for which the expertise is woefully lacking.[67]

In view of the very limited response to the various court decisions by state legislatures, many began to view litigation as "counterproductive, unproductive, unwarranted, unnecessary, and undesirable."[68] Yet, as explained by Turnbull in 1975, "Litigation is a last-ditch action. It stems from the failure to effect change by persuading legislatures and administrators to change. As a last-ditch effort, it is, paradoxically, only a door-opener, a catalyst to change by others. It changes the ground rules and procedures by which institutions may operate. Unfortunately, it is not likely to alter the power relationship between the institutions and society on the one hand and the resident or the retarded person on the other. But if, as a result of litigation, legislators and administrators comply with specified standards of care and treatment that are for the most part desirable; if litigation precipitates new programs, new public awareness of the residents' needs, and new professional awareness of the residents' rights; and if litigation draws into the mental retardation field concerned and sensible law reformers, then litigation will be, in historical perspective, laudable, just as many of the changes produced by litigation over the last twenty years in other problem areas now are laudable . . . ."[69]

To protect mentally retarded residents in institutions, on May 23, 1980, President Carter signed into law an act that gave to the U.S. Justice Department the standing authority to sue states for alleged violations of the rights of institutionalized people.[70] Yet, the act was so convoluted with political and bureaucratic considerations, for all practical purposes it proved of little value; in later years, the Justice Department would be severely criticized for its absence of activity.[71]

TITLE XIX:
IMPACT AND LIMITATIONS

While litigation did have its impact, the *tour de force* of institutional reform was the inclusion of residential facilities for mentally retarded persons under the 1971 amendments to Title XIX (Medicaid) of the Social Security Act. Though several states qualified their institutions for federal funding under the nursing home provisions of Social Security as early as 1969, it was not until 1974 that the federal government created two categories specifically intended to aid states in improving their residential programs for mentally retarded persons—the intermediate care facility and the skilled nursing care facility. The more common of the two was the intermediate care facility, which was defined as an "institution (or distinct part thereof) primarily for the diagnosis, treatment, or rehabilitation of the mentally retarded or persons with related conditions, which provides in a protected residential setting, individualized ongoing evaluation, planning, 24-hour supervision, coordination, and integration of health or rehabilitative services to help each individual reach his maximum of functioning capacities."[72]

One of the first and foremost expectations was that each funded facility was to provide active treatment, which included:

a) regular participation, in accordance with an individual plan of care in professionally developed and supervised activities, experiences, or therapies; and

b) an individual "plan of care" which is a written plan setting forth measurable goals or behaviorally stated objectives and prescribing an integrated program of individually designed activities, experiences, or therapies necessary to achieve such goals or objectives. The overall objective of the plan is to attain or maintain the optimal physical, intellectual, social, or vocational functioning of which the individual is presently or potentially capable; and

c) an interdisciplinary professional evaluation consisting of complete medical, social, and psychological diagnosis and evaluation, and an evaluation of the individual's need for institutional care, prior to, but not to exceed 3 months before admission to the institution or, in the case of individuals who make application while in such institution, before requesting payment under the plan;

d) re-evaluation medically, socially, and psychologically at least annually . . . including review of the individual's progress . . . , the appropriateness of the individual plan of care, assessment of continuing need for institutional care, and consideration of alternative methods of care; and

e) an individual postinstitutionalization plan (as part of the individual plan of care) developed prior to discharge by a Qualified Mental Retardation Professional and other appropriate professionals, including provision for appropriate services, protective supervision, and other follow-up services in the resident's new environment.[73]

Institutions participating in this program, and by 1980, that included all but a few, were also subject to an Independent Professional Review team that determined whether quality services were being rendered to each participating resident and if continued residential placement was required. This evaluation by external personnel was most critical. If, in the judgment of the team, a resident did not require extended placement in a residential facility, it was incumbent upon the administration of that facility to seek an alternative, less restrictive placement. Participating facilities were also required to satisfy 563 standards collated under the following headings, with subheadings similar to those of the Accreditation Council: 1) Administrative Policies and Practices, 2) Resident Living, 3) Professional and Special Programs and Services, 4) Records, 5) Research, 6) Safety and Sanitation, 7) Administrative Support Services, and 8) Engineering and Maintenance.

Over the years, the standards were upgraded and greater emphasis was placed on safeguarding individual rights, including those related to choice, correspondence, privacy, and confidentiality of records and other personal data.

The standards, however, were not without their problems. A number of concerns and questions were raised shortly following their release:

1. While many of the standards could be readily met by new, relatively small residential facilities, they could not be satisfied by some of the larger facilities constructed prior to 1965 without a significant financial outlay.

2. Should one set of standards apply equally to all residential facilities throughout the United States?

3. The federal regulations were too medically oriented.

4. Many of the surveyors were not professionally qualified in the field of mental retardation.

5. Some of the standards were vague and subject to individual interpretation.

6. Federal and Accreditation Council standards were not always compatible.

7. Rigid fire and safety codes would make it extremely difficult to create a normal physical environment.[74]

Of particular concern was the fact that the federal standards were based solely on professional judgment, and their validity in terms of actually increasing programmatic effectiveness and facilitating the return of mentally retarded persons to the community had not, in the opinion of many, been evaluated adequately. Subsequently, a number of organizations again requested further research:

> Any standards governing programs for the developmentally disabled person should be evaluated in a rigorous, scientifically acceptable manner. To date, the majority of standards reflect professional judgment. Their validity now needs to be established. Further, many questions have been raised about the reliability of assessment instruments and raters. Reliability studies are most essential to increasing acceptability of standards and related procedures established by many agencies.[75]

Regrettably, such critical research was not conducted with the ultimate results that the "standards" often consisted of vaguely stated requirements subject to the discretionary interpretation of the individual surveyor. Consequently, in 1984, many persons responsible for institutional programming and physical environment were still not certain as to exactly what was expected.

Nevertheless, considerable progress was made, at least in certain areas. New fire safety regulations were implemented; programming was expanded to all residents, including those most severely affected; and staffing ratios improved significantly. In 1964, for example, the overall staff/resident ratio was .40:1; in 1984, it was 1.69:1[76] Not only did the total number of staff increase, but so did the variety of their experience and background. Thus, many facilities offered therapeutic services previously unavailable to their residents.[77]

Institutions grew smaller in size. In 1960, there were 107 state-sponsored residential facilities.[78] In 1984, there were 267 such facilities, down from a maximum of 282 in 1981.[79] The additional institutions enabled a significant reduction in the average daily population per facility, which in 1984 was 383 as compared to 1,139 in 1964.[80] Regardless of size,

however, facilities that opened during the sixties and early seventies still retained many of the undesirable features of older institutions—congregate, ward-style living arrangements; terrazzo floors; and tiled walls.

Another trend, influenced by a variety of factors, ranging from abortion to PL 94-142, was the dramatic change in populations served. In 1964, 51% of the residents were less than 21 years of age, and 60% were classified as either severely or profoundly mentally retarded.[81] In contrast, the population served in 1984 was composed primarily of adults (82%), severely or profoundly mentally retarded (82%).[82]

Also, over the years, the trend was for fewer new admissions and readmissions as well as increased community placements. Yet, in 1984, the total activity level in all three categories was repressed. To illustrate, in 1984, there were only 4,627 new admissions, as compared to 11,173 in 1974; but, the total number of alternative placements during 1984 was only 8,823, as compared to 13,771 in 1974.[83]

In addition, 90% of the public residential facilities extended a wide range of programs to youngsters and adults from the community, often with the intent of averting the need for extended residential care. Such outreach services, which ranged from diagnosis, program planning, and counseling to direct home support and training for parents and offspring, were often successful.[84]

Naturally, additional staff, expenditures for physical plant improvements, and inflation over the years all contributed to a substantial increase in the daily cost per resident, which rose from $4.55 in 1960 to $115.88 in 1984.[85]

But the gains were not enough to keep abreast of growing knowledge, changing philosophies, and everyone's expectations. Fire systems were improved, living environments often were not; paperwork abounded, new programs did not; staffing ratios improved, but remained insufficient: in 1982, 50% of the public residential facilities still needed additional personnel to meet all resident needs.[86]

Thus, it was not uncommon still to see such glaring headlines as:

Plymouth Center is 'Disastrous' Court is Told[87]
'Hogtied', Shackled, and Left[88]
9 Employees Indicted for Abusing Patients at Mental Institution[89]

In 1984, members of Congress and officials of the U.S. Department of Health and Human Services, perhaps to the surprise of no one but themselves, discovered that many institutions remained rife with problems and shortcomings. On July 31, Senator Lowell Weicker of Connecticut chaired a joint hearing of the Senate Subcommittee on the Handicapped and the Appropriations Subcommittee on Labor/Health and Human Services. A survey of seven institutions supported with Title XIX funds revealed:

1. Abuse and neglect of clients continue to persist despite a wide range of techniques and procedures utilized to attempt to eliminate this problem.
2. In all seven facilities visited, superintendents stated there were many mentally retarded individuals in the institutions who did not belong there, but belonged in less restrictive settings.
3. Basic rights such as freedom of movement, privacy, and exercising choice over daily activities are abridged.
4. A full program of active treatment appropriate to meet individual needs is not yet afforded to all individuals.
5. The federal mandate (PL 94-142) requiring a free appropriate education for all handicapped children (age 3–21) has not been achieved for many institutionalized mentally retarded children and youth.
6. Problems persist with the environment in institutions. These problems include barren living areas and lack of personal possessions and furnishings.[90]

Similar results were reported by Margaret Heckler, Secretary of the U.S. Department of Health and Human Services, following "look-behind" inspections of 17 institutions:

> The majority of institutions did not meet requirements concerning provision of active treatment, a requirement added to the law to avoid creating merely another custodial type of program. Let me explain here that the purpose of requiring active treatment services is to ensure that each client will be afforded the opportunity to gain as many independent skills as possible as well as to prevent further physical and mental deterioration or loss of already acquired skills . . . .
> In many facilities, these services simply were not provided to most of the clients because of insufficient and/or poorly trained staff, inadequate physical environments or management problems. Thus, from a services perspective, many of these clients are receiving essentially "custodial," nonaggressive care, the very type of care Congress sought to end by the ICF/MR program . . . .
> Some facilities were found to have Life Safety Code (fire protection) deficiencies, such as improper fire escape devices, broken or inadequate alarm systems, or improper fire walls and doors. In one case, we found large numbers of clients who were not capable of self-preservation living in residences that could not protect the clients in the event of fire. We decided this condition constituted an immediate threat to the clients' safety, and we terminated the facility's Medicaid agreement. The action has prompted the state to take immediate action to correct this life threatening situation.
> All of the 17 facilities inspected were substandard; nine had major health and safety deficiencies.[91]

Thus began a renewed effort to improve the quality of residential programming while, at the same time, encouraging deinstitutionalization.

DEINSTITUTIONALIZATION

Deinstitutionalization as a concept affecting mentally retarded persons gained recognition during the late sixties; acquired greater support during the seventies; and became a national political, professional, and parental goal during the eighties. Conceptually, deinstitutionalization represented a corollary of normalization, seeking greater emphasis on freedom, independence, individuality, mobility, personalized life experiences, and a high degree of interaction in a free society.

While the general mood of the sixties was for institutional reform, a few persons did call for deinstitutionalization. In 1962, for example, J. E. Wallace Wallin, renowned psychologist, special educator, and administrator, wrote an article entitled, "Psycho-social Considerations Militating Against Institutionalization, Particularly for Children,'' in which he observed

> It was now generally recognized:
>
> that a proper feeling tone is essential for effective learning and for wholesome personality development; . . .
>
> that a good home with the real parents is the best place for normal growth and development of all children, normal and abnormal, and that no institution, however good, can take the place of such a home; . . .
>
> that a warm, accepting, affectionate atmosphere is the sine qua non during the period of infancy for engendering the feelings of security, contentment, and satisfaction that are needed for normal psychophysical development; . . .
>
> that institutionalization, particularly at an early age, is fraught with grave psychic hazards, often referred to as "hospitalism," including intellectual retardation or disorganization, personality distortions, and social maladaptation; . . .
>
> and that many of the committed children rebel against their confinement and constantly yearn to return home.[92]

DEINSTITUTIONALIZATION IN PRINCIPLE

Despite such urgings, primary attention during the sixties was devoted to establishing small, specialized residential centers in contrast to the existing large, multipurpose facilities. In 1969, Dunn proposed the creation of such residential centers for four reasons:

1. Responsibility for the facility could be assigned specifically to the discipline that provides the specialized treatment (i.e., physicians for medical-nursing programs; educators or psychologists for developmental centers).
2. Specialization would eliminate interdisciplinary struggles and bickering.
3. Such centers would emphasize intensive, specialized treatment programs.
4. Small, specialized facilities would reduce manpower needs.[93]

Dunn's comments reflected an extreme degree of disappointment with the ability of representatives from various disciplines to work together collaboratively. While his observa-

tions concerning the desirability of smaller facilities were well received, few authorities were willing to abandon the concept of or need for a multidisciplinary approach.

By the seventies, the growing emphasis was on closing institutions. In 1971, Wolfensberger seriously challenged the need for residential facilities, at least as they then existed: "I can see no reason why small, specialized living units (mostly hostels) cannot accommodate all of the persons now in institutions."[94] This observation was based on five noted trends:

1. Development of nonresidential services, e.g., day care and public school programs.
2. New conceptualizations of and attitudes toward residential services, i.e., large, multipurpose residential facilities are undesirable and unnecessary.
3. Increased usage of individual rather than group residential placements, e.g., foster family placement and five-day boarding homes.
4. Provision of small, specialized residential placements, e.g., hostels.
5. A decline in the prevalance of severely and profoundly retarded through the continuing decline in birthrate among high-risk groups; preventive health services for high-risk groups; increased legalization and practice of abortion; improvement of health and preventive services generally; environmental betterment; and early childhood education.[95]

Similarly, the Association for Retarded Citizens of the United States, in their 1972 testimony concerning Willowbrook, observed: "Large institutions, like Willowbrook, must be phased out. They have proven over the years that they cannot adequately serve all ages and all degrees of handicap, with all the services required, from birth to death. Although millions might be spent, it is unlikely that they would meet even minimum standards."[96]

The positions of Dunn, Wolfensberger, and the Association for Retarded Citizens of the United States reflected the two most commonly expressed projected trends for residential programming during the late sixties and early seventies. Others, however, were somewhat more cautious in their predictions, and frequently expressed reservations over the proposed radical departures from existing residential patterns. In 1966, for example, Tarjan wrote:

> During the next decade much time will be spent on debating which type of institution is the "ideal" one. Single-purpose, highly specialized facilities will be contrasted with multi-purpose ones. Some people will advocate the establishment of separate facilities for children and adults. Others will favor a dichotomy along diagnostic lines. The advantages of a "generic" approach in residential care will be a popular subject of discussion, without a clear determination of the meaning of generic in this context. Many decisions will be made. Most will probably reflect emotionality or armchair thinking rather than scientific considerations. There are very few data available to pass judgment on the comparative efficiency of small or large, generic or specialized facilities. For a while residential stay is apt to remain long. A word of caution, therefore, is in order. The establishment of highly specialized facilities, by necessity, results in the frequent transfer of the retarded person. Each of these moves demands a new adjustment by the patient and his family . . . . It is rather easy to say that institutions are not needed; if this assumption was correct, residential services would be sought with decreasing frequency and the waiting lists would disappear. One should ask, therefore, of those who advocate the closing of institutions that they first create the community resources which might make institutions unnecessary, then prove that, in fact, institutions are no longer needed. Natural forces should then take care of the issues. Until that time, one must continue to believe that residential centers are necessary and viable. For this reason, professionals and the public should give our institutional system not unwarranted criticism, but energetic support in the pursuit of improvements.[97]

Inasmuch as these quotes were taken out of context, it should be noted that Tarjan was most alert to the need for and probability of change as related to residential services. At the same time, he warned that one could not simply close residential facilities until alternatives were available with some degree of demonstrated effectiveness.

During the seventies and early eighties, the movement for deinstitutionalization gained momentum for philosophical, legal, theoretical, and economic reasons.

Philosophical Influences

As noted, a key driving force of the period under review was the principle of normalization, which placed considerable emphasis on living in the community:

> For a (deviant) person, integration is achieved where he lives in a culturally normative community setting in ordinary community housing, can move and communicate in ways typical for his age, and is able to utilize, in typical ways, typical community resources: developmental, social, recreational, and religious facilities; hospitals and clinics; the post office; stores and restaurants; job placements; and so on.
>
> Ultimately, integration is only meaningful if it is social integration; i.e., if it involves social integration and acceptance, and not merely physical presence. However, social integration can only be attained if certain pre-conditions exist, among these being physical integration, although physical integration by itself will not guarantee social integration.[98]

Physical integration involved four factors— the home's location (in the community where the person is to be served), its adjacency to other facilities and settings, its accessibility, and its size (few residents). Again, however, even though foster or group homes might be located in the heart of a community in the midst of a nondeviant population, this alone would not necessarily guarantee social integration.

Legal Influences

The entire thrust for deinstitutionalization received considerable impetus as a result of early federal court decisions. First, they placed marked restrictions on who should be considered for admission:

> No borderline or mildly mentally retarded persons shall be a resident of the institution. (*Wyatt v. Stickney, 1972*)[99]
>
> No person classified as borderline, mildly, or moderately retarded according to the standards of classification at Cambridge shall be admitted unless that person suffers from psychiatric or emotional disorders in addition to his retardation . . . . (*Welsch v. Likens, 1974*)[100]

Second, mentally retarded persons, even those considered eligible under court orders, should not be admitted to a residential facility until all other community resources have been explored:

> No person shall be admitted to the institution unless a prior determination shall have been made that residence in the institution is the least restrictive habilitation setting. (*Wyatt* v. *Stickney,* 1972)[101]
>
> No mentally retarded person shall be admitted to Cambridge State Hospital on civil commitment if services and programs are available in the community. (*Welsch* v. *Likens,* 1974)[102]

These decisions again reflected upon the concept of the least restrictive environment. As explained in a report by the Mental Health Law Project, the least restrictive environment in the context of institutionalization:

> . . . means a person should not be hospitalized, with drastic curtailment of liberty involved, if he can be treated in a community at outpatient clinics or community mental health centers. . . . The right to be treated in a setting less restrictive than an institution [is] required by the constitutional principle of the least drastic means. The Constitution required that whenever a government is going to restrict a person's liberty against his will in order to accomplish a legitimate governmental objective, it must impose the least drastic restriction necessary to accomplish the legitimate governmental objective.[103]

Third, no mentally retarded person should remain in a residential facility longer than necessary:

> Residents shall have a right to the least restrictive conditions necessary to achieve the purposes of habilitation. To this end, the institution shall make every attempt to move residents from: (a) more to less structured living; (b) larger to smaller facilities; (c) larger to smaller living units; (d) group to individual residence; (e) segregated from the community to integrated living. (*Wyatt* v. *Stickney,* 1972)[104]

Neither should the individual be returned to the community indiscriminately:

> No resident may be transferred to a community residential facility or foster home unless it has been duly licensed; and the defendants are to make a written determination of the eligibility of each resident at Cambridge for community

placement and review such determination at least yearly. The defendants are to provide the court with a written plan to develop alternative residential care for all residents. (*Welsch* v. *Likens,* 1974)[105]

The intent of these decisions was clear. A residential facility should be used only as a last resort and only if the mentally retarded person's needs can be met.

Theoretical Influences

Many persons, professionals and parents alike, firmly believed that "smaller was better" and that community placement would automatically result in tremendous changes in behavior, development, and "normalization." The available research conducted throughout this period in time, however, did not fully support such contentions, and a rather mixed picture emerged.

Most—but not all—persons transferred from an institution to a small community setting, such as a supervised apartment, foster care, or a group home, found life most satisfying and pleasant.[106] A few of those relocated would have preferred to remain at the institution at least at the time of the study, primarily because they were separated from their friends of many years.[107]

As noted previously, however, placement per se did not automatically assure greater normalization, appropriate developmental experiences, or greater independence.[108] As reported by O'Connor in 1976, Butler and Bjaanes in 1978, and Flynn in 1980, many of the homes and/or their programs fell far short of meeting the criteria associated with normalization.[109] Butler and Bjaanes even concluded that many of the smaller community facilities were "socially isolated total institutions within the community."[110] Not surprisingly, in 1977, O'Connor cautioned that without proper study and planning, community facilities could simply represent a new version of the old institution without adequate public attention and resources.[111]

While many former residents did appreciate gains in life experiences, as already noted in the studies by Edgerton and Heshusius, mental retardation did not disappear with community placement, and many group home residents believed they had simply substituted one set of external decision-makers for another.[112]

Results concerning gains in intelligence or adaptive behavior varied significantly. In England, highly respected Jack Tizard reported that moderately and severely mentally retarded persons in small settings gained in verbal mental age but not in other areas normally measured by an intelligence test.[113] Rosen and colleagues in 1974 found no significant changes in intelligence quotients following placement.[114]

Measurements of adaptive behavior yielded more mixed results. Some studies demonstrated an increase in adaptive behavior, at least in some areas.[115] Others found no major change or difference between community-placed and institutionalized individuals, before or after placement, especially among those more severely affected.[116]

From these experiences and other related research, Sandler and Thurman in 1981 observed, "one can not conclude from these studies that positive changes in behavior resulted solely from movement out of large total institutions into smaller community based programs."[117] Their judgment was similar to that of Sharon Landesman-Dwyer, a highly respected researcher, in her extensive review of the research and report to the President's Committee on Mental Retardation: "Knowing that a given program benefits some individuals is not equivalent to understanding which features of residential programs are responsible for the encouraging results. Indiscriminate solutions, such as small family-style homes for everyone, will not long prove satisfactory."[118]

Others, however, examined the size question from a slightly different perspective, looking more closely at independence and community interaction. Under these circumstances, size may play an important role. Parental and foster homes were often found to be overprotective, creating a general atmosphere of dependence.[119] Conversely, "homes"

with eight or more residents tended to become "institutionalized," fostering dependence, compliance, group activity, and competition for attention. Mid-size homes (e.g., four to six persons) seemed to fare best.[120]

In the final analysis, therefore, normalization, independence, and community mobility were dependent upon many factors other than size. Yet, given such positive influences as encouraging individuality and independence as well as social interaction, the probability of success should be inversely related to size.

Economic Considerations

Perhaps the most common lobbying technique used by many organizations and groups when approaching various legislative bodies is to proclaim that their proposal would cost less money than currently being spent. So it was with many people promoting deinstitutionalization and alternative community living arrangements. Some studies tended to support that position: a sample of national facilities by the Center for Residential and Community Services of the University of Minnesota, in 1980, revealed that the average cost per day in the community setting was less than 50% of that of the institution. A number of state studies conducted in Pennsylvania, Minnesota, New York, and Nebraska yielded similar but less dramatic results: savings in community facilities ranged from 10% to 30%.[121] There were, however, many problems associated with studies of this nature since it was extremely difficult, and often impossible, to determine or monitor the detailed costs in the community since they were spread over so many individuals and agencies. Further, the studies usually failed to take into consideration the characteristics of the residents served, their program, or the degree to which their needs were met.

More definitive studies, such as that conducted in Oregon in 1982, indicated that group homes cost slightly more than an institution.[122] In 1983, Bensberg and Smith examined 16 group homes and compared their costs with 12 institutions, taking into consideration a number of variables and concluded,

"The costs of providing community-based residential services appear to be at least equal if not greater than those in the public residential facility."[123] In this, their conclusion was almost identical to that of Mayeda and Wai in 1975, following a study involving community and institutional costs in Washington, California, and Florida: "The cost of services to developmentally disabled persons in state hospitals do not differ significantly from the adjusted, true cost of services in community settings *provided* both groups are provided with a full array of needed services."[124]

By 1984, it was becoming increasingly clear that while the costs of noncomplicated cases involving school-age mildly or moderately mentally retarded persons living at home, in a foster home, or in a group home might cost less than similar institutional programs, meeting the needs of more medically and behaviorally involved persons, especially more severely mentally retarded persons, would cost considerably more.[125] As one person observed in 1983, while the cost of a special program in an institution is approximately $50,000 per year, a specialized group home for a similar population could cost as much as $130,000 per year per person.[126]

By the mid-eighties, most persons, regardless of their position or responsibility, recognized that cost savings would not be realized when appropriate programming was in place. As Conroy and Bradley, researchers and advocates for deinstitutionalization, opined, "we recommend that administrators and advocates at all levels avoid the claim that tax dollars can be 'saved' by switching to community-based services."[127]

While the question of institutional versus community costs was being investigated and debated, often overlooked were the comparative costs of providing for mentally retarded persons in the community with nondisabled youngsters and adults receiving similar services. Since most local agencies did not have financial commitments for institutional programs, the entire issue of institutional versus community cost was rather meaningless in their eyes. What they discovered was quite disconcerting: serving deinstitutionalized

mentally retarded persons in the community cost twice as much as did their other programs, and both their budgets and services were often inadequate.[128] Given these circumstances, many local communities and their representatives were hesitant to assume additional responsibilities.

The Shifting Emphasis

By the late seventies and early eighties, the mood among a growing segment of the professional, parental, and political communities had clearly shifted. Increasingly, more groups and individuals sought the complete closure of institutions for their continued failure to meet expectations:

> We must evacuate the institutions for the mentally retarded. There is no time any more for the new task forces and new evaluation teams. The time is long past for such nonsense. Joint accreditation commissions do no good. We need to empty the institutions. The quicker we accomplish that goal the quicker we will be able to repair the damage done to generations of innocent inmates. The quicker we get about converting our ideologies and resources to a community model, the quicker we will learn how to forget what we have perpetrated in the name of humanity.
>
> Those who fear that community placements will cause problems are quite right. To live with our retarded children, our handicapped friends, our aging parents does place burdens on us. What we must learn from the nightmare of institutions is that there are burdens which cannot be avoided or delegated: to have a decent society we must behave as decent individuals. Ultimately our society will discover that it is actually easier to meet than avoid the responsibilities we have as human beings.
>
> Thus, we demand that every institution for the mentally retarded in the United States be closed. We insist that a society which claims to be civilized can find the proper ways and means to include the people who have been institutional inmates in decent community environments. The inmates have suffered enough. Society has done enough damage.[129]

Increasing support for deinstitutionalization came from several influential groups. These included the Association for Persons with Severe Handicaps, which worked diligently for "the rapid termination of living environments . . . that segregate, regiment, and isolate persons from individualized attention . . ."[130] In 1980, Operation Real Rights, a network of persons with disabilities and advocates of institutional reform, was created with a single purpose: "The end of segregated living environments for all persons with severe disabilities."[131] This "Ad Hoc Committee to Make Real the Rights of All Persons with Disabilities" drafted federal legislation intended to provide alternative living arrangements, primarily through the transfer of Medicaid (Title XIX) dollars from institutions to the community.

In 1982, the Association for Retarded Citizens of the United States lent considerable support and weight to the deinstitutionalization movement when, in November of that year, it adopted the following policy:

WHEREAS, in the domain of Human Rights:
All people have fundamental moral and constitutional rights.
These rights must not be abrogated merely because a person has a mental or physical disability.
Among these fundamental rights is the right to community living, and
WHEREAS, in the domain of Educational Programming and Human Service:
All people, as human beings, are inherently valuable.
All people can grow and develop.
All people are entitled to conditions which foster their development.
Such conditions are optimally provided in community settings.
NOW THEREFORE BE IT RESOLVED that in fulfillment of fundamental human rights and in securing optimum developmental opportunities, all people, regardless of the severity of their disabilities, are entitled to community living.[132]

In 1983, these various groups found an ally in Senator John Chafee of Rhode Island, who supported the legislation drafted by Operation Real Rights and introduced it to the U.S. Senate. The intent and basic features of the resultant bill, the Community and Family Living Amendments of 1983, were to:

1. assure the right of persons who are severely disabled to live and be served in the community regardless of the degree of their disability;
2. shift of the federal share of Medicaid funds

from institutional to community-based environments, giving states 10 to 15 years (to be negotiated with the Health Care Financing Administration) to create family scale residences before losing Medicaid money for persons residing in institutions;
3. protect against "dumping" by mandating that an appropriate environment and program be created for each individual with the participation of the individual and, when appropriate, the individual's parent or guardian;
4. require that the residence in the community meet ICF/MR (Medicaid) standards and that it must be monitored regularly by an independent contractor (not by the state or a provider agency);
5. help states fund the establishment of community living arrangements by allowing Medicaid money to follow the individual into the community and by adding 5% "start up" money to the federal match for the first five years of the program;
6. assure quality of service for persons not yet living in the community by requiring that institutions and private facilities, including nursing homes, that serve persons with mental retardation must continue to meet federal standards or the state would face a percentage reduction in its federal Medicaid match for administrative expenses;
7. provide that services such as personal aides, domestic assistance, family support services, respite care, staff training, case management services, habilitation and rehabilitation be funded by Medicaid on a permanent basis for the first time. This would make services available to persons with severe disabilities who are living at home or in other community arrangements.[133]

Representatives of Operation Real Rights contended that if the bill were passed and signed into law, the "United States would become the world's leading advocate for community services for developmentally and physically disabled persons."[134] Other parents and advocates, as is discussed, were not equally as enthusiastic.

DEINSTITUTIONALIZATION IN PRACTICE

Deinstitutionalization as a process involved two basic phases: 1) preventing initial admission and 2) providing adequate community programs and resources for persons currently living in institutions. It was in the latter area that deinstitutionalization encountered some of its greatest difficulties.

Community services and deinstitutionalization had long been on the mind of the Association for Retarded Citizens of the United States, which, in 1979, outlined four desirable characteristics of an alternative living setting. It should:

> Provide a home environment with supervision and guidance as needed;
>
> Afford living experiences appropriate to the age, functioning level and learning needs of the individual;
>
> Provide access to necessary supportive, habilitative and rehabilitative programs based on a developmental model of programming; and
>
> Provide access to the mainstream of community life.[135]

The Association also advised its membership to be certain that basic services were available, including:

1. Services for infants and preschool children
   a. Diagnostic and evaluation services
   b. Special nursery and preschool classes
   c. Home training
   d. Home nursing
   e. Parent Counseling
   f. Parent discussion groups
   g. Trained babysitter pool
   h. Medical and dental management
   i. Child welfare services
   j. Foster home care and respite care
2. Services for school-age children
   a. Special school programs
   b. Developmental day programs for severely and profoundly retarded and/or multihandicapped children
   c. Homemaker services
   d. Special therapies such as speech, occupational, or physical therapy
   e. Recreation programs
   f. Scouting
   g. Foster home care
   h. Residential services, including respite care

3. Services for adolescents
   a. Special school programs
   b. Counseling services
   c. Prevocational evaluation and training
   d. Sheltered workshops
   e. Activity centers
   f. Advocacy program
   g. Sex education programs
   h. Youth groups, recreation and social clubs
   i. Premarital and genetic counseling
   j. Guardianship and protective services
   k. Residential services, including respite care
4. Services for adults
   a. Special adult education programs
   b. Vocational evaluation, training, and placement
   c. Social habilitation programs
   d. Sheltered employment
   e. Recreation and social activities
   f. Legal counsel
   g. Supportive services such as meals, homemaking, medical, and dental
   h. Advocacy program
   i. Guardianship and protective services[136]

Unfortunately, however, these conditions often were not met.

DEINSTITUTIONALIZATION OF MENTALLY ILL PERSONS

Before discussing deinstitutionalization experiences among mentally retarded persons, it should be noted that the entire movement had its inception a decade earlier with persons living in mental hospitals. The original idea of reducing institutional populations evolved from the findings of the Joint Commission on Mental Illness and Health. This Commission, originally established by Congress in 1955, reported its recommendations in 1960. The ideas proposed were included in President Kennedy's message to Congress, which, in turn, as already noted, resulted in the passage of the Mental Retardation Facilities and Community Mental Health Centers Construction Act of 1963.[137]

The movement gained almost immediate acceptance and within a relatively short period of time, tens of thousands of mentally ill persons were released from mental hospitals. Between 1970 and 1974, mental hospital populations fell by approximately 55%.[138] By 1984, over 75% of the population had been returned to the community.[139]

The results were often cruel and inhumane, and the entire effort became a national disgrace. Many of the individuals discharged were senior citizens with major psychiatric and neurological problems who were simply transferred to nursing homes, often ill prepared in terms of staffing, facilities, and resources to offer adequate programs. A number of cities started "psycho buses," vehicles used to transfer a person from the hospital to a vacant city street.[140] A wide range of welfare hotels were used, many of which did not begin to satisfy any semblance of decent or safe accommodations. It was estimated in 1975 that 25% of the 100,000 or more residents in New York City's welfare hotels were "severely mentally dysfunctional."[141] During that same year, a series of investigative news stories reported malnutrition, insect infestation, and dehydration among former state mental patients confined in board and care homes. Although 600 such homes existed in Philadelphia alone, the state had stopped licensing and inspecting them in 1967.[142]

A few groups, including the American Federation of State, County, and Municipal Employees, complained bitterly about such circumstances. In their 1975 publication, *Out of Their Beds and Into the Streets*, written by Henry Santiestevan, ample documentation was offered to highlight the sad plight of many patients from mental hospitals in Massachusetts, California, and New York. Though Santiestevan's primary attention was devoted to mentally ill persons, he also noted some of the undesirable practices involving former residents who were mentally retarded, returning from either a mental hospital or an institution.[143] While such reports received some attention, no national movement to modify the conditions occurred. Most of the newspaper reports dealt with local situations and many persons viewed Santiestevan's publication as simply reflecting union interests. By 1984, that situation had changed dramatically with frequent national scandals involving the millions of "street people," many of whom had gone through the deinstitutionalization process either by being returned to the community or not being admitted for help because they were not legally considered dangerous to themselves or to others. In 1984, the American Psychiatric Association released its first comprehensive report on the situation, labeling the practice of discharging mentally ill persons from state hospitals to poorly prepared communities, "a major social tragedy."[144]

In brief, "dumping" had become synonymous with deinstitutionalization, and those who were to be helped became "unwanted incompetents" who were "nobody's problem."[145] Unfortunately, despite increased media attention, street people remained politically ignored. The lesson for those responsible for deinstitutionalizing mentally retarded persons was clear—no transfer should occur until all basic community support systems were functioning well, and former residents should not be abandoned following placement.

DEINSTITUTIONALIZATION OF MENTALLY RETARDED PEOPLE

Deinstitutionalization of mentally retarded persons was a mixture of success, failure, and occasionally, unconscionable decision making. "Dumping" did occur, especially in the beginning.

While few mentally retarded persons became street people, early deinstitutionalization efforts often followed the same patterns that had become associated with the movement of mentally ill individuals. Partly in order to meet deinstitutionalization intents and partly to satisfy Title XIX requirements for substantially reduced rated bed capacities, thousands of mentally retarded persons, regardless of age or mental or physical abilities, were transferred to nursing homes, leading the Association for Retarded Citizens of the United States both to object and to set forth the following policy statement:

> Placement in any residential setting should be age appropriate. The nursing home setting is appropriate *only* for those mentally retarded individuals who require continuous, 24-hour skilled nursing care because of chronic and severe medical problems or physical and mental incapacitation due to advanced age. Mentally retarded children and adults must not be placed in nursing homes if they have principal habilitative needs which are not medically related . . . .[146]

Even following these early and often negative experiences, data provided by public residential facilities over the years consistently indicated that many alternative placements involved another institutional setting. Though between 1970 and 1983 the number of residents served daily in a public residential facility decreased by 37%, from 189,546 to 119,335, this did not mean that over 70,000 persons returned to the community, engaged in the mainstream of society, and readily fulfilled the social and physical expectancies associated with normalization.[147] Rather, approximately 25% returned to their immediate family or relatives, a pattern well established prior to the seventies. Another 25%–30% returned to the community and genuinely less restrictive settings, such as foster homes, apartments, or small group homes. The remaining 45%–50%, however, moved to other institutions, including nursing homes, county homes, private institutions, correctional facilities, and various hospitals.[148]

Also, in an effort to reduce institutional populations, some states and/or local agencies sought to defer all admissions. Thus, one state, long known as very progressive, conducted a survey in 1979 of developmentally disabled adults receiving some form of aided residential service. Of 8,183 adults, 1,483 were in a state center for developmentally disabled persons; 1,250 were in apartments or group homes with less than 9 persons; 319 were in group homes of 9–20 individuals; 510 were in small institutions of 20 or more (usually county homes); and the largest number,

4,622, were in nursing homes. Thus, only 15% of those studied were living in a more normalized setting; that is, one with less than nine persons.[149]

For those who hoped that all placements would involve a small, home-like community environment, actual experiences were somewhat disappointing. Yet, gains in alternative living situations were made, and some historical attitudes were altered, especially as they related to mentally retarded children.

Foster Care and Adoption

Prior to the sixties, foster care and adoption were rarely considered for mentally retarded children, because most social agencies believed such youngsters could not formulate normal relations within a typical family setting.[150] In fact, if children were placed with a family and later discovered to be mentally retarded, they frequently were returned to the placing agency and often ended up in an institution. During the sixties, an increasing number of mildly mentally retarded youngsters and a few of the more severely affected children began to be placed in foster settings. Adoption also began to be viewed as appropriate for a few mildly involved youngsters.[151]

During the seventies, many agencies, including institutions, launched rather large-scale foster family programs even for more severely affected children; they frequently encountered no difficulties in such placements and even had waiting lists of prospective foster parents. Adoption moved at a much slower pace, as illustrated by Krishef's study of 1977, which only requested information concerning mildly mentally retarded children. His results revealed that, by then, most social agencies considered mildly mentally retarded children to be fully adoptable and that neither special screening nor unique follow-up services were required.[152] Relatively few placements were made, however.

In 1978, the federal government, under the provisions of the Child Abuse Prevention and Treatment and Adoption Reform Act (PL 95-266), set out to encourage the adoption of special needs children by providing information, training, and technical assistance aimed at helping state and local groups eliminate barriers to the adoption of mentally retarded and other disabled youngsters. Two years later, the Adoption Assistance and Child Welfare Act of 1980 (PL 96-272) added direct financial support to the program.[153] During the spring of 1983, the federal government once more renewed its efforts in this direction by encouraging the movement of developmentally disabled children from foster homes and institutions into adoptive family settings.[154] Through efforts such as these, an increasing number of mentally retarded youngsters over the years found a genuine, secure home.

Group Homes and Public Sentiment

Nothing in the new scheme of providing for mentally retarded persons would test public attitudes as much as the possibility and, in some cases, the reality of placing a group home for mentally retarded individuals in one's immediate neighborhood. At the same time, with the exception of parental support, nothing was more important to successful placement and societal integration than neighborhood acceptance.

The media gave greater visibility to those who were mentally retarded than ever in the past. Television spots, encouraging community acceptance, were sponsored by the President's Committee on Mental Retardation and the Association for Retarded Citizens of the United States.

Major movies and television productions presented realistic portrayals of mentally retarded persons, including several that won national recognition and awards for their starring actors: "Charly" (1968), "Bill" (1981), and "Bill: On His Own" (1983). "Charly," which was based on the classic short story "Flowers for Algernon" by Daniel Keyes, depicted the fictional experiences of a mentally retarded young man whose intelligence, as a result of a scientific experiment, rose to the level of genius—only to return to its former level.[155] The two films about Bill presented the true story of a mentally retarded man released from a state institution. Other

films offered equally sensitive stories of mentally retarded persons and the turmoil surrounding their lives, including "No Other Love" (1979), about two mildly retarded young adults who married despite the marked reservations of their parents; "Two of a Kind" (1982), in which a mentally retarded young man brings renewed youth to his aging grandfather; "A Special Kind of Love" (1982), depicting the plight and anguish of a widowed truck driver who, much to his dread, decided to place his mentally retarded son in an institution; and "Welcome Home, Jelly Bean" (1982), describing the family difficulties in having a hyperactive severely retarded girl return home from an institutional placement. Perhaps the most outstanding film, appreciated more by those familiar with mental retardation and its history, as opposed to the public in general, was the marvelously conceived and acted film "The Wild Child" (1969), about Victor the Wild Boy of Aveyron, directed by the internationally renowned French director and artist, Francois Truffaut.

In addition to films, a number of books about mentally retarded offspring were published by notable persons, such as: *The Gifts They Bring* by Pearl S. Buck and Gweneth Zarfoss.[156] The most remarkable book, however, was by Nigel Hunt, an Englishman with Down syndrome, whose personal story was one of sensitive humor and a profound love of life.[157]

The Special Olympics

Of all activities that projected a positive image to the public, none garnered the support and affection of thousands of people from all walks of life as did the Special Olympics. This international activity, which in 1984 involved over a million mentally retarded persons, had its origins in a 1967 request by a Chicago civic committee to the Joseph P. Kennedy, Jr. Foundation to underwrite a special track meet. Spearheaded by the energetic and persuasive Eunice Kennedy Shriver, sister of President John F. Kennedy, the meet was held with an unanticipated 1,000 participants.[158] Interest in the program grew rapidly and within a few years, Special Olympic events were held in every state and in 52 countries around the world. In 1978, the first international competition was held.

From its inception, the Special Olympics drew national attention, and many former athletes, former coaches, and major companies directly participated in the training and/or financial support of the events. Naturally, it was a tremendous experience for the participants and their families.

While a few persons did question the Special Olympics in terms of normalization, nearly everyone believed the program completely fulfilled its goals "to contribute to the physical, social, and psychological development of the mentally retarded . . . [and to help them] gain confidence and self-mastery and start to build a self-image associated with success rather than failure."[159]

Other Support and Changing Attitudes

The United Nations also sought greater visibility for the problems of developmentally disabled persons, approximately 500 million people worldwide, by declaring the years of 1983–1992 to be the "Decade of the Disabled." It also encouraged a greater intensification of efforts on their behalf.[160] In response, President Reagan issued a proclamation calling forth a National Decade of Disabled Persons, corresponding to the same years and purposes as those set by the United Nations.[161]

All these events and activities, plus affirmative action, mainstreaming, and educational programs, did increase sensitivity to developmentally disabled persons, as reflected in various public opinion polls. Surveys conducted throughout the years revealed a gradual greater acceptance of those who were mentally retarded as well as their right to live and work in the community.[162] In 1975, a Gallup Poll commissioned by the President's Committee on Mental Retardation reported that 85% of their sample of 796 people indicated they would not object to a group home of six mildly or moderately retarded people located within 6 blocks of their home.[163] In 1983, Roth and Smith reported that their study of Arkansawyers found similar favorable attitudes toward community living.[164] The following year, Salend and colleagues noted that 82% of landlords contacted would rent to mentally retarded persons.[165]

Zoning Arguments

Nevertheless, many people objected strongly to locating a group home in their neighborhood. On occasion, negative reactions were aggressively expressed, including destroying group homes under construction and threatening employees and/or residents. More often, however, members of the community sought to prevent the development of a group home through legal means, relying on zoning ordinances and the definition of a family dwelling.

The first such case arose in New York in the early seventies. In essence, those who attempted to block the development of a group home relied on the interpretation that since there was no legal or biological relationship between residents, the home violated the family dwelling clause. In response, the New York Court of Appeals, in the landmark case of *City of White Plains* v. *Ferraioli* (1974), ruled:

Special Olympics

The city has a proper purpose in largely limiting the uses in a zone to single family units. But if it goes beyond to require that the relationships in the family unit be those of blood or adoption, then its definition of family might be too restrictive . . . . Zoning is intended to control the types of housing and living and not the generic or intimate internal family relations of human beings . . . .

Whether a family be organized along ties of blood or formal adoptions, or be a similarly structured group sponsored by the state, as is the group home, should not be consequential in meeting the test of the zoning ordinance. So long as the group home bears the generic character of a family unit as a relatively permanent household, and is not a framework for transients or transient living, it conforms to the purpose of the ordinance . . . .[166]

A number of such cases appeared throughout the country over the next few years, with most, but not all, ending in a decision similar to that just described.[167] In one notable case, the matter had to be referred to the U.S. Supreme Court for final resolution.

In 1980, Cleburne Living Centers, Inc. desired to lease a building in the city to operate a group home for 13 mentally retarded clients. The city informed the operators that they would have to obtain a special permit under a zoning regulation governing the construction of "hospitals for the insane or feebleminded, or alcoholic, or drug addicts, or penal or correctional institutions." The entrepreneurs complied, and on October 14, 1980, the City Council of Cleburne, Texas denied the permit, following a public hearing. Reasons cited included:

the attitude of a majority of the owners of property located within 200 feet of the proposed group home;
the location of a junior high school across the street from the proposed home;
fears of elderly residents of the neighborhood;
the size of the home and the number of residents to be housed;

concern over the legal responsibility of the operators for any actions the residents might take;
the home's location on a 500 year flood plain; and
in general, the presentations made before the city council at the hearing.[168]

Based on the permit denial, the operators filed suit in the U.S. District Court for the Northern District of Texas, claiming that the city of Cleburne was discriminating against handicapped persons in violation of the federal Revenue Sharing Act and the equal protection and due process clauses of the Fourteenth Amendment to the U.S. Constitution. On October 4, 1982, U.S. District Court Judge Robert W. Porter denied the plaintiff's contention that mentally retarded persons constitute a "suspect" or "quasi-suspect" class and, thus, deserve a higher level of judicial scrutiny in cases of alleged discrimination.

Judge Porter's decision, however, was overturned by a three-judge panel of the Fifth U.S. Circuit Court of Appeals on March 5, 1984. The appeals court found that the mentally retarded do, indeed, constitute a quasi-suspect class and, as such, deserve special judicial protection. The city of Cleburne then addressed the matter to the U.S. Supreme Court.*

The reasons people rejected group homes for mentally retarded persons varied widely, from the fear of family danger, including sexual assault, to concern over property values.[170] As regards the latter, research indicated that property values did not decrease by the appearance of a specialized group home.[171]

Fortunately, while neighborhood objections did exist and undoubtedly slowed the rate at which alternative living facilities were established, considerable progress was evident in that thousands of group homes were established. As of January 1, 1982, 57,494 men-

---

*On July 1, 1985, the U.S. Supreme Court rendered its ruling, which declared that the city of Cleburne had acted improperly in denying a license to establish the group home, indicating that "mere negative attitudes, or fear, unsubstantiated by factors which are properly cognizable in a zoning proceeding, are not permissible bases for treating a home for the mentally retarded differently from apartment houses, multiple dwellings, and the like."[169] At the same time, and to the consternation of many, the U.S. Supreme Court did not hold that mentally retarded persons had a quasi-suspect status in equal protection cases.

tally retarded persons lived in 6,302 group homes of which 73% were 15 beds or less. Remarkable was the fact that there had been a 900% growth in the number of facilities with 15 or less beds over the preceding 10-year period.[172] In fact, few such homes existed prior to the sixties.

When the group home appeared, neighbors reacted differently. Some were frightened:

> Ever since that day when 10 retarded men moved into the house behind hers in Altamonte Springs, [Ms. M.] said, she has kept her doors locked and her shades drawn.
> "I'm scared to death," she said.
> "The first time someone comes peeping in my door, we're going to have a funeral in three days. Not them, but me. I am going to have a heart attack."[173]

Some became passively accepting:

> "We never even think about it anymore. We really have no more contact with them. We were more concerned with the thought, but it's all worn off," said [Mr. E.], who lives down the street from the group home.[174]

Some became actively accepting:

> [Mrs. W.] of Orlando said she probably would have never bought next to a group home had she known it was there. "But now," she said, "I couldn't have nicer neighbors.
> They watch my house and if the car windows are down when it's raining, they will be closed.
> We have one that calls us mother and father. She visits us, well, it was seven days a week, but we got it down to three or four days a week. We were inundated for a while, but now it's no problem."[175]

After reviewing the situation and interviewing a number of neighbors, including those just cited, journalist Rosemary Goudreau could only conclude, "Whether the retarded will ever truly be accepted as an integral part of any neighborhood is still questionable."[176] Fortunately, in time, most neighbors (80%) came to accept, or at least not openly object, to the specialized group home.[177]

EXPERIENCES IN DEINSTITUTIONALIZATION

For many—especially the more mildly affected—deinstitutionalization, while rarely perfect in all aspects, did offer a new sense of freedom, self-worth, and happiness:

> There are many people like me who are in institutions. Today my life is so much better. I am free because I live in a group home. I also have a job that I work at fulltime. It's in the neighborhood and with a big company. They are happy with my work and I am happy there. Because of the group home there are many other people just like me who have jobs. And there could be more. I am told we make excellent, reliable workers. Think about that. I am not living in an institution. Now I have a purpose to my life. I am a happy person.[178]

Fortunately, there were early models upon which local, regional, and state agencies could develop their efforts. There was the foster home program of the Macomb-Oakland Regional Center intended to avert the need for institutionalization. Similarly, the Eastern Nebraska Community Office of Mental Retardation, better known as ENCORE, established a network of community-based services for mentally retarded persons, including those more severely affected. Formed as one of the state's regional programs in 1970, ENCORE encompassed a five-county area, primarily rural in nature, with the exception of the city of Omaha. Built on the normalization principle, ENCORE emphasized full social integration of all clients.[179]

But the deinstitutionalization experience, even among model programs, was not without its difficulties, programmatically and administratively. From the programmatic perspective, problems included proper matching of client and home; balancing independence and protection; providing adequate services, especially for the adult, delinquent, mentally troubled or difficult-to-manage individual; locating adequate medical and therapeutic services for the more severely affected; a general feeling of loneliness, sometimes resulting from breaking up long-standing friendships; little

A group home setting

active interaction with the general community or use of its social-recreational resources; frequent transferring between community facilities; inadequate parental participation; and transitional shock.[180]

Transitional shock was a poorly understood phenomenon, but if placements were not carefully planned, the adverse effects could range from a relatively minor, short-term loss in language usage to an increase in aggressive behavior, which might warrant return to the institution.[181] At its worst, poorly conceived movement could and did result in death.[182] Too many mentally retarded (and mentally ill) persons died in group home fires, most of whom had been placed in such facilities to avoid institutionalization.[183] Some of the homes were described as being "built to burn."[184]

The situation was succinctly summarized by Landesman-Dwyer in 1981:

> The number, quality, and diversity of residential programs and support services are inadequate . . . . Despite the emphasis on accountability and on individualized plans, many mentally retarded individuals and their families do not receive the help they need. Freedom of choice is seldom a reality when people try to find appropriate educational, training, social, recreational, vocational, or health-care services.[185]

Similarly, during the eighties, Dudley found that too many clients were still "captives" of the mentally retarded world.[186] Also, Conroy

and Bradley reported that former residents were "being fit into programs, rather than programs being designed specifically to meet individual needs."[187]

From an administrative perspective, community homes suffered from a host of problems, including closure rates (7.7% per year, according to one study); location in poorer sections of the community; inadequate community services; poor personnel salaries and high turnover rates; and insufficient staff training.[188] Again, in the words of Sharon Landesman-Dwyer, "Residential facilities are plagued by uncertainties in funding, high staff-turnover rates, low pay scales, resistance from local communities, problems in interagency coordination, fluctuations in the morale of the direct-care staff and administrators, and the perpetual fear of lawsuits or loss of licensure."[189]

As regards training of community direct-care personnel, a number of community colleges, as early as the mid-sixties, developed special 2-year programs, but salaries offered were not commensurate with student investment. Therefore, many graduates accepted other positions.[190]

While these inadequacies did not deter persons determined to provide community alternative living arrangements, they did, nevertheless, illustrate severe deficiencies, ones that would have to be addressed more seriously in the future. Further, the absence of an adequate number of well-trained staff resulted in too many individuals being returned to institutions because of behavioral/safety reasons.[191] Persons with medically related difficulties, especially among those more seriously affected, also found themselves at increased risk for readmission.[192]

One of the major problems confronting all concerned with deinstitutionalization was the lack of adequate funds. Support for alternative living situations came from a number of sources, including personal earnings, local and state agency grants, and a variety of third party payees (e.g., insurance companies).[193] Several federal programs also contributed, directly and indirectly. Among these were Title XX of the Social Security Act, passed in 1974, which had among its five objectives "preventing or reducing inappropriate institutional care through provision of less restrictive alternatives."[194] By 1981, $500 million were spent on community services for developmentally disabled persons through this legislation, devoted primarily to transportation, day care, and attendant care.[195] Another source of federal funding was Supplemental Security Income, originally intended to provide for the "creature" needs of developmentally disabled and other eligible persons. Such funds could be used for a variety of special purposes.

In 1981, the Secretary of Health and Human Services was granted the authority to waive Medicaid requirements to permit the transfer of Title XIX funds to support community services for individual institutional residents. By 1983, 16 states had successfully applied for the Medicaid waiver program and used the money to provide various community services to individuals, including: case management, homemaker services, home health aide services, personal care, habilitation, respite care, therapy, and counseling.[196] As of December 31, 1984, 17,000 disabled persons, not all of whom were mentally retarded, were being served under this provision.[197] It was also estimated that the program saved over $403 million compared to institutional costs.[198]

Another major federal funding resource was Section 202 of the Housing Act of 1959, administered by the Department of Housing and Urban Development. Between 1960 and 1985, approximately 15% of available funds were used to develop 6,000 group homes, serving approximately 46,000 mentally disabled persons, approximately 50% of whom were mentally retarded.[199] In 1984, $604.8 million were available for such purposes, which included construction, purchase, or renovation.[200]

Despite the diversity of financial resources, in the final analysis, available funds were woefully inadequate. It was for this reason that Senator Chafee sought to increase sub-

stantially the Medicaid waiver program with his Community Living Amendments of 1983.

DEINSTITUTIONALIZATION AND PARENTS

While much attention was devoted to mentally retarded persons affected by deinstitutionalization, less concern was devoted to their parents. And, as repetitive studies demonstrated, many parents objected vigorously to the placement of their offspring into the community.[201] The study of Spreat and colleagues reported in 1985 was rather typical: 58.2% of the parents contacted would not, under any circumstances, approve discharge of their offspring to the community; 36% would agree if there were adequate security, active programming, and adequate medical services.[202] Objecting parents were often knowledgeable about and supportive of the principle of normalization, but expected greater realization of its tenets in the institutional setting; however, Conroy and Bradley did find in their series of follow-up studies that many parents who initially disagreed with community placement came to accept it when permanence and stability were assured.[203]

Regardless of such findings, many parents of institutionalized persons continued to protest against deinstitutionalization. This was most evident as these parents reacted to the alternative living policy of the Association for Retarded Citizens of the United States and to the Community Living Amendments of 1983:

> It [the bill] reflects an arrogant, dictatorial, inflexible philosophy or policy of ARC in . . . denying the right of mentally retarded citizens and their parents and legal guardians to choose the most appropriate residence from a large variety of options, including state and community institutions . . . .
>
> It probably goes without saying that it is a slap in the face . . . to those of us who have sons and daughters in state or community institutions and who want said institutions to be a viable positive option and who have fought the long fight for the initiation and expansion of community services, including education, developmental achievement centers, work activity centers, workshops, employment, group homes, foster homes, inde-

pendent living facilities and family subsidies, and who have always believed that with few exceptions, each parent should have the right to decide whether his mentally retarded son or daughter should live at home, in a community group home, in a community independent living unit, or in a state or community-based institution.[204]

As a general rule, each person should reside in the situation needed for his or her progress, health, training, education, happiness, etc. Everything depends on which physical place contributes most to his or her welfare and benefit. If a group home is best for a person, that's where he or she should be. If an institution is best, then that's where he or she should be. The good of the person is decisive—not the institution . . . not a nursing home . . . not a group home![205]

. . . I object to this Bill because, in my opinion, it will create out of the profoundly and severely retarded a class of people, much like many of the mentally ill who today are dumped on the streets of our cities, shuttling between police stations, hospitals, and courts—unwanted by the society and a prey to thieves, rapists, and murderers.[106]

Research showed that seriously discussing deinstitutionalization produced a crisis in 50% of the families contacted, even when their offspring was not placed into an alternative setting.[207] For the older parent, the experience could be terrifying, as exemplified by a letter written to a parents' organization:

I am 65 years old and have had a total laryngectomy and right neck dissection for carcinoma of the larynx. I can't speak and am a total nervous wreck. I just can't seem to be able to cope, but God willing, everything will work out. My husband is 74 years old and has a heart condition. Our oldest son died four years ago. My youngest son has a family of his own, so no help can come from him as money is already spread too thin. I wonder if you could help me . . . .[208]

Perhaps Fern Kupfer, parent and author, best summarized the position of those who objected to their offspring being placed in the community:

Most retarded people do not belong in institutions any more than most people over 65 belong in nursing homes. What we need are options and alternatives for a heterogeneous population. We need group homes and halfway houses and government subsidies to families who choose to care for dependent members at home. We need accessible housing for independent handicapped people; we need to pay enough to foster-care families to show that a good home is worth paying for. We need institutions. And it shouldn't have to be a dirty word.[209]

Regardless of the merits of the positions expressed, one thing was certain: Those responsible for community services had failed to convince many parents of the quality and stability of such services.

The Future for Institutions

The final question arising from the various theoretical positions and the emphasis on deinstitutionalization related to the future of institutions: Would they be needed, and if so, what might be their role? To some, the day of the institution was over, and future generations would "look upon them as we today look upon the almshouses and poor farms of the past—societal institutions that once performed essential services, but whose ways became obsolete in time, so that what was once a positive contribution became a damaging entity no longer needed."[210] Others were less certain, including administrators of community services. A 1984 study of 550 agencies in 35 states reported that 66% of the respondents believed institutions in the future would provide short-term intensive care; 41%, respite care; 80%, intensive therapy or programming for special groups, such as the difficult-to-manage; and 46%, extended care for those most severely affected. Only 8% believed that there would be no need for the institution.[211] In the final analysis, the future of institutions would be dependent upon many factors, especially the success of community programming.

EPILOGUE

IF NOT IMPOSSIBLE, it would certainly be unwise to attempt to winnow through the various forces that interacted throughout the historical period reviewed in order to assign respective values. Only time and further experience may determine what ultimately was most beneficial and why. Yet, 1960 to 1985 was a time of promise, progress, and uncertainty.

Many promises were made: rights, special considerations, normalization, and a full partnership in that society unique to the United States. Some progress was made in all areas of human endeavor. Medical science developed the capacity to treat more successfully a host of ills and physical problems that historically would have resulted in the premature death of young mentally retarded persons. Yet, there were the "Baby Does."

Educational services opened their doors to more severely affected persons and sought greater integration for all through mainstreaming. Yet, in too many instances, genuine social integration remained unrealized and high dropout rates were all too evident.

Full participation of adults in the normal flow of societal life was promised. Yet, all too many adults lived and labored in specialized facilities, often isolated and lonely. While the needs of the mentally ill, norm-violating, and aging mentally retarded person were recognized, progress again trailed far behind both promise and knowledge.

Similarly, parents faced a new day with promises of strong decision-making roles in selecting from a wide range of service options for themselves and their family members. Yet, while some gains were made, many deficiencies persisted.

In essence, promise far outweighed progress. Yet, the promises were magnificent and entirely consistent with the reawakened social and legal conscience of the country. Many programmatic islands of excellence did appear and clearly established a foundation upon which future growth could be made.

It was a period of uncertainty. Would the new philosophies be accepted? Could they be realized? Would the public open its heart and arms to those who were mentally retarded, encouraging and supporting their ventures in an open society? Would the people urge their political representatives to expend the money necessary to meet the tremendous need? In most instances, the response was positive. Yet, the period ended with great uncertainty: Would funds be available in the future when the social and political climate had become increasingly conservative during the eighties with federal spending for social programs already decreasing?[1] Correspondingly, would those who were mentally retarded maintain high visibility and value among legislators confronted with new and equally serious social challenges, such as the ubiquitous drug and alcohol problem?

Only time will tell; however, persons who are mentally retarded have much to offer our

259

society, and their history is one of spirit and confidence. Their life, as demonstrated by a number of studies previously cited, is never easy, even under the best of circumstances. Edgerton and his colleagues, in reporting on their aging subjects, in 1984, made several observations that would justify whatever support mentally retarded persons receive. Though their subjects' days were filled with stress, the authors acknowledged with admiration, "There is a central theme to their lives, whether those lives have worsened, improved, or remained very much the same: that theme is hope. With the exception of one woman who was quite depressed, all the rest had an un-shakeable optimism; they still had hope that life would be rewarding, or more rewarding than it had been, and they believed that their own actions could help to bring this outcome to pass. . . . There is something indomitable about these people. They truly believed that somehow they would manage."[2]

Perhaps, in years to come, history will record that the quarter century of 1960 to 1985 rendered its greatest service from a democratic, humanitarian perspective. Yet, as President Kennedy once observed, "Our responsibility is not discharged by an announcement of virtuous ends."[3]

SUPPLEMENTAL READINGS

A number of fine books and articles have been prepared concerning nearly every topic reviewed in this history. The supplemental readings listed below are just a few items that correspond closely with the text and, at the same time, should be readily available in any university library.

The interested reader is also referred to two serial publications: *International Review of Research in Mental Retardation*, edited by Norman Ellis and published by Academic Press of New York; and *Mental Retardation and Developmental Disabilities*, edited by Joseph Wortis and published by Brunner/Mazel of New York.

Aging:

Janicki, M.P., & Wisniewski, H.M. (Eds.). (1985). *Aging and developmental disabilities: Issues and approaches*. Baltimore: Paul H. Brookes Publishing Co.

Definition, Classification, and Labeling:

Baumeister, A., & Muma, J. (1975). On defining mental retardation. *Journal of Special Education, 9*, 293–306.

Farber, B. (1968). *Mental retardation: Its social context and social consequences*. Boston: Houghton Mifflin.

Grossman, H. (Ed.). (1983). *Classification in mental retardation*. Washington, DC: American Association on Mental Deficiency.

Heber, R. (1961). *A manual on terminology and classification in mental retardation* (2nd ed.). Monograph Supplement to the *American Journal of Mental Deficiency*.

Hunt, J. (1961). *Intelligence and experience*. New York: Ronald Press.

Jensen, A. (1969). How much can we boost IQ and scholastic achievement? *Harvard Educational Review, 39*, 1–123.

Deinstitutionalization and Community Services:

Bruininks, R., Mayers, C., Sigford, B., & Lakin, K. (Eds.). (1981). *Deinstitutionalization and community adjustment of mentally retarded people*. Washington, DC: American Association on Mental Deficiency.

Edgerton, R. (1967). *The cloak of competence*. Berkeley: University of California Press.

Edgerton, R. (Ed.). (1984). *Lives in progress: Mildly retarded adults in a large city*. Washington, DC: American Association on Mental Deficiency.

Edgerton, R., & Bercovici, S. (1976). The cloak of competence: Years later. *American Journal of Mental Deficiency, 80*, 485–497.

Haywood, C. (1981). Presidential address: Reducing social vulnerability is the challenge of the eighties. *Mental Retardation, 19*, 190–195.

Landesman-Dwyer, S. (1981). Living in the community. *American Journal of Mental Deficiency, 86*, 223–234.

Novak, A.R., & Heal, L.W. (Eds.). (1980). *Integration of developmentally disabled individuals into the community*. Baltimore: Paul H. Brookes Publishing Co.

O'Connor, G. (1983). Presidential address 1983: Social support of mentally retarded persons. *Mental Retardation, 21*, 187–196.

President's Panel on Mental Retardation. (1962). *A proposed program for national action to combat mental retardation*. Washington, DC: U.S. Government Printing Office.

Willer, B., & Intagliata, J. (1984). *Promises and realities for mentally retarded citizens*. Baltimore: University Park Press.

Wolfensberger, W. (1972). *The principle of normalization in human services*. Toronto: National Institute on Mental Retardation.

Wolfensberger, W. (1983). Social role valorization: A proposed new term for the principle of normalization. *Mental Retardation, 21*, 234–239.

Federal Legislation:

Boggs, E. (1971). Federal legislation. In J. Wortis (Ed.), *Mental retardation: An annual review* (Vol. 3). New York: Grune & Stratton.

Boggs, E. (1978). A taxonomy of federal programs affecting developmental disabilities. In J. Wortis (Ed.),

Mental retardation and developmental disabilities (Vol. 10, pp. 214–241). New York: Brunner/Mazel.

Braddock, D. (1987). *Federal policy toward mental retardation and developmental disabilities*. Baltimore: Paul H. Brookes Publishing Co.

Litvin, M., & Browning, P. (1978). Public assistance in historical perspective. In J. Wortis (Ed.), *Mental retardation and developmental disabilities* (Vol. 10, pp. 196–213). New York: Brunner/Mazel.

Summary of Existing Legislation Relating to the Handicapped. (1980). (Publication No. E-80-22014). Washington, DC: U.S. Department of Education, Office of Special Education and Rehabilitative Services.

General Historical Overviews of Mental Retardation:

President's Committee on Mental Retardation. (1977). *Mental retardation: Past and present*. Washington, DC: U.S. Government Printing Office.

Rosen, M., Clark, G., & Kivitz, M. (Eds.). (1976). *The history of mental retardation* (Vols. 1 and 2). Baltimore: University Park Press.

Scheerenberger, R.C. (1983). *A history of mental retardation*. Baltimore: Paul H. Brookes Publishing Co.

Sloan, W., & Stevens, H. (1976). *A century of concern: A history of the American Association on Mental Deficiency, 1876–1976*. Washington, DC: American Association on Mental Deficiency.

Vitello, S., & Soskin, R. (1985). *Mental retardation: Its social and legal context*. Englewood Cliffs, NJ: Prentice-Hall.

Institutions:

Baumeister, A., & Butterfield, E. (1970). *Residential facilities for the mentally retarded*. Chicago: Aldine, 1970.

Blatt, B., & Kaplan, F. (1966). *Christmas in purgatory.* Boston: Allyn & Bacon.

Kugel, R., & Wolfensberger, W. (Eds.). (1969). *Changing patterns in residential services for the mentally retarded*. Washington, DC: U.S. Government Printing Office.

Rothman, D., & Rothman, S. (1984). *The Willowbrook wars: A decade of struggle for social justice*. New York: Harper & Row.

Scheerenberger, R. (1978). Public residential services for the mentally retarded. In: N. Ellis (Ed.), *International review of research in mental retardation* (Vol. 9, pp. 187–208). New York: Academic Press.

White, W., & Wolfensberger, W. (1969). The evaluation of dehumanization in our institutions. *Mental Retardation, 7*(3), 5–9.

Wolfensberger, W. (1974). *The origin and nature of our institutional models*. Syracuse, NY: Center on Human Policy.

Law and Advocacy:

Burgdorf, R.L., Jr. (Ed.). (1980). *The legal rights of handicapped persons: Cases, materials, and text*. Baltimore, MD: Paul H. Brookes Publishing Co.

Burgdorf, R.L., Jr., & Spicer, P.P. (1983). *The legal rights of handicapped persons: Cases, materials, and text (1983 Supplement)*. Baltimore, MD: Paul H. Brookes Publishing Co.

Wolfensberger, W. (1975). *Citizen advocacy for the handicapped, impaired, and disadvantaged: An overview*. Washington, DC: U.S. Government Printing Office.

Wolfensberger, W., & Zauha, H. (1973). *Citizen advocacy and protection services for the impaired and handicapped*. Toronto: National Institute on Mental Retardation.

Learning and Behavior:

Bailer, I., & Sternlicht, M. (1977). *The psychology of mental retardation*. New York: Psychological Dimensions.

Balthazar, E., & Stevens, H. (1975). *The emotionally disturbed mentally retarded: A historical and contemporary perspective*. Englewood Cliffs, NJ: Prentice-Hall.

Ellis, N. (Ed.). (1979). *Handbook of mental deficiency, psychological theory and research* (2nd ed.). Hillsdale, NJ: Lawrence Erlbaum Associates.

Menolascino, F. (Ed.). (1970). *Psychiatric approaches to mental retardation*. New York: Basic Books.

Stark, J., & Menolascino, F. (Eds.). (1984). *Handbook of mental illness and mental retardation*. New York: Plenum.

Medicine:

Harris, H., & Hirschhorn, K. (Eds.). (1983). *Advances in human genetics*. New York: Plenum.

Smith, D. (1982). *Recognizable patterns of human malformation* (3rd ed.). Philadelphia: W.B. Saunders.

Parents:

Turnbull, H., & Turnbull, A. (Eds.). (1978). *Parents speak out*. Columbus, OH: Charles E. Merrill.

Turnbull, H., & Turnbull, A. (Eds.). (1985). *Parents speak out: Then and now*. Columbus, OH: Charles E. Merrill.

Special Education:

Blatt, B., & Morris, R. (Eds.). (1984). *Perspectives in special education: Personal orientations*. Glenview, IL: Scott, Foresman.

Jordan, J. (Ed.). (1976). *Exceptional child education at the Bicentennial: A parade of progress*. Reston, VA: The Council for Exceptional Children.

PL 94-142, The Education for All Handicapped Children Act (1975).

Rostetter, D., Kowalski, R., & Hunter, D. (1984). Implementing the integration principle of PL 94-142. In N. Certo, N. Haring, & R. York (Eds.), *Public School Integration of Severely Handicapped Students: Rational issues and progressive alternatives* (pp. 293–320). Baltimore, MD: Paul H. Brookes Publishing Co.

Tests and Measurements:

Sattler, J. (1982). *Assessment of children's intelligence and special abilities* (2nd ed.). Boston: Allyn & Bacon.

REFERENCE NOTES

Introduction

1. In: Hayes, 1969, p. xvii.
2. In: *Four Days,* 1964, p. 31.
3. In: Commanger, 1973, pp. 654–656.
4. From: Friendly & Cronkite, 1970.
5. From: Friendly & Cronkite, 1970.
6. Commanger, 1973.
7. Commanger, 1973.
8. In: Commanger, 1973, p. 653.
9. In: Roberts, 1970, p. 568.
10. Executive Order 11776, 1974.
11. Sherrill, 1977, p. 2.
12. Miller, W., Miller, A., & Schneider, 1980.
13. White, T., 1982, p. 4.
14. In: White, T., 1982, pp. 317, 329.
15. Maloney, Walsh, & DeLouise, 1984.
16. Karmin & Morse, 1984.
17. "U.S. needs," 1984, p. 59; "Youth character," 1984.

Chapter 1

1. Heber, 1961.
2. Heber, 1962.
3. Doll, 1941.
4. e.g., Cantor, 1960.
5. Garfield & Wittson, 1960, p. 953.
6. Grossman, 1973, p. 11.
7. Grossman, 1973, p. 11.
8. Grossman, 1973, p. 18.
9. Grossman, 1973, p. 11.
10. Grossman, 1973.
11. Grossman, 1977, pp. 5–6.
12. Grossman, 1977, p. 6.
13. "An open letter," 1979, p. 74.
14. "An open letter," 1979, pp. 74–75.
15. Grossman, 1983a, p. 11.
16. Grossman, 1983a, p. 15.
17. Grossman, 1983a, pp. 11, 16.
18. Tarjan & Eisenberg, 1972, p. 17.
19. President's Panel, 1962, pp. 1, 4.
20. Masland, 1963, p. 286.
21. Bijou, 1963, p. 101.
22. Scheerenberger, 1964.
23. Luria, 1963a, pp. 5, 10.
24. Luria, 1963a, p. 10.
25. Tenny, 1960, p. 303.
26. Kirk & Bateman, 1962.
27. Myklebust, 1964; Siegel, 1968.
28. PL 91-517.
29. PL 94-103.
30. PL 95-602.
31. *Federal Register,* 1980.
32. Grossman, 1983a, pp. 213–214.
33. Dexter, 1958, pp. 920–921.
34. Dexter, 1960, p. 836.
35. Dexter, 1960, p. 839.
36. Mercer, 1970, p. 382.
37. Mercer, 1970, pp. 383–384.
38. Baumeister & Muma, 1975, p. 297.
39. President's Panel, 1962, p. 1.
40. President's Panel, 1962, p. 1.
41. President's Panel, 1962, p. 1.
42. Tarjan, 1965.
43. Kushlick, 1966; Mercer, 1973a.
44. Luckey & Neman, 1976.
45. Jacobson & Janicki, 1983.
46. President's Committee, 1970.
47. Baller, 1936; Charles, 1953; Miller, E., 1965.
48. Miller, E., 1965.
49. Kogel & Edgerton, 1984, pp. 170–171.
50. Conley, 1973, p. 16.
51. Jensen, 1969; Nagi, 1976; National Commission, 1983.
52. Balakrishnan & Wolf, 1976; Kaveggia, 1985.
53. Dingman & Tarjan, 1960; Zigler, 1967.
54. e.g., Miles, 1963.
55. Tarjan, 1966.
56. Scheerenberger, 1964.
57. Mercer, 1973b; Kauffman & Payne, 1975; Maloney & Ward, 1979; Baroff, 1982.
58. Wechsler, 1971, p. 50.
59. Humphreys, 1971, pp. 31–32.
60. Cattell, 1963.
61. Guilford, 1966.
62. Bruner, 1965, p. 1007.
63. Hunt, J., 1961, pp. 362–363.
64. Flavell, 1963; Tuddenham, 1966.
65. Flavell, 1963, p. 15.
66. Inhelder, 1953, p. 75.
67. Piaget, 1952, 1966.
68. Piaget, 1952, p. 407.
69. Scheerenberger, 1969a.
70. Cronbach, 1975; Scheerenberger, 1983b.
71. Anastasi, 1967.
72. In: Burgdorf, 1980.
73. Terman & Merrill, 1960.
74. Thorndike, R., 1973.
75. Wechsler, 1974.
76. Wechsler, 1967.
77. Bayley, 1969.
78. Užgiris & Hunt, 1975.
79. McCarthy, D., 1972.
80. Slosson, 1963.
81. French, 1964.
82. Lewis & Mercer, 1978, p. 211.
83. Sattler, 1982; Wodrich, 1984.
84. Kennedy, W., Moon, Nelson, Lindner, & Turner, 1961; Sattler, 1982.

85. Sattler, 1982, p. 285.
86. Doll, 1953.
87. e.g., Walls, Werner, Bacon, & Jane, 1977; Mayeda, 1977.
88. Grossman, 1983a, p. 11.
89. Meyers, Nihira, & Zetlin, 1979.
90. Nihira, K., Foster, Shellhaas, & Leland, 1969; Lambert Windmiller, Cole, & Figueroa, 1975.
91. Fogelman, 1974.
92. Morrow, H., & Coulter, 1978.
93. Sparrow, Balla, & Cicchetti, 1984.
94. *Camelot Behavioral Systems Checklist,* 1974; Bock & Weatherman, 1976; Gunsburg, 1976.
95. Cain, Levine, & Elzey, 1963.
96. Levine, Elzey, Thormahlen, & Cain, 1976.
97. Ross, R., 1969.
98. Balthazar, 1971, 1973; Song & Jones, 1980.
99. Levine & Elzey, 1968.
100. Clausen, 1967, 1972.
101. Clausen, 1967, pp. 742–743.
102. MacMillan & Jones, 1972; Adams, 1973.
103. Baumeister & Muma, 1975.
104. Mercer, 1975; Buck, M., 1975.
105. Gold, 1978.
106. Garrison, 1960, p. 510.
107. Gallagher, J., & Moss, 1964, pp. 1, 4.
108. Reynolds, M., 1965, p. 341.
109. Weiner, 1967, p. 367.
110. In: Filler, Robinson, Smith, Vincent-Smith, Bricker, & Bricker, 1975, p. 202.
111. Filler et al., 1975, p. 203.
112. PL 88-352.
113. Brayfield, 1965.
114. *Hobson* v. *Hansen,* 1967.
115. In: Burgdorf, 1980, p. 308.
116. Cleary, Humphreys, Kendrick, & Wesman, 1975.
117. Cleary et al., 1975, pp. 39–40.
118. Jackson, 1975, p. 92.
119. *Diana* v. *State Board of Education,* 1970.
120. Lippman & Goldberg, 1973.
121. *Griggs* v. *Duke Power Company,* 1971; "Guidelines," 1972, p. 12334.
122. *Larry P.* v. *Riles,* 1972.
123. In: Burgdorf & Spicer, 1983, p. 94.
124. In: Baumeister, 1981, p. 451.
125. "Teachers' union," 1983, p. 1.

126. "Teachers' union," 1983, p. 1.
127. PL 94-142.
128. *Mattie T.* v. *Holladay,* 1977.
129. *Parents in Action on Special Education (PSE)* v. *Hannon,* 1980.
130. In: Burgdorf & Spicer, 1983, pp. 96–98.
131. *Larry P.* v. *Riles,* 1972.
132. Sattler, 1982, p. 387.
133. Sattler, 1982, p. 387.
134. Dick, 1974, p. 672.
135. Gould, 1981, pp. 28–29.
136. Grossman, 1983a, p. 19.
137. In: Scheerenberger, 1983b, p. 112.
138. Binet & Simon, 1908, p. 2.
139. e.g., Doll, 1941; Sarason, 1959.
140. Edgerton & Edgerton, 1973, p. 223.
141. Blatt, 1972, p. 542.
142. Mercer, 1973a; Rowitz, 1974, 1981.
143. Mercer, 1973a, p. 33.
144. Blatt, 1972, pp. 542–543.
145. Baumeister & Muma, 1975, p. 305.
146. Gallagher, J.,1976, p. 3.
147. MacMillan, Jones, & Aloia, 1974, p. 241.
148. MacMillan et al., 1974, p. 241.
149. Guskin, 1974.
150. Guskin, 1962, p. 405.
151. Guskin, 1963.
152. Edgerton, 1967.
153. Edgerton, 1967, pp. 47, 147.
154. Edgerton, 1967, p. 50.
155. Edgerton & Bercovici, 1976, p. 490.
156. Edgerton & Bercovici, 1976, p. 490.
157. Edgerton & Bercovici, 1976, p. 491.
158. "They survive," 1983.

Chapter 2

1. Heber, 1961, pp. 10–12.
2. Grossman, 1983a, pp. 130–134.
3. Scheerenberger, 1983b.
4. Lejeune & Turpin, 1961.
5. Patau, Inhorn, Therman, & Wagner, 1960; Edwards, Harnden, Cameron, Nosse, & Wolfe, 1960; Lejeune et al., 1963.
6. Warkany, Lemire, & Cohen, 1981.
7. Steele, 1982.
8. Berg, 1972, p. 122.
9. Turner, 1983.

10. Hagerman, Smith, & Mariner, 1983; Turner, 1983.
11. Martin, J., & Bell, 1943.
12. Turner, 1983.
13. Sutherland, 1982.
14. Turner, 1983.
15. "Findings show," 1985.
16. Menolascino & Egger, 1978.
17. Moser, 1982, p. 9.
18. In: Scheerenberger, 1983b.
19. Bonner, 1961; Rich, 1963.
20. Raeburn, 1984.
21. Milunsky, 1983, p. 24.
22. Jensen, 1969.
23. Jensen, 1969, p. 115.
24. Jensen, 1969, p. 108.
25. Jensen, 1969, p. 117.
26. Hunt, J., & Kirk, 1971, p. 268.
27. Shockley, 1972, p. 307.
28. Shockley, 1972, p. 306.
29. Frost & Hawkes, 1966, p. 1.
30. Frost & Hawkes, 1966.
31. e.g., Wakefield, 1964; Heber & Garber, 1971.
32. *The nation's youth,* 1968; Mercer, 1970; Heber & Garber, 1971.
33. Birch & Gussow, 1970, p. 81.
34. President's Panel, 1962.
35. Kirk, 1966, p. xii.
36. Frost & Hawkes, 1966, p. 9.
37. Kugel & Parsons, 1967.
38. "U.S. poverty," 1969, p. 2.
39. Radin, 1968, pp. 174–175.
40. Black, 1966.
41. Metfessel, 1964/1966.
42. Kvaraceus & Miller, 1959.
43. e.g., Scheerenberger, 1969b.
44. Eisenberg, 1973, p. 482.
45. Harrington, 1962, 1984.
46. Murray, 1984.
47. Samuelson, 1984.
48. Samuelson, 1984.
49. Smith, 1984, p. 62; Fustero, 1984.
50. In: Carson, 1962, p. 8.
51. Commoner, 1972.
52. Sternglass & Bell, 1983, p. 545.
53. Heinrichs, 1983; Gibson, Colley, & Baghurst, 1983; Cordero & Oakley, 1983.
54. Heinrichs, 1983, p. 431; Trafford et al., 1984.
55. "High-tech," 1984.
56. Putnam, 1972.
57. Dodd, 1966; Birch & Gussow, 1970, p. 81.
58. Bacon, Froome, Gent, Cooke, & Sowerby, 1967; Alpert et al., 1969; Klein, Namer, Harpur, & Corbin, 1970.
59. Alpert et al., 1969.

60. Oberle, 1969.
61. "Lead poisoning," 1984.
62. Marlowe, Errera, & Jacobs, 1983.
63. "Newborn problems," 1984.
64. *Research profile #11,* 1965, pp. 4–5.
65. "Two sides," 1984.
66. "Dioxin," 1983.
67. "Agent Orange," 1984, p. 1.
68. "Dioxin causes," 1983.
69. Barnes, 1963; Connelly, 1964; Rayborn, Wible-Kant, & Bledsoe, 1982.
70. Rosen & Schimmel, 1983, p. 669.
71. Rosen & Schimmel, 1983, p. 671.
72. Rosen & Schimmel, 1983, p. 675.
73. Rossi, 1964.
74. "Acne drug," 1984.
75. Woody, Sistrunk, & Platou, 1964, p. 63.
76. "USA syphilis," 1983.
77. Centers for Disease Control, In: Bettoli, 1982, p. 924.
78. "Confusion," 1984.
79. *Herpes: The evasive invader,* undated.
80. *Herpes: The evasive invader,* undated.
81. Leary, 1969, p. 589.
82. Leary, 1969.
83. Connelly, 1964.
84. Ubell, 1984a.
85. Rayborn et al., 1982.
86. Greenland, Richwald, & Honda, 1983.
87. "Cocaine and motherhood," 1985.
88. "Narcotics booming," 1985.
89. Lawson & Wilson, 1980.
90. In: Abel, 1982, p. 421.
91. Streissguth, 1983.
92. Rouqette, 1957.
93. Lemoine, Haurrousseau, Borteyru, & Menuet, 1968.
94. Ulleland, 1972; Jones, K., & Smith, 1973.
95. Jones, K., & Smith, 1973; Abel, 1982, 1984.
96. Hardy, 1973; Russell, 1982.
97. Abel, 1984, p. 422.
98. Abel, 1984.
99. Abel, 1984.
100. Sokol, Miller, & Reed, 1980.
101. In: Streissguth, 1978.
102. "Surgeon General's advisory," 1981.
103. "Sad news," 1984.
104. "Sad news," 1984.
105. Fried & Oxorn, 1980.
106. Rantakallio, 1983; Wainright, 1984.

107. King & Fabro, 1983.
108. "Research ties," 1984.
109. The Boston Children's Medical Center, 1972; Fried & Oxorn, 1980.
110. [Barclay ad], 1984.
111. e.g., Groisser, Rosso, & Winick, 1982.
112. Berkowitz, Holford, & Berkowitz, 1982; Linn et al., 1982; Kurpa, Holmberg, Kuosma, & Saxen, 1983.
113. Luke, 1982; Bracken, Bryce-Buchanan, Silten, & Srisauphan, 1982.
114. Auletta, 1984.
115. Adler, 1985.
116. Miller, S., 1984.
117. Furstenberg, 1976; Miller, S., 1984.
118. Furstenberg, 1976.
119. Phipps-Yonas, 1980; Auletta, 1984.
120. Auletta, 1984, p. 5.
121. Auletta, 1984, p. 7.
122. Auletta, 1984, p. 7.
123. Wallis, 1984.
124. Rubin et al., 1983; Wallis, 1984.
125. Steele, 1982, p. 32.
126. Masland, 1965.
127. Tardieu, 1860, p. 361.
128. O'Doherty, 1964.
129. Wisconsin Statute 48.981, 1978.
130. Wisconsin Statute 48.981, 1978.
131. Office for Children, Youth, and Families, 1983, p. 8.
132. Boocock, 1975, p. 12.
133. Boocock, 1975, p. 12.
134. "What price day care?" 1984.
135. Brandwein, 1973.
136. Oliver, 1975; O'Neill & Bellamy, 1978; Tsai, Zee, & Apthrop, 1980; Merton & Osborne, 1983.
137. Caffey, 1974.
138. Collins, 1974; Merton & Osborne, 1983.
139. Oliver, 1975.
140. Morse, Sahler, & Friedman, 1970; Sandgrund, Gaines, & Green, 1974.
141. Johnson, 1984, p. 15.
142. Winick & Rosso, 1969; Barnet et al., 1978; Celedon, Csaszar, Middleton, & de Andraca, 1980; Chase, Canosa, Dabiere, Welch, O'Brien, 1984.
143. Galler, 1984.
144. "To protect," 1983.
145. Jacobson & Barter, 1967.

146. Powledge, 1983.
147. Kolata, 1984.
148. Irene, 1964.
149. "Fetus given," 1981.
150. *Birth defects,* 1983.
151. Brazier, 1962.
152. Smith, K., Cobb, & French, 1983.
153. Smith, K. et al., 1983.
154. Schriber, 1983; "NMR imaging," 1983.
155. Burr, 1983.
156. "Brain healing," 1983.
157. Young, P., 1983.
158. Moser, 1982.
159. Moser, 1982.
160. Moser, 1982.
161. Moser, 1982.
162. A disease gene, 1983; Clark, 1984; Carey, 1984; "Helping little people," 1984.
163. Ubell, 1984b.
164. Yannet, 1953, p. 449.
165. Vernon, 1969.
166. Vernon, 1969; Chess & Fernandez, 1980.
167. Centers for Disease Control, 1980.
168. Schmeck, 1984.
169. Schmeck, 1984.
170. Schmeck, 1984, p. 59.
171. Scriver, Mackenzie, Chow, & Delvin, 1971.
172. Turkel, 1963.
173. Harrell, Capp, Davis, Peerless, & Ravitz, 1981.
174. Rasmussen, 1983, p. 3.
175. e.g., Ellis, N., & Tomporowski, 1983; Ellman, Silverstein, Zingarelli, Schafer, & Silverstein, 1984.
176. Carney, 1984, p. 217.
177. Panati, 1980; Sinha, 1981; Menolascino, Neman, & Stark, 1983; Hall, 1984; Blonston, 1984.
178. Stark, 1983, p. 6.
179. In: Scheerenberger, 1983b, p. 15.
180. *Roe* v. *Wade,* 1973.
181. e.g., Patrick, 1978; Wolfensberger, 1980a, 1981.
182. Gest, 1983.
183. Gest, 1983.
184. Hansen, H., 1978.
185. *Speck* v. *Finegold,* 1981.
186. Furlow, 1973, p. 86.
187. *Harbeson* v. *Parke-Davis, Inc.,* 1983.
188. Duff & Campbell, 1973.
189. *Report of the Joseph P. Kennedy Foundation,* 1971.
190. *In re: Phillip B.,* 1979.
191. *Richard W. Bothman* v. *Warren B. and Patricia B.,* 1979;

Burgdorf & Spicer, 1983.
192. Will, 1980, p. 112.
193. Will, 1980, p. 112.
194. Biklen, 1981.
195. *Guardianship of Becker,* 1981.
196. Becker, W., & Becker, P., 1983, p. 17.
197. Grossman, 1983b.
198. "Death of 'Baby Doe,'" 1982, pp. 3–4.
199. Indiana Association for Retarded Children, 1982, p. 2.
200. "Death of 'Baby Doe,'" 1982, pp. 3–4.
201. Will, 1982, p. 14.
202. "Summary and analysis," 1982, p. 136.
203. "Reagan pens," 1983, p. 2.
204. "The Death of 'Baby Doe,'" 1982.
205. "Nondiscrimination," 1984.
206. "Nondiscrimination," 1983, p. 17588.
207. "Nondiscrimination," 1983, p. 17588.
208. "Nondiscrimination," 1983, p. 17588.
209. "Nondiscrimination," 1983, p. 17588.
210. American Association on Mental Deficiency, 1973a, p. 66.
211. Grossman, 1983b.
212. *Weber* v. *Stony Brook Hospital,* 1983; *United States* v. *University Hospital,* 1984.
213. *Otis R. Bowen* v. *American Hospital Association et al.,* 1986.
214. PL 98-457.
215. PL 98-457.
216. PL 98-457.
217. PL 98-457.
218. Patrick, 1978, p. 36.
219. In: Patrick, 1978, p. 35.
220. Shaw, 1977.
221. Gross, Cox, Tatyrek, Pollay, & Barnes, 1983.
222. Turnbull, H., 1983.
223. In: Patrick, 1978, p. 37.
224. In: Hentoff, 1983a, p. 6.
225. In: Hentoff, 1984b, p. 6.
226. In: Hentoff, 1984a, p. 8.
227. [Letters to the editor], 1983, p. 12.
228. In: Hentoff, 1984a, p. 8.
229. In: Hentoff, 1983b, p. 4.
230. Todres, Krane, Howell, & Shannon, 1977; Shaw, Randolph, & Manard, 1977.
231. Shaw et al., 1977.
232. [Letters], 1983, p. 6.
233. [Letters], 1983, p. 6.
234. In: Hentoff, 1984b, p. 6.

235. "MR right-to-life poll," 1983.
236. In: Hentoff, 1984b, p. 6.
237. In: Hentoff, 1984b, p. 6.
238. Bogdan & Taylor, 1976, pp. 47–51.
239. In: Gould, 1981, p. 31.

Chapter 3

1. President's Panel, 1962.
2. e.g., Stolurow, 1959, p. 332.
3. Zigler & Balla, 1982, pp. 3–4.
4. Lewin, 1935, 1936.
5. In: Zigler, 1962, p. 142.
6. In: Zigler, 1962, p. 142.
7. Zigler & Balla, 1982.
8. Zigler & Balla, 1982, p. 4.
9. e.g., Ellis, N., 1963, 1982.
10. Ellis, N., 1963, pp. 155–156.
11. Luria, 1963a, 1963b.
12. Zeaman & House, 1963, 1979.
13. Cole & Cole, 1979, p. 14.
14. Zeaman & House, 1979, p. 117.
15. Butterfield, 1983, p. 203.
16. Haywood, 1979, p. 431.
17. Kazdin, 1978, p. 61.
18. e.g., Ross, 1966.
19. Watson, 1913, p. 158.
20. Watson, 1924, p. 104.
21. Thorndike, 1913, p. 2.
22. Kazdin, 1978.
23. Skinner & Vaughn, 1983.
24. Skinner, 1938.
25. Leo, 1983, p. 42.
26. Skinner, 1975, p. 43.
27. Skinner, 1948.
28. Skinner, 1968.
29. Skinner, 1983, p. 32.
30. Bijou, 1963, p. 109.
31. Bijou, 1983, p. 238.
32. Bijou, 1983, p. 238.
33. Bijou, 1983, p. 238.
34. Whitman & Scibak, 1979.
35. e.g., Ellis, 1979a.
36. Bensberg, 1965.
37. Smeets, 1971; Ross, R., 1972.
38. Baumeister & Rollings, 1976, pp. 1–2.
39. Gardner, 1972; Baumeister & Rollings, 1976; Watson, L., 1977; Bates & Wehman, 1977; Schroeder, Mulick, & Schroeder, 1979; Ellis, 1979a.
40. Schroeder et al., 1979.
41. Schroeder et al., 1979, p. 341.
42. Schroeder et al., 1979, p. 359.
43. Spitz, 1976, p. 53.

44. Brooks, P., & Baumeister, 1977, p. 407.
45. Brooks, P., & Baumeister, 1977, p. 415.
46. Haywood, 1977, p. 317.
47. Stevens, 1964, p. 38.
48. In: Stevens, 1964, p. 43.
49. Stevens, 1964, pp. 50–51.
50. In: Scheerenberger, 1976a, pp. 228–229.
51. e.g., "Protection of human subjects," 1978; "Protection of human research subjects," 1979; President's Commission, 1981.
52. Zigler, 1978.
53. Zigler, 1978, pp. 2–3.
54. Baumeister & Berkson, 1982.
55. e.g., Baumeister, 1981.
56. McClelland, 1978, p. 201.
57. "A federal voice," 1983, p. 1.
58. Scheerenberger, 1983b.
59. Beier, 1964; Heber, 1964a, 1964b.
60. Beier, 1964, p. 464.
61. Heber, 1964a, p. 307.
62. Heber, 1961, p. 40.
63. Heber, 1961, pp. 65–66.
64. Chess, 1962.
65. Menolascino, 1969.
66. Bernstein & Rice, 1972.
67. Philips & Williams, 1975, pp. 139, 145.
68. Kanner, 1948, pp. 717–720.
69. American Psychiatric Association, 1982, p. 43.
70. Grossman, 1983a, p. 99.
71. Coleman, 1976.
72. Philips & Williams, 1975, p. 141.
73. Reiss, Levitan, & Szyszko, 1982.
74. Menolascino & Bernstein, 1970.
75. e.g., Szymanski, 1977.
76. Potter, 1927, pp. 691–692.
77. Potter, 1964, p. 360.
78. Snygg & Combs, 1949, p. 78.
79. Cobb, 1966, p. 74.
80. Guthrie, Butler, & Gorlow, 1961; Piers & Harris, 1964; Goldstein, H., 1964; Fitts, 1965.
81. Ringness, 1961; Meyerwitz, 1962; Guthrie, Butler, & Gorlow, 1963; Carroll, 1967; Harrison & Budoff, 1972.
82. Tymchuk, 1971.
83. e.g., Mayer, 1966; Lambeth, 1967; Knight, 1968.
84. e.g., Achenbach & Zigler, 1963; Katz & Zigler, 1967.
85. Kniss, Butler, Gorlow, &

Guthrie, 1962; McAfee, R., & Cleland, 1965.

86. Cochran & Cleland, 1963; Reger, 1964; Silverstein, 1966.
87. e.g., Bailer & Cromwell, 1965; Gardner, 1966.
88. Balla & Zigler, 1979, p. 154.
89. Chess, 1962; Ricker & Pinkard, 1964; Robertson, 1964; Nordoff & Robbins, 1965; Leland & Smith, 1965; Ucer, Goulden, & Mazzeo, 1968; Ross, D., 1970; Selan, 1976; Silvestri, 1977; Roth, E., & Barrett, 1977; Brier & Demb, 1980; Franzini, Litrownik, & Magy, 1980.
90. e.g., Chess, 1962.
91. Szymanski, 1977.
92. Himwich, Costa, Rinaldi, & Rudy, 1960; Bark & Menolascino, 1968; Davis, K., Sprague, & Werry, 1969; LeVann, 1971; Grabowski, 1973.
93. In: Scheerenberger, 1983b, pp. 226–227.
94. *Wouri* v. *Zitnay*, 1978.
95. In: Bruening & Poling, 1982, p. 241.
96. e.g., Bruening & Poling, 1982.
97. e.g., Lipman, 1970; Aman & Singh, 1980, 1983; Bruening & Davidson, 1981.
98. e.g., Christensen, 1975.
99. Kalachnik, 1984.
100. *Clites* v. *Iowa*, 1980.
101. In: Bruening & Poling, 1982, p. 241.
102. Heistad, Zimmerman, & Doebler, 1982.
103. Heavner, 1986.
104. Lipman, 1970.
105. Davis, Cullari, & Bruening, 1982.
106. Simmons, Tymchuk, & Valente, 1975, p. 20.
107. Schroeder, Mulick, & Schroeder, 1979, p. 357.
108. In: Scheerenberger, 1976a, pp. 227–228.
109. Roos, 1974, pp. 3–4.
110. Whiteside, 1983, p. 13.
111. Whiteside, 1983, p. 13.
112. Haywood, 1977, p. 316.
113. McGee & Menolascino, undated.
114. Gardner, 1977; Gardner & Cole, 1980.
115. Atlanta Association for Retarded Citizens, 1973.
116. "The mentally retarded offender," 1980.
117. Brown, B., & Courtless,

1971; MacEachron, 1979; South Carolina Department of Corrections, 1973; Haskins & Friel, 1973a; Kentucky Legislative Research Commission, 1975; Rockoff & Hofmann, 1977.
118. Levy, 1967; Olczak & Stott, 1976.
119. Haskins & Friel, 1973b; Dennis, 1976.
120. Thompson, Roberts, & Whiddon, 1979.
121. Brown & Courtless, 1971; *Services for developmentally disabled delinquents and offenders*, 1977; "The mentally retarded offender," 1980; Day & Joyce, 1982.
122. U.S. Bureau of the Census, 1983.
123. "The mentally retarded offender," 1980.
124. Brown & Courtless, 1971.
125. Ellis, A., & Brancale, 1965.
126. Rockoff & Hofmann, 1977.
127. Cull, Reuthebuck, & Pape, 1975.
128. *Services for developmentally disabled delinquents and offenders*, 1977, p. 10.
129. Sussman, 1974; Biklen, 1977.
130. Brown, Courtless, & Silber, 1970; Miller, C., Mayer, & Whitworth, 1973.
131. Smith, J., 1962; Santamour, 1982.
132. Brown et al., 1970; Miller, C. et al., 1973.
133. Smith, 1962; Rowan, 1972; Miller, C. et al., 1973; Menolascino, 1974, 1975; Dennis, 1976.
134. Rowan, 1972; Miller, C. et al., 1973; Krause, 1973; Atlanta Association for Retarded Citizens, 1976; Santamour, 1982.
135. Santamour, 1982, p. 137.
136. Sternlicht, 1966; MacEachron, 1979.
137. Beier, 1964, p. 468.
138. Begab, 1984, p. 461.
139. Begab, 1973; Dignan, 1973; Tymchuk, 1973; Huttenlocher, 1984; Spradlin & Saunders, 1984.
140. *University affiliated facilities*, undated.
141. UAF Long-Range Planning Task Force, 1976.
142. Ellis, 1966, p. vii.
143. Ellis, 1963, 1979a.
144. "Mental deficiency conference," 1960.

145. Stevens, 1985.
146. In: Scheerenberger, 1983b.
147. "Winners of the 1971 Kennedy International Awards," 1971.

Chapter 4

1. President's Panel, 1962, p. 196.
2. President's Panel, 1962.
3. President's Panel, 1962, pp. 14–15.
4. Kennedy, J., 1963, pp. 13–14.
5. Doyle, 1964, p. 9.
6. U.S. Department of Education, 1980.
7. Comptroller General, 1976.
8. Litvin & Browning, 1978.
9. Boggs, 1978, p. 214.
10. In: Coughlin, 1981.
11. Scheerenberger, 1983b.
12. President's Panel, 1962.
13. Coughlin, 1981.
14. Coughlin, 1981.
15. President's Panel, 1962, p. 76.
16. *Patterns for planning*, 1965; *Chapter II*, 1965; *Massachusetts plans for its retarded*, 1966; *Quiet revolution*, 1968.
17. *Florida's plan for comprehensive action*, 1965, p. 30.
18. Mooring, 1964.
19. Mooring, 1964.
20. Lippman, 1965.
21. President's Committee, 1977, p. 127.
22. President's Committee, 1977.
23. Executive Order 11776, 1974.
24. e.g., President's Committee, 1968, 1969a, 1971, 1972.
25. In: *Accommodating the spectrum of individual abilities*, 1983, p. 60.
26. Stedman, 1975, p. 4.
27. Boggs, 1971.
28. President's Committee, 1977.
29. U.S. Department of Health, Education, and Welfare, 1977, p. 1.
30. Bank-Mikkelsen, 1969, p. 234.
31. Wolfensberger & Kugel, 1969.
32. Nirje, 1969, pp. 181–184.
33. Nirje, 1969, p. 181.
34. International League, 1971, p. 2.
35. *From charity to rights*, 1968, p. 3.
36. Portray, 1968.
37. Warren & Jones, 1973, p. 3.
38. Wolfensberger, 1972, p. 28.

39. Wolfensberger, 1972, p. 28.
40. Wolfensberger, 1980b, p. 80.
41. Wolfensberger, 1980b, p. 80.
42. Wolfensberger, 1972, p. 48.
43. Wolfensberger, 1983a.
44. Wolfensberger, 1972, pp. 41–42.
45. Wolfensberger, 1980b, pp. 89, 100.
46. Fram, 1974, p. 32.
47. Dybwad, 1982, p. 1.
48. Ellis, 1979b, p. 26.
49. Thorne, 1975.
50. Schwartz, C., 1977, p. 39.
51. Kaplan, Schaaf, & Heath, 1982, p. 12.
52. Kaplan et al., 1982, p. 12.
53. Kaplan et al., 1982, p. 13.
54. Wolfensberger & Glenn, 1973, pp. 226–227.
55. Wolfensberger & Thomas, 1983.
56. Wolfensberger & Thomas, 1983.
57. Flynn & Nitsch, 1980, p. 3.
58. Wolfensberger & Zauha, 1973.
59. Gillis, 1978, p. 327.
60. International League, 1971, p. 2.
61. e.g., National Association for Retarded Citizens, 1972.
62. President's Committee, 1969a, Wolfensberger, 1969; e.g., Roos, 1971; International League, 1971.
63. In: Burgdorf, 1980, p. 278.
64. Shelton v. Tucker, 1960.
65. Burgdorf, 1980, p. 279.
66. Turnbull, H., 1981.
67. Halderman v. Pennhurst State School and Hospital, 1978.
68. Wolfensberger, 1980b, pp. 92, 108.
69. Cobb, 1968, p. 11.
70. United Nations, 1971.
71. American Association on Mental Deficiency, 1973b, pp. 56–57.
72. American Association on Mental Deficiency, 1973b, p. 58.
73. Joint Commission on Mental Health of Children, 1970, pp. 3–4.
74. Joint Commission on Mental Health of Children, 1970, p. 4.
75. "Florida's bill of rights," 1975, p. 1.
76. "Florida's bill of rights," 1975, p. 1.
77. Rehabilitation and develop-

mental legislation, 1976, p. 53.
78. Friedman, 1973, p. 595.
79. PL 93-112.
80. In: Cannon, 1983, p. 10.
81. In: Cannon, 1983, p. 11.
82. Gilhool, 1973, p. 53.
83. Accommodating the spectrum of individual abilities, 1983, pp. 86–88.
84. Wolfensberger, 1983b.
85. Ellis, 1979b.
86. e.g., Blatt, 1970, 1973, 1976, 1980.
87. "On the educability of intelligence," 1973.
88. Biklen & Winschel, 1985, p. 234.
89. Wolfensberger & Kugel, 1969.
90. Dale, 1960, p. 134.
91. Provencal, 1979, p. 214.
92. Kaplan et al., 1982.
93. "United together," 1982, p. 1.
94. "United together," 1982, pp. 1–2.
95. Browning, Thorin, & Rhoades, 1984.
96. Wolfensberger, 1975, p. 12.
97. Wolfensberger, 1975, p. 1.
98. Helsel, 1974, p. 32.
99. Holland, 1977.
100. Danker-Brown, Sigelman, & Bensberg, 1979, p. 139.
101. Strichart & Gottlieb, 1980.
102. Wolfensberger & Zauha, 1973.
103. Ad Hoc Committee on Advocacy, 1969; e.g., Hobbs, 1975; Kenney & Clemmens, 1975.
104. Wolfensberger, 1983c.
105. Villing, 1976, p. 286.
106. Ennis, 1972.
107. Amicus Curiae, 1980.
108. Helsel, 1974.
109. Helsel, 1974.
110. Helsel, 1974.
111. White, B., 1966, p. 20.
112. White, B., 1966, p. 22.
113. Levy, 1965, pp. 883–884.
114. Allen, 1968, p. 91.
115. Wolfensberger & Zauha, 1973, p. 28.
116. Rehabilitation and developmental legislation, 1976, p. 55.
117. Metzer & Rheingold, 1962, p. 828.
118. In: Scheerenberger, 1976a, p. 154.
119. Minnesota State Planning Agency, 1975, p. 25.

Chapter 5

1. Denhoff, 1981.
2. Scheerenberger, 1969b.
3. Murphy, 1983.
4. Mental Retardation, 1965, p. 45.
5. e.g., Wolraich, 1979; Retish, 1980.
6. e.g., Affleck, 1980.
7. Frohboese, Menolascino, & McGee, 1985.
8. In: "Harvard's president," 1984, p. 33.
9. Zorzi, Thurman, & Kistenmacher, 1980.
10. e.g., Koch & Dobson, 1971.
11. Michelmore, 1985.
12. President's Committee, 1975a.
13. e.g., Ehlers, 1966; Curfman & Arnold, 1967.
14. Baum, 1962; Cummings & Stock, 1962; Cummings, Bayley, & Rie, 1966; Ehlers, 1966.
15. Denhoff, 1981, p. 35.
16. President's Panel, 1962.
17. President's Panel, 1962.
18. Bender et al., 1981.
19. The role of higher education, 1976.
20. Bloom, 1964, p. 88.
21. Bruner, 1961, p. 33.
22. Heber and Garber, 1971; Garber and Heber, 1981, 1982; Garber, 1982.
23. In: Raspberry, 1972, p. 6.
24. Raspberry, 1972.
25. Garber, 1982.
26. In: Skerry, 1983, p. 19.
27. Skerry, 1983.
28. Skerry, 1983.
29. Coleman, J., 1966.
30. e.g., Ozer & Milgram, 1967; Hyman & Kliman, 1967.
31. Freeman, 1968, p. 10.
32. Omwake, 1969, pp. 130–131.
33. Blank, 1973; Karnes & Zehrbach, 1977; Allen, K., 1981; Gallagher, J., 1984.
34. Quick, Little, & Campbell, 1974.
35. e.g., Connor & Talbot, 1964; Linde & Kopp, 1973; Quick et al., 1974; United Cerebral Palsy, 1974.
36. Quick et al., 1974.
37. Bricker & Bricker, 1977, p. 102.
38. Bronfenbrenner, 1974, p. 15.
39. Skerry, 1983, pp. 18, 19.
40. U.S. Department of Health,

Education, and Welfare, 1975.

41. U.S. Department of Health, Education, and Welfare, 1978.
42. PL 94-142.
43. "State extends services," 1985.
44. Mullen & Sumner, In: Skerry, 1983.
45. Lazar & Darlington, 1978; Stickney & Plunkett, 1983; "Impact," 1983; "High grades," 1985.
46. Stickney & Plunkett, 1983, p. 289.
47. "Preschool," 1984, p. 4.
48. Clark, E., 1976; LaVeck & Brehm, 1978; Hanson & Schwartz, 1978; Fink & Sandall, 1978; Morgan, 1979; Cooke, Heron, Heward, & Test, 1982.
49. Kirk, 1972.
50. Graham, 1962, pp. 256, 258–259.
51. Graham, 1962, p. 259.
52. Doll, 1964, p. 207.
53. PL-94-142.
54. PL-94-142.
55. PL-94-142.
56. Roos, 1970.
57. Roos, 1970.
58. Birch, 1974.
59. Birch, 1974, p. 7.
60. Kirk, 1953.
61. Tenny, 1953.
62. Johnson, G., 1962, p. 66.
63. Johnson, G., 1962, p. 66.
64. Johnson, G., 1962, p. 68.
65. Reynolds, 1962, p. 368.
66. Reynolds, 1962, p. 368.
67. Dunn, 1968, p. 5.
68. Dunn, 1968, p. 6.
69. Dunn, 1968, p. 6.
70. Hobson v. Hansen, 1967.
71. In: Dunn, 1968, p. 7.
72. Dunn, 1968, p. 20.
73. Johnson, G., 1962, p. 63.
74. Gallagher, J., 1967, p. 441.
75. Gallagher, J., 1967, p. 443.
76. Gallagher, J., 1967, p. 443.
77. Gallagher, J., 1967, p. 444.
78. Scheerenberger, 1979a, pp. 212–213.
79. Brown v. The Board of Education, 1954.
80. Wolf v. Legislature of the State of Utah, 1969.
81. Pennsylvania Association for Retarded Children et al. v. Commonwealth of Pennsylvania et al., 1971.
82. See Scheerenberger, 1983b.

83. Pennsylvania Association for Retarded Children et al. v. Commonwealth of Pennsylvania et al., 1971.
84. Mills v. The Board of Education, 1972.
85. Mills v. The Board of Education, 1972.
86. Mills v. The Board of Education, 1972.
87. Harrison v. State of Michigan, 1972; North Dakota Association for Retarded Children v. Peterson, 1972; Lebanks v. Spears, 1973; Eaton et al. v. State of Arizona, 1974; Dembowski v. Knox Community School Corp., 1974; Beauchamp v. Jones, 1975; Rhode Island Society for Autistic Children, Inc. et al. v. Board of Regents for Education of the State of Rhode Island et al., 1975; Swain v. Barrington School Board, 1976; Cuyahoga County Association for Retarded Citizens and Adults et al. v. Essex, 1976; Rainey v. Tennessee Department of Education, 1976; Unified School District No. 1 v. Barbara Thompson, 1976; Mattie T. v. Holladay, 1977.
88. The National Advisory Committee on Handicapped Children, 1973, p. 4.
89. Andelamn, 1976.
90. Jordan, 1973, p. 222.
91. Soeffing, 1974, p. 202.
92. Martin, E., 1968, p. 494.
93. Martin, 1968, p. 494.
94. Martin, 1968, p. 496.
95. Martin, 1968, p. 496.
96. Martin, 1968, p. 498.
97. Kirk & Johnson, 1951.
98. "Kirk honored," 1963, p. 272.
99. Martin, E., 1968, p. 498.
100. Martin, E., 1968, p. 501.
101. In: Kirk, 1968, p. 481.
102. Kirk, 1968.
103. Kirk, 1968, p. 481.
104. PL 94-142.
105. Kirk, 1972.
106. Tisdall & Moss, 1962, p. 359.
107. Mackie & Robbins, 1960; Meer, 1984.
108. Mackie & Robbins, 1960; Meer, 1984.
109. Garrison, 1960; President's Panel, 1962.
110. Mackie & Robbins, 1960; Kirk, 1972.

111. Guskin & Spicker, 1968.
112. Kirk, 1972, p. 228.
113. Aquilina, 1976.
114. Kennedy & Danielson, 1978.
115. Vernon, 1981, p. 29.
116. Vernon, 1981, p. 24.
117. Vernon, 1981, p. 27.
118. e.g., Cronin, 1976.
119. "What's it all about?," 1976, p. 19.
120. Reynolds, M., 1973.
121. Childs, 1974.
122. MacMillan, Jones, & Meyers, 1976.
123. Kaufman, M., Gottlieb, Agard, & Kukic, 1975, p. 3.
124. Mainstreaming mentally retarded students, 1978, p. 3.
125. Paul, J., Turnbull, & Cruickshank, 1977, pp. vii–viii.
126. Mainstreaming mentally retarded students, 1978, p. 3.
127. Gan, Tymchuk, & Nishihara, 1977.
128. Stainback, S. & Stainback, 1975; e.g., Tenny, 1976; MacMillan et al., 1976; Horn, 1976; Flynn, Gack, & Sundean, 1978; Mainstreaming mentally retarded students, 1978.
129. Horn, 1976, p. 336.
130. e.g., Johnson, A. & Cartwright, 1979; Reynolds, B., Martin-Reynolds, J., & Marks, F., 1982.
131. "Teachers' experiences," 1976.
132. "Mainstreaming handicaps," 1983.
133. Childs, 1981.
134. e.g., Bensky et al., 1980; Weiskopf, 1980.
135. e.g., Alexander and Strain, 1978; Moore & Fine, 1978; Crisci, 1981.
136. e.g., Dixon, Shaw, & Bensky, 1980.
137. Davis, Cullari, & Bruening, 1982.
138. Barngrover, 1971; Guerin & Szatlocky, 1974.
139. Guerin & Szatlocky, 1974, p. 179.
140. Jaffe, 1966; Jones, 1967; Stamm & Gardner, 1969; Wilson, 1970; Lazar, Haughton, & Orpet, 1972; Goodman, H., Gottlieb, & Harrison, 1972; Gottlieb & Davis, 1973; Neer, Foster, Jones, & Reynolds, 1973; Gottlieb, Cohen, & Gold-

stein, 1974; Bruininks, Rynders, & Gross, 1974; Strichart, 1974; Smith, I., & Greenberg, 1975; Gillung & Rucker, 1977; Foster & Keech, 1977; Gerber, 1977; Newman, 1978; Budoff & Siperstein, 1978; Young, Algozzine, & Schmid, 1979; Siperstein, Budoff, & Bak, 1980; Gibbons & Gibbons, 1980; Palmer, 1980; Voeltz, 1980; Aloia, Maxwell, & Aloia, 1981; Budoff & Siperstein, 1982; Bates, Morrow, & Sedlak, 1984.

141. e.g., Bradfield, Brown, Kaplan, Rickert, & Stannard, 1973.

142. Safer, 1980, p. 35.

143. Iano, 1970; Shotel, Iano, & McGettigan, 1972; e.g., Stainback, W., Stainback, & Jaben, 1981.

144. Jones, R., 1967; Gerber, 1977.

145. Stroud, 1978.

146. "Handicapped girl," 1974, p. 7.

147. Johnson, D., & Johnson, 1975; Martino & Johnson, 1979; Stainback, W. et al., 1981; Salend, 1981.

148. Rucker, Howe, & Snider, 1969.

149. Hamre-Nietupski & Nietupski, 1981, pp. 31–38.

150. Meyerwitz, 1965; Rucker, 1968; Budoff, 1971; Gottlieb & Davis, 1973; MacMillan et al., 1974.

151. "What's being done," 1983, p. 64.

152. Melcher, personal communication, 1983; Gruenewald, personal communication, 1984.

153. Gruenewald & Schroeder, 1979, p. 22.

154. Gallagher, J., 1984, p. 230.

155. Gallagher, J., 1984, p. 229.

156. Kirk, 1984, p. 47.

157. U.S. Department of Education, 1982.

158. U.S. Department of Education, 1981, 1982; Rostetter, Kowalski, & Hunter, 1984.

159. Granger, 1985, pp. 38–39.

160. Granger, 1985, p. 39.

161. PL 94-142.

162. U.S. Department of Education, 1982.

163. U.S. Department of Education, 1982.

164. Budoff & Orenstein, 1982, p. 60.

165. Budoff & Orenstein, 1982, p. 61.

166. Budoff & Orenstein, 1982, p. 61.

167. Goldstein, Strickland, Turnbull, & Curry, 1980; National Committee for Citizens in Education, In: Turnbull, A., & Turnbull, 1982; Goldstein & Turnbull, 1982.

168. Turnbull, A., & Turnbull, 1982, p. 120.

169. Mattson, 1977, p. 358.

170. Retish, 1979; Childs, 1974.

171. Meyen, In: Thomas, 1979, p. 119.

172. Horn, 1976, p. 336.

173. *United States Department of Education News,* 1982; "Education regs," 1983.

174. *Armstrong* v. *Kline,* 1980.

175. *Board of Education of the Hendrick Hudson Central School District* v. *Rowley,* 1982.

176. McLure, Burnham, & Henderson, 1975.

177. Lamm, 1984.

178. e.g., Gottlieb, Alter, & Gottlieb, 1983.

179. *Mainstreaming mentally retarded students,* 1978.

180. *Mainstreaming mentally retarded students,* 1978.

181. Commission on the Reorganization of Secondary Education, 1918.

182. Kearney, 1953.

183. Kirk, 1972, p. 197.

184. Kirk, 1972, pp. 34–35.

185. Kirk, 1972, p. 192.

186. Sellin, 1979.

187. *Curriculum guide,* 1984.

188. Kirk, 1972; Waite, 1972; Bender & Valletutti, 1976; Berdine & Cegelka, 1980.

189. e.g., Brown, L., Jones, Troccolo, Heiser, & Bellamy, 1972; Ysseldyke & Salvia, 1974; Folk & Campbell, 1978.

190. e.g., Burton, 1976; Fink, 1982.

191. Sontag, 1977; Tawney, 1979; Wehman, 1979; Snell, 1982.

192. Brown et al., 1982, p. 3.

193. e.g., Delacato, 1959, 1963; Kephart, 1971.

194. Kephart, 1971, pp. 12–14.

195. Kephart, 1971, p. 42.

196. e.g., Delacato, 1959, 1963.

197. Delacato, 1963, pp. 4–6.

198. Delacato, 1963, p. 6.

199. Doman, Spitz, Zueman, Delacato, & Doman, 1960.

200. Robbins, 1966.

201. Kershner, 1968.

202. Cruickshank, 1968; Zigler & Weintraub, 1980.

203. Doman et al., 1960, p. 258.

204. Neman, McCann, Roos, Menolascino, & Heal, 1977.

205. In: Cruickshank, 1968, p. 365.

206. In: Cruickshank, 1968, p. 366.

207. In: Cruickshank, 1968, p. 366.

208. In: Cruickshank, 1968, p. 366.

209. Zigler & Weintraub, 1980, p. 249.

210. e.g., Cruickshank, Bentzen, Ratzburg, & Tannhauser, 1961; Myers & Hammill, 1969.

211. Strauss & Lehtinen, 1947.

212. Feuerstein, 1970, p. 346.

213. Feuerstein, 1970, pp. 347–348.

214. Feuerstein, 1979, 1980.

215. Olszowy, 1978; Burt-Astell, 1981; Brosnan, 1982; e.g., Levete, 1982; Crain, C., McLaughlin, & Eisenhart, 1983.

216. Cratty, 1969, p. 5.

217. Kirk & McCarthy, 1961; McCarthy, J., 1964; Olson, J., Hahn, & Hermann, 1965; Bateman & Wetherell, 1965; Kirk, McCarthy, & Kirk, 1968; Lombardi & Lombardi, 1977.

218. Dunn & Dunn, 1981.

219. Dunn et al., 1976; Dunn, Mith, Dunn, Horton, & Smith, 1981.

220. Schiefelbusch, 1984.

221. Schiefelbusch, 1984, p. 242.

222. Schiefelbusch, 1965, 1984; Schiefelbusch, Copeland, & Smith, 1967; Schiefelbusch & Lloyd, 1974.

223. e.g., Fristoe & Lloyd, 1978; Goodman, Wilson, & Bornstein, 1978; Kahn, 1981.

224. Bliss, 1966, p. 54.

225. Kates & McNaughton, 1974.

226. Pitman, 1961.

227. Downing, 1964, p. 114.

228. Mzurkiewicz, 1965.

229. Williams, 1965.

230. Bobath, K., 1964, 1980; Bobath, B., 1969; Seaman, 1967.

231. Kunzelmann, 1970, p. 12.
232. Haring, In: Kunzelmann, 1970, p. 11.
233. Skinner, 1968, p. 21.
234. Skinner, 1968, p. 22.
235. e.g., Miller, G., Galanter, & Pribam, 1960.
236. Stolurow, 1960, p. 83.
237. Behrmann, 1984.
238. Taber, 1981; Bennett, 1982; Budoff & Hutton, 1982; Browning & Nave, 1983.
239. e.g., Hannaford & Taber, 1982; Hannaford, 1983.
240. Lally, 1980, 1981; Frank, Wacker, Berg, & McMahon, 1985.
241. e.g., Foulds, 1982; "Bioengineering program." 1985.
242. Olshin, 1968.
243. "Handicapped children," 1975, p. 7409.
244. Harmon & Haring, 1976, p. 103.
245. President's Panel, 1962.
246. "Summer courses," 1964.
247. "Scholarships and fellowships," 1964.
248. Grant & Snyder, 1984.
249. Thurman & Hare, 1979, p. 292.
250. Schwartz, L., 1967a, 1967b; Fox, Egner, Paolucci, Perelman, & McKenzie, 1972; Prouty & McGarry, 1972; DeHoop, 1973; White, O., & Haring, 1976; Young, A., 1976; Stainback, S., Stainback, Schmid, & Courtnage, 1977; Lampner, 1979; Heller, H., 1979; Thurman & Hare, 1979.
251. Thiagarajan, Semmel, & Semmel, 1974; Peter, 1976; Berdine, Cegelka, & Kelly, 1977; Thurman & Hare, 1979; Milne, 1979; Stamm, 1980.
252. Brooks, 1975, p. 47.
253. Haring, In: Stamm, 1980.
254. Stamm, 1980, pp. 53–56.
255. e.g., Berdine et al., 1977.
256. Thurman & Hare, 1979, p. 292.
257. In: Thomas, 1979, p. 116.
258. Milne, 1979.
259. Roos, 1970; Young, C., & Kerr, 1979; Porcella, 1980; Jenkins, Stephens, & Sternberg, 1980; Escudero & Sears, 1982; Fenrick & Petersen, 1984.
260. President's Committee, 1976, p. 84.
261. Turnbull, H., & Turnbull, 1977; Ekstrand, 1979.
262. Turnbull, A., 1977.

Chapter 6

1. Lorber, 1974; e.g., Edgerton & Bercovici, 1976; Gan et al., 1977; Olley & Ramey, 1978; Moise, 1978; Green & Klien, 1980; Heshusius, 1981.
2. Crain, L., & Millor, 1978; Krishef & DiNitto, 1981.
3. MacAndrew & Edgerton, 1966; Clark, Kivitz, & Rosen, 1968; Gozali, 1971; Kokaska, 1972; Crnic & Pym, 1979; McAfee, J., & Mann, 1982; Sternlicht & Windholz, 1984; Landesman-Dwyer & Berkson, 1984.
4. Heshusius, 1981, pp. 120–121.
5. O'Connor, 1983, p. 187.
6. Edgerton, 1967, pp. 217–218.
7. e.g., Edgerton & Bercovici, 1976; O'Connor, 1983; Edgerton, Bollinger, & Herr, 1984.
8. Sales, Powell, Duizend, & Associates, 1982.
9. *Homan* v. *Homan*, 1967.
10. *Johnson* v. *Johnson*, 1960.
11. In: Sales et al., 1982, p. 10.
12. Gottwald, 1970; Lattimer, 1970; Scheerenberger, 1976a.
13. "Parent attitudes," 1976.
14. Kennedy, R., 1948, 1966.
15. Crain, E., 1980.
16. Edgerton et al., 1984.
17. Alvarez, 1969, p. 58.
18. Bass, 1978.
19. Ferster, 1966.
20. Ferster, 1966, p. 600.
21. Ferster, 1966.
22. In: Ferster, 1966, p. 604.
23. e.g., Bass, 1964, 1968, 1969, 1978.
24. Bass, 1968, pp. 1, 4.
25. Reed & Reed, 1965, p. 77.
26. *In re Simpson*, 1962.
27. In: Ferster, 1966, p. 609.
28. In: Ferster, 1966, p. 609.
29. *In re Andrada*, 1965.
30. *In the matter of Hernandez*, 1966.
31. *Relf et al.* v. *Weinberger*, 1973; *National Welfare Rights Organization* v. *Weinberger*, 1974.
32. "New cases," 1973.
33. "Restrictions applicable," 1974, pp. 13887–13888.
34. American Association on Mental Deficiency, 1974, p. 61.
35. *Matter of C.D.M.*, 1981.
36. *In re Terwilliger*, 1982.
37. e.g., *Matter of Guardianship of Hayes*, 1980; *In re Penny N.*, 1980; *Matter of A.W.*, 1981; *In re Truesdell*, 1983.
38. *Matter of A.W.*, 1981.
39. e.g., Whitcraft & Jones, 1974; David, Smith, & Friedman, 1976; Wolf & Zarfas, 1982.
40. Passer, Rauh, Chamberlain, McGrath, & Burket, 1984.
41. Vining & Freeman, 1978, p. 851.
42. Sabagh & Edgerton, 1962, p. 216.
43. Sabagh & Edgerton, 1962, p. 216.
44. *Buck* v. *Bell*, 1927.
45. Gould, 1981, p. 336.
46. Ferster, 1966; Robinson, F., Robinson, & Williams, 1979; Wolf & Zarfas, 1982.
47. Kanner, 1949, pp. 4–5.
48. Cohen, 1972; Brolin, 1973; Mithaug, Hagmeir, & Haring, 1977; Lynch, 1979; McInerney & Karan, 1981.
49. Doll, 1963, p. 278.
50. Doll, 1963, p. 275.
51. President's Panel, 1962; Mayo, 1963.
52. Mayo, 1963, p. 429.
53. President's Panel, 1962; Mayo, 1963.
54. President's Panel, 1962, pp. 13–14.
55. In: Fenton, Thompson, & Rose, 1964, p. 167.
56. Fenton et al., 1964; Posner, 1970.
57. Posner, 1970.
58. Fenton et al., 1964, p. 166.
59. Kidd, Cross, & Higginbottom, 1967.
60. PL 83-566.
61. PL 88-214; Geer, Connor, & Blackman, 1964.
62. Mackie, 1965, p. 254.
63. PL 93-112.
64. Comptroller General of the United States, 1976, p. 146.
65. Comptroller General of the United States, 1976, p. 146.
66. Comptroller General of the United States, 1976, p. 145.
67. Conley, 1973.
68. Hightower, 1976.
69. U.S. Department of Health

and Human Services, 1984, p. 1.

70. Bioengineering program, 1985.

71. Domino and McGarty, 1972; Nickelsburg, 1973; Guarnaccia, 1976; Stodden, Ianacone, & Lazar, 1979; Becker, R., Widener, & Soforenko, 1979; Greenspan & Shoultz, 1981; Foss & Peterson, 1981; Brickey, Browning, & Campbell, 1982; Cheney & Foss, 1984.

72. Fiester & Giambra, 1972; Malgady, Barcher, Towner, & Davis, 1979; Chadsey-Rusch, Karlan, Riva, & Rusch, 1984.

73. Klein, N., & Babcock, 1979; Fleming & Fleming, 1982; Bregman, 1984.

74. Rosen, M., Halenda, Nowakiwska, & Floor, 1970; Bellamy & Sontag, 1973; Goldberg, Katz, & Yekutiel, 1973; Morris, Martin, & Nowak, 1981.

75. Talkington & Overbeck, 1975.

76. Rosen, M. et al., 1970.

77. Gold, 1980a, 1980b.

78. Gold, 1977, p. 41.

79. Alper & Retish, 1978.

80. Kaufman, H., 1970; McKerracher & Orritt, 1972; Alper & Retish, 1978.

81. Gold, 1980a, 1980b.

82. e.g., "Attitudes toward," 1983.

83. Gold, 1980a, pp. 3–4.

84. Bellamy, G. T., Inman, & Yeates, 1978; O'Neill & Bellamy, 1978; Spooner, Weber, & Spooner, 1983.

85. e.g., Meadow & Greenspan, 1961; Flexer, Martin, & Friedenberg, 1977.

86. Commission on Accreditation of Rehabilitation Facilities, 1976, p. 5.

87. Walker, 1985, p. 268.

88. DeFazio & Flexer, 1983, pp. 162–163.

89. Brown et al., 1984, p. 1.

90. White, C., Hill, Lakin, & Bruininks, 1984.

91. Brown et al., 1984.

92. Brown et al., 1984, p. 9.

93. Bellamy, G. T. et al., 1984, p. 31.

94. "W.T. Grant Co.," 1968.

95. "Turnover," 1983.

96. Hire ability, 1984.

97. Hire ability, 1984, p. 6.

98. Hire ability, 1984, p. 6.

99. Bangser, 1985.

100. "Massachusetts enacts," 1984.

101. Bellamy, G. T. et al., 1984, pp. 27–28.

102. In: "OSERS pinpoint," 1984.

103. Gollay, 1976.

104. Jones, L., & Moe, 1980.

105. "What?," 1982.

106. In: Forbes, 1984.

107. Dybwad, 1962.

108. Hauber, Rotegard, & Bruininks, 1985.

109. Dybwad, 1985.

110. e.g., Kennedy, R., 1966; Baller, Charles, & Miller, 1967; Edgerton et al., 1984.

111. DiGiovanni, 1978; Janicki, Knox, & Jacobson, 1985.

112. e.g., Olson, M., & Shaw, 1969; Dalton & Crapper, 1977; Wisniewski & Merz, 1985.

113. Krieger, 1975; Report of the Committee on Aging and Developmental Disabilities, 1983; Stroud and Murphy, 1984; Hauber et al., 1985.

114. Hauber et al., 1985.

115. Krieger, 1975.

116. e.g., Cotten, Purzycki, Cowart, & Merritt, 1983.

117. "ARCs establish," 1983.

118. Report of the Committee on Aging and Developmental Disabilities, 1983, pp. 44–45.

119. President's Panel, 1962, p. iv.

120. President's Panel, 1962, p. 16.

121. Haggerty, Kane, & Udall, 1976, p. 66.

122. Haggerty et al., 1976, p. 60.

123. Biklen, 1977, pp. 52–53.

124. Krause, 1973, p. 1.

125. Marsh, Friel, & Eissler, 1975.

126. Reichard, Spencer, & Spooner, 1980.

127. Krause, 1973; Talent & Keldgord, 1975; e.g., Haggerty et al., 1976.

128. Schilit, 1979, p. 19.

129. The Tennessee Association for Retarded Citizens, 1976.

130. Gibbons, Gibbons, & Kassin, 1981, p. 241.

131. Durham v. United States, 1954.

132. Hinkle, 1961, p. 436.

133. In: Hinkle, 1961, p. 437.

134. In: Rowan, 1972, p. 342.

135. In: "Freed in slaying," 1960, p. 2.

136. DeSilva, 1980, p. 25.

137. DeSilva, 1980, p. 25.

138. United States ex rel. Peeples v. Greer, 1983.

139. Maloney, J., 1983, p. 13.

140. Correction Services, 1975, p. 110.

141. In: Menolascino, 1975, p. 63.

142. Weingold, 1966; Harbach, 1976; Biklen, 1977; DeSilva, 1980.

143. Biklen, 1977, pp. 45–46.

144. "The mentally retarded offender," 1980, pp. 18–19.

145. In: Boslow & Manne, 1966, p. 23.

146. Boslow, Rosenthal, Kandel, & Manne, 1961; Boslow, 1964; Boslow & Kandel, 1966; Boslow & Manne, 1966.

147. Boslow et al., 1961, p. 66.

148. Boslow et al., 1961, p. 69.

149. Prettyman, 1972; Rowan, 1976.

150. Jackson v. Indiana, 1972.

151. Baxstrom v. Herold, 1966.

152. McNeil v. Director, Paxutent Institution, 1972.

153. United States v. Ewell, 1966.

154. Rouse v. Cameron, 1966.

155. Conine & Machaclan, 1982; Pike, 1982.

156. Perel, 1982.

157. Allen, R., 1966, p. 5.

158. Allen, R., 1966, p. 6.

159. Morrow, C., 1976, p. 86.

160. Magrab & Williams, 1982, p. 242.

161. Schwartz, V., 1982.

162. Mabile, 1982.

163. Louisiana v. Brown, 1982.

164. Kansas v. Moss, 1982.

165. Talent & Keldgord, 1975.

166. Miller, C. et al., 1973.

167. In: Forget, 1980.

168. "Mentally retarded offenders," 1983.

169. Dennis, 1976, p. 171.

170. Dennis, 1976.

171. Friedman, E., 1961; Scheer & Sharpe, 1963; Lauchenmeyer, 1969; Saunders & Repucci, 1972.

172. Menolascino, 1974, p. 11.

173. Morton, 1983.

174. Denkowski, Denkowski, & Mabli, 1983.

175. e.g., Baumeister & Rollings, 1976.

176. President's Panel, 1962.

177. Dybwad, 1969, 1970.

178. Woodward, Jaffe, & Brown, 1964; Szurek & Philips, 1966; Bernstein, 1969; Dybwad, 1970; Szymanski, 1977.

179. American Psychiatric Association, 1966, p. 1303.
180. Group for the Advancement of Psychiatry, 1979, p. 611.
181. American Psychiatric Association, 1966, p. 1302.
182. American Psychiatric Association, 1966, p. 1309.
183. In: Dybwad, 1970, pp. 144–145.
184. Wortis, 1977, p. 5.
185. Matson, 1984, p. 170.
186. e.g., Renshaw, 1977.
187. Bernstein, 1969, pp. 81–82.
188. Szymanski, 1977.
189. e.g., Luecking, 1981; Casey, McGee, Stark, & Menolascino, 1985; Menolascino & McGee, undated.
190. Luecking, 1981.
191. Holmes, P., undated; Reiss & Trenn, 1984.
192. Sternlicht & Deutsch, 1972; Scheerenberger, 1980; Intagliata & Willer, 1982; Hill & Bruininks, 1984.
193. Wolfensberger, 1983b, p. 5.
194. Farber, 1959; Farber, Jenné, & Toigo, 1960; Farber & Jenné, 1963; Farber & Ryckman, 1965.
195. e.g., Roos, 1982; Murphy, 1983.
196. President's Committee, 1985.
197. e.g., Roos, 1982.
198. Cleveland & Miller, 1977, p. 40.
199. Paul, 1983, p. 37.
200. e.g., Iano, 1970; Bruininks et al., 1974; Peterson, 1974; Willer, Intagliata, & Wicks, 1979; Lei & Eyman, 1979.
201. Menolascino & Egger, 1978.
202. e.g., Beckman, 1983; Intagliata & Doyle, 1984.
203. "Siblings speak out," 1983, p. 3.
204. From: Loop & Hitzing, 1980.
205. Frohboese et al., 1985.

Chapter 7

1. National Association for Retarded Citizens, 1976.
2. Jacobs, 1962, p. 96.
3. President's Panel, 1962, pp. 132–133.
4. Klebanoff, 1964, p. 83.
5. President's Panel, 1962, pp. 137–138.
6. Elkin, 1976.
7. President's Panel, 1962, p. 146.
8. President's Committee, 1967, p. 29.

9. Shotwell, Dingman, & Tarjan, 1960; Scheerenberger, 1965; Noone, 1967; Butterfield, Barnett, & Bensberg, 1968; Hubbard, 1969; Kugel, 1969; Klaber, 1969.
10. U.S. Department of Health, Education, and Welfare, 1965.
11. Kugel, 1969.
12. Elkin, 1972, p. 4.
13. MacAndrew & Edgerton, 1964, pp. 312–314.
14. Blatt & Kaplan, 1966, p. 1.
15. Blatt & Kaplan, 1966, p. v.
16. President's Committee, 1970, [inside cover].
17. Gettings, personal communication, April 16, 1985.
18. President's Committee, 1970, p. 1.
19. National Association of Superintendents of Public Residential Facilities for the Mentally Retarded, 1984.
20. President's Committee, 1974, p. 8.
21. Kugel & Wolfsenberger, 1969; e.g., National Association for Retarded Citizens, 1972.
22. *Standards for State Institutions,* 1964.
23. Hubbard, 1969.
24. Joint Commission on Accreditation of Hospitals, 1971.
25. Joint Commission on Accreditation of Hospitals, 1971.
26. *Standards for Residential Facilities,* 1973; *Standards for Services,* 1978.
27. Schwindler, 1974, p. 201.
28. Amos, In: Boggs, 1966, p. 409.
29. *Wyatt* v. *Stickney,* 1972.
30. In: Scheerenberger, 1976a, pp. 220–223.
31. *Burnham* v. *Department of Public Health of the State of Georgia,* 1972.
32. *Wyatt* v. *Aderholt,* 1974.
33. *Donaldson* v. *O'Connor,* 1974.
34. *O'Connor* v. *Donaldson,* 1975, Part II.
35. *Rouse* v. *Cameron,* 1966.
36. Bazelon, 1969, p. 742.
37. "Cases to deinstitutionalize," 1981.
38. *New York State Association for Retarded Citizens et al.* v. *Carey et al.,* 1975.
39. Hansen, 1977.

40. Hansen, 1977.
41. *Halderman* v. *Pennhurst State School and Hospital,* 1978.
42. *Pennhurst State School and Hospital* v. *Halderman,* 1981.
43. *Youngberg* v. *Romeo,* 1982, pp. 14–15.
44. *Youngberg* v. *Romeo,* 1982, pp. 16–17.
45. *Youngberg* v. *Romeo,* 1982, pp. 1–3.
46. "Reynold's memo," 1983.
47. *Lessard* v. *Schmidt,* 1972.
48. Ruling, 1983.
49. *Lessard* v. *Schmidt,* 1972.
50. *Saville* v. *Treadway,* 1974.
51. *Saville* v. *Treadway,* 1974.
52. Tennessee Department of Mental Health, 1974.
53. Tennessee Department of Mental Health, 1974.
54. *O'Connor* v. *Donaldson,* 1975.
55. Hubbard, 1969.
56. *Townsend* v. *Treadway,* 1973.
57. *Souder* v. *Brennan,* 1973.
58. *Souder* v. *Brennan,* 1973.
59. *National League of Cities* v. *Usery,* 1976.
60. Turnbull, H., 1975.
61. In: Scheerenberger, 1976a, p. 217.
62. Turnbull, H., 1975.
63. *Labor, litigation,* 1975.
64. e.g., Hansen, C., 1977; Braddock, 1977; Marchetti, 1983.
65. Hansen, C., 1977, pp. 15–16.
66. Hansen, C., 1977, pp. 16–17.
67. Grunberg, 1977, p. 48.
68. Turnbull, H., 1975, p. 52.
69. Turnbull, H., 1975, p. 52.
70. PL 96-247; "President signs," 1980.
71. *Care of institutionalized mentally disabled,* 1985.
72. In: Scheerenberger, 1976a, p. 79.
73. In: Scheerenberger, 1976a, pp. 79–80.
74. Scheerenberger, 1976a, p. 82.
75. Scheerenberger, 1976a, p. 83.
76. Scheerenberger, 1965; 1986.
77. Scheerenberger, 1986.
78. Baumeister, 1970.
79. Scheerenberger, 1982; 1986.
80. Scheerenberger, 1965; 1986.
81. Scheerenberger, 1965.
82. Scheerenberger, 1986.
83. Scheerenberger, 1975; 1986.
84. Scheerenberger, 1975; Townsend & Flanigan, 1976; Ellis, Bostwick, Moore, & Taylor, 1981.
85. Baumeister, 1970; Scheerenberger, 1986.

86. Scheerenberger, 1982.
87. Magnusson & Watson, 1979, p. A3.
88. *Oklahoma shame,* 1982, p. 9.
89. Sniffen, 1983, p. 2.
90. "Senate testimony," 1984, pp. 93–94.
91. "Senate testimony," 1984, pp. 96–97.
92. Wallin, 1962, p. 89.
93. Dunn, 1969.
94. Wolfensberger, 1971, p. 32.
95. Wolfensberger, 1971.
96. Elkin, 1972, p. 4.
97. Tarjan, 1966, pp. 5–6.
98. Wolfensberger, 1972, pp. 28, 48.
99. *Wyatt* v. *Stickney,* 1972.
100. *Welsch* v. *Likens,* 1974.
101. *Wyatt* v. *Stickney,* 1972.
102. *Welsch* v. *Likens,* 1974.
103. Mental Health Law Project, 1973, pp. 27–28.
104. *Wyatt* v. *Stickney,* 1972.
105. *Welsch* v. *Likens,* 1974.
106. e.g., Scheerenberger & Felsenthal, 1977; Aninger & Bolinsky, 1977.
107. Scheerenberger & Felsenthal, 1977; e.g., Gollay, Freedman, Wyngaarden, & Kurtz, 1978.
108. Aninger & Bolinsky, 1977; Scheerenberger & Felsenthal, 1977; Birenbaum & Re, 1979.
109. O'Connor, 1976; Butler & Bjaanes, 1978; Flynn, R., 1980; Flynn, R., & Nitsch, 1980.
110. Butler & Bjaanes, 1978, p. 372.
111. O'Connor, 1976.
112. Edgerton, 1967; Heshusius, 1981.
113. King, R., Raynes, & Tizard, 1971.
114. Rosen, M., Floor, & Baxter, 1974.
115. Kushlick, 1975; Aninger & Bolinsky, 1977; Close, 1977; Conroy & Bradley, 1985.
116. e.g., Brereton & Robertson, 1979; Eyman, Demaine, & Lei, 1979; Scheerenberger, 1983a.
117. Sandler & Thurman, 1981, p. 247.
118. Landesman-Dwyer, 1981, p. 231.
119. Campbell, 1971; Bjaanes & Butler, 1974; Edgerton, 1975; Scheerenberger & Felsenthal, 1977; Landesman-Dwyer et al., 1980; Willer & Intagliata, 1984.

120. e.g., Willer & Intagliata, 1984.
121. Fitzgerald, 1983.
122. Templeman, Gage, & Fredericks, 1982.
123. Bensberg & Smith, 1983, p. 15.
124. Mayeda & Wai, 1975, p. 4.
125. e.g., Lei & Eyman, 1979; Braddock, 1981.
126. W.R.C., 1983.
127. Conroy & Bradley, 1985.
128. "Converting community residences," 1980.
129. Blatt, Ozolins, & McNally, 1979, pp. 143–144.
130. "TASH policy," 1983, p. 3.
131. "Disability groups," 1983, p. 1.
132. *The right to community service,* 1982.
133. Elkin, 1983, pp. 1–2.
134. "Community life amendments readied," 1983, p. 1.
135. *Bridges,* 1979, p. 7.
136. Residential Services & Facilities Committee, 1973; *Bridges,* 1979.
137. Bassuk & Gerson, 1978.
138. "Mental health reform fails." 1975.
139. Fustero, 1984.
140. Fustero, 1984.
141. "Mental health reform fails," 1975, p. 46.
142. "Mental health reform fails," 1975.
143. Santiestevan, 1975.
144. "Release of mentally ill," 1984 p. 1.
145. Smith, 1984, p. 62.
146. *ARC Action,* 1981, p. 1.
147. Scheerenberger, 1983c.
148. Scheerenberger, 1975, 1976b, 1978, 1979b, 1982, 1983c, 1986.
149. "Where have all the people gone?," 1980.
150. Krishef, 1977.
151. Gallagher, U., 1968.
152. Krishef, 1977.
153. "Legislation focuses," 1983.
154. Reece, 1983.
155. Keyes, 1959.
156. Buck & Zarfoss, 1965.
157. Hunt, N., 1967.
158. *Facts on Special Olympics,* 1977.
159. *Facts on Special Olympics,* 1977; Polloway & Smith, 1978; Mason, 1983; Gildea, 1984.
160. "UN declares," 1983.
161. "Proclamation," 1983.
162. e.g., Gottwald, 1970; Lattimer, 1970; Lewis, 1973.

163. President's Committee, 1975b.
164. Roth, E., & Smith, 1983.
165. Salend, Michael, Veraja, & Noto, 1983.
166. *City of White Plains* v. *Ferraioli,* 1974.
167. e.g., *Defoe* v. *San Francisco Planning Commission,* 1973; *Doe* v. *Damm,* 1973; *Boyd* v. *Gateways to Better Living, Inc.,* 1973; *Driscoll* v. *Goldberg,* 1974; *City of Los Angeles* v. *California Department of Health,* 1975; *Anderson* v. *City of Shoreview,* 1975; *State ex. rel. Thelan* v. *City of Missoula,* 1975; *Zarek* v. *Attleboro Area Human Services, Inc.,* 1975.
168. *City of Cleburne, Texas* v. *Cleburne Living Center, Inc.,* 1985.
169. *City of Cleburne, Texas* v. *Cleburne Living Center, Inc.,* 1985.
170. Berdiansky & Parker, 1977; Evans, 1983.
171. "Study shows group homes," 1979; Wiener, Anderson, & Nietupski, 1983.
172. Janicki, Mayeda, & Epple, 1983.
173. Goudreau, 1982, p. A-23.
174. Goudreau, 1982, p. A-23.
175. Goudreau, 1982, p. A-23.
176. Goudreau, 1982, p. A-23.
177. Sherman, Frenkel, & Newman, 1984; Conroy & Bradley, 1985.
178. President's Committee, 1975a, p. 25.
179. Galloway & Chandler, 1978; Casey et al., 1985.
180. e.g., Clark, G. et al., 1968; Redding, 1970; Barker, 1971; Shanyfelt, 1974; Bickersteth, 1978; Polivka, Marvin, Brown, & Polivka, 1979; Holmes, 1979; Skarnulis, In: Ellis, 1979b; Sitkei, 1980; Bruininks, Kudla, Wieck, & Hauber, 1980; Scheerenberger, 1980; Landesman-Dwyer, 1981; "Training needs in the community," 1982; Garrard, 1982; *Parents Association of St. Louis State School and Hospital et al.* v. *Bond et al.,* 1982; Gotowka, Johnson, Gotowka, 1982; Heller, 1982; Willer & Intagliata, 1984; Karan & Gardner, 1984; Jacobson, J., Silver, & Schwartz, 1984; Landesman-Dwyer & Berkson, 1984.

181. Karan & Gardner, 1984.
182. "Study probes," 1984.
183. "Around the country," 1981; "Fire at home," 1983; "14 killed," 1984; "Boarding home fires," 1984.
184. "14 killed," 1984, Section 1, p. 2.
185. Landesman-Dwyer, 1981, p. 223.
186. Dudley, 1983.
187. Conroy & Bradley, 1985, p. 8.
188. O'Connor, 1976; Dellinger & Shope, 1978; Polivka et al., 1979; Intagliata, Kraus, & Willer, 1980; Bruininks et al., 1980; Margolis, Heddock, & Fiorelli, 1980; Fiorelli, 1982; Janicki, Jacobson, Zigman, & Gordon, 1984; Bruininks, Lakin, & McGuire, 1984.
189. Landesman-Dwyer, 1981, p. 223.
190. "Community and junior colleges," 1976; Bilovsky &

Matson, 1977; "Aide-training plan," 1983.
191. Nihira & Nihira, 1974, 1975; Gollay, 1976; Pagel & Whitling, 1978; Sternlicht, 1978; Scheerenberger, 1980; Sutter, 1980; Eyman, Borthwick, & Miller, 1981; Schalock, Harper, & Genung, 1981; Kleinberg & Galligan, 1983.
192. Sternlicht, 1978; Pagel & Whitling, 1978; Scheerenberger, 1980.
193. Fiorelli, 1982.
194. "Washington report," 1975, p. 3.
195. Kilbourn & Molnar, 1981.
196. Lakin, Greenberg, Schmitz, & Hill, 1984; "Report cites savings," 1985.
197. "Report cites savings," 1985.
198. "Report cites savings," 1985.
199. President's Committee, 1985.
200. "HUD announces," 1985.

201. Willer & Intagliata, 1984; Conroy & Bradley, 1985.
202. Spreat, Telles, Conroy, Feinstein, & Colombatto, 1985.
203. Heckt, personal communication to ARC officials, August 23, 1983.
204. Spare, 1983, p. 4.
205. Mager, 1983, p. 3.
206. Heckt, personal communication to ARC officials, August 23, 1983.
207. Willer, Intagliata, & Atkinson, 1981.
208. In: Scheerenberger, 1984, p. 15.
209. Kupfer, 1982, p. 36.
210. Dybwad, 1983, p. 1.
211. Henning & Bartel, 1984.

Epilogue

1. Wineke, 1986.
2. Edgerton, et al., 1984, pp. 350–351.
3. In: Connor, 1964, p. 286.

BIBLIOGRAPHICAL
GUIDE TO
REFERENCE NOTES

Abel, E. (1982). Consumption of alcohol during pregnancy: A review of effects on growth and development of offspring. *Human Biology, 54,* 421–453.

Abel, E. (1984). *Fetal alcohol syndrome and fetal alcohol effects.* New York: Plenum.

Accommodating the spectrum of individual abilities. (1983). Washington, DC: U.S. Commission on Civil Rights.

Achenbach, R., & Zigler, E. (1963). *Social competence and self-image disparity in psychiatric and nonpsychiatric patients. Journal of Abnormal and Social Psychology, 67,* 197–205.

Acne drug triggers abortions, birth defects. (1984, April 6). *USA Today,* p. 4D.

Ad Hoc Committee on Advocacy. (1969). The social worker as advocate: Champion of social victims. *Social Work, 14*(2), 16–22.

Adams, J. (1973). Adaptive behavior and measured intelligence in the classification of mental retardation. *American Journal of Mental Deficiency, 78,* 77–81.

Adler, J. (1985, March 25). Teenage pregnancies. *Newsweek,* p. 90.

Affleck, G. (1980). Physicians' attitudes toward discretionary medical treatment of Down's syndrome infants. *Mental Retardation, 18,* 79–81.

Agent Orange study cites "minor" illnesses. (1984, February 25). *Wisconsin State Journal,* pp. 1–2.

Aide-training plan to help developmentally disabled. (1983, August 29). *Wisconsin State Journal,* Section 1, p. 7.

Alexander, C., & Strain, P. (1978). A review of educators' attitudes towards handicapped children and the concept of mainstreaming. *Psychology in the Schools, 15,* 390–396.

Allen, K. (1981). Curriculum models for successful mainstreaming. *Topics in Early Childhood Special Education, 1*(1), 45–55.

Allen, R. (1966). Towards an exceptional offenders court. *Mental Retardation, 4*(1), 3–6.

Allen, R. (1968). Legal norms and practices affecting the mentally deficient. In B. Richards (Ed.), *Proceedings of the First Congress of the International Association on the Scientific Study of Mental Deficiency* (pp. 89–97). London: Michael, Jackson.

Aloia, G., Maxwell, J., & Aloia, S. (1981). Influence of a child's race and the EMR label on initial impressions of regular classroom teachers. *American Journal of Mental Deficiency, 85,* 619–623.

Alper, S., & Retish, P. (1978). The influence of academic information on teachers' judgments of vocational potential. *Exceptional Children, 44,* 537–538.

Alpert, J., Bereault, H., Friend, W., Harris, V., Scherz, R., Semsch, R., Smith, H., & Coleman, A. (1969). Prevention, diagnosis, and treatment of lead poisoning in childhood. *Pediatrics, 44,* 291–298.

Alvarez, W. (1969). More tribes of paupers. *Modern Medicine, 37*(2), 57–58.

Aman, M., & Singh, N. (1980). The usefulness of thioridazine for treating childhood disorders—fact or folklore? *American Journal of Mental Deficiency, 84,* 331–338.

Aman, M., & Singh, N. (1983). Pharmacological intervention. In J. Matson & J. Mulick (Eds.), *Handbook of mental retardation* (pp. 317–337). New York: Pergamon.

American Association on Mental Deficiency. (1973a). The right to life. *Mental Retardation, 11*(6), 61.

American Association on Mental Deficiency. (1973b). Rights of mentally retarded persons. *Mental Retardation, 11*(5), 56–58.

American Association on Mental Deficiency. (1974). Sterilization of persons who are mentally retarded. *Mental Retardation, 12*(2), 59–61.

American Psychiatric Association. (1966). Psychiatry and

mental retardation: Official actions. *American Journal of Psychiatry, 122,* 1302–1314.

American Psychiatric Association. (1982). *Desk reference to the diagnostic criteria from Diagnostic and Statistical Manual of Mental Disorders* (3rd ed.). Washington, DC: Author.

Amicus Curiae. (1980). 5 (inside cover)

Anastasi, A. (1967). Psychology, psychologists, and psychological testing. *American Psychologist, 22,* 297–306.

Andelamn, F. (1976). Mainstreaming in Massachusetts under Law 766. *Today's Education, 65*(2), 20–22.

Anderson v. City of Shoreview, No. 401575, D. Ct., Second Judicial District, Minn. (June 24, 1975).

Aninger, M., & Bolinsky, K. (1977). Levels of independent functioning of retarded adults in apartments. *Mental Retardation, 15*(4), 12–13.

Aquilina, R. (1976). Revolutionary legislation for a bicentennial year. *Education and Training of the Mentally Retarded, 11,* 189–196.

ARC Action. (1981, winter). 1–2.

ARC's establish elderly DD programs. (1983, June). *New Directions,* pp. 1, 3.

Armstrong v. Kline, 629 F. 2d 269, 3rd Cir. (July 18, 1980).

Around the country. (1981, January). *Memo to Management,* p. 2.

Atlanta Association for Retarded Citizens. (1973). *A study of Georgia's criminal justice system as it relates to the mentally retarded.* Atlanta: Author.

Atlanta Association for Retarded Citizens. (1976). *The mentally retarded offender: Education in prison.* Atlanta: Author.

Attitudes toward people with disabilities. (1983, January). *Memo to Management,* p. 3.

Auletta, K. (1984, June 17). Children of children. *Parade Magazine,* pp. 4–7.

Bacon, A., Froome, K., Gent, A., Cooke, T., & Sowerby, P. (1967). Lead poisoning from drinking soft water. *Lancet, 1,* 264–266.

Bailer, I., & Cromwell, R. (1965). Failure as motivation with mentally retarded children. *American Journal of Mental Deficiency, 69,* 680–684.

Balakrishnan, T., & Wolf, L. (1976). Life expectancy of mentally retarded persons in Canadian institutions. *American Journal of Mental Deficiency, 80,* 650–662.

Balla, D., & Zigler, E. (1979). Personality development in retarded persons. In N. Ellis (Ed.), *Handbook of mental deficiency, psychological theory, and research* (2nd ed., pp. 143–168). Hillsdale, NJ: Lawrence Erlbaum Associates.

Baller, W. (1936). A study of the present social status of a group of adults, who, when they were in elementary schools, were classified as mentally deficient. *Genetic Psychology Monographs, 18*(13), 165–244.

Baller, W., Charles, D., & Miller, E. (1967). Mid-life attainment of the mentally retarded: A longitudinal study. *Genetic Psychology Monographs, 75,* 235–329.

Balthazar, E. (1971). *Balthazar Scales of Adaptive Behavior I: Scales for Functional Independence.* Champaign, IL: Research Press.

Balthazar, E. (1973). *Balthazar Scales of Adaptive Behavior II: Scales of Social Adaption.* Palo Alto, CA: Consulting Psychologists Press.

Bangser, M. (1985). *Lessons on transitional employment.* New York: Manpower Demonstration Research Corporation.

Bank-Mikkelsen, N. (1969). A metropolitan area in Denmark: Copenhagen. In W. Wolfensberger & R. Kugel (Eds.), *Changing patterns in residential services for the mentally retarded* (pp. 227–254). Washington, DC: President's Committee on Mental Retardation.

[Barclay ad]. (1984).

Bark, H., & Menolascino, F. (1968). Haloperidol in emotionally disturbed mentally retarded individuals. *American Journal of Psychiatry, 124,* 1589–1591.

Barker, E. (1971). *ENCORE—A community alternative to institutionalization. Education and Training of the Mentally Retarded, 6,* 185–190.

Barnes, A. (1963). Prevention of congenital anomalies from the point of view of the obstetrician. In *Papers and Discussions of the Second International Conference on Congenital Malformations* (pp. 104–109). New York: National Foundation—March of Dimes.

Barnet, A., Weiss, I., Sotillo, M., Ohrlich, E., Sokurovich, A., & Craviofo, J. (1978). Abnormal auditory evoked potential in early infancy malnutrition. *Science, 201,* 450–452.

Barngrover, E. (1971). A study of educator's preferences in special education programs. *Exceptional Children, 37,* 754–755.

Baroff, G. (1982). Predicting the prevalence of mental retardation in individual catchment areas. *Mental Retardation, 20,* 133–135.

Bass, M. (1964). Marriage for the mentally defective. *Mental Retardation, 2*(4), 198–202.

Bass, M. (1968). The prevention of conception for the mentally deficient. *International Mental Health Research Newsletter, 10*(3), 1, 3–5.

Bass, M. (1969, December). Pastoral counseling on voluntary sterilization for retarded individuals. *Pastoral Psychology.*

Bass, M. (1978). Surgical contraception: A key to normalization and prevention. *Mental Retardation, 16,* 399–404.

Bassuk, E., & Gerson, S. (1978). Deinstitutionalization and mental health services. *Scientific American, 238*(2), 46–53.

Bateman, B., & Wetherell, J. (1965). Psycholinguistic aspects of mental retardation. *Mental Retardation, 3*(2), 8–13.

Bates, P., Morrow, S., & Sedlak, R. (1984). The effect of functional vs. non-functional activities on attitudes/expectations of non-handicapped college students: What they see is what we get. *The Journal of the Association for the Severely Handicapped, 9,* 73–78.

Bates, P., & Wehman, P. (1977). Behavior management with the mentally retarded: An empirical analysis of the research. *Mental Retardation, 15*(6), 9–12.

Baum, M. (1962). Some dynamic factors affecting family adjustment to the handicapped child. *Exceptional Children, 29,* 387–392.

Baumeister, A. (1970). The American residential institution: Its history and character. In A. Baumeister & E. Butterfield (Eds.), *Residential facilities for the mentally retarded* (pp. 1–28). Chicago: Aldine.

Baumeister, A. (1981). Mental retardation policy and research: The unfulfilled promise. *American Journal of Mental Deficiency, 5,* 449–456.

Baumeister, A., & Berkson, G. (1982). Mental retardation research funding trends of the National Institute of Child Health and Human Development. *American Journal of Mental Deficiency, 87,* 119–121.

Baumeister, A., & Muma, J. (1975). On defining mental retardation. *Journal of Special Education, 9,* 293–306.

Baumeister, A., & Rollings, J. (1976). Self-injurious behavior. In N. Ellis (Ed.), *International Review of Research in Mental Retardation* (pp. 1–34). New York: Academic Press.

Baxstrom v. Herold, 383 U.S. 107 (1966).

Bayley, N. (1969). *Bayley Scales of Infant Development: Birth to Two Years.* New York: Psychological Corporation.

Bazelon, D. (1969). Implementing the right to treatment. *University of Chicago Law Review, 36,* 742–754.

Beauchamp v. Jones, No. 75-350 (D. Del., October 23, 1975).

Becker, R., Widener, Q., & Soforenko, A. (1979). Career education for trainable mentally retarded youth. *Education and Training of the Mentally Retarded, 14*(2), 101–105.

Becker, W., & Becker, P. (1983, May 30). Mourning the loss of a son. *Newsweek,* p. 17.

Beckman, P. (1983). Influence of selected child characteristics on stress in families of handicapped infants. *American Journal of Mental Deficiency, 88,* 150–156.

Begab, M. (1973). Guest editorial: Some perspectives on research in mental retardation research centers. *American Journal of Mental Deficiency, 77,* 483–484.

Begab, M. (1984). Guest editorial. *American Journal of Mental Deficiency, 88,* 461–464.

Behrmann, M. (1984). *Handbook of Microcomputers in Special Education.* San Diego: College Hill Press.

Beier, D. (1964). Behavior disturbances in the mentally retarded. In H. Stevens & R. Heber (Eds.), *Mental retardation: A review of research* (pp. 453–487). Chicago: University of Chicago Press.

Bellamy, G.T., Inman, D., & Yeates, J. (1978). Workshop supervision: Evaluation of a procedure for production management with the severely retarded. *Mental Retardation, 16,* 317–318.

Bellamy, G.T., Rhodes, L., Wilcox, B., Albin, J., Mank, D., Boles, S., Horner, R., Collins, M., & Turner, J. (1984). *Quality and equality in employment services for adults with severe disabilities.* Eugene: University of Oregon.

Bellamy, T., & Sontag, E. (1973). Use of group contingent music to increase assembly line production rates of retarded students in a simulated sheltered workshop. *Journal of Music Therapy, 10,* 125–136.

Bender, M., Gardner, T., Urbano, R., Forness, S., Lynch, E., Rothberg, J., & Zemanek, D. (1981). Identifying inservice training programs in university affiliated facilities. *Mental Retardation, 19,* 173–175.

Bender, M., & Valletutti, P. (1976). *Teaching the moderately and severely handicapped* (Vols. 1 and 2). Baltimore: University Park Press.

Bennett, R. (1982). Applications of microcomputer technology to special education. *Exceptional Children, 48,* 106–113.

Bensberg, G. (1965). *Teaching the mentally retarded: A handbook for ward personnel.* Atlanta: Southern Regional Education Board.

Bensberg, G., & Smith, J. (1983). *Comparative costs of public residential and community residential facilities.* Lubbock, TX: Research and Training Center.

Bensky, J., Shaw, S., Gouse, A., Bates, H., Dixon, B., & Beane, W. (1980). Public Law 94-142 and stress: A problem for educators. *Exceptional Children, 47,* 24–29.

Berdiansky, H., & Parker, R. (1977). Establishing a group home for the adult mentally retarded in North Carolina. *Mental Retardation, 15*(4), 8–11.

Berdine, W., & Cegelka, P. (1980). *Teaching the trainable retarded.* Columbus, OH: Charles E. Merrill.

Berdine, W., Cegelka, P., & Kelly, D. (1977). Practica evaluation: A competency based teacher education system. *Education and Training of the Mentally Retarded, 12*(4), 381–386.

Berg, J. (1972). Lionel Sharples Penrose. *American Journal of Mental Deficiency, 77,* 121–122.

Berkowitz, G., Holford, T., & Berkowitz, R. (1982). Effects of cigarette smoking, alcohol, coffee and tea consumption on preterm delivery. *Early Human Development, 7,* 239–250.

Bernstein, N. (1969). Psychiatric training in a state school for the retarded. *Journal of the American Academy of Child Psychiatry, 8,* 68–83.

Bernstein, N., & Rice, J. (1972). Psychiatric consultation in a school for the retarded. *American Journal of Mental Deficiency, 76,* 718–725.

Bettoli, E. (1982). Herpes: Facts and fallacies. *American Journal of Nursing, 82,* 924–929.

Bickersteth, P. (1978). There is a positive side to sheltering. *Education and Training of the Mentally Retarded, 13*(2), 206–208.

Bijou, S. (1963). Theory and research in mental (developmental) retardation. *The Psychological Record, 13,* 95–110.

Bijou, S.W. (1983). The prevention of mild and moderate retarded development. In F.J. Menolascino, R. Neman, & J. A. Stark (Eds.), *Curative aspects of mental retardation: Biomedical and behavioral advances* (pp. 223–241). Baltimore: Paul H. Brookes Publishing Co.

Biklen, D. (1977). Myths, mistreatment, and pitfalls: Mental retardation and criminal justice. *Mental Retardation, 15*(4), 51–57.

Biklen, D. (1981). The Supreme Court v. retarded children. *The Journal of the Association for the Severely Handicapped, 6,* 3–5.

Biklen, D., & Winschel, J. (1985). Burton Blatt. *American Journal of Mental Deficiency, 90,* 233–235.

Bilovsky, D., & Matson, J. (1977). *Community colleges and the developmentally disabled.* Washington, DC: American Association of Community and Junior Colleges.

Binet, A., & Simon, T. (1908). Sur la necessite d'establir un diagnostic scientifique des etats inferieurs de l'intelligence [The need for establishing a scientific diagnosis for conditions of inferior intelligence]. *Annee Psychologique, 11,* 1–28.

Bioengineering program scores first success. (1985). *Association for Retarded Citizens, 34*(4), 1–2.

Birch, J. (1974). *Mainstreaming: Educable mentally re-*

tarded children in regular classes. Reston, VA: The Council for Exceptional Children.

Birch, J., & Gussow, J. (1970). Disadvantaged children: Health, nutrition, and school failure. New York: Grune & Stratton.

Birenbaum, A., & Re, M. (1979). Resettling mentally retarded adults in the community—Almost 4 years later. American Journal of Mental Deficiency, 83, 323–329.

Birth defects: Tragedy and hope. (1983). White Plains, NY: March of Dimes Foundation.

Bjaanes, A., & Butler, E. (1974). Environmental variation in community care facilities for mentally retarded persons. American Journal of Mental Deficiency, 78, 429–439.

Black, M. (1966). Characteristics of the culturally disadvantaged child. In J. Frost & G. Hawkes (Eds.), The disadvantaged child (pp. 45–50). New York: Houghton Mifflin.

Blank, M. (1973). Teaching learning in the preschool: A dialogue approach. Cambridge, MA: Brookline Books.

Blatt, B. (1970). Exodus from pandemonium: Human abuse and reformation of public policy. Boston: Allyn & Bacon.

Blatt, B. (1972). Public policy and the education of children with special needs. Exceptional Children, 38, 537–545.

Blatt, B. (1973). Souls in extremis: An anthology on victims and victimizers. Boston: Allyn & Bacon.

Blatt, B. (1976). Revolt of the idiots: A story. Glen Ridge, NJ: Exceptional Press.

Blatt, B. (1980). Exodus from pandemonium. Boston: Allyn & Bacon.

Blatt, B., & Kaplan, F. (1966). Christmas in purgatory. Boston: Allyn & Bacon.

Blatt, B., Ozolins, A., & McNally, J. (1979). The family papers: A return to purgatory. New York: Longman.

Bliss, C. (1966). Semantography (2nd ed.). Sydney, Australia: Semantography (Blissymbolics) Publications.

Blonston, G. (1984). To build a worm. Science, 5(2), 62–70.

Bloom, B. (1964). Stability and change in human characteristics. New York: John Wiley & Sons.

Board of Education of the Hendrick Hudson Central School District v. Rowley, U.S. S.C. 102 S. Ct. 3034 (1982).

Boarding home fires. (1984, December). The Parents' Voice, pp. 3–4.

Bobath, B. (1969). The treatment of neuromuscular disorders by improving patterns of coordination. Physiotherapy, 55, 18–22.

Bobath, K. (1964). The early diagnosis of cerebral palsy and its differentiation from uncomplicated mental subnormality. In: J. Øster (Ed.), Proceedings of the International Copenhagen Congress on the Scientific Study of Mental Retardation (pp. 415–426). Copenhagen: Det Berlingske Bogtrykkeri.

Bobath, K. (1980). A neurophysiological basis for the treatment of cerebral palsy. London: William Heinemann Medical Books.

Bock, W., & Weatherman, R. (1976). Minnesota developmental programming system (rev. ed.). Minneapolis: University of Minnesota.

Bogdan, R., & Taylor, S. (1976). The judged, not the judges: An insider's view of mental retardation. American Psychologist, 31, 47–52.

Boggs, E. (1966). Legal aspects of mental retardation. In I. Phillips (Ed.), Prevention and treatment of mental retardation (pp. 407–428). New York: Basic Books.

Boggs, E. (1971). Federal legislation. In J. Wortis (Ed.), Mental retardation: An annual review (Vol. 3, pp. 103–127). New York: Grune & Stratton.

Boggs, E. (1978). A taxonomy of federal programs affecting developmental disabilities. In J. Wortis (Ed.), Mental retardation and developmental disabilities (Vol. 10, pp. 214–241). New York: Brunner/Mazel.

Bonner, D. (1961). Heredity. Englewood Cliffs, NJ: Prentice-Hall.

Boocock, S. (1975, February 18). Is U.S. becoming less child-oriented? National Observer, p. 12.

Boslow, H. (1964). The team approach in a psychiatrically oriented correctional institution. Prison Journal, 44(2), 37–42.

Boslow, H., & Kandel, A. (1966). Administrative structure and therapeutic climate. Prison Journal, 46(1), 23–31.

Boslow, H., & Manne, S. (1966). Treating adult offenders at Patuxent Institution. Crime and Delinquency, 12, 22–28.

Boslow, H., Rosenthal, D., Kandel, A., & Manne, S. (1961). Methods and experiences in group treatment of defective delinquents in Maryland. The Journal of Special Therapy, 7(2), 65–75.

The Boston Children's Medical Center. (1972). Pregnancy, birth, and the newborn baby. New York: Delacorte Press.

Richard W. Bothman v. Warren B and Patricia B, No. 79-698, U.S. Supreme Court (1979).

Boyd v. Gateways to Better Living, Inc., Case No. 73-CI-531, Mahoning County Court of Common Pleas (April 18, 1973).

Bracken, M., Bryce-Buchanan, C., Silten, R., & Srisauphan, W. (1982). Coffee consumption during pregnancy. The New England Journal of Medicine, 306, 1548–1549.

Braddock, D. (1977). Opening closed doors. Reston, VA: Council for Exceptional Children.

Braddock, D. (1981). Deinstitutionalization of the retarded: Trends in public policy. Hospital and Community Psychiatry, 32, 607–615.

Bradfield, R., Brown, J., Kaplan, R., Rickert, E., & Stannard, R. (1973). The special child in the classroom. Exceptional Children, 39, 384–390.

Brain healing. (1983, August 8). Time, p. 52.

Brandwein, H. (1973). The battered child: A definite and significant factor in mental retardation. Mental Retardation, 11(5), 50–51.

Brayfield, A. (1965). Editorial note. American Psychologist, 20(2), 121–122.

Brazier, M. (1962). The analysis of brain waves. Scientific American, 206(6), 125–133.

Bregman, S. (1984). Assertiveness training for mentally retarded adults. Mental Retardation, 22(1), 12–16.

Brereton, D., & Robertson, J. (1979). A comparison of institutional and community residents. Unpublished manuscript, University of Wisconsin–Madison.

Bricker, D., & Bricker, W. (1977). A developmentally integrated approach to early intervention. Education and Training of the Mentally Retarded, 12, 100–108.

Brickey, M., Browning, L., & Campbell, K. (1982). Vocational histories of sheltered workshop employees placed in projects with industry and competitive jobs. *Mental Retardation, 20,* 52–57.

Bridges. (Vol. 1). (1979). Arlington, TX: Association for Retarded Citizens of the United States.

Brier, N., & Demb, H. (1980). Psychotherapy with the developmentally disabled adolescent. *Developmental and Behavioral Pediatrics, 1,* 19–23.

Brolin, D. (1973). Vocational evaluation: Special education's responsibility. *Education and Training of the Mentally Retarded, 8*(1), 12–17.

Bronfenbrenner, U. (1974). *Is early intervention effective? A report on longitudinal evaluations of preschool programs.* Washington, DC: U.S. Government Printing Office, Superintendent of Documents, DHEW Publication.

Brooks, B. (1975). Applied teacher training—A consumer based approach. *Education and Training of the Mentally Retarded, 10,* 46–50.

Brooks, P., & Baumeister, A. (1977). A plea for consideration of ecological validity in the experimental psychology of mental retardation: A guest editorial. *American Journal of Mental Deficiency, 81,* 407–416.

Brosnan, B. (1982). *Yoga for handicapped people.* Cambridge, MA: Brookline.

Brown v. Board of Education, 349 U.S. 294 (1954).

Brown, B., & Courtless, T. (1971). *The mentally retarded offender.* Washington, DC: U.S. Government Printing Office.

Brown, B., Courtless, T., & Silber, D. (1970). Fantasy and force: A study of the dynamics of the mentally retarded offender. *The Journal of Criminal Law, Criminology, and Police Science, 61,* 71–77.

Brown, L., Fort, A., Nisbet, J., Sweet, M., Donnellan, A., & Gruenewald, L. (1982). Opportunities available when severely handicapped students attend chronological age appropriate regular schools. In *Educational programs for severely handicapped students* (pp. 1–16). Madison: University of Wisconsin–Madison.

Brown, L., Jones, S., Troccolo, E., Heiser, C., & Bellamy, T. (1972). Teaching functional reading to young trainable subjects: Towards longitudinal objectives. *Journal of Special Education, 6,* 237–246.

Brown, L., Shiraga, B., York, J., Kessler, K., Strohm, B., Sweet, M., Zanella, K., VanDeventer, P., & Loomis, R. (1984). *The direct pay waiver for severely intellectually handicapped workers.* Madison: University of Wisconsin–Madison.

Browning, P., & Nave, G. (1983). Computer technology for the handicapped. *The Computing Teacher, 10*(6), 56–59.

Browning, P., Thorin, E., & Rhoades, C. (1984). A national profile of self-help/self-advocacy groups of people with mental retardation. *Mental Retardation, 22,* 226–230.

Bruening, S., & Davidson, N. (1981). Effects of psychotropic drugs on intelligence test performance of institutionalized mentally retarded adults. *American Journal of Mental Deficiency, 85,* 575–579.

Bruening, S., & Poling, A. (1982). Pharmacotherapy. In J. Matson & R. Barrett (Eds.), *Psychopathology in the mentally retarded* (pp. 195–251). New York: Grune & Stratton.

Bruininks, R., Kudla, M., Wieck, C., & Hauber, F.

(1980). Management problems in community residential facilities. *Mental Retardation, 18,* 125–130.

Bruininks, R., Lakin, K., & McGuire, S. (1984). *Stability of mental retardation facilities for mentally retarded people: 1977–1982* (Brief No. 22). Minneapolis: University of Minnesota, Center for Residential and Community Services, Department of Educational Psychology.

Bruininks, R., Rynders, J., & Gross, J. (1974). Social acceptance of mildly retarded pupils in resource rooms and regular classes. *American Journal of Mental Deficiency, 78,* 377–383.

Bruner, J. (1961). *The process of education.* Cambridge, MA: Harvard University Press.

Bruner, J. (1965). The growth of mind. *American Psychologist, 20,* 1007–1017.

Buck v. Bell, 274 U.S. 200, 47 S. Ct. 584 (1927).

Buck, M. (1975). The multi-dimensional model for the assessment of children referred for classes for mental retardation. *Journal of Afro-American Issues, 3,* 91–102.

Buck, P., & Zarfoss, G. (1965). *The gifts they bring: Our debt to the retarded.* New York: John Day.

Budoff, M. (1971). The mentally retarded child in the mainstream of the public school: His relation to the school administration, his teachers, and his age-mates. In P. Mittler (Ed.), *Education and training* (pp. 307–313). Baltimore: University Park Press.

Budoff, M., & Hutton, L. (1982). Microcomputers in special education: Promises and pitfalls. *Exceptional Children, 49,* 123–128.

Budoff, M., & Orenstein, A. (1982). *Due process in special education: On going to a hearing.* Cambridge, MA: Ware Press.

Budoff, M., & Siperstein, G. (1974). Judgments of EMR students towards their peers: Effects of label and academic competency. *American Journal of Mental Deficiency, 78,* 377–383.

Budoff, M., & Siperstein, G. (1978). Low-income children's attitudes toward mentally retarded children: Effects of labeling and academic behavior. *American Journal of Mental Deficiency, 82,* 474–479.

Budoff, M., & Siperstein, G. (1982). Judgments of EMR students toward their peers: Effects of label and academic competence. *American Journal of Mental Deficiency, 86,* 367–371.

Burgdorf, R.L., Jr. (Ed.). (1980). *The legal rights of handicapped persons: Cases, materials, and text.* Baltimore: Paul H. Brookes Publishing Co.

Burgdorf, R.L., Jr., & Spicer, P.P. (1983). *The legal rights of handicapped persons: Cases, materials, and text (1983 Supplement).* Baltimore: Paul H. Brookes Publishing Co.

Burnham v. Department of Public Health of the State of Georgia, Civil Action No. 16385, U.S. District Court, Northern Division of Georgia (1972).

Burr, L. (1983, January 30). Stereotaxic neurosurgery: A new frontier. *Patient Care,* pp. 63–70.

Burt-Astell, C. (1981). *Puppetry for mentally handicapped people.* Cambridge, MA: Brookline.

Burton, T. (1976). *The trainable mentally retarded.* Columbus, OH: Charles E. Merrill.

Butler, E., & Bjaanes, A. (1978). Activities and the use of time by retarded persons in community care facilities. In G. P. Sackett (Ed.), *Observing behavior: Vol.*

1. Theory and applications in mental retardation (pp. 379–399). Baltimore: University Park Press.

Butterfield, E.C. (1983). To cure cognitive deficits of mentally retarded persons. In F.J. Menolascino, R. Neman, & J.A. Stark (Eds.), *Curative aspects of mental retardation: Biomedical and behavioral advances* (pp. 203–221). Baltimore: Paul H. Brookes Publishing Co.

Butterfield, E., Barnett,C., & Bensberg, G. (1968). A measure of attitudes which differentiates attendants from separate institutions. *American Journal of Mental Deficiency, 72,* 890–899.

Caffey, J. (1974). The whiplash syndrome: Manual shaking by the extremities with whiplash-induced intracranial and intraocular bleedings, linked with residual permanent brain damage and mental retardation. *Pediatrics, 54,* 396–403.

Cain, L., Levine, S., & Elzey, F. (1963). *Manual for the Cain-Levine Social Competency Scale.* Palo Alto, CA: Consulting Psychologists Press.

Camelot Behavioral Systems Checklist. (1974). Bellevue, WA: Edmark Associates.

Campbell, A. (1971). Aspects of personal independence of mentally subnormal and severely subnormal adults in hospital and in local authority hostels. *International Journal of Social psychiatry, 17,* 305–310.

Cannon, M. (1983). Contentious and burdensome litigation: A need for alternatives. *National Forum, 43*(4), 10–13.

Cantor, G. (1960). A critique of Garfield and Wittson's reaction to the revised manual on terminology and classification. *American Journal of Mental Deficiency, 64,* 954–956.

Care of institutionalized mentally disabled. (1985). (Joint Hearings before the Subcommittee on the Handicapped of the Committee on Labor and Human Resources.) Washington, DC: U.S. Government Printing Office.

Carey, J. (1984, August 6). New insight into genes: Now the payoff. *U.S. News & World Report,* p. 57.

Carney, M. (1984). Vitamin deficiencies and excesses: Behavioral consequences in adults. In J. Galler (Ed.), *Human nutrition* (pp. 193–222). New York: Plenum.

Carroll, A. (1967). The effects of segregated and partially integrated school programs on self-concept and academic achievement of educable mental retardates. *Exceptional Children, 34,* 93–99.

Carroll, L. (1986). *Alice in Wonderland.* New York: Putnam.

Carson, R. (1962). *Silent spring.* Boston: Houghton Mifflin.

Cases to deinstitutionalize mentally retarded persons. (1981). *Mental Disabilities Law Review, 5*(3), 142–143.

Casey, K., McGee, J., Stark, J., & Menolascino, F. (1985). *A community-based system for the mentally retarded: The ENCORE experience.* Lincoln: University of Nebraska Press.

Cattell, R. (1963). Theory of fluid and crystallized intelligence: A critical experiment. *Journal of Educational Psychology, 54,* 1–22.

Celedon, J., Csaszar, D., Middleton, J., & de Andraca, I. (1980). The effect of treatment on mental and psychomotor development of morasmic infants according to age of admission. *Journal of Mental Deficiency Research, 24,* 27–35.

Centers for Disease Control. (1980). Current status of rubella in the United States, 1969–1979. *The Journal of Infectious Diseases, 142,* 776–779.

Chadsey-Rusch, J., Karlan, G., Riva, M., & Rusch, F. (1984). Competitive employment: Teaching conversational skills to adults who are mentally retarded. *Mental Retardation, 22,* 218–225.

Chapter II: A report of Iowa's comprehensive plan to combat mental retardation. (1965). Des Moines, IA: Comprehensive Plan to Combat Mental Retardation.

From charity to rights. (1968). Brussels: International League of Societies for the Mentally handicapped.

Charles, D. (1953). Ability and accomplishments of persons earlier judged mentally deficient. *American Journal of Mental Deficiency, 58,* 337–341.

Chase, H., Canosa, C., Dabiere, C., Welch, N., & O'Brien, D. (1984). Postnatal undernutrition and human brain development. *Journal of Mental Deficiency Research, 18,* 355–366.

Cheney, D., & Foss, G. (1984). An examination of the social behavior of mentally retarded workers. *Education and Training of the Mentally Retarded, 19,* 216–221.

Chess, S. (1962). Psychiatric treatment of the mentally retarded child with behavior problems. *American Journal of Orthopsychiatry, 32,* 863–869.

Chess, S., & Fernandez, P. (1980). Neurologic damage and behavior disorder in rubella children. *American Annals of the Deaf, 125,* 998–1001.

Childs, R. (1974). A closer look at labeling children who are mentally retarded. *Education and Training of the Mentally Retarded, 9,* 179–182.

Childs, R. (1981). Perceptions of mainstreaming by regular classroom teachers who teach mainstreamed educable mentally retarded students in the public schools. *Education and Training of the Mentally Retarded, 6,* 225–227.

Christensen, D. (1975). Effects of combining methylphenidate and a classroom token system in modifying hyperactive behavior. *American Journal of Mental Deficiency, 80,* 266–276.

City of Cleburne, Texas v. Cleburne Living Center, Inc., No. 84-468, U.S. Sup. Ct. (July 1, 1985).

City of Los Angeles v. California Department of Health, No. 116571, Calif. Sup. Ct. (October 24, 1975).

City of White Plains v. Ferraioli, 34 N.Y. 2d 300, 357 N.Y.S. 2d 449, 313, N.E. 2d 756 (1974).

Clark, E. (1976). Teacher attitudes toward integration of children with handicaps. *Education and Training of the Mentally Retarded, 11,* 333–335.

Clark, G., Kivitz, M., & Rosen, M. (1968). *A transitional program for institutionalized mentally retarded adults.* Washington, DC: Department of Health, Education, and Welfare.

Clark, M. (1984, March 5). Medicine: A brave new world. *Newsweek,* pp. 64–70.

Clausen, J. (1967). Mental deficiency—Development of a concept. *American Journal of Mental Deficiency, 71,* 727–745.

Clausen, J. (1972). *Quo Vadis, AAMD? Journal of Special Education, 6,* 51–60.

Cleary, T., Humphreys, L., Kendrick, S., & Wesman, A. (1975). Educational uses of tests with disadvantaged students. *American Psychologist, 30,* 15–41.

Cleveland, D., & Miller, N. (1977). Attitudes and life

commitments of older siblings of mentally retarded adults: An exploratory study. *Mental Retardation, 15*(3), 38–41.

Clites v. Iowa, No. 46274 Pottawattamie County, Iowa (1980).

Close, D. (1977). Community living for severely and profoundly retarded adults: A group home study. *Education and Training of the Mentally Retarded, 12,* 256–262.

Cobb, H. (1966). The attitude of the retarded person toward himself. In *Stress on families of the mentally handicapped* (pp. 62–74). Brussels: International League of Societies for the Mentally Handicapped.

Cobb, H. (1968). Presidential address. In *From charity to rights* (pp. 11–12). Brussels: International League of Societies for the Mentally Handicapped.

Cocaine and motherhood. (1985, September 14). *Healthweek,* CNN.

Cochran, I., & Cleland, C. (1963). Manifest anxiety of retardates and normals matched as to academic achievement. *American Journal of Mental Deficiency, 67,* 539–542.

Cohen, J. (1972). Vocational rehabilitation concepts in the education of teachers of the retarded. *Education and Training of the Mentally Retarded, 7,* 189–194.

Cole, M., & Cole, S. (Eds.). (1979). *The making of mind: A personal account of Soviet psychology.* Cambridge, MA: Harvard University Press.

Coleman, J. (1966). *Equality of educational opportunity.* Washington, DC: U.S. Government Printing Office.

Coleman, M. (Ed.). (1976). *The autistic syndromes.* New York: American Elsevier.

Collins, C. (1974). On the dangers of shaking young children. *Child Welfare, 53,* 143–146.

Commanger, H. (Ed.). (1973). *Documents of American history* (9th ed., Vol. 2). Englewood Cliffs, NJ: Prentice-Hall.

Commission on Accreditation of Rehabilitation Facilities. (1976). *Standards manual for rehabilitation facilities.* Chicago: Commission on Accreditation Facilities.

Commission on the Reorganization of Secondary Education. (1918). *Cardinal principles of secondary education.* Washington, DC: U.S. Government Printing Office.

Commoner, B. (1972). *The closing circle.* New York: Alfred A. Knopf.

Community and junior colleges train mental retardation paraprofessionals. (1976). *Mental Retardation News, 25*(5), 1.

Community life amendments readied. (1983, November). *Community Living,* pp. 1, 8.

Comptroller General of the United States. (1976). *Report to the Congress: Returning the mentally disabled to the community: Government needs to do more.* Washington, DC: U.S. Government Printing Office.

Confusion over infant herpes. (1984, January 16). *Time,* p. 73.

Conine, A., & Machaclan, M. (1982). The special unit for developmentally disabled offenders. In M. Santamour & P. Watson (Eds.), *The retarded offender* (pp. 450–463). New York: Praeger.

Conley, R. (1973). *The economics of mental retardation.* Baltimore: Johns Hopkins University Press.

Connelly, J. (1964). Viral and drug hazards in pregnancy. *Clinical Pediatrics, 3,* 587–597.

Connor, F. (1964). Legislation: A responsibility. *Exceptional Children, 31,* 286–287.

Connor, F., & Talbot, M. (1964). *An experimental curriculum for young mentally retarded children.* New York: Columbia University, Teachers College.

Conroy, J., & Bradley, V. (1985). *The Pennhurst longitudinal study: Combined report of five years of research and analysis—Executive summary.* Philadelphia: Temple University.

Converting community residences into intermediate care facilities for the mentally retarded: Some cautionary notes. (1980). Albany: New York State Commission on Quality of Care for the Mentally Disabled.

Cooke, N., Heron, T., Heward, W., & Test, D. (1982). Integrating a Down's syndrome child in a classwide peer tutoring system: A case report. *Mental Retardation, 20,* 22–25.

Cordero, J., & Oakley, G. (1983). Drug exposure during pregnancy: Some epidemiologic considerations. *Clinical Obstetrics and Gynecology, 26,* 418–428.

Correction Services. (1975). *The developmentally disabled offender in the Illinois criminal justice system.* Chicago: Author.

Cotten, P., Purzycki, E., Cowart, C., & Merritt, F. (1983). Alternative living arrangements for elderly mentally retarded people. *Superintendents' Digest, 2,* 35–37.

Coughlin, D. (1981). *Placement and care of the mentally retarded: A service delivery assessment.* New York: Department of Health and Human Services, Region II.

Crain, C., McLaughlin, J., & Eisenhart, M. (1983). The social and physical effects of a 10-week dance program on educable mentally retarded adolescents. *Education and Training of the Mentally Retarded, 18*(4), 308–312.

Crain, E. (1980). Socioeconomic status of educable mentally retarded graduates of special education. *Education and Training of the Mentally Retarded, 15,* 90–94.

Crain, L., & Millor, G. (1978). Forgotten children: Maltreated children of mentally retarded parents. *Pediatrics, 61,* 130–132.

Cratty, B. (1969). *Motor activity and the education of retardates.* Philadelphia: Lea & Febiger.

Crisci, P. (1981). Competencies for mainstreaming: Problems and issues. *Education and Training of the Mentally Retarded, 16,* 175–182.

Crnic, K., & Pym, H. (1979). Training mentally retarded adults in independent living skills. *Mental Retardation, 17,* 13–17.

Cronbach, L. (1975). Five decades of public controversy over mental testing. *American Psychologist, 30,* 1–14.

Cronin, J. (1976). The federal takeover: Should the junior partner run the firm? *Phi Delta Kappan, 57,* 499–501.

Cruickshank, W. (1968). Position statement on Doman-Delacato method. *Exceptional Children, 34,* 365–366.

Cruickshank, W., Bentzen, F., Ratzburg, F., & Tannhauser, M. (1961). *A teaching method for brain-injured and hyperactive children.* Syracuse, NY: Syracuse University Press.

Cull, W., Reuthebuck, G., & Pape, N. (1975). *Mentally retarded offenders in adult and juvenile correctional institutions.* Frankfort, KY: Legislative Research Commission.

Cummings, S., Bayley, H., & Rie, H. (1966). Effects of the child's deficiency on the mother: A study of mothers of mentally retarded, chronically ill and neurotic children. *American Journal of Orthopsychiatry, 36,* 595–608.

Cummings, S., & Stock, D. (1962). Brief group therapy of mothers of retarded children outside the specialty clinic setting. *American Journal of Mental Deficiency, 66,* 739–748.

Curfman, H., & Arnold, C. (1967). A homebound therapy program for severely retarded children. *Children, 14*(2), 63–68.

Curriculum guide: Special education courses. (1984). Madison, WI: LaFollette High School.

Cuyahoga County Association for Retarded Children and Adults et al. v. Essex, No. C 74-587 (N.D. Ohio, April 5, 1976).

Dale, R. (1960). *A tribute to Herschel W. Nisonger.* Columbus: University of Ohio.

Dalton, A., & Crapper, D. (1977). Down's syndrome and aging of the brain. In P. Mittler (Ed.), *Research to practice in mental retardation: Biomedical aspects* (Vol. 3, pp. 391–400). Baltimore: University Park Press.

Danker-Brown, P., Sigelman, C., & Bensberg, G. (1979). Advocate-protege: Pairings and activities in three citizen advocacy programs. *Mental Retardation, 17,* 137–141.

David, H., Smith, J., & Friedman, E. (1976). Family planning services for persons handicapped by mental retardation. *American Journal of Public Health, 66,* 1053–1057.

Davis, K., Sprague, R., & Werry, J. (1969). Stereotyped behavior and activity level in severe retardates: The effects of drugs. *American Journal of Mental Deficiency, 73,* 721–727.

Davis, V., Cullari, S., & Bruening, S. (1982). Drug use in community foster-group homes. In S. Bruening & A. Poling (Eds.), *Drugs and mental retardation* (pp. 359–376). Springfield, IL: Charles C Thomas.

Day, E., & Joyce, K. (1982). Mentally retarded youth in Cuyahoga County Juvenile Court work research group. In M. Santamour & P. Watson (Eds.), *The retarded offender* (pp. 141–165). New York: Praeger.

Death of "Baby Doe." (1982, September). *Memo to Management,* pp. 3–4.

DeFazio, N., & Flexer, R. (1983). Organizational barriers to productivity, meaningful wages, and normalized work opportunity for mentally retarded persons. *Mental Retardation, 21,* 157–163.

Defoe v. San Francisco Planning Commission, Civ. No. 30789, Superior Ct., Calif. (1973).

DeHoop, W. (1973). Multilevel preparation of special education personnel. *Education and Training of the Mentally Retarded, 8,* 37–43.

Delacato, C. (1959). *The treatment and prevention of reading problems.* Springfield, IL: Charles C Thomas.

Delacato, C. (1963). *The diagnosis and treatment of speech and reading problems.* Springfield, IL: Charles C Thomas.

Dellinger, J., & Shope, L. (1978). Selected characteristics and working conditions of direct service staff in Pennsylvania CLA's. *Mental Retardation, 16,* 19–21.

Dembowski v. Knox Community School Corporation et al., Civil Action No. 74-210 (Starke County Ct., Ind., May 15, 1974).

Denhoff, E. (1981). Current status of infant stimulation or enrichment programs for children with developmental disabilities. *Pediatrics, 67,* 32–37.

Denkowski, G., Denkowski, K., & Mabli, J. (1983). A 50-state survey of the current status of residential treatment programs for mentally retarded offenders. *Mental Retardation, 5,* 197–203.

Dennis, H. (1976). A community approach to rehabilitation. In P. Browing (Ed.), *Rehabilitation of the mentally retarded offender* (pp. 164–178). Springfield, IL: Charles C Thomas.

DeSilva, B. (1980). The retarded offender: A problem without a program. *Corrections Magazine, 6,* 24–31.

Dexter, L. (1958). A social theory of mental deficiency. *American Journal of Mental Deficiency, 62,* 920–928.

Dexter, L. (1960). Research on problems of mental subnormality. *American Journal of Mental Deficiency, 64,* 835–838.

Diana v. State Board of Education, C-70-37, RFP District of Northern California (1970).

Dick, J. (1974). Equal protection and intelligence classifications. *Stanford Law Review, 26,* 647–672.

DiGiovanni, L. (1978). The elderly retarded: A little known group. *The Gerontologist, 18,* 262–266.

Dignan, P. (1973). Polydactyly in Down's syndrome. *American Journal of Mental Deficiency, 77,* 486–491.

Dinger, J. (1961). Post-school adjustment of former educable retarded pupils. *Exceptional Children, 27,* 353–360.

Dingman, H., & Tarjan, G. (1960). Mental retardation and the normal distribution curve. *American Journal of Mental Deficiency, 64,* 991–994.

Dioxin. (1983, July 4). *U.S. News and World Report,* p. 56.

Dioxin causes minor effects, tests indicate. (1983, March 17). *Wisconsin State Journal,* p. 15.

Disability groups back legislation. (1983, November). *Community Living,* p. 1.

A disease gene. (1983, December). *Discover,* p. 16.

Dixon, B., Shaw, S., & Bensky, J. (1980). Administrator's role in fostering the mental health of special services personnel. *Exceptional Children, 47,* 30–36.

Dodd, R. (1966). Lead industry. *Collier's Encyclopedia, 14,* 401–404.

Doe v. Damm, Complaint No. 627, U.S. D. Ct., (E.D. Mich., March 8, 1973).

Doll, E. (1941). The essentials of an inclusive concept of mental deficiency. *American Journal of Mental Deficiency, 46,* 214–219.

Doll, E. (1953). *Measurement of social competence: A manual for the Vineland Social Maturity Scale.* Minneapolis: Educational Publishers.

Doll, E. (1963). Adultation of the special child. *Exceptional Children, 29,* 275–280.

Doll, E. (1964). Yesterday, today, and tomorrow. *Mental Retardation, 2*(4), 203–208.

Doman, R., Spitz, E., Zueman, E., Delacato, C., & Doman, G. (1960). Children with severe brain injuries. *Journal of the American Medical Association, 174,* 257–262.

Domino, G., & McGarty, M. (1972). Personal and work adjustment of young retarded women. *American Journal of Mental Deficiency, 77,* 314–321.

Donaldson v. O'Connor, No. 73-1843, U.S. Court of Appeals, Fifth Circuit (1974).

Downing, J. (1964). The prevention of communication disorder by the use of a simplified alphabet. *Developmental Medicine and Child Neurology, 6,* 113–124.

Doyle, P. (1964). A national action to combat mental retardation. In J. Øster (Ed.), *International Copenhagen Congress on the Scientific Study of Mental Retardation* (pp. 8–14). Copenhagen: Der Berlingske Bogtrykkeri.

Driscoll v. Goldberg, Case No. 72-C1-1248, Mahoning County Ct. of Common Pleas, Ohio, 73 C.A. 59, Ohio Court of Appeals, 7th District (April 9, 1974).

Dudley, J. (1983). *Living with stigma: The plight of people who we label mentally retarded.* Springfield, IL: Charles C Thomas.

Duff, R., & Campbell, A. (1973). Moral and ethical dilemmas in the special-care nursery. *The New England Journal of Medicine, 289,* 890–894.

Dunn, L. (1968). Special education for the mildly retarded—Is much of it justifiable? *Exceptional Children, 35,* 5–22.

Dunn, L. (1969). Small special purpose residential facilities for the retarded. In R. Kugel & W. Wolfensberger (Eds.), *Changing patterns in residential services for the mentally retarded* (pp. 211–226). Washington, DC: U.S. Government Printing Office.

Dunn, L., Chun, L., Crowell, D., Dunn, L., Halevi, L., & Yackel, E. (1976). *Peabody Early Experiences Kit.* Circle Pines, MN: American Guidance Service.

Dunn, L., & Dunn, L. (1981). *Peabody Picture Vocabulary Test (Revised).* Circle Pines, MN: American Guidance Service.

Dunn, L., Mith, J., Dunn, L., Horton, K., & Smith, D. (1981). *Peabody Language Development Kits (Revised).* Circle Pines, MN: American Guidance Service.

Durham v. United States, 214 Fed. Rep. 2d Series 862 (1954).

Dybwad, G. (1962). Administrative and legislative problems in the care of the adult and aged mental retardate. *American Journal of Mental Deficiency, 66,* 716–722.

Dybwad, G. (1969, May 5). *The psychiatrist and the mental retardation movement: Divorce, separation, or remarriage—Comments.* Paper presented at the American Psychiatric Association's 125th Anniversary Meeting, Bal Harbour, Florida.

Dybwad, G. (1970). Psychiatry's role in mental retardation. In N. Bernstein (Ed.), *Diminished people* (pp. 123–149). Boston: Little, Brown.

Dybwad, G. (1982). Normalization and its impact on social and public policy. In G. Foss (Ed.), *Advancing your citizenship: Normalization revisited* (pp. 1–8). Eugene, OR: Rehabilitation Research and Training Center in Mental Retardation.

Dybwad, G. (1983, November). A society without institutions. *Community Living,* pp. 1, 8.

Dybwad, G. (1985). Thoughts on aging among persons with disabilities [Foreword]. In M.P. Janicki & H.M. Wisniewski (Eds.), *Aging and developmental disabilities: Issues and approaches* (pp. xi–xii). Baltimore: Paul H. Brookes Publishing Co.

Eaton et al. v. State of Arizona, Civil Action No. 329028, Superior Ct., Ariz. (December 10, 1974).

Edgerton, R. (1967). *The cloak of competence.* Berkeley: University of California Press.

Edgerton, R. (1975). Issues relating to the quality of life among mentally retarded persons. In M. Begab & S. Richardson (Eds.), *The mentally retarded and society: A social science perspective* (pp. 127–140). Baltimore: University Park Press.

Edgerton, R., & Bercovici, S. (1976). The cloak of competence: Years later. *American Journal of Mental Deficiency, 80,* 485–497.

Edgerton, R., Bollinger, M., & Herr, B. (1984). The cloak of competence: After two decades. *American Journal of Mental Deficiency, 88,* 345–351.

Edgerton, R., & Edgerton, C. (1973). Becoming mentally retarded in a Hawaiian school. In R. Eyman, C. Meyers, & G. Tarjan (Eds.), *Sociobehavioral studies in mental retardation* (pp. 211–233). Washington, DC: American Association on Mental Deficiency.

On the educability of intelligence and related issues—A conversation with Burton Blatt. (1973). *Education and Training of the Mentally Retarded, 8,* 219–227.

Education regs. (1983). *Superintendents' Digest, 2,* 27–28.

Edwards, J., Harnden, D., Cameron, A., Nosse, V., & Wolfe, O. (1960). A new trisomic syndrome. *Lancet, 1,* 787.

Ehlers, W. (1966). *Mothers of retarded children.* Springfield, IL: Charles C Thomas.

Eisenberg, L. (1973). Herbert G. Birch. *American Journal of Mental Deficiency, 77,* 481–482.

Ekstrand, R. (1979, March/April). Preparing for the due process hearing: What to expect and what to do. *Amicus,* pp. 91–96.

Elkin, E. (1972). Excerpts from NARC statement for HEW hearings on Willowbrook State School. *Mental Retardation News, 21*(5), 4.

Elkin, E. (1976). Historical perspectives. In *1976 national forum on residential services.* Arlington, TX: NARC Research and Demonstration Institute.

Elkin, E. (1983, November). [Operation Real Rights membership letter].

Ellis, A., & Brancale, R. (1965). *The psychology of sex offenders.* Springfield, IL: Charles C Thomas.

Ellis, N. (1963). The stimulus trace and behavioral inadequacy. In N. Ellis (Ed.), *Handbook of mental deficiency* (pp. 134–158). New York: McGraw-Hill.

Ellis, N. (Ed.). (1966). Preface. *International review of research in mental retardation.* New York: Academic Press.

Ellis, N. (1979a). *Handbook of mental deficiency, psychological theory and research.* Hillsdale, NJ: Lawrence Erlbaum Associates.

Ellis, N. (1979b). The Partlow case: A reply to Dr. Roos. *Law and Psychology Review, 5,* 15–49.

Ellis, N. (1982). A behavioral research strategy in mental retardation: Defense and critique. In E. Zigler & D. Balla (Eds.), *Mental retardation: The developmental difference controversy* (pp. 121–152). Hillsdale, NJ: Lawrence Erlbaum Associates.

Ellis, N., Bostick, G., Moore, S., & Taylor, J. (1981). A follow-up of severely and profoundly mentally retarded children after short-term institutionalization. *Mental Retardation, 19,* 31–35.

Ellis, N., & Tomporowski, P. (1983). Vitamin/mineral supplements and intelligence of institutionalized mentally retarded adults. *American Journal of Mental Deficiency, 88,* 211–214.

Ellman, G., Silverstein, C., Zingarelli, G., Schafer, E., & Silverstein, L. (1984). Vitamin-mineral supplement fails to improve IQ of mentally retarded young adults. *American Journal of Mental Deficiency, 88,* 688–691.

Ennis, B. (1972). National Council on the Rights of the Mentally Impaired. In *The rights of the mentally handicapped* (pp. 39–54). Arlington, VA: National Association of Coordinators of State Programs for the Mentally Retarded.

Escudero, G., & Sears, J. (1982). Teachers' and teacher aides' perceptions of their responsibilities when teaching severely and profoundly handicapped students. *Education and Training of the Mentally Retarded, 17*(3), 190–195.

Evans, D. (1983). *The lives of mentally retarded people.* Boulder, CO: Westview Press.

Executive Order 11776. (1974, March 28). *Continuing the President's Committee on Mental Retardation and broadening its membership and responsibilities.* Washington, DC: The White House.

Eyman, R., & Borthwick, S. (1980). Patterns of care of mentally retarded persons. *Mental Retardation, 18,* 63–66.

Eyman, R., Borthwick, S., & Miller, C. (1981). Trends in maladaptive behavior of mentally retarded persons placed in community and institutional settings. *American Journal of Mental Deficiency, 85,* 473–477.

Eyman, R., Demaine, G., & Lei, T. (1979). Relationship between community and resident changes in adaptive behavior. *American Journal of Mental Deficiency, 83,* 330–338.

Facts on Special Olympics. (1977). Washington, DC: Joseph P. Kennedy, Jr. Foundation.

Farber, B. (1959). Effects of a severely mentally retarded child on family integration. *Monographs of the Society for Research in Child Development* (Serial No. 71).

Farber, B., & Jenné, W. (1963). Family organization and parent-child communication: Parents and siblings of a retarded child. *Monographs of the Society for Research in Child Development* (Serial No. 93).

Farber, B., Jenné, W., & Toigo, R. (1960). Family crisis and the decision to institutionalize the retarded child. *Council for Exceptional Children, Research Monograph Series* (Series A, No. 1).

Farber, B., & Ryckman, D. (1965). Effects of severely mentally retarded children on family relationships. *Mental Retardation Abstracts, 2*(1), 1–17.

Federal Register, 1980, *45,* 31007.

A federal voice for behavioral and social sciences. (1983). *Newsletter, 12*(6), 1–2.

Fenrick, N., & Petersen, T. (1984). Developing positive changes in attitudes towards moderately/severely handicapped students through a peer tutoring program. *Education and Training of the Mentally Retarded, 19*(2), 83–90.

Fenton, J., Thompson, M., & Rose, F. (1964). Employment opportunities for the mentally retarded in government agencies. In J. Øster (Ed.). *Proceedings, International Copenhagen Congress on the Scientific Study of Mental Retardation* (Vol. 1, pp. 166–176). Copenhagen: Det Berlingske Bogtrykkeri.

Ferster, E. (1966). Eliminating the unfit—Is sterilization the answer? *Ohio State Law Journal, 27,* 591–633.

Fetus given a second chance by surgery. (1981, June 28). *The Milwaukee Journal,* p. 7.

Feuerstein, R. (1970). A dynamic approach to the causation, prevention, and alleviation of retarded performances. In C. Haywood (Ed.), *Social-cultural aspects of mental retardation* (pp. 341–377). New York: Appleton-Century-Crofts.

Feuerstein, R. (1979). *The dynamic assessment of retarded performers: The learning potential assessment device, theory, instruments, and techniques.* Baltimore: University Park Press.

Feuerstein, R. (1980). *Instrumental enrichment: An intervention program for cognitive modifiability.* Baltimore: University Park Press.

Fiester, A., & Giambra, L. (1972). Language indices of vocational success in mentally retarded adults. *American Journal of Mental Deficiency, 77,* 332–337.

Filler, J., Robinson, C., Smith, R., Vincent-Smith, L., Bricker, D., & Bricker, W. (1975). Mental retardation. In N. Hobbs (Ed.), *Issues in the classification of children* (Vol. 1, pp. 194–238). San Francisco: Jossey-Bass.

Findings show prevalence of Rett's syndrome greater. (1985). *ARC, 34*(4), 1,3.

Fink, W. (1982). Education and habilitation of the moderately and severely mentally retarded. In P. Cegelka & H. Prehm (Eds.), *Mental retardation: From categories to people* (pp. 260–286). Columbus, OH: Charles E. Merrill.

Fink, W., & Sandall, S. (1978). One-to-one vs. group academic instruction with handicapped and nonhandicapped preschool children. *Mental Retardation, 16,* 236–240.

Fiorelli, J. (1982). Community residential services during the 1980s: Challenges and future trends. *The Journal of the Association for the Severely Handicapped, 7*(4), 14–18.

Fire at home for mentally handicapped kills eight. (1983, September 1). *Wisconsin State Journal,* Section 1, p. 6.

Fitts, W. (1965). *Tennessee Self-Concept Scale.* Nashville: Counselor Recordings and Tests.

Fitzgerald, I. (1983, May/June). The cost of community residential care for mentally retarded people. *Programs for the Handicapped,* pp. 10–14.

Flavell, J. (1963). *The developmental psychology of Jean Piaget.* Princeton, NJ: Van Nostrand.

Fleming, E., & Fleming, D. (1982). Social skill training for educable mentally retarded children. *Education and Training of the Mentally Retarded, 17,* 44–50.

Flexer, R., Martin, A., & Friedenberg, W. (1977). Increasing the productivity of the severely retarded with monetary reinforcement: Developing a work ethic. *Mental Retardation, 15*(6), 44–45.

Florida's bill of rights sets precedent. (1975). *Mental Retardation News, 24*(7), 1, 4.

Florida's plan for comprehensive action to combat mental retardation: Report to the governor. (1965). Tallahassee, FL: Interagency Committee on Mental Retardation Planning.

Flynn, J., Gack, R., & Sundean, D. (1978). Are classroom teachers prepared for mainstreaming? *Phi Delta Kappan, 59,* 562.

Flynn, R. (1980). Normalization, PASS, and service quality assessment: How normalizing are current human services? In R. Flynn & K. Nitsch (Eds.), *Normalization, social integration, and community services* (pp. 323–359). Baltimore: University Park Press.

Flynn, R., & Nitsch, K. (Eds.). (1980). *Normalization,*

social integration, and community services. Baltimore: University Park Press.

Fogelman, C. (Ed.). (1974). *AAMD Adaptive Behavior Scale Manual, 1974 Revision*. Washington, DC: American Association on Mental Deficiency.

Folk, M., & Campbell, J. (1978). Teaching functional reading to the TMR. *Education and Training of the Mentally Retarded, 13,* 322–326.

Forbes, M. (1984, January 2). Not seekers but people to fill jobs will be. *Forbes,* pp. 25–26.

Forget, C. (1980). The mentally retarded person in the criminal justice system. *Journal of Offender Counseling Services and Rehabilitation, 4,* 285–295.

Foss, G., & Peterson, S. (1981). Social-interpersonal skills relevant to job tenure to mentally retarded adults. *Mental Retardation, 19,* 103–106.

Foster, G., & Keech, V. (1977). Teacher reactions to the label of educable mentally retarded. *Education and Training of the Mentally Retarded, 12,* 307–311.

Foulds, R. (1982). Applications of microcomputers in the education of the physically disabled. *Exceptional Children, 49,* 155–162.

Four Days. (1964). New York: American Heritage.

14 killed in fire in rooming house. (1984, July 5). *Wisconsin State Journal*, Section 1, p. 2.

Fox, W., Egner, A., Paolucci, P., Perelman, P., & McKenzie, H. (1972). An introduction to a regular classroom approach to special education. In E. Deno (Ed.), *Instructional alternatives for exceptional children* (pp. 22–46). Reston, VA: The Council for Exceptional Children.

Fram, J. (1974). The right to be retarded—normally. *Mental Retardation, 12*(6), 32.

Frank, A., Wacker, D., Berg, W., & McMahon, C. (1985). Teaching selected microcomputer skills to retarded students via picture prompts. *Journal of Applied Behavior Analysis, 18,* 179–185.

Franzini, L., Litrownik, A., & Magy, M. (1980). Training trainable mentally retarded adolescents in delay behavior. *Mental Retardation, 18,* 45–47.

Freed in slaying. (1960). *Children Limited, 9*(6), 2.

Freeman, R. (1968, July 8). Schools and the elusive "Average Children" concept. *Wall Street Journal*, p. 10.

French, J. (1964). *Manual: Pictorial Test of Intelligence*. Boston: Houghton Mifflin.

Fried, P., & Oxorn, H. (1980). *Smoking for two*. New York: The Free Press.

Friedan, B. (1963). *The feminine mystique*. New York: Ballantine.

Friedman, E. (1961). Individual therapy with a "defective delinquent." *Journal of Clinical Psychology, 17,* 229–232.

Friedman, L. (1973). *A history of American law*. New York: Simon & Schuster.

Friendly, F., & Cronkite, W. (Eds.). (1970). *I can hear it now: The sixties*. New York: Columbia Records.

Fristoe, M., & Lloyd, L. (1978). A survey of the use of non-speech systems with severely communication impaired. *Mental Retardation, 16,* 99–103.

Frohboese, R., Menolascino, F., & McGee, J. (Eds.). (1985). *Parent concerns and advice: A summary of interview findings*. Washington, DC: President's Committee on Mental Retardation.

Frost, J., & Hawkes, G. (1966). The disadvantaged child.

In J. Frost & G. Hawkes (Eds.), *The disadvantaged child* (pp. 1–12). New York: Houghton Mifflin.

Furlow, T. (1973). A matter of life and death. *Pharos, 1,* 84–90.

Furstenberg, F. (1976). *Parenthood: The social unplanned consequences of teenage childbearing*. New York: Macmillan.

Fustero, S. (1984). Home on the street. *Psychology Today, 18*(2), 57–63.

Gallagher, J. (1967). New directions in special education. *Exceptional Children, 33,* 441–447.

Gallagher, J. (1976). The sacred and profane uses of labeling. *Mental Retardation, 14*(6), 3–7.

Gallagher, J. (1984). The evolution of special education concepts. In B. Blatt & R. Morris (Eds.), *Perspectives in special education: Personal orientations* (pp. 210–232). Glenview, IL: Scott, Foresman.

Gallagher, J., & Moss, J. (1963). New concepts of intelligence and their effect on exceptional children. *Exceptional Children, 30,* 1–5.

Gallagher, U. (1968). Adoption can benefit a mildly retarded child. *Children Limited, 17*(4), 6.

Galler, J. (1984). Behavioral consequences of malnutrition in early life. In J. Galler (Ed.), *Human nutrition* (pp. 63–117). New York: Plenum.

Galloway, C., & Chandler, P. (1978). The marriage of special and generic early education services. In M. Guralnick (Ed.), *Early intervention and the integration of handicapped and nonhandicapped children* (pp. 261–287). Baltimore: University Park Press.

Gan, J., Tymchuk, A., & Nishihara, A. (1977). Mentally retarded adults: Their attitudes toward retardation. *Mental Retardation, 15*(5), 5–9.

Garber, H. (1982). The Milwaukee Project: Preventing mental retardation in children of families at risk. In *Mental retardation* [Proceedings of the Symposium Mental Retardation from a Neurobiological and Sociocultural Point of View, Lund, Sweden, May 1982] (pp. 35–65). Goteborg, Sweden: CIBA-GEIGY.

Garber, H., & Heber, R. (1981). The efficacy of early intervention with family rehabilitation. In M. Begab, H. Haywood, & H. Garber (Eds.), *Psychosocial influences in retarded performance: Strategies for improving competence* (Vol. II, pp. 71–87). Baltimore: University Park Press.

Garber, H., & Heber, R. (1982). Modification of predicted cognitive development in high-risk children through early intervention. In D. Detterman & R. Sternberg (Eds.), *How and how much can intelligence be increased* (pp. 121–137). Norwood, NJ: ABLEX.

Gardner, W. (1966). Effects of failure on intellectually retarded and normal boys. *American Journal of Mental Deficiency, 70,* 899–902.

Gardner, W. (1972). Use of punishment procedures with the severely retarded: A review. In E. Trapp & P. Himelstein (Eds.), *Readings on the exceptional child* (2nd ed., pp. 197–224). New York: Appleton-Century-Crofts.

Gardner, W. (1977). *Learning and behavior characteristics of exceptional children and youth*. Boston: Allyn & Bacon.

Gardner, W., & Cole, C. (1980). A cognitive-behavioral approach to conduct in the developmentally disabled. In E. Balthazar (Ed.), *Managing the aggressive, self-abusive and/or emotionally disturbed developmentally disabled individual* (pp. 92–114). Madison: Wisconsin Department of Health and Social Services.

Garfield, S., & Wittson, C. (1960). Some reactions to the revised "Manual on Terminology and Classification in Mental Retardation." *American Journal of Mental Deficiency, 64,* 951–953.

Garrard, S. (1982). Health services for mentally retarded people in community residences: Problems and questions. *American Journal of Public Health, 72,* 1226–1228.

Garrison, I. (1960). Developing potential of exceptional children. *Exceptional Children, 26,* 510.

Geer, W., Connor, L., & Blackman, L. (1964). Recent federal legislation—Provisions and implications for special education. *Exceptional Children, 30,* 411–421.

Gerber, P. (1977). Awareness of handicapping conditions and sociometric status in an integrated pre-school setting. *Mental Retardation, 15*(3), 24–25.

Gest, T. (1983, June 27). Anti-abortion groups have a bad day in court. *U.S. News & World Report,* p. 31.

Gibbons, F., & Gibbons, B. (1980). Effects of the institutional label on peer assessments of institutionalized EMR persons. *American Journal of Mental Deficiency, 84,* 602–609.

Gibbons, F., Gibbons, B., & Kassin, S. (1981). Reactions to the criminal behavior of mentally retarded and nonretarded offenders. *American Journal of Mental Deficiency, 86,* 235–242.

Gibson, G., Colley, D., & Baghurst, P. (1983). Maternal exposure to environmental chemicals and the aetiology of teratogenesis. *Australian New Zealand Journal of Obstetrics and Gynecology, 23,* 170–175.

Gildea, W. (1984, January). These olympics are truly special. *Reader's Digest,* pp. 107–110.

Gilhool, T. (1973). A commentary on the Pennsylvania right to education suit. In *The rights of the mentally handicapped* (p. 53). Washington, DC: National Association of State Coordinators of State Programs for the Mentally Retarded.

Gillis, V. (1978). 1978 leadership award presented to Wolf Wolfensberger. *Mental Retardation, 16,* 327.

Gillung, T., & Rucker, C. (1977). Labels and teacher expectation. *Exceptional Children, 43,* 464–465.

Gold, M. (1977). Factors affecting production by the retarded: Base rate. *Mental Retardation, 15*(4), 41–45.

Gold, M. (1978). An adaptive behavior philosophy: Who needs it? In W. Coulter & H. Morrow (Eds.), *Adaptive behavior* (pp. 234–235). New York: Grune & Stratton.

Gold, M. (1980a). *"Did I say that?"* Champaign, IL: Research Press.

Gold, M. (1980b). *Try another way.* Champaign, IL: Research Press.

Goldberg, J., Katz, S., & Yekutiel, E. (1973). The effects of token reinforcement on the productivity of moderately retarded clients in a sheltered workshop. *British Journal of Mental Subnormality, 19,* 80–84.

Goldstein, H. (1964). *The development of the Illinois Index of Self Derogation.* Washington, DC: U.S. Government Printing Office.

Goldstein, S., Strickland, B., Turnbull, A., & Curry, L. (1980). An observational analysis of the IEP conference. *Exceptional Children, 46,* 278–286.

Goldstein, S., & Turnbull, A. (1982). The use of two strategies to increase parent participation in the IEP conference. *Exceptional Children, 48,* 361–362.

Gollay, E. (1976). *A study of the community adjustment of deinstitutionalized mentally retarded persons: Vol. 5. An analysis of factors associated with community adjustment.* Cambridge, MA: Abt Associates.

Gollay, E. (1977). *A survey of higher education facilities and services for students with disabilities.* Cambridge, MA: Abt Associates.

Gollay, E., Freedman, R., Wyngaarden, M., & Kurtz, N. (1978). *Coming back: The community experiences of institutionalized mentally retarded people.* Cambridge, MA: Abt Books.

Goodman, H., Gottlieb, J., & Harrison, R. (1972). Social acceptance of EMRs integrated into a non-graded elementary school. *American Journal of Mental Deficiency, 76,* 412–417.

Goodman, L., Wilson, P., & Bornstein, H. (1978). Results of a national survey of sign language programs in special education. *Mental Retardation, 16,* 104–106.

Gotowka, T., Johnson, E., & Gotowka, C. (1982). Costs of providing dental services to adult mentally retarded: A preliminary report. *American Journal of Public Health, 72,* 1246–1250.

Gottlieb, J., Alter, M., & Gottlieb, B. (1983). Mainstreaming mentally retarded children. In J. Matson & J. Mulick (Eds.), *Handbook of mental retardation* (pp. 67–77). New York: Pergamon Press.

Gottlieb, J., Cohen, L., & Goldstein, L. (1974). Social contact and personal adjustment as variables relating to attitudes toward EMR children. *Training School Bulletin, 71,* 9–16.

Gottlieb, J., & Davis, J. (1973). Social acceptance of EMR children during overt behavioral interactions. *American Journal of Mental Deficiency, 78,* 141–143.

Gottwald, H. (1970). *Public awareness about mental retardation.* Arlington, VA: Council for Exceptional Children.

Goudreau, R. (1982, November 28). Neighbors divided on group homes. *The Orlando Sentinel,* p. A-23.

Gould, S. (1981). *The mismeasure of man.* New York: W. W. Norton.

Gozali, J. (1971). Citizenship and voting behavior of mildly retarded adults: A pilot study. *American Journal of Mental Deficiency, 75,* 640–641.

Grabowski, S. (1973). Safety and effectiveness of haloperidol for mentally retarded behaviorally disordered and hyperkinetic patients. *Current Therapeutic Research, 15,* 856–861.

Graham, R. (1962). Responsibility of public education for exceptional children. *Exceptional Children, 28,* 255–259.

Granger, B. (1985, August). Alec's song. *Reader's Digest,* pp. 33–39.

Grant, W., & Snyder, T. (1984). *Digest of education statistics 1983–84.* Washington, DC: National Center for Education Statistics.

Green, B., & Klien, N. (1980). The political values of mentally retarded citizens. *Mental Retardation, 18,* 35–38.

Greenland, S., Richwald, G., & Honda, G. (1983). The effects of marijuana use during pregnancy. *Drug and Alcohol Dependence, 11,* 359–366.

Greenspan, S., & Shoultz, B. (1981). Why mentally retarded adults lose their jobs: Social competence as a factor in work adjustment. *Applied Research in Mental Retardation, 2,* 23–28.

Griggs v. Duke Power Company, 401 U.S. 424, 431 (1971).

Groisser, D., Rosso, P., & Winick, M. (1982). Coffee consumption during pregnancy: Subsequent behavioral abnormalities of the offspring. *Journal of Nutrition, 112,* 829–832.

Gross, R., Cox, A., Tatyrek, R., Pollay, M., & Barnes, W. (1983). Early management and decision making for the treatment of myelomeningocele. *Pediatrics, 72,* 450–458.

Grossman, H. (Ed.). (1973). *Manual on terminology and classification in mental retardation.* Washington, DC: American Association on Mental Deficiency.

Grossman, H. (1977). *Manual on terminology and classification in mental retardation.* Washington, DC: American Association on Mental Deficiency.

Grossman, H. (Ed.). (1983a). *Classification in mental retardation.* Washington, DC: American Association on Mental Deficiency.

Grossman, H. (1983b, July 28). *To Newsweek, in response to the Becker editorial* [correspondence]. Washington, DC: The American Association on Mental Deficiency.

Group for the Advancement of Psychiatry. (1979). *Psychiatric consultation in mental retardation.* New York: Mental Health Materials Center.

Gruenewald, L., & Schroeder, J. (1979, February). *Integration of handicapped students in public schools: Concepts and processes.* Paper presented at the conference of the Organization for Economic Cooperation and Development on Integration, Paris, France.

Grunberg, F. (1977). Willowbrook: A view from the top. In J. Wortis (Ed.), *Mental retardation and developmental disabilities: An annual review* (Vol. IX, pp. 46–52). New York: Brunner/Mazel.

Guardianship of Becker, 1 Civ. 53419, Cal. Ct. App. (October 19, 1981).

Guarnaccia, V. (1976). Factor structure and correlates of adaptive behavior in noninstitutionalized retarded adults. *American Journal of Mental Deficiency, 80,* 543–547.

Guerin, G., & Szatlocky, K. (1974). Integration programs for the mildly retarded. *Exceptional Children, 41,* 173–179.

Guidelines on employee selection procedures. (1972). *Federal Register, 35,* 12333–12336.

Guilford, J. (1966). Intelligence: 1965 model. *American Psychologist, 21,* 20–26.

Gunsburg, H. (1976). *Progress Assessment Chart of Social and Personal Development, Manual* (4th ed.). Stratford-upon-Avon, England: Sefa Publications.

Guskin, S. (1962). The influence of labeling upon the perception of subnormality in mentally defective children. *American Journal of Mental Deficiency, 67,* 402–405.

Guskin, S. (1963). Measuring the strength of the stereotype of the mental defective. *American Journal of Mental Deficiency, 67,* 569–575.

Guskin, S. (1974). Research on labeling retarded persons: Where do we go from here? *American Journal of Mental Deficiency, 79,* 262–264.

Guskin, S., & Spicker, H. (1968). Educational research in mental retardation. In N. Ellis (Ed.), *International review of research in mental retardation* (Vol. 3, pp. 217–278). New York: Academic Press.

Guthrie, G., Butler, A., & Gorlow, L. (1961). Patterns of self-attitudes of retardates. *American Journal of Mental Deficiency, 66,* 222–229.

Guthrie, G. Butler, A., & Gorlow, L. (1963). Personality differences between institutionalized and noninstitutionalized retardates. *American Journal of Mental Deficiency, 67,* 543–548.

Hagerman, R., Smith, A., & Mariner, R. (1983). Clinical features of the fragile X syndrome. In R. Hagerman & P. McBogg (Eds.), *The fragile X syndrome* (pp. 17–54). Dillon, CO: Spectra.

Haggerty, D., Kane, L., & Udall, D. (1976). An essay on the legal rights of the mentally retarded. *Family Law Quarterly, 6,* 59–71.

Halderman v. Pennhurst State School and Hospital, 466 F. Supp. 1295, U.S. Third Circuit Court of Appeals (1978).

Hall, S. (1984). The LaCross file. *Science, 5(6),* 54–61.

Hamre-Nietupski, S., & Nietupski, J. (1981). Integral involvement of severely handicapped students within regular public schools. *The Journal of the Association for the Severely Handicapped, 6,* 30–39.

Handicapped children: (1975). HEW/OE regulates contracts and grants for education programs. *Federal Register, 40,* 7408–7430.

Handicapped girl seeks acceptance, writes letter which tells it all. (1974). *Mental Retardation News, 23(2),* 7.

Hannaford, A. (1983). Microcomputers in special education: Some new opportunities, some old problems. *The Computing Teacher, 10(6),* 11–17.

Hannaford, A., & Taber, F. (1982). Microcomputer software for the handicapped: Development and evaluation. *Exceptional Children, 49,* 137–142.

Hansen, C. (1977). Willowbrook. In J. Wortis (Ed.), *Mental retardation and developmental disabilities: An annual review* (Vol. IX, pp. 6–45). New York: Brunner/Mazel.

Hansen, H. (1978). Decline of Down's syndrome after abortion reform in New York state. *American Journal of Mental Deficiency, 83,* 185–188.

Hanson, M., & Schwartz, R. (1978). Results of a longitudinal intervention program for Down's syndrome infants and their families. *Education and Training of the Mentally Retarded, 13,* 403–407.

Harbach, R. (1976). An overview of rehabilitation alternatives. In P. Browning (Ed.), *Rehabilitation and the retarded offender* (pp. 123–141). Springfield, IL: Charles C Thomas.

Harbeson v. Parke-Davis, Inc., 51, U.S.L.W. 2421, Washington Sup. Ct. (1983).

Hardy, J. (1973). Clinical and developmental aspects of rubella. *Archives of Otolaryngology, 98,* 230–236.

Harmon, E., & Haring, N. (1976). Meet AAESPH—The new kid on the block. *Education and Training of the Mentally Retarded, 11,* 101–105.

Harrell, R., Capp, R., Davis, D., Peerless, J., & Ravitz, L. (1981). Can nutritional supplements help mentally retarded children? An exploratory study. *Proceedings of the National Academy of Sciences, 78,* 574–578.

Harrington, M. (1962). *The other Americans.* New York: Macmillan.

Harrington, M. (1984). *The New American poverty.* New York: Holt, Rinehart & Winston.

Harrison v. State of Michigan, 350 F. Supp. 846, E.D. Mich. (1972).

Harrison, R., & Budoff, M. (1972). Demographic, historical, and ability correlates of the Laurelton Concept Scale in an EMR sample. *American Journal of Mental Deficiency, 76,* 460–480.

Harvard's president calls medical school "far too narrow." (1984, April 20). *Wall Street Journal,* p. 33.

Harvey, J. (1979). The potential of relaxation training for the mentally retarded. *Mental Retardation, 17,* 71–76.

Haskins, J., & Friel, C. (1973a). *Project Cameo* (Vol. 4). Huntsville, TX: Sam Houston State University.

Haskins, J., & Friel, C. (1973b). *Project Cameo* (Vol. 5). Huntsville, TX: Sam Houston State University.

Hauber, F.A., Rotegard, L.L., & Bruininks, R.H. (1985). Characteristics of residential services for older/elderly mentally retarded persons. In M.P. Janicki & H.M. Wisniewski (Eds.), *Aging and developmental disabilities: Issues and approaches* (pp. 327–350). Baltimore: Paul H. Brookes Publishing Co.

Hayes, H. (Ed.). (1969). *Smiling through the apocalypse.* New York: McCall.

Haywood, H. (1977). The ethics of doing research . . . and of not doing it. *American Journal of Mental Deficiency, 81,* 311–317.

Haywood, H. (1979). What happened to mild and moderate mental retardation? *American Journal of Mental Deficiency, 83,* 429–431.

Heavner, G. (1986). Effects of graduated decrease and discontinuation of neuroleptics. *Superintendents' Digest, 5*(4), 75–83.

Heber, R. (1961). *A manual on terminology and classification in mental retardation* (2nd ed.). Monograph supplement to the *American Journal of Mental Deficiency.*

Heber, R. (1962). Mental retardation. In E. Trapp & P. Himelstein (Eds.), *Readings on the exceptional child* (pp. 69–81). New York: Appleton-Century-Crofts.

Heber, R. (1964a). Research on personality disorders and characteristics of the mentally retarded. *Mental Retardation Abstracts, 1,* 304–321.

Heber, R. (1964b). Personality. In H. Stevens & R. Heber (Eds.), *Mental retardation* (pp. 143–173). Chicago: University of Chicago Press.

Heber, R., & Garber, H. (1971). An experiment in prevention of cultural-familial mental retardation. In *Proceedings of the Second Congress of the International Association for Scientific Study of Mental Deficiency* (pp. 31–35). Warsaw: Polish Medical Publishers.

Heinrichs, W. (1983). Reproductive hazards of the workplace and the home. *Clinical Obstetrics and Gynecology, 26,* 429–436.

Heistad, G., Zimmerman, R., & Doebler, M. (1982). Long-term usefulness of thioridazine for institutionalized mentally retarded patients. *American Journal of Mental Deficiency, 87,* 243–251.

Heller, H. (1979). A suggested approach for the establishment of realistic goals of achievement for educable mentally retarded. *Education and Training of the Mentally Retarded, 14,* 156–158.

Heller, T. (1982). The effects of involuntary residential relocation: A review. *American Journal of Community Psychology, 10,* 471–492.

Heller, T., & Berkson, G. (1982). *Friendship and presidential relocation.* Paper presented at the Gatlinburg Conference on Research in Mental Retardation, Gatlinburg, TN.

Helping little people grow tall. (1984, May 6). *Parade,* unpaged.

Helsel, E. (1973). History and present status of protective services. In W. Wolfensberger & H. Zauha (Eds.), *Citizen advocacy and protective services for the impaired and handicapped* (pp. 131–146). Toronto: National Institute on Mental Retardation.

Helsel, E. (1974). Putting it together in Ohio: Parameters, definitions, and alternatives for protective services. In C. Sigelman (Ed.), *Protective services and citizen advocacy* (pp. 23–32). Lubbock: Texas Tech University.

Henning, D., & Bartel, N. (1984). *Deinstitutionalization: A study of community program directors' and superintendents' attitudes.* Philadelphia: Temple University.

Hentoff, N. (1983a, December 13). The baby who was starved to death for his own good. *Voice,* p. 6.

Hentoff, N. (1983b, December 20). "He was hungry. He cried. He moved. He was one of us." *Voice,* p. 7.

Hentoff, N. (1984a, January 3). Troublemaking babies and pious liberals. *Voice,* p. 8.

Hentoff, N. (1984b, January 10). "Did you ever get a letter from a vegetable?" *Voice,* p. 6.

Herpes: The evasive invader. (undated). Newport Beach, CA: Newport Pharmaceuticals International.

Heshusius, L. (1981). *Meaning in life as experienced by persons labeled retarded in a group home.* Springfield, IL: Charles C Thomas.

High grades for preschool. (1985, January). *Dis-data News,* p. 1.

High-tech firms can pose health hazards. (1984, July 24). *Wisconsin State Journal,* p. 10.

Hightower, M. (1976). Status quo is certain death. *Journal of Rehabilitation, 42,* 32–35.

Hill, B., & Bruininks, R. (1984). Maladaptive behavior of mentally retarded individuals in residential facilities. *American Journal of Mental Deficiency, 88,* 380–387.

Himwich, H., Costa, E., Rinaldi, F., & Rudy, L. (1960). Triflupromazine and trifluoperazine in the treatment of disturbed mentally defective patients. *American Journal of Mental Deficiency, 64,* 711–712.

Hinkle, V. (1961). Criminal responsibility of the mentally retarded. *American Journal of Mental Deficiency, 65,* 434–439.

Hire ability. (1984). Washington, DC: U.S. Government Printing Office.

Hobbs, N. (1975). *The futures of children.* San Francisco, CA: Jossey-Bass.

Hobson v. Hansen, 269 F. Supp. 401, District of Columbia (1967).

Holland, F. (1977). A survey of the status of citizen advocacy programs for mentally retarded persons. *Mental Retardation, 15*(4), 65.

Holmes, P. (undated). *Final report—Dual diagnosis program study: MR/MI state-of-the-art service delivery.* Ypsilanti: Eastern Michigan University.

Holmes, R. (1979). Characteristics of five community living arrangements serving mentally retarded adults in southwestern urban Pennsylvania. *Mental Retardation, 17,* 181–184.

Homan v. Homan, Supreme Court of Nebraska, 181 Neb. 259, 147 N. W. 2d 630 (1967).

Horn, C. (1976). Differentiation in special education. *Education and Training of the Mentally Retarded, 11,* 335–336.

Hubbard, J. (1969). *Results of team evaluations in 134*

state institutions in the United States. Washington, DC: U.S. Department of Health, Education, and Welfare.

HUD announces latest round of elderly handicapped housing loans. (1985, October 10). *Intelligence Report*, pp. 1, 3.

Humphreys, L. (1971). Theory of intelligence. In R. Cancro (Ed.), *Intelligence: Genetic and environmental influences* (pp. 31–42). New York: Grune & Stratton.

Hunt, J. (1961). *Intelligence and experience*. New York: Ronald Press.

Hunt, J., & Kirk, G. (1971). Social aspects of intelligence: Evidence and issues. In R. Cancro (Ed.), *Intelligence: Genetic and environmental influences* (pp. 262–306). New York: Grune & Stratton.

Hunt, N. (1967). *The world of Nigel Hunt: The diary of a Mongoloid youth*. New York: Garrett.

Huttenlocher, P. (1984). Synapse elimination and plasticity in developing human cerebral cortex. *American Journal of Mental Deficiency, 88*, 488–496.

Hyman, I., & Kliman, D. (1967). First grade readiness of children who have had summer Head Start programs. *Training School Bulletin, 63*, 163–167.

Iano, R. (1970). Social class and parental evaluation of educable retarded children. *Education and Training of the Mentally Retarded, 5*, 62–67.

Impact of Handicapped Children's Early Education Program. (1983). *Word from Washington, 14*(5), 7–9.

Indiana Association for Retarded Children. (1982, April 20). [News release].

Inhelder, B. (1953). Criteria of the stage of mental development. In J. Tanner and B. Inhelder (Eds.), *Discussions on child development* (pp. 75–85). New York: International University Press.

In re Andrada, 380 U.S. 953 (1965).

In re Penny N., 120 N.H. 269, 414 A. 2d 541 (1980).

In re Phillip B., Court of Appeals of the State of California, First Appellate District, Division Four, Civil Act. No. 4429 (1979).

In re Simpson, 180 N.E. 2d 206, Ohio P. Ct. (1962).

In re Terwilliger, 450 A. 2d 1376, Pa. Sup. Ct. (1982).

In re Truesdell, 304 S.E. 2d 793, N.C. Ct. App. (1983).

Intagliata, J., & Doyle, N. (1984). Enhancing social support for parents of developmentally disabled children: Training in interpersonal problem solving skills. *Mental Retardation, 22*, 4–11.

Intagliata, J., Kraus, S., & Willer, B. (1980). The impact of deinstitutionalization on a community based service system. *Mental Retardation, 18*(6), 305–307.

Intagliata, J., & Willer, B. (1982). Reinstitutionalization of mentally retarded persons successfully placed into family-care and group homes. *American Journal of Mental Deficiency, 87*, 34–39.

International League of Societies for the Mentally Handicapped: Report of Frankfurt Conference. (1971, Spring). *The Record*, p. 2.

In the matter of Hernandez, No. 76757 (Santa Barbara Sup. Ct., June 8, 1966).

Irene, S. (1964). Doctor researches new procedure for saving doomed "Rh babies." *Hospital Management, 98*(5), 47–49.

Jackson v. Indiana, 406 U.S. 715 (1972).

Jackson, G. (1975). On the report of the ad hoc committee on educational uses of tests with disadvantaged students: Another view from the Association of Black Psychologists. *American Psychologist, 30*, 88–93.

Jacobs, R. (1962). A survey of residents. *Training School Bulletin, 57*, 94–98.

Jacobson, C., & Barter, R. (1967). Intrauterine diagnosis and management of genetic defects. *American Journal of Obstetrics and Gynecology, 99*, 796–807.

Jacobson, J., & Janicki, M. (1983). Observed prevalence of multiple developmental disabilities. *Mental Retardation, 21*, 87–94.

Jacobson, J., Silver, E., & Schwartz, A. (1984). Service provision in New York's group homes. *Mental Retardation, 22*, 231–239.

Jaffe, J. (1966). Attitudes of adolescents toward the mentally retarded. *American Journal of Mental Deficiency, 70*, 907–912.

Janicki, M.P., Jacobson, J., Zigman, W., & Gordon, N. (1984). Characteristics of employees of community residences for retarded persons. *Education and Training of the Mentally Retarded, 19*(1), 35–44.

Janicki, M.P., Knox, L.A., & Jacobson, J.W. (1985). Planning for an older developmentally disabled population. In M.P. Janicki & H.M. Wisniewski (Eds.), *Aging and developmental disabilities: Issues and approaches* (pp. 143–159). Baltimore: Paul H. Brookes Publishing Co.

Janicki, M.P., Mayeda, T., & Epple, W. (1983). Availability of group homes for persons with mental retardation in the United States. *Mental Retardation, 21*, 45–51.

Jenkins, S., Stephens, B., & Sternberg, L. (1980). The use of parents as parent trainers of handicapped children. *Education and Training of the Mentally Retarded, 15*(4), 256–263.

Jensen, A. (1969). How much can we boost IQ and scholastic achievement? *Harvard Educational Review, 39*, 1–123.

Johnson v. Johnson, Supreme Court of North Dakota, 104 N.W. 2d 8 (1960).

Johnson, A. (1984, June 25). Breaking out of a vicious circle. *Newsweek*, p. 15.

Johnson, A., & Cartwright, C. (1979). The roles of information and experience in improving teachers' knowledge and attitudes about mainstreaming. *Journal of Special Education, 4*, 453–462.

Johnson, D., & Johnson, R. (1975). *Learning together and alone: Cooperation, competition, and individualization*. Englewood Cliffs, NJ: Prentice-Hall.

Johnson, G. (1962). Special education for the mentally handicapped—A paradox. *Exceptional Children, 8*, 62–69.

Joint Commission on Accreditation of Hospitals. (1971). *Standards for residential facilities for the mentally retarded*. Chicago: Joint Commission on Accreditation of Hospitals.

Joint Commission on Mental Health of Children. (1970). *Crisis in child mental health: Challenge for the 1970s*. New York: Harper & Row.

Jones, K., & Smith, D. (1973). Recognition of the fetal alcohol syndrome in early infancy. *Lancet, 2*, 999–1001.

Jones, L., & Moe, R. (1980). College education for mentally retarded adults. *Mental Retardation, 18*, 59–62.

Jones, R. (1966). Research on the special education teacher and special education training. *Exceptional Children, 33*, 251–257.

Jones, R. (1967). Early perception of orthopedic disability. *Exceptional Children, 34,* 42–44.

Jordan, J. (1973). On the educability of intelligence and related issues—A conversation with Burton Blatt. *Education and Training of the Mentally Retarded, 4,* 219–229.

Jordan, J. (Ed.). (1976). *Exceptional child education at the Bicentennial: A parade of progress* (p. 24). Reston, VA: The Council for Exceptional Children.

Kahn, J. (1981). A comparison of sign and verbal language training with nonverbal retarded children. *Journal of Speech and Hearing Research, 24,* 113–119.

Kalachnik, J. (1984). Tardive dyskinesia: A monitoring system. *Superintendents' Digest, 3,* 76–82.

Kanner, L. (1948). *Child psychiatry.* Springfield, IL: Charles C Thomas.

Kanner, L. (1949). *A miniature textbook of feeblemindedness.* New York: Child Care Publications.

Kansas v. Moss, No. 640 P. 2d 321 Kan. Ct. Apd. (1982).

Kaplan, S., Schaaf, V., & Heath, D. Normalization and the consumer. (1982). In G. Foss (Ed.), *Advancing your citizenship: Normalization re-examined* (pp. 9–20). Eugene: University of Oregon, Rehabilitation Research and Training Center in Mental Retardation.

Karan, O., & Gardner, W. (1984). Planning community services using the Title XIX waiver as a catalyst for change. *Mental Retardation, 22,* 240–247.

Karmin, M., & Morse, R. (1984, February 13). Drowning in debt. *U.S. News & World Report,* pp. 18–23.

Karnes, M., & Zehrbach, R. (1977). Alternative models for delivering services to young handicapped children. In J. Jordan, A. Hayden, M. Karnes, & M. Wood (Eds.), *Early childhood education for exceptional children: A handbook of exemplary practices* (pp. 20–65). Reston, VA: Council for Exceptional Children.

Kates, B., & McNaughton, S. (1974). *The first application of Blissymbolics as a communication medium for non-speaking children: History and development, 1971–74.* Toronto: Blissymbolics Communication Foundation.

Katz, P., & Zigler, E. (1967). Self-image disparity: A developmental approach. *Journal of Personality and Social Psychology, 5,* 186–195.

Kauffman, J., & Payne, J. (1975). *Mental retardation: Introduction and personal perspectives.* Columbus, OH: Charles E. Merrill.

Kaufman, H. (1970). Diagnostic indices of employment with the mentally retarded. *American Journal of Mental Deficiency, 74,* 777–779.

Kaufman, M., Gottlieb, J., Agard, J., & Kukic, M. (1975). Mainstreaming toward an explication of the construct. *Focus on Exceptional Children, 7*(3), 1–12.

Kaveggia, F. (1985). Survival analysis of the severely and profoundly mentally retarded. *American Journal of Medical Genetics, 21,* 213–223.

Kazdin, A. (1978). *History of behavior modification.* Baltimore: University Park Press.

Kearney, N. (1953). *Elementary school objectives.* New York: Russell Sage Foundation.

Kennedy, J. (1963). *Message from the President of the United States.* Washington, DC: House of Representatives (88th Congress), Document Number 58.

Kennedy, M., & Danielson, L. (1978). Where are un-

served handicapped children? *Education and Training of the Mentally Retarded, 13,* 408–413.

Kennedy, R. (1948). *The social adjustment of morons in a Connecticut city.* Hartford, CT: Mansfield-Southbury Training Schools.

Kennedy, R. (1966). *A Connecticut community revisited* [Abridged version]. Hartford: Connecticut State Department of Health.

Kennedy, W., Moon, H., Nelson, W., Lindner, R., & Turner, J. (1961). The ceiling of the new Stanford-Binet. *Journal of Clinical Psychology, 17,* 284–286.

Kenney, T., & Clemmens, R. (1975). *Behavior pediatrics and child development.* Baltimore: Williams & Wilkins.

Kentucky Legislative Research Commission. (1975). *Mentally retarded offenders in adult and juvenile correctional institutions.* Frankfort, KY: State Printers.

Kephart, N. (1971). *The slow learner in the classroom* (2nd ed.). Columbus, OH: Charles E. Merrill.

Kershner, J. (1968). Doman-Delacato's theory of neurological organization applied with retarded children. *Exceptional Children, 34,* 441–450.

Keyes, D. (1959). *Flowers for Algernon.* New York: Mercury Press.

Kidd, J., Cross, T., & Higginbottom, J. (1967). The world of work for the educable mentally retarded. *Exceptional Children, 33,* 648–649.

Kilbourn, B., & Molnar, J. (1981). *Developmental disabilities program: A service delivery assessment.* Washington, DC: U.S. Department of Health and Human Services, Office of Inspector General.

King, J., & Fabro, S. (1983). Alcohol consumption and cigarette smoking: Effect on pregnancy. *Clinical Obstetrics and Gynecology, 26,* 437–448.

King, R., Raynes, N., & Tizard, J. (1971). *Patterns of residential care: Sociological studies in institutions for handicapped children.* London: Routledge & Kegan, Paul.

Kirk honored by Kennedy Foundation. (1963). *Exceptional Children, 29,* 272.

Kirk, S. (1953). What is special about special education: The child who is mentally handicapped. *Exceptional Children, 19,* 138–142.

Kirk, S. (1966). [Foreword]. In J. Frost & G. Hawkes (Eds.), *The disadvantaged child* (pp. xi–xiii). New York: Houghton Mifflin.

Kirk, S. (1968). The National Advisory Committee on Handicapped Children. *Exceptional Children, 34,* 481–484.

Kirk, S. (1972). *Educating exceptional children* (2nd ed.) Boston: Houghton Mifflin.

Kirk, S. (1984). Introspection and philosophy. In B. Blatt & R. Morris (Eds.), *Perspectives in special education: Personal orientations* (pp. 25–55). Glenview, IL: Scott, Foresman.

Kirk, S., & Bateman, B. (1962). Diagnosis and remediation of learning disabilities. *Exceptional Children, 29,* 73–78.

Kirk, S., & Johnson, G. (1951). *Educating the retarded child.* Cambridge, MA: Riverside Press.

Kirk, S., & McCarthy, J. (1961). The Illinois Test of Psycholinguistic Abilities—An approach to differential diagnosis. *American Journal of Mental Deficiency, 66,* 399–412.

Kirk, S., McCarthy, J., & Kirk, W. (1968). *The Illinois Test of Psycholinguistic Abilities*. Urbana: University of Illinois Press.

Klaber, M. (1969). The retarded and institutions for the retarded—A preliminary report. In S. Sarason & J. Doris (Eds.), *Psychological problems in mental deficiency* (pp. 148–185). New York: Harper & Row.

Klebanoff, L. (1964). Out of mind—out of sight. *Journal of Education, 147*, 82–86.

Klein, M., Namer, R., Harpur, E., & Corbin, R. (1970). Earthenware containers as a source of fatal lead poisoning. *New England Journal of Medicine, 283*, 669–672.

Klein, N., Babcock, D. (1979). Assertiveness training for moderately retarded adults: A position. *Education and Training of the Mentally Retarded, 14*, 232–234.

Kleinberg, J., & Galligan, B. (1983). Effects of deinstitutionalization on adaptive behavior of mentally retarded adults. *American Journal of Mental Deficiency, 88*, 21–27.

Knight, O. (1968). The self-concept of educable mentally retarded children in special and regular classes. *Dissertation Abstracts International, 28*, 4483.

Kniss, J., Butler, A., Gorlow, L., & Guthrie, G. (1962). Ideal self-patterns of female retardates. *American Journal of Mental Deficiency, 67*, 245–249.

Koch, R., & Dobson, J. (Eds.). (1971). *The mentally retarded child and his family: A multidisciplinary handbook*. New York: Brunner/Mazel.

Kogel, P., & Edgerton, R. (1984). Black "six hour retarded children" as young adults. In R. Edgerton (Ed.), *Lives in progress: Mildly retarded adults in a large city* (pp. 145–171). Washington, DC: American Association on Mental Deficiency.

Kokaska, C. (1972). Voter participation of the EMR. *Mental Retardation, 10*, 6–8.

Kolata, G. (1984). Amnio alternative. *Science, 5*(6), 92.

Krause, F. (1973). *Police, courts, and the M.R. offender*. Washington, DC: Superintendent of Documents.

Krieger, S. (1975). On aging and mental retardation. In J. Hamilton & R. Segal (Eds.), *Proceedings on a consultation conference on the gerontological aspects of mental retardation* (pp. 75–83). Ann Arbor: University of Michigan.

Krishef, C. (1977). Adoption agency services for the retarded. *Mental Retardation, 15*, 38–39.

Krishef, C., & DiNitto, D. (1981). Alcohol abuse among mentally retarded individuals. *Mental Retardation, 19*, 151–155.

Kugel, R. (1969). Why innovative action? In R. Kugel & W. Wolfensberger (Eds.), *Changing patterns in residential services for the mentally retarded* (pp. 1–13). Washington, DC: U.S. Government Printing Office.

Kugel, R., & Parsons, M. (1967). *Children of deprivation*. Washington, DC: U.S. Government Printing Office.

Kugel, R., & Wolfensberger, W. (Eds.). (1969). *Changing patterns in residential services for the mentally retarded*. Washington, DC: U.S. Government Printing Office.

Kunzelmann, H. (1970). *Precision teaching: An initial training sequence*. Seattle: Special Child Publications.

Kupfer, F. (1982, December 13). Institution is not a dirty word. *Newsweek*, p. 36.

Kurpa, K., Holmberg, P., Kuosma, E., & Saxen, L. (1983). Coffee consumption during pregnancy and selected congenital malformations: A nationwide case-control study. *American Journal of Public Health, 73*, 1397–1399.

Kushlick, A. (1966). Assessing the size of the problem of subnormality. In J. Meade & A. Parkes (Eds.), *Genetic and environmental factors in human ability* (pp. 121–147). New York: Plenum.

Kushlick, A. (1975). Epidemiology and evaluation of services for the mentally handicapped. In M. Begab & S. Richardson (Eds.), *The mentally retarded and society: A social science perspective* (pp. 325–343). Baltimore: University Park Press.

Kvaraceus, W., & Miller, W. (1959). *Delinquent behavior: Culture and the individual*. Washington, DC: National Education Association.

Labor, litigation, and legal rights of residents. (1975). Madison, WI: National Association of Superintendents of Public Residential Facilities for the Mentally Retarded.

Lakin, K., Greenberg, J., Schmitz, M., & Hill, B. (1984). A comparison of Medicaid waiver applications for populations that are mentally retarded and elderly/disabled. *Mental Retardation, 22*, 182–192.

Lally, M. (1980). Computer-assisted development of number conservation in mentally retarded school children. *Australian Journal of Developmental Disabilities, 6*(3), 134–136.

Lally, M. (1981). Computer-assisted teaching of sight-word recognition for mentally retarded school children. *American Journal of Mental Deficiency, 4*, 383–388.

Lambert, N., Windmiller, M., Cole, L., & Figueroa, R. (1975). Standardization of a public school version of the AAMD Adaptive Behavior Scale. *Mental Retardation, 13*(2), 3–7.

Lambeth, H. (1967). The self-concept of mentally retarded children in relation to educational placement and developmental variables. *Dissertation Abstracts International, 27*, 3726.

Lamm, R. (1984, March 30). *Crossfire* [Film]. CNN.

Lampner, C. (1979). Special education teacher training: A cumulative development model. *Education and Training of the Mentally Retarded, 14*(3), 204–210.

Landesman-Dwyer, S. (1981). Living in the community. *American Journal of Mental Deficiency, 3*, 223–234.

Landesman-Dwyer, S., & Berkson, G. (1984). Friendship and social behavior. In J. Wortis (Ed.), *Mental retardation and developmental disabilities* (Vol. 13, pp. 129–154). New York: Plenum.

Landesman-Dwyer, S., Sulzbacher, S., Edgar, E., Keller, S., Wise, B., & Baatz, B. (1980). *Rainier school placement study*. Olympia, WA: Department of Social and Health Services.

Larry P. v. Riles, 495 F. Supp. 926, U.S. District Court for the Northern District of California (1972).

Lattimer, R. (1970). Current attitudes toward mental retardation. *Mental Retardation, 8*(5), 30–36.

Lauchenmeyer, C. (1969). Systematic socialization: Observations on a program for the rehabilitation of antisocial retardates. *Psychological Record, 19*, 247–257.

LaVeck, B., & Brehm, S. (1978). Individual variability among children with Down's syndrome. *Mental Retardation, 16*, 135–137.

Lawson, M., & Wilson, G. (1980). Parenting among

women addicted to narcotics. *Child Welfare, LIX*(2), 67–79.

Lazar, A., Haughton, D., & Orpet, R. (1972). A study of attitude acceptance and social adjustment. *Behavior Disorder, 2*(2), 85–88.

Lazar, I., & Darlington, R. (1978, October). *Lasting effects after preschool: A report of the consortium for longitudinal studies: Final report* (Grant No. 90C-1311). Denver: U.S. Department of Health, Education, and Welfare, Education Commission of the States.

Lead poisoning. (1984, March 19). *U.S. News and World Report*, pp. 79–80.

Leary, T. (1969). Turning on the world. In H. Hayes (Ed.), *Smiling through the apocalypse* (pp. 589–599). New York: McCall.

Lebanks v. Spears, 60 F.R.D., 135 E.D. La. (1973).

Legislation focuses on special needs adoption. (1983, November). *New directions*, p. 3.

Lei, T., & Eyman, R. (1979). Characteristics of individuals referred to services for the developmentally disabled. *Mental Retardation, 17*, 196–198.

Lejeune, J., Lafourcade, J., Berger, R., Vialette, J., Boeswillwalk, M., Seringe, P., & Turpin, R. (1963). Trois cas de letion partielle du bras court d'un chromosome 5 [Three cases of partial deletion of the short arm of a chromosome]. *Academy of Science of Paris, 257*, 3098.

Lejeune, J., & Turpin, R. (1961). Chromosomal aberrations in man. *American Journal of Human Genetics, 13*, 175–184.

Leland, H., & Smith, D. (1965). *Play therapy with mentally subnormal children*. New York: Grune & Stratton.

Lemoine, P., Haurrousseau, H., Borteyru, J., & Menuet, J. (1968). Les enfants de parents alcooliques. Anomalies observees: A propos de 127 cas [Children of alcoholic parents. Anomalies observed among 127 cases]. *Quest Medical, 1968, 21*, 476–482.

Leo, J. (1983, October 10). Still walking faster and longer. *Time*, pp. 42–43.

Lessard v. Schmidt, Civil Action No. 71-C-602, U.S. District Court, Eastern District of Wisconsin (1972).

[Letters]. (1983, December 5). *Time*, p. 6.

[Letters to the editor]. (1983, September 16). *Wisconsin State Journal*, p. 12.

LeVann, L. (1971). Clinical comparison of haloperidol and chlorpromazine in the mentally retarded. *American Journal of Mental Retardation, 75*, 719–723.

Levete, G. (1982). *No handicap to dance: Creative improvisation for people with handicaps*. Cambridge, MA: Brookline.

Levine, S., & Elzey, F. (1968). *Manual for the San Francisco Vocational Competency Scale*. New York: Psychological Corporation.

Levine, S., Elzey, F., Thormahlen, P., & Cain, L. (1976). *The T.M.R. School Competency Scales*. Palo Alto, CA: Consulting Psychologists Press.

Levy, R. (1965). Protecting the mentally retarded: An empirical survey and evaluation of the establishment of state guardianship in Minnesota. *Minnesota Law Review, 5*, 821–887.

Levy, R. (1967). Dimensions of mental retardation among wards of the Illinois Youth Council. *The Journal of Correctional Education, 19*, 125–132.

Lewin, K. (1935). *A dynamic theory of personality*. New York: McGraw.

Lewin, K. (1936). *Principles of topological psychology*. New York: McGraw.

Lewis, J. (1973). The community and the retarded: A study in social ambivalence. In G. Tarjan, R. Eyman, & C. Meyers (Eds.), *Sociobehavioral studies in mental retardation* pp. 164–183. Washington, DC: American Association on Mental Deficiency.

Lewis, J., & Mercer, J. (1978). The system of multicultural pluralistic assessment: SOMPA. In W. Coulter & H. Morrow (Eds.), *Adaptive behavior* (pp. 185–212). New York: Grune & Stratton.

Linde, T., & Kopp, T. (1973). *Training retarded babies and pre-schoolers*. Springfield, IL: Charles C Thomas.

Linn, S., Schoenbaum, S., Monson, R., Rosner, B., Stubblefield, P., & Ryan, K. (1982). No association between coffee consumption and adverse outcomes of pregnancy. *The New England Journal of Medicine, 306*, 141–145.

Lipman, R. (1970). The use of psychopharmacological agents in residential facilities for the retarded. In F. Menolascino (Ed.), *Psychiatric approaches to mental retardation* (pp. 387–398). New York: Basic Books.

Lippman, L. (1965). A state plans for its mentally retarded. *Children, 12*, 171–177.

Lippman, L., & Goldberg, I. (1973). *Right to education*. New York: Teachers College Press.

Litvin, M., & Browning, P. (1978). Public assistance in historical perspective. In J. Wortis (Ed.), *Mental retardation and developmental disabilities* (Vol. 10, pp. 196–213). New York: Brunner/Mazel.

Lombardi, T., & Lombardi, E. (1977). *ITPA: Clinical interpretation and remediation*. Seattle: Special Child Publications.

Loop, B., & Hitzing, W. (1980). *Family resource service and support systems for families with handicapped children*. Omaha: Meyer Children's Rehabilitation Institute.

Lorber, M. (1974). *Consulting the Mentally Retarded: An Approach to the Definition of Mental Retardation by Experts*. Unpublished doctoral dissertation, University of California–Los Angeles.

Louisiana v. Brown, 414 So. 2d 689 La. Sup. Ct. (1982).

Luckey, R., & Neman, R. (1976). Practices in estimating mental retardation prevalence. *Mental Retardation, 14*, 16–18.

Luecking, R. (1981, May 29). *Community based treatment of behaviorally disturbed developmentally disabled persons*. Summary of a presentation given at the 1981 International Association of Psycho-social Rehabilitation Services Conference, Washington, DC.

Luke, B. (1982). Coffee consumption. *The New England Journal of Medicine, 306*, 1549–1550.

Luria, A. (1963a). *The mentally retarded child*. New York: Pergamon Press.

Luria, A. (1963b). Psychological studies of mental deficiency in the Soviet Union. In N. Ellis (Ed.), *Handbook of mental deficiency* (pp. 353–387). New York: McGraw-Hill.

Lynch, K. (1979). Toward a skill oriented prevocational program for trainable and severely impaired students. In T. Bellamy, G. O'Connor, & O. Karan (Eds.), *Vocational rehabilitation of severely handicapped per-*

sons: Contemporary service strategies (pp. 253–265). Baltimore: University Park Press.

Mabile, W. (1982). The mentally retarded defendant program. In M. Santamour & P. Watson (Eds.), *The retarded offender* (pp. 434–443). New York: Praeger.

MacAndrew, C., & Edgerton, R. (1964). The everyday life of institutionalized idiots. *Human Organization, 23*, 312–318.

MacAndrew, C., & Edgerton, R. (1966). On the possibility of friendship. *American Journal of Mental Deficiency, 70*, 612–621.

MacEachron, A. (1979). Mentally retarded offenders: Prevalence and characteristics. *American Journal of Mental Deficiency, 84*, 165–176.

Mackie, R. (1965). Converging circles—Education of the handicapped and some general federal programs. *Exceptional Children, 31*, 250–255.

Mackie, R., & Robbins, P. (1960). Exceptional children in local public schools. *School Life, 43*(3), 14–16.

MacMillan, D., & Jones, R. (1972). Lions in search of more Christians. *Journal of Special Education, 6*, 81–91.

MacMillan, D., Jones, R., & Aloia, G. (1974). The mentally retarded label: A theoretical analysis and review of research. *American Journal of Mental Deficiency, 79*, 241–246.

MacMillan, D., Jones, R., & Meyers, C. (1976). Mainstreaming the mentally retarded: Some questions, cautions and guidelines. *Mental Retardation, 14*(1), 3–10.

Mager, A. (1983). [Statement on the draft of Community Living for Severely Disabled Individuals Act of 1982 at the ARC-CA Board of Directors meeting in Sacramento on June 18, 1983].

Magnusson, P., & Watson, S. (1979, September 21). Plymouth Center in 'diastrous' court is told. *Detroit Free Press*, p. A3.

Magrab, P., & Williams, V. (1982). The Georgetown University Child Development Center Regional Training and Technical Assistance Project. In M. Santamour & P. Watson (Eds.), *The retarded offender* (pp. 241–259). New York: Praeger.

Mainstreaming handicaps. (1983, January/February). *Reflections*, p. 9.

Mainstreaming mentally retarded students in public schools: Position statements by the National Association for Retarded Citizens. (1978). Arlington, TX: National Association for Retarded Citizens.

Malgady, R., Barcher, P., Towner, G., & Davis, J. (1979). Language factors in vocational education of mentally retarded workers. *American Journal of Mental Deficiency, 83*, 432–438.

Maloney, J. (1983, November/December). The J.B. factor. *Saturday Review*, 10–13.

Maloney, L., Walsh, M., and DeLouise, R. (1984, December 24). Welfare in America: Is it a flop? *U.S. News & World Report*, pp. 38–43.

Maloney, M., & Ward, M. (1979). *Mental retardation and modern society.* New York: Oxford University Press.

Marchetti, A. (1983). *Wyatt v. Stickney*: A historical perspective. *Applied Research in Mental Retardation, 4*, 189–206.

Margolis, H., Heddock, T., & Fiorelli, J. (1980). Train-

ing resident advisors: A product-process competency approach. *Journal of Special Education, 14*, 405–414.

Marlowe, M., Errera, J., & Jacobs, J. (1983). Increased lead and cadmium burdens among mentally retarded children and children with borderline intelligence. *American Journal of Mental Deficiency, 87*, 477–483.

Marsh, R., Friel, C., & Eissler, V. (1975). The adult MR in the criminal justice system. *Mental Retardation, 13*(2), 21–25.

Martin, E. (1968). Breakthrough for the handicapped: Legislative history. *Exceptional Children, 34*, 493–503.

Martin, J., & Bell, J. (1943). A pedigree of mental defect showing sex-linkage. *Journal of Neurology and Psychiatry, 6*, 154–157.

Martino, L., & Johnson, D. (1979). Cooperative and individualistic experiences among disabled and normal children. *Journal of School Psychology, 107*, 177–183.

Masland, R. (1963). Mental retardation. In M. Fishbein (Ed.), *Birth defects* (pp. 286–301). Philadelphia: J.B. Lippincott.

Masland, R. (1965). *Summary of progress in childhood disorders of the brain and nervous system.* Washington, DC: Superintendent of Documents.

Mason, J. (1983, July). Eunice Shriver gets the retarded on the right track. *Life*, pp. 121–124.

Massachusetts enacts ''Turning 22'' law. (1984, July). *New Directions, 1*, 3.

Massachusetts plans for its retarded: A ten year plan. The report of the Massachusetts Mental Retardation Planning Project. (1966). Boston: The Medical Foundation, Inc.

Matson, J. (1984). Psychotherapy with persons who are mentally retarded. *Mental Retardation, 22*, 170–173.

Matter of A.W., Colo., 637 P. 2d 366 (1981).

Matter of C.D.M., 627 P. 2d 607, Alaska (1981).

Matter of Guardianship of Hayes, 93 Wash. 228, 608 P. 2d 635 (1980).

Mattie T. v. Holladay, Civ. Action No. DC-75-31-S (N.D. Miss.) (April 25, 1977).

Mattson, B. (1977). Involving parents in special education: Did you really reach them? *Education and Training of the Mentally Retarded, 12*, 358–360.

Mayeda, T. (1977). *Performance measures of skill and adaptive competencies in the developmentally disabled.* Pomona: University of California, Los Angeles.

Mayeda, T., & Wai, F. (1975). *The cost of long term developmental disabilities care.* Pomona: University of California, Los Angeles.

Mayer, C. (1966). The relationship of early special class placement and the self-concepts of mentally handicapped children. *Exceptional Children, 34*, 77–81.

Mayo, L. (1963). Philosophy and recommendations of the President's Panel on Mental Retardation relating to education, vocational rehabilitation, and training. *Exceptional Children, 29*, 425–430.

McAfee, J., & Mann, L. (1982). The prognosis for mildly handicapped students. In T. Miller & E. Davis (Eds.), *The mildly handicapped student* (pp. 461–496). New York: Grune & Stratton.

McAfee, R., & Cleland, C. (1965). The discrepancy between self-concept and ideal-self as a measure of psychological adjustment in educable mentally retarded males. *American Journal of Mental Deficiency, 70,* 63–68.

McCarthy, D. (1972). *Manual for the McCarthy Scales of Children's Abilities.* New York: Psychological Corporation.

McCarthy, J. (1964). The importance of linguistic ability in the mentally retarded. *Mental Retardation, 2*(2), 90–96.

McClelland, D. (1978). Managing motivation to expand human freedom. *American Psychologist, 33,* 201–210.

McGee, J., & Menolascino, F. (Undated). *Gentle teaching techniques for severely retarded persons with severe behavior problems.* Unpublished manuscript.

McInerney, M., & Karan, O. (1981). Federal legislation and the integration of special education and vocational rehabilitation. *Mental Retardation, 19,* 21–23.

McKerracher, D., & Orritt, C. (1972). Prediction of vocational and social skills acquisition in a developmentally handicapped population: A pilot study. *American Journal of Mental Deficiency, 76,* 574–580.

McLure, W., Burnham, R., & Henderson, R. (1975). *Special education: Needs—cost—methods of financing.* Urbana: University of Illinois, College of Education.

McNeil v. Director, Patuxent Institution, 407 U.S. 245 (1972).

Meadow, L., & Greenspan, E. (1961). Employability of lower level mental retardates. *American Journal of Mental Deficiency, 65,* 623–628.

Meer, J. (1984). Civil rights indicators. *Psychology Today, 18*(6), 49–50.

Menolascino, F. (1969). Emotional disturbances in mentally retarded children. *American Journal of Psychiatry, 126,* 168–176.

Menolascino, F. (1974). The mentally retarded offender. *Mental Retardation, 1974, 12*(1), 7–11.

Menolascino, F. (1975). A system of services for the mentally retarded offender. *Crime and Delinquency, 21,* 57–64.

Menolascino, F., & Bernstein, N. (1970). Psychiatric assessment of the mentally retarded child. In N. Bernstein (Ed.), *Diminished people* (pp. 201–221). Boston: Little, Brown.

Menolascino, F., & Egger, M. (1978). *Medical dimensions of mental retardation.* Lincoln: University of Nebraska Press.

Menolascino, F., & McGee, J. (Undated). Mental illness in the mentally retarded: Toward bonding and interdependence. Omaha: University of Nebraska Medical Center.

Menolascino, F., McGee, J., Swanson, D., & Folk, L. (Undated). A continuum of care for mentally retarded—mentally ill. Omaha: University of Nebraska Medical Center.

Menolascino, F.J., Neman, R., & Stark, J.A. (1983). *Curative aspects of mental retardation: Biomedical and behavioral advances.* Baltimore: Paul H. Brookes Publishing Co.

Mental deficiency conference meets this July in London. (1960). *Exceptional Children, 26,* 310.

Mental Health Law Project. (1973). *Basic rights of the mentally handicapped.* Washington, DC: Author.

Mental health reform fails. (1975). *Modern Healthcare, 4*(6), 45–48.

Mental retardation: A handbook for the primary physician. (1965). Chicago: American Medical Association.

The mentally retarded offender. (1980, October). *Angolite,* pp. 17–36, 100.

Mentally retarded offenders. (1983, January). *Memo to Management,* pp. 2–3.

Mercer, J. (1970). Sociological perspectives on mild mental retardation. In H. Carl Haywood (Ed.), *Sociocultural aspects of mental retardation* (pp. 378–391). New York: Appleton-Century-Crofts.

Mercer, J. (1973a). *Labelling the mentally retarded.* Berkeley: University of California Press.

Mercer, J. (1973b). The myth of 3% prevalence. In R. Eyman, C. Meyers, & G. Tarjan (Eds.), *Sociobehavioral studies in mental retardation* (pp. 1–18). Washington, DC: American Association on Mental Deficiency.

Mercer, J. (1975). Sociocultural factors in educational labelling. In M. Begab and S. Richardson (Eds.), *The mentally retarded and society: A social science perspective* (pp. 141–157). Baltimore: University Park Press.

Mercer, J., & Lewis, J. (1978). *System of multicultural pluralistic assessment.* New York: Psychological Corporation.

Merton, D., & Osborne, D. (1983). Craniocerebral trauma in the child abuse syndrome. *Pediatric Annuals, 12,* 882–887.

Metfessel, N. (1964). Unpublished research. University of Southern California, Center for the Study of the Education of Disadvantaged Youth. (Cited in M. Black. [1966]. Characteristics of the culturally disadvantaged child. In J. Frost & G. Hawkes [Eds.], *The disadvantaged child* [pp. 45–50]. New York: Houghton Mifflin.)

Metzer, R., & Rheingold, H. (1962). Mental capacity and incompetency: A psycholegal problem. *American Journal of Psychiatry, 18,* 827–831.

Meyers, C., Nihira, K., & Zetlin, A. (1979). The measurement of adaptive behavior. In N. Ellis (Ed.), *Handbook of mental deficiency, psychological theory and research* (2nd ed, pp. 431–481). Hillsdale, NJ: Lawrence Erlbaum Associates.

Meyerwitz, J. (1962). Self-derogations in young retardates and special class placement. *Child Development, 33,* 443–451.

Meyerwitz, J. (1965). The neighborhood sociometric. In J. Moss & L. Jordan (Eds.), *The efficiency of special class training on the development of mentally retarded children* (Appendix F, unpaged). Urbana: University of Illinois.

Michelmore, P. (1985, July 14). They save babies. *Parade,* pp. 12–14.

Miles, C. (1963). Gifted children. In L. Carmichael (Ed.), *Manual on child psychology* (2nd ed., pp. 984–1063). New York: John Wiley & Sons.

Miller, C., Mayer, D., & Whitworth, W. (1973). A study of mentally retarded juvenile offenders in Corpus Christi, Texas. *Federal Probation, 37,* 54–61.

Miller, E. (1965). Ability and social adjustment at midlife of persons earlier judged mentally deficient. *Genetic Psychology Monographs, 72,* 139–198.

Miller, G., Galanter, E., & Pribam, K. (1960). *Plans and the structure of behavior.* New York: Henry Holt.

Miller, S. (1984). Childbearing and childrearing among the very young. *Children Today, 13*(3), 26–29.

Miller, W., Miller, A., & Schneider, E. (1980). *American national election studies data sourcebook, 1952–1978.* Cambridge, MA: Harvard University Press.

Millett, K. (1970). *Sexual politics.* Garden City, NY: Doubleday.

Mills v. The Board of Education, Civil Action No. 1939-71, U.S. District Court of the District of Columbia (1972).

Milne, N. (1979). Teachers of the severely and profoundly retarded students: What competencies are needed? *Mental Retardation, 17,* 87–88.

Milunsky, A. (1983). Genetic aspects of mental retardation: From prevention to cure. In F.J. Menolascino, R. Newman, & J.A. Stark (Eds.), *Curative aspects of mental retardation* (pp. 15–25). Baltimore: Paul H. Brookes Publishing Co.

Minnesota State Planning Agency. (1975). *Community alternatives and institutional reform.* St. Paul: Minnesota State Planning Agency.

Missouri unveils procedures for MR/MI clients. (1983, April). *New Directions,* p. 1.

Mithaug, D., Hagmeir, L., & Haring, N. (1977). The relationship between training activities and job placement in vocational education of the severely and profoundly handicapped. *AAESPH Review, 2*(2), 24–45.

Moise, L. (1978). In sickness and death. *Mental Retardation, 16,* 397–398.

Moore, J., & Fine, M. (1978). Regular and special class teachers' perceptions of normal and exceptional children and their attitudes toward mainstreaming. *Psychology in the Schools, 15,* 253–259.

Mooring, I. (1964). The mental retardation joint agencies project. In J. Øster (Ed.), *Proceedings, International Copenhagen Congress on the Scientific Study of Mental Retardation, Volume 1* (pp. 22–27). Copenhagen: Det Berlingske Bogtrykkeri.

Morgan, S. (1979). Development and distribution of intellectual and adaptive skills in Down syndrome children: Implications for early intervention. *Mental Retardation, 17,* 247–249.

Morris, J., Martin, A., & Nowak, M. (1981). Job enrichment and the mentally retarded. *Mental Retardation, 19,* 290–294.

Morrow, C. (1976). An attorney's experiences in a legal center for retarded persons. In P. Browning (Ed.), *Rehabilitation of the mentally retarded offender* (pp. 81–87). Springfield, IL: Charles C Thomas.

Morrow, H., & Coulter, W. (1978). A survey of state policies regarding adaptive behavior measurements. In W. Coulter & H. Morrow (Eds.), *Adaptive behavior: Concepts and measurement* (pp. 85–92). New York: Grune & Stratton.

Morse, C., Sahler, O., & Friedman, S. (1970). A three-year follow-up study of abused and neglected children. *American Journal of Diseases of Children, 120,* 439–446.

Morton, J. (1983). *The Special Offender Project training manual.* Lincoln, NE: Crime and Community, Inc.

Moser, H. (1982). Mental retardation due to genetically determined metabolic and endocrine disorders. In I. Jakob (Ed.), *Mental retardation* (pp. 2–26). New York: Karger.

MR right-to-life poll. (1983). *Superintendents' Digest, 2,* 28.

Murphy, A. (1983). Positive and supportive counseling of parents of infants with Down syndrome. In S. Pueschel & J. Rynders (Eds.), *Down syndrome: Advances in biomedicine and the behavioral sciences* (pp. 305–330). Cambridge, MA: Academic Guild.

Murray, C. (1984). *Losing ground, American social policy, 1950–1980.* New York: Basic Books.

Myers, P., & Hammill, D. (1969). *Methods for learning disorders.* New York: John Wiley & Sons.

Myklebust, H. (1964). Learning disorders: Psychoneurological disturbances in children. *Rehabilitation Literature, 25,* 354–360.

Mzurkiewicz, A. (1965). The initial teaching alphabet for Reading?—Yes! *Educational Leadership, 22,* 390–393.

Nagi, S. (1976, Fall). An epidemiology of disability among adults in the United States. *Health and Society,* 439–467.

Narcotics booming. (1985, February 2). *Wisconsin State Journal,* p. 8.

The National Advisory Committee on Handicapped Children. (1973). *Basic education rights for the handicapped.* Washington, DC: U.S. Government Printing Office.

National Association for Retarded Citizens. (1972). *Residential programming for mentally retarded persons.* Arlington, TX: Author.

National Association for Retarded Citizens. (1976). Dehumanization. *South Central Journal* [Bicentennial Issue], p. 11.

National Association of Superintendents of Public Residential Facilities for the Mentally Retarded. (1984). *Membership handbook* (Revised). Madison, WI: National Association of Superintendents of Public Residential Facilities for the Mentally Retarded.

National Commission on Excellence in Education. (1983, April 27). A nation at risk: The imperative for educational reform. *Education Week,* pp. 1–4.

National League of Cities v. Usery, 44 U.S. Law Week, 4974 (1976).

National Welfare Rights Organization v. Weinberger, Civil Action No. 74-243, U.S. District Court of the District of Columbia (1974).

The nation's youth. (1968). Washington, DC: U.S. Department of Health, Education, and Welfare.

Neer, W., Foster, D., Jones, J., & Reynolds, D. (1973). Socioeconomic bias in diagnosis of mental retardation. *Exceptional Children, 40,* 38–39.

Neman, R., McCann, B., Roos, P., Menolascino, F., & Heal, L. (1977). A survey of parents using sensorimotor home training programs. *Education and Training of the Mentally Retarded, 12,* 109–119.

Newborn problems linked to PCBs. (1984). *Science, 5*(8), 7–8.

New cases. (1973, October). *Mental Retardation and the Law,* 9–11.

Newman, R. (1978). *The effects of informational and experimental activities on the attitudes of regular classroom students toward severely handicapped children and youth.* Unpublished doctoral dissertation, University of Kansas.

New York State Association for Retarded Citizens et al.

v. Carey et al., U.S. District Court, Eastern Division of New York, 72C., 356 and 357 (1975).

Nickelsburg, R. (1973). Time sampling of work behavior to mentally retarded trainees. *Mental Retardation, 11*(6), 29–32.

Nihira, K., Foster, R., Shellhaas, M., & Leland, H. (1969). *AAMD Adaptive Behavior Scale.* Washington, DC: American Association on Mental Deficiency.

Nihira, L., & Nihira, K. (1974). From the shadows to success: A survey of successful adapting by community placed retardates. *Exchange 2*(3), 5–9.

Nihira, L., & Nihira, K. (1975). Jeopardy in community placement. *American Journal of Mental Deficiency, 79,* 538–544.

Nirje, B. (1969). The normalization principle and its human management implications. In R. Kugel & W. Wolfensberger (Eds.), *Changing patterns in residential services for the mentally retarded* (pp. 181–194). Washington, DC: President's Committee on Mental Retardation.

NMR imaging found to have advantages over CT scanning. (1983). *Hospitals, 57*(8), 43.

Nondiscrimination on the basis of handicap. (1983, April 24). *Federal Register,* p. 17588.

Nondiscrimination on the basis of handicap. (1984, January 12). *Federal Register,* pp. 1622–1654.

Noone, J. (Ed.). (1967). *Staffing at residential institutions for the mentally retarded in the United States.* Columbus, OH: The American Association on Mental Deficiency.

Nordoff, P., & Robbins, C. (1965). *Music Therapy for Handicapped Children.* Blauvelt, NY: Rudolph Steiner Publications.

North Dakota Association for Retarded Children v. Peterson, Civil No. 1196 (United States District Court, Southwestern Division) (November, 1972).

Oberle, N. (1969). Lead poisoning: A preventable childhood disease of the slums. *Science, 165,* 991–992.

O'Connor v. Donaldson, Supreme Court of the United States, No. 74-8 (1975).

O'Connor, G. (1976). *Home is a good place: A national perspective of community residential facilities for developmentally disabled persons.* Washington, DC: American Association on Mental Deficiency.

O'Connor, G. (1983). Presidential address 1983: Social support of mentally retarded persons. *Mental Retardation, 21,* 187–196.

O'Doherty, N. (1964). Subdural hematomas in battered babies. *Developmental Medicine and Child Neurology, 6,* 192–193.

Office for Children, Youth, and Families. (1983). *Annual report to the Governor and the legislature on the Wisconsin Child Abuse and Neglect Act.* Madison, WI: Department of Health and Social Services.

Oklahoma shame. (1982). Washington, DC: Gannett News Service.

Olczak, P., & Stott, M. (1976). Family Court placement of mentally retarded juvenile offenders and the use of intelligence testing. *Criminal Justice and Behavior, 3,* 23–27.

Oliver, J. (1975). Microcephaly following baby battering and shaking. *British Medical Journal, 2,* 262–264.

Olley, J., & Ramey, G. (1978). Voter participation of retarded citizens in the 1976 presidential election. *Mental Retardation, 16,* 255–258.

Olshin, G. (1968). Special education instructional materials center program. *Exceptional Children, 34,* 515–519.

Olson, J., Hahn, H., & Hermann, A. (1965). Psycholinguistic curriculum. *Mental Retardation, 3*(2), 14–19.

Olson, M., & Shaw, C. (1969). Presenile dementia and Alzheimer's disease in mongolism. *Brain, 92,* 147–156.

Olszowy, D. (1978). *Horticulture for the disabled and disadvantaged.* Springfield, IL: Charles C Thomas.

Omwake, E. (1969). From the President. *Young Children, 24,* 130–131.

O'Neill, J., & Bellamy, G. (1978). Evaluation of a procedure for teaching saw chain assembly to a severely retarded woman. *Mental Retardation, 16,* 37–41.

An open letter to the Committee on Terminology and Classification of AAMD from the Committee on Definition and Terminology of CEC-MR. (1979). *Education and Training of the Mentally Retarded, 14,* 74–76.

OSERS pinpoint transitions as priority. (1984, July). *New Directions,* pp. 3, 5.

Otis R. Bowen, Secretary of Health and Human Services, Petitioner v. American Hospital Association et al., U.S. Supreme Court, No. 85-225 (June 9, 1986).

Ozer, M., & Milgram, N. (1967). The effects of a summer Head Start program: A neurological evaluation. *American Journal of Orthopsychiatry, 37,* 331–332.

Pagel, S., & Whitling, C. (1978). Readmissions to a state hospital for mentally retarded persons: Reasons for community placement failure. *Mental Retardation, 16,* 164–166.

Palmer, D. (1980). The effect of educable mental retardation descriptive information on regular classroom teachers' attributions and instructional prescriptions. *Education and Training of the Mentally Retarded, 18,* 171–175.

Panati, C. (1980). *Breakthroughs: Astonishing advances in your lifetime in medicine, science, and technology.* Boston: Houghton Mifflin.

Parent attitudes on sterilization and marriage. (1976, October). *Mental Retardation News, 25*(7), p. 3.

Parents Association of St. Louis State School and Hospital, et al., v. Bond, et al., Case 82-0852-C(3), U.S. District Court, Eastern District of Missouri (Filed May 28, 1982).

Parents in Action on Special Education (PASE) v. Hannon, 506 F. Supp. 831, U.S. District Court for the Northern District of Illinois (1980).

Passer, A., Rauh, J., Chamberlain, A., McGrath, M., & Burket, R. (1984). Issues in fertility control for mentally retarded female adolescents: II. Parental attitudes towards sterilization. *Pediatrics, 73,* 451–454.

Patau, K., Inhorn, S., Therman, E., & Wagner, H. (1960). Multiple congenital anomaly caused by an extra chromosome. *Lancet, 1,* 790.

Patrick, J. (1978). Little murders. *New Times, 10*(7), 32–37.

Patterns for planning. (1965). Springfield: Illinois Department of Mental Health.

Paul, J. (1983). Families of handicapped children. In J. Paul (Ed.), *The exceptional child* pp. 37–63. Syracuse, NY: Syracuse University Press.

Paul, J., Turnbull, A., & Cruickshank, W. (1977). *Main-*

streaming: A practical guide. Syracuse, NY: Syracuse University Press.

Pennhurst State School and Hospital v. Halderman, Civil Act. No. 79-1489, U.S. Third Cir. Ct. of App. (1981).

Pennsylvania Association for Retarded Citizens et al. v. Commonwealth of Pennsylvania et al., 344 F. Supp. 1275, 3-judge Court, E.D. Pa. (1971).

Penrose, L. (1962). *The biology of defect* (3rd ed.). New York: Grune & Stratton.

Perel, I. (1982). The developmentally disabled offender: A program model. In M. Santamour & P. Watson (Eds.), *The retarded offender* (pp. 414–426). New York: Praeger.

Peter, L. (1976). *Competencies for teaching.* Belmont, CA: Wadsworth.

Peterson, G. (1974). Factors related to the attitudes of nonretarded children toward their EMR peers. *American Journal of Mental Deficiency, 79,* 412–416.

Philips, I., & Williams, N. (1975). Psychopathology and mental retardation: A study of 100 mentally retarded children. *American Journal of Psychiatry, 132,* 139–145.

Phipps-Yonas, S. (1980). Teenage pregnancy and motherhood: A review of the literature. *American Journal of Orthopsychiatry, 50,* 403–431.

Piaget, J. (1952). *The origins of intelligence in children* (Margaret Cook, Trans.). New York: W. W. Norton.

Piaget, J. (1966). *The psychology of intelligence.* Totowa, NJ: Littlefield, Adams.

Piers, E., & Harris, D. (1964). Age and other correlates of self-concept in children. *Journal of Educational Psychology, 55,* 91–95.

Pike, C. (1982). Sandhills' program for youthful offenders. In M. Santamour & P. Watson (Eds.), *The retarded offender* (pp. 444–449). New York: Praeger.

Pitman, I. (1961). Learning to read: An experiment. *Royal Society of Arts Journal, 109,* 149–180.

PL 83-566, *Vocational Rehabilitation Act of 1953.*

PL 88-164, *Mental Retardation Facilities and Community Mental Health Centers Construction Act* (1964).

PL 88-214, *The Manpower Development and Training Act of 1963.*

PL 88-352, *Civil Rights Act of 1964.*

PL 91-517, *The Developmental Disabilities Services and Facilities Construction Amendments* (1970).

PL 93-112, *Rehabilitation Act of 1973.*

PL 94-103, *Developmentally Disabled Assistance and Bill of Rights Act of 1975.*

PL 94-142, *The Education for All Handicapped Children Act* (1975).

PL 95-602, *The Rehabilitation Comprehensive Services and Developmental Disabilities Amendment* (1978).

PL 96-247, *Civil Rights of Institutionalized Persons Act* (1980).

PL 98-457, *Child Abuse Amendments of 1984.*

Polivka, C., Marvin, W., Brown, J., & Polivka, L. (1979). Selected characteristics, services and movement of group home residents. *Mental Retardation, 17,* 227–230.

Polloway, E., & Smith, J. (1978). Special olympics: A second look. *Education and Training of the Mentally Retarded, 13,* 432–435.

Porcella, A. (1980). Increasing parent involvement. *Education and Training of the Mentally Retarded, 15,* 155–157.

Portray, R. (1968). La Ligue Internationale des Associations d'Aide aux Handicapes Mentaux [The International League of Societies for the Mentally Handicapped]. In *From charity to rights* (pp. 31–37). Brussels, Belgium: International League of Societies for the Mentally Handicapped.

Posner, B. (1970). Federal survey shows retarded good workers. *Mental Retardation News, 19*(4), 3.

Potter, H. (1927). Mental deficiency and the psychiatrist. *American Journal of Psychiatry, 6,* 691–700.

Potter, H. (1964). The needs of mentally retarded children for psychiatry services. *Journal of the American Academy of Child Psychiatry, 3,* 352–374.

Powledge, T. (1983). Windows of the womb. *Psychology Today, 17*(5), 36–42.

Preschool special education questioned. (1984). *Insights, 11*(6), 4.

President's Commission for the Study of Ethical Problems in Medicine and Biomedical and Behavioral Research. (1981). *Protecting human subjects.* Washington, DC: Superintendent of Documents.

President's Committee on Mental Retardation. (1967). *MR 67: A first report to the President on the nation's progress and remaining great needs in the campaign to combat mental retardation.* Washington, DC: U.S. Government Printing Office.

President's Committee on Mental Retardation. (1968). *MR 68: The edge of change.* Washington, DC: U.S. Government Printing Office.

President's Committee on Mental Retardation. (1969a). *MR 69: Toward progress.* Washington, DC: U.S. Government Printing Office.

President's Committee on Mental Retardation. (1969b). *Residential services for the mentally retarded: An action policy proposal.* Washington, DC: U.S. Government Printing Office.

President's Committee on Mental Retardation. (1970). *Residential services for the mentally retarded: An action policy proposal.* Washington, DC: U.S. Government Printing Office.

President's Committee on Mental Retardation. (1971). *MR 70: The decisive decade.* Washington, DC: U.S. Government Printing Office.

President's Committee on Mental Retardation. (1972). *MR 71: Entering the era of human ecology.* Washington, DC: U.S. Government Printing Office.

President's Committee on Mental Retardation. (1974). *Residential programming: Position statement by the National Association of Superintendents of Public Residential Facilities for the Mentally Retarded.* Washington, DC: U.S. Department of Health, Education and Welfare.

President's Committee on Mental Retardation. (1975a). *MR 74: A friend in Washington.* Washington, DC: U.S. Government Printing Office.

President's Committee on Mental Retardation. (1975b, April). Gallup poll shows attitudes on MR improving. *President's Committee on Mental Retardation Message,* p. 1.

President's Committee on Mental Retardation. (1976). *Mental retardation: Century of decision.* Washington, DC: U.S. Government Printing Office.

President's Committee on Mental Retardation. (1977). *Mental retardation: Past and present.* Washington, DC: U.S. Government Printing Office.

President's Committee on Mental Retardation. (1985). *Mental retardation: Plans for the future*. Washington, DC: U.S. Government Printing Office.

President's Panel on Mental Retardation. (1962). *A Proposed Program for National Action to Combat Mental Retardation*. Washington, DC: Superintendent of Documents.

President signs institutional rights bill into law. (1980, May). *Capitol Capsule*, pp. 1, 3.

Prettyman, B. (1972). The indeterminate sentence and the right to treatment. *American Criminal Law Review, 11*, 18–21.

Proclamation: National Decade of Disabled Persons (1983).

To protect the unborn and the newborn [March of Dimes leaflet]. (1983).

Protection of human research subjects. (1979). *Federal Register, 44*(158), 47688–47729.

Protection of human subjects. (1978). *Federal Register, 43*(141), 31786–31794.

Protection of human subjects. (1982). *Federal Register, 47*(80), 13272–13305.

Prouty, R., & McGarry, F. (1972). The diagnostic/prescriptive teacher. In E. Deno (Ed.), *Instructional alternatives for exceptional children* (pp. 47–57). Reston, VA: The Council for Exceptional Children.

Provencal, G. (1979). AAMD leadership award: David Rosen. *Mental Retardation, 17*, 214.

Putman, J. (1972). Quicksilver and slow death. *National Geographic, 142*, 507–527.

Quick, A., Little, T., & Campbell, A. (1974). *Project MEMPHIS: Enhancing developmental progress in preschool exceptional children*. Belmont, CA: Fearon.

Quiet revolution: Wisconsin's plan for the mentally retarded. (1968). Madison: Wisconsin Mental Retardation Planning and Implementation Program.

Radin, N. (1968). Some impediments to the education of disadvantaged children. *Children, 15*, 171–176.

Raeburn, P. (1984, September 17). "Maps" trace gene defects. *Wisconsin State Journal*, Section A, pp. 1–2.

Rainey v. Tennessee Department of Education, Chancery Court, Davidson County, Tennessee, No. A-3100 (January 21, 1976).

Rantakallio, P. (1983). A follow-up study up to the age of 14 of children whose mothers smoked during pregnancy. *Acta Paediatrica Scand., 72*, 747–753.

Rasmussen, S. (1983, May). Nutritional supplements for the retarded. *Prevention Newsletter*, 1–4.

Raspberry, W. (1972). Wisconsin study may settle question of their effect on MR. *Mental Retardation News, 21*(5), 6. (Reprinted from the *Washington Post*)

Rayborn, W., Wible-Kant, J., & Bledsoe, P. (1982). Changing trends in drug use during pregnancy. *The Journal of Reproductive Medicine, 27*, 569–575.

Reagan pens anti-abortion 10-page item. (1983, April 29). *Wisconsin State Journal*, p. 2.

Redding, S. (1970). Life adjustment patterns of retarded and non-retarded low functioning students. *Exceptional Children, 1*, 5–7.

Reece, C. (1983, February-March). HHS announces major initiative to place special needs children in adoptive homes. *Human Development News*, pp. 1–2.

Reece, C. (1985). Head Start at 20. *Children Today, 14*(2), 6–9.

Reed, S., & Reed, E. (1965). *Mental retardation: A family study*. Philadelphia: W. B. Saunders.

Reger, R. (1964). Reading ability and CMAS scores in educable mentally retarded boys. *American Journal of Mental Deficiency, 68*, 652–655.

Rehabilitation and developmental legislation [A compilation prepared for the Subcommittee of the Handicapped of the Committee on Labor and Public Welfare, United States Senate]. (1976). Washington, DC: U.S. Government Printing Office.

Reichard, C., Spencer, J., & Spooner, F. (1980). The mentally retarded defendant-offender. *The Journal of Special Education, 14*, 113–119.

Reiss, S., Levitan, G., & Szyszko, J. (1982). Emotional disturbance and mental retardation: Diagnostic overshadowing. *American Journal of Mental Deficiency, 86*, 567–574.

Reiss, S., & Trenn, E. (1984). Consumer demand for outpatient mental health services for people with mental retardation. *Mental Retardation, 22*, 112–116.

Release of mentally ill called 'societal tragedy.' (1984, September 13). *Wisconsin State Journal*, pp. 1–2.

Relf et al. v. Weinberger, Civil Action No. 1557-73, U.S. District Court of the District of Columbia (1973).

Renshaw, D. (1977). Mentally retarded, hyperkinetic and psychotic. *Diseases of the Nervous System, 38*, 160–161.

Report cites savings of Medicaid waiver. (1985, November-December). *Word from Washington*, p. 11.

Report of the Committee on Aging and Developmental Disabilities. (1983). Albany: New York State Office of Mental Retardation and Developmental Disabilities.

Report of the Joseph P. Kennedy Foundation International Symposium on Human Rights, Retardation, and Research. (1971). Washington, DC: The Joseph P. Kennedy Foundation.

Research profile #11. (1965). Washington, DC: U.S. Government Printing Office.

Research ties infant deaths to cigarettes. (1984, February 24). *Wisconsin State Journal*, p. 10.

Residential Services & Facilities Committee. (1973). *The right to choose: Achieving residential alternatives in the community*. Arlington, TX: National Association for Retarded Citizens.

Restrictions applicable to sterilization procedures in federally funded assisted family planning projects. (1974). *Federal Register, 39*, 13887–13888.

Retish, P. (1979). Individual education programs in secondary schools for mainstreamed students. *Education and Training of the Mentally Retarded, 14*(3), 235–236.

Retish, P. (1980). Medical training and mentally retarded citizens: An enrichment program. *Mental Retardation, 18*, 253–254.

Reynold's memo. (1983, January). *Superintendents' Digest*, p. 3.

Reynolds, B., Martin-Reynolds, J., & Marks, F. (1982). Elementary teachers' attitudes toward mainstreaming educable mentally retarded students. *Education and Training of the Mentally Retarded, 17*, 171–176.

Reynolds, M. (1962). A framework for considering some issues in special education. *Exceptional Children, 28*, 367–370.

Reynolds, M. (1973). A framework for considering some

issues in special education. In J. Glavin (Ed.), *Major issues in special education* (pp. 13–16). New York: MSS Information Corporation.

Rhode Island Society for Autistic Children, Inc. et al. v. Board of Regents for Education of the State of Rhode Island et al., Civil Action File No. 5081 (D.R.I.) (September 19, 1975).

Rich, A. (1963). Polyribosomes. *Scientific American, 209,* 44–53.

Ricker, L., & Pinkard, C. (1964). Three approaches to group counseling involving motion pictures with mentally retarded adults. In J. Øster (Ed.), *Proceedings of the International Copenhagen Congress on the Scientific Study of Mental Retardation* (pp. 715–717). Copenhagen: Det Berlingske Bogtrykkeri.

Riechard, C., Spencer, J., & Spooner, F. (1980). The mentally retarded defendant-offender. *The Journal of Special Education, 14,* 113–119.

Riessman, F. (1962). *The culturally deprived child.* New York: Harper.

The right to community service. (1982). Arlington, TX: Association for Retarded Citizens of the United States.

The right to community service. (1983, November). *Community Living,* p. 2.

Ringness, T. (1961). Self-concept of children of low, average, and high intelligence. *American Journal of Mental Deficiency, 65,* 453–461.

Robbins, M. (1966). A study of the validity of Delacato's theory of neurological organization. *Exceptional Children, 32,* 517–523.

Roberts, S. (1970). United States: Presidency. In J. Paradise (Ed.), *Collier's 1970 Year Book* (pp. 568–569). New York: Crowell-Collier Educational Corporation.

Robertson, M. (1964). Shadow therapy. In J. Øster (Ed.), *Proceedings of the International Copenhagen Congress on the Scientific Study of Mental Retardation* (pp. 661–664). Copenhagen: Det Berlingske Bogtrykkeri.

Robinson, F., Robinson, S., & Williams, L. (1979). Eugenic sterilization: Medico-legal and sociological aspects. *Journal of the National Medical Association, 71,* 593–598.

Robinson, H., & Robinson, N. (1965). *The mentally retarded child.* New York: McGraw-Hill.

Rockoff, E., & Hofmann, R. (1977). The normal and the retarded offender: Some characteristic distinctions. *International Journal of Offender Therapy and Comparative Criminology, 21,* 52–56.

Roe v. Wade, 410 U.S. 113, 125 (1973).

The role of higher education in mental retardation and other developmental disabilities. (1976). Washington, DC: American Association of University Affiliated Programs for the Developmentally Disabled.

Roos, P. (1970). Trends and issues in special education for the mentally retarded. *Education and Training of the Mentally Retarded, 5,* 51–61.

Roos, P. (1971). Misinterpreting criticisms of the medical model. *Mental Retardation, 9*(2), 22–24.

Roos, P. (1974). Human rights and behavior modification. *Mental Retardation, 12*(3), 3–6.

Roos, P. (1982). Special trends and issues. In P. Cegelka & H. Prehm (Eds.), *Mental retardation: From categories to people* (pp. 355–381). Columbus, OH: Charles E. Merrill.

Rosen, M., Floor, L., & Baxter, D. (1974). IQ, academic achievement and community adjustment. *Mental Retardation, 12*(2), 51–53.

Rosen, M., Halenda, R., Nowakiwska, M., & Floor, L. (1970). Employment satisfaction of previously institutionalized mentally subnormal workers. *Mental Retardation, 8*(3), 35–40.

Rosen, T., & Schimmel, M. (1983). A short review of perinatal pharmacology. *Bulletin of the New York Academy of Medicine, 59,* 669–677.

Ross, D. (1970). Effect on learning of psychological attachment to a film model. *American Journal of Mental Deficiency, 74,* 701–707.

Ross, L. (1966). Classical conditioning and discrimination learning research with the mentally retarded. In N. Ellis (Ed.), *International review of research in mental retardation* (pp. 21–54). New York: Academic Press.

Ross, R. (1969). *Fairview Self-help Scale.* Fairview, CA: Fairview State Hospital.

Ross, R. (1972). Behavioral correlates of levels of intelligence. *American Journal of Mental Deficiency, 76,* 515–519.

Rossi, J. (1964). High risk babies: Determining the problem. *Connecticut Health Bulletin,* unpaged.

Rostetter, D., Kowalski, R., & Hunter, D. (1984). Implementing the integration principle of PL 94-142. In N. Certo, N. Haring, & R. York (Eds.), *Public school integration of severely handicapped students: Rational issues and progressive alternatives* (pp. 293–320). Baltimore: Paul H. Brookes Publishing Co.

Roth, E., & Barrett, R. (1977). Parallels in art and play therapy with a disturbed retarded boy. *The Arts in Psychotherapy, 4,* 195–197.

Roth, R., & Smith, T. (1983). A statewide assessment of attitudes toward the handicapped and community living programs. *Education and Training of the Mentally Retarded, 18,* 164–168.

Rouqette, J. (1957). *Influence de l'intoxication alcoolique parentele sur le developpement physique et psychique des jeune enfants* [The influence of parental alcoholism on the physical and psychological development of infants]. Unpublished doctoral dissertation, University of Paris.

Rouse v. Cameron, 373, F. 2d 451 (1966).

Rowan, B. (1972). The retarded offender. *The Florida Bar Journal, 46,* 338–343.

Rowan, B. (1976). The mentally retarded citizen and correctional institutions. In M. Kindred, J. Cohen, D. Penrod, & T. Shaffer (Eds.), *The mentally retarded and the law,* (pp. 649–680). New York: Free Press.

Rowitz, L. (1974). Sociological perspective on labeling [A reaction to MacMillan, Jones, and Aloia]. *American Journal of Mental Deficiency, 79,* 265–267.

Rowitz, L. (1981). A sociological perspective on labeling in mental retardation. *Mental Retardation, 19,* 47–52.

Rubin, G., Peterson, H., Dorfman, S., Layde, P., Maze, J., Ory, J., & Cates, W. (1983). Ectopic pregnancy in the United States. *Journal of the American Medical Association, 249,* 1725–1729.

Rucker, C. (1968). Acceptance of mentally retarded junior high children in academic and nonacademic classes. *Dissertation Abstracts, 28,* 3030–3039.

Rucker, C., Howe, C., & Snider, B. (1969). The participation of retarded children in junior high academic and nonacademic regular classes. *Exceptional Children, 35,* 617–623.

Ruling named for her angers Lessard. (1983, November 28). *The Capital Times,* p. 2.

Russell, M. (1982, July). Drinking and pregnancy. *New York State Journal of Medicine,* pp. 1218–1221.

Sabagh, G., & Edgerton, R. (1962). Sterilized mental defectives look at eugenic sterilization. *Eugenics Quarterly, 9,* 213–222.

Sad news for the happy hour. (1984, March 19). *Time,* p. 57.

Safer, N. (1980). Teacher experiences and their implications for teaching retarded students. In J. Gottlieb (Ed.), *Educating mentally retarded persons in the mainstream* (pp. 24–44). Baltimore: University Park Press.

Salend, S. (1981). Cooperative games promote positive student interactions. *Teaching Exceptional Children, 13,* 76–79.

Salend, S., Michael R., Veraja, M., & Noto, J. (1983). Landlords' perceptions of retarded individuals as tenants. *Education and Training of the Mentally Retarded, 18,* 232–234.

Sales, B., Powell, D., Duizend, R., & Associates. (1982). *Disabled persons and the law: State legislative issues.* New York: Plenum.

Samuelson, R. (1984, September 10). Escaping the poverty trap. *Newsweek,* p. 60.

Sandgrund, A., Gaines, R., & Green, A. (1974). Child abuse and mental retardation: A problem of cause and effect. *American Journal of Mental Deficiency, 79,* 327–330.

Sandler, A., & Thurman, S. (1981). Status of community placement research: Effects on retarded citizens. *Education and Training of the Mentally Retarded, 16,* 245–251.

Santamour, M. (1982). A functional discussion of mental retardation and criminal behavior. In M. Santamour & P. Watson (Eds.), *The retarded offender* (pp. 133–138). New York: Praeger.

Santiestevan, H. (1975). *Out of their beds and into the streets.* Washington, DC: American Federation of State, County, and Municipal Employees.

Sarason, S. (1959). *Psychological problems in mental deficiency.* New York: Harper & Row.

Sattler, J. (1982). *Assessment of children's intelligence and special abilities* (2nd ed.). Boston: Allyn & Bacon.

Saunders, J., & Repucci, N. (1972). Reward and punishment: Some guidelines for their effective application in correctional programs for youthful offenders. *Crime and Delinquency, 18*(3), 284–290.

Saville v. Treadway, 404 F. Supp., 430, 433, Middle District of Tennessee (1974).

Schalock, R., Harper, R., & Genung, T. (1981). Community integration of mentally retarded adults: Community placement and program success. *American Journal of Mental Deficiency, 85,* 478–488.

Scheer, R., & Sharpe, W. (1963). Social group work in day camping with institutionalized delinquent retardates. *Training School Bulletin, 60,* 138–147.

Scheerenberger, R. (1964). Mental retardation: Definition, classification, and prevalence. *Mental Retardation Abstracts, 1,* 1–10.

Scheerenberger, R. (1965). A current census of state in-

stitutions for the mentally retarded. *Mental Retardation, 3*(3), 4–6.

Scheerenberger, R. (1969a). Nursery school experiences for the trainable mentally retarded. In R. Scheerenberger (Ed.), *Mental retardation* (pp. 47–60). Springfield: Illinois Department of Mental Health.

Scheerenberger, R. (1969b). *A study of generic services for the mentally retarded and their families.* Springfield: Illinois Department of Mental Health.

Scheerenberger, R. (1975). *Current trends and status of public residential services for the mentally retarded, 1974.* Madison, WI: National Association of Superintendents of Public Residential Facilities for the Mentally Retarded.

Scheerenberger, R. (1976a). *Deinstitutionalization and institutional reform.* Springfield, IL: Charles C Thomas.

Scheerenberger, R. (1976b). *Public residential services for the mentally retarded, 1976.* Madison, WI: National Association of Superintendents of Public Residential Facilities for the Mentally Retarded.

Scheerenberger, R. (1978). *Public residential services for the mentally retarded, 1977.* Madison, WI: National Association of Superintendents of Public Residential Facilities for the Mentally Retarded.

Scheerenberger, R. (1979a). Presidential address: The past is not past. *Mental Retardation,* 211–213.

Scheerenberger, R. (1979b). *Public residential services for the mentally retarded, 1979.* Madison, WI: National Association of Superintendents of Public Residential Facilities for the Mentally Retarded.

Scheerenberger, R. (1980). *Community programs and services.* Madison, WI: National Association of Superintendents of Public Residential Facilities for the Mentally Retarded.

Scheerenberger, R. (1982). *Public residential services for the mentally retarded, 1981.* Madison, WI: National Association of Superintendents of Public Residential Facilities for the Mentally Retarded.

Scheerenberger, R. (1983a). An exploratory developmental study of adaptive behavior among profoundly mentally retarded persons. *Occasional Paper #17.* Madison, WI: Association of Superintendents of Public Residential Facilities for the Mentally Retarded.

Scheerenberger, R. (1983b). *A history of mental retardation.* Baltimore, MD: Paul H. Brookes Publishing Co.

Scheerenberger, R. (1983c). *Public residential services for the mentally retarded, 1982.* Madison, WI: National Association of Superintendents of Public Residential Facilities for the Mentally Retarded.

Scheerenberger, R. (1984). Community and Family Living Amendments of 1983. *Superintendents' Digest, 3,* 5–15.

Scheerenberger, R. (1986). *Public residential services for the mentally retarded, 1985.* Madison, WI: National Association of Superintendents of Public Residential Facilities for the Mentally Retarded.

Scheerenberger, R., & Felsenthal, D. (1977). Community settings for MR persons: Satisfaction and activities. *Mental Retardation, 15*(4), 3–7.

Schiefelbusch, R. (1965). A discussion of language treatment methods for mentally retarded children. *Mental Retardation, 3*(2), 4–7.

Schiefelbusch, R. (1984). The odyssey of a speech clinician. In B. Blatt & R. Morris (Eds.), *Perspectives in special education: Personal orientations* (pp. 233–262). Glenview, IL: Scott, Foresman.

Schiefelbusch, R., Copeland, R., & Smith, J. (Eds.). (1967). *Language and mental retardation*. New York: Holt, Rinehart and Winston.

Schiefelbusch, R., & Lloyd, L. (Eds.). (1974). *Language perspectives—Acquisition, retardation and intervention*. Baltimore: University Park Press.

Schilit, J. (1979). The mentally retarded offender and criminal justice personnel. *Exceptional Children, 45*, 16–22.

Schmeck, H. (1984, April 29). The new age of vaccines. *New York Times*, pp. 58–59.

Scholarships and fellowships in special education. (1964). *Exceptional Children, 30*, 379–387.

Schriber, J. (1983). Brain storms. *Forbes, 131*(12), 116–121.

Schroeder, S., Mulick, J., & Schroeder, C. (1979). Management of severe behavior problems of the retarded. In N. Ellis (Ed.), *Handbook of mental deficiency, psychological theory, and research* (2nd ed., pp. 341–366). Hillsdale, NJ: Lawrence Erlbaum Associates.

Schwartz, C. (1977). Normalization and idealism. *Mental Retardation, 15*(6), 38–39.

Schwartz, L. (1967a). An integrated teacher education program for special education—A new approach. *Exceptional Children, 33*, 411–416.

Schwartz, L. (1967b). Clinical teacher model for interrelated areas of special education. *Exceptional Children, 34*, 117–124.

Schwartz, V. (1982). A diversionary system of services for the mentally retarded offender. In M. Santamour & P. Watson (Eds.), *The retarded offender* (pp. 298–302). New York: Praeger.

Schwindler, W. (1974). *Court and constitution in the 20th century*. New York: Bobbs.

Scriver, C., MacKenzie, S., Chow, C., & Delvin, E. (1971). Thiamine responsive maple syrup urine disease. *Lancet, 1*, 310–312.

Seaman, S. (1967). The Bobath concept in treatment of neurological disorders. *American Journal of Physical Medicine, 46*, 477–483.

Selan, B. (1976). Psychotherapy with the developmentally disabled. *Health and Social Work, 1*, 73–85.

Sellin, D. (1979). *Mental retardation: Nature, needs, and advocacy*. Boston: Allyn & Bacon.

Senate testimony of Senator Weicker and Secretary Heckler. (1984). *Superintendents' Digest, 3*, 93–99.

Services for developmentally disabled delinquents and offenders. (1977). Columbus, OH: Department of Mental Health and Mental Retardation.

Shanyfelt, P. (1974, Winter). Occupational preparation of secondary educable students. *The Pointer*, pp. 20–24.

Shaw, A. (1977). Defining the quality of life. *Hastings Center Report, 7*, 11.

Shaw, A., Randolph, J., & Manard, B. (1977). Ethical issues in pediatric surgery: A national survey of pediatricians and pediatric surgeons. *Pediatrics, 60*, 588–599.

Shelton v. Tucker, 364, U.S. Supreme Court, 479, 483 (1960).

Sherman, S., Frenkel, E., & Newman, E. (1984). Foster family care for older persons who are mentally retarded. *Mental Retardation, 22*, 302–308.

Sherrill, R. (1977). Election '76. In J. Paradise (Ed.), *Collier's 1970 Year Book* (pp. 2–5). New York: Macmillan.

Shockley, W. (1972). Dysgenics, genecity, raceology: A challenge to the intellectual responsibility of educators. *Phi Delta Kappan, 53*, 297–307.

Shotel, J., Iano, R., & McGettigan, J. (1972). Teacher attitudes associated with the integration of handicapped children. *Exceptional Children, 38*, 677–683.

Shotwell, A., Dingman, H., & Tarjan, G. (1960). Need for improved criteria in evaluating job performance of state hospital employees. *American Journal of Mental Deficiency, 65*, 208–213.

Siblings speak out at seminar. (1983, September). *New Jersey Developmental Disabilities Newsletter*, pp. 2–3.

Siegel, E. (1968). Learning disabilities: Substance or shadow. *Exceptional Children, 34*, 433–438.

Silverstein, A. (1966). Anxiety and the quality of human-figure drawings. *American Journal of Mental Deficiency, 70*, 607–608.

Silvestri, R. (1977). Implosive therapy treatment of emotionally disturbed retardates. *Journal of Consulting and Clinical Psychology, 45*, 14–22.

Simmons, J., Tymchuk, A., & Valente, M. (1974). Treatment and care of the mentally retarded. *Psychiatric Annals, 4*(2), 38–69.

Simmons, J., Tymchuk, A., & Valente, M. (1975). Treatment considerations in mental retardation. *Current Psychiatric Therapies, 15*, 15–24.

Sinha, S. (1981). Progress in prevention of mental retardation caused by viral infections. In P. Mittler (Ed.), *Frontiers of knowledge in mental retardation* (Vol. 2, pp. 31–39). Baltimore: University Park Press.

Siperstein, G., Budoff, M., & Bak, J. (1980). Effects of the labels "mentally retarded" and "retard" on the social acceptability of mentally retarded children. *American Journal of Mental Deficiency, 84*, 596–601.

Siperstein, G., & Gottlieb, J. (1978). Parents' and teachers' attitudes toward mildly and severely retarded children. *Mental Retardation, 16*, 321–322.

Sitkei, E. (1980). After group home living—What alternatives? Results of a two year mobility followup study. *Mental Retardation, 18*, 9–13.

Skerry, P. (1983). The charmed life of Head Start. *The Public Interest, 73*, 18–36.

Skinner, B. (1938). *The behavior of organisms*. New York: Appleton-Century.

Skinner, B. (1948). *Walden two*. New York: Macmillan.

Skinner, B. (1968). *The technology of teaching*. New York: Appleton-Century-Crofts.

Skinner, B. (1975). The steep and thorny way to a science of behavior. *American Psychologist, 30*, 42–49.

Skinner, B. (1983). Origins of a behaviorist. *Psychology Today, 17*(9), 22–38.

Skinner, B., & Vaughn, M. (1983). *Enjoy old age*. New York: Norton.

Slosson, R. (1963). *Slosson Intelligence Test (SIT) for Children and Adults*. New York: Slosson Educational Publications.

Smeets, P. (1971). Some characteristics of mental defectives displaying self-mutilative behaviors. *Training School Bulletin, 68*, 131–135.

Smith, I., & Greenberg, S. (1975). Teacher attitudes and the labeling process. *Exceptional Children, 41,* 319–324.

Smith, J. (1962). Criminality and mental retardation. *Training School Bulletin, 59,* 74–80.

Smith, K., Cobb, C., & French, B. (1983). CAT scans: What do they tell us? *Journal of Neurosurgical Nursing, 15,* 222–227.

Smith, M. (1984). Psychology and the homeless. *Psychology Today, 18*(2), 62.

Snell, M. (1982). Education and habilitation of the profoundly mentally retarded. In P. Cegelka & H. Prehm (Eds.), *Mental retardation: From categories to people* (pp. 309–350). Columbus, OH: Charles E. Merrill.

Sniffen, M. (1983, November 3). 9 employees indicted for abusing patients at mental institution. *The Capitol Times,* p. 2.

Snygg, D., & Combs, A. (1949). *Individual behavior.* New York: Harper.

Soeffing, M. (1974). Normalization of services for the mentally retarded—A conversation with Dr. Wolf Wolfensberger. *Education and Training of the Mentally Retarded, 9,* 202–208.

Sokol, R., Miller, S., & Reed, S. (1980). Alcohol abuse during pregnancy: An epidemiologic study. *Alcohol Clinical and Experimental Research, 4,* 135–145.

Song, A., & Jones, S. (Eds.). (1980). *Wisconsin Behavior Rating Scale.* Madison: Central Wisconsin Center for the Developmentally Disabled.

Sontag, E. (Ed.) (1977). *Educational programming for the severely and profoundly handicapped.* Reston, VA: Council for the Exceptional Children.

Souder v. Brennan, Civil Action No. 482-73, U.S. District Court for the District of Columbia (1973).

South Carolina Department of Corrections. (1973). *The mentally retarded adult offender: A study of the problems of mental retardation in the South Carolina Department of Corrections.* Columbia: South Carolina Department of Corrections.

Spare, P. (1983, October 21). The state of the art: Community and Family Living Amendments of 1983. Unpublished manuscript.

Sparrow, S., Balla, D., & Cicchetti, D. (1984). *Vineland Adaptive Behavior Scales.* Circle Pines, MN: American Guidance Service.

Speck v. Finegold, No. 80-1-16, Pa. Sup. Ct. (1981).

Spitz, H. (1976). Toward a relative psychology of mental retardation with special emphasis on evaluation. In N. Ellis (Ed.), *International review of research in mental retardation* (Vol. 8, pp. 35–56). New York: Academic Press.

Spooner, F., Weber, L., & Spooner, D. (1983). The effects of backward chaining and total task presentation on the acquisition of complex tasks by severely retarded adolescents and adults. *Education and Treatment of Children, 6,* 401–420.

Spradlin, J., & Saunders, R. (1984). Behaving appropriately in new situations: A stimulus class analysis. *American Journal of Mental Deficiency, 88,* 574–579.

Spreat, S., Telles, J., Conroy, J., Feinstein, C., & Colombatto, J. (1985). *Attitudes toward deinstitutionalization: A national survey of families of institutionalized mentally retarded persons.* Philadelphia: Temple University.

Stainback, S., & Stainback, W. (1975). A defense of the concept of the special class. *Education and Training of the Mentally Retarded, 2,* 91–93.

Stainback, S., Stainback, W., Schmid, R., & Courtnage, L. (1977). Training teachers for the severely and profoundly retarded: An accountability model. *Education and Training of the Mentally Retarded, 12,* 170–173.

Stainback, W., Stainback, S., & Jaben, T. (1981). Providing opportunities for interaction between severely handicapped and nonhandicapped students. *Teaching Exceptional Children, 13,* 72–75.

Stamm, J. (1980). Teacher competencies: Recommendations for personnel preparation. *Teacher Education and Special Education, 3,* 52–57.

Stamm, J., & Gardner, W. (1969). Effectiveness of normal and retarded peers in influencing judgments of mildly mentally retarded adolescents. *American Journal of Mental Deficiency, 73,* 597–603.

Standards for residential facilities for the mentally retarded. (1973). Washington, DC: Accreditation Council for Services for Mentally Retarded and Other Developmentally Disabled Persons.

Standards for services for developmentally disabled individuals. (1978). Washington, DC: Accreditation Council for Services for Mentally Retarded and Other Developmentally Disabled Persons.

Standards for state institutions for the mentally retarded. (1964). Columbus, OH: American Association on Mental Deficiency.

Stark, J.A. (1983). The search for cures of mental retardation. In F.J. Menolascino, R. Neman, & J.A. Stark (Eds.), *Curative aspects of mental retardation: Biomedical and behavioral advances* (pp. 1–6). Baltimore: Paul H. Brookes Publishing Co.

State ex. rel. Thelan v. City of Missoula, No. 13192, Supreme Ct., Montana (December 8, 1975).

State extends services. (1985). *ARC, 34*(4), 4.

Stedman, D. (1975). The state planning and advisory council on developmental disabilities. *Mental Retardation, 13*(3), 4–8.

Steele, M. (1982). Genetics of mental retardation. In I. Jakab (Ed.), *Mental retardation* (pp. 27–37). New York: Karger.

Sternglass, E., & Bell, S. (1983). Fallout and SAT scores: Evidence for cognitive damage during early infancy. *Phi Delta Kappan, 64,* 539–545.

Sternlicht, M. (1966). Fantasy aggression in delinquent and nondelinquent retardates. *American Journal of Mental Deficiency, 70,* 819–821.

Sternlicht, M. (1978). Variables affecting foster care placement of institutionalized retarded residents. *Mental Retardation, 16,* 25–28.

Sternlicht, M., & Deutsch, M. (1972). *Personality development and social behavior in the mentally retarded.* Lexington, MA: Heath.

Sternlicht, M., & Windholz, G. (1984). *Social behavior of the mentally retarded.* New York: Garland.

Stevens, H. (1964). Use of human subjects for research. In J. Øster. *Proceedings, International Copenhagen Congress on the Scientific Study of Mental Retardation* (pp. 37–60). Copenhagen: Det Berlingske Bogtrykkeri.

Stevens, H. (1985). American Association on Mental Deficiency: Participation in international activities. *Mental Retardation, 23,* 215–218.

Stickney, B., & Plunkett, V. (1983). Closing the gap: A historical perspective on the effectiveness of compensatory education. *Phi Delta Kappan, 65*(4), 287–290.

Stodden, R., Ianacone, R., & Lazar, A. (1979). Occupational interests and mentally retarded people. *Mental Retardation, 17,* 294–298.

Stolurow, L. (1959). Requirements for research on learning in mental deficiency. *American Journal of Mental Deficiency, 64,* 323–332.

Stolurow, L. (1960). Automation in special education. *Exceptional Children, 27,* 78–83.

Strauss, A., & Lehtinen, L. (1947). *Psychopathology and education of the brain-injured child.* New York: Grune & Stratton.

Streissguth, A. (1978). Fetal alcohol syndrome: An epidemiological perspective. *American Journal of Epidemiology, 107,* 467–478.

Streissguth, A. (1983). Alcohol and pregnancy: An overview and update. *Substance and Alcohol Actions/Misuse, 4,* 149–173.

Strichart, S. (1974). Effects of competence and nurturance on imitation of nonretarded peers by retarded adolescents. *American Journal of Mental Deficiency, 78,* 665–673.

Strichart, S., & Gottlieb, J. (1980). Advocacy through the eyes of citizens. In J. Gottlieb (Ed.), *Educating mentally retarded persons in the mainstream* (pp. 231–250). Baltimore: University Park Press.

Stroud, M. (1978). Do students sink or swim in the mainstream? *Phi Delta Kappan, 60,* 316.

Stroud, M., & Murphy, M. (1984). *The aged mentally retarded/developmentally disabled in Northeast Ohio—1982.* Akron, OH: University of Akron.

Study probes high death rate. (1984, April). *New Directions,* pp. 1–2.

Study shows group homes don't hurt land values. (1979). *Mental Retardation News, 28*(5), 5.

Summary and analysis. (1982). *Mental Disabilities Law Reporter, 6,* 135–136.

Summer courses in special education. (1964). *Exceptional Children, 30,* 322–329.

Supreme Court refuses to order life-prolonging surgery for baby. (1983, December 14). *Wisconsin State Journal,* p. 1.

Surgeon General's advisory on alcohol and pregnancy. (1981). *FDA Drug Bulletin, 11,* 1–2.

Sussman, A. (1974). Psychological testing and juvenile justice: An invalid judicial function. *New York Law Journal in Criminal Law, 10,* 117–148.

Sutherland, G. (1982). Heritable fragile sites on human chromosomes: VII preliminary population cytogenetic data on the folic-acid-sensitive fragile sites. *American Journal of Human Genetics, 34,* 452–458.

Sutter, P. (1980). Environmental variables related to community placement failure in mentally retarded adults. *Mental Retardation, 18,* 189–191.

Swain v. Barrington School Board, No. Eq. 5750 Superior Ct., New Hampshire (March 12, 1976).

Swartz, L. (1967). Preparation of the clinical teacher for special education: 1866–1966. *Exceptional Children, 34,* 117–124.

Szurek, S., & Philips, I. (1966). Mental retardation and psychotherapy. In I. Philips (Ed.), *Prevention and treatment of mental retardation* (pp. 221–246). New York: Basic Books.

Szymanski, L. (1977). Psychiatric diagnostic evaluation of mentally retarded individuals. *Journal of the American Academy of Child Psychiatry, 16,* 67–87.

Taber, F. (1981). The microcomputer—Its applicability to special education. *Focus on Exceptional Children, 14*(2), 1–14.

Talent, A., & Keldgord, R. (1975). The mentally retarded probationer. *Federal Probation, 39*(3), 39–42.

Talkington, L., & Overbeck, D. (1975). Job satisfaction and performance with retarded females. *Mental Retardation, 13*(3), 18–19.

Tardieu, A. (1860). Etude medico-legale sur les services et Maurias traitments exerces on des infants [A medicolegal study of services and child abuse]. *Annual of Public Hygiene and Legal Medicine, 13,* 361–398.

Tarjan, G. (1965). The next decade: Expectations from the biological sciences. *Journal of the American Medical Association, 191,* 160–163.

Tarjan, G. (1966). The role of residential care—Past, present, and future. *Mental Retardation, 4*(6), 4–8.

Tarjan, G., & Eisenberg, L. (1972). Some thoughts on the classification of mental retardation in the United States of America. *American Journal of Psychiatry, 128*(11), 14–18.

TASH policy. (1983, November). *Community Living,* p. 3.

Tawney, J. (1979). *Programmed environments curriculum.* Columbus, OH: Charles E. Merrill.

Teachers' experiences in Massachusetts. (1976). *Today's Education, 65,* 23–27.

Teachers' union OKs standardized tests. (1983, August 8). *Wisconsin State Journal,* p. 1.

Tedrick, D. (1980, May 1). Retarded couple undefeated despite struggle. *The Milwaukee Journal,* Section 2, page 1.

Teenage pregnancies. (1985, March 18). *Wisconsin State Journal,* p. 12.

Templeman, D., Gage, M., Fredericks, H. (1982). Cost effectiveness of the group home. *The Journal of the Association for the Severely Handicapped, 6,* 11–16.

The Tennessee Association for Retarded Citizens. (1976). *The mentally retarded offender and the law enforcement official.* Nashville: Author.

Tennessee Department of Mental Health. (1974). *Regulation on voluntary admission.* Nashville: Author.

Tenny, J. (1953). The minority status of the handicapped. *Exceptional Children, 19,* 260–264.

Tenny, J. (1960). Special education in the Soviet Union. *Exceptional Children, 26,* 296–304.

Terman, L., & Merrill, M. (1960). *Stanford-Binet Intelligence Scale.* Boston: Houghton Mifflin.

They survive in this complex world. (1983, December 7). *Milwaukee Sentinel.*

Thiagarajan, S., Semmel, D., & Semmel, M. (1974). *Instructional development for training teachers of exceptional children: A sourcebook.* Reston, VA: The Council for Exceptional Children.

Thomas, M. (1979). Put the focus on instructional skills: A conversation with Edward L. Meyen about mildly retarded students. *Education and Training of the Mentally Retarded, 14,* 112–119.

Thompson, H., Roberts, R., & Whiddon, M. (1979).

Inadequacy of brief IQ measures in the classification of mentally retarded prisoners. *American Journal of Mental Deficiency, 83,* 416–417.

Thorndike, E. (1898). Animal intelligence: An experimental study of the associative processes in animals. *Psychological Review,* Monograph Supplement No. 8.

Thorndike, E. (1913). The psychology of learning. *Educational Psychology, 2,* 16, 17, 19–23, 45, 46, 204.

Thorndike, R. (1973). *Stanford-Binet Intelligence Scale, Form L-M, 1972 Norm Tables.* Boston: Houghton Mifflin.

Thorne, J. (1975). Normalization through the normalization principle: Right ends, wrong means. *Mental Retardation, 13*(5), 23–25.

Thurman, S., & Hare, B. (1979). Teacher training in special education: Some perspectives circa 1980. *Education and Training of the Mentally Retarded, 14,* 292–295.

Tisdall, W., & Moss, J. (1962). A total program for the severely mentally retarded. *Exceptional Children, 28,* 357–362.

Todres, I., Krane, D., Howell, M., & Shannon, D. (1977). Pediatricians' attitudes affecting decision-making in defective newborns. *Pediatrics, 60,* 197–201.

Townsend v. Treadway, Civil Action No. 6500, U.S. District Court, Northern District of Tennessee (1973).

Townsend, P., & Flanagan, J. (1976). Experimental preadmission program to encourage home care for severely and profoundly retarded children. *American Journal of Mental Deficiency, 80,* 562–569.

Trafford, A., Avery, P., Thornton, J., Carey, J., Galloway, J., & Sanoff, A. (1984, August 6). She's come a long way—or has she? *U.S. News and World Report,* pp. 44–51.

Training needs in the community. (1982, November). *Memo to Management,* p. 1.

Tsai, F., Zee, C., & Apthrop, J. (1980). Computed tomography in child abuse head trauma. *Journal of Computed Tomography, 4,* 277–285.

Tuddenham, R. (1966). Jean Piaget and the world of the child. *American Psychologist, 21,* 207–217.

Turkel, H. (1963). Medical treatment of mongolism. In O. Stur (Ed.), *Proceedings of the Second International Congress on Mental Retardation* (pp. 409–416). Bazel, Switzerland: S. Karger.

Turnbull, A. (1977). Citizen advocacy in special education training. *Education and Training of the Mentally Retarded, 12,* 166–169.

Turnbull, A., & Turnbull, H. (1982). Parent involvement in the education of handicapped children: A critique. *Mental Retardation, 20,* 115–122.

Turnbull, H. (1975). Effects of litigation on mental retardation centers. *Popular Government, 40*(3), 44–52.

Turnbull, H. (1981). *The least restrictive alternative: Principles and practices.* Washington, DC: American Association on Mental Deficiency.

Turnbull, H. (1983). Fundamental rights, Section 504, and Baby Doe. *Mental Retardation, 21,* 218–221.

Turnbull, H., & Turnbull, A. (1977). Implications of right-to-education movement for institutions of higher education. *Education and Training of the Mentally Retarded, 12,* 286–295.

Turner, G. (1983). Historical overview of X-linked mental retardation. In R. Hagerman & P. McBogg (Eds.),

The fragile X chromosome (pp. 1–16). Dillon, CO: Spectra.

Turnover among mentally retarded employees. (1983, January). *Memo to Management,* p. 3.

Two sides claim victory in Agent Orange fight. (1984, February 26). *Wisconsin State Journal,* Section 1, p. 3.

Tymchuk, A. (1971). Personality and sociocultural retardation. *Exceptional Children, 38,* 721–728.

Tymchuk, A. (1973). Effects of concept familiarization vs. stimulus enhancement on verbal abstracting in institutionalized retarded delinquent boys. *American Journal of Mental Deficiency, 77,* 551–555.

UAF Long-Range Planning Task Force. (1976). *The role of higher education in mental retardation and other developmental disabilities.* Washington, DC: American Association of University Affiliated Programs for the Developmentally Disabled.

Ubell, E. (1984a, March 4). How you can help turn off drug abuse. *Parade,* unpaged.

Ubell, E. (1984b, February 12). How vaccines may end infections. *Parade,* unpaged.

Ucer, E., Goulden, G., & Mazzeo, A. (1968). Utilizing film therapy with emotionally disturbed retardates. *Mental Retardation, 6*(1), 35–38.

Ulleland, C. (1972). The offspring of alcoholic mothers. *Annuals of the New York Academy of Science, 197,* 167–169.

UN declares 1983–1992 as the "Decade of Disabled Persons." (1983, March). *Memo to Management,* pp. 1–2.

Unified School District No. 1 v. Barbara Thompson, Case No. 146-488 (Cir. Ct., Dane County, WI) (May 21, 1976).

United Cerebral Palsy. (1974). *The first three years: Programming for atypical infants and their families.* New York: United Cerebral Palsy.

United Nations. (1971). Declaration of general and special rights of the mentally retarded. New York: Author.

United States Department of Education News. (1982, August 3).

United States ex rel. Peeples v. Greer, 566 F. Supp. 580 C.D. Ill. (1983).

United States v. Ewell, 383 U.S. 116 (1966).

United States v. University Hospital, State University of New York at Stony Brook. 729 F. 2d 144 (1984).

United together. (1982, July). *Memo to Management,* pp. 1–2.

University affiliated facilities. (Undated). Washington, DC: American Association of University Affiliated Programs.

USA syphilis rate up, gonorrhea cases drop. (1983, May 5). *USA Today,* p. 5.

U.S. Bureau of the Census. (1983). *Statistical abstract of the United States: 1981–1982.* Washington, DC: U.S. Government Printing Office.

U.S. Department of Education. (1980). *Summary of existing legislation relating to the handicapped.* Washington, DC: U.S. Government Printing Office.

U.S. Department of Education. (1981). *Third annual report to the Congress on the implementation of Public Law 94-142: The Education for All Handicapped Children Act.* Washington, DC: Author.

U.S. Department of Education. (1982). *Fourth annual report to Congress on the implementation of Public*

Law 94-142: The Education for All Handicapped Children Act. Washington, DC: Author.

U.S. Department of Health, Education, and Welfare. (1965, January). Provisional patient movement and administrative data: Public institutions for the mentally retarded in the United States, 1964. *Mental Health Statistics, Current Reports.*

U.S. Department of Health, Education, and Welfare. (1975). *Head Start services to handicapped children: Third annual report of the U.S. Department of Health, Education, and Welfare to the Congress of the United States on services provided to handicapped children in Project Head Start.* Washington, DC: Office of Human Development.

U.S. Department of Health, Education, and Welfare. (1977). *Developmental disabilities program.* Washington, DC: U.S. Government Printing Office.

U.S. Department of Health, Education, and Welfare. (1978). *The status of handicapped children in Head Start programs: Fifth annual report of the U.S. Department of Health, Education, and Welfare to the Congress of the United States on services provided to handicapped children in Project Head Start.* Washington, DC: Office of Human Development Services.

U.S. Department of Health and Human Services. (1980). *The status of handicapped children in Head Start programs: Seventh annual report of the U.S. Department of Health, Education, and Welfare to the Congress of the United States on services provided to handicapped children in Project Head Start.* Washington, DC: Office of Human Development Services.

U.S. Department of Health and Human Services. (1984). *Fact sheet.* Washington, DC: Author.

U.S. needs a "moral and social recovery." (1984, January 9). *U.S. News & World Report,* pp. 59–60.

U.S. poverty study begun. (1969). *Children Limited, 18*(5), 2.

Užgiris, I., & Hunt, J. (1975). *Assessment in infancy: Ordinal scales of psychological development.* Urbana: University of Illinois Press.

Vernon, M. (1969). *Multiply handicapped deaf children: Medical, educational, and psychological considerations.* Reston, VA: Council for Exceptional Children.

Vernon, M. (1981, October). Education's "Three Mile Island": P.L. 94-142. *Peabody Journal of Education,* pp. 24–29.

Villing, J. (1976). National Center for Law and the Handicapped. *Education and Training of the Mentally Retarded, 11,* 286.

Vining, E., & Freeman, J. (1978). Sterilization and the retarded female: Is advocacy depriving individuals of their rights? *Pediatrics, 62,* 850–853.

Vitamins bring gains for retarded children. (1981, July/August). *Upfront,* p. 6.

Voeltz, L. (1980). Children's attitudes toward handicapped peers. *American Journal of Mental Deficiency, 84,* 455–464.

Wainwright, R. (1984). Change in observed birth weight associated with change in maternal cigarette smoking. *American Journal of Epidemiology, 117,* 668–675.

Waite, K. (1972). *The trainable mentally retarded child.* Springfield, IL: Charles C Thomas.

Wakefield, R. (1964). An investigation of the family backgrounds of educable mentally retarded children in special classes. *Exceptional Children, 31,* 143–146.

Walker, M. (1985). *Beyond bureaucracy: Mary Elizabeth Switzer and rehabilitation.* New York: University Press of America.

Wallin, J. (1962). Psycho-social considerations militating against institutionalization, particularly for children. *Training School Bulletin, 59,* 89–104.

Wallis, C. (1984, September 10). The new origins of life. *Time,* pp. 46–50, 52–54.

Walls, R., Werner, T., Bacon, A., & Jane, T. (1977). Behavior checklists. In J. Cone & R. Hawkins (Eds.), *Behavioral assessment: New directions in clinical psychology* (pp. 77–146). New York: Brunner/Mazel.

Warkany, J., Lemire, R., & Cohen, M. (1981). *Mental retardation and congenital malformations of the central nervous system.* Chicago: Yearbook Medical Publishers.

Warren, S., & Jones, S. (1973). Survey of administrators of residential facilities for the mentally retarded. Unpublished manuscript. Boston University.

Washington report: New social services program to be launched in October. (1975). *Mental Retardation News, 24*(6), 3.

Watson, J. (1913). Psychology as the behaviorist views it. *Psychological Review, 20,* 158–177.

Watson, J. (1924). *Behaviorism.* Chicago: The People's Institute.

Watson, L. (1977). Issues in behavior modification of the mentally retarded individual. In I. Bialer & M. Sternlicht (Eds.), *The psychology of mental retardation: Issues and approaches* (pp. 493–549). New York: Psychological Dimensions.

Weber v. Stony Brook Hospital, No. 672 N.Y. Ct. App. (Oct. 28, 1983).

Wechsler, D. (1967). *Manual for the Wechsler Preschool and Primary Scale of Intelligence.* New York: Psychological Corporation.

Wechsler, D. (1971). Intelligence, theory, and IQ. In R. Cancro (Ed.), *Intelligence: Genetic and environmental influences* (pp. 50–55). New York: Grune & Stratton.

Wechsler, D. (1974). *Manual for the Wechsler Intelligence Scale for Children–Revised.* New York: Psychological Corporation.

Wechsler, D. (1981). *Manual for the Wechsler Adult Intelligence Scale–Revised.* New York: Psychological Corporation.

Wehman, P. (1979). *Curriculum design for the severely and profoundly handicapped.* New York: Human Sciences Press.

Weiner, B. (1967). Assessment: Beyond psychometry. *Exceptional Children, 33,* 367–370.

Weingold, J. (1966). Towards a new concept of the delinquent offender. *Mental Retardation, 4*(6), 36–38.

Weiskopf, P. (1980). Burnout among teachers of exceptional children. *Exceptional Children, 7,* 18–23.

Welsch v. Likens, Civil Action No. 451, U.S. District Court, District of Minnesota (1974).

What price day care? (1984, September 10). *Newsweek,* pp. 14–21.

What? Retarded people in college? (1982, September). *Newsletter,* p. 1.

What's being done about dropouts? (1983, June 2). *U.S. News and World Report,* p. 64.

What's it all about? (1976). *Today's Education, 65*(2), 18–19.

Where have all the people gone? (1980, August-September), *ARC,* p. 4.

Whitcraft, C., & Jones, J. (1974). A survey of attitudes about sterilization of retardates. *Mental Retardation, 12,* 30–33.

White, B. (1966). Protective services for the mentally retarded in New Jersey. In E. Helsel & S. Messner (Eds.), *Conference on protective supervision and services for the handicapped* (pp. 20–24). New York: United Cerebral Palsy Association.

White, C., Hill, B., Lakin, K., & Bruininks, R. (1984). Day programs of adults with mental retardation in residential facilities. *Mental Retardation, 22,* 121–127.

White, O., & Haring, N. (1976). *Exceptional teaching: A multimedia training package.* Columbus, OH: Charles E. Merrill.

White, T. (1982). *America in search of itself.* New York: Harper & Row.

Whiteside, M. (1983, September 12). A bedeviling new hysteria. *Newsweek,* p. 13.

Whitman, T., & Scibak, J. (1979). Behavioral modification research with the severely and profoundly retarded. In N. Ellis (Ed.), *Handbook of mental deficiency: Psychological theory and research* (pp. 289–400). Hillsdale, NJ: Lawrence Erlbaum Associates.

Wiener, D., Anderson, R., & Nietupski, J. (1982). Impact of community-based residential facilities for mentally retarded adults on surrounding property values using realtor analysis methods. *Education and Training of the Mentally Retarded, 17,* 278–282.

Will, G. (1980, April 14). The case of Phillip Becker. *Newsweek,* p. 112.

Will, G. (1982, April 22). Requium for infant Doe. *Washington Post,* p. 14.

Willer, B., & Itagliata, J. (1984). *Promises and realities for mentally retarded citizens: Life in the community.* Baltimore: University Park Press.

Willer, B., Intagliata, J., & Atkinson, A. (1981). De-institutionalization as a crisis event for families of mentally retarded persons. *Mental Retardation, 19,* 28–29.

Willer, B., Intagliata, J., & Wicks, N. (1979, March 16). *Return of retarded adults to natural families: Issues and results.* Paper presented at the Conference on Community Adjustment, Minneapolis, MN.

Williams, P. (1965). Initial Teaching Alphabet (ITA): Interim assessment. *The Winnower, 2*(1), 26–44.

Wilson, W. (1970). Social psychology and mental retardation. In N. Ellis (Ed.), *International review of research in mental retardation* (pp. 229–262). New York: Academic Press.

Wineke, W. (1986, February 2). Cut in block grants is nothing new. *Wisconsin State Journal,* Section 1, page 4.

Winick, M., & Rosso, P. (1969). Head circumference and cellular growth of the brain in normal and marasmic children. *Journal of Pediatrics, 74,* 774–778.

Winners of the 1971 Kennedy International Awards. (1971). *Mental Retardation, 9*(6), 14.

Wisconsin Statute 48.981. *The child abuse and neglect act* (1978).

Wisniewski, H.M., & Merz, G.S. (1985). Aging, Alzheimer's disease, and developmental disabilities. In M.P. Janicki & H.M. Wisniewski (Eds.), *Aging and*

developmental disabilities: Issues and approaches (pp. 177–184). Baltimore: Paul H. Brookes Publishing Co.

Wodrich, D.L. (1984). *Children's psychological testing: A guide for nonpsychologists.* Baltimore: Paul H. Brookes Publishing Co.

Wolf v. Legislature of the State of Utah. Civil No. 182646, 3rd. Jud. Distr. Ct., Utah (January 8, 1969).

Wolf, L., & Zarfas, D. (1982). Parents' attitudes toward sterilization of their mentally retarded children. *American Journal of Mental Deficiency, 87,* 122–129.

Wolfensberger, W. (1969). The origin and nature of our institutional models. In R. Kugel & W. Wolfensberger (Eds.), *Changing patterns in residential services for the mentally retarded* (pp. 59–177). Washington, DC: President's Committee on Mental Retardation.

Wolfensberger, W. (1971). Will there always be an institution? I. The impact of new service models. *Mental Retardation, 9*(5), 31–38.

Wolfensberger, W. (1972). *The principle of normalization in human services.* Toronto, Canada: National Institute on Mental Retardation.

Wolfensberger, W. (1975). *Citizen advocacy for the handicapped, impaired, and disadvantaged: An overview.* Washington, DC: U.S. Government Printing Office.

Wolfensberger, W. (1980a). A call to wake up to the beginning of a new wave of "euthanasia" of severely impaired people. *Education and Training of the Mentally Retarded, 15,* 171–173.

Wolfensberger, W. (1980b). The definition of normalization: Update, problems, disagreements, and misunderstandings. In R. Flynn & K. Nitsch (Eds.), *Normalization, social integration, and community services* (pp. 71–115). Baltimore: University Park Press.

Wolfensberger, W. (1981). *The extermination of handicapped people in World War II Germany. Mental Retardation, 19,* 1–7.

Wolfensberger, W. (1983a). Social role valorization: A proposed new term for the principle of normalization. *Mental Retardation, 21,* 234–239.

Wolfensberger, W. (1983b). *Voluntary associations on behalf of societally devalued and/or handicapped persons.* Toronto, Canada: National Institute on Mental Retardation.

Wolfensberger, W. (1983c). *Reflections on the status of citizen advocacy.* Ontario, Canada: National Institute on Mental Retardation.

Wolfensberger, W., & Glenn, L. (1973). *PASS: Program analysis of service systems.* Toronto, Canada: National Institute on Mental Retardation.

Wolfensberger, W., & Kugel, R. (Eds.). (1969). *Changing patterns in residential services for the mentally retarded.* Washington, DC: President's Committee on Mental Retardation.

Wolfensberger, W., & Thomas, S. (1983). *PASSING: Program analysis of service systems' implementation of normalization goals.* Toronto, Canada: National Institute on Mental Retardation.

Wolfensberger, W., & Zauha, H. (1973). *Citizen advocacy and protection services for the impaired and handicapped.* Toronto, Canada: National Institute on Mental Retardation.

Wolraich, M. (1979). Pediatric training in developmental disabilities. *Mental Retardation, 17,* 133–136.

Woodward, K., Jaffe, N., & Brown, D. (1964). Psychiatric program for very young retarded children. *American Journal of Diseases of Children, 108,* 221–229.

Woody, N., Sistrunk, W., & Platou, R. (1964). Congenital syphilis: A laid ghost walks. *Pediatrics, 64,* 63–67.

Wortis, J. (Ed.). (1977). Introduction: The role of psychiatry in mental retardation services. In J. Wortis (Ed.), *Mental retardation and developmental disabilities* (Vol. 9, pp. 1–5). New York: Brunner/Mazel.

Wouri v. Zitnay, No. 75-80-SD Maine (1978).

W.R.C. (1983). Commentary. *New England Journal of Human Services, 3*(4), 4–7.

W.T. Grant Company rates MR job performance good. (1968). *Children Limited, 17*(8), 5.

Wyatt v. Aderholt, No. 72-2634, U.S. Court of Appeals, Fifth Circuit (1974).

Wyatt v. Stickney, Civil Action No. 3195-N, U.S. District Court, Middle District of Alabama, North Division (1972).

Yannet, H. (1953). The progress of medical research in the field of mental deficiency. *American Journal of Mental Deficiency, 57,* 447–452.

Young, A. (1976). The dialectic teaching system: A comprehensive model. *Education and Training of the Mentally Retarded, 11,* 232–246.

Young, C., & Kerr, M. (1979). The effects of a retarded child's social initiations on the behavior of severely retarded school-aged peers. *Education and Training of the Mentally Retarded, 14*(3), 185–190.

Young, P. (1983). A conversation with Richard Jed Wyatt. *Psychology Today, 17*(8), 29–41.

Young, S., Algozzine, B., & Schmid, R. (1979). The effects of assigned attributes and labels on children's peer acceptance ratings. *Education and Training of the Mentally Retarded, 14*(4), 257–261.

Youngberg v. Romeo, 457 U.S. 307 (1982).

Youth character. (1984, November 21). *Wisconsin State Journal,* p. 2.

Ysseldyke, J., & Salvia, J. (1974). Diagnostic-prescrip-tive teaching: Two models. *Exceptional Children, 41,* 181–185.

Zarek v. Attleboro Area Human Services, Inc., No. 2450 Superior Ct., Massachusetts (November, 1975).

Zeaman, D., & House, B. (1963). The role of attention in retardate discrimination learning. In N. Ellis (Ed.), *Handbook on mental deficiency* (pp. 159–223). New York: McGraw-Hill.

Zeaman, D., & House, B. (1979). A review of attention theory. In N. Ellis (Ed.), *Handbook of mental deficiency, psychological theory, and research* (pp. 63–117). Hillsdale, NJ: Lawrence Erlbaum Associates.

Zigler, E. (1962). Rigidity in the feebleminded. In E. Trapp & P. Himelstein (Eds.), *Readings on the exceptional child* (pp. 141–162). New York: Appleton-Century-Crofts.

Zigler, E. (1967). Familial mental retardation: A continuing dilemma. *Science, 155,* 292–298.

Zigler, E. (1978). National crises in mental retardation research. *American Journal of Mental Deficiency, 83,* 1–8.

Zigler, E. (1982). A plea to end the use of the patterning treatment for retarded children. In S. Chess & A. Thomas (Eds.), *Annual progress in child psychiatry and child development* (pp. 502–506). New York: Brunner/Mazel.

Zigler, E., & Balla, D. (Eds.). (1982). *Mental retardation: The developmental difference controversy.* Hillsdale, NJ: Lawrence Erlbaum Associates.

Zigler, E., & Weintraub, E. (1980). Patterning: Unproven hope for brain-damaged children. *Education and Training of the Mentally Retarded, 15,* 247–249.

Zohn, C., & Bornstein, P. (1980). Self-monitoring of work performance with mentally retarded adults: Effects upon work productivity, work quality, and on-task behavior. *Mental Retardation, 18,* 19–26.

Zorzi, G., Thurman, S., & Kistenmacher, M. (1980). Importance and adequacy of genetic counseling information: Impressions of parents with Down's syndrome children. *Mental Retardation, 18,* 255–257.

INDEX